Visual QuickStart Guide

Illustrator CS

for Windows and Macintosh

Elaine Weinmann
Peter Lourekas

 **Peachpit Press**

For Simona

Visual QuickStart Guide
Illustrator CS for Windows and Macintosh
Elaine Weinmann and Peter Lourekas

Peachpit Press
1249 Eighth Street
Berkeley, CA 94710
510/524-2178
800/283-9444
510/524-2221 (fax)

Find us on the Web at: http://www.peachpit.com

Visual QuickStart Guide is a trademark of Peachpit Press, a
division of Pearson Education

Cover design: The Visual Group
Interior design: Elaine Weinmann
Production: Elaine Weinmann and Peter Lourekas
Illustrations: Elaine Weinmann and Peter Lourekas,
except as noted

Colophon
This book was created with QuarkXPress 5 on a Power
Macintosh G4 and a G5. The fonts used are Sabon, Gill Sans,
and CaflischScript from Adobe Systems Inc.

ISBN 0-321-19955-3
9 8 7 6 5 4 3

Printed and bound in the United States of America

Chris Spollen

Special thanks to

The creative and skilled *artists* whose work we're honored to feature in the color insert (for their contact information, see "The Artists" on the following page).

Nancy Aldrich-Ruenzel, Publisher, Peachpit Press; *Nancy Davis,* Editor-in-Chief; *Marjorie Baer,* Executive Editor; *Lisa Brazieal,* Production Editor; *Nathalie Valette,* cover designer; *Gary-Paul Prince,* Publicist; *Keasley Jones,* Associate Publisher; and the rest of the folks at Peachpit Press. They are truly a pleasure to work with.

Cary Norsworthy, our wonderful Editor at Peachpit Press.

Victor Gavenda, clever, thorough, and indispensible Technical Editor at Peachpit Press.

Adobe Systems, Inc., for designing software that's inspiring and fun to write about.

Malloy Lithographing, for a fine print job.

Mies Hora of Ultimate Symbol, for the Design Elements CD (www.ultimatesymbol.com).

Nathan Olson and *Jeff Seaver,* for helping us revise some chapters.

Rebecca Pepper, copy editor.

Leona Benten, proofreader.

Steve Rath, indexer.

Peter from *Elaine* and *Elaine* from *Peter*— two ships passing in the night.

Thanks

The Artists

Chris Spollen

Kenneth Batelman
128 Birch Leaf Drive
Milford, PA 18337
Voice 888-532-0612
kenneth@batelman.com
www.batelman.com
color section

Jeanne de la Houssaye
MardiDraw
2816 Coliseum Street
New Orleans, LA 70115
Voice 504-957-8981
Fax 504-899-2216
mardidraw@hotmail.com
www.mardidraw.com
color section

Jib Hunt
Jib Hunt Illustration
575 8th Avenue, Suite 1900
New York, NY 10018
Voice 212-489-2015
Fax 212-262-4512
Cell 908-868-2858
www.jibhunt.com
color section

Shane Kelley
Kelley Graphics
Voice 1-800-222-0753
www.kelley-graphics.com
color section

Diane Margolin
41 Perry Street
New York, NY 10014
Voice 212-691-9537
dimargolin@ixpres.com
*45, 59, 79, 80, 108, 128, 136,
162, 168, 272, 273, 276, 286,
330, 393*

Tom Nikosey
Nikosey Design, Inc.
www.tomnikosey.com
color section

Daniel Pelavin
80 Varick Street, #3B
New York, NY 10013
Voice 212-941-7418
Fax 212-431-7138
www.pelavin.com
*v, ix, xiii, xiv, xv, xvi, 65, 66,
67, 109, 140, 169, 172, 309,
324, 349, 529, 554, 560, 563,
color section*

Chris Spollen
Moonlightpress Studio
362 Cromwell Avenue
Staten Island, NY 10305-2304
Voice 718-979-9695
cjspollen@aol.com
www.spollen.com
iii, 1, 67, 139, 531, 565

Nancy Stahl
www.nancystahl.com
449, color section

Mark Stein
Mark Stein Studios
73–01 Juniper Valley Road
Middle Village, NY 11379
Voice 718-326-4839
steinstudios@att.net
257, color section

Carol Zuber-Mallison
Charts, maps, and informational
   graphics
Voice 214-906-4162
www.zmgraphics.com
color section

TABLE OF CONTENTS

Note! New features or substantially changed features are identified by this symbol: ■

4 VIEWS

5 OBJECT BASICS

6 SELECT/COPY

11 LAYERS

12 CREATE TYPE

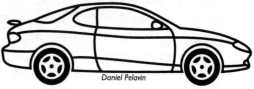

Daniel Pelavin

Table of Contents

21 DISTORT

22 EFFECTS & FILTERS

Daniel Pelavin

Table of Contents

Table of Contents

Daniel Pelavin

27 WEB

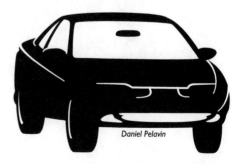

Daniel Pelavin

A KEYBOARD SHORTCUTS

Daniel Pelavin

Table of Contents

ILLUSTRATOR INTERFACE

This chapter is an introduction to Illustrator's tools, menus, palettes, and measurement systems.

Note: If you'd like to glance onscreen at the features discussed in this chapter as you read, launch Illustrator and create a new document (see pages 39–41).

Chris Spollen

Hide/show

Tab Hide/show all currently open palettes, including the Toolbox

Shift-Tab Hide/show all currently open palettes and tearoff toolbars, but not the Toolbox

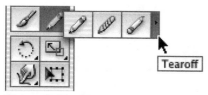

1 *Open a tearoff toolbar by choosing a tearoff bar.*

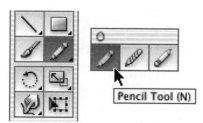

2 *A tearoff toolbar*

Tools
Using the Toolbox

The Toolbox contains **74 tools** that are used for object creation and editing. If the Toolbox is hidden, choose Window > Tools to display it. To move the Toolbox, drag the top bar. Click once on a visible tool to select it. Press on any tool that has a tiny arrowhead to choose a related tool from a pop-out menu. When you double-click some tools, an options dialog box opens for the tool.

To create a standalone **tearoff toolbar 1–2**, release the mouse when it's over the vertical tearoff bar on the far right side of any tool pop-out menu. Move a tearoff toolbar by dragging its top bar. To restore a tearoff toolbar to the Toolbox, click its close box.

To access a tool quickly, use its letter **shortcut** (see the letters in gray on the next two pages). Some tools can be accessed using a toggle key (e.g., pressing Cmd/Ctrl accesses the Selection tool when the Pen tool is chosen). You'll learn more toggles later.

To turn tool pointers into **crosshairs** for precise positioning, check Use Precise Cursors in Illustrator (Edit, in Windows) > Preferences > General. Or press Caps Lock to turn a tool pointer into a crosshair temporarily.

➤ You'll probably want to leave Disable Warnings unchecked in Preferences > General, at least if you're new to Illustrator. With this option unchecked, an alert prompt will appear when a tool is used incorrectly.

The Toolbox

Note: To assign your own shortcuts to tools, use the **Keyboard Shortcuts** dialog box (see pages 526–528).

Adobe Online access

V Selection — Selects entire objects

Direct Selection A — Selects parts of objects

Y Magic Wand — Selects objects by color

Lasso Q — Selects individual points or segments by lassoing

P Pen — Draws curved and straight line segments

Type T — Creates and edits horizontal type

\ Line Segment — Draws straight lines at any angle

Rectangle M — Draws rectangles and squares

B Paintbrush — Creates Calligraphic, Scatter, Art, and Pattern brush strokes

Pencil N — Creates freehand-style lines

R Rotate — Rotates objects

Scale S — Enlarges or shrinks objects

Shift-R Warp — Distorts shapes

Free Transform E — Rotates, scales, reflects, shears, distorts, or applies perspective

Shift-S Symbol Sprayer — Sprays symbol instances

Column Graph J — Creates graphs

U Mesh — Creates and edits multicolored mesh objects

Gradient G — Changes the direction of existing gradients

I Eyedropper — Samples paint and type attributes

Blend W — Creates shape and color blends between objects

Shift-K Slice — Defines slice areas

Scissors C — Cuts paths

H Hand — Moves the artboard in the document window

Zoom Z — Changes the magnification of the illustration

X Fill — The color, gradient, or pattern that fills the inside of a path

Swap Fill and Stroke Shift-X

D Default Fill and Stroke — (white fill, black stroke)

Stroke X — Color that's applied to the edge of a path (click to activate)

> Gradient — Reapplies last gradient fill

None / — No stroke or fill

< Color — Reapplies last solid color stroke or fill

Full Screen Mode F

F Standard Screen Mode

Full Screen Mode with Menu Bar F

The Toolbox

The tearoff toolbars

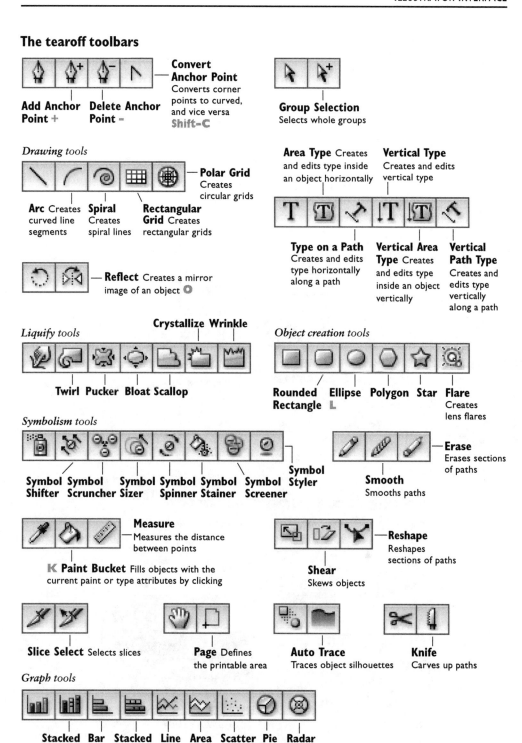

Add Anchor Point + **Delete Anchor Point =** **Convert Anchor Point** Converts corner points to curved, and vice versa **Shift-C**

Group Selection Selects whole groups

Drawing tools

Arc Creates curved line segments **Spiral** Creates spiral lines **Rectangular Grid** Creates rectangular grids **Polar Grid** Creates circular grids

Reflect Creates a mirror image of an object **O**

Area Type Creates and edits type inside an object horizontally **Vertical Type** Creates and edits vertical type

Type on a Path Creates and edits type horizontally along a path **Vertical Area Type** Creates and edits type inside an object vertically **Vertical Path Type** Creates and edits type vertically along a path

Liquify tools

Crystallize Wrinkle

Twirl Pucker Bloat Scallop

Object creation tools

Rounded Rectangle L Ellipse Polygon Star Flare Creates lens flares

Symbolism tools

Symbol Shifter Symbol Scruncher Symbol Sizer Symbol Spinner Symbol Stainer Symbol Screener Symbol Styler

Smooth Smooths paths **Erase** Erases sections of paths

Measure Measures the distance between points

K Paint Bucket Fills objects with the current paint or type attributes by clicking

Shear Skews objects

Reshape Reshapes sections of paths

Slice Select Selects slices

Page Defines the printable area

Auto Trace Traces object silhouettes

Knife Carves up paths

Graph tools

Stacked Column Bar Stacked Bar Line Area Scatter Pie Radar

The Toolbox

On the screen

The Illustrator screen in Macintosh

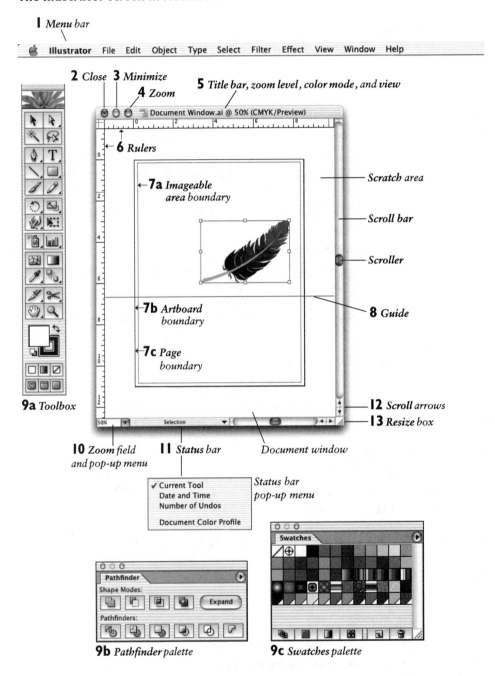

1 *Menu bar*

2 *Close* **3** *Minimize*

4 *Zoom*

5 *Title bar, zoom level, color mode, and view*

6 *Rulers*

7a *Imageable area boundary*

Scratch area

Scroll bar

Scroller

7b *Artboard boundary*

8 *Guide*

7c *Page boundary*

9a *Toolbox*

12 *Scroll arrows*

13 *Resize box*

10 *Zoom field and pop-up menu*

11 *Status bar*

Document window

✓ Current Tool
Date and Time
Number of Undos

Document Color Profile

Status bar pop-up menu

9b *Pathfinder palette*

9c *Swatches palette*

Illustrator Screen in Macintosh

Key to the Illustrator screen in Macintosh

1 *Menu bar*
Use the menu bar to open dialog boxes or palettes or to choose commands.

2 *Close button (red)*
To close a document or a palette, click its close button.

3 *Minimize button (yellow)*
Click the minimize button to shrink the document window to an icon in the Dock; click the icon in the Dock to restore the document window to its previous size.

4 *Zoom button (green)*
Click a document window zoom button to enlarge the window. Click again to restore the window to its previous size. (Click a palette zoom button to shrink the palette or restore it to its previous size.)

5 *Title bar, zoom level, color mode, and view*
The illustration's title, zoom level, color mode (CMYK or RGB), and view (Preview, Outline, Pixel Preview, or Overprint Preview) are listed on the title bar.

6 *Rulers*
The current position of the pointer is indicated by a marker on the horizontal and vertical rulers. Ruler increments can be displayed in any of these measurement units: points, picas, inches, millimeters, centimeters, or pixels.

7a–c *Imageable area, artboard boundary, and page boundary*
The imageable area within the margin guides is the area that will print on the paper size currently selected in File > Print (General). The artboard is the user-defined work area and the largest possible printable area. The nonprinting page boundary matches the current paper size. Objects located in the area outside the artboard will save with the file, but they won't print.

8 *Guide*
Drag from the horizontal or vertical ruler to create a guide. Guides are used only for aligning objects; they don't print.

9a–c *Palettes*
Pathfinder and Swatches are five of 31 moveable palettes that open from the Window menu. The Toolbox contains 74 (yes, 74!) drawing and editing tools, as well as color controls and screen mode buttons.

10 *Zoom field*
Enter a new zoom percentage in this field or choose a preset zoom percentage from the pop-up menu.

11 *Status bar*
Depending on which category you choose from the pop-up menu, the status bar displays the name of the Current Tool, the current Date and Time from System Preferences > System > Date & Time, the Number of available Undos/Redos, or the Document Color Profile. Option-press the status bar pop-up menu to learn the Moon Phase, Shopping Days 'til Christmas, and other vital statistics.

12 *Scroll arrows*
Click the downward-pointing scroll arrow to move the illustration upward in the document window. Click the upward-pointing scroll arrow to move the illustration downward in the document window.

13 *Resize box*
To resize a document window, drag its resize box diagonally.

The Illustrator screen in Windows

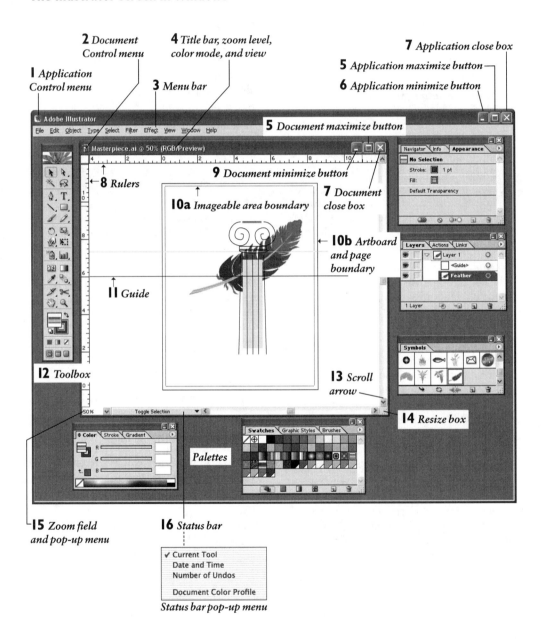

2 *Document Control menu*

4 *Title bar, zoom level, color mode, and view*

7 *Application close box*

5 *Application maximize button*

6 *Application minimize button*

1 *Application Control menu*

3 *Menu bar*

5 *Document maximize button*

9 *Document minimize button*

8 *Rulers*

7 *Document close box*

10a *Imageable area boundary*

10b *Artboard and page boundary*

11 *Guide*

12 *Toolbox*

13 *Scroll arrow*

14 *Resize box*

15 *Zoom field and pop-up menu*

16 *Status bar*

Current Tool
Date and Time
Number of Undos

Document Color Profile

Status bar pop-up menu

Palettes

Key to the Illustrator screen in Windows

1 *Application Control menu box*
The Application Control menu box commands are Restore, Move, Size, Minimize, Maximize, and Close.

2 *Document Control menu box*
The Document Control menu box commands are Restore, Move, Size, Minimize, Maximize, Close, and Next.

3 *Menu bar*
Use the menu bar to open dialog boxes or palettes or choose commands.

4 *Title bar, zoom level, color mode, view*
The illustration's title, zoom level, color mode (CMYK or RGB), and view (Preview, Outline, Pixel Preview, or Overprint Preview) are listed on the title bar.

5 *Maximize/restore down button*
Click the document or application maximize button to enlarge either window to fill the available space completely. When a window is maximized, the button turns into a restore down button. Click this button to shrink the window to its former size.

6 *Application minimize button*
Click the application minimize button to shrink the application to an icon on the taskbar. Click the icon on the taskbar to restore the application window to its previous size.

7 *Close box*
To close a document or a palette, click its close box.

8 *Rulers*
The current position of the pointer is indicated by a marker on the horizontal and vertical rulers. Ruler increments can be displayed in any of these measurement units: points, picas, inches, millimeters, centimeters, or pixels.

9 *Document minimize button*
Click the document minimize button to shrink the document to an icon at the bottom left corner of the application window. To restore the document to its previous size, double-click the icon or click the restore up button.

10a–b *Imageable area, artboard boundary, and page boundary*
The imageable area within the margin guides is the area that will print on the paper size currently selected in File > Print (General). The artboard is the user-defined work area and the largest possible printable area. The nonprinting page boundary matches the current paper size. Objects outside the artboard save with the file but don't print.

11 *Guide*
Drag from the horizontal or vertical ruler to create a guide. Guides are used only for aligning objects; they don't print.

12 *Toolbox*
The Toolbox contains 74 (yes, 74!) drawing and editing tools, as well as color controls and screen mode buttons. It's one of the 31 moveable palettes that open from the Window menu.

13 *Scroll arrows*
Click the downward-pointing scroll arrow to move the illustration upward in the document window. Click the upward-pointing scroll arrow to move the illustration downward in the document window.

14 *Resize box*
To resize a document window, drag its resize box diagonally or drag the edge of the window.

15 *Zoom field*
Enter a new zoom percentage in this field or choose a preset zoom percentage from the pop-up menu.

16 *Status bar*
Depending on which category you choose from the pop-up menu, the status bar displays the name of the Current Tool, the current Date and Time from the computer's internal clock, the Number of available Undos/Redos, or the Document Color Profile (RGB or CMYK). Alt-press the status bar pop-up menu to learn the Moon Phase, Shopping Days 'til Christmas, and other vital statistics.

Illustrator Screen in Windows

The Illustrator menus

Illustrator menu

Illustrator

About Illustrator...
About Plug-ins...

Preferences ▶

Services ▶

Hide Illustrator
Hide Others ⌥⌘H
Show All

Quit Illustrator ⌘Q

In Windows, the
Preferences *command*
is on the ***Edit*** *menu*
and the ***Exit*** *command*
is on the ***File*** *menu.*

File menu

File

New... ⌘N
New from Template... ⇧⌘N
Open... ⌘O
Open Recent Files ▶

Close ⌘W
Save ⌘S
Save As... ⇧⌘S
Save a Copy... ⌥⌘S
Save as Template...
Save for Web... ⌥⇧⌘S
Save a Version...
Revert F12

Place...

Save for Microsoft Office...
Export...

Scripts ▶

Document Setup... ⌥⌘P
Document Color Mode ▶
File Info...
Versions...

Print... ⌘P

Edit menu

Edit

Undo Paste ⌘Z
Redo ⇧⌘Z

Cut ⌘X
Copy ⌘C
Paste ⌘V
Paste in Front ⌘F
Paste in Back ⌘B
Clear

Find and Replace...
Find Next
Check Spelling... ⌘I
Edit Custom Dictionary...

Define Pattern...

Edit Original

Transparency Flattener Presets...
Print Presets...
PDF Presets...

Color Settings... ⇧⌘K
Assign Profile...

Keyboard Shortcuts... ⌥⇧⌘K

Object menu

Object

Transform ▶
Arrange ▶

Group ⌘G
Ungroup ⇧⌘G
Lock ▶
Unlock All ⌥⌘2
Hide ▶
Show All ⌥⌘3

Expand...
Expand Appearance
Flatten Transparency...
Rasterize...
Create Gradient Mesh...

Slice ▶

Path ▶
Blend ▶
Envelope Distort ▶
Text Wrap ▶

Clipping Mask ▶
Compound Path ▶
Crop Area ▶
Graph ▶

Type menu

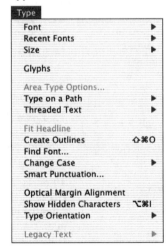

Type

Font ▶
Recent Fonts ▶
Size ▶

Glyphs

Area Type Options...
Type on a Path ▶
Threaded Text ▶

Fit Headline
Create Outlines ⇧⌘O
Find Font...
Change Case ▶
Smart Punctuation...

Optical Margin Alignment
Show Hidden Characters ⌥⌘I
Type Orientation ▶

Legacy Text ▶

Select menu

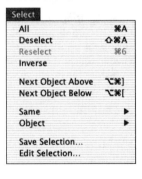

Select

All ⌘A
Deselect ⇧⌘A
Reselect ⌘6
Inverse

Next Object Above ⌥⌘]
Next Object Below ⌥⌘[

Same ▶
Object ▶

Save Selection...
Edit Selection...

Filter menu

Filter

Apply Free Distort	⌘E
Free Distort...	⌥⌘E
Colors	▶
Create	▶
Distort	▶
Stylize	▶
Artistic	▶
Blur	▶
Brush Strokes	▶
Distort	▶
Pixelate	▶
Sharpen	▶
Sketch	▶
Stylize	▶
Texture	▶
Video	▶

Effect menu

Effect

Apply Ellipse	⇧⌘E
Ellipse...	⌥⇧⌘E
Document Raster Effects Settings...	
3D	▶
Convert to Shape	▶
Distort & Transform	▶
Path	▶
Pathfinder	▶
Rasterize...	
Stylize	▶
SVG Filters	▶
Warp	▶
Artistic	▶
Blur	▶
Brush Strokes	▶
Distort	▶
Pixelate	▶
Sharpen	▶
Sketch	▶
Stylize	▶
Texture	▶
Video	▶

View menu

View

Outline	⌘Y
Overprint Preview	⌥⇧⌘Y
Pixel Preview	⌥⌘Y
Proof Setup	▶
Proof Colors	
Zoom In	⌘+
Zoom Out	⌘-
Fit in Window	⌘0
Actual Size	⌘1
Hide Edges	⌘H
Hide Artboard	
Show Page Tiling	
Show Slices	
Lock Slices	
Hide Template	⇧⌘W
Show Rulers	⌘R
Hide Bounding Box	⇧⌘B
Show Transparency Grid	⇧⌘D
Hide Text Threads	⇧⌘Y
Guides	▶
Smart Guides	⌘U
Show Grid	⌘"
Snap to Grid	⇧⌘"
Snap to Point	⌥⌘"
New View...	
Edit Views...	

Window menu

Window

New Window	
Minimize Window	⌘M
Bring All To Front	
Actions	
Align	⇧F7
Appearance	⇧F6
Attributes	F11
Brushes	F5
Color	F6
Document Info	
Flattener Preview	
Gradient	F9
Graphic Styles	⇧F5
Info	F8
Layers	F7
Links	
Magic Wand	
Navigator	
Pathfinder	⇧F9
Stroke	F10
SVG Interactivity	
Swatches	
Symbols	⇧F11
Tools	
Transform	⇧F8
Transparency	⇧F10
Type	▶
Variables	
Brush Libraries	▶
Graphic Style Libraries	▶
Swatch Libraries	▶
Symbol Libraries	▶

Help menu

Help

Illustrator Help...	F1
Welcome Screen...	
Tutorials...	
System Info...	
Online Support...	
Updates...	
Registration...	
Illustrator Online...	

The Help > About Illustrator and About Plug-ins commands are available only in Windows.

The Window > Cascade, Tile, and Arrange Icons commands are available only in Windows.

Using dialog boxes

Dialog boxes are like fill-in forms with multiple choices. They are opened from the menu bar or via shortcuts.

In Windows: To activate a menu, type Alt plus the underlined letter, then release Alt and type the underlined letter on the submenu.

Some modifications are made by entering a number in an entry field. Press **Tab** to highlight the next field in a dialog box; press **Shift-Tab** to highlight the previous field. Press or click on a pop-up menu to choose further options.

Click **OK** or press **Return/Enter** to accept modifications and exit a dialog box. To cancel out of a dialog box, click Cancel or press Esc.

Many Illustrator dialog boxes have a **Preview** option that when checked will apply the effect while the dialog box is open. Take advantage of this great timesaver.

Illustrator dialog boxes, like all the other features in the program, function the same way on the Mac as in Windows, though they look slightly different because the graphic interfaces are different.

In Windows, you can type an underlined letter to activate that field (e.g., "U" for "Uniform"). If a field is already highlighted, type Alt plus the underlined letter. In Windows XP, you have to press Alt for the underlines to show up.

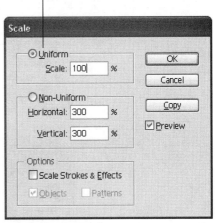

A dialog box in Windows

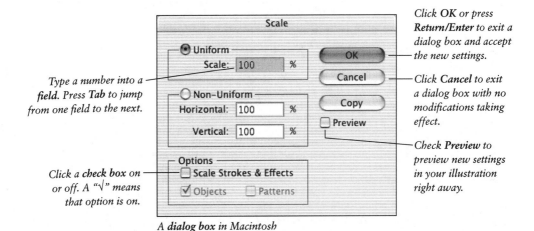

Type a number into a field. Press Tab to jump from one field to the next.

Click a check box on or off. A "√" means that option is on.

Click OK or press Return/Enter to exit a dialog box and accept the new settings.

Click Cancel to exit a dialog box with no modifications taking effect.

Check Preview to preview new settings in your illustration right away.

*A **dialog box** in Macintosh*

Using the palettes

Illustrator has 31 movable palettes, all of which can be opened from the **Window** menu, and many of which can be opened and closed via assigned shortcuts. To save screen space, the palettes are organized into these default **groups**: Appearance/Layers; Actions/Links; Navigator/Info; Character Styles/Paragraph Styles; Swatches/Color; Document Info/Attributes; Flattener Preview; Glyphs; Stroke/Gradient/Transparency; Tabs; Graphic Styles/Brushes/Symbols; Magic Wand; Transform/Align/Pathfinder; SVG Interactivity/Variables; Character/Paragraph/Open Type; and Tools. The palette name you choose from the Window menu will appear in front within its group when the group opens.

You can compose your own groups or separate a palette from its group. To **separate** a palette, drag its tab (palette name) away from the group **1**–**2**. To **add** a palette to any group, drag the tab over the group.

➤ When you compose a palette group, start with one of the resizable palette windows.

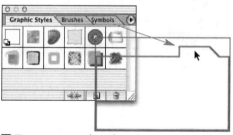

1 *To separate a palette from its group, drag the tab (palette name) out of the group.*

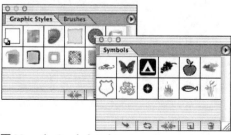

2 *Now the Symbols palette is on its own.*

To **dock** (hook up) one palette to the bottom of another palette or palette group, drag the tab to the bottom of the target palette, and release the mouse when the thick black line appears **3**. To undock, drag a palette tab out of the dock group.

To **display** an open palette at the front of its group, click its tab. Palettes with an up/down arrow on the tab (such as the Color palette) have more than one **panel**. Click this arrow or the tab name to cycle through the palette configurations: tab only, two option panels, or one option panel. Another way to display a full palette is to choose Show Options from the palette menu. To shrink a palette group to just the tabs, on the Mac, click the palette zoom button (green) in the upper left corner; in Windows, click the minimize/maximize button. Click the button again to restore the palette's previous size.

➤ Press Tab to **hide/show all** currently open palettes, including the Toolbox; press Shift-Tab to hide/show all open palettes except the Toolbox.

Palettes that are open when you quit/exit Illustrator will reappear in the same location when the application is relaunched.

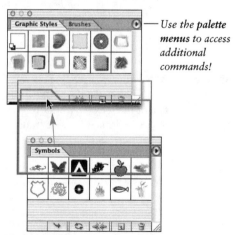

— *Use the palette menus to access additional commands!*

3 *To dock palettes together, drag the tab name of one palette to the bottom of another palette, and release the mouse when the thick black line appears across the bottom of the target palette.*

The color controls

The current fill and stroke colors display in color squares on the Toolbox **1** and on the Color palette **2**. The **Color** palette displays the color model and breakdown of the fill or stroke in the currently selected object or objects; use it to choose Web-safe colors or process colors or to adjust global process or spot color tints.

The **Stroke** palette displays the weight and style of the stroke in the currently selected object or objects, and can be used to change those attributes. If no object is selected, changes made on the Color or Stroke palette will apply to subsequently drawn objects.

Color palette F6

Use the Color palette to mix, choose, and switch between fill and stroke colors. Choose a color model for the palette from the palette menu. Quick-select a color, black, white, or None from the bar at the bottom of the palette.

Whichever box (Fill or Stroke) is currently active (is on top on the Color palette and the Toolbox) will be affected by changes on the Color palette.

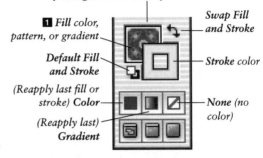

1 *Fill color, pattern, or gradient*

Swap Fill and Stroke

Default Fill and Stroke

Stroke color

(Reapply last fill or stroke) **Color**

None (no color)

(Reapply last) **Gradient**

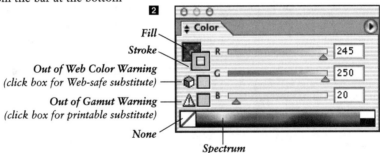

2

Fill

Stroke

Out of Web Color Warning (click box for Web-safe substitute)

Out of Gamut Warning (click box for printable substitute)

None

Spectrum

Stroke palette F10

Use the Stroke palette to edit the stroke weight and style of the selected object or objects, and to create dashed lines or frames.

Join (bend) styles

Cap (end) styles

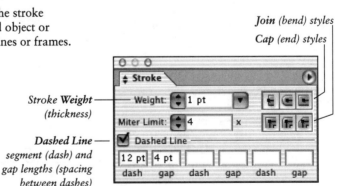

Stroke Weight (thickness)

Dashed Line segment (dash) and gap lengths (spacing between dashes)

Swatches palette

Use the Swatches palette to choose and store default and user-defined colors. If you click a swatch, it becomes the current fill or stroke color, depending on whether the Fill or Stroke box is currently active on the Toolbox and Color palette.

Drag from the Fill or Stroke color box on the Toolbox or the Color palette to the Swatches palette to save that color as a swatch in the current file. You can merge swatches and perform other tasks via the palette menu.

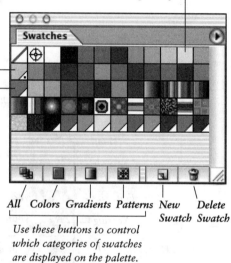

A nonglobal process color

A spot color

A global process color

All   Colors Gradients Patterns New   Delete
                                        Swatch Swatch

Use these buttons to control which categories of swatches are displayed on the palette.

Gradient palette

Use the Gradient palette to create new gradients and edit existing gradients. You can move a color by dragging its stop; choose a different color for a stop from the Color palette; click below the gradient slider to add a new color; move a midpoint diamond to adjust how adjacent colors are distributed; or change the gradient angle.

The gradient Type: Linear or Radial

*The **Midpoint** diamond marks the point where two adjacent colors are at an equal, 50/50 mix.*

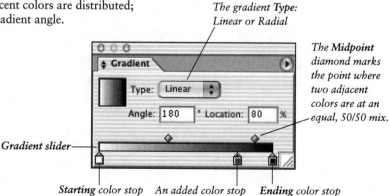

Gradient slider

Starting color stop   An added color stop   Ending color stop

Character palette

Use the Character palette to apply type attributes: font, size, leading, kerning, tracking, horizontal scale, vertical scale, baseline shift, character rotation, and foreign language options. To apply an attribute to currently highlighted text, choose a value from the pop-up menu; or click the up or down arrow; or enter a value in the field and press Return/Enter.

Text-related palettes

The palettes that are used for formatting text are opened from the Window > **Type** submenu: Character, Character Styles, Glyphs, OpenType, Paragraph, Paragraph Styles, and Tabs. Four of these palettes can be opened via a shortcut:

Character Cmd-T/Ctrl-T

OpenType Cmd-Option-Shift-T/ **NEW**
Ctrl-Alt-Shift-T

Paragraph Cmd-Option-T/Ctrl-Alt-T **NEW**

Tabs Cmd-Shift-T/Ctrl-Shift-T

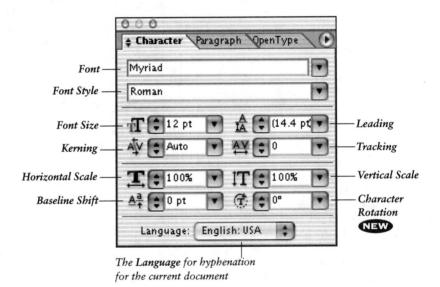

The **Language** for hyphenation
for the current document

Character Styles palette NEW

Character styles are collections of character attributes, such as font, point size, leading, tracking, and kerning. Unlike paragraph styles, which are applied to whole paragraphs, character styles are applied to bits and pieces here and there—bullets, boldfaced words, italicized words, large initial caps, etc. When character styles are applied to highlighted text within a paragraph, multiple attributes are applied at a time; when you edit a style, the text that it's associated with updates accordingly. Using the Character Styles palette, you can create, apply, edit, store, duplicate, and delete character styles.

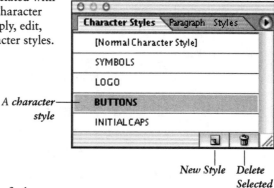

A character style

New Style   Delete Selected Styles

Glyphs palette NEW

Using the Glyphs palette, you can find out which character variations (alternate glyphs) are available for any given character in a specific font, and use the palette to insert glyphs from any font into your text (some of which can't be inserted via the keyboard).

Via the Show pop-up menu, you can control whether the palette displays glyphs of a specific category or for an entire font.

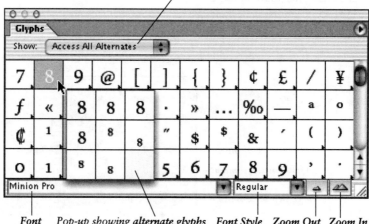

Font   *Pop-up showing **alternate glyphs** for an individual character*   *Font Style*   *Zoom Out*   *Zoom In*

Magic Wand palette

The Magic Wand tool selects objects that have the same or similar fill color, stroke color, stroke weight, opacity, or blending mode as the currently selected object. Using the Magic Wand palette, you can choose parameters for the tool. The Tolerance is the range within which the tool selects that attribute. For example, if you check Opacity, choose an opacity Tolerance of 10%, then select an object that has an opacity of 50%, the tool will find and select all objects that have an opacity between 40% and 60%.

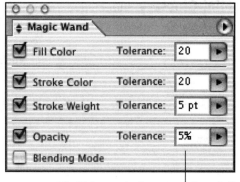

The Tolerance is the range within which the Magic Wand will find that attribute.

Symbols palette Shift-F11

Any Illustrator object can be stored on the Symbols palette for potential reuse in any document. To place one symbol onto the artboard, all you have to do is drag it out of the Symbols palette. A placed symbol is called an instance. The Symbol Sprayer tool is used to place multiple instances of a symbol in a document. Multiple instances form what is called a symbol set. Using symbols lets you create complex art quickly and easily.

Using any of the other symbolism tools (Symbol Shifter, Scruncher, Sizer, Spinner, Stainer, Screener, or Styler), you can change the closeness (density), position, stacking order, size, rotation, transparency, color tint, or style of multiple symbol instances in a symbol set, while still maintaining the link to the original symbol. If you edit the original symbol, any instances of that symbol in the document will update automatically.

Note: For a very brief synopsis of what the **Variables** palette does, see page 514. For more information about this advanced feature, refer to the Illustrator Help file or get ahold of *Real World Adobe Illustrator CS* by Deke McClelland (Peachpit Press).

Read about the **Flattener Preview** palette in Illustrator Help.

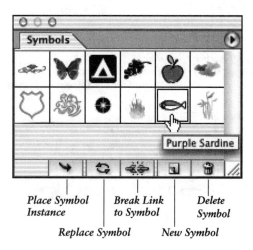

Place Symbol Instance

Break Link to Symbol

Delete Symbol

Replace Symbol

New Symbol

Magic Wand Palette; Symbols Palette

Mini-Glossary
A brief introduction to some of the terms that you'll encounter as you read this book.

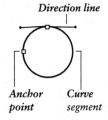

Objects

Closed path   *Open path*

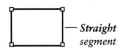

Direction line

Anchor point   *Curve segment*

— *Straight segment*

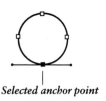

Selected object

Selected anchor point

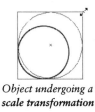

Object undergoing a scale transformation

Path (Or "object") Any individual shape that's created in Illustrator. A path can be open (a line with two endpoints) or closed (no endpoints). Path segments are joined together by smooth and/or corner anchor points.

Smooth anchor points have a pair of direction lines that move in tandem and form a straight line. Corner points can have no direction lines, one direction line, or a pair of direction lines that can be moved independently.

A curve segment can join two smooth points, or a corner point and a smooth point. A straight segment always joins two corner points. You can reshape any path by modifying its anchor points and/or segments.

Direction lines The pair of antennae that stick out from every smooth point. To reshape a curved segment, you'll rotate, lengthen, or shorten a direction line on the anchor point that connects the segment.

Select To highlight an object in the document window for editing. Only selected objects can be modified. When a whole object is selected, its anchor points are solid (not hollow). The Selection tool selects whole objects or groups; the Group Selection tool selects nested groups; the Direct Selection tool and Lasso tool select parts of objects; and the Magic Wand tool selects objects based on such criteria as fill color, stroke color, stroke weight, opacity, or blending mode.

Layer A tier of a document that holds a stack of objects. An illustration can contain multiple top-level layers and sublayers. The actual objects that make up an illustration (paths, type, mesh objects, etc.) are nested within top-level layers or sublayers.

Group Two or more objects that are united via the Group command so they can be moved or modified in unison.

Transform To rotate, scale, reflect, or shear an object, or create a blend between two objects.

Fill The color, pattern, or gradient that's applied to the inside of an object.

Stroke The solid color that's applied to the edge of an object.

Blend A multistep color and shape progression between two or more objects. If you reshape, recolor, or move any of the individual objects in a blend or reshape, move, or transform the path that controls the whole blend, the blend updates automatically.

Blend created using a circle and a star

Brush stroke A Calligraphic, Art, Scatter, or Pattern embellishment that's either applied to an existing path or drawn using the Paintbrush tool.

Art brush stroke

Gradient A gradual blending of two or more colors within an object. A gradient fill can be linear (side to side) or radial (radiating outward from a center point).

Mesh An editable object fill, composed of multicolored gradients along mesh lines, that's created by using either the Mesh tool or the Create Gradient Mesh command.

Radial gradient

Compound shape An editable (and reversible) union of overlapping objects produced via the Shape Mode buttons on the Pathfinder palette. If individual objects within a compound shape are moved, restacked, or reshaped, the overall compound shape readjusts accordingly.

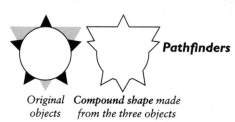

Mesh

Compound path Two or more objects combined into one object— that is, until or unless the compound path is released. Where the original objects overlapped, a transparent hole is created, through which shapes or patterns behind the object are revealed.

Pathfinders Commands on the Pathfinder palette that determine where selected paths overlap and then divide, trim, merge, crop, outline, or subtract from them to produce nonoverlapping (flattened) closed paths. These commands aren't reversible, except by using Undo.

Original objects   *Compound shape made from the three objects*

Clipping mask A command that uses an object to trim (clip) away parts of other objects that extend beyond its border. The clipped areas don't display or print. An opacity mask applies a mask based on opacity values.

(Continued on the following page)

Original objects   *Compound path made from the circle and star*

Mini-Glossary

Drop shadow effect

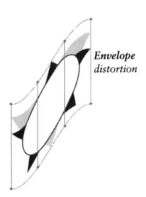

Symbol

Symbol set

Envelope distortion

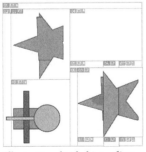

Illustration divided into slices

Appearances   Editable and removable attributes, such as multiple fills, strokes, effects, blending modes, transparency values, patterns, and brush strokes.

Style   A set of graphic appearance attributes that's saved to, and applied via, the Graphic Styles palette; a set of character attributes that's created and applied via the Character Styles palette; or a set of paragraph and character attributes that's created and applied via the Paragraph Styles palette.

Effects   Commands on the Effect menu that modify the appearance of an object without actually changing its path shape. Effects can be edited or removed at any time via the Appearance palette.

Symbol   Reusable objects that are stored on the Symbols palette and can be placed into any document. A placed symbol is called an instance; multiple instances form symbol sets. Instances can be modified by using the symbolism tools.

Liquify   Seven tools—Warp, Twirl, Pucker, Bloat, Scallop, Crystallize, and Wrinkle—that are used to reshape an object or objects. By pushing and pulling on an object's edges with one of these tools, you can reshape the object as you might sculpt a piece of clay. Many of the Effect commands also produce distortion.

Envelope   A special kind of container that's used for applying distortion. When you distort an envelope, everything within the envelope conforms to the distortion. Both an envelope and the object(s) it contains are fully editable.

Action   A recorded sequence of editing events that can be replayed on any object, file, or batch of files.

Optimization   The process in which file format, storage size, and color parameters are chosen for an image in order to maximize its quality yet enable it to download and display quickly on the Web.

Slicing   The division of areas in an illustration. When exporting an illustration using Illustrator's Save for Web dialog box, you can choose different optimization formats and settings for each slice in order to achieve faster download speeds. A separate export file is generated for each slice and the object or objects that it contains. Three types of slices can be created in Illustrator: object slices, text slices, and user slices.

Division the easy way

Let's say you want to reduce an object's width by 25%. Select the object, highlight the *entire* W field on the Transform palette, type "75%", then press Return/Enter. The width will be reduced to three-quarters of its current value (e.g., 4p becomes 3p). You could also click to the right of the current entry, type an asterisk (*), type a percentage value, then press Return/Enter.

Symbols you can use

Unit	Symbol
Picas	**p**
Points	**pt**
Inches	**" or in**
Millimeters	**mm**
Centimeters	**cm**
Q *(a type unit)*	**q**
Pixels	**px**

Points 'n' picas

12 pt = 1 pica

6 picas = 1 inch

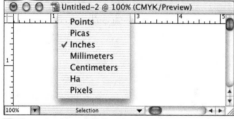

1 *You can choose* **Units** *via a* **context menu** *in the document window...*

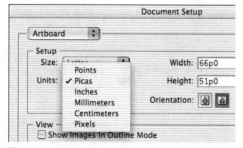

2 *...or from the* **Units** *pop-up menu in the* **Document Setup** *dialog box.*

Measuring up

The measurement unit that you choose for an individual document (instructions below) overrides the measurement unit that's chosen for the application in Illustrator (Edit, in Windows) > Preferences > Units & Display Performance. The current unit is used as the default value in entry fields in most palettes and dialog boxes, and on the rulers.

You can enter values in dialog boxes and palettes in any of the measurement units listed in the sidebar at left, regardless of the current default units. If you enter a value in a nondefault unit, it will be translated into the default unit when you press Tab or Return/Enter.

➤ If you enter the symbol for subtraction (-), addition (+), multiplication (*), division (/), or percent (%) after the current value in any field, Illustrator will do the math for you (see the sidebar).

➤ To enter a combination of picas and points, separate the two numbers by a "p". For example, 4p2 equals 4 picas plus 2 points, or 50 pt. Be sure to highlight the entire entry field first.

Follow the instructions below to change the measurement units just for the current document. To choose a measurement unit for the current and future documents, go to Illustrator (Edit, in Windows) > Preferences > Units & Display Performance.

To change the units for the current document:

If the rulers aren't showing, choose View > Show Rulers (Cmd-R/Ctrl-R), then Control-click/right-click either ruler and choose a unit from the context menu **1**.
or
Choose File > Document Setup (Cmd-Option-P/Ctrl-Alt-P); choose Artboard from the pop-up menu; choose Units: **Points, Picas, Inches, Millimeters, Centimeters,** or **Pixels 2**; then click OK.

➤ The current location of the pointer is indicated by a dotted line on both rulers. The higher the zoom level, the finer the ruler increments.

Multiple undos

To undo an operation, choose Edit > Undo (Cmd-Z/Ctrl-Z). To undo the second-to-last operation, choose Edit > Undo again, and so on. To reverse an undo, choose Edit > Redo (Cmd-Shift-Z/Ctrl-Shift-Z). You can also Control-click/right-click on the artboard and choose either command from the context menu. You can undo or redo after saving your document, but not after you close and reopen it.

Contextual menus

Contextual menus allow you to choose a command from an onscreen menu without having to mouse to the menu bar or even to a palette. To open a contextual menu (or "context menu," for short), Control-click/right-click on the artboard.

Context menu offerings change depending on which tool is selected and whether any objects are selected in your illustration **1**–**3**. Not all of the commands that appear on a context menu may be applicable to, or available for, the currently selected objects.

And don't forget

Use **tool tips** to help you identify palette buttons, swatch names, tool names, tool shortcuts, and other application features. Simply rest the pointer without clicking on a button, swatch, or icon, and a tip will pop up onscreen **4**.

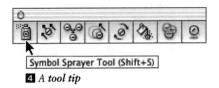

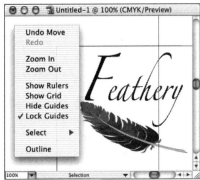

4 *A tool tip*

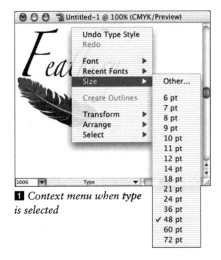

1 *Context menu when **type** is selected*

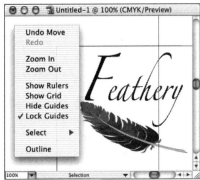

2 *Context menu when **nothing** is selected*

3 *Context menu when two **paths** are selected*

Undos; Contextual Menus

HOW ILLUSTRATOR WORKS 2

In this chapter you'll learn the basic differences between object-oriented and bitmap applications and you'll get a broad overview of how objects are created and modified in Illustrator.

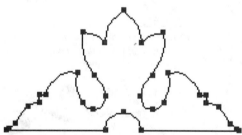

1 *Object-oriented graphics are sharp and crisp.*

2 *Objects in an object-oriented program are mathematically defined paths (this object is selected).*

Vectors and rasters

There are two main types of picture-making applications: bitmap (or "raster") and object-oriented (or "vector"), and it's important to know their strengths and weaknesses. Bitmap programs are ideal for creating soft, painterly effects, whereas object-oriented programs are ideal for creating sharp, smooth shapes and typographic designs (logos and the like).

Drawings created in **object-oriented** programs, such as Adobe Illustrator and Macromedia FreeHand, are composed of separate, distinct, mathematically defined objects or groups of objects. The vector objects that you create in Illustrator can be recolored, resized, and reshaped without diminishing their sharpness or smoothness, and can be moved around or restacked onto other layers or sublayers without disturbing other objects.

Vector objects have smooth and sharp edges regardless of the size at which they're displayed or printed **1**–**2**, and the higher the resolution of the printer, the sharper and finer the printed image. And thankfully, vector file sizes tend to be relatively small, so you can save multiple versions of a document without eating up too much disk space.

Images created in **bitmap** programs such as Photoshop, on the other hand, are composed of one or more layers of tiny squares on a grid, called pixels; each layer can be stacked above or below any other layer. When you edit a bitmap image, only the currently selected layer or areas you paint on are affected; you can't isolate independent objects, as you can in a vector program. If you zoom way in on a bitmap image, you'll see the checkerboard of tiny squares **1–2**. Bitmap files tend to be quite large, and their printout quality is dependent on their resolution. However, bitmaps are the way to go when you want to produce digital paintings, montages, or photorealistic images, or if you need to edit or retouch some photographs.

Although your Illustrator images will mostly consist of vector shapes, you can place or open raster images in Illustrator and apply some commands to them. You can also **rasterize** vector objects (convert them into bitmap images) and then apply filters to them.

How objects are made

In Illustrator, the key building blocks that you'll be using to compose an illustration are Bézier objects, type, and placed bitmap images. Bézier objects are composed of **anchor points** connected by **curved** or **straight segments.** The edge of an object that defines its shape is called its **path.** A path can be open (with two endpoints) or closed and continuous. You can close an open path by joining its endpoints or open a closed path with the Scissors tool.

Some Illustrator tools—such as the **Rectangle, Ellipse, Polygon, Star, Rectangular Grid, Polar Grid,** and **Flare**— produce complete, closed paths simply by clicking on the artboard. As a beginner, a good way to start is to create simple geometric objects, such as polygons or circles, with one of these tools, and then reshape them or combine them with other objects.

Other tools let you draw shapes "from scratch" by clicking or dragging with the mouse. The **Pencil** tool creates open freeform lines. The **Paintbrush** tool **3** can be used with its four categories of brushes to create **Calligraphic, Scatter, Art,** or **Pattern** brush strokes (start by experimenting with the brushes that Illustrator supplies, then later create some of your own). To draw straight lines quickly, you can draw with the **Line Segment** tool, or to draw partial curves, use the **Arc Segment** tool.

1 *A bitmap image*

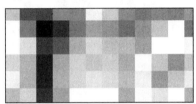

2 *Extreme closeup of a bitmap, showing the individual pixels that make up the image*

3 *Strokes drawn with the Paintbrush tool, using various brushes*

1 *Adobe Illustrator CS symbols, applied via the Symbol Sprayer tool*

2 *Horizontal path type*

3 *Vertical path type*

4 *Horizontal path type*

By using the most versatile tool of all, the **Pen,** you can create as many corner or curve anchor points as you need to form an object of virtually any shape imaginable. (It's not the easiest tool to master, so save it for a day when you're feeling peppy and clear-headed!)

If you want to use a scanned image as a starting point, you can place it onto a standard layer or a **template** layer and then trace its shapes, either manually with a drawing tool or automatically using the Auto Trace tool. You can also build documents by using one of the layout **templates** that Illustrator supplies, or by creating your own.

Another way to build graphics efficiently is by using **symbols** **1**. You'll use the Symbols palette or the Symbol Sprayer tool to place repetitive instances of a symbol into a document, and then use other symbolism tools (Shifter, Scruncher, Sizer, Spinner, Stainer, and Screener) to modify those instances.

The written word

Illustrator has six tools for creating **type,** a smorgasbord of features with which type can be styled and formatted, and many word processing features. Type can be freestanding (point type), it can flow along the edge of an object (path type) **2**–**4**, or it can fill the inside of an object of any shape (area type). Depending on which tool it was created with, type can flow (and be read) vertically or horizontally.

Once created or imported, your type can be repositioned, edited, restyled, recolored, transformed, or warped, and it can be threaded from one type object to another. You can even design your own characters by converting standard type into paths, called **outlines,** and then reshaping the outlines.

Editing tools

Objects must be **selected** before they can be modified, and there are five tools that let you do this mechanically (**Selection, Direct Selection, Group Selection, Lasso,** and **Magic Wand**), as well as a host of useful commands that let you select objects by criteria such as color, style, blending mode, etc.

How Illustrator Works

Objects can be modified by using an assortment of menu commands, filters, dialog boxes, 31 movable palettes, and 74 tools (see Chapter 1 for a full rundown). For fast access, you can use keyboard shortcuts to open and close many of the palettes; and you can shrink down or close the ones that you use infrequently to get them out of the way.

How it all shapes up

An object's contour can be reshaped by moving its anchor points or segments or by converting its curve **anchor points** 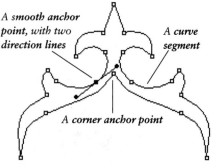 into corner anchor points (or vice versa). A curve segment can be reshaped by rotating, lengthening, or shortening its **direction lines**.

Some tools are specifically designed for modifying paths, such as the **Add Anchor Point** tool, which adds points to a path; the **Delete Anchor Point** tool, which deletes points from a path; the **Scissors** tool, which splits a path; and the **Convert Anchor Point** tool, which converts corner points into curve points, and vice versa.

Other tools are used like sculptors' utensils to change the contour of an object. The **Knife** tool carves out sections of an object; the **Smooth** tool removes points to create smoother curves; the **Erase** tool removes whole chunks of a path; and the **Pencil** and **Reshape** tools reshape an object by pushing or pulling on its contour.

And there are yet other ways to combine objects. For example, you could use the **Compound Path** command to cut a hole through an object to reveal underlying shapes, or use an object as a **clipping mask** to hide parts of other objects that extend beyond its edges. The **shape mode** buttons 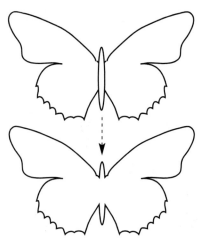 on the Pathfinder palette produce an editable compound shape from selected, overlapping objects; the **Pathfinder** buttons on the same palette divide areas where objects overlap into separate objects.

Still other modifications can be made using the **transformation** tools: the **Scale** tool enlarges or shrinks an object (**1**, next page) the **Rotate** tool rotates an object; the **Reflect**

A smooth anchor point, with two direction lines

A curve segment

A corner anchor point

1 *An object can be reshaped by manipulating its **anchor points and segments**.*

2 *The **Add to Shape Area** shape mode command combines multiple shapes into an editable compound shape.*

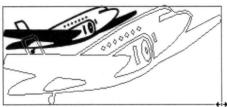

1 *Illustrator objects are very elastic: They can be rotated, reflected, sheared, or, as in this case, scaled.*

The original formation

2 *After applying the Transform Each command*

tool creates a mirror image of an object; the **Shear** tool slants an object; and the **Blend** tool or command transforms one object into another by creating a series of transitional shapes. Multiple transformations can be performed at once using the **Free Transform** tool, the **Transform Each** command **2**, or the **Transform** palette.

If you go in for extreme distortions, you'll enjoy using the **Warp, Twirl, Pucker, Bloat, Scallop, Crystallize,** or **Wrinkle** tool to mold or twist existing objects. Another option is to put an object or objects (even type) into an **envelope** and then manipulate points in the envelope mesh to reshape the object(s) inside it.

If you're the type that hates to do the same thing twice, you can automate repetitive tasks by saving a series of editing steps and commands as an **action** and then replaying your action in any file, or batch of files.

And finally, if you're the nervous type, relax—Illustrator has **multiple undo**s!

Gilding the lily

Using the **Color, Swatches, Gradient, Stroke, Transparency,** and **Brushes** palettes, you can apply colors, control stroke attributes, and add various kinds of embellishments to your objects.

You can **fill** the inside of any open or closed object with a **solid** color, a **gradient** (a smooth gradation between two or more colors), or a **pattern** of repeating tiles. You can also apply a solid-color (plain or dashed) **stroke** or a **brush stroke** to the edge of any object. The stroke and fill colors that you apply to objects can be from a matching system, such as PANTONE, or you can mix your own CMYK, HSB, or RGB colors. As for the patterns and gradients, you can use the ones that Illustrator supplies or you can create your own.

The **Transparency** palette lets you assign **opacity** levels to any type of object (even to placed raster images and type characters); apply **blending modes** to control how objects and layers interact; or use an object as an **opacity mask** in order to control the transparency of other objects.

Want more? If you've got a painter's touch, you'll enjoy using Illustrator's **gradient mesh** features. First you create a flexible, elastic armature, and then you apply multiple colors to it. The colors will blend smoothly and seamlessly from one area to the next, and can be edited at will.

How it all stacks up

The **Layers** palette exhibits and lists the complete stacking configuration of every top-level layer, sublayer, group, and object in an illustration. You can use this palette to select objects; target layers, groups, or objects for appearance changes; restack objects within the same layer; move or copy objects between layers; and turn lock, display, template, and print options on and off for individual layers, sublayers, groups, and objects.

Keeping up with appearances

Attributes that are listed on the **Appearance** palette change an object's appearance without changing its actual underlying path. Appearance attributes that can be applied to objects include multiple fills and strokes, transparency settings, blending modes, brush strokes, and Effect menu commands. Appearances, bless them, can be reedited, restacked, or removed at any time.

Whole sets of object attributes can be applied quickly using **graphic styles** . A graphic style can include just about any command that you would apply to a path, such as effects, fill and stroke attributes, opacity values, blending modes, and brush strokes. (Graphic styles are stored on the Graphic Styles palette, but are edited with the Appearance palette.)

On the **Effect** menu you'll find commands that change an object's appearance without changing its actual path, such as Feather, Drop Shadow, Inner Glow, Outer Glow, the **3D** effects (Extrude & Bevel, Revolve, and Rotate) as well as effect versions of most of the commands that are on the **Filter** menu. The vector filters and effects randomly

1 *Some Adobe Illustrator CS* *graphic styles applied to an object*

1 *Preview view*

2 *Outline view*

distort an object's shape or modify its color; the bitmap filters and effects add artistic, painterly touches or textures. The Filter menu commands permanently alter an object, whereas effects can be edited or removed from an object without causing the object to become permanently changed—only the object's appearance changes. There's even a **Convert to Shape** effect that allows you to change an object's contour (e.g., from round to square) without actually reshaping it. If you're a Web designer, you use this feature to create resizable buttons for type.

Onscreen

You can draw shapes "by eye" or you can use a variety of Illustrator features to help you work with more precision, such as **smart guides, ruler guides, grids,** the **Measure** tool, the **Move** dialog box, the **Align** palette, and the transform commands and palette, which we mentioned before.

You can zoom in on a small detail in an illustration as you work to facilitate editing and reduce eyestrain, then zoom back out to see the overall scheme. Illustrator does everything but squint for you. If a drawing is magnified onscreen, you can move it around in the document window by using the **Hand** tool or the **Navigator** palette.

An illustration can be displayed and edited in **Preview** view **1**, in which all the fill and stroke colors are displayed. Or to speed up editing and screen redraw and to make it easier to select anchor points, you can display your illustration in **Outline** view **2**, in which objects are displayed as wireframe outlines. **Pixel preview** mode lets you see how your vector objects will look when they're rasterized for the Web.

When all is said and done

There are many options for outputting your Illustrator artwork. They can be **color-separated** right from Illustrator or printed on an output device, such as a laser printer or imagesetter. Or if you want to **export** an Illustrator file to a page layout application (e.g., QuarkXPress, InDesign, or Microsoft Office), or to an image-editing application

How Illustrator Works

(e.g., Photoshop), you can save it in a wide assortment of file formats, such as Photoshop, EPS, and TIFF. Not surprisingly, Illustrator offers full support for the PDF format.

As for **Web** output, the goal is to make your page look as good as possible while minimizing its download time. Illustrator's **slicing** tools can be of help in this regard. First you define slice areas in a document **1**, and then you can choose different optimization (compression) options for each slice.

Illustrator's **Save for Web** dialog box offers an impressive collection of optimization features **2**. Here you can choose compression, transparency, and other options for a file, save it in an appropriate file format, such as GIF, JPEG, or PNG, and then preview it in a browser. Illustrator also lets you assign a URL to an object to create an image map, and then export the file for use as a clickable element on a Web page.

In addition to the standard output options mentioned above, you can also save files in the **SVG** format, a vector file format based on XML. This format allows for interactivity and scalability; stores shapes, paths, text, and SVG filter effects; and preserves color quality, all in a small, efficient file size. Illustrator also has a command for saving multiple layers in a document as **cascading style sheets** (CSS) to control how they're organized and displayed on the Web page, as well as a command that releases groups and objects to individual layers for export to an animation program.

Hopefully, this comprehensive description of features has whetted your appetite (and not scared you away!). Remember, unless you're very compulsive (or you mistakenly signed up for a four-semester course), you don't have to master every stinking feature. Start by creating some simple shapes, then expand into more complex objects as you broaden your repertoire. Many of the program features and commands will let you distort, reshape, recolor, embellish, transform, and combine paths with little effort or angst on your part. **Time to start drawing!**

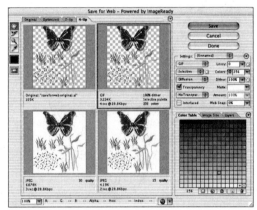

1 *An illustration divided into **slices***

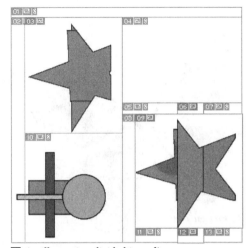

2 *This is the **Save for Web** dialog box with the 4-Up tab chosen. The original illustration is shown in the upper left corner; different optimization settings preview in the other three sections.*

STARTUP 3

In this chapter you'll learn how to launch Illustrator; create a new document; preview, open, and create templates; define the working and printable areas of a document; save a document in three different file formats; open an existing document; close a document; and quit/exit Illustrator.

1 *Click the Illustrator application icon in the Dock (or drag a file icon over the application icon).*

Creating files

A new document window doesn't appear automatically when you **launch** Illustrator. To create a new document after launching the application, see page 41.

To launch Illustrator in Macintosh:

Open the Adobe Illustrator CS folder in the Applications folder on the startup drive, then double-click the Illustrator CS application icon.

or

Click the Illustrator application icon in the Dock **1**.

or

Drag any Illustrator file icon **2** over the application icon in the Dock to both launch Illustrator and open that file.

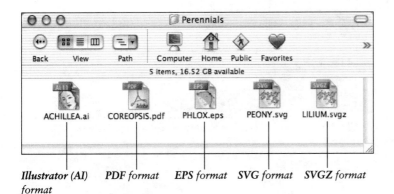

Illustrator (AI)   *PDF format*   *EPS format*   *SVG format*   *SVGZ format*
format

2 *You can open (and save) a file in any of these formats in Illustrator.*

A new document window doesn't appear automatically when you **launch** Illustrator. To create a new document after launching the application, see the instructions on the next page.

To launch Illustrator in Windows:

Open My Computer, double-click the hard drive icon where you installed Illustrator (the default is C:), follow the path Program Files/Adobe/Illustrator CS, then double-click the Adobe Illustrator CS icon to start the program.

or

Double-click an Illustrator file icon **1**.

or

Click the Start button on the taskbar, choose All Programs, then click the Adobe Illustrator CS shortcut **2**.

1 *Double-click an Illustrator file icon.*

2 *Click the Start button, then locate and click the application.*

Launch Illustrator in Windows

Layers as templates

You'll learn more about tracing images on pages 269–270, but here's a sneak preview. To trace a bitmap image, create or open an Illustrator document, then use File > **Place** with the **Template** option checked to import a TIFF, PICT, PSD, or EPS image. The image will appear on its own template layer, dimmed and uneditable. On another layer, use the **Pen, Pencil,** or **Auto Trace** tool to produce path shapes above the template.

To convert an existing top-level layer into a template layer, click the layer name on the Layers palette, then choose Template from the Layers palette menu; or double-click a top-level layer name, click Template, then click OK.

To create a new document:

1. Choose File > New (Cmd-N/Ctrl-N).

2. Type a Name for the new document **1**.

3. In the Artboard Setup area, choose dimensions for the document:

   From the Size pop-up menu, choose a preset size. For Web output, choose 640 x 480, 800 x 600, or 468 x 60. For print output, choose Letter, Legal, Tabloid, A4, A3, B5, or B4.
   or
   To enter custom dimensions, choose a measurement unit from the Units pop-up menu (use Pixels for Web output), then enter Width and Height values.

4. Click an Orientation button: Portrait (vertical) or Landscape (horizontal). This can be changed later.

5. Click a Color Mode for the document: CMYK Color for print output, or RGB Color for video or Web output.

6. Click OK. A new document window will open, at the maximum window size and zoom level for your monitor.

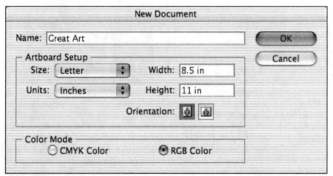

1 *In the* **New Document** *dialog box, type a name, choose dimensions for the artboard, and choose a color mode.*

Create New Document

Illustrator CS ships with 200 professionally designed **templates** that can be used as a starting point for creating industry-standard illustration layouts and projects. The templates include layers, styles, symbols, custom swatches, and more. If you're a new Illustrator user, seeing these features used in the templates will also give you a good idea of how they can be used in actual projects.

NEW **To preview the Illustrator templates:**

1. By default, a welcome screen **1** opens when Illustrator is launched. If you unchecked "Show this dialog at startup" to prevent it from opening upon launching, choose Help > Welcome Screen to make it appear onscreen.

2. In the welcome screen, click Cool Extras. Adobe Acrobat will launch, if it isn't already open, and a PDF file containing preview images of each template will open **2**. Take a look.

➤ The actual PDF file, named Additional Content.pdf, is located in the Adobe Illustrator CS application folder.

➤ You can't open a template directly from the PDF preview. To open a template file, follow the steps below.

The **New from Template** command opens a template file as a new, untitled document—content, specifications, and all—which can be edited like any other document; the original file is left intact.

On the following page we show you how to save a file as a template. You can also simply open any existing Illustrator file as an untitled document via the New from Template command, which is discussed in the following instructions. In either case, you're not limited to using the templates that ship with Illustrator.

NEW **To open a template or an existing file as an untitled document:**

1. Choose File > New from Template (Cmd-Shift-N/Ctrl-Shift-N).

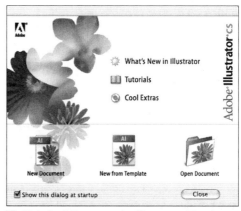

1 *Click* **Cool Extras** *on the Illustrator CS welcome screen.*

2 *The template preview document (Additional Content.pdf) as viewed in Adobe Acrobat. Click a bookmark button to preview template files in that category.*

1 *These two templates (CD label and disk label) are found in the Business Sets folder.*

2. To open an Illustrator template, in Macintosh, locate a template category folder in Applications/Adobe Illustrator CS/Templates; in Windows, locate a template category folder in Program Files\Adobe\Illustrator CS\Templates.

Open a template category folder, click a template name, then click New from Template. The template will open in a new document window **1**.

or

Select an existing Illustrator file, then click New from Template to open the file as an untitled document.

You can go the extra mile and **save** any of your own files as a **template.** Regardless of what kind of project you're working on—CD labels, business cards, book covers, Web graphics—a template can serve as a useful labor- and time-saving foundation. In creating a template, you can choose settings and layout aids such as guides, zoom level, and artboard dimensions; and also create swatches, symbols, graphic styles, and, of course, path objects.

To create a template: **NEW**

1. Create a new file. Create any path objects, swatches, graphic styles, symbols, etc. that you want saved in the template. You can also choose specifications for the artboard; choose a zoom level or custom views; create layers and guides; and create transparency flattener, PDF, or print presets. You can even create text boxes containing instructions for anyone who will be using the template.

2. Save the file by following steps 1–5 on page 46. In step 4, choose Illustrator Template (ait) from the Format (Mac)/ Save as Type (Windows) pop-up menu. Click Save. That's all there is to it.

Create Template

In the center of every Illustrator document is one nonmovable **artboard** work area 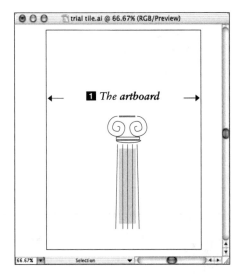. The dimensions of the artboard are chosen in the Size area of the New Document dialog box.

 Whatever Media (paper) Size is chosen in File > Print > General is what Illustrator considers to be the current printable page size. Letter size, for example, is 8½ x 11. You're not limited to an 8½ x 11 artboard or to the portrait format, though. That is, the artboard doesn't have to match the current media size or orientation.

To change the artboard dimensions or orientation:

1. Choose File > Document Setup (Cmd-Option-P/Ctrl-Alt-P).

2. Choose Artboard from the topmost pop-up menu.

3. From the Setup: Size pop-up menu, choose a preset size 2. For Web output, choose 640 x 480, 800 x 600, or 468 x 60. For print output, choose Letter, Legal, Tabloid, A4, A3, B5, or B4.
   or
   To enter custom dimensions, choose a measurement unit from the Units pop-up menu (use Pixels for Web output), then enter Width and Height values. Custom will become the selection on the Size pop-up menu. The maximum work area is 227 x 227 inches. *Note:* For the current document, the Units chosen here override the Units chosen in Illustrator (Edit,

in Windows) > Preferences > Units & Display Performance.

4. Click a different Orientation icon, if desired (1, next page).

5. Click OK.

➤ Objects (or parts of objects) outside the artboard will save with the illustration.

➤ Double-click the Hand tool to display the entire artboard in the document window.

➤ If you change the orientation, be sure to reset the ruler origin by double-clicking the upper left corner of the document, where the two rulers meet.

The artboard — caption within figure.

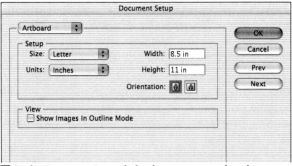

2 *In the Document Setup dialog box, you can either choose a preset Size or enter custom Width and Height values.*

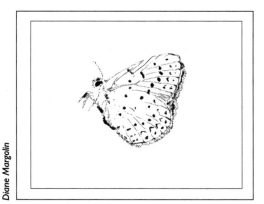

Diane Margolin

1 *The artboard in landscape orientation*

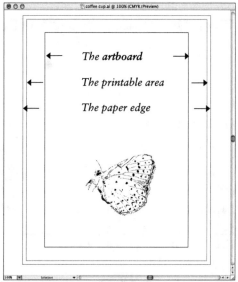

2 *Page Tiling showing. The size and/or orientation of the printable page doesn't have to match the size and/or orientation of the artboard.*

The artboard and printing NEW

In the default setup for printing, only objects (or parts of objects) that are within the artboard area will print.

You can use the Setup panel in File > Print to reposition the printable page in relation to the artboard. If the illustration is oversized, in the Setup panel you can specify that it be tiled (subdivided) into a grid so it will print in sections on the paper size for the currently chosen printer (see pages 452–453).

To view the relationship between the current artboard and the paper size for the currently chosen printer, choose View > Fit in Window and View > Show Page Tiling. The outer dotted rectangle that you see onscreen represents the paper size; the inner dotted rectangle represents the actual printable area, which accounts for the printer's nonprintable margins on the edge of the paper **2**.

➤ The Page tool can be used to reposition the printable page in relation to the artboard, but we prefer to use the Setup options in the Print dialog box.

For more information about printing from Illustrator CS, see Chapter 26.

Artboard and Printing

Saving files

You can choose from six formats when **saving** an Illustrator file: Illustrator (ai), Illustrator EPS (eps), Illustrator Template (ait), **NEW** Illustrator PDF (pdf), SVG Compressed (svgz), and SVG (svg). Files in all of these formats can be reopened and edited in Illustrator.

If you're going to print your file directly from Illustrator, we suggest using the **Illustrator** format (ai). One advantage of using this format is that it's based on the PDF format, so these files can also be opened in any application that reads PDF files.

If you're going to export your file to another application (e.g., a layout application for print or Web output), you'll need to choose one of the other formats, as not all applications can read native Illustrator (ai) files. Other export formats are discussed on pages 49–54 and pages 473–478; the SVG format is discussed on pages 509–511.

To save a file in the Illustrator format:

1. If the file has never been saved, choose File > Save (Cmd-S/Ctrl-S). If the file has already been saved in a different format, choose File > Save As.

2. Enter a name in Save As (Mac) 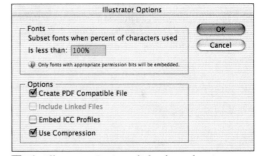/ File Name (Win) 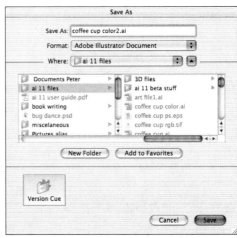. (Panther is shown in , next page.)

3. On the Mac, navigate to the desired folder or disk.

   In Windows, use the Save in pop-up menu to navigate to the folder in which you want to save the file.

4. On the Mac, make sure Adobe Illustrator Document is chosen from the Format pop-up menu.

   In Windows, choose Save as Type: Adobe Illustrator (*.AI).

5. Click Save. The Illustrator Options dialog box opens.

NEW 6. Under Fonts , enter a percentage in the "Subset fonts when percentage of characters used is less than" field to save fonts used in the illustration as part of the document. Characters in embedded fonts

1 *The Save As dialog box in Mac OS X, Jaguar*

2 *The Save As dialog box in Windows*

3 *The **Illustrator Options** dialog box, showing options for the native Illustrator format*

shortcuts for saving files

	Mac	Windows
Save	Cmd-S	Ctrl-S
Save As	Cmd-Shift-S	Ctrl-Shift-S
Save a Copy	Cmd-Option-S	Ctrl-Alt-S

1 *The Save As dialog box in Mac OS X, Panther*

will display and print on any system, even where they aren't installed, but keep in mind that this option increases the file storage size. At 100%, all font characters will be embedded.

If not all the characters in a particular font are used in your artwork, you can choose to embed just a subset of characters, as opposed to the whole font. This will help reduce the file size. For example, at a setting of 50%, the entire font will be embedded only if you use more than 50% of its characters in the file, and the Subset option will be used if you use fewer than 50% of its characters in the file.

7. Under Options, you can check:

Create PDF Compatible File to save a PDF-compatible version of the file for use in other Adobe applications. Checking this option increases the file storage size.

Include Linked Files to save a copy of any linked files with the illustration. (Read about linking on pages 261–265.)

If a profile was chosen in Edit > Assign Profile, check **Embed ICC Profiles** to embed those profiles in the file in order to color-manage the file.

Use Compression compresses vector data and PDF data (if included) to help reduce the file storage size.

8. Click OK.

➤ If Version Cue is enabled in Preferences > File Handling & Clipboard, you can click the Version Cue button in the Save dialog box to utilize the Version Cue file management features in the Adobe Creative Suite applications. Read about Version Cue in Illustrator Help.

The prior version of a file is overwritten whenever the **Save** command is executed. Do yourself a favor and save often—don't be shy about it! And be sure to create backups of your work, too.

To save an existing file:

Choose File > Save (Cmd-S/Ctrl-S).

You can use the **Save As** or **Save a Copy** command to save an existing file in a different format, such as Illustrator AI, Illustrator PDF, or Illustrator EPS. When you use Save As (discussed on the previous two pages), the new version of the file stays open onscreen; the original file closes but is preserved on disk. With Save a Copy, discussed below, the original version of the file stays open onscreen, and a copy of it is saved to disk.

To save a copy of an existing file:

1. Choose File > Save a Copy (Cmd-Option-S/Ctrl-Alt-S).

2. To save the file in the Illustrator (ai) format, follow the instructions starting on page 46. Other file formats are discussed on pages 49–54 and 473–478.

To revert to the last saved version:

1. Choose File > Revert.

2. Click Revert.

Include linked files?

If you check **Include Linked Files** in the EPS Options dialog box for an Illustrator file that contains a linked, placed EPS image, you won't need that original EPS image if you print the file from another program (e.g., QuarkXPress or InDesign). You'll still need the original EPS image to print the file from Illustrator, though. Also be aware that including linked files will increase the file storage size of the EPS.

If your Illustrator file contains linked, placed images and you *don't* check the Include Linked Files option when saving, you'll get a second chance to save with placed files, because an alert box will open. Just say yes.

Not all applications can read Illustrator (ai) files, and no preview options are available for this format. To prepare an Illustrator file for export to a page layout application or another drawing application, you'll need to save it in either the Illustrator EPS format or the PDF format. First, we'll discuss **EPS**.

The EPS (Encapsulated PostScript) format saves both vector and bitmap objects and is supported by most illustration and page layout programs. This makes it a good choice for files that are going to be printed from another application. Also, EPS files can be reopened and edited in Illustrator.

To save a file as EPS:

1. If the file hasn't yet been saved, choose File > Save (Cmd-S/Ctrl-S). If the file has already been saved in a different format, choose File > Save As or Save a Copy.

2. Choose Format/Save as Type: Illustrator EPS (eps) **1**, choose a location, then click Save. The EPS Options dialog box opens.

(Continued on the following page)

1 *In the Save As dialog box, choose Format/Save as Type: Illustrator EPS (eps).*

3. Choose a Preview Format **1**:

None for no preview. The image won't display onscreen in any other application, but it will print.

TIFF (Black & White) for a black-and-white preview.

TIFF (8-bit Color) for a color preview.

On the Mac, you can also choose **Macintosh (Black & White)** for a black-and-white PICT preview; or **Macintosh (8-bit Color)** for a color preview in the PICT format.

Note: Regardless of which preview option you choose, color information will be saved with the file and the illustration will print normally from Illustrator or any other application into which it's imported.

If you chose the TIFF (8-bit Color) format, click **Transparent** to save the file with a transparent background, or click **Opaque** to save it with a solid background. Choose Opaque if you're going to import the file into a Microsoft Office application.

4. From the Transparency: **Overprints** pop-up menu, choose **Preserve** to maintain the overprint information in the EPS file, or choose **Discard** to save the EPS file without any overprint information.

From the **Preset** pop-up menu, choose [High Resolution], [Medium Resolution], or [Low Resolution] to specify which flattening preset will be used when flattening is necessary (see page 462). For the Custom option, see Illustrator Help.

Take a minute to read any information messages 🛈 that you see in the dialog box to see if the document contains transparency that will require flattening, and also to learn how overprints in transparent areas will be handled.

5. Under Fonts, check **Embed Fonts (for other applications)** to save any fonts used in the file as a part of the file so they'll display and print properly on any system, even where they aren't installed. Check this option if your Illustrator file contains type and you're going to import it into a layout application.

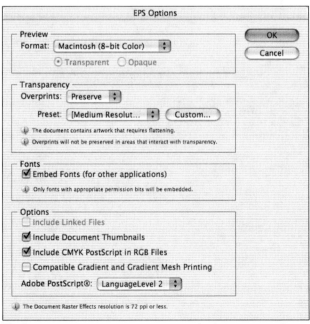

1 *Choose Preview, Transparency, Font, and other options in the* **EPS Options** *dialog box.*

6. *Check any of these optional boxes:*

Include Linked Files to save a copy of any linked, placed files with the illustration (see the sidebar on page 49).

Include Document Thumbnails to save a thumbnail of the file for previewing in Illustrator's Open or Place dialog box.

Include CMYK PostScript in RGB Files to enable RGB files to print from programs that output only CMYK color. RGB colors will be preserved as RGB if the EPS file is reopened in Illustrator.

Compatible Gradient and Gradient Mesh Printing to include instructions to help older PostScript printers print gradients and meshes. If your printer isn't having problems printing gradient and meshes, leave this option unchecked.

7. Choose **Adobe PostScript®:** LanguageLevel 2 or LanguageLevel 3, whichever option conforms to your printing device. Choose LanguageLevel 3 if the file contains gradient meshes and will be output to a Level 3 printer.

8. Click OK. If you didn't check Include Linked Files and your file contains placed, linked images, an alert dialog box will appear. Click Embed Files or Preserve Links **1**.

9. If your illustration is in CMYK mode (File > Document Color Mode > CMYK Color) and it contains a placed, linked RGB TIFF or EPS image, an alert dialog box will appear **2**.

➤ RGB color objects are saved as RGB in an Illustrator EPS file if its Document Color Mode is RGB Color.

➤ Images that are dragged and dropped or copied and pasted from Photoshop to Illustrator are converted to the illustration's current Document Color Mode setting.

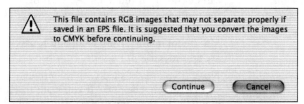

1 *This prompt will appear if you **didn't** check **Include Linked Files** in the EPS Format Options dialog box and your file contains placed, linked images. Here's your second chance to include those placed files.*

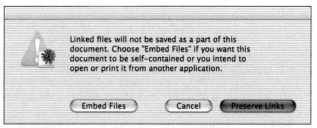

2 *This prompt will appear if you save, as EPS, an Illustrator file in CMYK Color mode that contains linked RGB images from other applications.*

Adobe PDF (Portable Document Format) is a good choice when preparing an Illustrator file for display on the Web. It's also useful when transferring files to another application or computer platform that reads PostScript-based Adobe PDF files. The only software users will need in order to view a PDF file is either Acrobat Reader or Adobe Reader 6 (both free of charge!)—they won't need the Illustrator application. The artwork will look as it was originally designed, as this format preserves all object attributes, groups, fonts, and text, and saves RGB colors as RGB and CMYK colors as CMYK. In the Acrobat 6 format, Illustrator layers can be saved as Acrobat layers. PDF files can also be viewed and edited using Acrobat, and this format supports document text search and navigation features.

You can open one page of a multipage PDF file in Illustrator, edit vector graphics or bitmap images on the page, if you like, and then resave the page in PDF format. If you save an Illustrator file as PDF and then reopen or place it in Illustrator, you'll still be able to edit individual objects as usual.

NEW **To save a file as an Adobe PDF:**

1. If the file has never been saved, choose File > Save (Cmd-S/Ctrl-S). If the file has already been saved, choose File > Save As or Save a Copy (see page 48).

2. Type a name in Save As/File Name field, choose a location in which to save the file, choose Format/Save as Type: Adobe PDF (pdf), then click Save. The Adobe PDF Options dialog box opens.

3. *Optional:* From the **Preset pop-up menu** 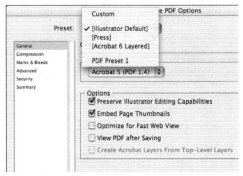, choose one of these predefined settings:

   [**Illustrator Default**] preserves all the data from an Illustrator document so it can be reopened in Illustrator without any data loss. The resulting file is Acrobat 5-compatible, fonts are embedded, the resolution of any bitmap images is left unchanged, and no compression is applied.

Reopening a PDF

Because PDF is the basis for the Illustrator (ai) file format, if you save a file in Adobe PDF format and then reopen it in Illustrator CS, all object attributes will be preserved and be fully editable, and image links will be preserved.

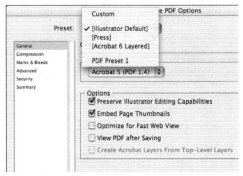

1 *The Preset pop-up menu in the Adobe PDF Options dialog box*

[**Press**] for print output. The resulting file is Acrobat 4-compatible, all fonts are automatically embedded, compression is JPEG, the quality is Maximum, and custom color and high-end image options are preserved. This preset produces the highest image quality, but in order to accommodate the included data, the resulting file size is larger.

[**Acrobat 6 Layered**] for an Acrobat 6-compatible file (obviously!). Top-level layers from Illustrator are preserved and can be shown or hidden in Acrobat 6; the resolution of any bitmap images is downsampled; JPEG compression, with Maximum quality, is applied; and fonts are embedded.

Note: If you're satisfied with the preset you've chosen, click OK. If you want to manually change any of the settings and create a custom preset, proceed with the remaining steps.

Save as PDF

The following is a summary of available features:

4. Click one of the five categories at the left of the dialog box to display that panel.

5. In the General panel **1**, choose Compatibility: **Acrobat 4, Acrobat 5,** or **Acrobat 6.** The Acrobat 6 format preserves top-level layers. Acrobat 5 and Acrobat 6 preserve transparency. The Acrobat 4 format requires that areas of transparency be flattened in order to preserve the appearance of transparency. *Note:* Not all applications can read Acrobat 6 files yet.

Check **Preserve Illustrator Editing Capabilities** if you want the option to reopen and edit the file in Illustrator. This option will limit how much the file can be compressed.

For the Acrobat 6 Compatibility option, check Create Acrobat Layers From Top-level Layers to preserve the ability to work with layers when the file is opened in Acrobat 6.

Check **Embed Page Thumbnails** to save a thumbnail of the file (or the page).

For the other Options check boxes, see Illustrator Help.

6. In the Compression panel (**1**, next page) choose a downsampling option from all of the leftmost pop-up menus:

If your PDF will output to print, choose **Do Not Downsample** to retain all pixel data. If your PDF will be placed in a Web-page creation program, choose a **compression** method. Downsampling reduces the image resolution by averaging nearby pixels and combining them to form one pixel. If an image is downsampled too much, its quality will also be diminished too much. Enter the desired final resolution and enter the resolution value that a placed bitmap image must have to be downsampled. For onscreen output, keep the final value at 72 ppi.

Choose a compression type from the pop-up menus. Choose Automatic to have

(Continued on the following page)

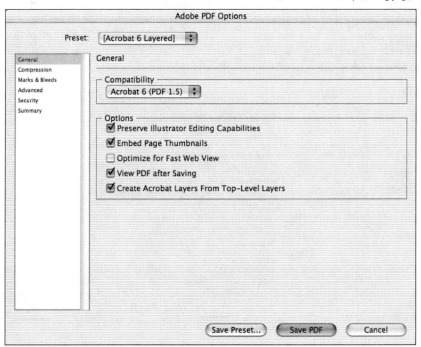

1 *The General panel in the Adobe PDF Options dialog box*

Illustrator choose the appropriate compression and quality settings for your file. (For information about the compression methods, see Illustrator Help.)

Leave Compress Text And Line Art checked to have ZIP compression, a lossless method, be used on all text and line art in the file.

7. In the **Marks & Bleeds** panel, specify printer marks and bleed options for the PDF file. For information about these features, see page 454–455.

8. In the Advanced panel (**1**, next page) if profiles were chosen in Edit > Assign Profile, check **Embed ICC Profiles** to embed those profiles into the file in order to color-manage the file.

The PDF format automatically embeds all the fonts used in the file. If not all the characters in a particular font were actually used in your artwork, you can choose to embed just a subset of characters to help reduce the file size of the PDF. To do this, enter a percentage in the "Subset fonts when percentage of characters used is less than" field. If you enter 50%, for example, the entire font will be embedded if you use more than 50% of its characters in the file; and the Subset

Saving PDF settings NEW

Now there's a way to preserve all the choices you've made in the Adobe PDF Options dialog box. Click **Save Preset** in that dialog box to create a preset of the current PDF settings, enter a name for the preset, then click OK. Saved presets can be chosen from the Preset pop-up menu at the top of the dialog box. What's more, PDF presets can also be created and edited by choosing Edit > PDF Presets (see page 467).

option will be used if you use fewer than 50% of its characters.

When Acrobat 4 is chosen as the Compatibility option, you also need to choose Overprint and Transparency Flattener options. Choose to preserve or discard overprint areas in the PDF file. For information on the Transparency Flattener feature, see pages 462–465. Acrobat 5 and 6 automatically preserve overprinting and transparency.

9. The Summary panel will list the settings you've chosen for each category, for your perusing pleasure. Expand any category to view its settings.

10. Click OK.

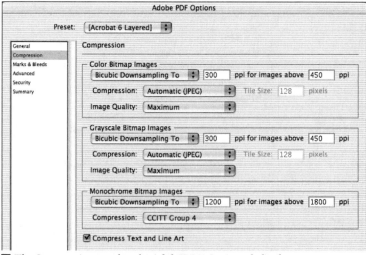

1 *The Compression panel in the Adobe PDF Options dialog box*

Save as PDF

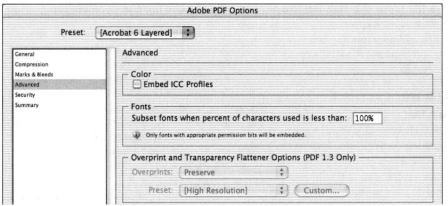

1 *The Advanced panel in the Adobe PDF Options dialog box*

2 *The Open dialog box in Mac OS X, Panther*

Opening files

Follow these instructions to **open** a file in Illustrator (ai) format. (Follow the instructions on page 259 to open other types of files.)

To open a file from within Illustrator:

1. Choose File > Open (Cmd-O/Ctrl-O).

2. On the Mac, choose Show: All Readable Documents to list only files in the formats Illustrator can read. In Windows, choose Files of Type: All Formats.

3. Locate and highlight a file name **2**–**4**, then click Open or double-click a file name. If you get an alert dialog box about a linked file, see page 264. To learn about updating legacy text (text from earlier program versions), see pages 222–223.

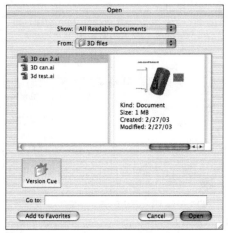

3 *The Open dialog box in Mac OS X, Jaguar*

4 *The Open dialog box in Windows*

To open a file from the Mac Desktop or from Windows Explorer:

Double-click an Illustrator file icon. Illustrator will launch if it hasn't already been launched **1**.

Ending a work session

To close a file:

On the Mac, click the close (red) button in the upper left corner of the document window (Cmd-W).

In Windows, click the close box in the upper right corner of the document window (Ctrl-W).

If the illustration was modified since it was last saved, an alert dialog box will appear **2**. You can close the file without saving (click Don't Save); save the file (click Save); or cancel the close operation (click Cancel).

➤ Hold down Option/Alt and choose Close (or Option-click the close button/Alt-click the close box) to close all currently open Illustrator files.

To quit/exit Illustrator:

On the Mac, choose Illustrator > Quit Illustrator (Cmd-Q).

In Windows, choose File > Exit (Ctrl-Q) or click the application window's close box.

All open Illustrator files will close. If changes were made to any open files since they were last saved, an alert dialog box will appear. To save the file(s), click Save, or to quit/exit without saving, click Don't Save.

A message for the [Converted]

By default, Illustrator CS automatically appends the word **[Converted]** to files from an earlier version of Illustrator that are opened in CS. If you want to prevent this from happening, go to Preferences > General and uncheck Append [Converted] Upon Opening Legacy File. If you do uncheck this option, remember to rename your file yourself by using the Save As command—don't open a legacy file for editing and use the Save command to save over the original.

Missing fonts

If you open a file that uses a font that's unavailable to the system, the **Font Problems** dialog box will appear **3**. Click Open to open the document as is, or click Cancel. If a missing font subsequently becomes available to the system, it will become available on Illustrator's font lists and the type will redisplay correctly without any action required on your part.

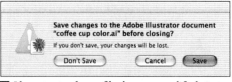

1 *Double-clicking an existing Illustrator file icon will cause the application to launch, if it hasn't already been launched.*

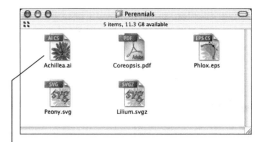

2 *If you try to close a file that was modified since it was last saved, this prompt will appear.*

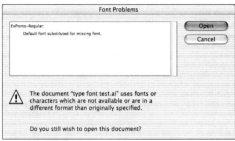

3 *The Font Problems alert dialog box will appear if you open a file that uses fonts that aren't available.*

VIEWS 4

In this chapter you'll learn how to change zoom levels, change views (Preview, Outline, or Pixel Preview), create custom view settings, change screen display modes, and move an illustration in its window.

Changing views

To use the Navigator palette to change the zoom level of an illustration:

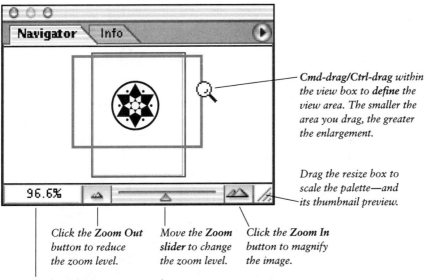

Cmd-drag/Ctrl-drag *within the view box to define the view area. The smaller the area you drag, the greater the enlargement.*

Drag the resize box to scale the palette—and its thumbnail preview.

*Click the **Zoom Out** button to reduce the zoom level.*

*Move the **Zoom slider** to change the zoom level.*

*Click the **Zoom In** button to magnify the image.*

*Enter the desired **zoom percentage** between 3.13% and 6400%, then press Return/Enter. To zoom to a percentage and keep the field highlighted, press Shift-Return/Shift-Enter.*

➤ You can also change the zoom level by double-clicking the zoom field in the lower left corner of the document window, typing the desired zoom percentage (up to 6400%), and then pressing Return/Enter.

➤ To separate the Navigator from its palette group, drag its tab (palette name).

Within the document window, you can display the entire artboard, an enlarged detail of an illustration, or any zoom level in between. The **zoom level** (3.13%–6400%) is indicated as a percentage both on the title bar and in the lower left corner of the document/application window. 100% is actual size. An illustration's zoom level has no bearing on its printout size.

To choose a preset zoom level:

Choose View > Zoom In (Cmd-+/Ctrl-+). Repeat to magnify further.
or
Choose View > Zoom Out (Cmd--/Ctrl--). Repeat, if desired.
or
Make sure no objects are selected, Control-click/right-click on the image, then choose Zoom In or Zoom Out from the context menu **1**.
or
Choose a preset percentage from the zoom pop-up menu in the lower left corner of the document/application window **2**. Or choose Fit On Screen from the pop-up menu to make the artboard fit within the current document window size.
or
Double-click in the zoom field in the lower left corner of the document/application window, type in the desired magnification, then press Return/Enter.

➤ Choose View > Fit In Window (Cmd-0/Ctrl-0) or double-click the Hand tool to display the entire artboard in the document window.

➤ To apply a new Zoom value without exiting the zoom field, press Shift-Return/Shift-Enter.

1 *Make sure no objects are selected, then Control-click/right-click on an image and choose* **Zoom In** *or* **Zoom Out** *from the context menu.*

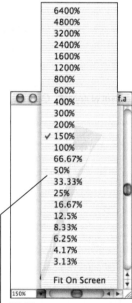

2 *Choose a* **preset percentage** *from the zoom pop-up menu in the lower left corner of the document/application window.*

Brush by Diane Margolin

1 *Drag with the* **Zoom** *tool.*

2 *The illustration is* **magnified.**

To change the zoom level using the Zoom tool:

1. Choose the Zoom tool (Z).

2. Click on the illustration in the center of the area that you want to enlarge, or drag a marquee across an area to magnify that area **1**–**2**. The smaller the marquee, the greater the degree of magnification. (To move the illustration in the document window, see pages 63–64.)
   or
   Option-click/Alt-click in the illustration to reduce the zoom level.
   or
   Drag a marquee, and then, without releasing the mouse, press and hold down the Spacebar, move the marquee over the area you want to magnify, then release the mouse.

➤ To display an illustration at actual size (100%), double-click the Zoom tool or choose View > Actual Size (Cmd-1/Ctrl-1). *Note:* If you double-click the Zoom tool when your illustration is at a small zoom level, the white area around the artboard may appear in the document window instead of the illustration. Use the Navigator palette or the Hand tool to reposition the illustration in the document window.

➤ You can click to change the zoom level while the screen is redrawing.

This method for changing the **zoom level** using the **keyboard** makes for speedier picture editing.

To change the zoom level using the keyboard:

To magnify the illustration with any tool other than Zoom selected, Cmd-Spacebar-click/Ctrl-Spacebar-click or -drag in the document window.
or
To reduce the zoom level, Cmd-Option-Spacebar-click/Ctrl-Alt-Spacebar-click.

Zoom Tool; Zoom Shortcuts

An illustration can be displayed and edited in four different **views:** Preview, Outline, Pixel Preview, or Overprint Preview. In all views, the other View menu commands—Hide/Show Edges, Artboard, Page Tiling, Slices, Guides, and Grid—are accessible, and any selection tool can be used. (Overprint Preview view is discussed on page 457.)

To change the view:

From the View menu, choose Preview (Cmd-Y/Ctrl-Y) to display all the objects with their fill and stroke colors as well as all placed images, or choose Outline (Cmd-Y/Ctrl-Y) to display all the objects as wireframes with no fill or stroke colors. The screen redraws more quickly in Outline view.

or

Make sure no objects are selected (click in a blank area of the artboard), then Control-click/right-click and choose Outline or Preview from the context menu **1**–**2**.

or

Choose Pixel Preview (Cmd-Option-Y/Ctrl-Alt-Y toggles it on and off) to turn on a 72 ppi display **3**. Use this view for Web graphics work.

➤ Let's say you've got a large file on a slow machine and you start to view it in all its glory in Preview view—nah, on second thought, you decide to preview it later. Press Esc to cancel the preview.

➤ You won't learn much about layers until you get to Chapter 11, but just to give you a little hint of what's to come, you can Cmd-click/Ctrl-click an eye icon for a layer (not an object) on the Layers palette to toggle between Preview and Outline views just for that layer.

(Overprint Preview view is discussed on page 457.)

It's a snap

In **Pixel Preview** view, you can get a good inkling of what your vector graphics will look like when they're rasterized for the Web (choose View > Actual Size first). But Pixel Preview is more than just a preview. When you choose this view, View > **Snap to Pixel** is turned on automatically. When Snap to Pixel is on (and Use Preview Bounds is off in Preferences > General), the edges of objects will snap to the nearest pixel edge as they're moved or reshaped. Snap to Pixel reduces the need for anti-aliasing and helps keep edges crisp. (Anti-aliasing adds pixels along the edges of objects to make them look smoother but can also diminish their crispness.)

1 *Deselect all objects, then choose* **Outline** *(or* **Preview***) from the context menu. This is* **Preview** *view.*

| Undo Move |
| Redo |
| Zoom In |
| Zoom Out |
| Show Rulers |
| Show Grid |
| Hide Guides |
| ✓ Lock Guides |
| Select ▶ |
| Outline |

2 *Outline view*

3 *Pixel Preview view*

Change Views

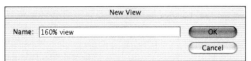

1 *Type a* ***Name*** *for the view in the* ***New View*** *dialog box.*

2 *Choose a* ***custom*** *view from the bottom of the* ***View*** *menu.*

You can define and save up to 25 **custom views** that you can switch to quickly using an assigned shortcut, and you can specify whether your illustration will be in Preview view or Outline view for each setting that you define.

To define a custom view:

1. Choose a zoom level for your illustration and choose scroll bar positions.
2. Put your illustration into Preview or Outline view (Cmd-Y/Ctrl-Y).
3. Choose View > New View.
4. Type a descriptive name for the new view in the Name field, as in "160% view" **1**.
5. Click OK.

To choose a custom view:

Choose the view name from the bottom of the View menu **2**.

➤ You can switch views at any time, even after choosing a custom view. For example, if your illustration is at a custom view for which you chose Outline view but you want to display your illustration in Preview view, choose View > Preview.

To rename or delete a custom view:

1. Choose View > Edit Views.
2. Click the name of the view you want to rename or delete **3**.
3. Change the name in the Name field.
   or
   Click Delete to delete the view.
4. Click OK. The View menu will update to reflect the changes.

➤ If you want to rename more than one view, you have to click OK, and then reopen the dialog box for each one.

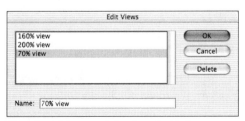

3 *In the* ***Edit Views*** *dialog box, highlight a view, then change the* ***Name*** *or click* ***Delete****.*

Custom Views

The number of Illustrator documents that can be open at a time is limited only by the amount of RAM (random access memory) currently available to Illustrator. To activate a currently open window, you can either click in it or choose the document name from the list of open documents at the bottom of the Window menu **1**.

To facilitate editing, an illustration can be displayed simultaneously in **two windows.** You could choose a high zoom level for one window (such as 200%) to edit small details and a lower zoom level for the other so you can see the whole illustration. Or in one window you could hide individual layers or display individual layers in Outline view and in another window you could preview all the layers together.

Note: The illustration in the window for which Preview view is selected will redraw each time you modify the illustration in the window for which Outline view is chosen. In this case, you won't save processing or redraw time when you work in the Outline window.

To display an illustration in two windows:

1. Open an illustration.

2. Choose Window > New Window. A new window of the same size will appear on top of the first window. It will bear the same title, followed by ":2" **2**.

3. On the Mac, reposition the new window by dragging its title bar so the original and new windows are side by side, and resize one or both of them.

   In Windows, you can choose any of these Window menu commands: **Cascade** arranges the currently open illustrations in a stair-step configuration; **Tile** arranges the open windows side by side; and **Arrange Icons** moves the minimized windows to the bottom of the application window.

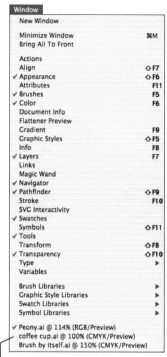

1 *The **currently open** documents are listed at the bottom of the Window menu.*

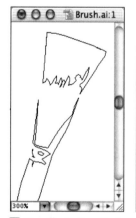

2 *One illustration displayed in **two windows***

One Illustration in Two Windows

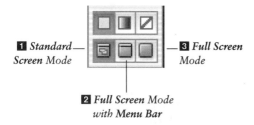

1 *Standard Screen Mode*

3 *Full Screen Mode*

2 *Full Screen Mode with Menu Bar*

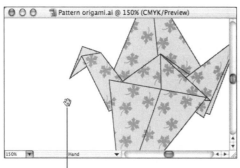

4 *Spacebar-drag in the document window to move the illustration.*

To change the screen display mode:

Click the **Standard Screen Mode** button at the bottom of the Toolbox **1** to display the image, menu bar, and scroll bars in the document window. This is the default mode.

or

Click the **Full Screen Mode with Menu Bar** (second) button **2** to display the image and the menu bar but not the scroll bars. The area around the image will be white.

or

Click the **Full Screen Mode** (third) button **3** to display the image but not the menu bar and scroll bars. The area around the image will be white.

➤ Press "F" to cycle through the three modes.

➤ Press Tab to hide (or show) all currently open palettes, including the Toolbox; press Shift-Tab to hide (or show) all the palettes, leaving the Toolbox.

➤ Choose View > Hide Artboard. Choose the command again to redisplay the artboard.

Getting around

To move an illustration in its window using the Hand tool:

Click any of the scroll arrows on the edge of the document window.

or

Choose the Hand tool (H) 🖐 (or hold down the Spacebar to turn any other tool into the Hand tool temporarily), then drag the illustration to the desired position **4**.

➤ Double-click the Hand tool to fit the entire artboard in the document window.

Screen Display Modes; Move the Illustration

To move the illustration in its window using the Navigator palette:

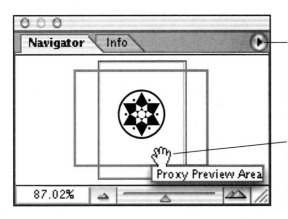

*Choose **View Artboard Only** from the palette menu to have the palette display only objects that are on the artboard. This is like a quick print preview.*

*Move the illustration in its window by dragging the **view box**. Or **click** the illustration thumbnail to display that area of the illustration.*

➤ To change the color of the view box frame from its default red, choose Palette Options from the Navigator palette menu, then choose a preset color from the Color pop-up menu or double-click the color swatch and choose a color from the system Color palette. Check "Draw dashed lines as solid lines" if you want dashed lines to display as solid lines on the palette.

➤ The proportions of the view box match the proportions of the document window. Resize the document window and you'll see what we mean.

➤ The Navigator palette will display multiple pages, if any, and tiling of the imageable area.

➤ To halt a slow screen redraw, press Esc. The display will change to Outline view. Choose View > Preview (Cmd-Y/Ctrl-Y) to restart the redraw.

Move Illustration in Window

In Illustrator, paths (objects) are composed of anchor points connected by straight and/or curved line segments. Paths can be open or closed. Rectangles and ovals are closed paths (they have no endpoints); lines are open paths. As you'll learn in Chapter 8, any path can be reshaped.

In this chapter, you'll first learn how to delete objects, for future reference. Then you'll learn how to create objects quickly using the Rectangle, Rounded Rectangle, Ellipse, Polygon, Star, Flare, Line Segment, Arc, Spiral, Rectangular Grid, and Polar Grid tools. And finally, you'll learn how to draw in a freehand style using the Pencil tool. Once you've learned the basics in this chapter, don't miss these other important chapters: 6, Select/Copy; 7, Transform; 8, Reshape; and 9, Fill & Stroke.

Danny Pelavin builds crisp, effective illustrations using basic geometric shapes.

Deleting objects

You'll be creating lots of different shapes in this chapter, and your artboard may start to get crowded with junk. To remove an object that you've just created, Undo (Cmd-Z/Ctrl-Z). To **remove** an object that's been lying around, follow these instructions.

To delete one object:

1. Choose the Selection tool (V), ▶ then click the object you want to delete.

2. Press Delete/Backspace or Del or choose Edit > **Cut** (Cmd-X/Ctrl-X) or Edit > **Clear.**

➤ If you're using the Direct Selection tool and only some of the object's points are selected, press Delete/Backspace or Del twice to delete the whole object.

To delete a bunch of objects:

1. Marquee the objects you want to remove, using the Selection tool (V), ▶ or use any of the other methods for selecting multiple objects that are described in the next chapter.

2. Press Delete/Backspace or Del.

Drawing geometric objects

To create a rectangle or an ellipse by dragging:

1. Choose the Rectangle tool (M) 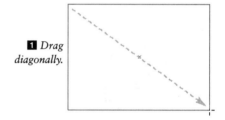 or the Ellipse tool (L).

2. Drag diagonally **1**. As you drag, you'll see a wireframe representation of the rectangle or oval. When you release the mouse, the rectangle or oval will be selected, and it will be colored with the current fill and stroke settings (Preview view).

➤ To create a series of perfectly aligned, equal-size rectangles, create or select a rectangle, then use Object > Path > Split into Grid (see page 423).

To create a rectangle or an ellipse by specifying dimensions:

1. Choose the Rectangle tool (M) or the Ellipse tool (L).

2. Click on the artboard where you want the object to appear.

3. In the Rectangle or Ellipse dialog box, enter dimensions in the Width and Height fields **2**. To create a circle or a square, enter a number in the Width field, then click the word Height (or vice versa)—the value in one field will copy into the other field.

4. Click OK.

➤ Values in dialog boxes in the current illustration are displayed in the measurement units currently chosen from the Setup: Units pop-up menu in File > Document Setup.

Extras

Draw a rectangle or oval from its **center**	Option-drag/Alt-drag
Move a rectangle or ellipse as you draw it	Spacebar-drag
Draw a **square** with the Rectangle tool or a **circle** with the Ellipse tool	Shift-drag

Recoloring: Sneak preview

You'll learn all about Illustrator's fill and stroke controls in Chapter 9, but here's a sneak preview. Select an object, click the **Fill** or **Stroke** box (square) on the **Toolbox** or the **Color** palette, then click a swatch on the **Swatches** palette or click the color bar on the **Color** palette.

1 *Drag diagonally.*

2 *Enter Width and Height values in the Rectangle (or Ellipse) dialog box. The dimensions of the last-drawn object will display when the dialog box opens.*

Circles, rectangles, and polygons (triangles)

Daniel Pelavin

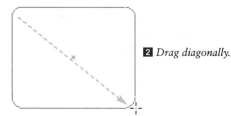

1 Rounded Rectangle Tool

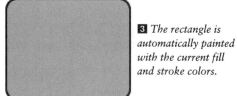

2 *Drag diagonally.*

3 *The rectangle is automatically painted with the current fill and stroke colors.*

To create a rounded rectangle:

1. Choose the Rounded Rectangle tool **1**. 🔲

2. Drag diagonally. As you drag, you'll see a wireframe representation of the rounded rectangle **2**. When you release the mouse, the rounded rectangle will be selected and colored with the current fill and stroke colors (Preview view) **3**.

➤ As you create an object with the Rounded Rectangle tool, keep the mouse button down and press the up arrow to make the corners rounder, or the down arrow to make them more square. Press (don't hold) the left or right arrow to toggle between square and round corners.

➤ To draw a rounded rectangle of a specific size, choose the Rounded Rectangle tool, click on the artboard, then enter Width, Height, and Corner Radius values.

➤ The Corner Radius value, which controls the degree of curvature in the corners of rounded rectangles, can be specified in Illustrator (Edit, in Windows) > Preferences > General: Corner Radius or in the Corner Radius field in the Rounded Rectangle dialog box. When this value is changed in one location, it automatically updates in the other.

Rounded Rectangle Tool

Chris Spollen

*Great uses for **rounded rectangles!***

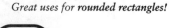

Daniel Pelavin

Daniel Pelavin

Here's a quick introduction to one of the many Illustrator filters: **Round Corners.** For other ways to reshape objects, see Chapter 8, Reshape.

To round the corners of an existing object:

1. Select an object.

2. Choose Filter > Stylize > Round Corners (on the top portion of the Filters menu).
   or
   Choose Effect > Stylize > Round Corners to create an editable appearance (not a permanent change to the object). You'll learn lots more about effects in Chapter 22.

3. Enter a Radius value (the radius of the curve, in points). When using an effect, you can check Preview, then make adjustments before closing the dialog box.

4. Click OK 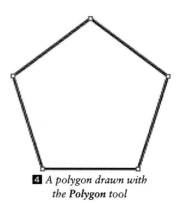.

1 *Top row: the original objects; second row: after applying the* **Round Corners** *filter (30pt)*

There are a number of tools, such as **Polygon, Star,** and **Spiral,** that make light work of drawing geometric objects. All you have to do is draw a marquee in the artboard or enter values in a dialog box. As you can see from the wonderful graphics by Daniel Pelavin and Chris Spollen in this chapter, you can create illustrations using basic geometric objects as building blocks.

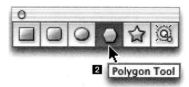

2 Polygon Tool

To create a polygon by clicking:

1. Choose the Polygon tool **2**. ⬡

2. Click where you want the center of the polygon to be.

3. Enter a Radius value (0–8192 pt) for the distance from the center of the object to the corner points **3**.

4. Choose a number of Sides for the polygon by clicking the up or down arrow or by entering a number (3–1000). The sides will be of equal length.

5. Click OK **4**. A polygon will appear where you clicked on the artboard; the current fill and stroke colors are applied automatically (see Chapter 9).

3 *In the* **Polygon** *dialog box, enter a Radius distance and choose a number of Sides.*

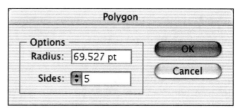

4 *A polygon drawn with the* **Polygon** *tool*

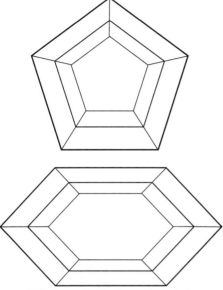

1 *Polygons (multiples made with the Scale tool, and then connecting lines added with the Line Segment tool)*

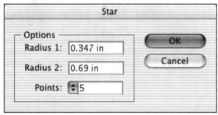

2 *Choose Radius and Points values in the **Star** dialog box.*

3 *On the left is a classic five-pointed star. On the right is the result of putting circles on top of the points and then clicking the Add to Shape Area button on the Pathfinder palette to join the shapes.*

To create a polygon by dragging:

1. Choose the Polygon tool. ⬡
2. Drag on the artboard, starting from where you want the center of the polygon to be.

   While dragging, do any of the following:

   Drag away from or toward the center to **resize** the polygon.

   Drag in a circular fashion to **rotate** the polygon.

   Hold down Shift while dragging to **constrain** the bottom side of the polygon to the horizontal axis.

   With the mouse still held down, press or hold down the up or down arrow key to **add** or **delete sides** from the polygon.

   Hold down the Spacebar and drag to **move** the polygon without resizing it.
3. When you release the mouse, the polygon will be selected, and it will be colored with the current fill and stroke settings **1**.
➤ To align a new object with an existing object as you draw it, use smart guides (see pages 90–91).

To create a star by clicking:

1. Choose the Star tool. ☆
2. Click where you want the center of the star to be.
3. Enter a value (0–8192 pt) in the Radius 1 and Radius 2 fields **2**. Whichever value is higher will become the distance from the center of the star to its outermost points. The lower value will become the distance from the center of the star to the innermost points. The greater the difference between the Radius 1 and Radius 2 values, the thinner the arms of the star will be.
4. Choose a number of Points for the star by clicking the up or down arrow or entering a number (3–1000).
5. Click OK **3**.
➤ To rotate the completed star, use the Rotate tool (see pages 99–100).

To create a star by dragging:

I. Choose the Star tool. ☆

2. Drag on the artboard, starting from where you want the center of the star to be 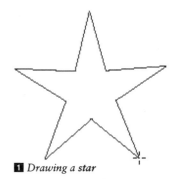.

While dragging, do any of the following:

Drag away from or toward the center to **resize** the star.

Drag in a circular fashion to **rotate** the star.

Hold down Shift while dragging to **constrain** two points to the horizontal axis.

With the mouse still held down, press the up or down arrow key to **add** or **delete** **points** from the star.

Hold down the Spacebar while dragging to **move** the star.

Hold down Option/Alt to make the shoulders (opposite segments) **parallel** to each other 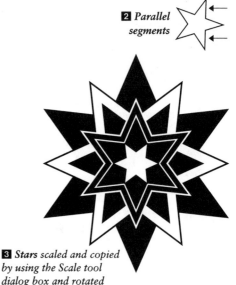.

Hold down Cmd/Ctrl and drag away from/toward the center to increase/ decrease the **length** of the **arms** of the star, while keeping the inner radius points constant.

3. When you release the mouse, the star will be selected and it will be colored with the current fill and stroke settings ▓–▓.

➤ Hold down ~ (tilde) while dragging quickly with the Star or Polygon tool to create progressively larger copies of the shape ▓. You can apply a stroke color to the copies afterward.

▓ *Drawing a star*

▓ *Parallel* *segments*

▓ *Stars scaled and copied by using the Scale tool dialog box and rotated by using the Rotate tool dialog box (no drawing!)*

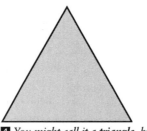

▓ *You might call it a **triangle**, but actually it's a three-pointed **star**!*

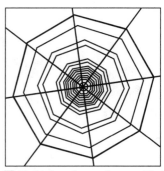

▓ *Multiple polygons drawn with the **Polygon** tool with ~ held down*

Star Tool

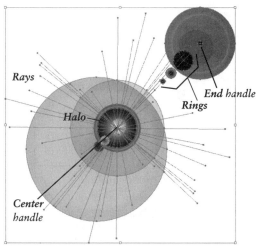

1 A selected flare

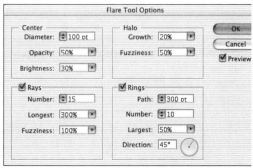

2 Choose **Center, Halo, Rays,** and **Rings** options for a flare in the **Flare Tool Options** dialog box.

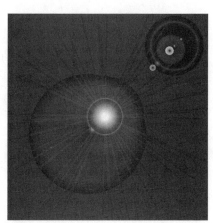

3 It's not easy to print a flare well in this type of book.

The **Flare** tool creates soft glow circles that consist of four components: a center, a halo, rays, and rings **1**, like a camera lens flare. The components are filled automatically with the current fill color at various opacity settings. Creating flares probably won't be your top priority as an illustrator, but the instructions will be here if you ever need them.

To create a flare by entering values:

1. Choose the Flare tool (it's on the Rectangle tool pop-out menu).

2. Click on the artboard where you want the flare to appear. The Flare Tool Options dialog box will open **2**.

3. For the Center portion (inner circle) of the flare, choose the Diameter, Opacity, and Brightness values.

4. For the Halo, choose the Growth (radius) as a percentage of the overall size, and choose or enter a Fuzziness value.

5. *Optional:* Check Rays, then specify the Number of rays, the length of the Longest ray as a percentage of the average ray, and the Fuzziness of the rays.

6. *Optional:* Check Rings, then specify the overall length of the flare Path, the Number of rings, the Largest ring as a percentage of the average ring, and the Direction (angle) of the rings. The Rings feature produces randomized results.

7. Click OK. Put your flare on top of a dark object—it will show up better **3**.

To create a flare using the current Flare tool settings:

1. Choose the Flare tool.

2. Option-click/Alt-click where you want the flare to appear (no dialog box will open).

Flare Tool; Edit Flare

To create a flare by dragging:

1. Choose the Flare tool.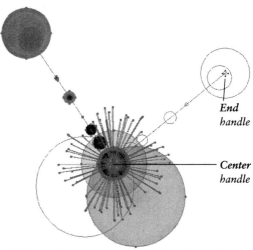

2. Position the tool on the artboard where you want the center handle of the flare to appear, then drag. The further you drag, the larger the center and the halo will be.

Before releasing the mouse, you can do any of the following:

Move in a **circular** direction to change the angle of the rays.

Press **Shift** to constrain the rays to the nearest 45° angle.

Press the **up arrow** to add rays.

Press the **down arrow** to remove rays.

Hold down **Cmd/Ctrl** to maintain the size of the center halo as you scale the flare.

3. Without deselecting the flare, drag in another spot to create an end handle and rings.

To edit a flare:

To change the **length** or **direction** of the rays on an existing flare and also move its rings, select the flare, choose the Flare tool, 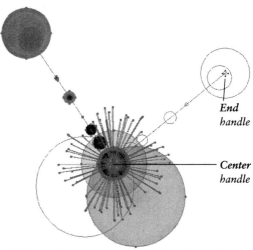 click the exact centerpoint of the center or end handle **1** of the flare (tiny arrowheads will appear on the flare cursor), then drag the handle. Locating the center points is a little tricky, and Smart Guides won't be of help.
or
To edit any of the components of a flare using its **options** dialog box, select the flare, double-click the Flare tool on the Toolbox, then change any of the settings in the Flare Tool Options dialog box (see the previous page). The Preview option will be checked.
or
To edit the **individual** components of a flare, you first have to expand it into individual objects. The individual shapes from an expanded flare can be edited as standard paths but not by using the Flare tool or Flare Tool Options dialog box. Choose the Selection tool, select the flare, choose Object > Expand, check the three Expand boxes, leave the Specify setting as is, then click OK.

➤ Choose View > Hide Edges to help you judge more easily how your edits look.

1 *Drag the* **center** *or* **end** *handle to change the length of the overall flare.*

End handle

Center handle

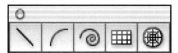

1 *The* ***Line Segment*** *tool on its tearoff toolbar*

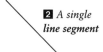

2 *A single line segment*

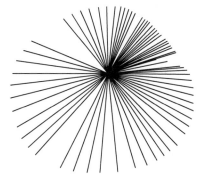

3 *Lines drawn with the* ***Line Segment*** *tool with ~ (tilde) held down*

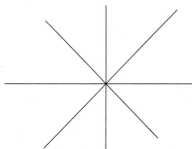

4 *Lines drawn with the* ***Line Segment*** *tool with Shift-~ (tilde) held down*

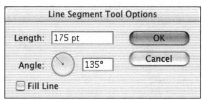

5 *Choose settings for the* ***Line Segment*** *tool in its options dialog box.*

The **Line Segment, Arc, Spiral, Rectangular Grid,** and **Polar Grid** tools **1** on the Line Segment tool pop-out menu create independent objects or groups of objects.

The **Line Segment** tool (and the Arc tool, which is discussed on the next page), create either one line or multiple, separate lines. Each time you drag with either tool, a new, separate path is created.

To draw using the Line Segment tool:

1. Choose the Line Segment tool.

2. Click to start the line, then drag in any direction to finish it **2**. As you drag, you can do any of the following:

Press **Option/Alt** to extend the line outward from both sides of the origin point.

Press **Shift** to constrain the line to the nearest increment of 45°.

Press the **Spacebar** to move the line.

Press ~ (tilde) to create multiple lines of varied lengths, from the same center point, at any angle **3**. Move the mouse quickly to spread the lines apart.

Press **Shift-~** (tilde) to create multiple lines at increments of 45° **4**.

To draw a line segment by entering values:

1. Choose the Line Segment tool.

2. Click where you want the segment to appear.

3. In the Line Segment Tool Options dialog box **5**, enter the desired line Length.

4. Enter an Angle or move the dial.

5. *Optional:* Check Fill Line to assign the current fill color to the line (see Chapter 9). If the line is subsequently joined to another line or segment, that color will be used as the fill. With this option unchecked, the line's fill will be None, though it can be changed later.

6. Click OK.

➤ Normally, the last used values will display in the Line Segment Tool Options dialog box. To restore the default values, Option/Alt-click Reset.

The **Arc** tool creates quick curves.

To draw an arc segment:

1. Choose the Arc tool.

2. Click where you want the arc to begin, then drag to create the arc **1**. As you drag, you can do any of the following:

   Press **C** to toggle between an open and closed arc **2**–**3**.

   Press **F** to flip the arc, keeping the origin point constant.

   Press (or press and hold) the **up arrow** or **down arrow** to increase or decrease the angle of the arc.

   Press **Option/Alt** to extend the arc outward from both sides of the origin point.

   Press the **Spacebar** to move the arc.

   Press ~ (tilde) to create multiple arc segments from the same origin point.

   Press and release **X** to toggle between a concave and convex arc.

To draw an arc segment by entering values:

1. Choose the Arc tool.

2. Click where you want the arc segment to appear.

3. In the Arc Segment Tool Options dialog box **4**, enter a Length X-Axis value for the width of the arc and a Length Y-Axis value for the height of the arc. Click a corner on the square icon to change the origin point.

4. From the Type pop-up menu, choose whether the arc will be Open or Closed.

5. From the Base Along pop-up menu, choose whether the arc will be measured from the X Axis or the Y Axis.

6. Move the Slope slider or enter a value for the steepness of the curve.

7. *Optional:* Check Fill Arc to have the arc fill with the current fill color.

8. Click OK.

➤ To restore the default values to the Arc Segment Tool Options dialog box, Option/Alt-click Reset.

Using arc segments

In Chapter 10 you'll learn how to draw curves "from scratch" using the Pen tool. You can use the Join command (see page 131) to combine pen and arc segments into a single object, or you can add segments to an arc using the Pen tool.

1 *We used **ruler guides** and **smart guides** to position the starting and ending points in an **arc segment**.*

2 *Drawing a closed **arc segment***

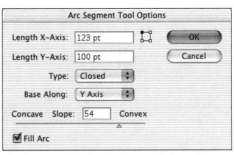

3 *After releasing the mouse, the arc **fills** with the current fill color (see Chapter 9).*

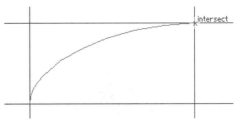

4 *Choose options for the **Arc** tool in its options dialog box.*

Arc Tool

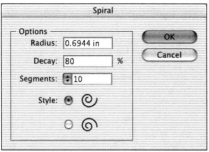

1 In the **Spiral** dialog box, enter Radius and Decay values, choose a number of Segments, and click a Style button.

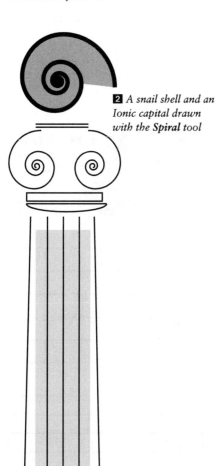

2 A snail shell and an Ionic capital drawn with the **Spiral** tool

To create a spiral by entering values:

1. Choose the Spiral tool. ◎

2. Click roughly where you want the center of the spiral to be.

3. Enter a Radius value for the distance from the center of the spiral to the outermost point **1**.

4. Enter a Decay percentage (5–150) to specify how tightly the spiral will wind.

5. Choose the number (2–1000) of Segments (quarter revolutions around the center point) for the spiral by clicking the up or down arrow or by entering a number.

6. Click a Style button for the direction the spiral will wind from the center point.

7. Click OK **2**.

8. Apply a stroke color to the spiral (see page 142).

To create a spiral by dragging:

1. Choose the Spiral tool. ◎

2. Drag in the document window, starting from where you want the center of the spiral to be.

3. While dragging, do any of the following:

Drag away from or toward the center to **resize** the spiral.

Option-drag/Alt-drag outward to **add segments** from the center of the spiral as you change its size. Option-drag/Alt-drag inward to **delete segments**.

Hold down Cmd/Ctrl and drag slowly away from or toward the center to control how **tightly** the spiral winds (the Decay value).

Keep the mouse button down, then press the up or down arrow key to **add segments** to or **delete segments** from the center of the spiral.

Drag in a circular fashion to **rotate** the spiral.

Hold down Shift while dragging to **constrain** the rotation of the entire spiral to an increment of 45°.

(Continued on the following page)

Spiral Tool

Hold down the Spacebar while dragging to **move** the spiral.

4. When you release the mouse, the spiral will be selected and it will be colored with the current fill and stroke colors **1**–**3**.

A **rectangular grid** can be created by dragging (instructions on this page) or by entering values in a dialog box (instructions on the following page). The grid is composed of a group of separate lines and a rectangle. You can't put anything into it, but you can put it on its own layer (lock it to make it uneditable), and then create objects or type on a layer above it (see Chapter 11).

To create a rectangular grid by dragging:

1. Choose the Rectangular Grid tool (it's on the Line Segment tool pop-out menu). 🔳

2. Drag diagonally. After you start dragging, you can press any of the following keys:

   Shift to constrain the grid to a square **4**.

   Option/Alt to draw the grid from the center.

   Shift-Option/Shift-Alt to draw a square grid from the center.

   Spacebar to move the grid as you draw.

   To adjust the grid **dividers,** press any of the following key modifiers:

   Up arrow or **down arrow** to add or remove horizontal dividers.

   Right arrow or **Left arrow** to add or remove vertical dividers.

   X to skew the vertical dividers to the left by increments of 10% **5** or **C** to skew the vertical dividers to the right (the dividers will be progressively closer together).

   F to skew the horizontal dividers to the bottom by increments of 10% or **V** to skew the horizontal dividers to the top.

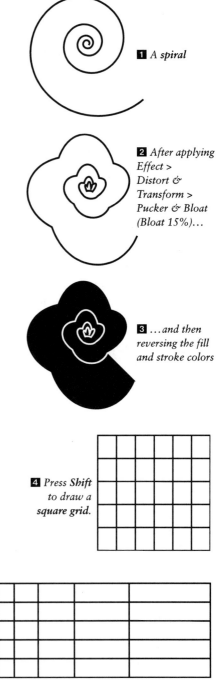

1 *A spiral*

2 *After applying Effect > Distort & Transform > Pucker & Bloat (Bloat 15%)…*

3 *…and then reversing the fill and stroke colors*

4 *Press Shift to draw a square grid.*

5 *Press X to draw a* **grid** *in which the vertical dividers are* **skewed** *to the left.*

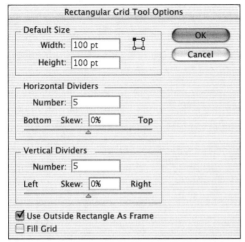

1 *Choose parameters for the **Rectangular Grid** tool in its **Options** dialog box.*

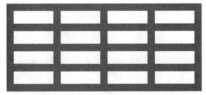

2 *Use Outside Rectangle As Frame* on: *The outer segment is a single rectangle.*

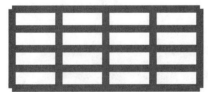

3 *Use Outside Rectangle As Frame* off: *Each of the four outer segments is a separate object.*

4 *A polar grid*

To create a rectangular grid by entering values:

1. Choose the Rectangular Grid tool (it's on the Line Segment tool pop-out menu). ▦

2. Click in the document window to establish an origin point for the grid.

3. In the **Default Size** area **1**, enter Width and Height values for the overall grid, and to specify the point the grid will be drawn from, click a corner on the square Origin Point icon.

4. Enter the Number of **Horizontal Dividers** to be inserted between the top and bottom edges of the grid. *Optional:* Choose a Skew value above or below 0 to cluster the dividers toward the bottom or top.

5. Enter the number of **Vertical Dividers** to be inserted between the left and right edges of the grid. *Optional:* Choose a Skew value above or below 0 to cluster the dividers toward the right or left.

6. *Optional:* Check Use Outside Rectangle As Frame to have the top, bottom, left, and right segments be a separate rectangular object instead of a line **2**–**3**.

7. *Optional:* Check Fill Grid to fill the grid with the current fill color.

8. Click OK.

➤ Hold down Option/Alt and click Reset to restore the tool's default values.

You can draw a **polar** (elliptical) **grid** by dragging (instructions on this page) or via a dialog box (instructions on the following page).

To create a polar grid by dragging:

1. Choose the Polar Grid tool (it's on the Line Segment tool pop-out menu). ⊕

2. Choose fill and stroke colors (see Chapter 9), then drag diagonally **4**. As you drag, you can do any of the following:

   Press **Shift** to constrain the grid to a circle.

   Press **Option/Alt** to resize the grid from all sides of the origin point.

   Press the **Spacebar** to move the grid.

(Continued on the following page)

Rectangular Grid, Polar Grid Tools

3. To adjust the grid dividers, do any of the following as you drag:

Press the **up arrow** or **down arrow** to add or remove concentric circles.

Press the **right arrow** or **left arrow** to add or remove radial lines.

Press **X** to skew the concentric dividers toward the center.

Press **C** to skew the concentric dividers toward the outer edge.

Press **F** to skew the radial dividers counterclockwise, or press **V** to skew the dividers clockwise.

To create a polar grid by entering values:

1. Choose fill and stroke colors (see Chapter 9).

2. Choose the Polar Grid tool, then click to establish the grid's origin point.

3. In the **Default Size** area ▌1▐, enter Width and Height values for the overall grid, and to specify the point the grid will be drawn from, click a corner on the square Origin Point icon.

4. Enter the Number of curved **Concentric Dividers** to appear inside the grid ▌2▐. *Optional:* Choose a Skew value above or below 0 to cluster the concentric dividers toward the edge or center of the grid ▌3▐.

5. Enter the number of straight-line **Radial Dividers** to appear in the grid. *Optional:* Choose a Skew value above or below 0 to cluster the straight dividers in a clockwise or counterclockwise direction around the grid ▌4▐.

6. Check Create Compound Path From Ellipses to have each concentric circle be converted into a separate compound path.

7. Click Fill Grid to have the whole grid be filled with the current fill color. If Create Compound Path From Ellipses is checked, alternating circles will be filled ▌5▐.

8. Click OK.

➤ Hold down Option/Alt and click Reset to restore the default tool values.

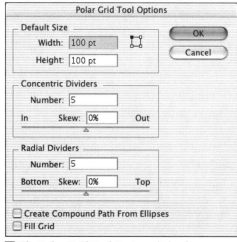

▌1▐ *The Polar Grid Tool Options dialog box*

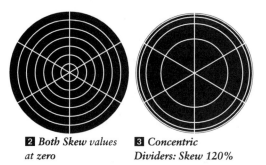

▌2▐ *Both Skew values at zero*

▌3▐ *Concentric Dividers: Skew 120%*

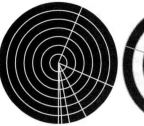

▌4▐ *Radial Dividers: Skew -128%*

▌5▐ *Create Compound Path From Ellipses and Fill Grid on: The white rings are see-through. The fill color is applied to the opaque rings automatically, and the stroke color is applied to the dividers.*

Diane Margolin

1 *Blue-footed booby, drawn with the Pencil tool*

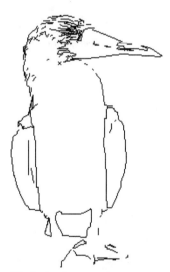

2 *The booby in Outline view*

Sketching

If you enjoy sketching objects "by hand," you'll gravitate to the **Pencil** tool, especially if you have a stylus. Pencil paths can be reshaped like any other paths (see Chapter 8). *Note:* If you need to draw straight lines or smooth curves, you'll go mad trying to do it with the Pencil tool; use the Line Segment, Arc, or Pen tool instead!

The Pencil tool performs three distinctly different functions. If you drag in an empty area of the artboard with the Pencil, you'll create a new, open path. If you drag along the edge of an existing, selected path (open or closed), the Pencil will reshape the path (see page 125). And if you drag from an endpoint on an existing open path, you will add a new segment to the path (see page 123).

To draw using the Pencil tool:

1. Choose the Pencil tool (N).

2. Display the Color palette (F6), click the Stroke color box on the palette, then choose a stroke color. Also choose stroke attributes from the Stroke palette (see Chapter 9).

3. Click the Fill Color box on the Color palette, then click the None button at the bottom of the palette so the curves on the path won't fill in.

4. Draw a line. A dotted line will appear as you draw. When you release the mouse, the line will be colored with the current fill and stroke settings and its anchor points will be selected (Preview view) **1**. In Outline view, you'll see only a wireframe representation of the line **2**.

   Note: To create a closed path with the Pencil tool, hold down Option/Alt before and as you release the mouse.

➤ Read about the Pencil tool preferences on the next page.

➤ To close an existing Pencil line, choose the Selection tool (V), select the line, then choose Object > Path > Join (Cmd-J/ Ctrl-J). The two endpoints will be joined by a straight segment.

The **Fidelity** and **Smoothness** settings for the Pencil tool control the number of anchor points and the size of the curve segments the tool produces. If you change these settings, only subsequently drawn lines will be affected—not existing lines.

To choose Pencil tool settings:

1. Double-click the Pencil tool (or press N to choose the tool, then press Return/ Enter).

2. Choose a **Fidelity** value (0.5–20) **1**–**4**. The lower the Fidelity, the more closely the line will follow the movement of the mouse and the greater the number of anchor points will be created. The higher the Fidelity, the smoother the path.

3. Choose a **Smoothness** value (0–100). The higher the Smoothness, the smoother the curves; the lower the smoothness, the more bends and twists in the path.

4. *Optional:* Leave **Keep selected** checked to keep a Pencil path selected after it's created. This is handy if you like to add to a path after it's drawn.

5. We'll discuss the reshaping function of the Pencil tool on page 125. Checking **Edit selected paths** activates this function. In the Within: [ ] pixels field, enter the minimum distance the pointer must be from a path in order for the tool to re-shape it. Uncheck "Edit selected paths" if you want to be able to draw multiple Pencil lines near each other without reshaping any existing selected paths.

6. Click OK.

➤ Click Reset in the Pencil Tool Preferences dialog box to restore the tool's default preferences.

➤ To smooth an existing path, use the Smooth tool (see page 126).

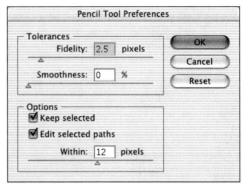

1 *The* **Pencil** *tool has its own* **Preferences** *dialog box.*

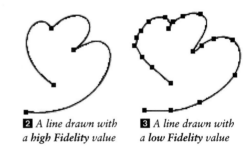

2 *A line drawn with a* **high Fidelity** *value*

3 *A line drawn with a* **low Fidelity** *value*

4 *An illustration drawn with the* **Pencil** *tool*

Diane Margolin

SELECT/COPY 6

In Chapter 5 you learned basic methods for creating objects. In later chapters you'll learn how to reshape, recolor, transform, and distort objects. Objects can't be modified unless they're selected, though, so the first thing you'll learn in this chapter is how to select and deselect objects. You'll also learn how to move objects; use smart guides to align objects; hide/show an object's anchor points and direction lines; hide/show whole objects; lock/unlock objects; copy objects within the same file or between files; and offset a copy of a path.

If you like to move or position objects by entering values or measuring distances, after you learn the fundamental techniques in this chapter, read Chapter 23, Precision Tools.

Selection Tools

A few pointers

The pointer over an
unselected segment

The pointer over a
selected segment

The pointer over a
selected point

Selection
tool

Direct
Selection
tool

Selecting Objects

The five selection tools

Use the **Selection** tool (**V**) to select or move whole paths and to resize or rotate a path using its bounding box. If you click the edge of an object with the Selection tool, all the points on that object will become selected. You can also select an object by clicking its fill, provided Object Selection by Path Only is unchecked (the default setting) in Illustrator (Edit, in Windows) > Preferences > General and the illustration is in Preview view. Note that this preference option replaces, and works the opposite way from, the Use Area Select preference in Illustrator 10.

Use the **Direct Selection** tool (**A**) to select one or more individual anchor points or segments of a path. If you click a curve segment with the Direct Selection tool, that segment's direction lines and anchor points will become visible. (Straight segments don't have direction lines—they only have anchor points.) If Object Selection by Path Only is unchecked in Preferences > General and you click an object's fill in Preview view using this tool, all the points on the object will become selected.

(Continued on the following page)

81

Although the **Group Selection** tool can be used to select all the anchor points on a single path, its primary purpose is for selecting groups of objects that are nested inside larger groups. Click once to select an object; click twice to select that object's group; click three times to select the next group that was added to the larger group, and so on.

Group Selection tool

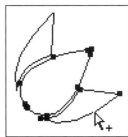

➤ The easiest way to access the Group Selection tool is by holding down Option/Alt when the Direct Selection tool is active (note the plus sign in the pointer).

Use the **Lasso** tool (**Q**) to select path points and segments by dragging a freeform marquee around them.

Note: The Lasso tool performs the function of the now defunct Direct Select Lasso tool; it no longer selects whole paths.

Lasso tool

Use the **Magic Wand** tool (**Y**) to select objects of the same or similar fill color, stroke color, stroke weight, opacity, or blending mode as those of the object you click on. You can choose options for this tool from the Magic Wand palette.

➤ If Use Precise Cursors is checked in Preferences > General, you'll see a crosshair pointer onscreen -¦- instead of an icon for the current tool.

Magic Wand tool

Quick select

To select all the objects on a **layer** or **sublayer** (even in a one-layer document), click the selection area for that layer at the far right side of the **Layers palette** (a colored square will appear). You can also click the selection area for an individual object or group. Read all about layers in Chapter 11!

Object selection by path only NEW

With **Object Selection by Path Only** unchecked in Illustrator (Edit, in Windows) > Preferences > General, you can select an object in Preview view by clicking with a selection tool anywhere within the object's bounding box. With this option checked, you must click on a path segment or anchor point with the Selection, Direct Selection, or Magic Wand tool in order to select an object.

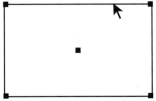

1 *Selecting a path (and all its anchor points) with the Selection tool*

2 *Marqueeing two paths with the Selection tool*

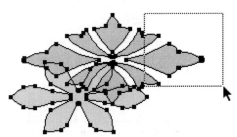

3 *One of two selected objects is marqueed with the Selection tool in order to deselect it.*

To select an object or objects:

1. Choose the Selection tool (V) ▸ or the Group Selection tool. ▸⁺

2. Click the edge of the path **1**.
   or
   If the path has a color fill, your illustration is in Preview view, and the Object Selection by Path Only option is off (see the sidebar), click on the fill.
   or
   Position the pointer outside the path(s) you want to select, then drag a marquee across all or part of it **2**. The whole path will be selected, even if you marquee only a portion of it.
   or
   If the illustration is in Outline view, click the edge of the path.

➤ Hold down Option/Alt to use the Group Selection tool while the Direct Selection tool is chosen, and vice versa.

You can **add** or **subtract** whole objects from a selection with the Selection tool.

To add or subtract objects from a selection:

Choose the Selection tool (V), ▸ then Shift-click or Shift-drag (marquee) any selected objects to deselect them **3**–**4**, or do the same for any unselected objects to add them to the selection.

4 *One path is deselected.*

Select an Object; Add, Subtract Objects

You will learn how to reshape objects in Chapter 8. But before you can proceed to reshaping, you have to know how to **select** individual **points** and **segments**. It's important to be precise about which components you select.

To select/deselect anchor points or segments with the Direct Selection tool:

1. Choose the Direct Selection tool (A).

2. Click the edge of the path (not the fill!). A **segment** will become selected. If you click a curve segment, the direction lines for that segment will become visible.

   or

   If the path isn't selected, click the edge of the path (not the fill!), then click an **anchor point** –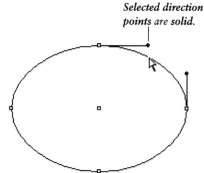.

   or

   Position the pointer outside the object or objects whose **anchor points** you want to select, then drag a marquee across them (a dotted marquee will define the area as you drag over it). Only the points you marquee will be selected –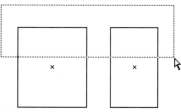.

3. To select additional anchor points or segments or to deselect selected anchor points or segments individually, Shift-click or Shift-marquee those points or segments with the Direct Selection tool.

➤ If you've got a nonselection tool selected and you need to use either the Selection tool or the Direct Selection tool, hold down Cmd/Ctrl instead of switching tools. The pointer will temporarily function like whichever of those two selection tools was last used (note the pointer icon).

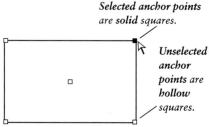

Selected anchor points are solid squares.

Unselected anchor points are hollow squares.

1 *One anchor point is selected with the **Direct Selection** tool (Outline view).*

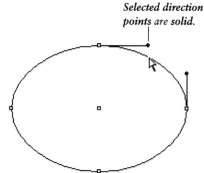

Selected direction points are solid.

2 *A segment is selected with the **Direct Selection** tool.*

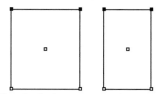

3 *A marquee selection is being made with the **Direct Selection** tool.*

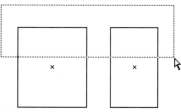

4 *Only the four points within the marquee become selected.*

Reselect

Let's say you just used a Select > Same submenu command and you love it so much you want to choose it again. Just press **Cmd-6/Ctrl-6**. And unlike the Undo command, this command doesn't need to be executed right away; you can perform other operations, and Illustrator will still remember which Select > Same submenu command was last used. Watch out, though. You may get unexpected results, depending on what object is selected.

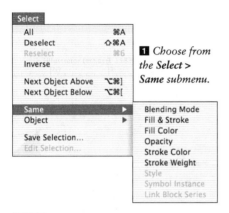

1 *Choose from the Select > Same submenu.*

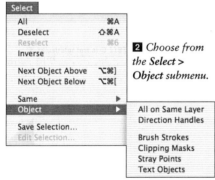

2 *Choose from the Select > Object submenu.*

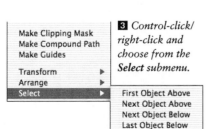

3 *Control-click/ right-click and choose from the Select submenu.*

The **Select commands** select objects whose characteristics are similar to those of the last selected (or currently selected) object. Each command is aptly named for the attributes it searches for.

To select using a command:

Do any of the following:

Select an object to base the search on, or deselect all objects to have the search be based on the last object that was selected, then from the Select > **Same** submenu **1**, choose **Blending Mode, Fill & Stroke, Fill Color, Opacity, Stroke Color, Stroke Weight, Style, Symbol Instance,** or **Link Block Series.** NEW

or

Select an object or objects, then from the Select > **Object** submenu **2**, choose **All on Same Layer** to select all the objects on the layer the object resides on (or layers, if objects from more than one layer are selected). Or choose **Direction Handles** to select all the points on the currently selected object or objects.

or

With or without an object selected, from the Select > Object submenu, choose **Brush Strokes** to select objects that have the same brush strokes; **Clipping Masks** to select masking objects (helpful for getting the edges of a masking object to display on screen); **Stray Points** to select lone points that aren't part of any path (so they can be deleted easily); or **Text Objects** to select all the text objects in the illustration.

or

Control-click/right-click an object where it overlaps the one you want to select, and choose Select > **First Object Above, Next Object Above, Next Object Below,** or **Last Object Below 3**.

or

Select an object, then from the menu bar, choose Select > **Next Object Above** (Cmd-Option-]/Ctrl-Alt-]) or **Next Object Below** (Cmd-Option-[/Ctrl-Alt-[). The next object above or below in the stacking order will become selected (look on the Layers palette) —not necessarily the one under the pointer.

Select Using a Command

Let's say you need to select a few points on one path and a couple of points on a nearby path. You could grab the Direct Selection tool and click the points individually (tedious) or you could marquee them (works only if the points in question fall conveniently within the rectangular marquee). With the **Lasso** tool, you can weave an irregular pathway around just the points and segments you want to select. This tool is especially helpful when you need to create selections among overlapping paths.

NEW *Note:* The Lasso tool performs the function of the now defunct Direct Select Lasso tool; it no longer selects whole paths.

To select/deselect points or segments with the Lasso tool:

1. Deselect (click on a blank area of the artboard).

2. Choose the Lasso tool (Q), 𝄞 then encircle the segments or points you want to select 1–2. You can drag right across a path. You don't need to "close" the lasso path.

3. *Optional:* Shift-drag around any unselected points or segments to select them, or Option-drag/Alt-drag around any selected points or segments to deselect them.

1 *Wend your way around parts of objects with the **Lasso** tool.*

2 *Only the **points** and **segments** you marquee will become selected.*

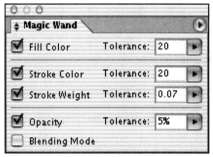

1 *The* **Magic Wand** *palette*

The **Magic Wand** tool selects all objects in a document with the same or similar fill color, stroke color, stroke weight, opacity, or blending mode as those of the object you click on. First you need to choose options for the tool. To use the Magic Wand tool, see the instructions on the following page.

To choose options for the Magic Wand tool:

1. To open the Magic Wand palette, double-click the Magic Wand tool ✕ or choose Window > Magic Wand.

   If the three panels aren't visible (as shown in **1**), click the up/down arrow on the palette tab until all the panels are visible, or choose Show Stroke Options and Show Transparency Options from the palette menu.

2. On the left side of the dialog box, check the attributes you want the tool to select: Fill Color, Stroke Color, Stroke Weight, Opacity, or Blending Mode.

3. For each option you checked in the previous step (except Blending Mode), choose a Tolerance range. Choose a low value to select only colors, weights, or opacities that match or are very similar to the pixel you click; or choose a high value to allow the tool to select a broader range of colors, weights, or opacities. For Fill Color or Stroke Color, choose a value (the range will be 0 to 255 for RGB or 0 to 100 for CMYK, depending on the document color mode); for Stroke Weight, choose a width Tolerance (0–1000 pt); for Opacity, choose a percentage (0 to 100).

4. To permit the Magic Wand tool to select objects on all layers, make sure the Use All Layers command on the palette menu has a checkmark. To allow the tool to select objects on only the current layer, leave this option unchecked.

➤ To reset the Magic Wand palette to its default values, choose Reset from the palette menu.

Magic Wand Palette

To use the Magic Wand tool:

1. Choose the Magic Wand tool (Y).

2. To create a **new** selection, click a color in the document window. Depending on which options are checked on the Magic Wand palette, other objects with the same or a similar fill color, stroke color, stroke weight, opacity, or blending mode may become selected **1**–**2**.

3. To **add** to the selection, Shift-click a color in the document window with the Magic Wand tool.

To **subtract** from the selection, Option-click/Alt-click a color in the document window with the Magic Wand tool.

To select all the objects in an illustration:

Choose Select > **All** (Cmd-A/Ctrl-A). All unlocked objects in your illustration will be selected, whether they're on the artboard or on the scratch area. Hidden objects or objects on hidden layers (eye icon off on the Layers palette) won't become selected.

➤ If the text cursor is flashing in a text block when the Select > All command is executed, the entire text block will become selected—not all the objects in the illustration.

To prevent objects from being modified, you must **deselect** them.

To deselect all objects:

Choose Select > **Deselect** (Cmd-Shift-A/Ctrl-Shift-A).
or
Choose any selection tool, then click on a blank area of the artboard.

➤ To deselect an individual object within a multiple-object selection, Shift-click it with the Selection tool. To deselect an object within a group, Shift-click it with the Direct Selection tool (the Group command is discussed on page 181).

To select all the deselected objects, and vice versa:

Choose Select > **Inverse**.

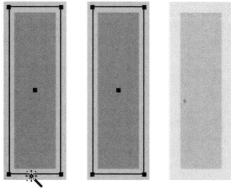

1 *These objects have the same **stroke** color, but the square on the far right has a lower **opacity** (50%). The Opacity option is **on** for the Magic Wand tool, and the tool is clicked on the stroke of the leftmost object. Only the objects with the same stroke color **and opacity** become selected.*

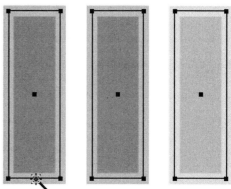

2 *This time the Magic Wand tool is used with the **Opacity** option off. All three objects become selected, and **opacity** is **ignored** as a factor.*

Give it a nudge

Press any arrow key to move a selected object or objects by the current Keyboard Increment: **Keyboard Increment** value in Illustrator (Edit, in Windows) > Preferences > General. The default increment is 1 pt.

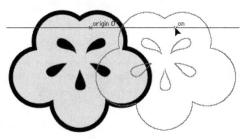

1 *You can drag the edge of an object using the Selection tool.*

2 *Or if the object has a fill, the illustration is in Preview view, and the Object Selection by Path Only option is off, you can drag an object's fill. Here, Smart Guides are being used to move the object along the horizontal axis.*

Moving objects

There are many ways to **move objects:** By dragging, nudging (arrow keys), or using a dialog box. Precise methods for positioning objects, such as the Move dialog box, the Transform palette, and Transform Each, are covered in Chapter 23, Precision Tools. We'll start with the most direct approach first.

To move an object by dragging:

1. Choose the Selection tool (V).

2. Drag the object's **edge** (you can do this in Outline or Preview view) **1**.
   or
   If the illustration is in Preview view, the object has a fill, and Object Selection by Path Only is off in Illustrator (Edit, in Windows) > Preferences > General, drag the object's **fill 2**. This can also be done with the Direct Selection tool.

➤ Use smart guides to guide you (see the following two pages).

➤ If View > Snap To Point is on (Cmd-Option-"/Ctrl-Alt-") and there are ruler guides on your artboard, the part of an object that is directly underneath the pointer will snap to a guide if it comes within 2 pixels of it (the pointer becomes hollow when it's over a guide). The pointer will also become hollow and snap to any anchor point it passes over.

➤ Hold down Shift while dragging an object to constrain the movement either to a multiple of 45° or to the current Constrain Angle in Illustrator (Edit, in Windows) > Preferences > General, if the latter value isn't 0.

Move an Object

Smart guides are temporary guides that appear when you draw, move, duplicate, or transform an object. They are designed to help you align objects with one another or along a particular axis. And smart guides have magnetism: Drag an object near one, and the pointer will snap to it.

To turn smart guides on or off, choose View > Smart Guides (Cmd-U/Ctrl-U). Smart guides settings are chosen in Illustrator (Edit, in Windows) > Preferences > Smart Guides & Slices **1**. You'll understand pretty quickly how smart guides work once you start working with them—they're easier done than said.

To start with, try using smart guides to move an object along an axis or to align one object with points on another object. Here's how it works.

To use smart guides to align objects:

1. Make sure View > Smart Guides (Cmd-U/Ctrl-U) is on (has a check mark), and make sure View > Snap to Grid is off.

2. Go to Illustrator (Edit, in Windows) > Preferences > Smart Guides & Slices, make sure Text Label Hints **2** and Object Highlighting **3** are checked, then click OK. (Construction Guides, Transform Tools, and other smart guides options are discussed on page 445.)

3. Choose the Selection tool (V). ▶

4. To use angle lines to position an object: Start dragging an object. Smart guide angle line guides will appear as you move the object (e.g., 0°, 45°, 90°). Release the mouse any time the word "**on**" appears next to the pointer, to position the object along that angle. You don't need to hold down Shift to constrain the movement— that's the whole point!
   or
   To align one object to another, start dragging an object, position the pointer over the edge of another path, and release

Use them for finding

Smart guides aren't just used for aligning objects. With **Text Label Hints** checked in Smart Guides & Slices Preferences, you can use smart guides to help you locate individual points on any object, whether the object is selected or not. With **Object Highlighting** checked, you can use smart guides to locate the edges of objects —irregularly-shaped objects, objects in a group, objects in a mesh, etc. Object Highlighting works even when View > Hide Edges is chosen.

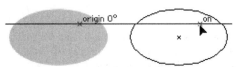

1 *The **Snapping Tolerance** is the farthest distance the pointer can be from an object for the snap function to work.*

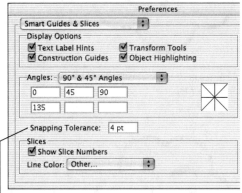

2 *Text label hints display when an object is moved along one of the axes.*

3 *The edge of an **object** highlights when the pointer is moved over it (with the mouse button up).*

Interesting angle

You can specify the angle for smart guides in Illustrator (Edit, in Windows) > Preferences > Smart Guides & Slices. You can choose a predefined **Angles** set from the pop-up menu or you can enter your own angles. If you switch from Custom Angles to a predefined set and then switch back to Custom Angles at a later time, the last-used custom settings will be restored.

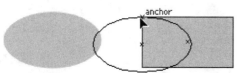

1 *An ellipse is moved over a rectangle. As the mouse is dragged over the rectangle's path, the word "path" appears on the unselected object.*

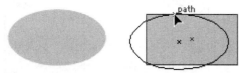

2 *An ellipse is dragged by an anchor point and is aligned with an anchor point on the rectangle (as revealed by the word "anchor") on the rectangle.*

the mouse when the word "**anchor**" or "**path**" appears next to the pointer **1**. You can also align an object's **center** point or path to another object's center point or path. The word "center" will appear. *Note:* In order for the center point to show up as a smart guide, the object's center point must be visible (see the following page).

or

To align objects by anchor points: Make sure the object you want to move is not selected, then position the pointer over one of its anchor points (the word "anchor" will appear). Drag the object over an anchor point on another object, and release the mouse when the word "anchor" appears on the second object **2**.

You can also align a path of one object to an anchor point or the center point on another object or an anchor point of one object to the path of another object.

➤ You can't lock smart guides—they vanish as quickly as they appear. To create guides that stay on screen, drag from the horizontal or vertical ruler into the artboard (see page 420).

➤ Smart guides are the same color as the current Guides color, which is chosen in Illustrator (Edit, in Windows) > Preferences > Guides & Grid.

Use Smart Guides

Hiding and locking objects

When the **Hide Edges** feature is on, anchor points and direction lines are invisible, yet objects are still fully editable. Try hiding edges to see how different stroke attributes, effects, flares, etc. look in Preview view or to make distracting points invisible when you're working in Outline view.

Note: The Hide Edges command won't hide the bounding box. To hide the bounding boxes of all objects in a document, choose View > Hide Bounding Box (Cmd-Shift-B/Ctrl-Shift-B). 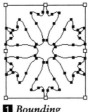–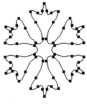. Choose the command again to redisplay the boxes.

To hide the anchor points and direction lines of an object or objects:

1. Select an object or objects.

2. Choose View > **Hide Edges** (Cmd-H/Ctrl-H). To redisplay the anchor points and direction lines, choose View > Show Edges.

You can use an object's **center point** as a handle to drag the object. You can also align objects via their center points using smart guides, but in order to do this, the objects' center points must be visible.

To hide/show an object's center point:

1. Select the object (or objects) whose center point you want to show or hide. Or to show or hide the center point for all the objects in the illustration, choose Select > All (Cmd-A/Ctrl-A).

2. Show the Attributes palette (F11) .

3. If the Show Center options aren't visible on the palette, choose Show All from the palette menu.

4. Click the Don't Show Center button ▣ 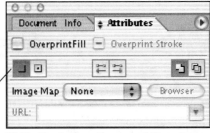.
   or
   Click the Show Center button ▣ 5.

5. Deselect the object(s).

1 *Bounding box on*   **2** *Bounding box off*

3 *The **Don't Show Center** and **Show Center** buttons on the Attributes palette*

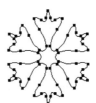 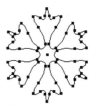

4 *Center point hidden*   **5** *Center point showing*

Use the Layers palette!

Here we go again, singing the praises of the **Layers** palette. It can be used to quickly show/hide or lock/unlock a layer, a group, or an individual object. For show/hide, see page 197. For lock/unlock, see page 196.

If your illustrations tend to be complex, you'll find the **Hide > Selection** command to be useful for isolating the objects you want to work on and for boosting screen redraw. Hidden objects don't print, and they are invisible in both Outline and Preview views. When you save, close, and reopen a file, hidden objects remain hidden. We generally prefer to use the Layers palette to show/hide (and lock/unlock) objects, but here it is, for whatever it's worth.

To hide an object or objects:

1. Select the object or objects to be hidden.

2. Choose Object > Hide > **Selection** (Cmd-3/Ctrl-3).

The **Show All** command redisplays all hidden objects in an illustration. (To selectively redisplay individual hidden objects, you have to use the Layers palette; see page 197.)

To redisplay all hidden objects:

Choose Object > **Show All** (Cmd-Option-3/ Ctrl-Alt-3).

Locked objects can't be selected or modified. If you save, close, and reopen the file, locked objects remain locked. For other lock commands, see page 196.

To lock an object or objects:

1. Select the object or objects to be locked. You can't lock or hide part of a path.

2. Choose Object > Lock > **Selection** (Cmd-2/Ctrl-2).

The **Unlock All** command unlocks all the locked objects in an illustration. (To unlock locked objects individually, you have to use the Layers palette; see page 196.)

To unlock all locked objects:

Choose Object > **Unlock All** (Cmd-Option-2/ Ctrl-Alt-2). The newly unlocked objects will be selected and any previously selected, unlocked objects will be deselected.

Hide/Show Objects; Lock, Unlock Objects

Copying

On this page we discuss two straightforward methods for copying: dragging and nudging. These are some other methods to explore:

➤ Copy an object using the Clipboard (page 95).

➤ Copy an object using a Transform tool (Chapter 7).

➤ Copy an object to a different layer (page 192).

➤ Copy a layer and all the objects on it (page 192).

➤ Copy an object using the Move dialog box (page 425).

To drag-copy an object:

1. Choose the Selection tool (V).

2. Option-drag/Alt-drag the fill or edge of an object (don't drag a bounding box handle) **1**–**2**. You can release the mouse in the same document or in another document window. The pointer will turn into a double arrowhead. Release the mouse before releasing Option/Alt.

   or

   To constrain the position of the copy to the horizontal or vertical axis (or to the Constrain Angle in Illustrator [Edit, in Windows] > Preferences > General), start dragging the object, then hold down Option-Shift/Alt-Shift and continue to drag. You could also use smart guides for positioning.

➤ To create another copy of the object, choose Object > Transform > Transform Again (Cmd-D/Ctrl-D). Repeat, if desired.

To copy an object by nudging:

1. Choose the Selection tool (V).

2. Select an object or objects.

3. Press Option-arrow/Alt-arrow to copy the object and move the copy the Keyboard Increment from the Preferences > General dialog box. The default unit is 1 pt.

   or

   Press Option-Shift-arrow/Alt-Shift-arrow to copy the object and move it 10 times the current Keyboard Increment.

Copying grouped objects

If you copy an object in a group by dragging (start dragging with the Direct Selection tool, then continue dragging with Option/Alt held down), the copy will be a **member** of that group.

If you use the **Clipboard** to copy and paste an object that was in a group, the object will paste **outside** the group. The Group command is discussed on page 181.

1 *To copy an object, **Option-drag/Alt-drag** it. Note the double-arrowhead pointer.*

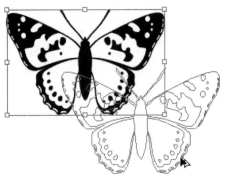

2 *A copy is made.*

If you select an object or a group and then choose the **Cut** or **Copy** command, that object or group will be placed onto the Clipboard, a temporary storage area in memory. The previous contents of the Clipboard are replaced each time you choose Cut or Copy.

The Paste command places the current Clipboard contents in the center of the active layer in the currently active document window. The Paste in Front and Paste in Back commands paste the object in its original *x/y* location in front of or behind the current selection. The Paste in Front and Paste in Back commands are handy for positioning the Clipboard contents in a particular stacking position.

Objects are copied to the Clipboard in the PDF and/or AICB format, depending on which of those options is currently chosen in Illustrator (Edit, in Windows) > Preferences > File Handling & Clipboard (see page 448). The same Clipboard contents can be pasted an unlimited number of times.

To copy or move objects from one document to another using the Clipboard:

1. Open two documents.

2. Select the object or group that you want to copy or move.

3. Choose Edit > Cut (Cmd-X/Ctrl-X). The object or group will be removed from the current document.
   or
   To move a copy of the object or group, choose Edit > Copy (Cmd-C/Ctrl-C).

4. Click in the target document, and click a layer name on the Layers palette (see Chapter 11).

5. *Optional:* Select an object that you want to paste the copied object in front of or behind.

6. Choose Edit > Paste (Cmd-V/Ctrl-V).
   or
   If you've selected an object in the target document, you can choose Edit > Paste in Front (Cmd-F/Ctrl-F) or Paste in Back (Cmd-B/Ctrl-B).

Use the Clipboard

The **Offset Path** command copies a path and offsets the copy around or inside the original path by a specified distance. The copy is also reshaped automatically so it fits nicely around the original path; its fill and stroke attributes will match those of the original.

To offset a copy of a path:

1. Select an object **1**. You can try using this command on a path that has a stroke, but no fill.

2. Choose Object > Path > Offset Path.

3. In the Offset field, enter the distance you want the offset path to be from the original path **2**. Be sure your Offset value is larger or smaller than the stroke weight of the original path so the copies will be visible. A positive value will create a path that's larger than the original; a negative value will create a smaller path.

4. Choose a Joins (bend) style: Miter (pointed), Round (semicircular), or Bevel (square-cornered).

5. *Optional:* Enter a different Miter limit for the maximum amount the offset path's line weight (as measured from the inside to the outside of the corner point) can be enlarged before the miter join becomes a bevel join. The Miter limit value times the stroke weight value equals the maximum inner-to-outer corner measurement. What?! Here's a simple rule of thumb: Use a high Miter limit to create long, pointy corners; use a low Miter limit to create bevel joins.

6. Click OK **3**–**4**. The offset path will be a separate path from, and stacked behind, or in front of, the original path. And regardless of whether the original object was open or closed, the offset path will be closed.

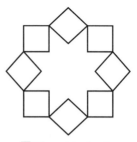

1 *The original path*

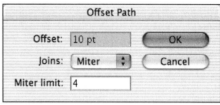

2 *In the **Offest Path** dialog box, choose Offset, Joins, and Miter limit options.*

3 *After applying the **Offset Path** command*

4 *After recoloring the objects*

TRANSFORM 7

This chapter covers methods for transforming an object. You'll learn how to use the five individual transformation tools (Rotate, Scale, Reflect, Shear, and Blend), the Free Transform tool, an object's bounding box, the Transform Each command, the Transform Effect command, and the Make Blend command. The Transform palette is discussed on page 426, the Move command on page 425.

The tools

Basic transformations

The **Rotate** tool rotates an object around its center or around another specified point.

The **Scale** tool enlarges or reduces the size of an object proportionally or nonproportionally.

The **Reflect** tool creates a mirror image of an object across a specified axis.

The **Shear** tool slants an object at a specified angle.

The **Free Transform** tool can be used to rotate, scale, reflect, or shear, or to apply perspective or distortion.

The **Blend** tool transforms one object into another by creating a multistep color and shape progression between the two objects.

Using the transformation tools

Before we delve into the individual transformation tools in detail, here's a summary of the basic ways they are used.

Dialog box method

Select the whole object, then double-click the Rotate, Scale, Reflect, or Shear tool to open the tool's dialog box, or Control-click/right-click in the document window and choose a command from the Transform submenu on the context menu **1**. The default point of origin at the object's center will now be visible. Check the Preview box in the tool dialog box, enter numbers (press Tab to apply a value and move to the next field), then click OK or Copy.

To use a point of origin other than the object's center, select the object, choose a transformation tool, then click on or near the object to establish a new point of origin (no need to **NEW** hold down Option/Alt). A dialog box will open.

Dragging method

Select the whole object; choose the Rotate, Scale, Reflect, Shear, or Free Transform tool; position the pointer outside the object; then drag.

➤ Once the point of origin is established, for finer control position the pointer (arrowhead) far from the point of origin before dragging. You can use Smart Guides (Cmd-U/Ctrl-U) for positioning.

To use a point of origin other than the object's center **2**, select the object, choose an individual transformation tool (not the Free Transform tool), and click to establish a new point of origin **3**, reposition the mouse **4**, then drag to complete the transformation **5**. The point of origin can also be dragged to a different location using a transformation tool.

Hold down Option/Alt while dragging with an individual transformation tool to transform a copy of the original (release the mouse first).

To transform an object using its bounding box, see page 105.

➤ The rotate angle and other readouts will appear on the Info palette as you transform an object.

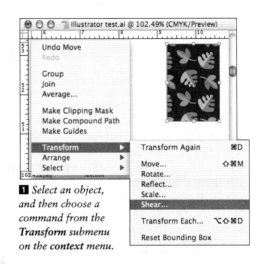

1 Select an object, and then choose a command from the **Transform** submenu on the **context menu**.

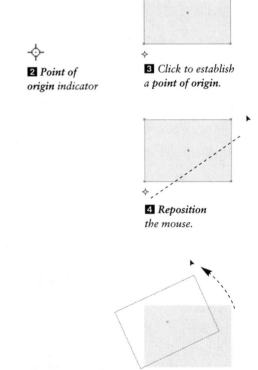

2 Point of origin indicator

3 Click to establish a point of origin.

4 Reposition the mouse.

5 Drag to transform.

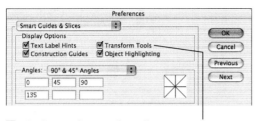

1 *Check* **Transform Tools** *in Illustrator (Edit, in Windows) > Preferences > **Smart Guides & Slices**.*

2 *Using Smart Guides with the* **Reflect** *tool*

3 *Using Smart Guides with the* **Scale** *tool*

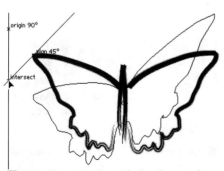

4 *Using Smart Guides with the* **Shear** *tool*

Repeating a transformation

Once you have performed a transformation on an object (except for a blend), you can repeat the transformation using the same values by choosing Object > Transform > **Transform Again** (Cmd-D/Ctrl-D). If you make a copy of an object while transforming it and then apply Transform Again, you'll get yet another copy, transformed.

➤ To constrain all transformations to a custom angle, change the Constrain Angle in Illustrator (Edit, in Windows) > Preferences > General (Cmd-K/Ctrl-K).

Transforming fill patterns

If you transform an object that contains a pattern fill and **Patterns** is checked in the transformation tool's dialog box or Transform Pattern Tiles is checked in Illustrator (Edit, in Windows) > Preferences > General, the pattern will also transform. Checking or unchecking this option in either location automatically resets it in the other.

To transform a pattern but not the object that contains it, uncheck **Objects** and check Patterns in the transformation tool's dialog box. Or with any individual transformation tool except Free Transform, click to establish the point of origin, then hold down ~ (tilde) and drag.

To use smart guides as you rotate, scale, or shear an object:

1. Choose Illustrator (Edit, in Windows) > Preferences > Smart Guides & Slices, and make sure Transform Tools is checked **1**. You can also choose a different Angles set or enter custom angles, if you like.

2. Make sure View > Smart Guides is on (Cmd-U/Ctrl-U).

3. Select the object to be transformed with the Selection (V) tool or Lasso tool.

4. Choose any individual transformation tool except Free Transform.

5. As you drag the mouse to transform the object, smart guides will appear temporarily **2**–**4**. Move the pointer along a smart guide to transform along that axis (more about smart guides on page 90).

To rotate an object using a dialog box:

1. Select an object (or objects) using the Selection tool .

2. Double-click the Rotate tool if you want to rotate the object around its center.
   or
   Choose the Rotate tool, then click near the object to establish a new point of origin.

3. Check Preview.

4. Enter a positive Angle (then press Tab) to rotate the object counterclockwise or a negative Angle to rotate the object clockwise (–360 to 360) **2**.

5. *Optional:* If the object contains a pattern fill and you check Patterns, the pattern will rotate with the object. Uncheck Objects to scale only the pattern and not the object.

6. Click Copy to rotate a copy of the object (not the original object) and close the dialog box.
   or
   Click OK to rotate the original object **3**.

To rotate an object by dragging:

1. Select an object (or objects) using the Selection tool.

2. Choose the Rotate tool (R).

3. Drag around the object to use the object's **center** as the point of origin.
   or
   Click to establish a new **point of origin** (the pointer will turn into an arrowhead), reposition the mouse as far from the origin as possible for better control, then drag to rotate the object.
   or
   To rotate a **copy** of the object, start dragging, then press Option/Alt (release the mouse before you release Option/Alt) **4**.

➤ Hold down Shift while dragging to rotate in 45° increments. Release the mouse before you release Shift.

➤ Press Cmd-D/Ctrl-D to repeat the last transformation on any selected object **5**.

1 *The shadow object is selected.*

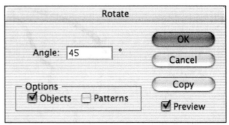

2 *Enter an Angle in the Rotate dialog box.*

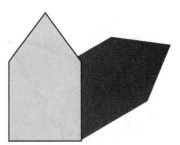

3 *The shadow was rotated –60° and then moved*

4 *An object is copy-rotated.*

5 *And then the Transform Again command is applied twice (Cmd-D/Ctrl-D).*

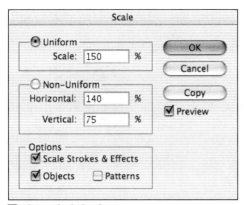

1 *The Scale dialog box*

2 *The original object*

3 *The object scaled **uniformly**, **Patterns** box **checked***

4 *The original object scaled **non-uniformly**, Patterns box **checked***

5 *The original object scaled **non-uniformly**, Patterns box **unchecked***

To scale an object using a dialog box:

1. Select an object (or objects) using the Selection tool.

2. To scale the object from its center, double-click the Scale tool.
   or
   Choose the Scale tool, then click near the object to establish a new point of origin.

3. Check Preview **1**.

4. To scale the object proportionally, click **Uniform,** then enter a Scale percentage (–20000 to 20000!), then press Tab to apply.
   or
   To scale the object nonproportionally, click **Non-Uniform,** enter in the Horizontal and Vertical percentages, then press Tab to apply.

   Note: Enter 100 to leave a dimension unchanged.

5. *Optional:* Check Scale Strokes & Effects to also scale the stroke thickness(es) and any effects from the Effects menu by the same percentage. This option can also be chosen in Illustrator (Edit, in Windows) > Preferences > General.

6. *Optional:* Check Patterns if the object contains a pattern fill and you want the pattern to scale with the object. Uncheck Objects to scale only the pattern and not the object.

7. Click Copy to scale a copy of the original (not the original object) and close the dialog box.
   or
   Click OK to scale the original object **2**–**5**.

When you scale an object using the **Scale** tool, the stroke may or may not scale accordingly, depending on whether Scale Strokes & Effects is checked in either Illustrator (Edit, in Windows) > Preferences > General or the Scale dialog box. Checking or unchecking this option in one location automatically resets it in the other location.

To scale an object by dragging:

1. Select an object (or objects) using the Selection tool.

2. Choose the Scale tool (S).

3. To scale from the object's **center,** drag (without clicking first) away from or toward the object.
   or
   Click near the object to establish a **point of origin** (the pointer will turn into an arrowhead), reposition the mouse **2**, then drag away from the object to enlarge it or drag toward the object to shrink it **3**.
   or
   To scale a **copy** of the object, start dragging, then press Option/Alt **4** (release the mouse first).

   Shift-drag diagonally to scale the object proportionally. Release the mouse before you release Shift.

➤ To scale a copy proportionally, hold down Option-Shift/Alt-Shift as you drag.

➤ To flip and scale an object simultaneously, drag completely across it with the Scale tool.

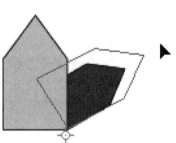

1 *Click to establish a point of origin.*

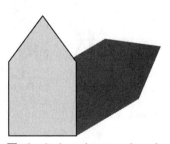

2 *Reposition the mouse…*

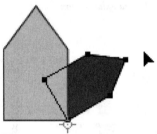

3 *…then drag away from the object.*

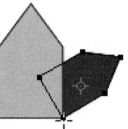

4 *The shadow object is **enlarged.***

Default angle

The default Horizontal angle is 0°; the default Vertical angle is 90°. The default starting point for measuring the degree of an angle is the horizontal *(x)* axis (the three o'clock position) A custom Constrain Angle can be entered in Preferences > General.

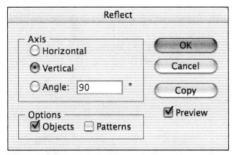

1 In the **Reflect** dialog box, click **Horizontal** or **Vertical** or enter an **Angle**.

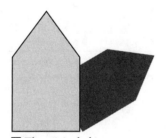

2 The original objects

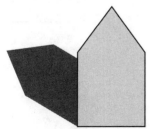

3 The shadow reflected across the **vertical axis** (90°)

To reflect (flip) an object using a dialog box:

1. Select an object (or objects) using the Selection tool.

2. To reflect from the object's center, double-click the Reflect tool (O) 🔲 (it's on the Rotate tool pop-out menu).
   or
   Choose the Reflect tool, then click near the object to establish a new point of origin.

3. Check Preview.

4. Click Axis: **Horizontal** or **Vertical** (the axis the mirror image will flip across) **1**.
   or
   Enter an **Angle** (360 to –360) for the object to flip over, then press Tab. A positive value is measured counterclockwise from the horizontal *(x)* axis; a negative value is measured clockwise from the horizontal axis.

5. *Optional:* Check Patterns if the object contains a pattern fill and you want it to be transformed.

6. Click Copy to reflect a copy of the original (not the original object) and close the dialog box.
   or
   Click OK to reflect the original object **2**–**3**.

➤ You can enter any Angle. Illustrator will substitute the nearest acceptable value.

To reflect an object by dragging:

1. Select the object (or objects) using the Selection tool.

2. Choose the Reflect tool (O). 🔲

3. Click near the object to establish a new **point of origin** (the pointer will turn into an arrowhead), reposition the mouse, then drag horizontally or vertically toward, across, or around the point of origin. The object will flip across the axis you create by dragging.

   Start dragging, then press Option/Alt to reflect a **copy** of the object.

   Shift-drag to **reflect** the object along a multiple of 45°. Release the mouse first.

To shear (slant) an object using a dialog box:

1. Select an object (or objects) using the Selection tool **1**.

2. To shear the object from its center, double-click the Shear tool (it's on the Scale tool pop-out menu).
   or
   Choose the Shear tool, then click near the object to establish a new point of origin.

3. Check Preview.

4. Enter a Shear Angle (360 to –360) **2**, then press Tab.

5. Click Axis: **Horizontal** or **Vertical** (the axis along which the object will be sheared) **3**.
   or
   Click Axis: **Angle,** enter an Angle value, then press Tab. The angle will be calculated clockwise relative to the horizontal *(x)* axis **4**.

6. *Optional:* Check Patterns to shear a pattern fill with the object.

7. Click Copy to shear a copy of the original (not the original object) and close the dialog box.
   or
   Click OK to shear the original object.

To shear an object by dragging:

1. Select an object (or objects) using the Selection tool or the Lasso tool.

2. Choose the Shear tool.

3. To slant from the object's **center,** without clicking first, position the pointer outside the object, then drag away from the object.
   or
   Click near the object to establish a new **point of origin,** reposition the mouse, then drag.

   Start dragging, then press Option/Alt to shear a **copy** of the object. To shear the object to a multiple of 45°, start dragging, then hold down Shift. Release the mouse button first.

Sidebar: Shear Tool

Get the numbers

Each transformation dialog box continues to display the **last-used** values for that type of transformation (whether a tool or a dialog box was used) until those values are changed or you quit/exit Illustrator.

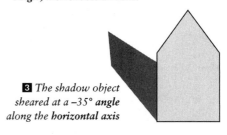

1 *The shadow object is selected.*

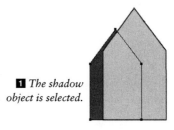

2 *In the Shear dialog box, enter a Shear Angle, then choose an Axis.*

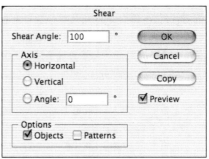

3 *The shadow object sheared at a –35° angle along the* **horizontal axis**

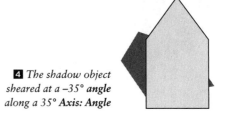

4 *The shadow object sheared at a –35° angle along a 35° Axis: Angle*

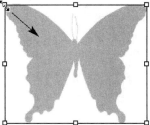

1 *Option-drag/Alt-drag to scale an object from its center.*

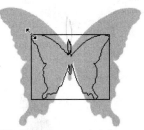

2 *The object is scaled down.*

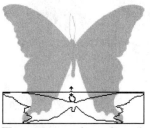

3 *To reflect an object, drag a bounding box handle all the way across it.*

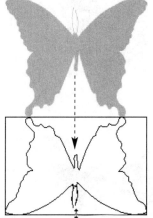

4 *A reflection of the object is made.*

The fastest way to transform an object is by using its **bounding box.**

To transform an object using its bounding box:

1. If bounding boxes are currently hidden, choose View > Show Bounding Box (Cmd-Shift-B/Ctrl-Shift-B).

2. Select an object (or objects) using the Selection tool. A rectangular box with eight handles will surround the object(s). The handles and box will be the color of the object's layer.

3. To **scale** the object along two axes, drag a corner handle; to resize along one axis, drag a side handle. Shift-drag to resize proportionally. Option-drag/Alt-drag to scale the object from its center **1**–**2**. Option-Shift-drag/Alt-Shift-drag to do both. *Note:* You can't choose a point of origin.
   or
   To create a **reflection** (mirror image) of the object, drag a side handle all the way across it **3**–**4**.
   or
   To **rotate** the object, move the pointer slightly outside of a corner handle, (the pointer will be a *curved* double arrow), then drag in a circular direction.
   or
   To **rotate** the object 180°, drag a corner handle all the way across the object or Shift-drag a side handle. Option-drag/Alt-drag to do this from the object's center.

After you rotate an object by using a tool or by dragging the corner of its bounding box, the bounding box will no longer align with the *x/y* axes of the page. The **Reset Bounding Box** command resets the orientation of the bounding box but not the orientation of the object.

To square off the bounding box:

With the object selected, choose Object > Transform > Reset Bounding Box, or Control-click/right-click and choose Transform > Reset Bounding Box.

The **Free Transform** tool does everything the transformation tools do, plus it can also apply distortion and perspective. You can't choose a different point of origin with this tool (it always works from the center of the object or objects), and you can't use it to make copies.

To use the Free Transform tool:

1. Select one or more objects or a group. The Free Transform tool won't make a clone, so copy the object now if you want to transform a copy of it.

2. Choose the Free Transform tool (E).

3. To **scale** in two dimensions, drag a corner handle. Shift-drag to scale proportionally; Option-drag/Alt-drag to scale the object from its center; Option-Shift-drag/Alt-Shift-drag to do both. To resize the object in one dimension, drag a side handle.

   To **rotate** the object, position the pointer outside it, then drag in a circular motion. Shift-drag to rotate in 45° increments.

   To **shear**, drag a side handle then hold down Cmd/Ctrl and continue to drag **1**–**2**. To constrain the movement, drag a side handle, then Cmd-Shift-drag/Ctrl-Shift-drag. To shear along the *x* or *y* axis from the object's center, start dragging, then hold down Cmd-Option-Shift/Ctrl-Alt-Shift and continue to drag.

   To **reflect**, drag a side handle all the way across the object. To rotate the object 180°, drag a corner handle all the way across it. To reflect or rotate from the object's center, Option-drag/Alt-drag a side or corner handle. Include the Shift key to reflect or rotate proportionally.

   To **distort**, drag a corner (not a side) handle, then hold down Cmd/Ctrl and continue to drag **3**–**4**. *Note:* This doesn't work on editable type.

   To apply **perspective**, drag a corner handle, then hold down Cmd-Option-Shift/Ctrl-Alt-Shift and continue to drag **5**–**6**. The perspective will occur along the *x* or *y* axis, depending on which direction you drag. *Note:* You can't apply perspective to editable type.

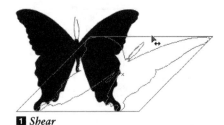

1 *Shear*

2 *The sheared object*

3 *Distort*   **4** *The distorted object*

5 *Perspective*

6 *The object with applied **perspective***

The original formation

The formation rotated 15° via the Rotate tool

*The formation rotated 15° via the **Transform Each** command with the **Random** option **unchecked***

1 *The **Transform Each** command vs. the **Rotate** tool*

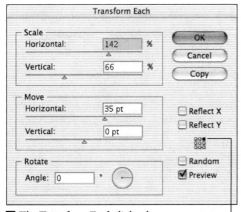

2 *The **Transform Each** dialog box*

Point of origin

(See also the first two figures on the following page.)

The **Transform Each** command modifies one or more selected objects relative to their *individual* center points. The transformation tools, by contrast, transform multiple objects relative to a single, *common* center point **1**. To make your illustration look less regular and more hand-drawn, apply the Transform Each command to a bunch of objects with the Random option checked.

To perform multiple transformations via Transform Each:

1. Select one or more objects. Objects in a group can't be transformed individually.

2. Choose Object > Transform > Transform Each (Cmd-Option-Shift-D/Ctrl-Alt-Shift-D).
   or
   Control-click/right-click and choose Transform > Transform Each.

3. Check Preview, and move the dialog box out of the way, if necessary.

4. Do any of the following **2**:

   Move the Horizontal or Vertical **Scale** slider (or enter a percentage and press Tab) to scale the objects horizontally and/or vertically from their center point.

   Choose a higher Horizontal **Move** value to move the objects to the right or a lower value to move them to the left, and/or choose a higher Vertical Move value to move the objects upward, or vice versa.

   Enter a number in the **Rotate: Angle** field and press Tab, or rotate the dial.

   Check the **Reflect X** or **Reflect Y** box to create a mirror reflection of the objects.

   Check **Random** to have Illustrator apply random transformations within the range of the values you've chosen for Scale, Move, or Rotate. For example, at a Rotate Angle of 35°, a different angle between 0° and 35° will be used for each selected object. Check Preview on and off to get different random effects.

   Click a different **point of origin** (the point that will remain stationary).

5. Click OK or Copy (**1**–**2**, next page).

1 *The original objects*

2 *After applying* **Transform Each** *(Horizontal Scale 120, Vertical Scale 80, Horizontal Move 13, Vertical Move –13, and Rotate 17°—nonmatching Horizontal and Vertical Scale values)*

Transform Effect

If you apply transformations via the **Transform Effect** dialog box, you will be able to edit (not just undo) those transformations long after you've closed the dialog box, and even after you close and reopen the file.

To use the Transform Effect dialog box to apply editable effects:

1. Select one or more objects.

2. Choose Effect > Distort & Transform > Transform.

3. Follow the instructions for the Transform Each dialog box on the previous page. The Transform Effect dialog box looks and behaves just like the Transform Each dialog box, with one exception: In the Transform Effect dialog box, you can specify how many copies you want **3**.

4. To edit the transformation, select the object, then double-click Transform on the Appearance palette **4**. That reopens the Transform Effect dialog box. This is a sneak preview of what's to come in Chapter 19, Appearances/Styles.

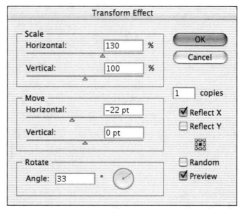

3 *Use the* **Transform Effect** *dialog box to apply editable effects.*

4 *To edit a transform effect, double-click* **Transform** *on the Appearance palette.*

Creating blends
Blends are live!

Both the **Blend** tool and the **Make Blend** command create a multistep color and shape progression between two or more objects. Using the Blend tool, you can control which parts of the objects are calculated for the blend, whereas the Make Blend command controls this function automatically.

If you reshape, recolor, or reposition any of the individual objects in a blend or reshape, reposition, or transform the path that controls the whole blend, the blend will update automatically. You can also alter the appearance of an existing blend by reshaping the straight path (spine) that the Blend tool or command creates, using any path-editing tool or by selecting the blend and changing the number of steps or other options in the Blend Options dialog box.

Before you create a blend, keep these guidelines in mind:

➤ You can blend nonmatching shapes and shapes that have different fill and stroke attributes (even brush strokes).

➤ You can blend gradients or other blends, but not mesh objects.

➤ You can blend two open paths, two closed paths, or a closed path and an open path.

➤ Illustrator lets you blend symbol instances, but the results aren't as fully functional as blends created with ordinary objects. Symbol sets can be blended too, but they require an excessive amount of time to process.

Note: To blend colors between objects without blending their shapes, use a Blend filter (see page 164).

Process or spot?

■ If one of the original blend objects contains a **process** color and another object contains a **spot** color, the intermediate objects will be painted with **process** colors.

■ If you blend objects containing more than one **spot** color, the intermediate objects will be painted with **process** colors.

■ If you blend **tints** of the **same spot** color, the intermediate objects will be painted with graduated **tints** of that color. To blend between a spot color and white, change the white fill to 0% of the spot color.

*Daniel Pelavin used a **blend** to create the shading on this lighthouse.*

Blends

To blend between objects using the Make Blend command:

1. Position two or more objects or groups, allowing room for the transition shapes that will be created between them, and select all the objects using the Selection tool or the Lasso tool **1**. You can blend **NEW** an editable type object, but not a mesh object.

2. Choose Object > Blend > Make (Cmd-Option-B/Ctrl-Alt-B) **2**–**3**.

3. To change the appearance of the blend, read the instructions on the following three pages.

➤ If you don't like the blend, you can Undo it, or you can release it (instructions below).

➤ To prevent banding when printing a blend, see page 113.

To release a blend:

1. Select the blend with the Selection tool (or using the Layers palette).

2. Choose Object > Blend > Release (Cmd-Option-Shift-B/Ctrl-Alt-Shift-B). The original objects and the *path* that was created by the blend will remain; the transitional blend objects will be deleted.

Recoloring blend objects

To recolor **all** the objects in a blend, use Filter > Colors > **Adjust Colors.**

To recolor one of the **original** blend objects, deselect the blend, choose the **Direct Selection** tool, select one of the **original** objects, then choose a color from the Color or Swatches palette. The transitional objects can't be recolored individually.

To recolor a blend of **symbols,** use the **Symbol Stainer** tool on a selected instance (see Chapter 16).

1 *The original objects: A white butterfly on top of a black butterfly*

2 *After choosing Object >* ***Blend > Make,*** *with Spacing: **Smooth Color** chosen in the Blend Options dialog box (see the following page)*

3 *The original objects after choosing Object > **Blend > Make,** with Spacing: **Specified Steps** (7) chosen in the Blend Options dialog box (see the following page)*

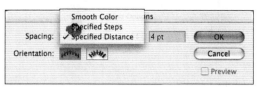

1 *Choose Spacing and Orientation options for existing and future blends in the Blend Options dialog box.*

2 *Spacing: Smooth Color*

3 *Spacing: Specified Steps (7)*

4 *Orientation: Align to Page*

5 *Orientation: Align to Path*

If you change the settings in the **Blend Options** dialog box, the new settings will be applied automatically to any and all currently selected blends as well as to any subsequently created blends.

To choose or change blend options:

1. *Optional:* To change the blend options for any existing blends, select them now.

2. Double-click the Blend tool (W) (not the Gradient tool!).
   or
   Select an existing blend and choose Object > Blend > Blend Options.

3. Check Preview to preview changes on any currently selected blends.

4. From the Spacing pop-up menu **1**:

   Choose **Smooth Color** to have Illustrator automatically calculate the necessary number of blend steps (transition shapes) to produce smooth, nonbanding color transitions **2**. This option may take a moment to preview on existing objects.

   Choose **Specified Steps,** enter the desired number of transition steps for the blend (1–1000), then press Tab to preview. Use this option if you want to create distinct, discernible transition shapes **3**.

   Choose **Specified Distance,** then enter the desired distance between the transition shapes in the blend. The Specified Distance has no effect on the overall length of the blend.

5. Click Orientation: **Align to Page** (the first button) to keep the blend objects perpendicular to the page (on the horizontal axis) **4**.
   or
   Click Orientation: **Align to Path** (the second button) to keep the blend objects perpendicular to the blend path **5**.
   (To place blend objects on a user-drawn spine, see page 115.)

6. Click OK.

Blend Options

Editing blends

➤ To recolor any of the original objects in a blend, use the Direct Selection tool.

➤ To recolor all the objects in a blend, use a filter on the Filter > Colors submenu.

➤ To transform an entire blend, use a transformation tool or the Free Transform tool.

➤ To reshape a blend path, move one of the original objects (Direct Selection tool) or use any of the path-reshaping tools (e.g., Reshape, Direct Selection, Add Anchor Point, or Convert Anchor Point tool).

➤ Use the liquify tools to reshape a blend object or blend path.

The original blend

The same blend after recoloring the rightmost snowflake, adding points to the blend path, and reshaping the path

Editing Blends

The 39 steps

To **print** a Smooth Color blend, Illustrator automatically calculates the number of steps needed to produce a smooth blend based on the difference in CMYK color-component percentages between the blend objects (e.g., changes in the percentage of magenta between each object), and based on the assumption that the blend will be output on a high-resolution device (1200 dpi or higher). To specify the number of steps for a blend, choose Object > Blend > Blend Options, choose Spacing: Specified Steps, then enter the desired number (1–1000) in the field. Banding is more likely to occur in a color blend if it spans a wide distance (wider than 7 inches). For better results, use Adobe Photoshop to create a wide color blend, then place it into Illustrator.

Outputting blends to the Web is a whole different story. See page 491.

The **Reverse Front to Back** command changes the stacking order of blend objects—not their *x/y* locations.

To reverse the stacking position of objects in a blend:

1. Select the blend with the Selection tool (or by using the Layers palette; more about layers later) **1**.

2. Choose Object > Blend > Reverse Front to Back **2**. The original and transitional objects will now be in their reverse stacking order (e.g., what was originally the backmost object will now be the frontmost object, and vice versa).

The **Reverse Spine** command swaps the *x/y* location of all the blend objects, but it doesn't change their stacking position.

To reverse the location of objects in a blend:

1. Select the blend with the Selection tool (or by using the Layers palette) **1**.

2. Choose Object > Blend > Reverse Spine. The blend objects will swap locations **3**.

1 *The original blend*

2 *After applying the **Reverse Front to Back** command*

3 *The previous figure after applying the **Reverse Spine** command*

Reverse Front to Back; Reverse Spine

To blend objects using the Blend tool:

1. Position two or more different-shaped open paths or two or more closed paths, allowing room for the transition shapes that will be created between them. You can apply different colors or gradients to each object.

2. Choose the Blend tool (W).

3. To let Illustrator decide which anchor points to use for the blend, click the **fill** of the first object (not on the center point!).
   or
   If you want to control which anchor point will be used, click an **anchor point** on the first object . The little square on the Blend tool pointer will change from hollow to filled when it's over an anchor point.

4. Click either the fill or an anchor point on the next object . If the path is open, click an endpoint. For the smoothest shape transitions, click corresponding points on all the objects (e.g., the top left corner point of all the objects but not the top left corner point of one object and the lower right corner point of another object). You can add points in advance so the objects have an equal number of points. The blend will appear 3–4.

   Repeat this step for any other objects that you want to include in the blend. The blend will update automatically! See "Blends are live!" on page 109.

5. To change the appearance of the blend, (e.g., change Specified Steps to Smooth Color), see page 111.

➤ If you don't like the blend, use Undo or choose Object > Blend > Release.

➤ If the original objects contain different pattern fills, the transition shapes will be filled automatically with the pattern fill from the topmost object.

➤ Apply a stroke color to the blend if you want the transition shapes to be clearly delineated. To do this after the blend is created, use the Selection tool, click the blend, then apply a stroke.

1 *With the Blend tool, click the fill or an anchor point of one object…*

2 *…then click the fill or an anchor point of another object.*

3 *The blend appears.*

4 *This is what happens if you click on non-corresponding points.*

Blend Tool

114

1 *The original user-drawn path and blend*

2 *After choosing* **Replace Spine,** *the blend flows along the user-drawn path.*

To apply an existing blend to a path:

1. Create a blend, then draw a separate path along which you want the blend to flow. The path you draw can be closed or open. If it's closed, the blend will wrap around the object as best as it can.

2. Select both the blend and the path, using the Selection tool or the Lasso tool **1**.

3. Choose Object > Blend > Replace Spine. The blend will now follow along the user-drawn path **2**.

➤ If you release a blend that is associated with a user-drawn path (Object > Blend > Release), the path (former spine) will be preserved, with no stroke color. You can locate the path in Outline view or using Smart Guides (Object Highlighting).

➤ To change the orientation of the blend objects, select the blend, choose Object > Blend > Blend Options, then click the Orientation: Align to Page or Align to Path icon, whichever one isn't currently highlighted (see the last two figures on page 111).

➤ Appearances and effects can be applied to blend objects, either before or after the blend is created. To learn more about blends and appearances, see page 338.

Apply Blend to Path

Use a blend to create a 3D effect:

I. Select an object **1**, and apply a fill color and a stroke of None.

2. Double-click the Scale tool.

3. Click Uniform, enter a number between 60 and 80 in the Scale field, then click Copy.

4. With the copy still selected, choose a lighter or darker variation of the original fill color (or black or white) **2**. (For a process color, you can Shift-drag a process color slider on the Color palette to lighten or darken the color.)

5. Move the smaller object in front of the larger object, then select both objects, using the Selection tool or the Lasso tool.

6. Choose Object > Blend > Make (Cmd-Option-B/Ctrl-Alt-B) **3**–**4**. If the resulting blend doesn't look smooth, select it, double-click the Blend tool, choose Smooth Color from the Spacing pop-up menu, then click OK.

➤ You can modify either blend object at any time. Select the object using the Direct Selection tool, and then reposition or recolor it. You can scale the selected object using the Free Transform tool, the Scale tool, or the object's bounding box. The blend will redraw automatically.

➤ A similar effect can be achieved on a single object by using Object > Create Gradient Mesh (choose Appearance: To Center). See pages 325–326.

1 *The original object*

2 *A reduced-size copy of the object is created, and a white fill is applied.*

3 *The two objects are blended together.*

4 *Here's another variation.*

A 3D Blend Effect

In Chapter 5 you learned how to draw closed and open paths without thinking about their individual components. In this important chapter, you'll learn how to reshape paths using the nuts and bolts that all paths are composed of: direction lines, direction points, anchor points, and segments. Once you learn how to alter the profile of an object by changing the number, position, or type of anchor points on its path, you'll be able to create just about any shape imaginable.

In this chapter, you'll learn how to move anchor points, direction lines, or path segments to reshape a path; convert a corner point into a smooth point (or vice versa) to reshape the segments that it connects; add or delete anchor points and segments; and use the Erase, Pencil, Paintbrush, Smooth, and Reshape tools to quickly reshape all or part of a path. You'll also learn how to average anchor points; join endpoints; combine paths; split a path; cut paths using the Divide Objects Below command; and carve away parts of a path using the Knife tool. Three practice exercises are also included in this chapter.

Corners and curves
The path building blocks

Paths can be open or closed, and are made up of anchor points connected by straight and/or curved **segments** **1**. **Smooth** anchor points have a pair of direction lines that move in tandem; **corner** anchor points have no direction lines, one direction line, or a pair of direction lines that move independently. At the end of each **direction line** is a **direction point** that controls the shape of the curve **2**–**3**.

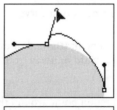

2 The **angle** of a direction line affects the **slope** of the curve into the anchor point.

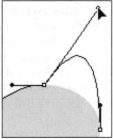

3 The **length** of a direction line affects the **height** of the curve.

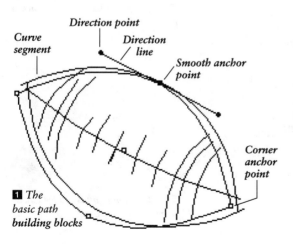

Direction point

Curve segment

Direction line

Smooth anchor point

Corner anchor point

1 *The basic path building blocks*

Move Point or Segment; Reshape Curve

If you **move** an **anchor point,** the segments that are connected to it will reshape. If you move a curve **segment,** the connecting anchor points will remain stationary. If you move a straight segment, connecting anchor points will move.

To move an anchor point or a segment:

1. Choose the Direct Selection tool (A).
   Note: You can move more than one point at a time, even points on different paths. To select them, Shift-click them individually or drag a marquee around them.

2. Drag an anchor point , or drag the middle of a segment , or press an arrow key. You can use Smart Guides for precise positioning (View > Smart Guides or Cmd-U/Ctrl-U).

➤ Shift-drag to constrain the movement of an anchor point to a multiple of 45°.

➤ If all the anchor points on a path are selected, you won't be able to move any individual points or segments. Deselect the object, then reselect an individual point.

In the instructions above, you learned that you can drag a curve segment or an anchor point to reshape a curve. A more precise way to **reshape** a **curve** is to lengthen, shorten, or change the angle of its direction lines.

To reshape a curve segment:

1. Choose the Direct Selection tool (A).

2. Click an anchor point or a curve segment 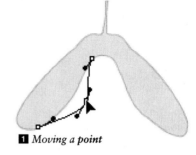.

3. Drag a direction point (the end of the direction line) toward or away from the anchor point .
   or
   Rotate the direction point around the anchor point. The anchor point will remain selected when you release the mouse. Use Shift to constrain the angle.

➤ Direction line antennae on a smooth point always move in tandem, and will stay in a straight line even if you move the segment or anchor point they're connected to.

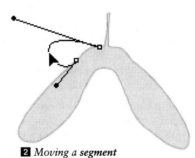

1 *Moving a point*

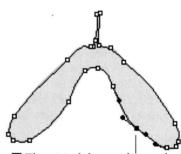

2 *Moving a segment*

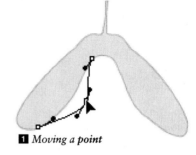

3 *The original shape with an anchor point selected*

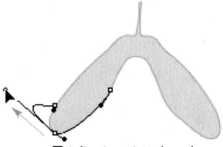

4 *A direction point is dragged away from its anchor point.*

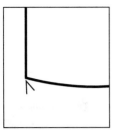

1 *To convert a corner point into a smooth point, press with the* **Convert Anchor Point** *tool on the anchor point...*

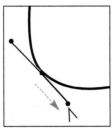

2 *...then drag away from the point.*

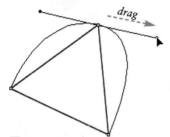

3 *Converting a* **corner** *point into a* **smooth** *point*

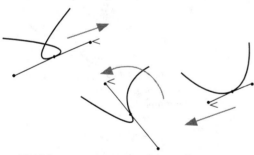

4 *If the curve twists around the anchor point, rotate the direction line to untwist it.*

To convert a corner anchor point into a smooth anchor point:

1. Choose the Convert Anchor Point tool. It's on the Pen tool pop-out menu. (Shift-C is the shortcut, but it works better for right-handed mousers than left-handed mousers—grrr...).
or
Choose the Pen tool (P).

2. Cmd-click/Ctrl-click the edge of the object to display its anchor points.

3. If you're using the Convert Anchor Point tool, press on an anchor point **1**, then drag away from it **2**. Direction lines will appear as you drag. If you're using the Pen tool, do the same thing with Option/Alt held down.

4. *Optional:* To further modify the curve, choose the Direct Selection tool (A), then drag the anchor point or a direction line **3**.

Note: If the new curve segment twists around the anchor point as you drag, keep the mouse button down, rotate the direction line back around the anchor point to undo the twist, then continue to drag in the new direction **4**.

➤ To reshape paths using a vector filter, try Filter > Stylize > Round Corners. To reshape paths using an effect, try Effect > Stylize > Round Corners (to remove the rounded corners, remove the effect).

Tearoff toolbar

While you're practicing the techniques in this chapter, we recommend tearing off the toolbar for the Pen tool so the Pen and its related tools are visible and easily accessible. Once you memorize the shortcuts for accessing these tools, you won't need to use the toolbar.

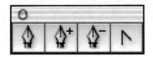

Convert Corner Point into Smooth Point

To convert a smooth anchor point into a corner anchor point:

1. Choose the Convert Anchor Point tool (Shift-C).
   or
   Choose the Pen tool (P).

2. Cmd-click/Ctrl-click the edge of an object to display its anchor points.

3. If you're using the Convert Anchor Point tool, click on a smooth point—don't drag! Its direction lines will disappear **1**–**2**. If you're using the Pen tool, do the same thing with Option/Alt held down.

In these instructions, you'll learn how to convert a point so its direction lines, instead of remaining in a straight line, can be **rotated independently** of each other.

To rotate direction lines independently:

1. Choose the Direct Selection tool (A).

2. Click the edge of an object to display its anchor points, then click a point **3**.

3. Choose the Convert Anchor Point tool (Shift-C).
   or
   Choose the Pen tool (P) and hold down Option/Alt.

4. Drag a direction point at the end of one of the direction lines. The curve segment will reshape as you drag **4**. Release Option/Alt, if it's pressed down.

5. Choose the Direct Selection tool (if it isn't already chosen), click the anchor point, then drag the other direction line for that anchor point **5**.

➤ To revert an independently rotating direction line pair back to its previous straight-line alignment and produce a smooth, unpinched curve segment, choose the Convert Anchor Point tool, then press on, and drag away from, the anchor point (if you just click on it, you'll create a corner).

1 *Click with the* **Convert Anchor Point** *tool on a smooth point...*

2 *...to convert it into a corner point.*

3 *A point is selected on an object.*

4 *A* **direction line** *is moved independently using the* **Convert Anchor Point** *tool.*

5 *The second* **direction line** *is moved.*

Nice curves

It's hard to get a symmetrical curve if you place points at the high point of a curve.

You'll get a more symmetrical curve if you place points only at the ends.

1 *Click a segment to add a new point...*

2 *...and then move the new point, if desired.*

Adding points

Another way to reshape a path is to manu-ally **add** or delete anchor points from it. Adding or deleting points from a closed path won't split or open it.

To add anchor points to a path manually:

1. Choose the Selection tool (V), then select the object you want to add a point or points to.

2. Choose the Add Anchor Point tool (+). It's on the Pen tool pop-out menu.
   or
   Choose the Pen tool (P). Also make sure Disable Auto Add/Delete is unchecked in Illustrator (Edit, in Windows) > Preferences > General.

3. Click the edge of the object. A new, selected anchor point will appear **1**. Repeat, if desired, to add more points.

   An anchor point that's added to a curve segment will be a smooth point with direction lines; an anchor point that's added to a straight segment will be a corner point.

4. *Optional:* Use the Direct Selection tool (A) to move the new anchor point (or its direction lines) **2**.

➤ Hold down Shift to disable the Auto Add/Delete function of the Pen tool. Release Shift before releasing the mouse.

➤ If you don't click precisely on a segment with the Add Anchor Point tool, a warn-ing prompt may appear. Click OK, then try again.

➤ Hold down Option/Alt to use the Delete Anchor Point tool when the Add Anchor Point tool is selected, and vice versa.

Add Anchor Points

The **Add Anchor Points** command inserts one point midway between every pair of existing anchor points in a selected object.

To add anchor points to a path using a command:

1. Choose the Selection tool (V), then select the object or objects that you want to add points to.

2. Choose Object > Path > Add Anchor Points **1**–**3**. Repeat, if desired.

1 *The original object*

Handy shortcuts

Pen tool	P
Add Anchor Point tool	+
Delete Anchor Point tool	-
Convert Anchor Point tool	Shift-C
Pencil tool	N
Paintbrush tool	B
Scissors tool	C
Lasso tool	Q
Pen tool to Convert Anchor Point tool	Option/Alt
Disable Auto Add/Delete function of Pen tool	Shift
Pen tool into last-used selection tool	Cmd/Ctrl
Add Anchor Point tool into Delete Anchor Point tool, and vice versa	Option/Alt
Pencil or Paintbrush tool into Smooth tool	Option/Alt
Average endpoints	Cmd-Option-J/ Ctrl-Alt-J
Join endpoints	Cmd-J/Ctrl-J
Average and join endpoints	Cmd-Option-Shift-J/ Ctrl-Alt-Shift-J

2 *After applying the Add Anchor Points command to the original object and then applying Filter > Distort > Pucker & Bloat (Pucker –70%)*

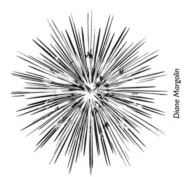

Diane Margolin

3 *After reapplying the Add Anchor Points command, and applying the Pucker & Bloat filter (Bloat 70%)*

1 *The pointer is positioned over an **endpoint** of an arc that was created with the Brush tool.*

2 *The path is added onto.*

3 *The pointer is positioned over an **endpoint**. Note the slash next to the pen.*

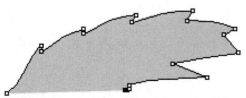

4 *After the endpoint is clicked, it becomes solid.*

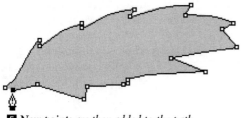

5 *New points are then added to the path.*

You can use the **Pencil** tool to **add** to any open path. It doesn't matter which tool was used to draw the path initially, and the path can have a brush stroke. The addition will have the same attributes as the original path.

To add to an open path using the Pencil tool:

1. Choose the Selection tool (V), then select an open path.

2. Choose the Pencil tool (N).

3. Position the pointer directly over an endpoint, then draw an addition to it. When you release the mouse, the path will remain selected.

➤ If you end up with a separate path instead of an addition to an existing path, delete the new path and try again.

To add to a brush stroke path using the Paintbrush tool:

1. Choose the Selection tool (V), then select an open path that has a brush stroke.

2. Choose the Paintbrush tool (B).

3. Position the pointer directly over an endpoint, then draw an addition to it **1**. When you release the mouse, the path will remain selected **2**.

To add a segment to an open path:

1. Choose the Pen tool (P).

2. Position the pointer over the endpoint of one of the paths to which you want to add a segment (the path doesn't have to be selected). A slash will appear next to the Pen pointer when the tool is positioned correctly **3** (use Smart Guides!).

3. Click the endpoint to make it a corner point or drag to make it a smooth point. The point will become solid **4**.

4. Position the pointer where you want the additional anchor point to appear.

5. Again, click to create a corner point or drag to create a smooth point **5**.

6. Continue to add points, if desired. Choose another tool when you're done.

➤ To close a path or join two separate paths by using the Pen tool, see page 132.

Deleting points
To delete anchor points from a path:

1. Choose the Delete Anchor Point tool (-). It's on the Pen tool pop-out menu.
   or
   Choose the Pen tool (P). And make sure Disable Auto Add/Delete is unchecked in Illustrator (Edit, in Windows) > Preferences > General.

2. Cmd-click/Ctrl-click the edge of the object that you want to delete anchor points from.

3. Click an anchor point (don't press Delete!). The point will be deleted and an adjacent point will become selected **1**–**2**. Repeat to delete other anchor points, if desired.

➤ Hold down Shift to disable the add/ delete function of the Pen tool. Release Shift before releasing the mouse button.

➤ If you don't click precisely on an anchor point with the Delete Anchor Point tool, an alert dialog box will appear. If you want to use Smart Guides to help you find anchor points, check Text Label Hints in Illustrator (Edit, in Windows) > Preferences > Smart Guides & Slices > Display Options.

1 *Click an anchor point with the* **Delete Anchor Point** *tool (or the Pen tool).*

2 *The point is removed.*

1 *The original objects*

2 *Using the Erase tool to erase points*

3 *Reshaping a path with the **Pencil** tool. (To get a crosshair pointer, check Use Precise Cursors in Preferences > General or press Caps Lock.)*

4 *The path is reshaped.*

Quick reshaping

The **Erase** tool deletes points, too—but you don't have to click on them individually.

To erase part of a path using the Erase tool:

1. Choose the Erase tool. It's on the Pencil tool pop-out menu.

2. Cmd-click/Ctrl-click an object to select it (not a gradient mesh or a text path).

3. Position the eraser tip of the pencil pointer directly over the area that you want to remove points from, then drag once across that area **1**–**2**. If you erase points from a closed path, you'll end up with an open path. If you erase points from an open path (not endpoints), you'll end up with two separate paths.

You already know how to use the **Pencil** and **Paintbrush** tools to draw freehand shapes. Now we'll show you how they can be used for quick-'n'-easy reshaping.

To reshape a path using the Pencil or Paintbrush tool:

1. To reshape a path that doesn't have a brush stroke, choose the Pencil tool (N).
   or
   To reshape a path that does have a brush stroke, choose the Pencil tool (N) or the Paintbrush tool (B).

2. Cmd-click/Ctrl-click a path to select it.

3. Position the pointer **directly** over the edge of the path, then start dragging **3**. If you want the path to close up or stay closed, finish up over another edge of the path. The path will reshape instantly **4**. *Note:* Be sure to position the pointer precisely on the edge of the path. If you don't, you'll create a new path instead of reshaping the existing one.

➤ Press Caps Lock to turn the pointer into a Precise Cursor (crosshair). Press Caps Lock again to restore the default cursors.

➤ To add to an open path using the Pencil or Paintbrush tool, see page 123.

To smooth part of an existing path:

1. Choose the Selection tool (V), select an open or closed path, then choose the Smooth tool ✎ (it's on the Pencil tool pop-out menu).

   or

   If the Pencil or Paintbrush tool is currently chosen, Cmd-click/Ctrl-click an open or closed path to select it, then hold down Option/Alt to access the Smooth tool.

2. Drag along the path. Any bumps on the path will be smoothed out ◼1. Some anchor points may be removed. Next, read about the Smooth Tool preferences, which affect how drastic an effect this tool may have on a path.

To choose settings for the Smooth tool:

1. Double-click the Smooth tool ◼2. ✎

2. Choose a Fidelity value (0.5–20) ◼3–◼4. The higher the Fidelity, the more anchor points will be removed.

3. Choose a Smoothness value (0–100%). The higher the Smoothness value, logically, the greater the amount of smoothing; the lower the Smoothness, the less drastic the reshaping.

4. Click OK.

➤ Click Reset to reset the preferences to their defaults.

◼1 *Using the* **Smooth** *tool*

◼2 *The* **Smooth Tool Preferences** *dialog box*

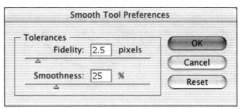

◼3 *The Smooth tool used with* **high Fidelity** *and* **Smoothness** *settings*

◼4 *The Smooth tool used on the original object with* **moderate Fidelity** *and* **Smoothness** *settings*

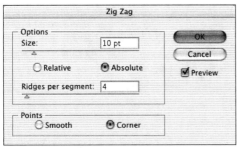

1 *The Zig Zag dialog box*

2 *The original star*

3 *After applying the Zig Zag effect (Size 45, Ridges 4, Smooth)*

4 *The original circle*

5 *After applying the Zig Zag effect (Size 24, Ridges 20, Corner)*

Some of the Illustrator filters and effects can be used to explode a simple shape into a more complex one in one fell swoop. The **Zig Zag** filter, for example, adds anchor points to a path or line and then moves those points to produce waves or zigzags. The Effect menu version applies the Zig Zag effect without actually altering the path. Effect menu commands are reeditable; Filter menu commands are not. (This is just a preview. Read more about effects and filters in Chapter 22.)

To apply the Zig Zag effect:

1. Select a path.

2. Choose Effect > Distort & Transform (upper part of the menu) > Zig Zag.

3. Check Preview **1**–**5**.

4. Click Points: **Smooth** (bottom of the dialog box) to make curvy waves, or **Corner** to create sharp-cornered zigzags.

5. To move the added points by a percentage of the size of the object, click **Relative,** then choose a **Size** percentage (0–100%).
   or
   To move the added points a specified distance, click **Absolute,** then choose or enter that distance (0–100 pt) via the **Size** slider or field (the increment is chosen in File > Document Setup: Units).

6. Choose a number of Ridges per segment (0–100) for the number of anchor points to be added between existing points. If you enter a number, press Tab to preview.

7. Click OK.

Zig Zag Effect

The **Reshape** tool is hard to describe in words. It's the best tool for gentle reshaping because it causes the least amount of distortion. Our favorite way to use this tool is to select a handful of points with it, then drag. That portion of the path will keep its overall contour while it elongates or contracts, and the rest of the path will stay put.

To use the Reshape tool:

1. Choose the Direct Selection tool (A), then click the edge of a path. Only one point or segment should be selected.

2. Choose the Reshape tool (it's on the Scale tool pop-out menu).

3. Drag any visible point. A square border will display around the point when you release the mouse.
    or
    Drag any segment of the path. A new square border point will be created.
    or
    Try this: Shift-click or marquee multiple points on the path using the Reshape tool (squares will display around these points), then drag. For smooth reshaping, leave at least one point on the path unselected (with no square around it) to act as an anchor for the shape **1**–**2**.

➤ Option-drag/Alt-drag with the Reshape tool to make a copy of the object as it's reshaped.

➤ Choose Edit > Undo to undo the last Reshape edits.

➤ To reshape multiple paths at a time, leave at least one point on each path unselected by the Reshape tool (with no square around it) to act as an anchor. For fun, try this on a series of lines. Their endpoints will remain stationary.

➤ Compare the Reshape tool, which adds one new point a time, with the liquify tools, which add many new points as they perform a more drastic reshaping function (see Chapter 21). Try using the Warp tool with a small brush and a low intensity.

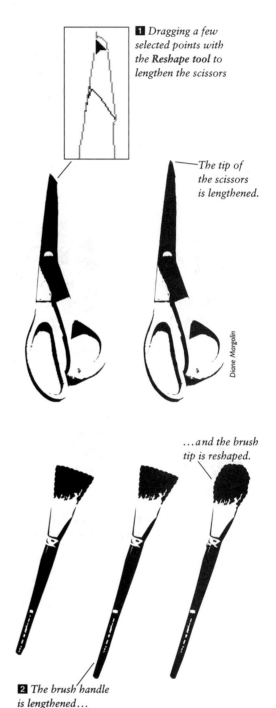

1 *Dragging a few selected points with the Reshape tool to lengthen the scissors*

The tip of the scissors is lengthened.

Diane Margolin

…and the brush tip is reshaped.

2 *The brush handle is lengthened…*

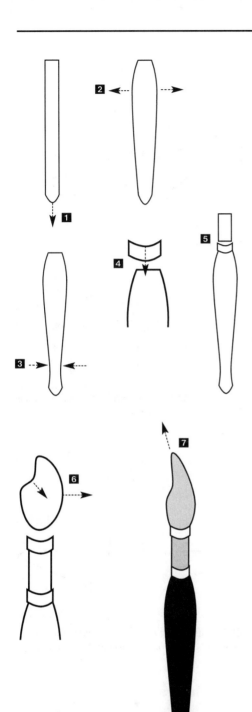

Exercise

Draw a paintbrush using the Reshape tool

1. Using the Rectangle tool, draw a narrow vertical rectangle. Give it a white fill and a black stroke (press D).

2. Choose the Direct Selection tool (A), deselect the path, then click on its edge.

3. Choose the Reshape tool, then drag downward from the middle of the bottom segment ▊.

4. Drag the upper middle of the right vertical segment slightly outward, and drag the upper middle part of the left vertical segment outward the same distance ▊.

5. Drag each side of the bottom vertical segments inward to pinch the stem ▊.

6. Using the Rectangle tool, draw a small horizontal rectangle. Then choose the Direct Selection tool, deselect the rectangle, then click its edge.

7. Choose the Reshape tool again, click the middle of the top segment, Shift-click the middle of the bottom segment, then drag downward ▊.

8. Choose the Selection tool (V), move the rectangle over the top of the brush stem, and scale it to fit.

9. Draw a slightly thinner vertical rectangle above the horizontal rectangle, then Control-click/right-click and choose Arrange > Send to Back ▊.

10. Using the Selection tool, Option-Shift/Alt-Shift drag the horizontal rectangle up to the top of the vertical rectangle.

11. Using the Ellipse tool, ⬭ draw an oval for the brush tip. Choose the Direct Selection tool (A), deselect the oval, then click the edge of the oval path.

12. Choose the Reshape tool, drag the right middle point outward, drag the upper left segment inward ▊, and drag the top point upward to lengthen the tip ▊.

13. With the Selection tool, move the brush tip over the brush stem, then Control-click/right-click and choose Arrange > Send to Back.

Averaging points

The **Average** command reshapes one or more paths by precisely realigning their endpoints or anchor points along the horizontal and/or vertical axis.

To average points:

1. Choose the Direct Selection tool (A) or the Lasso tool (Q).

2. Shift-click or marquee two or more anchor points 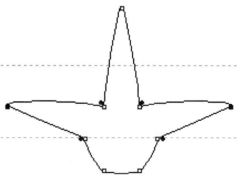. They can be on the same path or different paths.

3. Choose Object > Path > Average (Cmd-Option-J/Ctrl-Alt-J).
   or
   Control-click/right-click the artboard and choose Average from the contextual menu.

4. Click **Horizontal** to align the points along the horizontal *(x)* axis 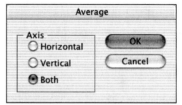. Points will move vertically.
   or
   Click **Vertical** to align the points along the vertical *(y)* axis. Points will move horizontally.
   or
   Click **Both** to overlap the points along both the horizontal and vertical axes. Choose this option if you're going to join them into one point (instructions on the following page).

5. Click OK **3**.

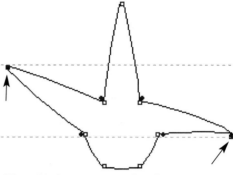

1 *Two anchor points are selected.*

2 *Click an **Axis** button in the **Average** dialog box.*

3 *After averaging the selected points, **Axis: Horizontal,** the points now align horizontally.*

Average Anchor Points

All at once

To **average** and **join** two selected endpoints, press Cmd-Option-Shift-J/ Ctrl-Alt-Shift-J. Don't apply this to a fully selected path.

1 *Two endpoints are selected.*

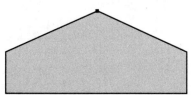

2 *The Join command joins the endpoints, adding a segment between them.*

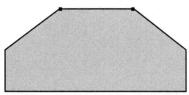

3 *If you choose the Join command when selected endpoints are right on top of each other, the Join dialog box will open.*

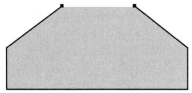

4 *This is figure* **1** *after the two endpoints were averaged and then joined into one point.*

Joining

If you align one endpoint on top of another, select the endpoints, and then execute the **Join** command, they'll be combined into one anchor point (that's method 1, below). If the endpoints aren't right on top of each other, the command will create a new straight segment between them. The Join command won't add direction lines to the new anchor point.

Note: The endpoints you join can be on separate open paths or on one open path. If you join an open path with a path in a group that's on a lower layer, the resulting path will appear on the higher of the two layers.

To join two endpoints:

Method 1 (Join command)

1. Choose the Direct Selection tool (A) or the Lasso tool (Q).

2. *Optional:* If you want to combine two endpoints into one, move one endpoint on top of the other manually, or use the Average command (Axis: Both) to align them (instructions on the previous page).

3. Marquee two endpoints **1**.

4. Choose Object > Path > Join (Cmd-J/ Ctrl-J), or Control-click/right-click the artboard and choose Join from the contextual menu. If one endpoint *isn't* on top of the other, the Join command will connect them with a straight segment **2**.

   If one endpoint *is* right on top of the other, the Join dialog box will open **3**. In the Join dialog box:

   Click **Corner** to join corner points into one corner point with no direction lines; or to connect two smooth points into one smooth point with independently moving direction lines; or to connect a corner point and a smooth point into a smooth point with one direction line.
   or
   Click **Smooth** to connect two smooth points into a smooth point with direction lines that move in tandem.

5. Click OK **4**.

   (Continued on the following page)

Method 2 (Pen tool)

1. Choose the Pen tool (P).

2. Position the pointer over the endpoint of one of the paths you want to join. A small slash will appear next to the Pen pointer when the tool is positioned correctly **1** (and the word "anchor," if you're using Smart Guides and Text Label Hints is checked in Preferences > Smart Guides & Slices).

3. Click the endpoint.

4. Position the pointer over the other endpoint of the same path (a small hollow circle will appear next to the Pen pointer) or over an endpoint on another path (a small square with a line behind it will appear next to the pointer) **2**.

5. Click the second endpoint. A new segment will appear between the two points you clicked **3**.

➤ If the path has an effect applied to it that makes it hard to locate its actual endpoints, use Smart Guides to help you.

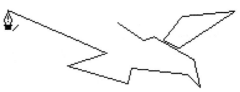

1 To join two endpoints, position the **Pen** over one **endpoint** and click...

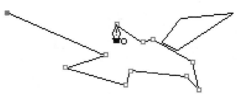

2 ...then click the other **endpoint**.

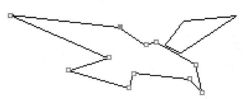

3 The two points are joined by a **new segment**.

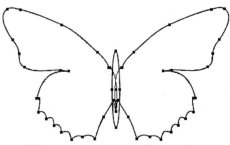

1 *Arrange two or more objects so they overlap, and then select them.*

2 *Clicking the Add to Shape Area button on the Pathfinder palette unites the individual shapes into a single shape.*

3 *The original objects*   **4** *After applying the Add to Shape Area command*

5 *The original objects*    **6** *After applying the Add to Shape Area command*

Using the tools that create shapes, such as the Rectangle, Ellipse, Star, or even the Pencil or Paintbrush, together with the reshaping functions covered in this chapter and occasionally some of the **Pathfinder** palette commands that are discussed in Chapter 17, you can create complex objects without having to draw with the Pen tool.

Rather than joining individual points, the shape mode commands on the Pathfinder palette combine whole objects. Here's an introduction to one of the most straightforward and useful shape mode commands: Add to Shape Area.

To combine objects using a command:

1. Position two or more objects so they overlap **1**.

2. Choose any selection tool.

3. Marquee at least some portion of all the objects.

4. Display the Pathfinder palette (Shift-F9).

5. Click the Add to Shape Area (first) button on the palette. The individual objects will combine into one closed compound shape **2**–**6** and will be colored with the paint attributes of the topmost object. To learn more about compound shapes, see Chapter 17.

➤ A stroke color that's applied to the new object will appear only on the perimeter of the overall combined shape, not on the interior segments. The interior segments are editable, but you can't apply a stroke color to them. If at some point you want to delete those interior segments, select the object, then click Expand on the Pathfinder palette.

➤ You can use the new closed object as a masking object. (You could not have created a single mask with the original objects before they were united.)

Slicing and dicing

The **Scissors** tool can be used either to open a closed path or to split an open path into two paths. A path can be split either at an anchor point or in the middle of a segment.

To split a path using the Scissors tool:

1. Choose any selection tool.

2. Click on an object to display its points. *Note:* You can split a closed path that contains text (area text), but not an open path that has text on it or inside it.

3. Choose the Scissors tool (C). ✂

4. Click on the object's path 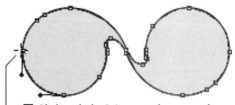. If you click once on a **closed** path, it will turn into a single, open path. If you click in **two** different spots on a closed path, the object will be split into two open paths. If you click once on an **open** path, it will split into two paths.

   If you click on a **segment**, two new endpoints will appear, one on top of the other. If you click on an anchor **point**, a new anchor point will appear on top of the existing one, and it will be selected.

5. To move the two new endpoints apart, choose the Direct Selection tool (A), ⬆ then drag the selected point away to reveal the other one underneath 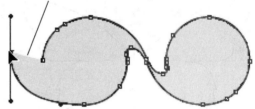. (To move the bottom endpoint instead, marquee both endpoints, Shift-click the top one, then press and hold an arrow key.)

The method for **splitting** a path described below is quick, but the results are not as controllable as in the method described above. If you delete a point from a closed path, the adjacent segments will be deleted; if you delete an endpoint from an open path, the adjacent segment will be deleted; and if you delete a point or segment within an open path, it will split into two shorter paths.

To split a path by deleting a point or a segment:

1. Deselect the object you want to split.

2. Choose the Direct Selection tool (A). ⬆

3. Click an anchor point or segment.

4. Press Delete/Backspace.

1 Click with the Scissors tool on an anchor point or a segment.

There is no segment, and thus no stroke, between the endpoints.

2 After moving the new endpoint. If you apply a stroke color to an open path, you'll be able to see where the missing segment is. An open path can have a fill.

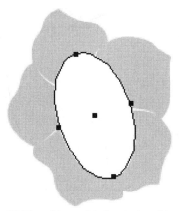

1 *The white oval is the cutting object.*

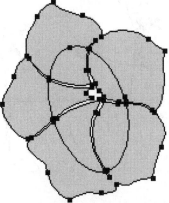

2 *After **Divide Objects Below** is chosen, all the resulting objects become selected.*

3 *After recoloring the five separate paths that originally formed an oval*

The **Divide Objects Below** command uses an object like a cookie cutter to cut the objects underneath it, and then deletes the cutting object.

To cut objects using the Divide Objects Below command:

1. Create or select an object (not a group) to be used as a cutting shape. The Slice command will cause this object to be deleted, so make a copy of it now if you want to preserve it.

2. Place the cutting object on top of the object(s) you want to cut **1**.

3. Make sure only the cutting object is selected.

4. Choose Object > Path > Divide Objects Below. The topmost shape (cutting object) will be deleted automatically and the underlying objects will be cut into separate paths where they meet the edge of the cutting object **2**–**3**. All the objects will become selected. Any objects that were in a group will remain grouped. **NEW**

➤ To prevent an object from being affected by the Divide Objects Below command, hide or lock it (see pages 196–197).

Divide, or Divide Objects Below?

Compare the **Divide Objects Below** command, discussed on this page, with the **Divide** command on the Pathfinder palette, which is discussed on pages 311–312. With Divide Objects Below, the top cutting object is deleted and the resulting objects aren't grouped. With Divide, the paint attributes of the topmost object are preserved, though the object is divided, and the resulting objects are grouped. You'll usually end up with smaller pieces with Divide than with Divide Objects Below.

Divide Objects Below

The **Knife** tool reshapes paths as a carving knife would, and is a wonderful tool for artists who have a freehand drawing style.

To cut an object into separate shapes:

1. *Optional:* If you select an object (or objects) before using the Knife tool, the tool won't cut any of the unselected objects. This is useful if there are many objects close together in the illustration and you don't want them all to be cut. If you don't select any objects first, any object the Knife passes across is fair game.

   Note: The Knife tool works on a closed path or a filled, open path, but not on an unfilled open path. To carve up type, you must convert it to outlines first (select it, then choose Type > Create Outlines).

2. Choose the Knife tool (it's on the Scissors tool pop-out menu). Don't confuse it with the Slice tool!

3. Starting from outside the object(s), drag completely across it to divide it in two, or carve off a chunk of it **1**–**3**.
   or
   Option-drag/Alt-drag to cut in a straight line. (Press and hold Option/Alt before dragging.) Option-Shift-drag/Alt-Shift-drag to constrain the cutting strokes to an increment of 45°.

➤ If you make a "closed" cut (drag back over the starting point) with the Knife tool completely inside an object, you'll create a new, separate object. You can move the new object with the Selection tool to expose the hole.

➤ Choose Object > Group to group the newly separated shapes together, and then use the Direct Selection tool if you need to select individual shapes within the group.

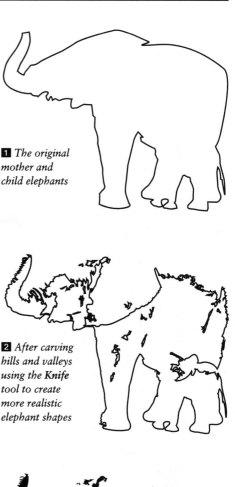

1 *The original mother and child elephants*

2 *After carving hills and valleys using the **Knife** tool to create more realistic elephant shapes*

3 *The final image, after applying a black fill*

Diane Margolin

Knife Tool

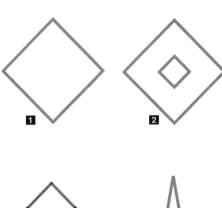

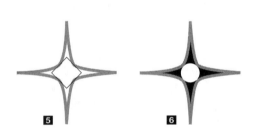

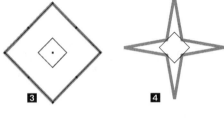

Exercise

Change a square into a star

1. Choose the Rectangle tool (M). Choose a fill of None and a 2 pt. stroke (see Chapter 9).

2. Click on the artboard.

3. In the Rectangle dialog box, enter 2″ in the Width field, click the word Height, then click OK.

4. Double-click the Rotate tool, enter 45 in the Angle field, then click OK **1**.

5. Double-click the Scale tool, enter 30 in the Uniform Scale field, then click Copy **2**.

6. Choose View > Guides > Make Guides (Cmd-5/Ctrl-5) to turn the small diamond into a guide.

7. Choose the Selection tool (V), then select the large diamond shape. Choose Object > Path > Add Anchor Points **3**.

8. Choose the Direct Selection tool (A). Deselect, then click on the edge of the diamond.

9. Drag each of the new midpoints inward until it touches the guide shape. Use Smart Guides to drag at a 45° angle **4**.

10. Choose the Convert Anchor Point tool (Shift-C), and drag each of the inner midpoints to create a curve. Drag clockwise and along the edge of the guide shape **5**.

11. Choose the Ellipse tool (L), position the pointer over the center point of the star shape, then Option-Shift-drag/Alt-Shift-drag until the circle touches the curves of the star.

12. To the circle, apply a white fill and a stroke of None; to the star shape, apply a black or dark fill and a lighter stroke **6**.

13. *Optional:* Select the circle. Choose the Scale tool (S). Start dragging, hold down Option-Shift/Alt-Shift, and continue to drag until the copy of the circle touches the outer tips of the star. Fill the large circle with None, and apply a 2 pt. stroke **7**.

Exercise
Draw a light bulb

1. Draw a **circle** about 1 inch in diameter and a **rectangle** about .5 inch square. Apply a fill of None and a 4 pt. black stroke to both objects.

2. Choose the **Direct Selection** tool (A), select the bottom point of the circle, then drag the point downward. Using the Selection tool (V), select **both** objects.

3. Option-click/Alt-click the **Add to Shape Area** button on the Pathfinder palette. Use the **Add Anchor Point** tool (+) to add a point on the bottom-most segment (1), then use the **Direct Selection** tool to drag the new point downward.

(1)

4. Click on each point where the curve meets the straight segment (2). Using Smart Guides to assist you, rotate the direction line upward to 90° vertical.

5. Apply a fill of white to the bulb.

6. Create a rounded rectangle or an oval that's wider than the base of the bulb. Rotate it using the **Rotate** tool (R). Choose the Selection tool, and Option-Shift/Alt–Shift drag two copies downward.

7. Apply a fill color and a stroke of None to the ovals, and place them on the bottom part of the bulb.

8. Use the Star tool to create a 20-point star (Radius 1: .4″, Radius 2: .69″). Apply a light fill color and a stroke of None. Scale the star, if necessary, so it's larger than the bulb.

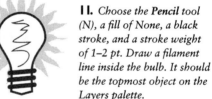

9. Position the star over the bulb. On the Layers palette, drag the star object below the bulb object.

10. Select the star. Apply Effect > Distort & Transform > Roughen (Size: 2, Relative, Detail: 3–6). Deselect.

11. Choose the **Pencil** tool (N), a fill of None, a black stroke, and a stroke weight of 1–2 pt. Draw a filament line inside the bulb. It should be the topmost object on the Layers palette.

12. Select the bulb. On the Transparency palette, set the Opacity slider to 60–70%, Normal mode.

13. Select the bulb, star, and filament. Apply Effect > Stylize > Drop Shadow (Opacity 50–60%, Blur 1–3 pt.).

FILL & STROKE | 9

In this chapter you'll learn to fill the inside or stroke the edge of an object with a solid color or pattern and choose stroke attributes, such as dashes and joins. You'll also learn how to change a document's color mode and choose colors for print or Web output; save, copy, edit, load, replace, delete, merge, move, and duplicate color swatches; select objects for recoloring; globally replace and edit colors; apply fill and stroke colors simultaneously using the Paint Bucket tool; sample colors using the Eyedropper tool; blend fill colors between objects; and invert, adjust, convert, and saturate/desaturate colors. Finally, you'll learn how to create and modify fill patterns.

Related topics

Gradients, Chapter 18
Appearance palette, Chapter 19

Opening the palettes

Color palette   F6
Stroke palette   F10

Chris Spollen

Mixing and applying colors
Fills and strokes

The flat color, pattern, or gradient that's applied to the inside of a closed or open path is called the **fill.** The color or brush stroke that's applied to the edge of a closed or open path is called the **stroke.** A stroke can be solid or dashed, and it can have an applied brush stroke, but it can't be filled with a gradient.

Colors and patterns can be applied using the **Color** or **Swatches** palette, buttons on the **Toolbox,** or the **Paint Bucket** tool. Using the **Stroke** palette, you can change the stroke thickness (weight), style (dashed or solid), and endcaps. When an object is selected, its color attributes display on the Toolbox and the Color and Appearance palettes. The current fill and stroke colors are automatically applied to any new object you create. You can store any color, pattern, or gradient on the Swatches palette for later use.

Note: Before you start working with color, you should calibrate your monitor. Then, for the instructions in this chapter, open the Color, Stroke, and Swatches palettes. And, of course, work with your illustration in Preview view so you can see colors onscreen as you apply them.

Here's a **quick** method for **applying color,** just to get you started. The beauty of this method is that you don't need to choose any particular tool or select anything in your document. Try this method, then keep on reading—there's lots more to learn in this chapter!

QuickStart drag-color:

1. Click the Fill box **1** or Stroke **2** box on the Toolbox or the Color palette.

2. Click a color on the color bar on the Color palette **4**.

3. Drag from the Fill or Stroke box (whichever box you clicked in step 1) over an object. The object doesn't have to be selected.

   If an object is already selected, simply clicking a color swatch or a color on the color bar will automatically change its fill or stroke, depending on whether the Fill or Stroke box is currently active.

➤ You can also apply a color by dragging a swatch from the Swatches palette over an object, or apply a gradient fill by dragging the gradient box on the expanded Gradient palette over an object.

➤ Shift-drag to apply a stroke color if the Fill box is active, or to apply a fill color if the Stroke box is active.

To apply a fill or stroke of black or white:

1. Select an object.

2. Click the Fill or Stroke box on the Color palette **1**–**2**, then click the white or black selector at the right end of the color bar on the Color palette **5** or click the white or black swatch on the Swatches palette **6**.
   or
   To apply a white fill *and* a black stroke, click the Default Fill and Stroke button (D) on the Toolbox **3**–**4**

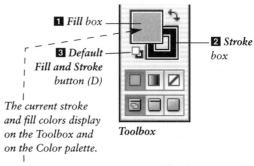

1 *Fill box*

2 *Stroke box*

3 *Default Fill and Stroke button (D)*

The current stroke and fill colors display on the Toolbox and on the Color palette.

Toolbox

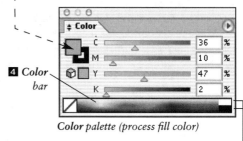

4 *Color bar*

Color palette (process fill color)

5 *White and black selectors*

White swatch **6** *Black swatch*

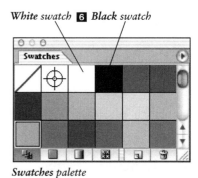

Swatches palette

4 *White fill, black stroke, full moon?*

Daniel Pelavin

Drag-Color; Apply Black or White

Fill color   Stroke color   Color models

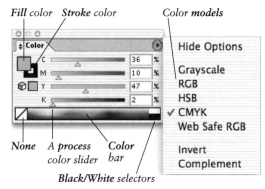

Hide Options

Grayscale
RGB
HSB
✓ CMYK
Web Safe RGB

Invert
Complement

None   A process   Color
       color slider bar
       Black/White selectors

1 The Color palette

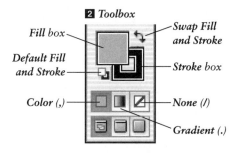

2 Toolbox

Fill box ——

Default Fill
and Stroke ——

Color (,) ——

Swap Fill
and Stroke

Stroke box

None (/)

Gradient (.)

A global process
color has a white   A nonglobal
corner with no dot.   process color   A spot color
                        (see page 144)   has a dot.
— None

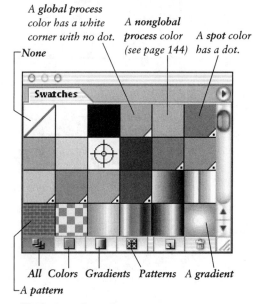

Swatches

All Colors Gradients Patterns A gradient
— A pattern

3 The Swatches palette

The palettes you'll use for coloring

Color palette

The **Color** palette (F6) is used to mix and choose solid colors. The color boxes on the Color palette display the current fill and stroke colors of the currently or most recently selected object **1**. The palette options change depending on whether the Grayscale, RGB, HSB, CMYK, or Web Safe RGB color model is chosen from the palette menu. You can click a color on the color bar or mix a process color using exact percentages. Choosing a color model for the palette doesn't change the document color mode (see page 146).

Toolbox

The Fill and Stroke boxes on the **Toolbox** **2** display the attributes of the currently or most recently selected object, and will update if the current fill or stroke color is changed via the Color or Swatches palette. Click the Color or Gradient button to reapply the last chosen solid color or gradient.

Swatches palette

The **Swatches** palette contains process color (RGB or CMYK, depending on the current document color mode), spot color, pattern, and gradient swatches **3**. You can append additional swatches from other libraries (e.g., PANTONE). If you click a swatch, that color will appear on the current Fill or Stroke box (whichever is currently active) on the Toolbox and on the Color palette, and it will apply immediately to all currently selected objects. If a selected object contains a color or colors from the Swatches palette, those swatches will be highlighted on the palette.

Illustrator supplies default process color, spot color, pattern, and gradient swatches as well as other swatch libraries. You can also create your own swatches, which will save with the file in which they're created.

None

The None button is located on the Color palette, the Swatches palette, and the Toolbox. Select an object and then click this button to remove any fill or stroke color, depending on which color box is currently active on the Color palette and Toolbox.

Basic coloring steps

Open the Toolbox and the Color (F6), Swatches, and Stroke (F10) palettes.

1. Select the objects whose color attributes you want to change.

2. Make sure the box for the attribute that you want to change (Fill or Stroke) is active on the Color palette or Toolbox.

3. To choose a solid color, choose a color model from the Color palette menu, then click the color bar on the palette or choose or enter specific color percentages.
   or
   Click a color, pattern, or gradient swatch on the Swatches palette. (You can also drag a swatch over an unselected object.)

4. Adjust the stroke weight and other attributes using the Stroke palette (see pages 150–152).

5. *Optional:* To save the current color as a swatch, follow the instructions below.

Swatches that are **stored** on the Swatches palette save only with the current file.

To save the current fill or stroke color as a swatch:

Drag the Fill or Stroke box from the Color palette or the Toolbox to an empty area of the Swatches palette to make it the last swatch **1** or release the mouse between two colors to insert the new color between them.
or
On the Color palette, activate whichever box (Fill or Stroke) contains the color you want to save as a swatch, then click the New Swatch button ▣ on the Swatches palette.
or
To choose options for the new swatch as you save it, Option-click/Alt-click the New Swatch button, ▣ enter a Swatch Name, choose a Color Type (Process Color or Spot Color), check or uncheck Global, leave the Color Mode as is, then click OK.
or
To save the color as a spot color, Cmd-click/Ctrl-click the New Swatch button, or Cmd-drag/Ctrl-drag from the Fill or Stroke box to the Swatches palette.

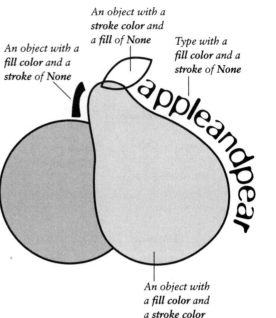

An object with a
fill color and a
stroke of None

An object with a
stroke color and
a fill of None

Type with a
fill color and a
stroke of None

An object with
a fill color and
a stroke color

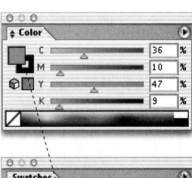

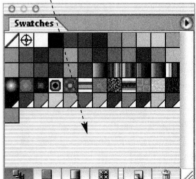

1 *To save a color as a **swatch**, drag a color from the Color palette onto the Swatches palette.*

Don't be fooled

Illustrator's **Color Settings** command works with the system's color management software to ensure more accurate color matching between the onscreen display of CMYK or RGB colors and the printed version of those colors. This command utilizes monitor and printer device profiles and output intents chosen by the user to better translate color between particular devices. However, the profiles won't produce a perfectly reliable onscreen proof.

You shouldn't mix or choose process colors or choose spot colors (e.g., PANTONE) for print output based on how they look onscreen, because screen colors won't look like the printed colors. Instead, you should use **matching system books** to choose spot colors or mix process colors, and be sure to run a color **proof** (or two or three) of your document. Really.

1 *The [Registration] color appears on every plate when a file is color-separated.*

Global process colors have a white triangle, with no dot, in the lower right corner (see the next page).

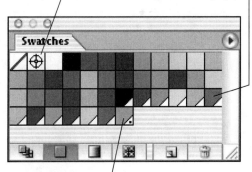

Spot colors have a dot in the lower right corner.

Colors for print

Spot colors are used for offset printing. Each **spot** color appears on its own plate after color separation. On rare occasions you might mix a spot color yourself, but normally you'll pick a named, numbered, premixed spot color from a matching system book (e.g., PANTONE). You can use spot colors exclusively if your illustration doesn't contain any continuous-tone (raster) images—as many spot colors as your budget permits.

➤ If you mix your own spot color, to ensure that it will color-separate onto its own plate, double-click the swatch for the color on the Swatches palette, choose Color Type: **Spot Color,** then click OK.

➤ You can achieve a pleasing range of tints using a black plate and a single spot color plate by applying an assortment of tint percentages of that spot color throughout your illustration.

Process colors are printed from four plates, one each for Cyan (C), Magenta (M), Yellow (Y), and Black (K). You can enter process color percentages yourself or you can choose premixed process colors from a matching system, such as TRUMATCH or PANTONE Process. (FOCOLTONE, DIC Color, and Toyo aren't normally used in the United States.)

Process printing *must* be used for any document that contains continuous-tone images, because it's the only way to print a range of graduated tones. Budget permitting, you can use both: four-color process and a handful of spot color plates.

➤ The [Registration] color is used for crop marks and the like **1**. To change the [Registration] color (let's say your illustration is very dark and you need white Registration marks), double-click the swatch and adjust the sliders.

➤ Double-click a spot color swatch to display its process color breakdown.

Note: Normally, Illustrator converts all spot colors into process colors when they're color-separated. To make your spot colors separate

(Continued on the following page)

properly to their own plates, choose File > Print, go to the Output pane, choose a Separations option from the Mode pop-up menu, then check **Convert All Spot Colors to Process.**

To define a color as process or spot, double-click the swatch on the Swatches palette, choose Color Type: Process Color or Spot Color, check or uncheck Global, choose a Color Mode **1**, then click OK.

➤ The Info palette displays the color breakdowns for the currently selected object. The breakdown on the left is the current fill color; the breakdown on the right is the current stroke color **2**. (If the bottom portion of the palette is hidden, choose Show Options from the palette menu.) If two or more objects with different color values are currently selected, no readouts will appear on the palette.

Global colors

If a process color is **global** (that is, the Global box is checked for that color in the Swatch Options dialog box) and you modify its swatch, the color will update on all objects to which it is currently applied. If you modify a **nonglobal** color (Global box unchecked), that color will update only on currently selected objects. See page 160.

Colors for the Web

For Web viewers whose monitors can display millions of colors, you can choose colors freely, with confidence that they'll display accurately. If your target viewers have 8-bit monitors, on the other hand, we recommend choosing colors using the **Web Safe RGB** color model on the Color palette **3**. (When this model is chosen, the sliders align with the vertical notches.) Web-safe colors won't shift (substitutes won't be chosen for them) when viewed in a browser.

If you mix an RGB color that isn't Web-safe, the **Out of Web** color warning button 🔲 will appear on the palette, and the closest Web-safe version of that color will appear in the little swatch next to it. You can click the cube or the swatch to convert the color to its closest Web-safe cousin.

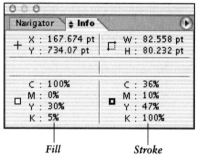

1 *Use the CMYK color model for print output.*

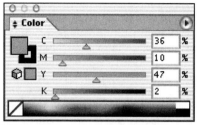

Fill   Stroke

2 *Color breakdowns on the Info palette*

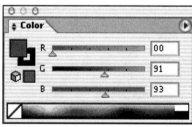

3 *Use the Web Safe RGB color model for Web graphics. The sliders have **notches.***

Selecting type for recoloring

➤ To recolor **all** the type in a block, highlight it with the Selection tool.

➤ To recolor only a **portion** of a type block, select it with a Type tool.

➤ To recolor a **type object** (not the type), click on its edge or fill with the Direct Selection tool. See pages 219 and 221.

1 *Fill box* **2** *Stroke box* *Tint slider*

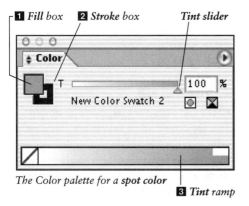

The Color palette for a spot color

3 *Tint ramp*

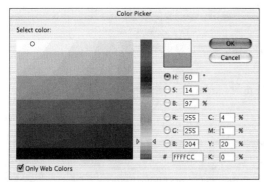

4 *In the Color Picker, you can enter HSB, RGB, or CMYK percentages. Check Only Web Colors to choose Web-safe colors. This is the Adobe Color Picker on the Mac.*

To choose a fill or stroke for a path before or after you create it:

1. Select an existing object (not all the anchor points have to be solid).
or
Choose the tool with which you want to draw a new object.

2. Click the Fill **1** or Stroke **2** box on the Color palette or the Toolbox. To toggle between these two boxes, press X.

3. Click a color or pattern swatch on the Swatches palette. If you chose a spot color swatch or a global process color swatch, you can move the tint (T) slider on the Color palette or click or drag inside the tint ramp to adjust the percentage of that color **3**.
or
Choose a color model from the Color palette menu, then choose color percentages (the models are discussed on page 147).
or
Double-click the Fill or Stroke box on the Color palette, then mix a color using the Color Picker **4**.

To choose a color from a matching system, such as PANTONE, see page 149.

4. If you're applying a stroke color, define the stroke weight and other attributes using the Stroke palette (see pages 150–152).

5. Your color is chosen. If you chose a drawing tool in step 1, now you're ready to use it. The current Color and Stroke palette attributes will be applied as you use the tool.

➤ You can fill an object with any of the patterns that are supplied with Illustrator or you can create and use your own patterns (see pages 166–168). Just remember not to apply a path pattern as a fill—it won't look right.

➤ A gradient can't be applied as a stroke. To work around this limitation, see page 313.

Document Color Mode

When you created your new document, you were asked to choose a Color Mode: CMYK or RGB. (The current color mode displays in the document title bar.) Any colors you mix or choose in a document automatically conform to the current **document color mode.** If you want to create two versions of an illustration, one for Web output (RGB mode) and one for print output (CMYK mode), you can make a copy of the file and then change the color mode for the copy.

Changing the color mode changes all colors in the illustration to the new mode, and will cause color shifts, particularly if you go in the direction of RGB to CMYK. That's why we suggest you copy your file first and leave the original file unchanged. To reverse a document mode change, *don't* rechoose the prior color mode. Instead, to restore the original colors, use Edit > Undo.

To change a document's color mode:

1. Use File > Save As to create a copy of your illustration.

2. Choose File > Document Color Mode > CMYK Color or RGB Color.

In the mode

➤ Any process or spot colors you create in a document will conform to the current document color mode, regardless of which mode you choose from the Color Mode pop-up menu in the Swatch Options dialog box (see page 165). You can create CMYK or RGB colors in an illustration but not both.

➤ When a spot color is displayed on the Color palette, a current document color mode indicator **1** also displays on the palette.

➤ The Swatches palette displays swatches for the current document color mode only: CMYK or RGB.

➤ Blend and gradient colors conform automatically to the current document color mode: all CMYK or all RGB.

➤ Placed and pasted images, linked or embedded, are converted to the current document color mode automatically.

➤ Available color mode options in the Rasterize dialog box will vary depending on the current document color mode.

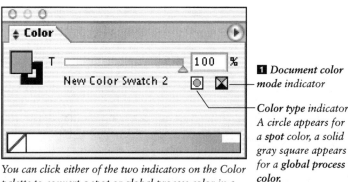

1 *Document color mode indicator*

Color type indicator: A circle appears for a spot color, a solid gray square appears for a global process color.

You can click either of the two indicators on the Color palette to convert a spot or global process color in a selected object to the current **document color mode** *(both buttons produce the same result). You can also convert colors on selected objects by choosing Filter > Colors > Convert to CMYK or Convert to RGB (depending on the current document color mode).*

What's the gamut?

If your document is in CMYK color mode and an exclamation point appears below the Color boxes on the Color palette **3**, it means the current RGB or HSB color has no **CMYK** equivalent, and thus **isn't printable** on a four-color press. If you click the exclamation point, Illustrator will substitute the closest CMYK (printable) equivalent.

If you're outputting your document **online,** your document color mode is **RGB,** and the exclamation point appears on the palette, it means the current color isn't within the Web-safe gamut.

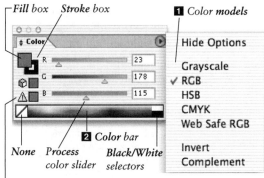

Fill box   Stroke box   **1** Color models

Hide Options

Grayscale

✓ RGB

HSB

CMYK

Web Safe RGB

Invert

Complement

2 Color bar

None   Process   Black/White
color slider   selectors

3 An exclamation point will appear if you mix a color that's outside the printable **gamut.**

If the fill or stroke colors differ among currently selected objects, a question mark will appear in the corresponding Fill or Stroke box on the Color palette and the Toolbox, but you can go ahead and apply a new fill and/or stroke color to all the selected objects.

Follow these instructions to **mix** your own **process color.** (To apply a color from a color matching system, such as TRUMATCH or FOCOLTONE, see page 149.)

To mix a process color:

1. Select the object or objects you want to recolor.
   or
   To choose a color for an object that you're about to draw, make sure no objects are selected.

2. On the Color palette (F6), click the Fill or Stroke box (X toggles between them).

3. Choose a color model from the Color palette menu **1**:

   Grayscale to convert colors in any selected objects to grayscale or to choose a gray shade.

   RGB to mix colors for video or Web output.

   HSB to adjust a color's hue (location on the color wheel), saturation (purity), or brightness values.

   CMYK to create process colors for output on a four-color printing press.

   Web Safe RGB to choose colors for Web output.

4. If you don't need to be precise about your color choice, click a color on the color bar at the bottom of the Color palette **2**.
   and/or
   To mix a color using specific color values, move the available sliders (0–255 for RGB; 0–100 for CMYK; 0, 33, 66, CC, or FF for Web). For a CMYK color, use values from a matching system book!

5. *Optional:* To save the newly mixed color as a swatch, drag the Fill or Stroke box on the Color palette to the Swatches palette.

➤ Grayscale, global, and spot colors that are applied to objects remain associated with their color model. So if you click a swatch or an object to which such a color is applied, the Color palette will reset to reflect that color's model.

Mix a Process Color

Color editing shortcuts

➤ To open the Color palette, press **F6**; to open the Stroke palette, press **F10**. There is no default shortcut for the Swatches palette.

➤ Shift-click the color bar on the Color palette to cycle through the color **models**. Or to display the color values for the current color in a different model, choose that model from the palette menu.

➤ To toggle between the Fill and Stroke boxes on the Toolbox and the Color palette, press **X**.

➤ To make the fill color the same as the stroke color, or vice versa, drag one box **over** the other on the Toolbox or the Color palette.

➤ To swap the fill and stroke colors, press **Shift-X** or click the Swap Fill and Stroke button on the Toolbox **1**.

➤ To apply a white fill and black stroke, press **D** or click the Default Fill and Stroke button on the Toolbox.

➤ If you apply a fill or stroke of None to a path and then decide you want to restore the last-applied color to the path, click the **Last Color** button **⌐⬛** on the Color palette.

➤ To invert the current color (produce its opposite on the color scale), choose **Invert** from the Color palette menu; to convert the current color to its complement within the same color model, choose **Complement**.

➤ If you **Shift-drag** an RGB or a CMYK **slider** on the Color palette, the other sliders will readjust automatically.

➤ To modify the stroke while the Fill box is active, or vice versa, **Option-drag/Alt-drag** in the **color bar**.

➤ To select objects with the same **paint attributes** via a command, see page 159.

To use the Color, Gradient, and None buttons:

If the Fill box is active, you can click the **Color** button (,) **⬛** on the Toolbox to reselect the last solid color that was chosen; or click the **Gradient** button (.) **▮** to reselect the last gradient that was chosen; or click the **None** button (/) **⬚** to apply a fill of None. If the Stroke box is active, only the Color and None buttons will be available.

If an object is selected and you click any of these buttons, the last fill or stroke color that was applied to that object will be reapplied (or if you click the None button, its current color will be removed).

For example, let's say the Fill box on the Toolbox is active and you want to apply a stroke of None to a selected object. You would press X, then press /.

➤ If you click the Color button on the Toolbox, the Color palette and any other palettes that it's grouped or docked with will display.

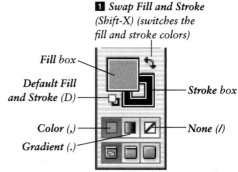

1 *Swap Fill and Stroke (Shift-X) (switches the fill and stroke colors)*

Fill box

Default Fill and Stroke (D)

Stroke box

Color (,)

None (/)

Gradient (.)

The color controls on the Toolbox

Quick-append

If you apply a color to a path directly from some library palettes, the color will be added to the current document's Swatches palette automatically. This doesn't work for some libraries (e.g., Pastels, Web). If you want to keep a color that you've applied to a path that didn't copy to the Swatches palette automatically, but you've already closed the library palette, select the object, then drag the Fill or Stroke box from the Color palette to the Swatches palette.

Beach
Brights
Camouflage
Cold
Default_CMYK
Default_RGB
Desert
Diccolor
Earthtones
FOCOLTONE
Forest
Fruits and Vegetables
Garden
Harmonies
HKS E
HKS K
HKS N
HKS Z
Hot
Jeweltones
Metals
Neutrals
PANTONE Metallic Coated
PANTONE Pastel Coated
PANTONE Pastel Uncoated
PANTONE Process Coated
PANTONE Process Uncoated
PANTONE Solid Coated
PANTONE Solid Matte
PANTONE Solid Uncoated
Pastels
Skintones
System (Macintosh)
System (Windows)
Tints and Shades
Toyo
Trumatch
Victorian
VisiBone2
Web

Other Library...

1 *These choices appear on the **Open Swatch Library** submenu on the Swatches palette menu and on the Window > **Swatch Libraries** submenu.*

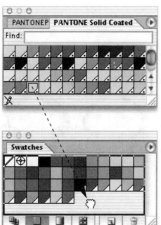

2 *Dragging a spot color from a swatch library to the Swatches palette in the current document*

In order to apply a color from a **matching system,** such as PANTONE or TRUMATCH, or from the Web palette, you must open that swatch library and then drag a swatch from the library palette onto your document's Swatches palette; it will be converted to the current document color mode. The Web palette contains 216 Web-safe RGB colors.

To add matching system or Web colors to the Swatches palette:

I. Display the Swatches palette.

2. From either the Open Swatch Library **NEW** submenu on the Swatches palette menu or the Window > Swatch Libraries submenu, choose a color matching system **1**.

3. For some types of libraries, all you have to do is click a swatch, and that color will appear on your document's Swatches palette. If this isn't the case with the library you've opened, do one of the following:

Click a swatch on the library palette (scroll downward or expand the palette, if necessary), then choose Add to Swatches from the library palette menu. Or to add multiple swatches, Cmd-click/Ctrl-click them individually or click, then Shift-click a contiguous series of them, then choose Add to Swatches.
or
Drag any swatch (or multiple swatches) from the library palette onto your document's Swatches palette **2**.

➤ To locate a color, if the Find field isn't visible, choose Show Find Field from the Swatches or library palette menu, then start typing the color number (or name) in the field. The swatch will become highlighted on the palette.

➤ If multiple swatch libraries are grouped in the same palette and you want to remove one of them, drag its tab out of the palette, then click its close box.

➤ You can't modify swatches on a library palette (note the non-edit icon in the palette's lower left corner); the Swatch Options dialog box won't be available. However, you can edit any swatch once it's been added to the Swatches palette.

Use Matching System or Web Colors

Changing stroke attributes

Next, you'll learn to change a **stroke's weight** (width) and **style** (dashed or solid, rounded or sharp corners, flat or rounded ends). First, the width.

To change the width of a stroke:

1. Select an object or objects.

2. On the Stroke palette (F10):

   Click the up or down arrow on the palette to change the current stroke weight one unit at a time. Or click in the Weight field, then press the up or down arrow on the keyboard (press Shift-arrow to change the weight by 6 units at a time).
   or

   Choose a preset weight from the Weight pop-up menu.
   or

   Enter a width in the Weight field (.01 to 1000 pt) **1**. *Note:* A stroke narrower than .25 pt. may not print. A weight of 0 produces a stroke of None. The stroke will be balanced on the path, with half the stroke width on one side of the path and the other half on the other side of the path **2**–**3**.

➤ Don't apply a wide stroke to small type—it will distort the letterforms.

➤ You can enter a number in inches (in), millimeters (mm), centimeters (cm), picas (p), or pixels (px) in the Weight field. When you click Return/Enter or Tab, it will be converted automatically to the Stroke unit currently chosen in Illustrator (Edit, in Windows) > Preferences > Units & Display Performance.

1 *To change a stroke's width, on the Stroke palette, enter a value in the stroke Weight field, or click the up or down arrow, or choose from the pop-up menu.*

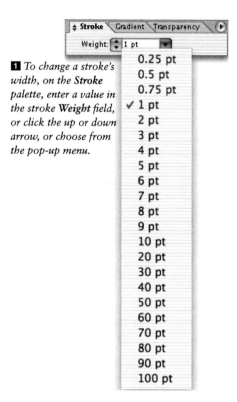

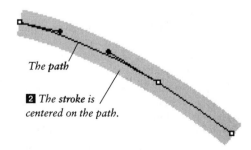

The path

2 *The stroke is centered on the path.*

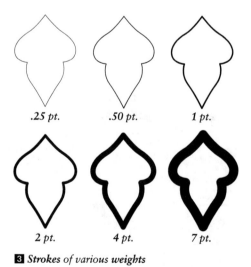

.25 pt.   .50 pt.   1 pt.

2 pt.   4 pt.   7 pt.

3 *Strokes of various weights*

Stroke Width

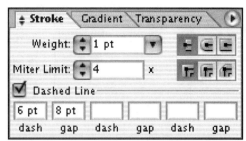

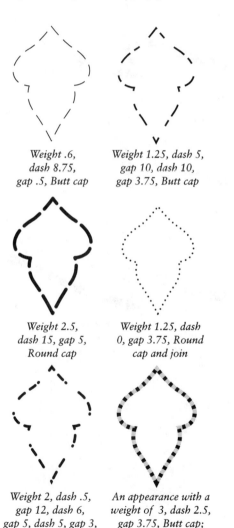

1 *Stroke palette settings for a **dashed line** with a 6 pt. dash **length** and an 8 pt. **gap** between dashes*

*Weight .6,
dash 8.75,
gap .5, Butt cap*

*Weight 1.25, dash 5,
gap 10, dash 10,
gap 3.75, Butt cap*

*Weight 2.5,
dash 15, gap 5,
Round cap*

*Weight 1.25, dash
0, gap 3.75, Round
cap and join*

*Weight 2, dash .5,
gap 12, dash 6,
gap 5, dash 5, gap 3,
Round cap*

*An appearance with a
weight of 3, dash 2.5,
gap 3.75, Butt cap;
and a separate path with
a gray stroke, 3 pt.*

Using the **Dashed Line** feature, you can easily create dashed strokes.

To create a dashed stroke:

1. Select an object. Make sure it has a stroke color and its stroke is wider than zero.

2. Display the Stroke palette (F10). If all the options aren't visible, choose Show Options from the palette menu.

3. Click a Cap button for the dash shape (see the following page) **1**.

4. Check Dashed Line.

5. Enter a value in the first dash field (the length of the first dash, in points), then press Tab to proceed to the next field. If you don't enter values in any of the other dash fields, the first dash value will be used for all the dashes. The default first dash unit is 12 pt.

6. *Optional:* Enter a value in the first gap field (the length of the first gap after the first dash), then press Tab to proceed to the next field or press Return/Enter to exit the palette. If you don't enter a gap value, the dash value will also be used as the gap value.

7. *Optional:* To create dashes of varying lengths, enter values in the other dash fields. The more different values you enter, the more irregular the dashes will look.

8. *Optional:* Enter different amounts in the other gap fields to create gaps of varying lengths. If you enter an amount in only the first gap field, that amount will be used for all the gaps.

➤ To create a dotted line, click the second Cap button, enter 0 for the dash value, and enter a gap value that is greater than or equal to the stroke Weight.

➤ You can enter a value in inches (in), millimeters (mm), centimeters (cm), picas (p), or pixels (px) in the dash or gap fields. That number will be translated automatically into the Stroke unit currently chosen in Illustrator (Edit, in Windows) > Preferences > Units & Display Performance.

➤ User-defined values remain in effect until you change them or quit/exit Illustrator.

Dashed Stroke

To modify stroke caps and/or joins:

1. Select an object. Make sure it has a stroke color and its stroke is wider than zero.

2. Display the Stroke palette (F10). If all the options aren't visible, choose Show Options from the palette menu.

3. To modify the endpoints of a solid line or all the dashes in a dashed line:

   Click the **Butt** (left) **Cap** button ⓵ to create square-cornered ends in which the stroke stops at the endpoints, or to create thin rectangular dashes. Use this option if you need to align your paths very precisely.

   Click the **Round** (middle) **Cap** button to create semicircular ends or dashes that end in a semicircle.

   Click the **Projecting** (right) **Cap** button to create square-cornered ends in which the stroke extends beyond the endpoints or to create rectangular dashes.

4. To modify the bends on corner points (not curve points) of the path:

   Click the **Miter** (left) **Join** button to produce pointed bends (miter joins) ⓶.

   Click the **Round** (middle) **Join** button to produce semicircular bends (round joins).

   Click the **Bevel** (right) **Join** button to produce square-cornered bends (bevel joins). The sharper the angle, the wider the bevel.

5. *Optional:* Change the Miter Limit (1–500) value for the point at which a miter (pointed) corner becomes a bevel corner. When the measurement from the inside to the outside of the corner point becomes greater than the miter limit value times the stroke weight, the miter corner is replaced with a bevel corner. Incomprehensible? Don't worry about how it works, just use a high Miter Limit to create long, pointy corners or a low Miter Limit to create bevel join corners.

➤ You can save a dashed stroke by dragging a path to which that stroke is applied into the Graphic Styles palette (see pages 342–343).

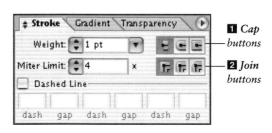

⓵ *Cap buttons*

⓶ *Join buttons*

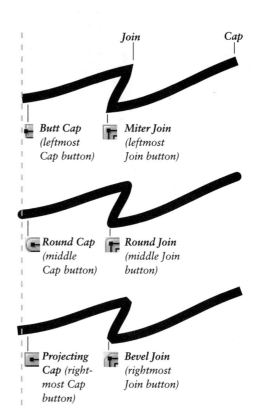

Join   *Cap*

Butt Cap *(leftmost Cap button)* **Miter Join** *(leftmost Join button)*

Round Cap *(middle Cap button)* **Round Join** *(middle Join button)*

Projecting Cap *(rightmost Cap button)* **Bevel Join** *(rightmost Join button)*

Global process colors have a white corner with no dot.

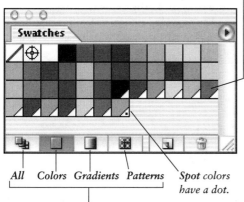

All   Colors   Gradients   Patterns   Spot colors have a dot.

1 *Use the **display** buttons on the Swatches palette to control which categories of swatches are displayed on the palette at a given time (in this figure, only the solid color swatches are displayed).*

RGB document color mode

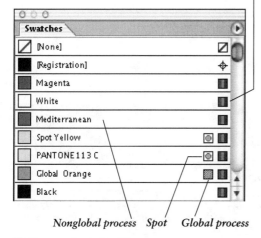

Nonglobal process   Spot   Global process

2 *The swatches in List View*

Using the Swatches palette

You can control whether the **Swatches palette displays** all types of swatches or only certain categories of swatches, and also whether the swatches are large or small.

To choose swatch display options:

1. Click a display button at the bottom of the Swatches palette to control which category of swatches is displayed **1**: **Show All** for all types (colors, gradients, and patterns); **Show Color** for solid colors only; **Show Gradient** for gradients only; or **Show Pattern** for patterns only.

2. From the palette menu, choose a view for the currently chosen category of swatches: **Small Thumbnail View, Large Thumbnail View,** or **List View.** In List View **2**, the palette also displays an icon for the color's color model.

   ➤ Choose Large Thumbnail View for gradients and patterns, to help you identify them more easily.

3. From the palette menu, choose **Sort by Name** to sort the swatches alphabetically by name.
   or
   Choose **Sort by Kind** to sort swatches into color, then gradient, then pattern groups (use when all the categories of swatches are displayed).

   ➤ To choose a swatch by typing, choose Show Find Field from the palette menu, click in the field, then start typing. A matching swatch, if found, will become selected.

   ➤ If you've chosen different views for the different categories of swatches (colors, gradients, and patterns) and you want to force all the categories of swatches to display in the same view, hold down Cmd-Option/Ctrl-Alt as you choose Small Thumbnail View, Large Thumbnail View, or List View from the palette menu.

Whatever swatches you **load** onto the Swatches palette will save with the current file. (To load matching system colors, see page 149.)

To copy swatches between Illustrator files:

1. Open the file that you want to load swatches into, then from the Swatches **NEW** palette menu, choose Open Swatch Library > Other Library.

2. Locate the Illustrator file you want to copy swatches from (that file shouldn't be open), then click Open.

3. Drag a swatch from the newly opened swatch library into the current document's Swatches palette **1**. To load multiple swatches, before dragging, Cmd/Ctrl click them individually or click, then Shift-click, a contiguous series of them.
   or
   Click the swatch(es) you want to load, then choose Add to Swatches from the swatch library menu. The selected color will appear on the current document's Swatches palette.

➤ Pattern library files are stored in Adobe Illustrator CS/Presets/Patterns; gradients are stored in the Gradients folder.

If you **drag and drop** an object from one file to another, any global or spot color swatches that are applied to that object will also appear in the target file.

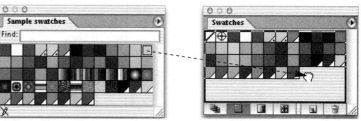

1 *Open a swatch library from another file, then* ***drag*** *a swatch or swatches from one swatch palette to another.*

2 *A copy of the swatch shows up on the Swatches palette.*

Swatches at launch time

If you want to control which colors appear on the Swatches palette when the application is launched, add those colors to the **Startup** file (see page 439).

If you enable the **Persistent** command on a swatch library palette menu, that swatch library palette will reopen automatically when you relaunch Illustrator, with the same tab in front.

There's no simple way to restore the **Swatches palette** to its **default** state. You have to manually drag swatches from either of the two default palettes.

To restore default swatches to the Swatches palette:

1. *Optional:* To clear your document's Swatches palette before restoring the default palette, choose Select All Unused from the palette menu, click the Delete Swatch button, 🗑 then click Yes.

2. From the Swatches palette menu, choose **(NEW)** Open Swatch Library > Default_CMYK or Default_RGB (depending on the current document color mode).

3. On the Default_CMYK or Default_RGB palette that you just opened, select the swatches that you want to restore to your document (click, then Shift-click to select contiguous swatches or Cmd-click/Ctrl-click to select multiple individual swatches).

4. Choose Add to Swatches from the Default_CMYK or Default_RGB palette menu **1**–**2**.
   or
   Drag the selected swatches to your document's Swatches palette.

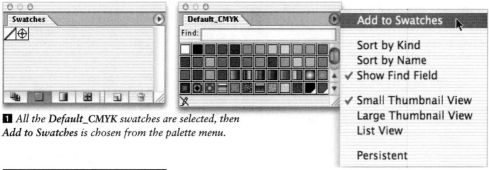

1 *All the Default_CMYK swatches are selected, then Add to Swatches is chosen from the palette menu.*

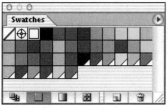

2 *The Default_CMYK swatches appear on the current document's Swatches palette.*

To delete swatches:

1. Click the swatch you want to delete. Or click, then Shift-click a series of contiguous swatches or Cmd-click/Ctrl-click individual swatches.
   or
   To select only the swatches that aren't currently applied to objects in your document, choose Select All Unused from the Swatches palette menu. To limit the selection to a particular category (e.g., patterns or gradients), make sure only those swatches are displayed on the palette before choosing Select All Unused.

2. Click the Delete Swatch button 🗑 at the bottom of the Swatches palette, then click Yes **1**.
   or
   Choose Delete Swatch from the Swatches palette menu, then click Yes.
   or
   To bypass the alert dialog box, Option-click/Alt-click the Delete Swatch button.
   or
   Drag the swatch(es) you want to delete over the Delete Swatch button (you won't get a prompt with this method, either).

➤ If you delete a global process color or a spot color that's currently applied to an object or objects, those objects will be recolored with the nonglobal process color equivalent to the deleted colors.

➤ To restore a deleted swatch or swatches, choose Undo right away. To restore swatches from a default library or any other library, see the instructions on the previous page.

Quick fix

If you inadvertently delete a color, gradient, or pattern swatch that was applied to an object in the current file, you can retrieve it by selecting the object and then dragging the Fill box from the Toolbox or the Color palette onto the Swatches palette.

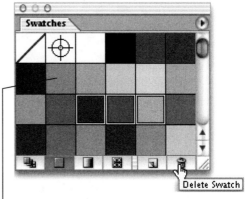

1 *Select the swatch or swatches that you want to delete from the Swatches palette, then click or Option-click/Alt-click the **Delete Swatch** button.*

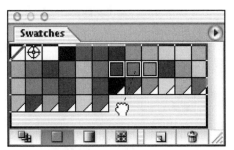

1 *Three swatches are **selected**, then they're **moved** to a new location on the palette.*

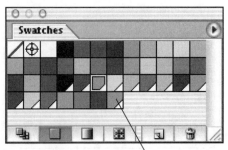

2 *Drag the swatch you want to **duplicate** over the New Swatch button.*

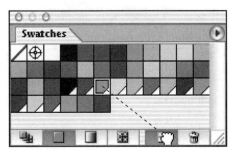

3 *The **duplicate** appears on the palette.*

To move a swatch or swatches:

Drag a swatch to a new location on the palette **1**. A dark vertical line will show the swatch location as you drag it. (To select multiple swatches, click a swatch, then Shift-click the last swatch in a series of contiguous swatches, or Cmd-click/Ctrl-click to select individual swatches.)

To duplicate a swatch:

Select the swatch you want to duplicate, then choose Duplicate Swatch from the Swaches palette menu or click the New Swatch button. **3** The duplicate swatch will appear next to the last swatch on the palette.
or
Drag the swatch to be duplicated over the New Swatch button **2**–**3**.

➤ If no swatch is selected when you click the New Swatch button, a new swatch will be created for the current fill or stroke color.

➤ Option-drag/Alt-drag one swatch over another to replace the existing swatch with the one you're dragging.

Move Swatch; Duplicate Swatch

Resolving swatch conflicts

If you copy and paste or drag and drop an object from one document window to another, the object's colors will appear as swatches on the target document's Swatches palette. If a global process or spot color on the copied object contains the same name, but different color percentages, as an existing global process or spot color swatch in the target document, the Swatch Conflict dialog box will open **1**. Choose from these options:

Click **Merge swatches** to apply the swatch of the same name in the target document to the copied objects. Or click **Add swatches** to add the new swatch to the Swatches palette in the target document; a number will be appended to the swatch name (choosing this option will prevent colors in the copied objects from changing).

Check **Apply to all** to have the current Options setting apply to any other name conflicts that crop up for other objects being copied. This will prevent the alert dialog box from opening repeatedly if more than one name conflict crops up.

Normally, if two spot colors have the same color percentages but different names, Illustrator will color-separate each of those colors to a separate sheet of film. You can use the **Merge Swatches** command to selectively merge colors into the same swatch so it will print from one plate.

To merge spot color swatches:

1. The first swatch you select will replace all the other selected swatches, regardless of its location on the palette, so take a minute to strategize. On the Swatches palette, select the swatches to be merged. Click, then Shift-click to select contiguous swatches or Cmd-click/Ctrl-click to select noncontiguous swatches **2**.

2. Choose Merge Swatches from the Swatches palette menu **3**. If any of the merged swatches were applied to objects in the file, the first swatch that was selected for merging will be applied to all of those objects.

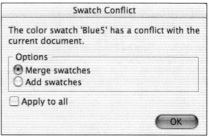

1 Use the **Swatch Conflict** dialog box to resolve name conflicts.

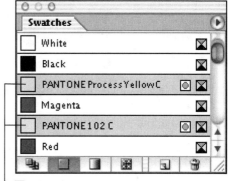

2 Select the spot colors you want to merge.

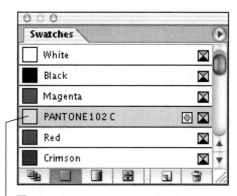

3 After choosing **Merge Swatches** from the palette menu, the swatches are merged into the first swatch that was selected.

(sidebar) Swatch Conflicts; Merge Spot Color Swatches

Select same tint percentage

When **Select Same Tint %** is checked in Illustrator (Edit, in Windows) > Preferences > General, the Select > Same > Fill Color and Stroke Color commands will select only colors that have the same tint percentage (spot color percentage) as the selected object.

1 *Choose from the Select > Same submenu.*

2 *The original group of objects*

3 *All the colors **inverted***

Changing colors

To select objects based on their color attributes:

1. Select an object whose paint or other attributes you want to change.
or
With no object selected, choose the attributes that you want to search for from the Swatches palette, the Color palette, or the Stroke palette.

2. Choose Select > Same > Fill & Stroke, Fill Color, Opacity, Stroke Color, or Stroke Weight to select objects with the same paint attributes as you chose in the previous step **1**. All objects with those paint attributes will now be selected. A spot color in different tint percentages is treated as the same color.

3. Now that the objects are selected, you can mix a new color using the Color palette, click a new swatch on the Swatches palette, choose a new Weight or other attributes from the Stroke palette, or perform other edits.

➤ To globally change a spot color or a global process color by replacing its swatch, see the next page.

The **Invert** command converts each color in an object into its color negative.

To invert colors:

1. Select the object or objects that contains the colors you want to invert.

2. Choose Filter > Colors > Invert Colors **2**–**3**. This filter converts only **nonglobal process colors**. It won't convert spot colors, global process colors, gradients, or patterns.
or
To invert only the object's **fill** or **stroke** color, click either box on the Color palette, then choose Invert from the Color palette menu. This command will convert **any** kind of solid color—spot, global process, or nonglobal process.

This is what happens when **colors** are replaced:

➤ If you replace a spot or global process color swatch with a different swatch, that color (or a tint of that color) will automatically update in *all* the objects to which it is currently applied—whether or not those objects are selected. The object's original tint percentage will be preserved.

➤ If you remix a nonglobal process color swatch, only the currently *selected* object or objects containing that color will be recolored.

To replace a swatch globally:

On the Color palette, mix a brand new color (not merely a tint variation of the global process or spot color that you want to replace). Then Option-drag/Alt-drag the Fill or Stroke box from the Color palette over the swatch on the Swatches palette that you want to replace 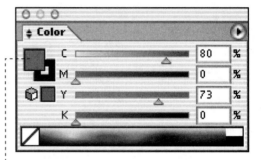.

or

Option-drag/Alt-drag one swatch over another swatch.

or

To edit a gradient swatch, use the Gradient palette (see pages 320–321). To edit a pattern swatch, follow the instructions on page 167.

Follow these instructions to **edit a process color globally.** To change spot colors in multiple objects, use the method described in the sidebar instead (that is, select the objects, then choose a new swatch).

To edit a color globally:

1. Double-click a global process swatch on the Swatches palette. Check Preview.

2. Modify the color using the Color Type menu or the Color Mode menu, or by moving the sliders, then click OK. The color will update in all objects to which it's currently applied; individual tint variations will be preserved.

Change without changing

If you want to globally change a color without changing the swatch from which it originated, use a command on the Select > Same submenu to select all the objects that contain that color (see the previous page), then choose a new swatch or mix a new color for the selected objects.

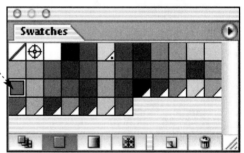

1 *Option-drag/Alt-drag the current color from the Fill or Stroke box over the spot or global process swatch you want to replace. Objects to which that color is currently applied will update.*

Replace, Edit Colors Globally

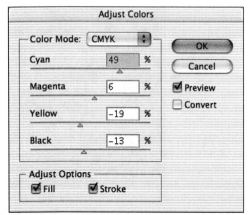

1 *Use the Adjust Colors filter to adjust solid colors in any kind of object.*

Use the **Adjust Colors** filter to adjust color percentages or convert color modes in one o more selected path objects; text objects; or an opened or placed Photoshop TIFF, EPS, PDF, JPEG, or PSD image—but not gradients or patterns. To adjust individual PSD layers, convert them into separate Illustrator objects first (see pages 267–268).

To adjust or convert colors:

1. Select the object or objects that contains the colors you want to adjust or convert.

2. Choose Filter > Colors > Adjust Colors.

3. Check Preview to preview color adjustments in your illustration while the dialog box is open **1**.

4. Check Adjust Options: Fill and/or Stroke to adjust one or both of those attributes.

5. If the selected objects contain colors from more than one mode, the sliders will represent the first mode that's present, in the following order: Global mode, then either CMYK or RGB mode, then Grayscale mode. Make sure Convert is unchecked, then to **adjust** the colors, move the sliders or enter new percentages in the fields. Only colors in that mode will be adjusted. After you adjust colors in one mode, you can choose another mode and continue adjusting colors. Only color modes that are present in the selected objects will be available on the pop-up menu.
   or
   To **convert** all the currently selected objects to the same color mode, regardless of their original mode, check Convert, choose a Color Mode from the pop-up menu, then move the sliders.

6. Click OK.

To convert an object's colors to a different mode:

1. Select the object or objects that contains the colors you want to convert.

2. Choose Filter > Colors > Convert to Grayscale, or choose either Convert to CMYK or Convert to RGB. If you choose Convert to CMYK, any spot colors will be converted into process colors.

If you click with the **Paint Bucket** tool on an object, the current colors and settings from the Color and Stroke palettes will be applied to that object. Neither palette has to be displayed for you to use the Paint Bucket.

To use the Paint Bucket tool:

1. With no objects selected, choose the Paint Bucket tool (K).

2. Choose fill and stroke colors from the Color or Swatches palette.
   or
   Option-click/Alt-click on a color anywhere in any open Illustrator window (this is a temporary Eyedropper).

3. Choose a stroke weight, and choose other stroke options, if desired.

4. Click an object (the object does not have to be selected). The object will become colored with the current Color and Stroke palette attributes 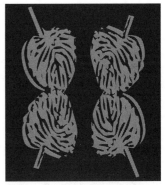–**2**. If the object you click doesn't have a fill color or if the illustration is in Outline view, position the black spill of the Paint Bucket pointer on the path outline before clicking.

Using the **Eyedropper/Paint Bucket Options** dialog box, you can specify which paint attributes the Eyedropper will pick up and which attributes the Paint Bucket will apply.

To choose Eyedropper/Paint Bucket options:

1. Double-click the Eyedropper or Paint Bucket tool.

NEW 2. Expand the Appearance list **3**, if necessary, as well as the Focal Fill and Focal Stroke lists, then check the paint attributes you want the Eyedropper tool to pick up and/or the Paint Bucket to apply.

NEW 3. Choose a Raster Sample Size: Point Sample, 3 x 3 Average, or 5 x 5 Average to specify how large an area you will allow the Eyedropper tool to sample from.

4. Click OK.

1 *The original illustration*

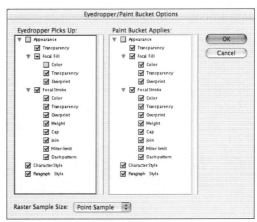

2 *After using the Paint Bucket to apply a white fill and a dashed stroke to the leaves on the left side*

Diane Margolin

3 *Eyedropper/Paint Bucket Options*

Paint Bucket Tool

Grab a color from another application

Open the application that you want to sample colors from. Move the window or palette from which you want to sample over to one side of the screen, and move the Illustrator document window so you can see the other application window behind it. Choose the **Eyedropper** tool (I), drag from the Illustrator document window over to a color in another application window or on the Desktop, then release the mouse (the color will appear on Illustrator's Toolbox and Color palette). Save the color as a swatch. Repeat for other colors.

If you click a path or a placed image with the **Eyedropper** tool, it will sample the object's paint attributes (not graphic styles), display them on the Toolbox and the Color and Stroke palettes, and apply them to any currently selected objects—all in one step.

To use the Eyedropper tool:

1. *Optional:* Select an object or objects if you want them to be recolored immediately with the attributes you pick up with the Eyedropper.

2. Choose the Eyedropper tool (I).

3. Click an object in any open Illustrator window that contains the color, gradient, or pattern you want to sample. The object doesn't have to be selected.
   or
   If you want the tool to pick up only the color it clicks on within a gradient, pattern, mesh objects, or placed image, Shift-click the color.

   The color will be copied to the fill or stroke of any selected objects, depending on whether the Fill or Stroke box is currently active on the Color palette.

   If you selected any objects before using the Eyedropper tool, the paint attributes of the object you click on with the tool will be applied to the selected objects automatically.

➤ Hold down Option/Alt to turn the Eyedropper into a temporary Paint Bucket tool, and vice versa.

➤ To preserve the sampled color to use again, drag the Fill or Stroke box from the Toolbox or the Color palette onto the Swatches palette.

Eyedropper Tool

The **Saturate** filter deepens or fades colors in selected objects (or placed images) by a relative percentage.

To saturate or desaturate colors:

1. Select the object(s) whose solid colors you want to saturate or desaturate.

2. Choose Filter > Colors > Saturate.

3. Check Preview to preview color changes in your illustration.

4. Move the Intensity slider or enter a percentage for the amount you want to intensify or fade the color or colors . A 100% tint can't be further saturated.

5. Click OK.

To blend fill colors between objects:

1. Select three or more objects that contain a fill color. Objects with a fill of None won't be recolored. The more objects you use, the more gradual the blend will be.

Note: The two objects that are farthest apart (or frontmost and backmost) can't contain gradients, patterns, global colors, or different spot colors. The frontmost and backmost objects can contain different tints of the same spot color. Objects will stay on their respective layers.

2. From the Colors submenu under the Filter menu, choose:

Blend Front to Back to create a color blend using the fill colors of the frontmost and backmost objects as the starting and ending colors.

Blend Horizontally to create a color blend using the fill colors of the leftmost and rightmost objects as the starting and ending colors.

Blend Vertically to create a color blend using the fill colors of the topmost and bottommost objects as the starting and ending colors **2**–**3**.

Any selected objects that are stacked between the frontmost and backmost objects (or between the leftmost and rightmost or topmost and bottommost objects) will be assigned intermediate blend colors. Stroke colors won't change.

1 *Change a color's intensity in the **Saturate** dialog box.*

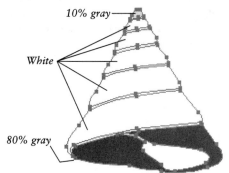

10% gray

White

80% gray

2 *Seven objects are selected.*

3 *After applying the **Blend Vertically** filter*

Saturate/Desaturate; Blend Fill Colors

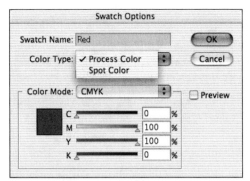

1 *Choose* **Swatch Options.** *Note: Regardless of whether CMYK or RGB is chosen from the Color Mode pop-up menu, only the option that matches the document's current color mode will be applied when you click OK.*

Quick conversion

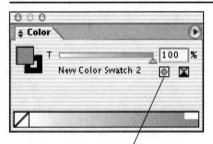

Click this button to convert the spot color on the currently selected object to the current document color mode (CMYK or RGB). This won't change the original spot swatch.

Drag and drop, to colorize

If you want to colorize a 1-bit image that you've dragged and dropped into Illustrator, first you must do the following: expand the image's group on the Layers palette, delete any clipping paths and paths from the group, click the circle ⬭ for the image layer to target the image, and then, on the Appearance palette, click the Fill icon. Now you can apply a fill color to it.

To convert a process color into a spot color or vice versa:

1. Deselect all objects, then mix a color on the Color palette.
   or
   Select the object that contains the color you want to convert.
2. If the color isn't already on the Swatches palette, drag the Fill or Stroke box from the Color palette or the Toolbox onto the Swatches palette.
3. Double-click the swatch to open the Swatch Options dialog box.
4. Choose Color Type: Process Color or Spot Color **1**, and rename the color, if desired.
5. For a process color, check or uncheck Global. If you edit a global process color that's been applied to objects in a file, the color will update on those objects; not so for a nonglobal color.
6. Choose Color Mode: Grayscale, RGB, HSB, CMYK, or Web Safe RGB.
7. Click OK.
➤ By default, spot colors are converted to process colors during color separation. To prevent this conversion from occurring, uncheck Convert to Process in the File > Print > Output panel.

You can **colorize** any **1-bit** TIFF, PSD, PCS, OS2, or BMP **image** that you've opened or placed in an Illustrator document. Black areas in the TIFF will be recolored; transparent areas will not (1-bit images contain only black and transparent areas).

To colorize a 1-bit image:

1. Use File > Open or Place to open and embed a 1-bit image. (See also the sidebar at left.)
2. Display the Layers palette (F7), then click the Image listing on the palette.
3. Apply a fill color (not a stroke color).
➤ To make transparent areas in a 1-bit image look as if they're colorized, create an object with the desired background color and send it behind the image.

Convert Process to Spot; Colorize an Image

Creating fill patterns

To create a fill pattern:

1. Draw an object or objects to be used as the pattern **1**. The objects can contain brush strokes but not a gradient, mask, blend, mesh, pattern, or bitmap image. Simple shapes are least likely to cause a printing error.

2. *Strictly optional:* Apply Filter > Distort > Roughen or Effect > Distort & Transform > Roughen at a low setting to make the pattern shapes look more hand drawn.

3. Marquee all the objects with the Selection tool (V).

4. Choose Edit > Define Pattern.
   or
   Drag the selection onto the Swatches palette, deselect the objects, then double-click the new swatch.

5. Type a name in the Swatch Name field.

6. Click OK **2**–**3**.

You can use a **rectangle** to control the amount of white space around a **pattern** or to crop parts of the objects that you want to eliminate from a pattern.

To use a rectangle to define a fill pattern:

1. Draw objects to be used as the pattern.

2. Choose the Rectangle tool (M).

3. Drag a rectangle or Shift-drag a half-inch to 1-inch square around the objects (use the Info palette to check the dimensions). Fit the rectangle closely around the objects if you don't want any blank space to be part of the pattern (use Smart Guides to assist you) **4**. If the pattern is complex, using a small rectangle will help to facilitate printing.

4. Choose Object > Arrange > Send to Back (Cmd-Shift-[/Ctrl-Shift-[). The rectangle must be behind the pattern objects.

5. Apply a fill and stroke of None to the rectangle if you don't want it to become

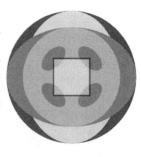

1 *Select one or more objects. You can use anything from geometric objects to free-hand lines. The simpler, the better.*

2 *After dragging the selected objects onto the Swatches palette*

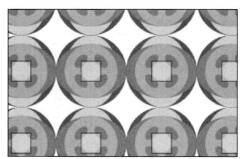

3 *An object is filled with the pattern from figure* **1***.*

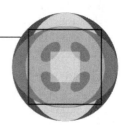

4 *Draw a rectangle around the objects, then send the rectangle to the back.*

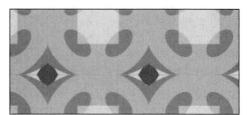

5 *An object is filled with the pattern from the previous figure.*

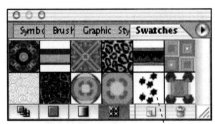

1 *Drag the pattern that you want to modify out of the Swatches palette.*

2 *The original pattern swatch*

3 *The pattern is modified, selected, and then dragged back over the original swatch.*

4 *The modified pattern used as a fill*

part of the pattern. Apply a fill color to the rectangle if you want it to become the background color in the pattern.

6. Follow steps 3–6 in the previous set of instructions (**5**, previous page).

You can **modify** any **pattern**, including any pattern that's supplied with Illustrator. To change an existing pattern, you first have to drag its swatch back into a document.

Note: Patterns are fun, patterns are beautiful, patterns choke printers. Try to keep it simple.

To modify a fill pattern:

1. Display a blank area in your document window, then drag the pattern swatch out of the Swatches palette **1**. It will consist of a group with a bounding rectangle (with a fill and stroke of None) as the bottommost layer in the group **2**.

2. Modify the pattern objects. Use the Direct Selection tool (A) to select individual components **3**. The pattern will be listed as one or more nested groups on the Layers palette.

3. Choose the Selection tool (V).

4. Click any object in the pattern; the whole group will become selected.

5. Option-drag/Alt-drag the selected pattern shapes over the original pattern swatch. Objects already filled with the pattern in the file will update automatically **4**.

Note: If you don't want to save over the original pattern, drag the selection onto the Swatches palette without holding down Option/Alt, then double-click the new swatch to rename it. The original swatch won't change, and the pattern won't update in any objects.

➤ Read about transforming patterns on page 99.

Read about transforming patterns on page 99.

Modify Fill Pattern

To create a geometric fill pattern:

1. Create a symmetrical arrangement of geometric objects ▮–▮ using the Rectangle, Ellipse, Polygon, Spiral, Star, or any other tool.

   To copy an object, Option-drag/Alt-drag it using a selection tool. Add Shift to constrain the movement horizontally or vertically. Position objects so they abut each other. You can use the grid or smart guides to help you align the objects (see pages 90–91).

2. *Optional:* Apply assorted fill colors to add variety to the pattern.

3. Choose the Rectangle tool (M).

4. Choose a fill and stroke of None, then carefully draw a rectangle around the objects, preserving the symmetry so the pattern will repeat properly ▮.

5. With the rectangle still selected, choose Object > Arrange > Send to Back.

6. Marquee all the objects with the Selection tool (V), drag the selection onto the Swatches palette, and use it as a fill in any object ▮.

➤ For instructions and pointers on how to create a pattern that repeats seamlessly, see Adobe Illustrator Help.

To expand a pattern fill into individual objects:

1. Select an object that contains a pattern fill ▮–▮.

2. Choose Object > Expand.

3. Leave the check boxes as is, and click OK ▮. The pattern fill will be divided into the original shapes that made up the pattern tile. Any stroke will become a compound path, and the expanded shapes will become nested groups inside a clipping mask. You can release the mask (it's listed on the Layers palette as <clipping path>), change the mask shape, or delete it.

Geometric Fill Pattern; Expand Pattern

---

shifting patterns

To reposition the pattern fill in an object without moving the object itself, hold down ~ (tilde) and drag inside it with the Selection tool.

1 *Draw geometric objects.*

2 *Copy the object(s) and arrange the copies symmetrically.*

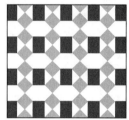

3 *Draw a rectangle, and position it so it will create symmetry in the pattern tile.*

4 *The* **geometric** *pattern fill*

5 *The original pattern*

Diane Margolin

6 *A detail of the pattern expanded (Outline view)*

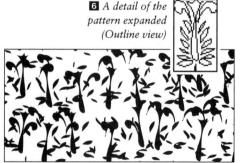

7 *After applying the* **Expand** *command, releasing the mask, and applying Effect > Distort & Transform > Roughen (low settings)*

Mastering the Pen tool—Illustrator's most difficult tool—requires patience and practice. Once you become comfortable creating Pen tool paths, refer to Chapter 8 to learn how to reshape them. If you find the Pen tool too difficult to use, remember that you can always transform or combine simple shapes into a complex shape or draw a freehand shape using the Pencil or Paintbrush tool and then reshape it. Simpler methods for creating shapes are covered in Chapter 5.

Daniel Pelavin

1 *This* **corner** *point joins two* **straight** *segments. It has* **no** *direction lines.*

2 *A* **smooth** *point always has a pair of direction lines that move in* **tandem.** *This is a smooth curve.*

3 *This* **corner** *point has direction lines that move* **independently.** *This is a nonsmooth curve.*

Drawing with the Pen tool
What the Pen tool does

The Pen tool creates precise curved and straight segments connected by anchor points. If you click with the Pen tool, you'll create corner points and straight segments *without* direction lines **1**. If you drag with the Pen tool, you'll create smooth points and curve segments *with* direction lines **2**–**3**. The distance and direction in which you drag the mouse determine the shape of the curve segment.

In the instructions on the following pages, you'll learn how to draw straight segments, smooth curves, and nonsmooth curves using the Pen tool. Once you master all three techniques, you'll naturally combine them without really thinking about it as you draw illustrations. Drag-drag-click, drag, click-click-drag…

Pen Tool

Click with the **Pen** tool to create an open or closed **straight-sided** polygon.

To draw a straight-sided object using the Pen tool:

1. If a solid color, gradient, or pattern (not None) is chosen as the fill (look at the Fill box on the Color palette), the Pen path will be filled as soon as you create your first three points. You'll see this only in Preview view, of course. To create segments that appear as lines only, choose a stroke color and a fill of None now or at any time while drawing a path.

2. Choose the Pen tool (P).

3. Click to create an anchor point.

4. Click to create a second anchor point. A straight segment will now connect the two points.

5. Click to create additional anchor points. They will be also connected by straight segments.

6. To complete the shape as an **open** path:

Click the Pen tool or any other tool on the Toolbox.
or
Hold down Cmd/Ctrl and click outside the new shape to deselect it.
or
Choose Select > Deselect (Cmd-Shift-A/Ctrl-Shift-A).

Or to complete the shape as a **closed** path, position the Pen pointer over the starting point (a small circle will appear next to the pointer), and click on it **1**.

➤ Hold down Shift while clicking with the Pen tool to constrain a segment to an increment of 45°.

➤ Use smart guides to help you align points and segments (see pages 90–91) **2**.

➤ If the artboard starts to get filled with extraneous points, use the Object > Path > Clean Up command with only the Stray Points option checked.

(see pages 90–91)

1 *The **Pen** tool pointer is positioned over the starting point to close the new shape.*

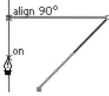

2 *You can use **Smart Guides** to align points as you create them.*

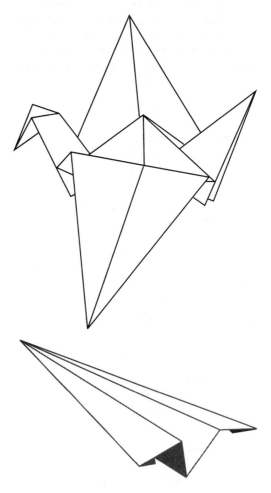

Draw a Straight-Sided Object

1 *Drag to create the first anchor point.*

2 *Release and reposition the mouse, then drag in the direction you want the curve to follow.*

3 *Continue to reposition and drag the mouse.*

Follow these instructions to create **smooth curves** with the **Pen** tool. The anchor points that connect smooth curve segments have a pair of direction lines that move in tandem. The longer the direction lines, the steeper or wider the curve. You can practice drawing curves by tracing over a placed image that contains curved shapes or by converting curved objects into guides and then tracing the guide lines (see pages 270 and 421).

To draw smooth curves using the Pen tool:

1. Choose the Pen tool (P). *Optional:* Turn on Smart Guides (Cmd-U/Ctrl-U toggle).

2. Drag to create the first anchor point **1**. The angle of the pair of direction lines that you create will be determined by the direction you drag.

3. **Release** the mouse, **move** it away from the last anchor point, then drag a short distance in the direction you want the curve to follow to create a second anchor point **2**. A curve segment will connect the first and second anchor points, and a second pair of direction lines will be created. The shape of the curve segment will be defined by the length and direction in which you drag the mouse.

Remember, you can always reshape the curves later (see Chapter 8). When you drag a direction line after it's drawn, only one of the curves that the smooth point connects will be reshaped.

4. Drag to create additional anchor points and direction lines **3**–**4**. The points will be connected by curve segments.

(Continued on the following page)

4 *Continue to reposition and drag.*

5. To complete the object as an **open** path:

Choose a different tool.
or
Hold down Cmd/Ctrl, then click away from the new object to deselect it.
or
Choose Select > Deselect (Cmd-Shift-A/Ctrl-Shift-A).

Or to complete the object as a **closed** path, position the Pen pointer over the starting point (a small loop will appear next to the pointer; if Text Label Hints is on in Illustrator (Edit, in Windows) > Preferences > Smart Guides & Slices, the word "anchor" will appear), drag, then release the mouse.

➤ The fewer the anchor points, the smoother the shape. Too many anchor points will produce bumpy curves, and also could cause printing errors. Also, make your direction lines relatively short at first—you can always lengthen them later.

Daniel Pelavin

Adjust as you go

➤ If the last-created anchor point was a **smooth** point and you want to convert it to a **corner** point, click on it with the Pen tool, release and move the mouse, then continue to draw. One direction line from that point will disappear.

➤ If the last point you created was a **corner** point and you want to add a direction line to it, position the Pen tool pointer over it, then drag. One direction line will appear. Continue to draw.

➤ To move a point as it's being created, keep the mouse button down, hold down the **Spacebar,** and drag the point.

Favorite toggles (Pen tool selected)

Convert Anchor Point tool   Option/Alt

Last-used selection tool   Cmd/Ctrl

Be smart with your pen

If you want Smart Guide angle lines for existing points to appear as you click or drag with the Pen tool to produce a new point **1**, check **Construction Guides** in Illustrator (Edit, in Windows) > Preferences > Smart Guides & Slices.

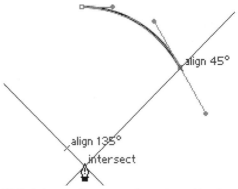

1 *To help you align new anchor points with existing, unselected anchor points, use* **Smart Guides.**

1 *Drag to create the first anchor point.*

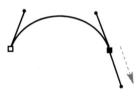

2 *Release the mouse, reposition it, then drag to create a second anchor point.*

3 *Option-drag/Alt-drag from the last anchor point in the direction you want the new curve to follow. The direction lines are on the same side of the curve segment.*

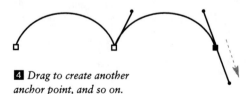

4 *Drag to create another anchor point, and so on.*

You can use the Pen tool to create corner points that join nonsmooth curves, which are segments that curve on the same side of an anchor point. (Segments curve on both sides of a smooth anchor point.) If you move one direction line from a corner point, only the curve on that side of the point will reshape. Smooth points and corner points can be combined in the same path, of course. You can **convert** smooth points into corner points (or vice versa) as you draw them (instructions on this page) or after you draw them (instructions on the next page).

To convert smooth points into corner points as you draw them:

1. Choose the Pen tool (P).

2. Drag to create the first anchor point **1**.

3. **Release** the mouse, **move** it away from the last anchor point, then drag to create a second anchor point **2**. A curve segment will connect the first and second anchor points, and a second pair of direction lines will be created. The shape of the curve segment will be determined by the length and direction you drag.

4. Position the pointer over the last anchor point, Option-drag/Alt-drag from that point to create a new direction line (it will be the type that can be moved independently), then drag in the direction you want the curve to follow **3**.
    or
    Click the last anchor point to remove one of the direction lines from that point.

5. Repeat steps 3 and 4 to draw a series of anchor points and curves **4**.

6. To close the shape:

    Drag on the starting point to keep it as a smooth point.
    or
    To convert the starting point to a corner, click on it.

This is a recap of the various ways to use the **Convert Anchor Point** tool. These techniques were covered in three separate sets of instructions in Chapter 8.

To convert points in an existing object:

1. Choose the Direct Selection tool (A).

2. Click on a path.

3. Choose the Convert Anchor Point tool (Shift-C).
or
Choose the Pen tool (P), then hold down Option/Alt.

4. Position the pointer over the anchor point that you want to convert.

5. Drag new direction lines from a corner point to convert it into a smooth point ■.
or
To convert a smooth point into a corner point with a nonsmooth curve, rotate a direction line from the anchor point so it forms a V shape with the other direction line ■.
or
Click on a smooth point to convert it into a corner point with no direction lines ■–■.

6. Repeat steps 4 and 5 to convert other anchor points.

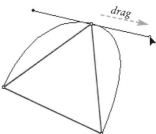

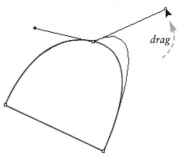

■ *Converting a **corner** point into a **smooth** point*

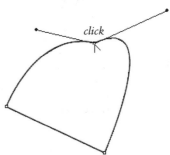

■ *Converting a **smooth** point into a corner point (creating a **nonsmooth** curve)*

■ *Converting a **nonsmooth** curve into a **corner** point with **no direction lines***

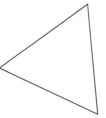

■ *Back to the original triangle*

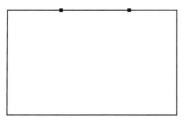

1 *Click to add two anchor points at the ⅓ points along the rectangle's top segment.*

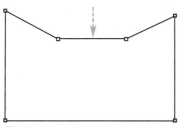

2 *Drag the segment between the new points downward.*

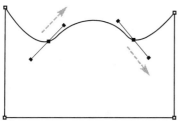

3 *Convert each new point into a smooth point.*

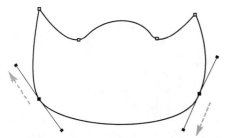

4 *Convert the rectangle's bottom corner points into smooth points.*

Exercise
Convert a rectangle into a costume mask

The outer part of the face mask

1. Draw a rectangle with a fill of None and a 1 pt. black stroke, and select it using the Direct Selection tool (A).

2. Choose the Pen tool (P), and make sure Disable Auto Add/Delete is unchecked in Illustrator (Edit, in Windows) > Preferences > General.

3. Click to add two anchor points at the points along the rectangle's top segment, dividing it into thirds **1**.

4. Cmd-drag/Ctrl-drag the segment between the new points downward **2**.

5. Option-drag/Alt-drag the new point on the left upward and to the right to convert it into a smooth point, and Option-drag/Alt-drag the new point on the right downward and to the right **3**.

6. Option-drag/Alt-drag the bottom left corner point upward and to the left and the bottom right corner point downward and to the left **4**.

7. Release Option/Alt, then click to add a point in the middle of the bottommost segment.

8. Hold down Cmd/Ctrl, click on the new center point, then drag it slightly upward **5**.

(Continued on the following page)

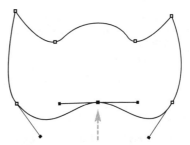

5 *Add a point in the center of the rectangle's bottom segment, then drag the new center point upward.*

The eye holes

1. Choose the Ellipse tool (L), ⬭ then draw a small ellipse for an eye hole **1**.

2. Choose the Direct Selection tool (A). ▶ Deselect, click on the leftmost anchor point of the ellipse, then drag it upward to form an eye shape **2**.

3. Click the bottommost anchor point of the ellipse, then drag the left handle of that point to the left to widen the bottom segment **3**.

4. Click the top middle point of the ellipse, then drag the right handle (direction point) of that point upward and to the right to widen the top right segment **4**.

5. Choose the Selection tool (V), ▶ then move the ellipse to the left side of the mask shape.

6. Choose the Reflect tool (O). ✖

7. Option-click/Alt-click the center of the face mask. In the dialog box, check Preview, click Vertical, enter 90° in the Angle field, then click Copy **5**.

8. Use the Selection tool to marquee all three shapes, and fill the shapes with a color. Leave them selected.

9. Choose Object > Compound Path > Make (Cmd-8/Ctrl-8) or click the Subtract from Shape Area button ▣ on the Pathfinder palette to create a compound shape. The eye holes, which now cut through the face mask **6**, can be modified with the Direct Selection tool.

1 *Create a small ellipse for the eye holes.*

2 *Drag the leftmost anchor point upward with the Direct Selection tool.*

3 *Drag the left direction handle of the bottommost anchor point to the left.*

4 *Drag the right handle of the top middle anchor point upward and to the right.*

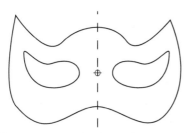

5 *To create the second eye hole, Option-click/ Alt-click in the center of the mask shape with the Reflect tool. Check Preview, click Vertical, enter 90° in the Angle field, then click Copy.*

6 *All the shapes are selected and made into a compound shape. A fill color is applied to the compound shape. (The gray rectangle behind reveals the transparency.)*

In this chapter you'll learn how to create top-level layers and sublayers; highlight layers; select objects using the Layers palette; create and edit groups; restack, duplicate, and delete layers and objects; choose layer options such as hide/show, lock/unlock, view, and print; and finally, merge and flatten layers.

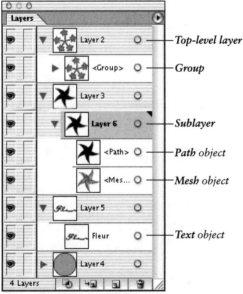

Top-level layer

Group

Sublayer

Path object

Mesh object

Text object

1 The objects in this illustration (paths, texts, images, meshes, etc.) are on top-level layers and sublayers at various stacking levels.

2 The Layers palette for this illustration is shown in the previous figure.

Layer upon layer

Until now (unless you snuck ahead to this chapter!), you've been creating objects on a single, default layer that was created automatically when you created your document. Each new path you drew was added above the next path in your document's stacking order.

Now it's time to get acquainted with the feature that displays the stacking order—the Layers palette. You can open the palette by pressing **F7.** With a document open, click the Layer 1 arrowhead on the Layers palette to reveal the list of objects on that layer. Layer 1 is called a **top-level layer** (meaning it's not nested within another layer) **1**–**2**.

You can add as many layers as you like to an illustration (memory permitting). You can also create **sublayers** (indented layers) within any top-level layer. The actual objects that make up the illustration—paths, text, images, etc.—are nested within one or more top-level layers (or on sublayers within top-level layers). You can highlight, restack, show/hide, or lock/unlock any layer, sublayer, group, or individual object.

Unless it's moved to a different layer, each object in an illustration is nested within whichever layer was highlighted when that object was created. Each top-level layer can hold up to 29 indent levels.

(Continued on the following page)

By default, each new vector object you create is assigned the name **<path>**; each placed raster image or rasterized object is assigned the name **<image>**; each new mesh object is assigned the name **<mesh>**; each new symbol is assigned the name of that symbol (e.g., "Button"); and each new text object is assigned the first few characters in that object (e.g., "The planting season has begun" might be shortened to "The plan").

➤ Double-click an object or layer name to assign a custom name to it. But leave the word "group" or "path" in the name to help you identify it later.

You may say "Whoa!" when you first see the long list of names on the Layers palette. Once you get used to working with it, though, you may become enamored with its clean, logical design, and you'll enjoy how easy it makes even simple tasks, such as selecting and restacking objects.

➤ Layers and sublayers are numbered in the order in which they are created, regardless of their position in the stacking order or whether they're at the top level or indented.

You can choose different **Layers palette options** for each document.

To choose Layers palette options:

1. Choose Palette Options from the bottom of the Layers palette menu.

2. Do any of the following **1**–**2**:

   Check **Show Layers Only** to have the palette list only top-level layers and sublayers—not individual objects.

   For the layer and object thumbnail size, click a **Row Size:** Small (12 pixels), Medium (20 pixels), or Large (32 pixels). Or click Other and enter a custom size (12–100 pixels).

   Check which **Thumbnails** are to be displayed: Layers, Groups, or Objects. For the Layers option, check Top Level Only to have thumbnails display for top-level layers, but not for sublayers.

3. Click OK.

One catchall name

In this book, we refer to paths, images, mesh objects, and text objects collectively as **objects.** If we need to refer to one of these categories individually for some reason, we will.

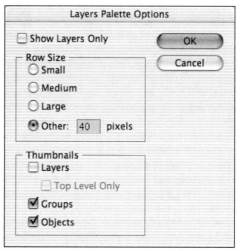

1 *You can customize the Layers palette for each file.*

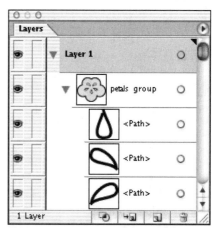

2 *For this document, we chose a large, custom Row Size (Other: 40 pixels), with Thumbnails: Layers off.*

Layers Palette Options (side tab)

Quick layer

To insert a new top-level layer in the topmost layer palette position, **Cmd-click/Ctrl-click** the New Layer button. ▣

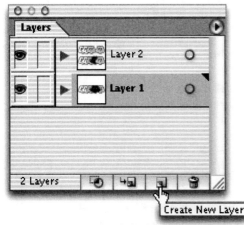

1 *Option-click/Alt-click the **New Layer** button on the **Layers** palette to choose options for or rename a new layer as you create it.*

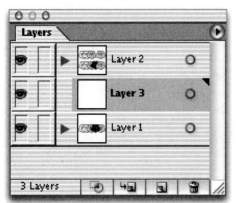

2 *The new Layer 3 appears above Layer 1.*

Creating layers

In these instructions, you'll learn how to create the granddaddy of layers—top-level layers.

To create a new top-level layer:

Method 1 (quick, no options)

1. On the Layers palette (F7), highlight the top-level layer name that you want the new layer to appear above.

2. To create a layer without choosing options for it, click the New Layer button ▣. Illustrator will assign to the new layer the next number in order and the next available color from the Color pop-up menu in the Layer Options dialog box.

Method 2 (choose options)

1. On the Layers palette (F7), highlight the top-level layer name that you want the new layer to appear above.

2. Option-click/Alt-click the New Layer button ▣ **1**–**2**.
   or
   Choose New Layer from the Layers palette menu.

3. Do any of the following:

   Change the layer **Name**.

   Choose a different selection border color for objects on the layer via the **Color** pop-up menu. The various selection colors are there to help you identify which layer or sublayer a selected object is on. Colors are assigned to new layers in the order in which they appear on this pop-up menu. If the fill or stroke colors are similar to the selection border colors, it may be difficult to distinguish among them. In that case, choosing a different selection color helps.

   Choose other layer options (for information about these options, see pages 194–195).

4. Click OK.

➤ A group or object will always be nested within a top-level layer or sublayer—it can't float around by itself.

Create a Top-Level Layer

Once you become accustomed to adding and using top-level layers, you're ready for the next level of intricacy: **sublayers.** Each sublayer is nested within (indented under) either a top-level layer or another sublayer, and layer options can be chosen separately for each individual sublayer. If you create a new object or group of objects while a sublayer is selected, the new object or group will be nested within that sublayer.

By default, every sublayer has the same shading and the same name ("Layer") as its top-level layer, which can be very confusing. To make it easier to distinguish between layers and sublayers, you can rename them (e.g., "poem" or "order form" or "tyrannosaurus").

To create a sublayer:

Method 1 (quick, no options)

1. On the Layers palette (F7), highlight the top-level layer (or sublayer) name that you want the new sublayer to appear in.

2. To create a new layer without choosing options for it, click the New Sublayer button **1**–**2**.

Method 2 (choose options)

1. On the Layers palette (F7), highlight the top-level (or sublayer) layer that you want the new sublayer to appear in.

2. To create a new sublayer and choose options for it, Option-click/Alt-click the New Sublayer button or choose New Sublayer from the Layers palette menu.

3. Enter a Name for the new sublayer.

4. *Optional:* Change the selection Color for the sublayer, and check or uncheck any of the Template, Show, Preview, Lock, Print, or "Dim Images to" options (see pages 194–195).

5. Click OK.

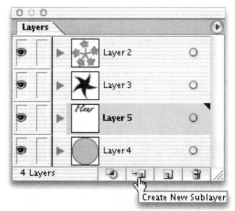

1 *Highlight a layer name, then click the New Sublayer button.*

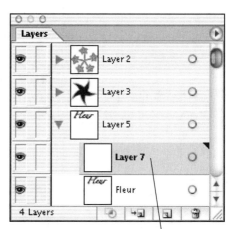

2 *A new sublayer name (in this case, Layer 7) appears within Layer 5.*

Create a Sublayer

1 *First, select the objects to be grouped. You can draw a marquee around them...*

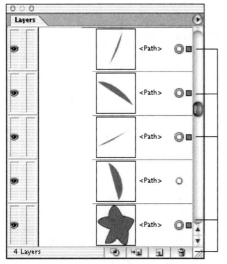

2 *...or Shift-click the selection area on the Layers palette for each object.*

If you **group** objects together, you can easily select, cut, copy, paste, transform, recolor, or move them as a unit. When objects are grouped, they're automatically placed on the same top-level layer (the top-level layer of the frontmost object in the group) and are assigned the same selection color. You can group any types of objects together (e.g., text objects with placed images) and you can select and edit individual objects in a group without having to ungroup them.

To create a group:

1. Choose the Selection tool (V). ▶ Then, in the document window, Shift-click or marquee all the objects to be grouped **1**.
   or
   Shift-click the selection area or the target circle ○ at the far right side of the Layers palette for each object you want to be part of the group. A selection square will appear for each of those objects **2**. (You'll learn more about the selection squares later in this chapter.)

2. Choose Object > Group (Cmd-G/ Ctrl-G) **3**.
   or
   Control-click/right-click the artboard and choose Group from the context menu.

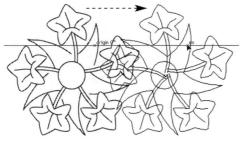

3 *If you move a group using the Selection tool, all the objects in the group will move in unison.*

Create a Group

Highlighting layers

If you want to control where a newly created (or pasted) object will be positioned within the overall stacking order of an illustration, you need to **highlight** (click the name of) a top-level layer, sublayer, group, or object on the Layers palette before pasting or drawing the object.

Highlighting a top-level layer or sublayer doesn't cause objects on those layers to become selected—selecting objects via the Layers palette is a separate step, and targeting items for appearance attributes is yet another step (see the sidebar on the next page). Think of highlighting as a layer management technique, and selecting as an essential first step when editing actual objects. To learn how to select objects using the Layers palette, see pages 184–185.

➤ If a **top-level** layer is highlighted when an object is created but no sublayer or group is highlighted, the new object (e.g., "<Path>" or "<Mesh>") will be listed in that top-level layer.

➤ If a **sublayer** or **group** is highlighted when an object is created or placed but no objects in that sublayer or group are selected, the new object will become a part of that sublayer or group.

➤ If an **object** is selected and a new object is created or placed, the new object will appear directly above the selected one within the selected object's sublayer or group, if indeed it belongs to one.

Note: What we call highlighting (for the sake of brevity and clarity), Adobe calls "selecting a layer listing."

To highlight a layer, sublayer, group, or object:

Click a top-level layer, sublayer, group, or object name—not the selection area at the far right side of the palette. The Current Layer indicator **1** will appear at the far right side of the palette for that layer, sublayer, or whatever. (To highlight multiple layers, groups, or objects, follow the instructions on the next page.)

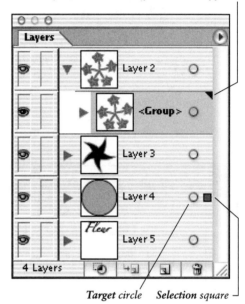

1 *When you highlight a layer, sublayer, group, or object, the* ***Current Layer*** *indicator appears.*

Target circle   *Selection* square

Circles and squares

The column of little circles on the right side of the Layers palette is used for **targeting** an object, group, or layer when applying appearance attributes (read about appearances in Chapter 19).

When you click the **target** circle or the **selection area** at the far right side of the palette for a group or object, the object or group becomes **selected** and becomes a listing on the Appearance palette (you'll learn more about selection methods on the next page).

For a top-level layer or sublayer, it's a different story. To select all the objects on a top-level layer or sublayer, click the selection area. To target a top-level layer or sublayer and have it become a listing on the Appearance palette, click the target circle. You can't target a top-level layer or sublayer using its selection area.

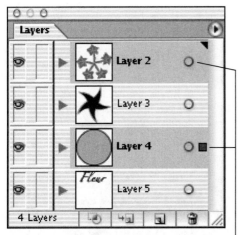

1 *Two noncontiguous top-level layer names are highlighted.*

When **more than one layer**, sublayer, or object is **highlighted**, they can be restacked on the palette en masse and the same layer options can be applied to them.

First, a few rules:

➤ You can highlight more than one sublayer within the same top-level layer, provided they're at the same nesting level, but you can't highlight sublayers from different top-level layers.

➤ You can highlight more than one item of the same category (e.g., all top-level layers), but you can't highlight items from different nesting levels at the same time (e.g., not top-level layers with sublayers).

➤ You can highlight multiple objects (e.g., paths) in the same top-level layer, but you can't highlight objects from different top-level layers.

Note that highlighting and selecting serve different functions. When objects are selected, their anchor points and segments become visible in the document window, and they're ready for editing. When an object is selected, its top-level layer becomes highlighted automatically, but simply highlighting a name on the Layers palette won't cause any objects to become selected.

To highlight multiple items:

1. On the Layers palette (F7), highlight a top-level layer, sublayer, or object name.

2. Shift-click another layer, sublayer, or object name. The items you clicked on and all items in between them of a similar kind will become highlighted.
   or
   Cmd-click/Ctrl-click noncontiguous layer, sublayer, or object names **1**.

   Note that although you can activate any number of layers, only one layer will have the Current Layer indicator (little black triangle) at a time.

➤ Cmd-click/Ctrl-click to unhighlight an item (name) when more than one item is highlighted.

Selecting objects

As we explored in Chapter 6, objects can be selected in the document window using a variety of selection tools and Select menu commands. We also like to use the **Layers palette** to **select** paths or groups. Here, we're talking about selecting for the purpose of editing or reshaping—selection handles and all—not just highlighting, which we showed you how to do on the previous two pages.

To select all the objects in a layer:

Click the **selection area** for a top-level layer or sublayer at the far right side of the Layers palette. A colored selection square will appear for every sublayer, group, and object on that layer; every object on the layer, regardless of its indent level, will become selected in the document window; and the target circle for each item will also become selected (a double ring), unless the items are within a group **1**–**2**.

➤ If you click a layer or sublayer that doesn't contain any objects, no selection square will appear.

➤ To deselect any selected object individually, expand the object's top-level layer or sublayer list, then Shift-click its selection square.

To deselect all the objects in a layer:

Shift-click a layer's **target circle** or **selection square.** All the objects in the layer will be deselected, including any objects contained in any of its sublayers or groups.

To select one object:

1. Make sure the name of the object that you want to select is visible on the Layers palette. Expand any top-level layer, sublayer, or group list, if necessary.

2. At the far right side of the Layers palette, click the **selection area** or **target circle** for the object you want to select **3**.

   To select multiple objects on different layers, follow the instructions on the next page.

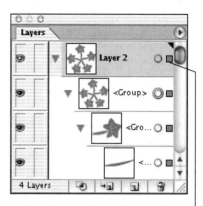

1 *Click the **selection area** for a layer to select all the paths and groups on that layer.*

2 *All the paths and path groups on our "flowers" layer became selected in the document window.*

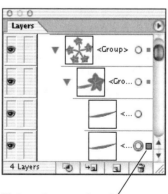

3 *One object is **selected.***

Select Objects

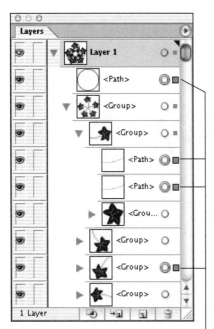

1 *Objects from **nonconsecutive** stacking levels are **selected** (note the selection squares).*

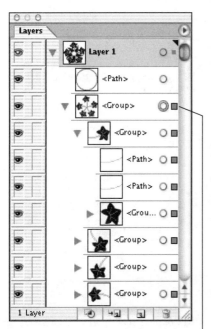

2 *If you click the selection area for a **group**, all the objects in the group will become selected.*

Using the **Layers palette,** you can **select multiple** groups or objects on different—even nonconsecutive—top-level layers or sublayers.

To select multiple objects on different layers:

Method 1
Expand any layer or group lists so the names of all the nested objects that you want to select are visible. Click the **selection area** or **target circle** for any object, then Shift-click any other individual groups or objects that you want to add to the selection **1**. They don't have to be listed consecutively.

Method 2
Option-drag/Alt-drag upward or downward through a series of consecutive top-level or sublayer **names** (not the selection areas) to select all the objects on those layers.
or
Expand a sublayer or group list, then Option-drag/Alt-drag upward or downward through a series of consecutive object **names.** They can be on different layers.

➤ To deselect any selected object individually, Shift-click its selection square or target circle.

Working with groups
To select all the objects in a group:
Method 1 (Layers palette)
1. Expand a top-level layer on the palette that contains a nested group.

2. To select all the objects in a group, (including any objects in groups that may be nested inside it), click the group's selection area or target circle at the far right side of the Layers palette **2**.
or
To select all the objects in a group that's nested inside another group, expand the list for the larger group, then click the selection area for just the nested group.

(Method 2 is on the following page.)

Select Multiple Objects; Select Grouped Objects

Method 2 (document window)

To select an entire group, click any item in the group with the Selection tool (V).

or

To select an object in a group—or individual anchor points or segments on an object in a group—click the object, point, or segment with the Direct Selection tool (A).

or

To select a group that's nested within a larger, parent group, you can either use the Direct Selection tool while holding down Option/Alt or use the Group Selection tool (it's on the Direct Selection tool pop-out menu). Click once to select an object in a group **1**; click again on the same object to select the whole group that the object is part of **2**; click a third time on the object to select the next larger group that the newly selected group is a part of **3**, and so on.

➤ To display the bounding box around a selection, make sure Show Bounding Box is chosen from the View menu, keep the object(s) selected, and choose the Selection tool.

1 *Click once to select an object in a group (in this case, the topmost flower).*

2 *Click again to select the remaining objects in the same group.*

3 *Continue clicking to select other groups, if any, that are nested inside the larger group.*

1 *To **select** multiple objects in a group, expand the group list, then Shift-click the **selection area** for each object. A **selection square** will appear for each object.*

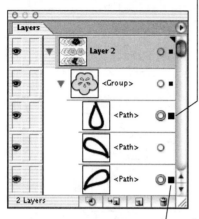

2 *To **deselect** an object in a group, Shift-click its selection square.*

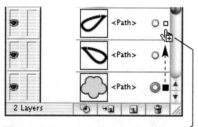

3 *To **copy** an object in a group, Option-drag/Alt-drag its selection square upward or downward (note the plus sign).*

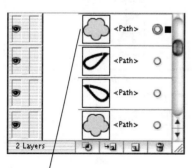

4 *The duplicate appears.*

To select some objects in a group:

1. Deselect all (Cmd-Shift-A/Ctrl-Shift-A).
2. Expand the group's list on the Layers palette, then Shift-click the selection area or target circle at the far right side of the palette for each object in the group that you want to select **1**.
   or
   Choose the Group Selection tool (on the Direct Selection tool pop-out menu), then Shift-click objects in a group (or nested groups) in the document window.
   or
   Choose the Direct Selection tool (A), then Cmd-Shift-click/Ctrl-Shift-click multiple items (or nested groups) in the document window.

To deselect an object in a group:

On the Layers palette, expand the group list, then Shift-click the selection square or target circle for an object in the group **2**.
or
Choose the Direct Selection tool (A), then Shift-click an object in the document window.

To copy an object in a group:

Method 1 (Layers palette)

1. Expand the group list.
2. Click the selection area for the object you want to copy.
3. Option-drag/Alt-drag the selection square upward or downward, then release the mouse when the little outline square is at the desired stacking position either inside the same group or in another sub-layer or top-level layer **3**–**4**.

Method 2 (document window)

1. Choose the Direct Selection tool (A), then select the object you want to copy.
2. To keep the copy inside the group, Option-drag/Alt-drag the object.
   or
   To have the copy appear outside the group, copy the object (Cmd-C/Ctrl-C), deselect, click the layer that you want the object to appear on, then paste (Cmd-V/Ctrl-V).

Select Grouped Objects; Copy Object in Group

Follow these instructions to **add** an existing object to a **group.** The object will stay in its original *x/y* position.

To move an existing object (or group) into a group:

1. Make sure the name of the object you want to add to the group is visible on the Layers palette.

2. Drag the object name upward or downward in the palette. Release the mouse when the large, black arrowheads point to the name of the group that you want to move the object into **1**. The group list will expand, if it isn't already expanded **2**.

➤ You can also move an object into a group by selecting it in the document window, choosing Edit > Cut (Cmd-X/Ctrl-X), selecting an object in the target group, then choosing Edit > Paste in Front (Cmd-F/Ctrl-F) or Paste in Back (Cmd-B/Ctrl-B).

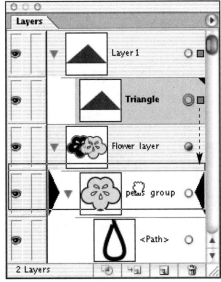

1 *The "Triangle"* **object** *is dragged downward to the "petals group."*

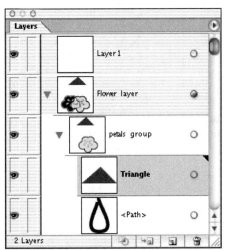

2 *The "petals group" list expands, and the "Triangle" object is on the list.*

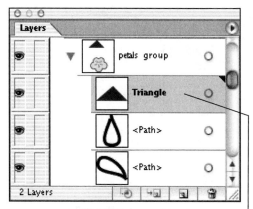

1 *Highlight an object in a group.*

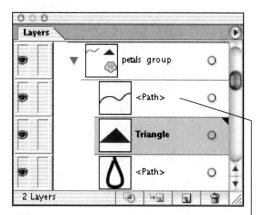

2 *A new path is drawn in the document window, and appears within the same group.*

You can **choose** a **group** for an object before it's created. *Note:* This works only for path objects drawn in Illustrator—not placed images.

To add a new object to a group:

1. Deselect all (Cmd-Shift-A/Ctrl-Shift-A).

2. On the Layers palette, expand the list for the group that you want to add a new object to.

3. Highlight the object (don't click its selection area) above which you want the new object to appear **1**.

4. Draw a new object. The new object will be listed directly above the one you clicked in the previous step, within the same group **2**.

There comes a time when a group has to be disbanded (**ungrouped**).

To ungroup a group:

1. If the group isn't already selected:
   Choose the Selection tool (V), ▶ then click the group in the document window.
   or
   Click the selection area or target circle for the group on the Layers palette.

2. Choose Object > Ungroup (Cmd-Shift-G/ Ctrl-Shift-G).
   or
   Control-click/right-click on the artboard and choose Ungroup from the context menu. If the command isn't available, it means no group is selected.

➤ Keep choosing the same command again to ungroup nested groups.

Add New Object to Group; Ungroup

Restacking layers

The order of objects (and layers) on the Layers palette matches the front-to-back order of objects (and layers) in the illustration. You can move a group or object to a different stacking position within the same layer, move a group or object to a different top-level layer or sublayer, or even move a whole top-level layer or sublayer upward or downward on the list.

On this page you'll use the **Layers palette** for **restacking**. On the next page, you'll use commands. Shop and compare.

To restack a layer, group, or object:

Drag a top-level layer, sublayer, group, or object name upward or downward on the Layers palette (the pointer will turn into a hand icon). Release the mouse between layers or objects to keep the object on the same indent level (e.g., keep a path within a group) **1**–**2**. Or release the mouse when the large black arrowheads point to a different group or layer **3**–**4**. The illustration will redraw with the objects in their new stacking position.

Beware! If you move an object that's part of a group or clipping mask to a different top-level layer, the object will be released from the group or mask.

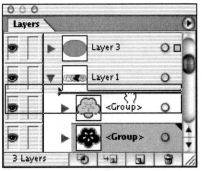

1 *Drag a layer, sublayer, group, or object name upward or downward on the list. Here the mouse is released at the* **same indent level.**

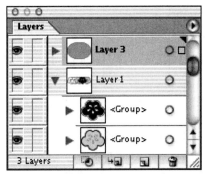

2 *The dark flower group is restacked.*

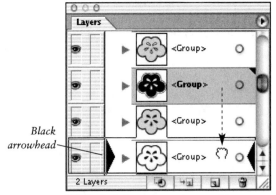

Black arrowhead →

3 *The dark flower group is moved into a different group.*

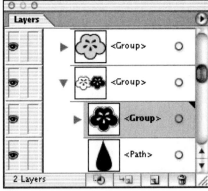

4 *The dark flower group is in a new stacking position and indent level.*

Upside down

To reverse the order of sublayers, groups, and objects within a layer, on the Layers palette, highlight (don't select) all the elements that you want to reverse. To highlight noncontiguous items, Cmd-click/Ctrl-click them; to highlight contiguous items, click the first and then Shift-click the last. Then choose **Reverse Order** from the Layers palette menu.

1 *Select the object that you want to restack, then choose Edit > Cut.*

2 *Select the object that you want to paste directly in front of or directly behind.*

3 *Choose Edit > Paste in Front or Paste in Back (we chose Paste in Back.)*

The **Paste in Front** and **Paste in Back** commands paste the Clipboard contents directly in front of or directly behind the currently selected object within the selected object's layer in the same horizontal and vertical *(x/y)* position from which it was cut.

To restack an object in front of or behind another object:

1. Choose the Selection tool (V), ⬦ then select an object **1**.

2. Choose Edit > Cut (Cmd-X/Ctrl-X).

3. Select the object (in the same document or a different document) that you want to paste directly in front of or directly behind **2**. If you don't select an object, the Clipboard contents will be pasted to the top or bottom of the currently highlighted top-level layer.

4. Choose Edit > Paste in Front (Cmd-F/Ctrl-F).
   or
   Choose Edit > Paste in Back (Cmd-B/Ctrl-B) **3**.

➤ If you restack an object in a group, it will stay in the group.

➤ To restack another way, use the Selection tool (V) to select an object or group, then to move it to the bottom or top of the same layer, Control-click/right-click and choose Arrange > Send to Back or Bring to Front; or to shift the object one level at a time within the same layer, Control-click/right-click and choose Arrange > Bring Forward or Send Backward.

Duplicating layers

If you **duplicate** an entire top-level layer, all the sublayers and objects in that layer will also appear in the duplicate. The duplicate layer will be stacked directly above the original from which it was made.

To duplicate a layer, sublayer, or object:

On the Layers palette, highlight the layer, sublayer, or object that you want to duplicate, then choose Duplicate "[layer or object name]" from the Layers palette menu.

or

Drag a layer, sublayer, or object name over the New Layer button **🗔** **■**–**■**. If you duplicate a top-level layer or sublayer, the word "copy" will appear in the duplicate name.

Follow these instructions to **copy** all the **objects** from a top-level layer, and any sublayers or groups that it contains, to an existing layer or sublayer of your choice. (In the previous set of instructions, the duplicate objects appeared in a new layer.)

To copy objects between layers:

1. Click the selection area for a top-level layer, sublayer, group, or object.

2. Option-drag/Alt-drag the selection square for the layer, sublayer, group, or object upward or downward on the list. Release the mouse when the selection square is in the desired location **■**. The duplicate objects will appear in the same *x/y* location as the original objects.

➤ If you Option-drag/Alt-drag a <clipping path> (a mask) into a different top-level layer, the mask copy won't clip any objects below it. It will be a basic path with a fill and stroke of None.

Duplicate Layer; Copy Objects

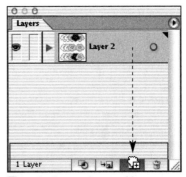

■ *To duplicate a layer, sublayer, group, or object, drag it over the New Layer button (note the plus sign).*

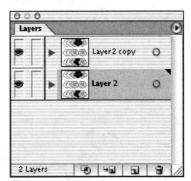

■ *A copy of Layer 2 is made.*

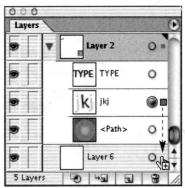

■ *To copy an object to another layer, Option-drag/Alt-drag its selection square upward or downward to the desired location.*

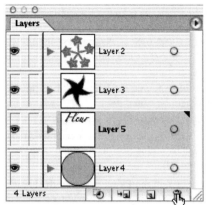

1 *Highlight a layer, sublayer, group, or object, then click the **Delete Selection** button.*

Deleting layers

You know how to make 'em. Now you need to learn how to **get rid of 'em**.

Beware! If you delete a top-level layer or a sublayer, any and all objects on that layer will be removed from the document.

To delete a layer, sublayer, group, or object:

1. On the Layers palette, highlight all the layers, sublayers, groups, and objects that you want to delete (Cmd-click/Ctrl-click to highlight more than one). Remember, you can highlight items only in the same indent level (e.g., all top-level layers), not from different indent levels (e.g., not a top-level layer and objects from a different top-level layer).

2. Choose Delete "[layer or object name]" from the Layers palette menu or click the Delete Selection button 🗑 at the bottom of the palette **1**. If there are any objects on a layer or sublayer that you're deleting, an alert dialog box will appear. Click Yes.
   or
   Drag the highlighted layers or objects over the Delete Selection button.🗑 No alert dialog box will appear.

➤ To retrieve a deleted layer and the objects it contained, choose Edit > Undo Deletion (Cmd-Z/Ctrl-Z) immediately.

Delete Layer or Object

Choosing layer options

To choose multiple options (e.g., color, lock, show/hide, and print) for a layer or object from one central dialog box, use the Layer Options dialog box, which is discussed on this page and the next (one-stop shopping). To choose individual options for a layer or an object (e.g., hide a layer or change its view mode), see pages 196–199.

If you choose **Layer Options** for a top-level layer, those options will apply to all the sublayers, groups, and objects within that layer. You can also choose options for a sublayer, group, or individual object.

To choose layer or object options:

1. Double-click a layer, sublayer, group, or object on the Layers palette.
   or
   Highlight a layer, sublayer, group, or object on the Layers palette, then choose Options for "[   ]" from the palette menu.
   or
   Highlight more than one layer, sublayer, group, or object, then choose Options for Selection from the palette menu.

2. For the highlighted layer, sublayer, group, or object, do any of the following **1**–**2**:

   Type a different **Name** for the layer, sublayer, group, or object.

   Check **Show** to display that object or all the objects on the layer or sublayer; uncheck to hide the object or objects. Hidden layers won't print.

   Check **Lock** to prevent that object or all the objects on that layer or sublayer from being edited; uncheck to allow the objects to be edited.

   ➤ Other (and faster) methods for locking layers and sublayers are discussed on page 196.

   For a layer or sublayer, do any of the following:

   Choose a different **Color** for the object's selection border in the illustration and its selection square on the Layers palette.

Making layers nonprintable

There are three ways to make a layer nonprintable, and there are significant differences among them:

➤ If you **hide** a layer, the layer can't be printed, exported, or edited.

➤ If you turn a layer into a **template,** it can't be printed or exported, but it can be edited and will be visible (images on the layer can be dimmed).

➤ If you turn off the **Print** option in the Layer Options dialog box, the layer won't print, but it can be exported and edited, and it will be visible.

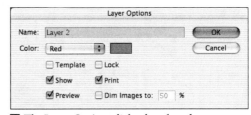

1 *The Layer Options dialog box for a* **layer**

2 *The Options dialog box for a* **path**

Choose Layer/Object Options

This is handy if the current selection color is very similar to the artwork color, and thus is hard to distinguish. You can choose a color from the pop-up menu or double-click the color swatch and mix a color yourself using the color picker.

Click **Template** to convert a layer or sub-layer into a nonprintable tracing layer. Any images and raster objects on the layer will be dimmed by default (more about templates on page 199).

➤ Bug: If you choose Template from the Layer palette menu, the layer will be locked and its name will become italicized; if you choose Template from the Layer Options dialog box, the layer won't be locked and its name won't be italicized. Who knew?!

Check **Preview** to have the layer display in Preview view; uncheck it to have the layer display in Outline view.

➤ To switch views for a layer without opening the Layer Options dialog box, see "To change the view for a top-level layer" on page 198.

Check **Print** to make the layer printable; uncheck it to prevent all the objects on that layer from printing. Nonprintable layers are listed in italics.

➤ Another way to make a layer non-printable is to hide it (click the eye icon on the Layers palette).

To dim any placed images or rasterized objects on that layer, check **Dim Images to** and specify a percentage by which you want those images dimmed (use this for tracing); uncheck this option to display placed images normally. Unlike template layers, dimmed images are editable and print normally.

Choose Layer/Object Options

Locked objects can't be selected or edited. When a whole layer is locked, none of the objects on that layer are editable. Locked layers remain locked even when you close and reopen a file.

To lock/unlock layers or objects:

Click in the edit column for a layer **1**, sublayer, group, or object **2**—the padlock icon 🔒 will appear. Click the padlock icon to unlock.

or

To lock multiple layers, sublayers, groups, or objects, drag upward or downward in the edit column. Drag back over the padlock icons to unlock.

or

Option-click/Alt-click in the edit column for a top-level layer to lock or unlock all the other top-level layers except the one you're clicking on.

or

Highlight the layer(s) that you want to keep unlocked—then to lock all the unhighlighted layers, choose Lock Others from the Layers palette menu.

or

Select the layer that you want to keep unlocked (or a nested object on that layer), then choose Object > Lock > Other Layers.

Note: You can't unlock an object individually if the top-level layer in which the object is nested is locked; you have to unlock the top-level layer before you can unlock the object.

➤ To lock a selected object via a command, choose Object > Lock > Selection (Cmd-2/Ctrl-2). There is no Object menu command for unlocking individual objects. To unlock all objects that were locked via the command, press Cmd-Option-2/Ctrl-Alt-2.

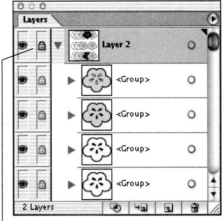

1 *If you **lock** an entire **layer**, none of the objects on that layer will be editable.*

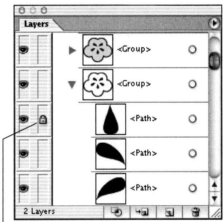

2 *Click in the edit column to **lock** a layer, group, or **object** (the padlock icon will appear).*

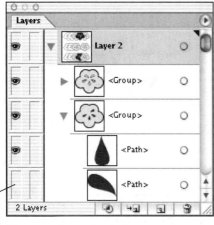

1 *You can hide individual **objects** or **groups**...*

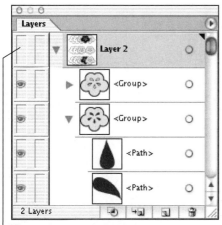

2 *...and you can hide whole **layers**.*

Do it via a command

Lock artwork directly above the selected object in the same layer	Select object, then Object > Lock > All Artwork Above
Hide artwork directly above the selected object in the same layer	Select object, then Object > Hide > All Artwork Above

What have you got to hide? Well, for one thing, if your illustration is crowded with objects, **hiding** the **objects** you're not working on will make your screen redraw faster. For another thing, it will make it easier to locate and focus on the areas and objects in your illustration that you are working on. You can hide a top-level layer and all its nested layers, hide a group, or just hide an individual object. What's hidden won't print.

To hide/show layers or objects:

Note: If you want to show an object, but its top-level layer is hidden, you must show its top-level layer first.

Click the eye icon 👁 (in the first column) for a top-level layer, a sublayer, a group, or an object **1**–**2**. If you hide a top-level layer or a sublayer, any objects nested within that layer or sublayer will be hidden, whether or not they are selected. To redisplay what was hidden, click where the eye icon was.

or

Drag upward or downward in the eye column to hide multiple, consecutive top-level layers, sublayers, groups, or objects. To redisplay what was hidden, drag again.

or

Option-click/Alt-click the eye column 👁 to hide/show all the top-level layers except the one you're clicking on.

or

Make sure all the layers are visible (choose Show All Layers from the Layers palette menu if they're not), highlight the top-level layer or layers that you want to remain visible, then choose Hide Others from the Layers palette menu.

➤ To hide a selected object via a command, choose Object > Hide > Selection (Cmd-3/Ctrl-3). There is no command for showing an individual object.

➤ To make a visible layer nonprintable, uncheck Print in the Layer Options dialog box. You can also show or hide an entire layer via that dialog box.

Hide Layer or Object

If you change the **view** for a top-level layer, all nested layers and objects within it will be displayed in that view.

To change the view for a top-level layer:

To display a top-level layer in Outline view when the illustration is in Preview view, Cmd-click/Ctrl-click the eye icon 👁 for that layer. The eyeball will become hollow **1**. To redisplay the layer in Preview view, Cmd-click/Ctrl-click the eye icon again.
or
Double-click the layer name, then check or uncheck Preview.

To display all top-level layers in Outline view except one:

Cmd-Option-click/Ctrl-Alt-click a top-level layer eye icon 👁 to display all layers in Outline view except the one you're clicking on. (Repeat to redisplay all layers in Preview view.)
or
Highlight the top-level layer that you want to display in Preview view, then choose Outline Others from the Layers palette menu.

➤ To display all layers in Preview view, choose Preview All Layers from the Layers palette menu.

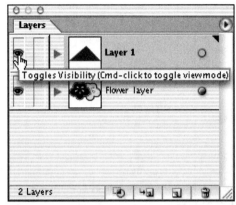

1 *Cmd/Ctrl click the eye icon to toggle between* **Outline** *and* **Preview** *views for that top-level layer.*

Change View for Layer

Show or hide 'em

To **show/hide** all **template layers** in a document, press Cmd-Shift-W/Ctrl-Shift-W.

1 *The template layer icon. The template layer name is in italics.*

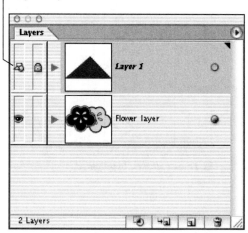

Objects on **template layers** are locked, nonprintable, and nonexportable, and any images on template layers are dimmed. You can use template layers either to trace objects or placed images using the Auto Trace tool, or as a guide to help you draw new objects. Read about tracing on pages 269–270.

Note: If you choose Template from the Layer palette menu, the layer will be locked and its name will become italicized; if you choose Template from the Layer Options, the layer won't be locked and its name won't be italicized. This may be a bug.

To create a template layer:

Method 1 (choose options)

1. Double-click an existing top-level layer name.
   or
   To create a new top-level layer to become the template layer, Option-click/Alt-click the New Layer button at the bottom of the Layers palette.

2. Check Template.

3. Choose a "Dim Images to" percentage for any placed images or rasterized objects on the template layer.

4. Click OK. A template icon will appear in place of the eye icon for the layer and any nested layers or objects in that layer are supposed to be locked **1**.

Method 2 (quick)

1. Highlight an existing layer.

2. Choose Template from the Layers palette menu.

Method 3 (as an image is placed)

To create a template layer as you place an image into Illustrator, check Template in the File > Place dialog box.

Create Template Layer

Layer management

With the abundance of information on the Layers palette comes one minor drawback: Sometimes it's hard to find things. Luckily, Adobe built in a **locator** command. Now, how 'bout a locator command for the contents of Elaine's handbag?

To locate an object on the Layers palette:

1. Choose the Selection tool (V).

2. Select the object in the document window that you want to locate on the Layers palette. You can select more than one object; they'll all be found. (To select an object in a group, use the Direct Selection or Group Selection tool.)

3. Choose Locate Object from the Layers palette menu. The selected object's top-level layer list will expand, if it isn't already expanded (the selection square for the object will be visible).

➤ If "Locate Layer" appears on the palette menu instead of "Locate Object," choose Palette Options from the palette menu and uncheck the Show Layers Only option. The Locate Object command will then become available.

The **Collect in New Layer** command moves all the currently highlighted top-level layers, sublayers, groups, or objects into a brand new layer.

To move layers, sublayers, groups, or objects to a new layer:

1. Cmd-click/Ctrl-click the layer, group, or object names that you want to gather together 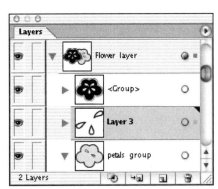. They all have to be at the same indent level (e.g., all objects from the same sublayer, or a series of consecutive sublayers). Don't click the selection area.

2. From the Layers palette menu, choose Collect in New Layer. The sublayers, groups, or objects you chose will be nested inside a new sublayer within the same top-level layer 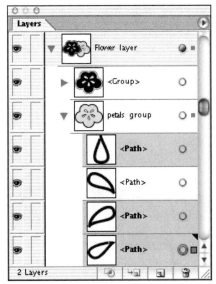. Highlighted top-level layers will be nested as sublayers within a new top-level layer.

1 *Three paths are **highlighted**.*

2 *After **Collect in New Layer** is chosen, the three highlighted paths are gathered into a new sublayer (Layer 3, in this case).*

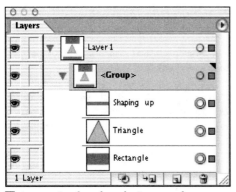

1 *A group is selected on the Layers palette.*

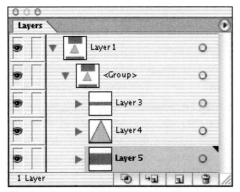

2 *After choosing Release to Layers (Sequence)*

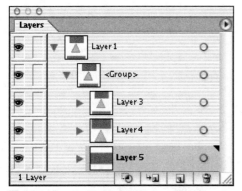

3 *After choosing Release to Layers (Build)*

The **Release to Layers** command disperses all the objects or groups that are nested within the currently highlighted layer onto separate layers within that layer.

If you're planning to export your Illustrator file to an animation program (e.g., Macromedia Flash) to use as the contents of an object or frame animation, you'll first need to release any groups and expand any appearances or blends in the file, and then release those objects to individual layers (nested within a top-level layer) via one of the Release to Layers commands. Then, in the animation program, you'll be able to convert the layers from the placed file into separate objects or into a sequence. See pages 477–478.

Read step 2 carefully before deciding which of the two commands you're going to use.

To move objects to new, separate layers:

1. On the Layers palette, highlight or select a top-level layer, sublayer, or group (not an object) **1**.

2. From the Layers palette menu, choose:

   Release to Layers (Sequence) **2**. Each object in the highlighted layer or group will be nested in its own new layer within the original layer. The objects' original stacking order will be preserved.
   or
   If you want to build a cumulative animation sequence, choose Release to Layers (Build) **3**. The bottommost layer will contain only the bottommost object; the next layer above that will contain the bottommost object plus the next object above it; the next layer above that will contain the two previous objects plus the next object above, and so on. If you're going to use another application to create a frame animation of objects that are added in succession, choose this option.

➤ If you release a layer or a sublayer that contains a clipping mask that was created using the Layers palette, the mask will

(Continued on the following page)

Release to Layers

still clip the objects within the same layer or sublayer.

➤ If you release a layer or group that contains a scatter brush, the brush object will remain as a single <Path>. If, on the other hand, you highlight only the brush object and release to layers, each object in the scatter brush will be moved to a separate layer; the original scatter brush path will be preserved.

Remembering layers

If you want to paste an object to the top of its own layer or sublayer rather than to a different layer, turn the **Paste Remembers Layers** option on via the Layers palette menu. If this option is on and the original layer is deleted after the object is copied, but before the Paste command is used, the object(s) will paste onto a brand new layer.

Release to Layers

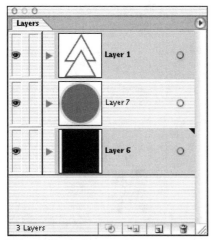

1 *Highlight the layers, sublayers, groups, or objects that you want to merge.*

2 *After* **Merge Selected** *is chosen, the two highlighted layers are merged into one.*

Merging and flattening

Dire warning! If there's a chance you're going to want to work with any individual layers in your file again, save a copy of the file, using File > Save As, before applying the **Merge Selected** or **Flatten Artwork** command.

If you have more layers and sublayers on the Layers palette than you can comfortably handle, you can consolidate the list by **merging** some of them together. You can also merge two or more groups or merge a group with individual nongrouped objects. In the latter case, the objects will become part of the group and will appear at the top or bottom of the group.

To merge layers, sublayers, groups, and objects:

1. Highlight two or more layers, sublayers, or groups. Cmd-click/Ctrl-click to highlight noncontiguous top-level layers or sublayers. Whatever you highlight will be merged into the item that has the Current Layer indicator (look for the little black triangle at the far right side of the Layers palette).

   The ground rules: Locked and/or hidden layers can be merged. A nongrouped object can be merged with a sublayer or a group, but not with another object.

2. Choose Merge Selected from the Layers palette menu **1**–**2**.

➤ If you merge two groups and one of the groups contains a clipping path, that clipping path may be released, depending on the original stacking order of the groups.

Merge

203

Warning! The **Flatten Artwork** command **discards** hidden top-level layers (read that again) and flattens **all** layers in the file into **one top-level layer,** with any sublayers and groups nested within it. Actually, you'll get an alert dialog box that will give you the option to keep the hidden artwork when layers are flattened, but you still need to think ahead.

One more warning! Flatten Artwork also **removes** transparency, effects, paint attributes, and any layer clipping sets that have been applied to any top-level layers. Otherwise, the appearance of the artwork in the document window won't change. The objects will be fully editable after the command is chosen. If you flatten the artwork into a highlighted layer that has appearances attached to it, those appearances will be applied to all the objects.

To flatten artwork:

1. Redisplay any hidden top-level layers that you want to keep **1**.

2. By default, if no layers are highlighted, the Flatten Artwork command merges all the currently visible layers into whichever top-level layer is displaying the Current Layer indicator. To flatten into a layer of your choice, highlight it now.

3. Choose Flatten Artwork from the Layers palette menu. If there are any hidden layers that contain artwork, an alert dialog box will appear **2**–**3**. Click Yes to discard the hidden artwork or click No to preserve the artwork, in the flattened document. You can choose Undo right away, if need be.

Note: If you try to flatten artwork into a hidden, locked, or template layer, Illustrator will flatten all the layers into the topmost top-level layer that isn't hidden, locked, or a template.

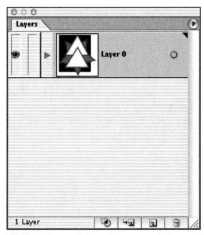

1 *In this original four-layer illustration, at least one layer is hidden and contains artwork (Layer 7), so an alert dialog box will appear when the **Flatten Artwork** command is chosen.*

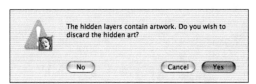

2 *It's always nice to get a second chance!*

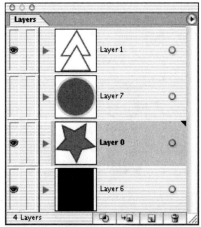

3 *The **Flatten Artwork** command flattened all the layers into the currently highlighted layer (Layer 0, in this case).*

This chapter is an introduction to Illustrator's type tools. First you'll learn how to create point type, type inside an object, and type along a path. Then you'll learn how to import type from another application, thread type between objects, copy type and a type object, and convert type into graphic outlines. Typographic attributes are modified using the Character, Paragraph, Character Styles, Paragraph Styles, and OpenType palettes, which are discussed in the next chapter, along with methods for selecting type.

The Type tool creates point type or type inside a rectangle.

1 *Type tool*

The Area Type tool enters type into a path of any shape. The Area Type tool enters type into a path of any shape. The Area Type tool enters type into a path of any shape, The Area

2 *Area Type tool*

The Type on a Path tool enters type along a path.

3 *Type on a Path tool*

```
T T T
Y Y H
P P E
E E
  T V
T T E
H O R
I O T
S L I
  C
W E A
A N L
Y T
  E
  R
  S
```
T H E V E R T I C A L P A T H T Y P E

4 *Vertical Type tool*   **5** *Vertical Type on a Path tool*

Creating type
The type tools

There are three horizontal type tools: The Type tool, the Area Type tool, and the Type on a Path tool. Each of these tools has a counterpart for creating vertical type: the Vertical Type tool, the Vertical Area Type tool, and the Vertical Type on a Path tool. Some of these tools' functions overlap, but each one has unique characteristics for producing a particular kind of type object.

T——The **Type** tool creates a block of type that isn't associated with a path **1**. You can also draw a rectangle with it and enter type inside the rectangle; you can use it to enter type along the edge of an open path; or you can use it to enter type inside a closed path. It's the most versatile of all the type tools.

T——The **Area Type** tool creates type *inside* an open or closed path. Lines of type that are created with the Area Type tool automatically wrap inside the path **2**.

T——The **Type on a Path** tool creates a line of type along the outer *edge* of an open or closed path **3**.

T——The **Vertical Type** tool has the same function as the Type tool, except it creates vertical type **4**.

T——The **Vertical Area Type** tool creates vertical type *inside* an open or closed path.

T——The **Vertical Type on a Path** tool creates vertical type along the outer *edge* of an open or closed path **5**.

205

Point type stands by itself—it's neither inside an object nor along a path. This kind of type is appropriate for small amounts of text that stand independently, such as headlines, titles, and button names.

To create point type:

1. Choose the Type tool (T) **T** or Vertical Type tool. **T**

2. Click on a blank area of the artboard where you want the type to start (not on an object). A flashing insertion marker will appear.

3. Enter type. Press Return/Enter each time you want to start a new line **1**.

4. Choose a selection tool on the Toolbox (don't use a keyboard shortcut to select the tool), then click outside the type block to deselect it.
   or
   Click the Type tool again to complete the type block and start a new one.

➤ To align separate blocks of point type, use the Align palette (see pages 428–429.)

➤ If you open a file containing text from a previous version of Illustrator into Illustrator CS, an alert dialog box will appear, offering you choices for updating the legacy text (see pages 222–223).

Choose type attributes first?

If you'd like to choose character and paragraph attributes before you create type, use the **Character** and **Paragraph** palettes, or click a paragraph style on the Paragraph Styles palette (don't worry, you'll learn all about styles in the next chapter!).

Recolor after?

When type is entered inside an object or on a path, a fill and stroke of None is applied to the object automatically. After the type is entered, if you want to apply fill and/or stroke colors to the **type object,** deselect it, then click the edge of the object with the Direct Selection tool. To recolor the **type** itself, first select it using a type tool or a selection tool (methods for selecting type are discussed in the next chapter).

I DON'T KNOW THE KEY TO SUCCESS, BUT THE
KEY TO FAILURE IS TRYING TO PLEASE EVERYBODY.

Bill Cosby

1 *Point type created using the Type tool*

No going back

Once you place type inside or along a graphic object, it becomes a type object, and it can be converted back into a graphic object only via the Undo command. To preserve the original graphic object, Option-drag/Alt-drag it to copy it, then convert the copy into a type object. You can't enter type into a compound path, a mask object, a mesh object, or a blend; also, you can't make a compound path from a type object. If you create type on a path that has a brush stroke, the brush stroke will be removed.

'It spoils people's clothes to squeeze under a gate; the proper way to get in, is to climb down a pear tree.'

1 *Drag with the* **Type** *tool to create a rectangle, then enter type. To see the edges of the rectangle, go to Outline view or use Smart Guides with Object Highlighting.*

2 *Drag with the* **Vertical Type** *tool, then enter type. Type flows from top to bottom and from right to left.*

A P E A R   T R E E .   .   .

C L I M B   D O W N

'It spoils people's clothes to squeeze under a gate; the proper way to get in, is to climb down a pear tree.'

3 *After reshaping the type rectangle using the Direct Selection tool*

Use this method if you want to define the shape of the **type container** before creating the type. To enter type in a nonrectangular object, see the instructions on the next page.

To create a type rectangle:

1. Choose the Type tool (T) **T** or the Vertical Type tool. **|T**

2. Drag to create a rectangle. When you release the mouse, a flashing insertion marker will appear.

   ➤ To draw a square, start dragging, then hold down Shift and continue to drag. To create vertical type using the Type tool or horizontal type using the Vertical Type tool, hold down Shift before and while dragging.

3. Enter type. Press Return/Enter only when you need to create a new paragraph. The type will wrap automatically to fit into the rectangle **1**–**2**.

4. Choose a selection tool on the Toolbox (don't use a keyboard shortcut to select the tool), then click outside the type block to deselect it.
   or
   To keep the type tool selected so as to create another, separate type rectangle, press Cmd/Ctrl to temporarily access the last-used selection tool, then click outside the type block to deselect it. Release Cmd/Ctrl, then click again to start the new type block. (You can also complete a type object by clicking the type tool.)

   Note: If the overflow symbol appears on the edge of the rectangle (a tiny red cross in a square) and you want to reveal the hidden type, deselect the rectangle, then reshape it using the Direct Selection tool. You can use Smart Guides (with Object Highlighting) to locate the edge of the rectangle. The type will reflow to fit the new shape **3**. Another option is to thread the overflow type into another object (see page 213).

Type Rectangle

Use the **Area Type** or **Vertical Area Type** tool to place type inside a rectangle or an irregularly shaped path, or onto an open path. The object will turn into a type path.

To enter type inside an object:

1. If the object is a closed path, choose the Area Type tool ⊤, Vertical Area Type tool ⊤, or either one of the Type tools (⊤ or ⊤). For an open path, choose either one of the Area Type tools.

2. Click precisely on the edge of the path. A flashing insertion marker will appear, and any fill or stroke on the object will be removed. The object will now be listed as <Type> (not <Path>) on the Layers palette.

3. Enter type in the path, or copy and paste text from a text editing application into the path. The text will stay inside the object and conform to its shape **1**–**2**. Vertical area type flows from top to bottom and from right to left.

   ➤ The smaller the type, the more snugly it will fit inside the shape. Click a Justify button on the Paragraph palette to make it hug both sides of the object, and also turn on hyphenation.

4. Choose a selection tool, then click outside the type object to deselect it.
   or
   To keep the type tool selected so as to enter type in another object, press Cmd/Ctrl to temporarily access the last-used selection tool, click away from the type block to deselect it, release Cmd/Ctrl, then click the next type object. Or you can click again on the type tool that you used to create the type object.

   ➤ The Area Type Options, which control the placement of type inside a type object, are discussed on page 250.

To make a whole horizontal type block vertical, or vice versa:

1. Choose the Selection tool.

2. Click on a type block.

3. Choose Type > Type Orientation > Horizontal or Vertical.

Switcheroo **NEW**

To rotate vertical area type characters, highlight only the characters that you want to convert, display the Character palette (Window > Type > Character), and then, on the Character palette menu, choose **Standard Vertical Roman Alignment** to uncheck or check that option.

To rotate just the type characters, select the type object, then choose or enter a positive or negative **Character Rotation** value 𝕋 on the Character palette.

This is text in a copy of a light bulb shape. You can use the Area Type tool to place type into any shape you can create. When fitting type into a round shape, place small words at the top and the bottom. This is text in a copy of a light bulb shape. You can use the Area Type tool to place type into any

1 *Area type*

The kiss of memory made pictures of love and light against the wall. Here was peace. She pulled in her horizon like a great fish-net. Pulled it from around the waist of the world and draped it over her shoulder. So much of life in its meshes! She called in her soul to come and see. ZORA NEALE HURSTON

2 *Type in a circle*

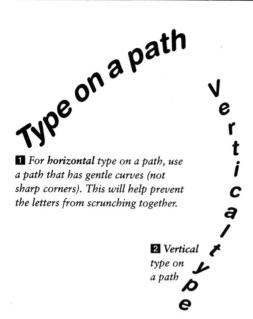

1 For *horizontal* type on a path, use a path that has gentle curves (not sharp corners). This will help prevent the letters from scrunching together.

2 *Vertical type on a path*

These pointers will display when the pointer is placed over a bracket on a selected type path.

▶┠   ▶⊥   ▶┥
Left bracket   *Center bracket*   *Right bracket*

3 When selected with the Selection tool, the left, center, and right brackets become visible.

4 The *left bracket is dragged to the left.*

5 After moving the *left bracket to the left*

Use the **Type on a Path** tool to place type on the inner or outer edge of a path. Type can't be placed on both sides of the same path, but it can be moved from one side to the other after it's created. Only one line of type can be created per path.

To place type along an object's path:

1. Choose the Type on a Path 🔧 or Vertical Type on a Path tool, 🔧 then click the top or bottom edge of a closed path. Or choose the Type, **T** or Vertical Type **⊺T** tool, then click an open path. The path can be selected, but it doesn't have to be.

2. When the flashing insertion marker appears, enter type. Don't press Return/Enter. The type will appear along the edge of the object, and the object will now have a fill and stroke of None **1**–**2**.

3. Choose a selection tool (or hold down Cmd/Ctrl), then click outside the type object to deselect it.
   or
   If you want to create a new type block, click the type tool again.

To adjust the position of type on a [NEW] path:

1. Choose the Selection tool (V) ▶ or Direct Selection tool (A). ▶

2. Click on the type. Center, left, and right brackets will appear **3**.

3. As you do any of the following, be sure to drag the bracket (the vertical bar)—not the little square! If your tool switches to a type tool, choose a selection tool and try again.

   Drag the **center** bracket to the left or right to reposition the type block along the path.

   Drag the **left** bracket **4**–**5** to reposition the starting point of the type on the path.

   Drag the **right** bracket back across the existing type. This will shorten the amount of type that's visible on the path and produce a type overflow.

   To **flip** the type to the other side of the path, drag the center bracket across to the other side of the path.

In the **Type on a Path Options** dialog box, you can change the orientation of type on a path by choosing from an assortment of distortion, alignment, and letterspacing options. These settings can be changed at any time.

NEW **To apply Type on a Path options:**

1. Click on type on a path with the Selection tool.

2. Choose Type > Type on a Path > Type on a Path Options.

3. Check Preview ◼.

4. Do any of the following:

   From the **Effect** pop-up menu, choose Rainbow, Skew, 3D Ribbon, Stair Step, or Gravity (◨, next page).

   Choose **Align to Path:** Ascender, Descender, Center, or Baseline to specify which part of the text will touch the path (◨, next page).

   Check (or uncheck) **Flip.**

   Choose or enter a new letter **Spacing** value.

5. Click OK. If you want to change or reverse any of the settings you've chosen, reselect the object and reopen the dialog box.

➤ Individual type effects can also be applied via the Type > Type on a Path submenu.

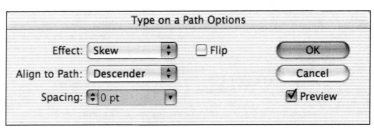

◼ *Use the* Type on a Path Options *dialog box to choose effect, alignment, orientation, and spacing options for type on a path.*

Type on a Path Options

2 *Type on a Path effects*

Rainbow effect

Skew effect

3D Ribbon effect

Stair Step effect

Gravity effect

3 *Align to Path options*

Ascender

flower

Descender

flower

Center

flower

Baseline

flower

Importing text

Using the Place command, you can **import** text files in the Microsoft Word (doc), Microsoft RTF (rtf, short for rich text format), or plain (ASCII) text format into an Illustrator document. The text will appear in a new rectangle.

Note: To place text onto a custom path, first place it by following the instructions on this page, then copy and paste it into or onto the custom path (see "To move type from one object to another" on page 215).

To import text:

1. Choose File > Place.

2. Click the name of the text file that you want to import.

3. Click Place.

For a Microsoft Word (doc) or Microsoft RTF (rtf) file, the Microsoft Word Options dialog box will open 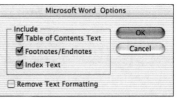. For a plain text format file, the Text Import Options dialog box will open 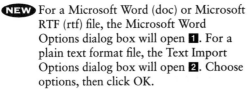. Choose options, then click OK.

The imported text will appear in a rectangle 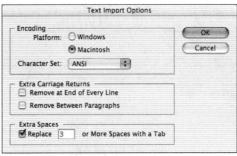. Formatting and styling is preserved by the Microsoft Word and Microsoft RTF formats, but not by the plain text format.

Be sure to learn about threading, starting on the following page.

➤ To export text from Illustrator, see pages 215 and 478.

➤ To create columns and rows of type, see page 252.

1 *For text in Microsoft Word or Microsoft RTF, choose settings in the **Microsoft Word Options** dialog box.*

2 *For text in the ASCII format, choose settings in the **Text Import Options** dialog box.*

May the day come (soon perhaps) when I'll flee to the woods on an island in Oceania, there to live on ecstasy, calm, and art. With a new family by my side, far from this European scramble for money. There, in Tahiti, in the silence of the beautiful tropical nights, I will be able to listen to the soft murmuring music of the movements of my heart in amorous harmony with the mysterious beings around me. Free at last, without financial worries and able to love, sing, and die.
Paul Gauguin

3 *Placed text appears in a rectangle.*

In port

Here was peace. She pulled in her horizon like a great fish-net. Pulled it from around the waist of the world and draped it over her

Out port

1 *To thread text, first click* **Out** *port with the Selection tool...*

Here was peace. She pulled in her horizon like a great fish-net. Pulled it from around the waist of the world and draped it over her

2 *...then drag (or click) elsewhere with the* **Loaded Text** *pointer.*

Here was peace. She pulled in her horizon like a great fish-net. Pulled it from around the waist of the world and draped it over her

shoulder. ?So much of life in its meshes! She called in her soul to come and see.

Zora Neale Hurston

3 *The overflow type spills from the first object into the second, in the direction shown by the* **thread** *arrowheads.*

Not all is copied

If you click to create a duplicate of a type object (step 4 on this page), only the object's shape will be copied, not its fill and stroke **attributes.** To copy the attributes afterward, choose the Direct Selection tool, click the edge of the duplicate object, choose the Eyedropper tool (I), then click the background of the original text object (before you click with the Eyedropper, make sure the pointer doesn't have a little "t").

Threading type

Illustrator CS boasts some new methods for linking overflow text, and has even given the process a new name: threading. But before we explore threading, if your type object is almost—but not quite—large enough to display all the type on or inside it, a simple solution is to enlarge the object to reveal the hidden type. You can do this in either of the following ways:

➤ Click the type block with the **Selection** tool, then drag a handle on its **bounding box** (choose View > Show Bounding Box if the box isn't visible).

➤ Or select only the rectangle—not the type—with the **Direct Selection** tool (turn on Smart Guides with Object Highlighting or go to Outline view to locate the rectangle), then **Shift-drag** a **segment.**

If your type overfloweth, you can spill, or **thread,** it into a different object or into a copy of the same object. Text can be threaded between path objects or area type objects, or between an area type object and a path object.

To thread overflow type to another **NEW** object:

1. Choose the Selection tool (V).

2. Select the original type object.

3. Click the Out port ⊞ on the selected object. The pointer will turn into a Loaded Text pointer ⊞ **1**.

4. To create a **new** object for the overflow text, either click where you want a duplicate of the **currently selected** text object to appear, or drag to create a **rectangular** type object **2**–**3**.
   or
   Position the pointer over an **existing** object—the pointer will change to ▶▨—then click the object's path. A fill and stroke of None will be applied to the path.

   Overflow type from the first object will flow into the second one.

5. Deselect the objects.

➤ If you double-click an Out port, Illustrator will link to a copy of the text object automatically, in a default location.

Thread Type

213

If you're curious to see what's threaded to what, you can **display** the text **threads.**

NEW **To display text threads:**

Select a linked type object. If the threads aren't showing, choose View > Show Text Threads (Cmd-Shift-Y/Ctrl-Shift-Y). *Note:* The stacking order of type objects on the Layers palette has no impact on how text flows from one object to another.

When you **unthread** two objects, you break the chain and the overflow text gets sucked back into the first object of the two.

NEW **To unthread two type objects:**

1. Choose the Selection tool (V), then click a threaded type object.

2. Double-click the object's In port or Out port **1**–**2**.
   or
   Click an In port or Out port, **▶** move the pointer slightly (the Unthread cursor 🐍 displays), then click the port again to cut the thread.

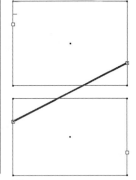

The Hike
Me and my class were on a hike on a very warm day at a campsite. As soon as the golden morning sun peeked over the trees, we were on our way. My best

friend Maggie was lugging all the books. They were the silly ones we would use for when we took observation breaks. It was unfair that Maggie had to carry them, because all she did was

whisper "Is there chorus tomorrow?" I hated hearing her whine, "oww" and "this hurts." But our teacher, Ms. Bretchin, the grouchy blob, didn't care at all. S.L.

The Hike
Me and my class were on a hike on a very warm day at a campsite. As soon as the golden morning sun peeked over the trees, we were on our way. My best

1 *An Out port is double-clicked...*

2 *...which causes the first type object to become **unthreaded**.*

Follow these instructions if you want to keep the remaining links intact as you **release** one object from a **thread.** The type will reflow.

NEW **To release an object from a thread and preserve the remaining threads:**

1. Choose the Selection tool (V), then click the type object to be released **3**.

2. To unthread the object but also preserve it, choose Type > Threaded Text > Release Selection **4**.
   or
   To delete the threaded object, press Delete/Backspace.

And finally, follow these instructions if you want to **disconnect threaded objects** from one another, but keep the type where it is.

NEW **To remove all threading between objects and leave the type in place:**

1. Choose the Selection tool (V), then click a threaded type object.

2. Choose Type > Threaded Text > Remove Threading.

Friends
Once there was a mousey, so cute and helpless.He had a friend named Cheesecake. It was shocking to hear the mousey didn't eat cheesecake, never ever, but

Cheesecake said okay for being friends together. This is a story about them playing parcheesi, which was Cheesecake's favorite game! Mousey's favorite game was Mousetrap, he loved it so

dearly! So meanwhile, they're in a parcheesi game and Boom!—Cheesecake beat mousey for the 9,999,999th time at the game, but mousey didn't care one bit! A.L.

Friends
Once there was a mousey, so cute and helpless.He had a friend named Cheesecake. It was shocking to hear the mousey didn't eat cheesecake, never ever, but

Cheesecake said okay for being friends together. This is a story about them playing parcheesi, which was Cheesecake's favorite game! Mousey's favorite game was

3 *The middle type object is selected...*

4 *...and then **released** from the thread.*

Moving type

1 *Point type is highlighted, put on the Clipboard via Edit > Cut...*

2 *...and then pasted into a rectangle.*

Copying type

To **copy** or move type with or without its object, you can use the Clipboard, a temporary storage area in memory. The Clipboard commands are Cut, Copy, and Paste. You could also use the drag-and-drop method to move a whole type object (see page 266).

To copy type and its object between Illustrator files or between Illustrator and Photoshop:

1. Choose the Selection tool (V).
2. Click on the edge of the object, on the type, or on the baseline of the type you want to copy.
3. Choose Edit > Copy (Cmd-C/Ctrl-C).
4. Click in another Illustrator document window, then choose Edit > Paste (Cmd-V/Ctrl-V). The type and its object will appear.
   or
   Click in a Photoshop document window, choose Edit > Paste, click Pixels, then click OK. The type and its object will appear as imagery on a new layer.
➤ If you copy a threaded text object, only that object and the text it contains will be copied.

To move type from one object to another:

1. Choose the Type tool **T** or Vertical Type tool. **|T**
2. Select (drag across) the type that you want to move **1**. To move all the text in a thread, click in one of the objects, then choose Select > All (Cmd-A/Ctrl-A).
3. Choose Edit > Cut (Cmd-X/Ctrl-X). The object you cut the type from will remain a type object.
4. Cmd-click/Ctrl-click the object you want to paste into, then click the edge of that object. A blinking insertion marker will appear. (To create path type, Option-click/Alt-click the object).
   or
   Drag to create a type rectangle.
5. Choose Edit > Paste (Cmd-V/Ctrl-V) **2**.

Creating outlines

The **Create Outlines** command converts each character in a type object into a separate graphic object. As outlines, the paths can then be reshaped, used in a compound or as a mask, or filled with a gradient or mesh, like any nontype object.

Before you proceed, a warning: once type is converted into outlines, unless you Undo the conversion immediately, you won't be able to change fonts, apply other typographic attributes, or convert the outlines back into type.

To create type outlines:

1. Create type using any type tool. *All* the characters in the type object or on the path are going to be converted.

2. Choose the Selection tool (V).

3. If the type isn't already selected, click a character or the baseline.

4. Choose Type > Create Outlines (Cmd-Shift-O/Ctrl-Shift-O) **1**–**3**.
    or
    Control-click/right-click and choose Create Outlines from the context menu.

    The characters' original fill and stroke attributes will be preserved, but the path object, if any, will be deleted.

➤ Type characters become separate compound paths when converted to outlines. If any of the characters you converted have an interior shape (known as a "counter")—as in an "A" or a "P"—those outside and inside shapes will also form a compound path. To release the compound into separate objects, choose Object > Compound Path > Release, then choose Object > Ungroup. To reassemble the parts at any time as a compound, select them, then choose Object > Compound Path > Make.

Converter beware

An advantage to creating type outlines is that printer fonts aren't required in order to print them from other applications. This command is appropriate for logos and other large characters that require reshaping, but it shouldn't be used on smaller type, as it removes the hinting information that preserves character shapes during printing. Furthermore, outline shapes are slightly heavier than their preoutline counterparts, and thus are less legible (especially if a stroke is applied to them), and they also take up more file storage space than type characters.

1 *The original type*

2 *The type converted into* ***outlines***

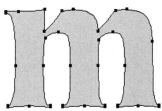

3 *The outlines are reshaped and filled with a gradient. The arrows point to sections that were reshaped.*

Don't space out!

If you press the Spacebar to access the Hand tool when type is selected, you'll end up adding spaces to your text instead of moving the illustration in the window. Instead, press Cmd-Spacebar/Ctrl-Spacebar, then quickly release Cmd/Ctrl, and you'll have your Hand tool. This may take some getting used to.

And another thing: keep an eye on your pointer. If it's in a palette field, you'll edit palette values instead of your type!

1 *Create an ellipse.*

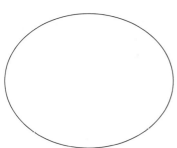

2 *Create path type at the top of the inner ellipse. The ellipse will have a stroke of None.*

Exercise

Putting type on both sides of an ellipse, and having all of it read vertically, requires creating two ellipses.

Type on an ellipse

Type on the top

1. Open the Character palette (Cmd-T/ Ctrl-T) and the Color palette (F6).

2. Choose Illustrator (Edit, in Windows) > Preferences > Units & Display Performance, choose General: Inches, then click OK. Set the fill color to None and the stroke color to black.

3. Choose the Ellipse tool (L), then click on the artboard (don't drag).

4. Enter 3.6 in the Width field, enter 2.8 in the Height field, then click OK **1**.

5. Double-click the Scale tool. Enter 70 in the Uniform: Scale field, then click Copy.

6. On the Character palette, enter 24 in the Size field and 150 in the Horizontal Scale field, and choose a font.

7. Choose the Type on a Path tool.

8. Click the top of the inner ellipse, then type the text that you want to appear at the top of the ellipse (*"type on top,"* in our example) **2**.

9. Choose the Selection tool, then drag the center bracket (it's near the bottom of the circle) left or right to reposition the type. Be aware that the left and right brackets are practically on top of each other near the starting point of the type. Don't move the left bracket over the right bracket; doing so could cause an overflow. If you like, you can move the right bracket all the way around, close to where the type characters end.

Type on the bottom

1. With the inner ellipse selected, double-click the Selection tool. In the Move dialog box, enter –0.1 in the Vertical field, then click Copy.

(Continued on the following page)

2. In the ellipse copy (which should still be selected), drag the center bracket into the ellipse. The type will now be positioned on the inside of the ellipse .

3. Double-click the bottom type with the Selection tool (the Type tool will be chosen automatically), select the type, type the words that you want to appear there, then click the Selection tool.

   Click the type on the bottom to reveal the center bracket. Center the bottom type by moving the center bracket **2**.

4. On the Layers palette (F7), click and then Shift-click the selection area of each type object to select both of them.

5. *Optional:* To recolor the type, apply a fill color and a stroke of None to the selected type objects.

6. Choose Type > Type on a Path > Gravity to slant the type for better orientation on the ellipse. (The default Rainbow path orientation would work better on a circle.)

7. Choose Object > Group (Cmd-G/Ctrl-G). To recolor either ellipse path, select it first with the Direct Selection tool.

8. *Optional:* To produce the hair ball as shown in **3**, choose the Ellipse tool (L), click to the left of center of the current type objects, enter 2 in the Width field, enter 1 in the Height field, then click OK. Choose the Selection tool, drag the new ellipse into the center of the type objects, and then, on the Graphic Styles palette, click the Hair Ball style (or another style of your choosing).

➤ Set the Horizontal Scale field back to zero (with no type selected) to prevent the scale value from being applied to any subsequently created type.

➤ Turn on Smart Guides (Cmd-U/Ctrl-U) to assist you when selecting either one of the type blocks manually, or click its selection area on the Layers palette.

1 *Use the Move dialog box to copy the type object, then drag the center bracket into the ellipse.*

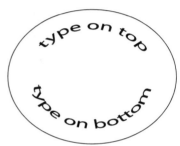

2 *Select the type on the bottom of the ellipse, and type the words that you want to appear there. Center the type at the bottom of its ellipse.*

3 *This is the final type. The type object ellipses still have a stroke of None. The Hair Ball graphic style was applied to another ellipse, which was placed in the center.*

Exercise: Type on an Ellipse

STYLE & EDIT TYPE 13

In this chapter, first and foremost, you'll learn how to select type. Next, you'll learn how to use the Character palette to apply typographic attributes, the Glyphs and OpenType palettes to insert alternate glyphs in lieu of standard characters, the Paragraph palette to apply paragraph formatting attributes, and the Paragraph Styles and Character Styles palettes to quickly apply and edit those attributes.

Lots of new stuff in this chapter!

You'll also learn how to use word processing features to check spelling, and find and replace fonts or text; create text rows and columns; apply professional typesetter's marks; turn on hyphenation; and apply tabs. And last but not least, you'll learn a few nifty tricks, such as how to wrap text around an object, create type with a shadow, and create slanted type. To apply styles or appearances to type, see Chapter 19; to change type opacity, see Chapter 20.

Selecting type

Before you can modify type, you must select it. If you use the **Selection** tool, both the type and its object will be selected **1**. If you use the **Direct Selection** tool, you can select the type object alone or select the type object *and* the type **2**. If you use a **type** tool to select type, only the type itself will be selected, not the type object **3**.

If we
shadows
have
offended,
Think but
this—
and all is
mended—

1 *Type and type object selected with the Selection tool*

If we
shadows
have
offended,
Think but
this —
and all is
mended—

2 *Type object selected with the Direct Selection tool*

If we
shadows
have
offended,
Think but
this —
and all is
mended—

William Shakespeare

3 *Type (but not its object) selected with the Type tool*

Use the **selection** method described here to move, transform, restyle, or recolor a whole type **block.** To reshape or recolor a type *object,* use the first selection method on the next page. To edit type or to restyle or recolor *part* of a type *block,* use the second selection method on the next page.

To select type and its object:

1. Choose the Selection tool (V).

2. Turn on Smart Guides (Cmd-U/Ctrl-U), with Object Highlighting on in Illustrator (Edit, in Windows) > Preferences > Smart Guides & Slices.

3. For type **inside** an object:

   If Type Object Selection by Path Only is checked in Preferences > Type & Auto Tracing, click either the type baseline or the edge of the type object. If this option is unchecked, click any part of the type character or type object **1**. If the object has a fill other than None, you could also click inside the object to select it.
   or
   Using object highlighting, click the edge of the type object (the word "path" will appear too, if Text Label Hints is on in Smart Guides & Slices preferences) **2**–**3**.

   For **point** or **path** type:
   Click the type or its path **4**. If View > Show Bounding Box is on, the bounding box will also display.

➤ If you select a threaded type object, all the other objects in the thread will also become selected.

➤ To modify the paint attributes of type, use the Color palette (see the sidebar on page 206).

➤ To move, scale, rotate, shear, or reflect type, use a command on the Object > Transform submenu or a transform tool.

Hot tip

If you double-click a type character in an existing type object with the Selection or Direct Selection tool, the **Type tool** will become selected automatically and an insertion point will appear where you clicked.

Appearances and type

The relationship between type color and appearances may be confusing at first. If you select a type object with the Selection tool, "Type" will be listed at the top of the Appearance palette and "Characters" will be listed among the attributes.

If you highlight text characters using a type tool or if you double-click the word "Characters" on the Appearance palette, the Stroke and Fill attributes for those characters will be listed on the palette. If you want to redisplay the type object's attributes, click the word "Type." To learn more about the Appearance palette, see Chapter 19. To work with type color and appearances, see steps 1–3 on pages 333–334, and see also page 358.

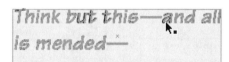

1 *To select type and its object, click the type...*

2 *...or click the type object's* ***path.***

4 *Point type is selected.*

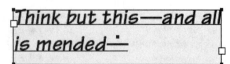

3 *The* ***type*** *and* ***type object*** *are selected.*

Inserting and deleting

To **add** type to an existing block, choose a type tool, click to create an insertion point, then start typing.

To **delete** one character at a time, choose a type tool, click to the right of the character you want to delete, then press Delete/Backspace. To delete a text string, select it with a type tool, then press Delete/Backspace.

Think but this—and all is mended—

1 *The type object is selected; the type is not.*

Think but this— and all is mended—

2 *The type object is reshaped and recolored.*

My line drawing is the purest and most direct translation of my emotion.

Henri Matisse

3 *Two words are selected.*

Use this **selection** method if you want to reshape a **type object** (and thus reflow the type) or recolor a type object.

To select a type object but not the type:

1. Choose the Direct Selection tool (A).

2. Click the edge of a type object (area or path type) **1**. Use Smart Guides (with Object Highlighting on) to assist you. Now modifications you make will affect only the type object—not the type **2**.

Use this selection method to **select** only the **type**—not the object—so you can edit the text or change its character, paragraph, or paint attributes.

To select type but not its object:

1. Choose any type tool.

2. For horizontal type, drag horizontally with the I-beam cursor to select and highlight a word or a line of type **3**. For vertical type, drag vertically.
or
For horizontal type, drag vertically to select whole lines of type. For vertical type, drag horizontally to select lines.
or
Double-click to select a word.
or
Triple-click to select a paragraph.
or
Click in the text block, then choose Select > All (Cmd-A/Ctrl-A) to select all the type in the block or on the path, and any other type it's threaded to.
or
Click to start a selection, then Shift-click where you want it to end (Shift-click again, if desired, to extend the selection).

3. After modifying the type:
Click in the type block to create a new insertion point for further editing.
or
Cmd-click/Ctrl-click outside the type object to deselect it.

➤ If you recolor type with Smart Guides on and text characters highlighted, choose a selection tool afterward if you want to see how the new color looks.

Select Type Object; Select Type

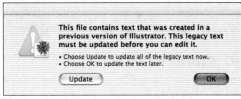Updating legacy text

Illustrator CS boasts a new text engine that allows text to be formatted with OpenType fonts, new composition commands, and character and paragraph styles. If you open a file from an earlier version of Illustrator in Illustrator CS, any text in the file from the earlier version must be updated before it can be edited **1**. Nonupdated text is called **legacy** text.

Updating may change text as follows:

➤ Line and character **spacing,** such as leading, tracking, and kerning, may be altered.

➤ Words may **wrap** to the next line.

➤ Text may **overflow** in an area type object, or words may flow into the next threaded type object.

If you **open** a file that contains **legacy text,** an alert dialog box will appear. You can update all the legacy text right away, or you can do it after opening the file at any time, either one object at a time or all at once.

To respond to a legacy text warning:

1. Using File > Open, open a file from an earlier version of Illustrator.

2. When the alert dialog box displays **2**:

   Click **Update** to update all legacy text now.
   or
   Click **OK** if you'd rather update the legacy text at a later time.

1 *Selected legacy text objects can be identified easily by the big X across the box.*

2 *This alert dialog box displays if a file that contains text from a previous version of Illustrator is opened.*

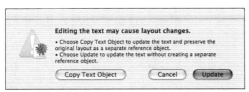

1 *This alert dialog box appears if you double-click a legacy text object.*

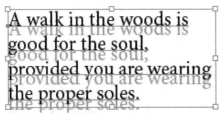

2 *After **Copy Text Object** is clicked, the updated text displays at its original opacity and the legacy text copy displays below it at 40% opacity. (We moved the updated text object upward a bit.)*

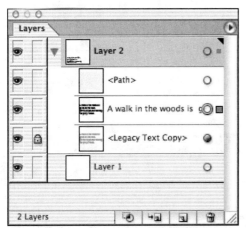

3 *On the Layers palette, the updated text layer is directly above the **Legacy Text Copy** layer. The Legacy Text Copy layer is locked automatically.*

Find 'em or get rid of 'em

To select and unlock all copies of legacy text objects, choose Type > Legacy Text > **Select Copies.** To delete all copies of legacy text objects, (they don't have to be selected), choose Type > Legacy Text > **Delete Copies.**

You can **update legacy text objects** after opening a file, either individually or en masse.

For individual objects, you can update either a copy of the legacy text object or the original. If you elect to update a copy, the updated object will appear on top of the legacy object. The legacy object will be placed on its own locked layer and will be assigned an opacity of 40% automatically. You can move the copy upward and compare the two for any threading or wrapping changes.

To update legacy text objects: NEW

1. Open a file that contains text from an earlier version of Illustrator.

2. Do one of the following:

   Choose the Selection tool or Type tool, double-click a legacy text object (or select more than one object, then double-click one of them). An alert dialog box will appear **1**. Click **Copy Text Object** or **Update.** If you click Copy Text Object, a copy of the legacy text will appear on its own layer, directly below the updated object **2**; choose the Selection tool, move the updated text object upward a bit, and compare it with the legacy text.
   or
   To update all the legacy text in the file (with no copies being made), choose Type > Legacy Text > **All Legacy Text** (you don't have to select anything).
   or
   Choose the Selection tool, click a legacy text object in the document window (or multiple-select more than one legacy object), then choose Type > Legacy Text > **Update Selected Legacy Text** (here too, no copy will be made).

➤ On the Layers palette, legacy text objects are listed as <Legacy Text>, and the copies are listed as <Legacy Text Copy> **3**.
   Note: You can't specify an opacity value for the legacy copies ahead of time.

Character and Paragraph palettes

In this section, we'll show you how to use the Character and Paragraph palettes to apply type attributes. Later in this chapter we'll show you how to use two power palettes to do the same thing more efficiently: Character Styles and Paragraph Styles.

You'll use the **Character palette** (**Cmd-T/Ctrl-T** or Window > Type > Character) to modify font, style, point size, kerning, leading, and tracking values for one or more highlighted text characters **1**. To access the horizontal scale, baseline shift, vertical scale, character rotation, and language options, choose Show Options from the palette menu or click the double arrowheads ⬍ on the palette tab twice.

You'll use the **Paragraph palette** (**Cmd-Option-T/Ctrl-Alt-T**) to modify paragraph attributes, such as alignment and indentation **2**. To access the Space Before Paragraph, Space After Paragraph, and hyphenation options, choose Show Options from the palette menu.

As we explained on pages 220–221, when you want to change the paragraph attributes of all the text in a type object or on a path, select the object or path with the Selection tool; to isolate a paragraph or series of paragraphs, select just those paragraphs with a type tool.

➤ A paragraph is created whenever the Return/Enter key is pressed within a type block. To reveal the symbols for line breaks and spaces, choose Type > Show Hidden Characters (Cmd-Option-I/Ctrl-Alt-I).

Changing fonts

If you want to choose a **font** before entering your text, skip step 1 below.

To change fonts:

1. Choose any type tool, then select the type you want to modify.
   or
   Choose the Selection tool, then click the type object.

*You can use **tool tips** to learn about any feature (just rest the mouse over the icon).*

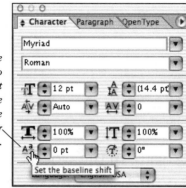

1 *The **Character** palette*

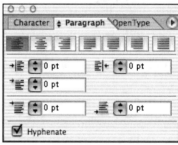

2 *The **Paragraph** palette*

3 *Select the type you want to modify...*

Font change

*...then choose a font from the **context menu**.*

Font change

4 *The **font** is changed from Gill Sans Bold to Bodoni Poster.*

Fast info

The size, font, and tracking info for selected type are listed on the **Info** palette **1**.

Type palette shortcuts

When entering values on the Character and Paragraph palettes:

Apply value and highlight **next** field	Tab
Apply value and highlight **previous** field	Shift-Tab
Apply value and **exit** palette	Return/Enter

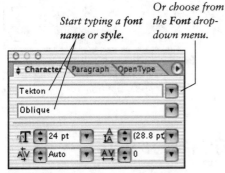

1 *The Info palette when the Type tool is selected*

Start typing a font name or style. *Or choose from the Font drop-down menu.*

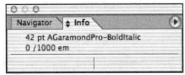

2 *The Character palette on the Mac*

2. Control-click/right-click the type and choose a font from the **Font** submenu (**3**–**4**, previous page) or **Recent Fonts** **NEW** submenu on the context menu.
   or
   On the Character palette on the Mac, choose a font from the Font pop-up menu (and from a submenu if the font name has an arrowhead next to it). In Windows, choose from the Font and Style pop-up menus.
   or
   On the Mac, double-click the Font field on the Character palette; in Windows just click the Font field. Then start typing the first few characters of the desired font name. When the name appears, press Tab. In addition, for a style other than Roman (or Regular), start typing the style name in the next field, then press Return/ Enter. You need enter only the first few letters of the font name or style—the name or style with the closest spelling match will appear in the field **1**–**2**.

➤ To have font families display in the actual typeface (WYSIWYG) on the Character **NEW** palette and the Type > Font submenu on the Mac, and on the Type > Font submenu in Windows, go to Preferences > Type & Auto Tracing, check the box next to Preview Size, then choose a size (Small, Medium, or Large) for the preview from the pop-up menu.

➤ Power tip: Press Cmd-Option-Shift-M/ Ctrl-Alt-Shift-M to quickly highlight the Font field on the Character palette. The palette will open, if it isn't open already.

Change Fonts

225

Changing point sizes

To resize type:

1. Choose any type tool, then highlight the type you want to modify.
   or
   Choose the Selection tool (V), then click the type object.

2. On the **Character palette** (Cmd-T/Ctrl-T):

   Enter a point size in the Font Size field (.1–1296 pt), then press Return/Enter to apply and exit the palette or press Tab to apply the value and highlight the next field **2**. You don't need to reenter the unit of measure.

   ➤ If the selected type contains more than one point size, the Font Size field will be blank, but the new size you enter will apply to all selected type.
   or
   Choose a preset size from the Font Size pop-up menu or click the up or down arrow. Or click in the Font Size field, then press the up or down arrow on the keyboard.

To resize type using the **keyboard:**

Hold down Cmd-Shift/Ctrl-Shift and press > to enlarge or < to reduce the point size **3**. The type will resize by the increment specified in the Size/Leading field in Preferences > Type & Auto Tracing. The default increment is 2 pt. Hold Cmd-Option-Shift/Ctrl-Alt-Shift and press > or < to change the point size by five times the current Size/Leading increment.

To choose a size via a **context menu:**

Control-click/right-click the type and choose a preset size from the context menu. Choosing Other from the context menu highlights the Font Size field on the Character palette.

scale type manually

To scale point or path type, select it using the Selection tool, then drag a handle on its **bounding box** (choose View > Show Bounding Box if the box isn't visible). You can also scale type with the **Scale** tool. Shift-drag to scale type proportionally using either tool **1**.

1 *Shift-drag a handle on the type object's bounding box to scale the type proportionally.*

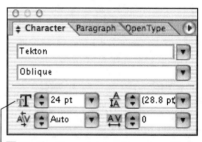

2 *On the Character palette, enter a Font Size, or click the up or down arrow, or choose a preset size from the pop-up menu.*

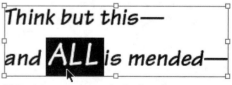

3 *Resizing type using the keyboard*

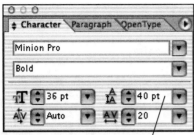

1 On the *Character* palette, enter a *Leading* value, or click the up or down arrow, or choose a preset value from the drop-down menu.

ACT III

Scene I

The Wood. The QUEEN OF FAIRIES *lying asleep.*

Enter QUINCE, SNUG, BOTTOM, FLUTE, SNOUT, *and* STARVELING.

Bot. Are we all met?

Quin. Pat, pat; and here is a marvellous convenient place for our rehearsal. This green plot shall be our stage, this hawthorn brake our tiring-house; and we will do it in action, as we will do it before the duke.

---

2 *"Loose" leading (8 pt. type; 12 pt. leading, in this case)*

ACT III

Scene I

The Wood. The QUEEN OF FAIRIES *lying asleep.*

Enter QUINCE, SNUG, BOTTOM, FLUTE, SNOUT, *and* STARVELING.

Bot. Are we all met?
Quin. Pat, pat; and here is a marvellous convenient place for our rehearsal. This green plot shall be our stage, this hawthorn brake our tiring-house; and we will do it in action, as we will do it before the duke.

---

3 *"Tight" leading (8 pt. type; 8.75 pt. leading, in this case)*

Leading

Leading, the distance from baseline to baseline between lines of type, is traditionally measured in points. Each line of type in a block can have a different leading value. (To adjust the spacing between whole paragraphs, follow the instructions on page 238.)

Note: To change the vertical spacing in vertical type, change the horizontal tracking (see the next page). Changing the leading for vertical type changes the horizontal spacing between vertical columns.

To change leading using the Character palette:

1. Select the horizontal type that you want to modify:

Click anywhere in a type block with the Selection tool to change the leading of the entire block.
or
Highlight an entire paragraph with a type tool (triple-click anywhere in the paragraph) to change the leading of all the lines in that paragraph.
or
Highlight (drag across) an entire line with a type tool, including any space at the end, to change the leading of just that line.

2. On the Character palette (Cmd-T/Ctrl-T), enter a Leading value (press Return/Enter or Tab to apply) **1**–**3**; or choose a preset leading value from the Leading pop-up menu; or click the up or down arrow. If you choose Auto from the pop-up menu, the leading will be 120% of the largest type size on each line.

To change leading using the keyboard:

1. Select the type you want to modify as per step 1, above.

2. Option-press/Alt-press the up arrow on the keyboard to decrease the leading or the down arrow to increase the leading by the Size/Leading increment specified in Preferences > Type & Auto Tracing.

Hold down Cmd-Option/Ctrl-Alt as you press an arrow to change leading by five times the current Size/Leading increment.

Leading

Kerning and tracking

Kerning is the addition or removal of space between **pairs** of adjacent characters. Kerning values for specific character pairs (e.g., an uppercase "T" next to a lowercase "a") are built into all fonts. The built-in kerning values are adequate for small text (e.g., body type), but not for large type (e.g., headlines and logos). This awkward spacing can be remedied by careful manual kerning. To kern a pair of characters, you must insert the cursor between them.

Note: Built-in kerning can be turned on or off for individual groups of characters. Before kerning text manually, turn built-in kerning off for your selected type by choosing Auto from the Kerning pop-up menu on the Character palette ■, then choosing or entering 0.

Tracking is the simultaneous adjustment of the space between each of **three or more characters**. Normally, it's applied to a whole line of type, or occasionally to a whole paragraph. To apply tracking, you'll first highlight some type using a type tool, or select an entire type block with a selection tool.

To apply kerning or tracking:

1. Zoom in on the type that you want to apply kerning or tracking to. Choose a type tool, then click to create an insertion point between two characters for kerning, or highlight a range of text for tracking.
or
To track all the type in an object, choose the Selection tool, then click the object.

2. In the Kerning or Tracking field on the Character palette (Cmd-Option-K/Ctrl-Alt-K), enter a positive number to add space between characters or a negative number to remove space, then press Return/Enter or Tab to apply ■–■.
or
Choose a preset kerning or tracking amount from the pop-up menu or click the up or down arrow.
or

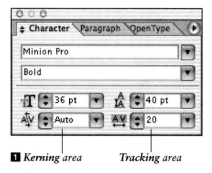

1 *Kerning area*   *Tracking area*

2 *Normal type*

3 *After adding space between the first two characters (**kerning**)*

Simone

4 *After removing space between the last five characters (kerning or **tracking**)*

Kerning, Tracking

Auto or Optical? NEW

You can choose from two different types of automatic (nonmanual) kerning in Illustrator. The "all-purpose" default method, **Auto** kerning (or "metrics" kerning), is applied to new or imported text based on the information for kern pairs (e.g., To, Ta, We, Wo, Yo) that's included with each font.

For fonts that have less than adequate or no built-in kerning or for a line that contains multiple typefaces or point sizes, you can give the new **Optical** kerning option a try: Choose Optical for the type from the Kerning pop-up menu on the Character palette. Illustrator will adjust the spacing between adjacent characters as it sees fit. See if you like it.

1 *The original, selected characters*

Fit Headline

2 *The* **Fit Headline** *command adds space* **between** *characters to fit the type object.*

Hold down Option/Alt and press the right arrow on the keyboard to add space between letters or the left arrow to remove space. The amount of space that is added or removed each time you press an arrow is specified in the Tracking field in Illustrator (Edit, in Windows) > Preferences > Type & Auto Tracing. Hold down Cmd-Option/Ctrl-Alt and press an arrow to track in larger increments.
or
Use this shortcut: Cmd-Shift-[or]/ Ctrl-Shift-[or].

➤ Tracking/kerning changes the vertical spacing of characters in vertical type.

➤ To adjust the overall word or letter spacing in a text block, use the Word Spacing and Letter Spacing fields on the Paragraph palette (see page 238).

The **Fit Headline** command uses tracking to fit a one-line paragraph of horizontal or vertical area type to the edges of its container.

To fit type to its container:

1. Choose any type tool.

2. Highlight a one-line paragraph (not a line in a larger paragraph; we're talking about a stand-alone line).

3. Choose Type > Fit Headline **1**–**2**.

Fit Headline

Horizontal scaling

The **Horizontal Scale** command extends (widens) or condenses (narrows) type. The Vertical Scale command makes type taller or shorter. The default scale is 100%.

Note: In typefaces that are narrow or wide by design (e.g., Univers Extended or Helvetica Narrow), the weight, proportions, and counters (interior spaces) are adjusted along with the width. For this reason, they look better than Regular or Roman style characters that are extended or narrowed via Illustrator's Horizontal or Vertical Scale command. That being said…

To scale type horizontally and/or vertically:

Select the type that you want to modify, change the Horizontal or Vertical Scale value on the Character palette, then press Return/ Enter or Tab to apply **1**–**2**. Or choose a preset value from the pop-up menu or click the up or down arrow.

or

To scale point or path type manually **3**, select it using the Selection tool, then drag a side handle of the bounding box without holding down Shift.

or

To scale a selected type block by a percentage, double-click the Scale tool, then change the Non-Uniform: Horizontal or Vertical value.

Back we go!

To restore normal scaling:

Select the type, then choose 100% from both Scale fields on the Character palette (Cmd-Shift-X/Ctrl-Shift-X). *Note:* If you applied scaling via an object's bounding box or via the Scale tool, restoring normal scaling to the type won't restore the object's original dimensions.

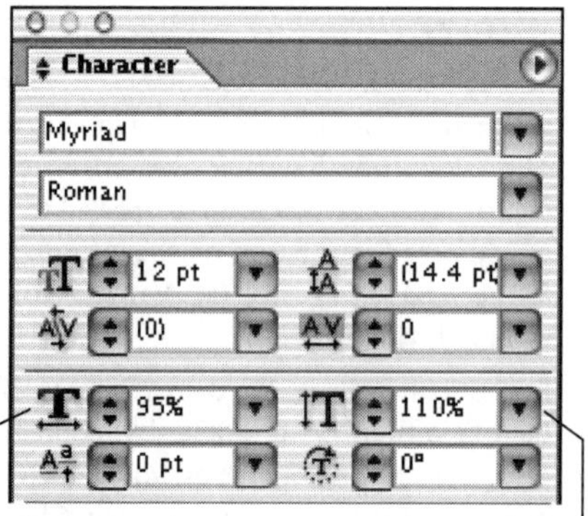
Character
Myriad
Roman
12 pt
(14.4 pt
(0)
0
95%
110%
0 pt
0°

Vertical Scale area **1** *Horizontal Scale area*

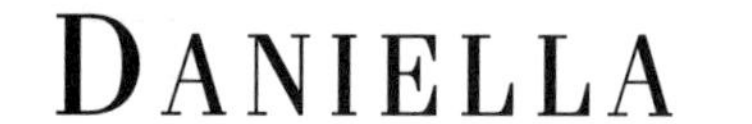
DANIELLA
DANIELLA
DANIELLA

Normal type (no scaling)

75% horizontal scale

125% horizontal scale

2 *Various horizontal scale values*

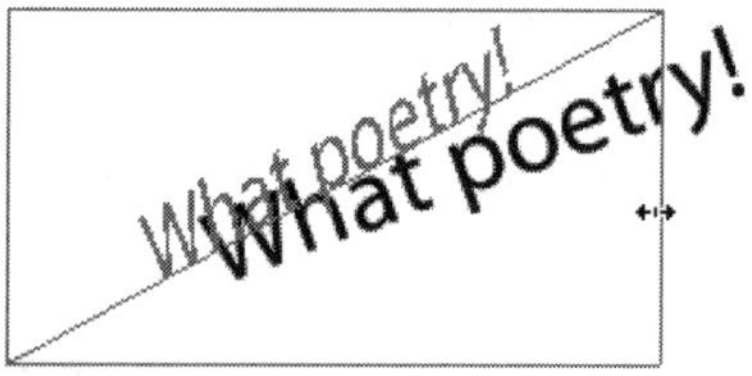
What poetry!
What poetry!

3 ***Scaling** path type by dragging a handle on the **bounding box***

Scale Type

Dialog box option	Keyboard	Smart punctuation
ff, fi, ffi Ligatures	ff, fi, ffi	ﬀ, ﬁ, ﬃ
ff, fl, ffl Ligatures	ff, fl, ffl	ﬀ, ﬂ, ﬄ
Smart Quotes	' "	' " " '
Smart Spaces (one space after a period)	. T	. T
En [dashes]	--	–
Em Dashes	---	—
Ellipses	...	...
Expert Fractions	1/2	½

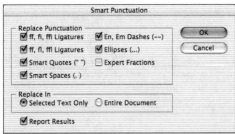

1 Check **Replace Punctuation** options in the Smart Punctuation dialog box.

Smart punctuation

The **Smart Punctuation** command converts existing keyboard punctuation into professional typesetter's marks.

To create smart punctuation:

1. *Optional:* Select text with a type tool to smart-punctuate that text only. Otherwise, the command will affect the entire document.

2. Choose Type > Smart Punctuation.

3. Check any of the Replace Punctuation boxes **1** (and see the sidebar).

4. Click Replace In: Selected Text Only if you selected text for step 1; otherwise click Entire Document.

5. *Optional:* Check Report Results to display a list of your changes.

6. Click OK **2**–**3**.

To specify a quotation marks style for **NEW** future type:

1. Choose File > Document Setup.

2. Display the Type panel, choose a Double Quotes style and a Single Quotes style, and check Typographers Quotes. You can also choose an alternate Language, if desired.

3. Click OK.

He supposed Miss Pettigrew might have leaned over the sugar bowl and said, "Mayor," which Daddy said was all she ever called him anymore, "I'd be pleased to have a chimpanzee." And Daddy supposed the mayor frumped himself up a little and muddied his expression and said, "Sister darling, your chimpanzee is just around the corner."

"Louis!" Momma said. Daddy was hardly ever a very big hit with Momma.

2 Dumb punctuation: Straight quotes and two spaces after each period

He supposed Miss Pettigrew might have leaned over the sugar bowl and said, "Mayor," which Daddy said was all she ever called him anymore, "I'd be pleased to have a chimpanzee." And Daddy supposed the mayor frumped himself up a little and muddied his expression and said, "Sister darling, your chimpanzee is just around the corner."

"Louis!" Momma said. Daddy was hardly ever a very big hit with Momma.

T. R. Pearson

3 Smart punctuation: Curly quotes and one space after each period

Smart Punctuation

NEW Inserting alternate glyphs

OpenType, a font format that was developed jointly by Adobe and Microsoft, allows the same fonts to be used on both the Mac and Windows systems. When these fonts are used, the problem of font substitution and text reflow when transferring files between platforms is virtually eliminated. Illustrator CS supplies you with 24 Roman-language OpenType font families. The ones with extra characters are labeled "Pro" **1**.

The OpenType format also allows for a broad expansion in the number of stylistic variations for any given character in a font file. These character variations are called **glyphs** (sounds like something out of *The Hobbit!*). For each individual character in an OpenType font, an assortment of glyphs may be substituted, such as ligatures, swashes, titling characters, stylistic alternates, ordinals, and fractions. Alternate glyphs can be inserted manually by using the **Glyphs palette** (see below), or automatically by using the OpenType palette (see the next page). The Glyphs palette isn't just for OpenType fonts, though—you can use this palette to locate and insert characters in any font.

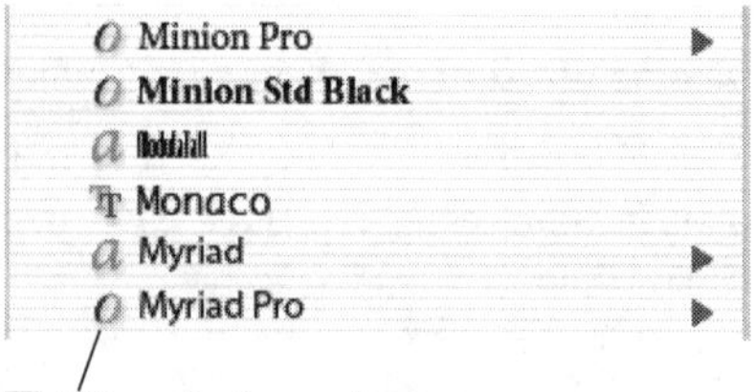

1 *When the font submenus are set to display font families in the actual font face (WYSIWYG), OpenType ("Pro") fonts are assigned this symbol* .

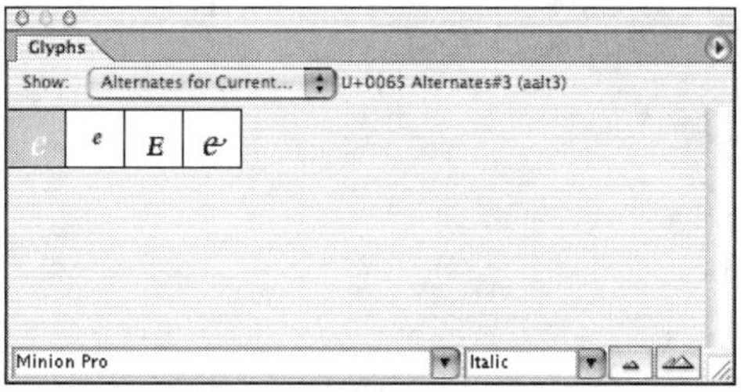

2 *The* ***Glyphs*** *palette with the letter "e" highlighted and* ***Alternates for Current Selection*** *chosen from the Show pop-up menu*

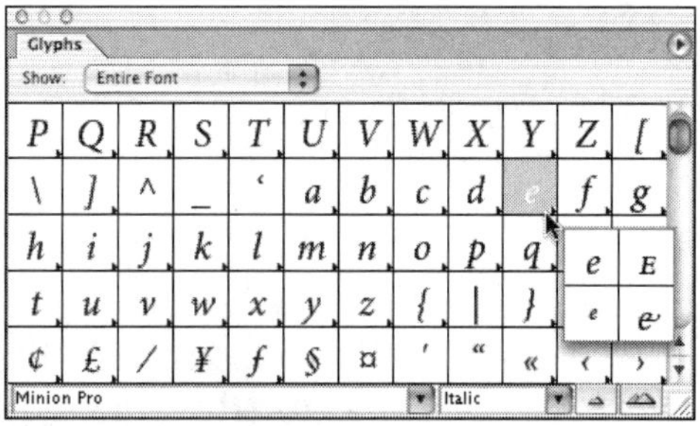

3 *The Glyphs palette displaying the pop-up menu of alternates for a highlighted glyph*

NEW To replace a character with an alternate glyph manually:

1. Using a Type tool, select a character or character pair in your text.
2. To open the Glyphs palette, choose Glyphs from the Type menu or the Window > Type submenu. The character you selected will be highlighted on the palette.
3. Choose Show: Alternates for Current Selection **2**, then double-click the glyph that you want the selected character to be replaced with.
   or
   Choose Show: Entire Font, and if the square containing the currently highlighted glyph has a triangle in the lower right corner, press the triangle and choose an alternate glyph for the character from the pop-up menu **3**.

➤ You can also choose a font from the bottom of the Glyphs palette.

Spot the glyph!

To have any substituted glyphs automatically be highlighted in the current document, choose File > Document Setup, display the Type panel, then check Highlight: **Substituted Glyphs.** To have any font substitutions (due to a missing font) be highlighted automatically as well, check Highlight: **Substituted Fonts.**

1 *The Show pop-up menu on the Glyphs palette*

2 *The OpenType palette*

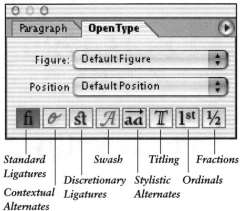

Standard Ligatures
Contextual Alternates
Discretionary Ligatures
Swash
Titling
Stylistic Alternates
Ordinals
Fractions

The button states

1st	Available
1st	Selected
1st	Not available

Swash
Fluffy
1st 2nd
Ordinal
Fraction
5/8 Fact
Discretionary ligature
Sylistic alternates
friend &

To insert a glyph into text manually: NEW

1. Choose a type tool, then click in the text to position the text insertion marker.

2. From the **Show** pop-up menu on the Glyphs palette **1**, choose a category of glyphs to be displayed on the palette.

   You can also choose a **font** from the pop-up menu at the bottom of the palette, and a type style from the pop-up menu to its right.

3. Double-click the desired glyph, or click a mini arrowhead and choose a glyph from the pop-up menu. It will appear in the text.

▶ Click the Zoom Out or Zoom In button in the lower right corner of the Glyphs palette to change the display size of the glyphs on the palette.

Using the OpenType palette, you can decide ahead of time or for existing text whether **alternate glyphs** will be inserted **automaticaly** in lieu of standard characters, based on the context of the text situation. For example, you can choose to have a glyph for a properly formatted fraction be inserted automatically when you type 1/2 or 1/4. Other available options, as shown on the Open Type palette **2**, include ligature glyphs for specific letter pairs (e.g., ff, ffl, and st), and swash, titling, and other special characters.

To specify or insert alternate glyphs NEW automatically:

1. Display the OpenType palette (Cmd-Option-Shift-T/Ctrl-Alt-Shift-T).

2. To change existing text, either select a text object to change all appropriate text occurrences in the object, or select specific text to limit the change to that text.
   or
   To specify alternate glyph options for future text to be entered in an OpenType font, deselect all type.

3. Click any of the available buttons on the palette.

▶ To see the alternate glyphs in your chosen font, from the Show pop-up menu on the Glyphs palette, choose a category of the same name as an available button on the OpenType palette.

Insert, Specify Alternate Glyphs

Some OpenType fonts also contain alternate glyphs for **numerals.** From the Figure pop-up menu on the Open Type palette, you can choose a style for numeral glyphs for existing or future text; or from the Position pop-up menu, you can choose a position for numeral glyphs relative to the baseline.

Note: If the currently chosen font contains numeral glyphs, such categories as Denominators, Numerators, Oldstyle Figures, Tabular Figures, etc. will be listed on the Show menu on the Glyphs palette.

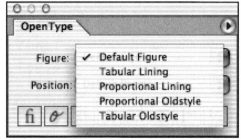

1 *The* **Figure** *pop-up menu on the OpenType palette*

NEW **To choose an alternate numeral style:**

1. Select a text object to change all the appropriate numerals in that object.
   or
   Select specific text that contains numerals to limit the change to just that text.
   or
   Deselect all to specify numeral options for future text.

2. On the OpenType palette, choose from the **Figure** pop-up menu **1–2**:

   Default Figure to keep (or revert to) the selected font's default numeral style.

   Tabular Lining to create full-height numerals of equal width. A good option when creating tables, as these numerals can be lined up in columns.

   Proportional Lining to create full-height numerals of different widths. Appropriate if you want numerals that are the same height as all caps text.

   Proportional Oldstyle to create old-fashioned numerals of nonuniform heights and widths. Beautiful, but not always appropriate.

   Tabular Oldstyle to create old-fashioned, varying-height numerals, but in uniform widths so they can be lined up in columns.

3. To choose whether the numerals can be raised or lowered relative to the baseline, choose an option from the **Position** pop-up menu (**1–2**, next page):

   Default Position to use the font's default position for numerals.

123456789

Default or **Tabular Lining**

123456789

Proportional Lining

123456789

Proportional Oldstyle

123456789

Tabular Oldstyle

2 *These are numbers in the Adobe Caslon Pro font. Note that tabular glyphs are wider than proportional glyphs, and some Oldstyle numerals sit below the baseline.*

Alternate Numeral Styles

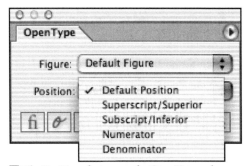

1 *The Position choices on the OpenType palette*

123456789

Default Position on baseline

123456789

Superscript/Superior

123456789

Subscript/Inferior

123456789

Numerator

123456789

Denominator

2 *Position options for numerals in an OpenType font*

1/2 4/5

3 *Standard numerals, entered with slashes in the Adobe Garamond Pro font*

½ ⅘

4 *The numerals and slashes reformatted as proper fractions—much better!*

Superscript/Superior to use glyphs that sit above the baseline.

Subscript/Inferior to use glyphs that sit below the baseline.

Numerator or **Denominator** to create small numerals that are raised or lowered relative to adjacent characters/numerals.

If you selected numerals in step 1 in a font that contains the alternate numeral glyphs that you chose from the Figure and/or Position pop-up menus, the new glyphs will appear in your selected text.

To produce good-looking fractions: NEW

1. Select a text object in which to change all appropriate numerals (e.g., 1/2, 2/3, 3/4).
or
Highlight text that contains numerals, to limit the change to just that text.

In either case, make sure an OpenType font is chosen for the numerals you want to restyle.

2. Click the Fractions button ½ on the OpenType palette. If the font used in the selected text contains glyphs for numerators, superscripts, denominators, or subscripts, the proper number glyphs will appear in your text **3**–**4**.

The **Change Case** commands change selected text to all UPPERCASE, lowercase, Title Case, or Sentence case.

To change case: NEW

1. Highlight the text you want to modify with a type tool.

2. Choose Type > Change Case > **UPPERCASE; lowercase; Title Case** (the first character in each word is uppercase, the other characters are lowercase); or **Sentence case** (only the first character in each sentence is uppercase).

➤ Some fonts, such as Lithos and Castellar, don't contain lowercase characters.

Paragraph alignment and spacing

Alignment and indentation values affect whole paragraphs. But before you learn how to apply paragraph formatting, you need to know what a paragraph is, at least as far as Illustrator is concerned:

➤ To create a new paragraph (hard return) in a text block, press **Return/Enter.** The type that precedes a return belongs to one paragraph; the type that follows a return belongs to the next paragraph. Type that wraps, automatically belongs to the same paragraph.

➤ To create a line break (soft return) within a paragraph in nontabular text, press **Shift-Return.**

To change paragraph alignment:

1. Choose a type tool, then click in a paragraph or drag through a series of paragraphs.
or
Choose a selection tool, then select a type object.

2. At the top of the Paragraph palette (Cmd-Option-T/Ctrl-Alt-T), click an alignment button **1**–**2**.
or
Use one of the keyboard shortcuts listed in the sidebar on this page.

➤ Don't apply any of the justify alignment options to path type or to freestanding type (type that's not in an object or block). Such objects don't have edges, so there's nothing to justify type to.

Paragraph alignment shortcuts

Align Left	Cmd-Shift-L/Ctrl-Shift-L
Align Center	Cmd-Shift-C/Ctrl-Shift-C
Align Right	Cmd-Shift-R/Ctrl-Shift-R
Justify Last Line Left	Cmd-Shift-J/Ctrl-Shift-J
Justify All Lines	Cmd-Shift-F/Ctrl-Shift-F

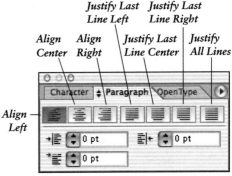

1 *The seven **alignment** buttons on the Paragraph palette*

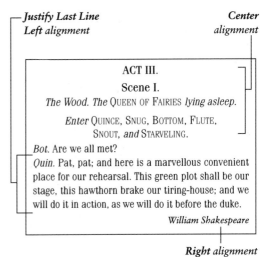

2 *A few paragraph alignment options*

What to select

If you want to change paragraph attributes for *all* the text in a type object or on a path, select the object or path with the Selection tool. To isolate a paragraph or series of paragraphs, select just those paragraphs with a type tool.

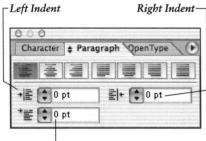

Left Indent   *Right Indent*

First-Line Left Indent

1 *If you forget which **Indent** field on the Paragraph palette is which, rest the mouse over an icon—the tool tip will remind you.*

You can apply **Left Indent** and/or **Right Indent** values to area type; use only a Left Indent value for point type.

To change paragraph indentation:

1. Choose a type tool, then select the paragraph(s) you want to modify or click to create an insertion point in a single paragraph.
or
Choose a selection tool, then select a type object.

2. On the **Paragraph** palette (Cmd-Option-T/Ctrl-Alt-T):

Change the Left and/or Right Indent value, then press Return/Enter or Tab to apply **1**–**2** or click the up or down arrow. (Strangely, this value also affects any lines that follow a soft return.)
or
To indent only the first line of each paragraph, enter a positive First-Line Left Indent value.

➤ You can enter a negative value in the Left Indent, First-Line Left Indent, or Right Indent field to expand the measure of each line. The type will be pushed outside its object, but it will still display and print **3**.

The Mock Turtle sighed deeply, and began, in a voice choked with sobs, to sing this:—

> *Beautiful Soup, so rich and green,*
> *Waiting in a hot tureen!*
> *Who for such dainties would not stoop?*
> *Soup of the evening, beautiful Soup!*
> *Soup of the evening, beautiful Soup!*
> *Beau—ootiful Soo-oop!*
> *Beau—ootiful Soo-oop!*
> *Soo—oop of the e—e—evening,*
> *Beautiful, beautiful Soup!*
> — *Lewis Carroll*

2 *Left indentation*

ACT III.

Scene I.

The Wood. The QUEEN OF FAIRIES *lying asleep.*

Enter QUINCE, SNUG, BOTTOM, FLUTE, SNOUT, *and* STARVELING.

Bot.   Are we all met?

Quin. Pat, pat; and here is a marvellous convenient place for our rehearsal. This green plot shall be our stage, this hawthorn brake our tiring-house; and we will do it in action, as we will do it before the duke.

— *William Shakespeare*

3 *To create a **hanging indent**, as in the last paragraph shown here, enter a value in the **Left Indent** field and the same value with a minus sign in front of it in the **First-Line Left Indent** field.*

Paragraph Indents

Use the **Space Before Paragraph** field or the **Space After Paragraph** field on the Paragraph palette to add or subtract space *between* paragraphs in area type. Point type isn't modified by this feature. To adjust the spacing between lines of type *within* a paragraph (leading), see page 227.

To adjust inter-paragraph spacing:

1. Select the type you want to modify. To modify the space before only one paragraph in a type block, select the paragraph with a type tool. To change all the type in an object, select the object with the Selection tool.

2. In the **Space Before Paragraph** or **Space After Paragraph** field on the Paragraph palette **1**, enter a positive value to move paragraphs apart or a negative value to move them closer together (press Return/Enter or Tab to apply) **2**, or click the up or down arrow.

➤ Keep in mind that the space before a paragraph is combined with the spacing from the paragraph above it (you could end up with more space between paragraphs than you intend).

Spacing and scaling defaults **NEW**

To change the horizontal word or letter spacing for justified paragraphs, choose Justification from the Paragraph palette menu, then change the Minimum, Desired, or Maximum **Word Spacing** or **Letter Spacing** values in the Justification dialog box **3**–**5**. Nonjustified paragraphs are affected only by the Desired value. Headlines usually look better with slightly reduced word spacing. **Glyph Scaling** (50%–200%) affects the width of all characters.

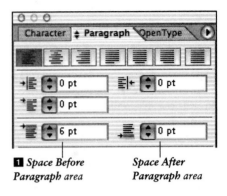

1 *Space Before Paragraph* area   *Space After Paragraph* area

ACT III.

Scene I.

The Wood. The Queen of Fairies *lying asleep.*

Enter QUINCE, SNUG, BOTTOM, FLUTE, SNOUT, *and* STARVELING.

Bot. Are we all met?

Quin. Pat, pat; and here is a marvellous convenient place for our rehearsal. This green plot shall be our stage, this hawthorn brake our tiring-house; and we will do it in action, as we will do it before the duke.

William Shakespeare

2 *Higher Space Before Paragraph values were applied to these paragraphs to add space above them.*

Ocean

Body more immaculate than a wave, salt washing away its own line, and the brilliant bird flying without ground roots.   *Pablo Neruda*

3 *Normal **word** and **letter** spacing*

Ocean

Body more immaculate than a wave, salt washing away its own line, and the brilliant bird flying without ground roots.

4 *Loose **letter** spacing*

Ocean

Body more immaculate than a wave, salt washing away its own line, and the brilliant bird flying without ground roots.

5 *Tight **word** spacing*

Your favorite composer **NEW**

On the Paragraph palette menu, you have a choice of two line composer options for selected type. **Adobe Every-line Composer** examines all the lines within a paragraph first, and then arranges line lengths and endings in order to optimize the appearance of the overall paragraph. **Adobe Single-line Composer** examines and arranges text and hyphenation one line at a time without regard to other lines.

1 *Set parameters for auto hyphenation in the* **Hyphenation** *dialog box.*

```
AN
OVER-
ABUN-
DANCE
OF HY-
PHENS
MAKES  2
FOR
TIR-
ING
READ-
ING.
```

Hyphenation

To choose hyphenation options: **NEW**

1. Auto hyphenation affects only currently selected or subsequently created text. If you want to hyphenate existing text, select it with a type tool or selection tool now.

2. On the Paragraph palette, check Hyphenate to enable hyphenation. (If this option isn't visible, choose Show Options from the palette menu.)

3. To choose hyphenation options, choose Hyphenation from the Paragraph palette menu.

4. In the **Words Longer Than [ ] letters** field, enter the minimum number of characters a word must contain in order to be hyphenated **1**.

   In the **After First [ ] letters** field, enter the minimum number of characters that can precede a hyphen (we use a value of 3).

   In the **Before Last [ ] letters** field, enter the minimum number of characters that can be carried over onto the next line following a hyphen.

   In the **Hyphen Limit** field, enter the maximum allowable number of hyphens in a row. More than two hyphens in a row makes the type hard to read, and looks ugly to boot **2**.

   When using Adobe Single-line Composer (see the sidebar), you can enter a value in the **Hyphenation Zone** field to specify the distance from the right margin within which hyphenation can't occur.

   Decide whether you want to permit the program to **Hyphenate Capitalized Words.**

5. Click OK. Look over the newly hyphenated text, and correct any awkward breaks manually.

➤ To hyphenate a word manually, press Cmd-Shift--(hyphen)/Ctrl-Shift--.

➤ In Preferences > Hyphenation, you can enter hyphenation exceptions, specify how particular words are to be hyphenated, and choose a different language for hyphenation (see page 446).

The **Roman Hanging Punctuation** command, mimicking a traditional typesetting technique, forces punctuation marks that fall at the beginning and/or end of a line of type in an area type block (period, comma, quotation mark, apostrophe, hyphen, dash, colon, or semicolon) to hang slightly outside the block. Why? It looks better!

NEW **To hang punctuation:**

1. With a type tool, select a paragraph in an area type object; or with a selection tool, select the whole object.

2. Choose Roman Hanging Punctuation from the Paragraph palette menu ▮.

➤ For more pleasing alignment of letters, such as W, O, or A (not punctuation), at the beginning and/or end of lines in a whole type object, choose Type > **Optical Margin Alignment**. Some characters will shift ever so slightly outside the block.

NEW **Character and paragraph styles**

Now that you know how to style type manually by using the Character and Paragraph palettes, you're ready to learn how to create and apply character and paragraph styles, which accomplish the same thing with much less sweat.

Paragraph ▮ styles include paragraph formats, such as leading and indentation, and character attributes, such as font and point size. When a paragraph style is applied, the whole paragraph or paragraphs are reformatted.

Character styles contain only character attributes, and are applied to selectively highlighted text within a paragraph (e.g., bullets, or boldfaced or italicized words), not to whole paragraphs ▮. Character styles can be applied in addition to paragraph styles—they're the icing on the cake.

Not only do styles make light work of typesetting, they also help to ensure consistency within and among multiple documents. Styles are created, modified, and applied by using the **Character Styles** and **Paragraph Styles** palettes ▮.

Roman Hanging
Punctuation

'Lo! all these trophies of affections hot,
Of pensiv'd and subdued desires the tender,
Nature hath charg'd me that I hoard them not,
But yield them up where I myself must render,
That is, to you, my origin and ender:
For these, of force, must your oblations be,
Since I their altar, you enpatron me.

—*William Shakespeare*

▮ *Let it hang out.*

This **ahimsa** is the basis of the search for truth. ⸆ I am realizing every day that the search is vain unless it is founded on **ahimsa** as the basis. ⸆ It is quite proper to resist and attack a system, but to resist and attack its author is tantamount to resisting and attacking **oneself.** ⸆ For we are all tarred with the same brush, and are children of one and the same Creator, and as such the divine powers within us are infinite. ⸆ To slight a single human being is to slight those divine powers, and thus to harm not only that being but with him the whole **world.**

Mohandas K. Gandhi

▮ *Paragraph style* ▮ *Character styles*

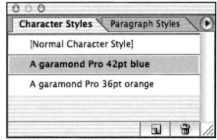

▮ *The Character Styles and Paragraph Styles palette group*

To create or modify a character or paragraph style: **NEW**

1. Choose Window > Type > Character Styles or Paragraph Styles.

2. To create a new style, we recommend selecting some text in your document that contains the attributes that you want to save in the style. Next, Option-click/ Alt-click the New Style button at the bottom of the Character or Paragraph Styles palette. If this is your first foray into styles, we recommend creating a paragraph style first.

or

To edit an existing style, deselect all, then double-click a style name on the palette. (Or if text is selected, Cmd-Option/Ctrl-Alt double-click a style name. The modifier keys will prevent the style from being applied to any text.)

3. An options dialog box will open for the chosen style type.

4. Change the default **Style Name** to a more descriptive name—say, the font name or the type of formatting that it will contain.

5. The options dialog box has several panels, which you can access by clicking a category on the left side. If text was selected in step 2, some panels will already contain information. Display any panel to choose attributes for the style.

Check **Preview** to preview the chosen options in any currently selected text.

Click **General** to display a list of the current settings for all the categories **1**.

Click **Basic Character Formats** to choose basic character attributes, such as font, point size, kerning, leading, and tracking.

Click **Advanced Character Formats** to choose scaling, baseline shift, and rotation values.

Click **Character Color,** click the Fill or Stroke square, then choose a fill and/or stroke color for the type. Colors from the Swatches palette will be listed here (nonglobal colors first, then global colors). For a stroke, you can also choose a Weight.

Click **OpenType Features** to choose options to be applied when OpenType fonts are used (**1**, next page).

6. In the Paragraph Style Options dialog box, you can also choose settings in the **Indents and Spacing** (**2**, next page), **Tabs, Composition** (Composer), **Hyphenation,** and **Justification** panels.

7. Click OK. To apply styles, see page 243.

(Continued on the following page)

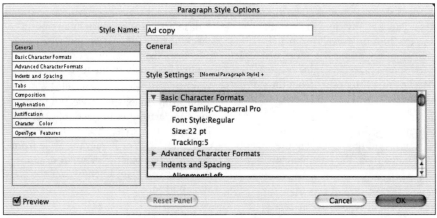

1 *The **General** panel of the **Paragraph Style Options** dialog box*

Create, Modify Character or Paragraph Style

Create, Modify Character or Paragraph Styles

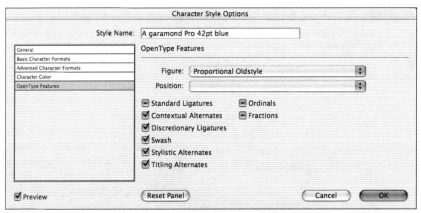

1 *Checking an option in the* **OpenType Features** *panel of the* **Character Style Options** *dialog box is equivalent to clicking a button on the OpenType palette.*

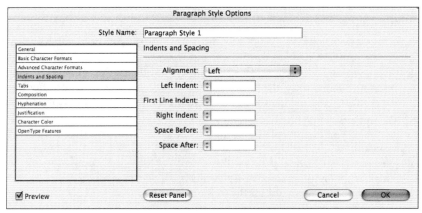

2 *The* **Indents and Spacing** *panel of the* **Paragraph Style Options** *dialog box*

➤ Click Reset Panel at any time to clear all settings in the currently displayed panel. Some individual nonnumeric options can be reset to a blank state (no value or effect) by choosing "(Ignore)" from the pop-up menu.

➤ You can also open the Paragraph or Character Style Options dialog box by selecting a style and then choosing the dialog box name from the palette menu.

➤ To change the palette view, from the palette menu, choose Small List View for style names in small type or Large List View for style names in large type.

➤ A dash/green check mark in an option check box means that option won't override any existing attributes that were applied manually to the text.

➤ You can also create a new style by duplicating an existing style and then changing attributes in the duplicate. To duplicate a style, choose Duplicate Character Style or Paragraph Style from the respective palette menu, or drag the style that you want to copy over the New Style button.

What if...

If you inadvertently apply a character style to a whole type object and then apply a paragraph style, only the paragraph style's formats will be applied (not its character attributes); the paragraph style name won't display a "+". To force a paragraph style to completely override a character style, select the type object, then click **[Normal Character Style]** on the Character Styles palette.

GEORGES BRAQUE (1882–1963)

THERE IS ONLY ONE VALUABLE THING IN ART: THE THING YOU CANNOT EXPLAIN.

REPORTED IN **SATURDAY REVIEW**, MAY 28, 1966

1 *Type styled with paragraph styles*   *Type styled with character styles*

GEORGES BRAQUE (1882–1963)

THERE IS ONLY ONE **VALUABLE** THING IN ART: THE THING YOU CANNOT EXPLAIN.

REPORTED IN **SATURDAY REVIEW**, MAY 28, 1966

2 *The boldfacing in the word "valuable" was applied manually, so is considered an* **override**.

GEORGES BRAQUE (1882–1963)

THERE IS ONLY ONE VALUABLE THING IN ART: THE THING YOU CANNOT EXPLAIN.

REPORTED IN **SATURDAY REVIEW**, MAY 28, 1966

3 *Option-clicking/Alt-clicking the paragraph style for the main paragraph on the Paragraph Styles palette* **removes** *the boldfacing (override).*

Removing overrides

Option-clicking/Alt-clicking a paragraph style removes **manual** overrides for the paragraph style, but doesn't remove character styling. To remove overrides from a character style, you have to Option-click/Alt-click that style, too. Overrides are removed from selected characters—or from the whole object, if no characters are selected.

To apply a style to text: NEW

1. For **paragraph** styling, select a type object, or select some paragraphs in a type object.

For **character** styling, select some text (not a whole object).

2. Click a style name on the Paragraph Styles or Character Styles palette **1**.

Note: If the text doesn't adopt the style sheet attributes, follow the next set of instructions.

➤ To choose a style for text before it's entered, deselect all, click a character or paragraph style name on the palette, then create your text.

A + (plus) sign after a style name signifies that some text in the selected type was styled manually using the Character or Paragraph palette after a style was assigned to it; that is, the text attributes no longer exactly match the attributes as defined in the applied style. Adobe calls this situation an **override.**

Follow these instructions if you you want to **clear overrides** in your text. The text will readopt the character attributes as defined in the style.

To remove overrides from styled text: NEW

1. Select the characters or paragraphs that contain overrides to be removed **2**–**3**. Or to "fix" the whole object, select the object but not any characters.

2. Option-click/Alt-click a name on the Character Styles or Paragraph Styles palette. The manually applied attributes in your text will disappear, and the "+" sign will disappear from the style name on the palette (see also the sidebar at left).

To redefine a style: NEW

1. Select the characters or paragraphs that contain the desired overrides. The applied style name will be automatically selected.

2. Choose Redefine Character Style from the Character Styles palette menu, or choose Redefine Paragraph Style from the Paragraph Styles palette menu. The selected style's settings will be modified to reflect the custom styling in the chosen text.

Apply, Redefine Style; Remove Overrides

When you **delete** a **style,** the text attributes don't change in the document—the text merely ceases to be associated with a style name.

NEW **To delete a style:**

1. Deselect all.

2. Click a style name (or select more than one name) on the Character Styles or Paragraph Styles palette, then click the Delete Selected Styles button 🗑 or choose Delete Character Style or Paragraph Style from the palette menu.
   or
   Drag a style name over the Delete Selected Styles button. If an alert dialog box appears, click Yes.

➤ To delete all unused styles in the current document, choose Select All Unused from the palette menu, then click the Delete Selected Styles button.

When **loading styles,** an incoming style will overwrite any style that bears a matching name in the current document. Text styled with an older style will adopt the attributes of the incoming style.

NEW **To load styles from another Illustrator document:**

1. From the Character Styles or Paragraph Styles palette menu:
   Choose Load Character Styles or Load Paragraph Styles.
   or
   Choose Load All Styles to load both character and paragraph styles from another document.

2. Locate the desired Illustrator document name, then click Open; or double-click the document name.

Delete, Load Styles

Finding and replacing text

You can use the **Find and Replace** command to search for and replace characters (not attributes).

To find and replace text: NEW

1. *Optional:* Click with a type tool to create an insertion point from which to start the search. If you don't do this, the search will begin from the most recently created object.

2. Choose Edit > Find and Replace.

3. Enter a word or phrase to search for in the **Find** field **1**.

4. Enter a replacement word or phrase in the **Replace With** field **2**, or leave this field blank to delete instances of the Find text altogether.

5. *Check any of these optional boxes:*

    Match Case to find only those instances that match the exact uppercase/lowercase configuration of the Find text. With this box unchecked, case will be ignored as a criterion.

    Find Whole Word to find only instances of the complete Find text by itself, not

when it's within a larger word (e.g., "go" but not "going").

   Search Backwards to search from the bottom to the top of the stacking order.

   Check Hidden Layers to search hidden layers.

   Check Locked Layers to search locked layers.

6. Click **Find Next** to search for the first instance of the Find word or phrase, or at any time to skip over a word **3**.

7. Click **Replace** to replace only the currently found instance of the Find text.
   or
   Click **Replace & Find** to replace the current instance and search for the next instance.
   or
   Click **Replace All** to replace all instances at once **4**.

8. Click Done (Return/Enter or Esc).

Find and Replace Text

1 *In the Find field, type the text that you want to search for.*

2 *In the Replace With field, type the text that you want to change the found text to.*

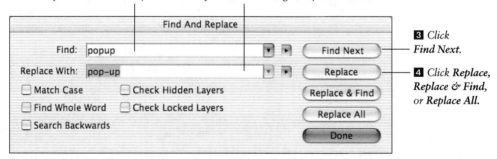

3 *Click Find Next.*

4 *Click Replace, Replace & Find, or Replace All.*

Use the Find And Replace dialog box to find and change text characters.

Checking spelling

The **Check Spelling** command checks spelling in an entire document, using a built-in dictionary and user dictionary.

NEW To check spelling:

1. Choose Edit > Check Spelling (Cmd-I/ Ctrl-I).

2. In the Check Spelling dialog box, click **Start.** The first word that isn't found in the application or user dictionary will appear in the Word Not Found window (**1**, next page), and will also be highlighted in the document window.

3. *Optional:* To refine the search, click the Options arrowhead to access Find and Ignore options for numerals, capitalization, and repeated words (words that are repeated right next to each other).

4. Do any of the following:

   If the correctly spelled word appears, highlighted or not, on the **Suggestions** list, double-click it. This will fix just the current instance of the word.
   or
   To change all instances of the misspelled word, click the correctly spelled word, then click **Change All.** The next misspelled word will now become highlighted.
   or

   If the correct word doesn't appear on the list, or if no words appear there at all (because no similar words were found in either dictionary), start typing the correctly spelled word. Your typing entry will replace the highlighted word in the Word Not Found window. Then click **Change** to change only the first instance of the highlighted misspelled word, or click **Change All** to change all instances of the misspelled word.

   For any word, you can click **Ignore** to leave the current instance of the word as is (no change), or click **Ignore All** to leave all instances of the current word as is.

   Click **Add** to add the currently highlighted word (from the Word Not Found window) to the user dictionary and move on to the next misspelled word. Clicking this button will create a user dictionary, if none already exists for this document.

5. Click Done (Return/Enter or Esc) when no more mispelled words are found, or at any time to end the spell check.

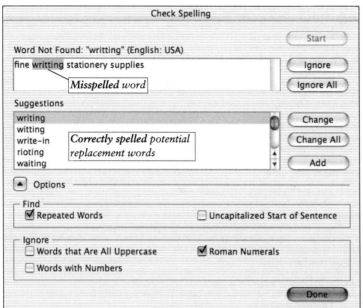

1 *The Check Spelling dialog box, with the Options pane displayed*

To edit the custom dictionary: **NEW**

1. Choose Edit > Edit Custom Dictionary.

2. In the Edit Custom Dictionary dialog box **2**, click a word in the list, correct it in the Entry field at the top of the dialog box, then click **Change**.
or
Click a word, then click **Delete**.
or
Type an entirely new word in the Entry field at the top of the dialog box, then click **Add**. Hyphenated words, such as "pop-up," are permitted.

Click a word, retype it in the Entry field, then click **Change**.

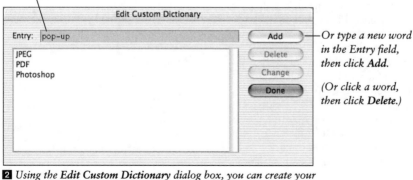

Or type a new word in the Entry field, then click **Add**.

(Or click a word, then click **Delete**.*)*

2 *Using the* **Edit Custom Dictionary** *dialog box, you can create your own word list or edit any words that were added to the list.*

Finding and replacing fonts

The **Find Font** command can be used to generate a list of the fonts currently being used in an illustration, or it can be used to replace fonts (not characters). When fonts are replaced, the type color, kerning, tracking, and other attributes are retained.

To find and replace a font:

1. Choose Type > Find Font.

2. Check any of the boxes in the **Include in List** area at the bottom of the dialog box (OpenType, Type 1, TrueType, Roman, CID, Multiple Master, or Standard) to have fonts of just those types appear on the scroll lists.

3. To display only fonts of the types checked in the previous step that are currently being used in your document, on the **Replace With Font From** list, leave the pop-up menu choice as **Document**.
   or
   Choose **System** from the Replace With Font From pop-up menu to display all the fonts that are currently available in your system (■, next page). If you choose this option, be patient while the list updates (take a quick snooze, call a friend).

4. On the **Fonts in Document** scroll list, click a font to search for. The first instance of that font will be highlighted in your document.

5. Click a replacement font on the replacement font list.

6. Click **Change** to change only the current instance of the currently highlighted font.
   or
   Click **Change All** to change all instances of the currently highlighted font. Once all the instances of a font are replaced, that font will be removed from the Fonts in Document list.
   or
   Click **Find** to search for the next instance of the currently highlighted font, or click the font name on the Fonts in Document list again.

7. *Optional:* To save a list of the fonts currently being used in the illustration as a text document, click Save List, enter a name, choose a location in which to save the file, then click Save. The text document can later be opened directly from the Desktop or it can be imported into a text editing or layout application.

8. Click Done.

➤ Use Undo to undo font changes made in your illustration using Find Font.

1 *Choose* **System** *from the* **Replace With Font From** *pop-up menu to display on the replacement font list all available fonts in the system of the types checked, or choose* **Document** *to list only the fonts currently being used in your illustration.*

Click a font to be searched for on the **Fonts in Document** *scroll list.*

Click **Change All**; *or click* **Change**, *then click* **Find**.

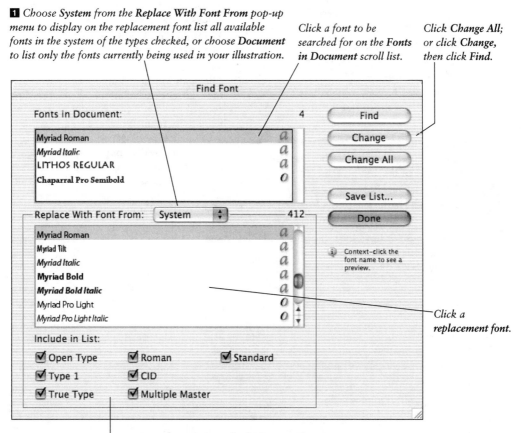

Uncheck any **font types** *to narrow the selection of replacement fonts.*

Choosing area type options

The **Area Type Options** dialog box lets you specify the inset spacing between area type and the type object and the position of the first line of type, and also lets you divide a type block into columns and/or rows.

NEW **To choose area type options:**

1. Select an area type object with a selection tool or type tool **1**.

2. Choose Type > Area Type Options.

3. Check Preview **2**.

4. In the Offset area, choose an **Inset Spacing** value for the space between the type and the type object.

5. To control the distance between the first line of text and the top edge of the object, choose a **First Baseline** option:

   Ascent to have the top of the tallest characters touch the top of the object.

   Cap Height to have uppercase letters touch the top of the object.

   Leading to make the distance between the first baseline of the text and the top of the object be equal to the leading value.

   x Height to have the top of the font's "x" character touch the top of the object.

   Em Box Height to have the top of the em box in Asian fonts touch the top of the object (available only when the

Show Asian Options preference is enabled).

Fixed to have the Min value you enter be the location of the first line's baseline.

Legacy to use the method from previous versions of Illustrator.

Enter a minimum baseline offset value in the **Min** field. Illustrator will use either this minimum value or the **First Baseline** option value, whichever is greater.

6. To arrange text in linked rows and columns, in the **Rows** and **Columns** areas, click an up or down arrow or enter values in the fields to choose:

   The total **Number** of rows and columns to be produced.

   and

   The **Span** for the height of each row and the width of each column. Check **Fixed** to control whether a row or column remains fixed in its span. When checked, resizing the overall type object will add or delete columns as needed, but the span of the rows or columns won't change. When unchecked, existing rows or columns will resize to adapt to changes in the type object size and no new rows or columns will be added.

   and

Hey! diddle, diddle,
The cat and the Fiddle,
The cow jumped over the moon;
The little dog laugh'd
To see such sport,
And the dish ran away with the spoon.

1 *The original text object*

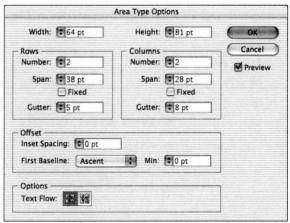

2 *Use the **Area Type Options** dialog box to position type within an object and to arrange type into columns or rows.*

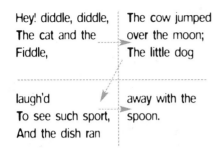

Hey! diddle, diddle,
The cat and the
Fiddle,

laugh'd
To see such sport,
And the dish ran

The cow jumped
over the moon;
The little dog

away with the
spoon.

1 *The object converted into two **rows** and two **columns**. In this case, the text is flowing from row to row.*

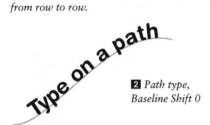

2 *Path type, Baseline Shift 0*

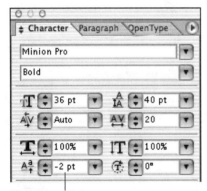

3 *Baseline Shift area*

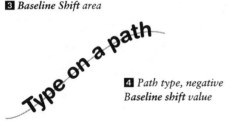

4 *Path type, negative Baseline shift value*

5 *The "A" has a Baseline Shift value of –9 pt.*

The **Gutter** (space) between the rows and the columns.
and
The total **Width** and total **Height** of the entire type object. If you change these dimensions, the height or width, or number (if Fixed is checked) of rows or columns will change, but the gutter values will remain constant.

7. Click one of the two **Text Flow** buttons to control the direction of the text flow—row to row or column to column.

8. Click OK **1**.

➤ If you select the type object and then reopen the Area Type Options dialog box, the current settings for that type object will be displayed.

By adjusting the **Baseline Shift** value, you can shift characters upward or downward from the baseline, or offset type from a path.

To baseline-shift type:

1. Select the type that you want to shift **2**.

2. Make sure the Baseline Shift area is showing on the Character palette (Cmd-T/Ctrl-T) **3**. If it's not, click the double arrowheads on the palette tab twice. Enter a positive Baseline Shift value to shift characters upward or a negative value to shift them downward **4**–**5**; or choose a preset amount from the pop-up menu; or click the up or down arrow.
or
Option-Shift-press/Alt-Shift-press the up arrow on the keyboard to shift highlighted characters upward or the down arrow to shift them downward as per the Baseline Shift increment specified in Preferences > Type & Auto Tracing. Cmd-Option-Shift-press/Ctrl-Alt-Shift-press to shift in larger increments.

➤ To insert superscript and subscript characters in OpenType fonts, use the OpenType palette.

Baseline Shift

Setting tabs

To align columns of text correctly, you must use **tabs**—not spaces. The default tab stops are half an inch apart. You can use the Tabs palette to set custom left-, center-, right-, and decimal-justified tabs in horizontal type, and top-, center-, bottom-, and decimal-justified tabs in vertical type.

To insert tabs into text:

Press Tab **once** as you input copy before typing each new column. The cursor will jump to the next tab stop.

or

To add a tab to existing text, click just to the left of the text that is to start a new column, then press Tab. The text will move to the next default tab stop.

To set custom tab stops, see the next page.

Out of hiding

To show the tab characters that are hidden in your text, along with other nonprinting characters, such as paragraph returns, soft returns, and spaces, choose Type > **Show Hidden Characters** (Cmd-Option-I/Ctrl-Alt-I). Tab characters display as right-pointing arrows. The nonprinting characters display in the color that's assigned to the layer the objects reside in **1**. Choose the command again at any time to turn off the display.

	Front.9	Back.9	Total
Tiger	34	34	68¶
Jack	38	44	82¶
David	34	38	72¶
Phil	35	38	73

1 *Text aligned using custom tab stops*

To set or modify custom tab stops: NEW

1. Choose the Selection tool, then click a text object.
   or
   Choose a type tool and select some text.

2. Choose Window > Type > Tabs (Cmd-Shift-T/Ctrl-Shift-T).

3. *Optional:* Choose **Snap to Unit** from the palette menu to have tab markers snap to the nearest ruler tick mark as you insert or move them. You can also turn the Snap feature on and off temporarily (the opposite of the current Snap to Unit state) by Shift-dragging a marker.

4. Do any of the following:

   Click just above the Tabs palette ruler to **insert** a new stop (the selected text will align to that stop) ∎, then click a tab **alignment** button in the top left corner of the palette. Repeat to insert more stops. You can change the alignment of any stop at any time; Option-click/Alt-click a tab stop to cycle through the alignment types.

   To **delete** a tab stop, drag the tab marker upward and out of the ruler. Cmd-drag/Ctrl-drag to delete a marker and all markers to its right.

   To **move** a tab stop: Drag the marker to the left or the right, or enter an exact location in the X field for horizontal type,

   the Y field for vertical type. Cmd-drag/Ctrl-drag a marker to move all the markers to the right of it along with it.

5. *Optional:* Click a tab stop in the ruler, then enter a character (up to 8 characters, actually) in the **Leader** field to have that character be repeated between tab stops ∎. Attributes must be applied to leader characters manually in the text object (use a character style!).

6. *Optional:* For the Decimal-Justified tab alignment option, you can enter a character for numerals to align on in the **Align On** field ∎. For this to work, the type object must contain that character.

➤ If you move the Tabs palette, you can click the Position Palette Above Text button ∎ to realign the tab ruler with the left and right margins of the selected text for horizontal type, or the top and bottom margins for vertical type.

➤ To create a series of tab stops that are equidistant from one another, click one tab stop, then choose Repeat Tab from the palette menu. Beware! This command deletes all other stops.

➤ The Tabs palette ruler units display in the increment currently chosen in File > Document Setup (Artboard: Units).

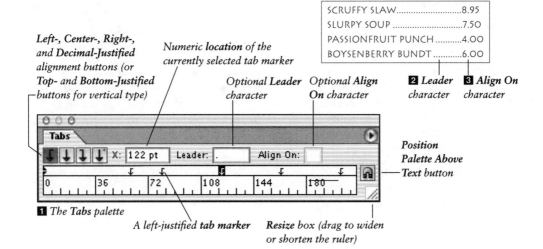

Left-, Center-, Right-, and Decimal-Justified alignment buttons (or Top- and Bottom-Justified buttons for vertical type)

*Numeric **location** of the currently selected tab marker*

*Optional **Leader** character*

*Optional **Align On** character*

*∎ **Leader** character*

*∎ **Align On** character*

SCRUFFY SLAW...........................8.95
SLURPY SOUP 7.50
PASSIONFRUIT PUNCH 4.00
BOYSENBERRY BUNDT 6.00

Position Palette Above Text button

∎ *The Tabs palette*

*A left-justified **tab marker***

Resize box (drag to widen or shorten the ruler)

Custom Tab Stops

253

Creating special effects with type

Type can wrap around an Illustrator path, Illustrator text, or a placed bitmap image.

NEW **To wrap type around an object:**

1. Create area type (type inside an object).

2. Choose the Selection tool.

3. Follow this instruction carefully, or the wrap won't work: Make sure the object that the type is going to wrap around (the "wrap object") is **above** the text that you want to wrap around it, in the **same** top-level layer, sublayer, or group. You can use the Layers palette to restack the wrap object if necessary. It can be a vector object or a bitmap (placed) image.

4. Select the wrap object **1** (click its selection square on the Layers palette).

5. Choose Object > Text Wrap > Make Text Wrap. If an alert dialog box appears, click OK.

6. In the Text Wrap Options dialog box **2**, click Preview, then enter or choose an Offset value for the distance between the wrap object and any type that wraps around it. If the wrap object is a placed image, the type will wrap around opaque or partially opaque pixels in the image.

   Optional: For entertainment on a rainy or snowy day, check Invert Wrap. This option will force the text to wrap inside the path rather than outside it.

7. Click OK **3**.

➤ To prevent a text object from being affected by the wrap object, move it above the wrap object via the Layers palette (or to a different top-level layer).

➤ To modify the options for an existing wrap object, select it, then choose Object > Wrap > Text Wrap Options; the dialog box reopens.

NEW **To release a text wrap:**

1. Select the wrap object.

2. Choose Object > Text Wrap > Release Text Wrap.

*Just picture a large sparrow cage made of bamboo grillwork and having a coconut-thatch roof, divided off into two parts by the curtains from my old studio. One of the two parts makes a bedroom, with very little light, so as to keep it cool. The other part, with a large window up high, is my studio. On the floor, some mats and my old Persian rug; and I've decorated the rest with fabrics, trinkets, and drawings. **Paul Gauguin***

1 *Select the object that the type is going to wrap around.*

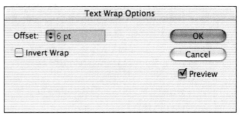

2 *In the **Text Wrap Options** dialog box, enter an Offset value and check Preview.*

*Just picture a large sparrow cage made of bamboo grillwork and having a coconut-thatch roof, divided off into two parts by the curtains from my old studio. One of the two parts makes a bedroom, with very little light, so as to keep it cool. The other part, with a large window up high, is my studio. On the floor, some mats and my old Persian rug; and I've decorated the rest with fabrics, trinkets, and drawings. **Paul Gauguin***

3 *The type **wraps** around the palm tree.*

Text Wrap

254

Another idea

Use the Layers palette to select the shadow object, choose the **Free Transform** tool, then vertically scale or shear the object by moving its top center handle. Or to reflect the shadow block using the same tool, drag the top center handle downward all the way across the object.

shadow

1 *Create the shadow and send it to the back.*

shadow

2 *Shorten the shadow by dragging the top center handle on its bounding box.*

shadow

3 *Slant the shadow using the Shear tool.*

shadow

4 *Reflect the shadow using the Reflect tool.*

An advantage of using the following method instead of Effect > Drop Shadow is that here the shadow is an independent vector object that can be modified by using effects, the transform tools, and other techniques.

To create type with a shadow:
1. Create point type (see page 206).
2. *Optional:* Select the type with the Type tool, then apply positive tracking (Cmd-Shift-]/Ctrl-Shift-]).
3. Choose the Selection tool; click the type.
4. Apply a dark fill color, stroke of None.
5. Option-drag/Alt-drag the type block slightly to the right and downward. Release the mouse, then Option/Alt.
6. With the copy of the type block still selected, lighten its shade.
7. On the Layers palette, drag the copy of the type below the original **1**, and make sure it still has a selection square.
8. Choose Effect > Stylize (on the upper part of the menu) > Feather, check Preview, choose a Radius value (try a low value), click OK, and then, via the Transparency palette, lower the transparency.

To slant the shadow:
1. Select the shadow object using the Layers palette.
2. Choose the Selection tool. Drag the top center handle downward a bit to shorten the type **2**.
3. With the shadow type still selected, double-click the Shear tool.
4. Enter 45 in the Shear Angle field, click Axis: Horizontal, then click OK.
5. Use the arrow keys to move the baseline of the shadow text so it aligns with the baseline of the original text **3**.

To reflect the shadow:
1. Select the shadow type.
2. Double-click the Reflect tool, click Axis: Horizontal, then click OK.
3. Move the two blocks of type together so their baselines meet **4**.

Type with a Shadow

To slant a type block:

1. Choose the Rectangle tool (M), ▢ then draw a rectangle.

2. Choose the Area Type tool. 🆃

3. Click the edge of the rectangle, then enter some type **2**.

4. With the rectangle still selected, double-click the Rotate tool. ⟳

5. Enter 30 in the Angle field, then click OK **3**.

6. Make sure Smart Guides is on (Cmd-U/Ctrl-U) with Object Highlighting (Preferences > Smart Guides & Slices).

7. Choose the Direct Selection tool (A), ▸ deselect the object, then Shift-drag the top segment diagonally to the right until the side segments are vertical **4**–**5**.

8. *Optional:* Drag the right segment of the rectangle a little to the right to enlarge the object and reflow the type.

➤ To rotate just the type characters and not slant the whole baseline (as in the steps above), select the type object, then choose or enter a positive or negative Character Rotation value 🔄 on the Character palette.

Use the shears

You can use the **Shear** tool 🗗 (on the Scale tool pop-out menu) to slant a block of type **1**.

1 *Select the type, click with the **Shear** tool on the center of the type, then drag upward or downward from the edge of the type block. (Shift-drag to constrain the shear to the vertical or horizontal axis.)*

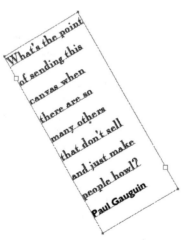

2 *The original type object*

3 *The type rotated 30°*

4 *The top segment dragged diagonally to the right*

5 *The final type object in Preview view*

In this chapter you'll learn how to get images into Illustrator via the Open command, the Place command, and drag-and-drop. You will also learn how to work with the Links palette to edit, locate, update, relink, and convert linked images, and how to trace objects manually and by using the Auto Trace tool.

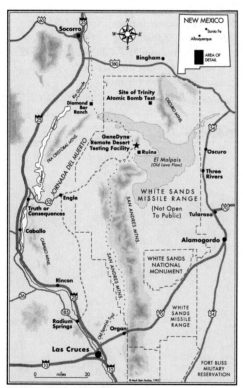

©Mark Stein, Mark Stein Studios

Opening and placing images
How images are acquired

You can use Illustrator to open or import objects or images in a variety of file formats, which means you can work with imagery that was originally created in other applications. Methods for acquiring images from other applications include the Open command, the Place command, and drag-and-drop. Your method of choice will depend on which file formats are available for saving the file in its original application and how you intend to use the imagery in Illustrator.

If you open a document from another drawing (vector) application using the **Open** command, a new Illustrator file will be created, and the acquired objects can then be manipulated using any Illustrator tool, command, filter, or effect. If you open a document from a bitmap program other than Photoshop by using the Open command, the image won't be converted into separate objects; it will stay as one object in its outlined box.

The **Place** command inserts imagery or text into an existing Illustrator document. For print output, the best formats for saving an image for placement into Illustrator are EPS and TIFF. Both of these formats preserve the color, detail, and resolution of the original image.

For Web output, an image saved in .psd (Photoshop) format works fine. If you place a layered .psd image in Illustrator, you can

(Continued on the following page)

(Continued on the following page)

Open and Place

have it appear either as a single flattened object or as separate objects on separate layers. If you want to put the image on a template layer for tracing, check Template in the Place dialog box. The Template option for a layer can be turned on or off at any time (double-click the layer on the Layers palette, then check or uncheck Template).

A bitmap image that's acquired in Illustrator via the Open, Place, or drag-and-drop method can be moved, placed on a different layer, masked, modified using any transformation tool, or modified using any color or raster (bitmap) filter.

➤ If you reduce the scale of an opened or placed TIFF or EPS image, its resolution will increase accordingly. Conversely, if you enlarge such an image, its resolution will decrease.

Both the Open and Place commands preserve the resolution of the original image, regardless of whether the image is linked or embedded when it's imported.

(The Clipboard commands, Cut, Copy, and Paste, are covered on page 95.)

File formats

File formats you can **Open** in Illustrator:

Native formats: Illustrator (ai) versions 1.0 through CS, Illustrator .ait, Illustrator EPS and PDF.

File formats you can **Open** or **Place** in Illustrator:

Raster (bitmap) formats: BMP, FLM (Mac only), GIF, JPEG, JPEG2000, Kodak PhotoCD, PCX, PIXAR, PNG, Photoshop, TGA, and TIFF.

Vector formats: CorelDRAW versions 5 through 10.

Graphics (vector) formats: CGM; DXF and DWG (AutoCAD drawing and export); Free-Hand (up to version 9); PICT; SVG and SVGZ; EMF; and WMF. Illustrator CS can't open Macromedia Flash SWF files.

Text formats: Plain text (ASCII), RTF, and MS Word (up to version 2002 in Windows, and on the Mac).

Open and Place

Easy reopen

From the File > **Open Recent Files** submenu, you can choose from a list of up to ten of the most recently opened files.

1 *Click a file name...*   *...then click* **Open.**

2 *For a* **multipage PDF,** *choose the page you want to open.*

A list of file formats that can be **opened** in Illustrator appears on the previous page.

To open a file from within Illustrator:

1. Choose File > Open (Cmd-O/Ctrl-O).

2. On the Mac, choose Show: **All Documents** to list files in all formats, or choose **All Readable Documents** to dim the files that are in formats that Illustrator can't read.

   In Windows, you can filter out files by choosing from the **Files of Type** pop-up menu, or you can choose **All Formats** (the default setting) to display files in all formats.

3. Locate and highlight a file name, then click Open (Return/Enter) **1**.
   or
   Double-click a file name.

   Note: If you get an alert dialog box concerning a linked file, see page 264.

4. If you're opening a multipage PDF, another dialog box will open **2**. Click an arrow to locate the desired page (or click the "1 of [ ]" button, enter the desired page), then click OK.

➤ If you open an EPS that contains a clipping path, the image will be nested inside a <Group> on the Layers palette (the words "<Clipping Path>" will appear directly above the <Image> listing). If the clipping path is composed of several paths, it will be listed as "<Compound Clipping Path>" instead. To select the clipping path, use the Layers palette; to move or reshape it, select the layer that contains the path, and use the Direct Selection tool.

➤ You can also delete the selected clipping path, in which case the entire image will become visible.

Open a File

An image from another application that's **placed** into an Illustrator file can be moved to a different *x/y* location, restacked within the same layer or to a different layer, masked, transformed, or modified using either effects or filters. You can also change its opacity and blending mode. For a list of file formats that can be placed into Illustrator, see page 258.

To place an image into an Illustrator document:

1. Open an Illustrator file. Highlight the layer name that you want the image to appear on.

2. Choose File > Place.

3. Locate and click the name of the file that you want to place .

4. Check Link to place a **screen** version of the image into your Illustrator document, with a link to the original image file. The original image file won't be affected by your Illustrator edits, but in order to print properly, it must be available on your hard disk. You can set an Illustrator preference so that if you modify and resave linked images in their original application, they'll automatically update in the Illustrator document (see page 264).
or
Uncheck Link to **embed** the actual image into the Illustrator file. This option will increase the storage size of your Illustrator document.

Read more about linking on pages 261–265.

5. *Optional:* Check Template to place a dimmed version of the image on a template layer for tracing.

6. Click Place. In Preview view, an X will appear across the box of all linked images 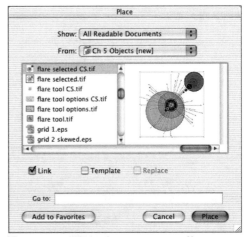 except TIFFs and GIFs.

In Outline view, placed image boxes are blank unless View: Show Images In Outline Mode is checked in File > Document Setup (Artboard panel) –.

1 *Locate and click a bitmap or vector file name in the Place dialog box, then click Place.*

2 *A selected, linked, placed image*

3 *A placed (linked or embedded) bitmap image in Outline view, with Show Images In Outline Mode unchecked*

4 *A placed (linked or embed-ded) bitmap image in Outline view, with Show Images In Outline Mode checked*

Place an Image

Update options

To specify how linked images are updated when the original files are modifed, choose one of these options from the **Update Links** pop-up menu in Illustrator (Edit, in Windows) > Preferences > File Handling & Clipboard:

Automatically: Illustrator will update linked images automatically whenever the original files are modified.

Manually: Linked images won't be updated automatically when the original files are modified. You can use the Links palette at any time to update links.

Ask When Modified: A dialog box will appear if the original files are modified and you return to Illustrator or reopen the file (click Yes or No to update the files or not).

Missing Linked Image indicator   Modified Linked Image indicator

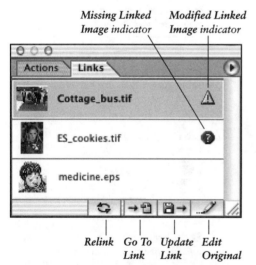

Relink   Go To Link   Update Link   Edit Original

1 *The Links palette lets you keep track of linked images, link to new files, and convert linked images into embedded ones.*

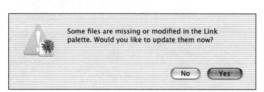

2 *This prompt will appear if you edit a link in its original application via the* **Edit Original** *button.*

Linking images

To keep your Illustrator file from becoming too large, you can link imported images (e.g., BMP, EPS, GIF, JPEG, PICT, PNG, PSD, or TIFF files) to the file instead of embedding them. A copy of each image will act as a placeholder in your Illustrator document, but the actual image will remain separate from the Illustrator file. If you revise a linked image via the Edit Original button, the image can be updated in the Illustrator document (this can't be done with embedded images).

To link a file, use the File > Place command with the **Link** option checked (for more about placing and linking images, see page 260).

Illustrator's **Links palette** **1** helps you and your service bureau or print shop keep track of linked files. It lists all the linked and embedded files in your Illustrator document and puts a number of useful controls at your fingertips.

Raster filters can be applied to any embedded image, or to a linked GIF, JPEG, or TIFF image. Effect menu filters can be applied to both types of images, and the effects will be editable. To embed a linked image, see page 265. The Object > Rasterize command automatically embeds linked images; the Effect > Rasterize command does not. Linked images can be transformed (moved, rotated, sheared, or reflected).

To edit a linked image in its original application:

1. Display the Links palette, then click the image name on the palette.

2. Click the Edit Original button at the bottom of the palette or choose Edit Original from the palette menu. The application in which the linked image was created will launch, if it isn't already open, and the image will open. *Note:* Edit Original may not work in Windows, depending on where the linked file is located.

3. Make your edits, resave the file, and then return to Illustrator. If a warning prompt appears, click Yes (see the sidebar) **2**. The linked image will update.

If you **replace** one **linked image** with another, any transformations that were applied to the original image, such as scaling or rotating, will be applied to the new one.

To replace one linked image with another:

1. On the Links palette, click the name of the file that you want to replace .

NEW 2. Click the Relink button ⟳ at the bottom of the Links palette (the button name is new).

or

Choose Relink from the Links palette menu.

3. Locate the replacement file, then click Place **2**.

➤ Another way to replace a linked image is to select the placed image in the document window, choose File > Place, locate the replacement image, check Replace, then click Place.

When a linked image is located using the **Go To Link** command, it becomes selected in the document window, centered onscreen.

To locate a linked image in an Illustrator file:

1. Open the illustration that contains the linked image.

2. Click the name of the linked image on the Links palette list.

3. Click the Go To Link button →🗇 at the bottom of the palette.

or

Choose Go To Link from the Links palette menu.

Linked and embedded files **NEW**

To a linked image that displays an "X" across it (when selected), you can apply opacity and blending modes, the Feather command, and some filters on the Effect menu. These attributes will become appearances on the image object. The linked image will be listed on the Layers palette as <Linked File> (or, for a PSD file, as the file name) within the currently active layer.

To a linked image that doesn't have an "X" across it, you can perform almost any Illustrator edits, much as you can to an embedded image.

For any linked image, any clipping path in the file will be applied, and it won't be listed separately.

An embedded image will be listed on the Layers palette as a nested image object within a group sublayer within the current layer. If a clipping path is included, it will be active and will be listed on the Layers palette as a clipping path within the group sublayer, stacked above the image object.

1 *Click the linked image that you want to replace, then click the **Relink** button.*

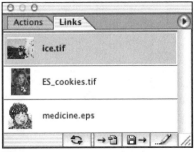

2 *The linked image is **replaced.***

1 *The **Link Information** dialog box lists the name of, and other information about, the linked image.*

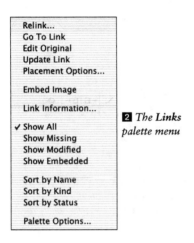

2 *The Links palette menu*

Embedded images are identified by this icon.

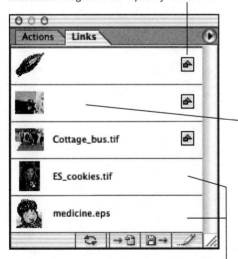

Linked images don't have an Embedded icon.

To view file information for a linked image:

1. Double-click an image thumbnail on the Links palette.
or
Click a file name on the Links palette, then choose Link Information from the palette menu.

A dialog box listing information about the image, such as its file format, location, size, modifications, and transform information, will appear **1**.

2. Click OK.

To choose Links palette display options:

To change the size of the thumbnail images that are displayed in the Links palette, choose **Palette Options** from the Links palette menu, click the preferred size, then click OK. To display just the file icons without the thumbnails, click None.

To change the order of links on the palette, from the Links palette menu, choose **Sort by Name** (alphabetical order), **Sort by Kind** (file format), or **Sort by Status** (missing, then modified, then embedded, then fully linked) **2–3**. To sort only selected links, first click, then Shift-click consecutive names or Cmd-click/Ctrl-click nonconsecutive names.

To control which type of links display on the palette, choose **Show All, Show Missing, Show Modified,** or **Show Embedded** from the Links palette menu.

With the exception of TIFF and JPEG files, the names of embedded images aren't listed on the palette.

3 *The Links palette with the Show All and Sort by Status display options chosen*

Links Palette

263

If an exclamation mark icon appears to the right of a link on the Links palette, it means the original file has been **modified** and the link is outdated. To **update** a **linked file,** follow the instructions below.

If you edit a linked image via the Edit Original button, you'll need to update it this way if Manually is chosen from the Update Links pop-up menu in Illustrator (Edit, in Windows) > Preferences > File Handling & Clipboard. If Automatically is chosen as the setting, the image will be updated automatically; if Ask When Modified is chosen, you'll get a warning prompt to update the file.

To update a modified linked image:

I. Click the name of the modified image on the Links palette 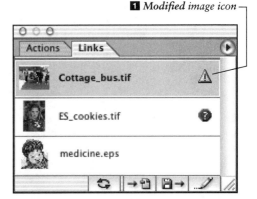.

2. Click the Update Link button ⬜➔ at the bottom of the palette.
   or
   Choose Update Link from the Links palette menu.

Unfortunately, Illustrator doesn't provide a method for updating **missing linked images** (missing linked images have a question mark). Your options are to either physically move it back to its original location or **replace** it.

To replace images upon opening a file:

If you move an actual linked image from its original location after saving the Illustrator file into which it was placed, you'll be prompted to relink the image when you reopen the Illustrator file. Click **Replace** , relocate the same image file or a different one, then click Replace again.

If you click **Ignore,** the linked image won't display, but a question mark icon will display for the file on the Links palette and its bounding box will still be visible in the Illustrator file in Outline view or, if Smart Guides is turned on, when the cursor passes over the bounding box. To completely break the link and prevent any alert prompts from appearing in the future, delete the bounding box and resave the file.

1 *Modified image icon* ⌐

2 *If a linked file was **moved** to another folder or is otherwise **missing**, Illustrator will alert you with this dialog box when you open the illustration. To reestablish the link, click **Replace**, then locate the file.*

The **Embed Image** command will cause a file that's separate from, but linked to, your Illustrator document to become embedded into (become a part of) your Illustrator document. Keep in mind that embedding images increases the size of your Illustrator file.

To convert a linked image to an embedded image:

1. On the Links palette list, click the name of the image that you want to embed **1**.

2. Choose Embed Image from the Links palette menu **2**.

   Note: There is no command to turn an embedded image into a linked image. If you're quick on your toes, you can choose Undo immediately, or at any time you can use the Relink button or the Relink command on the Links palette menu to replace the embedded image with a linked image.

3. *Optional:* If the linked image is a multi-layer Photoshop file, the Photoshop Options Import dialog box will open. Follow the instructions on pages 267–268.

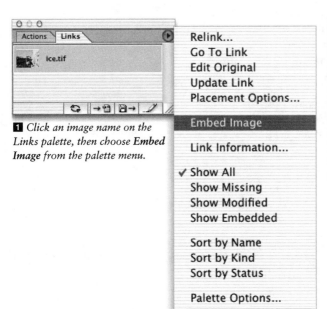

1 *Click an image name on the Links palette, then choose* **Embed Image** *from the palette menu.*

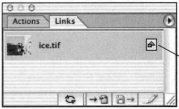

2 *The embedded image icon appears. The file name is preserved for TIFF, JPEG or flattened PSD images when such files are embedded.*

Convert Linked Image to Embedded

Drag-and-drop

Drag-and-drop is a quick method for copying images between applications or files (the copy is made automatically for you).

Here are a few pointers before you begin:

➤ You can drag and drop objects between Illustrator documents or between Illustrator and Adobe GoLive, Adobe InDesign, or any other drag-aware application. You can drag and drop a path from Photoshop to Illustrator; the Paste Options dialog box will open. Choose Paste As: Compound Shape or Compound Path. To drag and drop bitmap imagery, see the instructions on the following page. (You could also copy a path from Photoshop and paste it into Illustrator; the pasted path will be editable in Illustrator.)

➤ Drag-and-drop doesn't use the Clipboard; whatever is currently on the Clipboard is preserved.

➤ On the Mac, if you drag an Illustrator object to the Desktop, a Picture Clipping file will be created. Desktop clippings are stored on the Mac in PICT format. These intermediate files can be dragged back into an Illustrator file (with paths intact) or into any drag-aware applications.

Frankly, if you're going to print an Illustrator file that contains an acquired image, we recommend going to Photoshop first, converting the image to be acquired to CMYK Color mode, saving it as a TIFF or EPS, and then acquiring it in Illustrator using the Place or Open command.

Illustrator to Photoshop

You can also drag and drop files from Illustrator into Photoshop. In Photoshop, the Illustrator object will become a new layer of **pixels** in the color mode and resolution of the Photoshop image. If you want to preserve the object as a **path,** Cmd-drag/Ctrl-drag the Illustrator object. To position the object in the **center** of the Photoshop document window, hold down Shift after you start dragging.

When layers don't become objects

Adjustment layers and placed images (NEW)
In Photoshop, the position of an adjustment layer in the layer stack affects how these layers are converted into objects when the file is placed and embedded (not linked) into Illustrator. Any layers above an adjustment layer in the Photoshop file will be converted into separate objects in Illustrator. Any layers below an adjustment layer in the Photoshop file will be flattened with the adjustment layer into one object in Illustrator.

Shape layers and placed images (NEW)
When placing or opening a Photoshop EPS file, any Photoshop shape layers will be made into separate layers in Illustrator. All other Photoshop layers will be flattened into one object, which will be placed below the shape layer(s). In contrast, each layer from a Photoshop PSD file will be converted to a separate object layer, regardless of whether the fill contains any shape layers.

Pixels off the edge

If the active layer in a Photoshop file contains pixels that extend outside the live canvas area, those pixels won't appear in the Illustrator file, regardless of which method you use to acquire it—drag-and-drop, place, or open. Before acquiring the image, in Photoshop make sure the pixels that you want to import are within the live canvas area.

Photoshop to Illustrator

To drag and drop from Photoshop

If you **drag and drop** a Photoshop selection or layer into Illustrator, here's what results:

➤ The dragged image will be embedded at the resolution of the original image and will adopt the document color mode of the Illustrator file. Type and shape objects will be rasterized.

➤ The image will be nested within a new <Group> layer within the currently active layer.

➤ Any clipping paths in the Photoshop file will be ignored. Also, a generic clipping path will be created within the image group; it can be deleted and the image will remain clipped. You can create your own clipping mask in Illustrator if you want to further mask the acquired image.

➤ The opacity of the selection or layer will become 100%, regardless of its original opacity. If a lower transparency is desired, apply it in Illustrator.

➤ Layer masks and vector masks from Photoshop will be applied to the image (meaning the image will be clipped) and then will be discarded.

➤ Photoshop blending modes will be ignored.

To drag and drop Photoshop imagery into Illustrator:

1. In Photoshop, select some pixels or activate a layer.

2. Open the Illustrator file to which you want to copy the imagery.

3. Choose the Move tool in Photoshop, then drag the selection or layer into the target Illustrator document window. Presto! The target window will become active and a copy of the image pixels will appear inside it.

To place from Photoshop

If you **place** a Photoshop image with **Link** checked in the Place dialog box, it will appear on the Layers palette as one image nested inside the currently active layer—not

(Continued on the following page)

a group—and no clipping path will be generated by Illustrator. Any Photoshop clipping path will remain in effect.

If you **embed** a Photoshop image as you place it (Link unchecked), the **Photoshop Import Options** dialog box will open ∎. In this dialog box, you can choose from two options for how the Photoshop layers will be treated: layers can either be converted into separate objects or flattened into one image. (This dialog box also appears if you open a Photoshop image in Illustrator.)

If you click **Convert Photoshop layers to objects and make text editable where possible,** each object will be nested within an image group within the currently active layer. All transparency levels, blending modes, and layer and vector masks will be preserved. They'll be listed as editable appearances (see page 335), and will be targeted to the appropriate converted object in Illustrator. Layer sets will be preserved. Any clipping path that was saved with the Photoshop file will remain in effect and will be placed at the top of the stack of objects in the group.

If you click **Flatten Photoshop layers to a single image and preserve text appearance,** that image will be nested within the currently active layer. All transparency levels, blending modes, and layer mask effects will be applied to the flattened image, but those attributes won't be listed as editable appearances in Illustrator. Any clipping path saved with the Photoshop file will remain in effect and will be stacked above the nested image within a group.

Photoshop text into Illustrator NEW

If a Photoshop file that contains editable text is placed into Illustrator (Link option unchecked) and the **Convert Photoshop layers to objects** button is clicked, the text objects will remain editable, provided the text layer in Photoshop was neither warped nor had any effects applied to it. If you want to import a text layer as vector outlines instead, in Photoshop, use Layer > Type > Convert to Shape, save the file, then open the file in Illustrator via the Open or Place command.

If a Photoshop image containing multiple layers is opened or placed into Illustrator with the Link option unchecked and you choose to convert Photoshop layers to objects in the Photoshop Import Options dialog box, the Background layer from the Photoshop file will become one of the nested objects within Illustrator, and it will be opaque (you can change its opacity). If you don't want the background object, you can either delete it in Photoshop before opening or placing the image in Illustrator, or delete it afterwards using the Layers palette in Illustrator.

Also, in the Photoshop Import dialog box, check **Import Image Maps** and/or **Import Slices**, if these options are available, to bring in any image maps or slices that were saved with the Photoshop file.

➤ Each converted layer from a Photoshop image will be listed as a separate item on the Links palette.

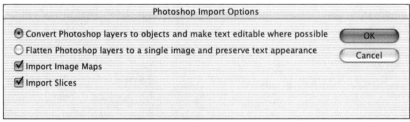

∎ *In the **Photoshop Import Options** dialog box, choose whether Photoshop layers will be converted into individual objects or flattened.*

1 *Placed artwork in a document window. (When placing an EPS for tracing, don't link the file, as this will produce either an inferior screen image or no screen image at all. A template layer isn't required when auto-tracing a placed image.)*

2 *After **tracing** the outer path*

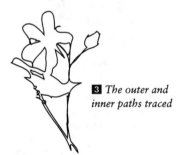

3 *The outer and inner paths traced*

4 *The final objects after applying black and white fills*

Tracing

You can use the **Auto Trace** tool to trace any image that's acquired via File > Place, such as a scanned photo or drawing. This tool tends to create extraneous anchor points and also places points in inappropriate locations, so you'll need to do some cleanup afterwards. If your artwork is simple (high contrast) or if you want a rough, hand-drawn look, this is the tool to use. For photographs, you'll be better off tracing with the Pen or Pencil tool (see the next page). P.S.: Adobe Streamline traces more accurately and offers many more options than Illustrator's Auto Trace tool.

Note: To control how exactly the Auto Trace tool traces a path, go to Illustrator (Edit, in Windows) > Preferences > Type & Auto Tracing. The higher the Auto Trace Tolerance (0–10 pt), the less precisely an object will be traced, and the fewer anchor points will be created. The Tracing Gap (0–2 pt) is the minimum width a gap in linework must have in order to be traced. A high Tracing Gap setting will probably produce a lot of extraneous points.

To use the Auto Trace tool:

1. Open a file, then choose File > Place.

2. Locate and highlight an EPS, PDF, TIFF, or PSD file of a silhouetted image, then click Place **1**. (For a PSD file, click the "Flatten..." option, then click OK.) Lock the image using the Layers palette.

3. Above the image, create a layer or click an existing layer.

4. For now, choose a fill of None and a black stroke.

5. Choose the Auto Trace tool ▧ (it's on the Blend tool pop-out menu).

6. To trace, click on or drag over the interior or edges of the image. The shapes will be traced automatically **2**–**3**. Apply a fill of None to prevent the new tracing shapes from obscuring the placed image.

7. Fill the traced shapes as desired **4**. To check your progress, hide the image by clicking its eye icon ⬙ on the Layers palette.

Auto Trace

Using the Pen or Pencil tool, you can **manually trace** over any placed image. When you trace an image manually, you can organize and simplify path shapes as well as control their stacking order. If you create separate paths on separate layers, you'll be able to restack and edit them more easily later on.

To trace over a placed image manually:

1. Create or open an Illustrator document, then choose File > Place .

2. Locate and highlight the image you want to trace, check Template if desired, then click Place. If you checked Template, the image will appear dimmed on its own uneditable layer. You can change the layer options at any time by double-clicking the top-level layer name.

   ➤ If you place the image without checking the Template option, you can lower the opacity of the image object at any time to make your tracing lines stand out better.

3. Create a new layer above the placed image layer.

4. Choose the Pen (P) tool or the Pencil (N) tool.

5. Trace the placed image . You can periodically hide the image or the template to check your progress. To hide the template, click the template icon on the Layers palette; or choose View > Hide Template; or press Cmd-Shift-W/ Ctrl-Shift-W. Redisplay it when you're ready to resume tracing.

   ➤ If you're using the Pencil tool, you can double-click the tool and change its Tolerances: Smoothness and/or Fidelity settings.

   ➤ You can transform a placed image before you trace it.

1 *A placed image*

2 *After **tracing the image using the Pen** tool, filling and stroking the paths with various shades of black, applying the Roughen effect at low Size and Detail settings to give the path strokes a more hand-made appearance, and adding a radial gradient*

In this chapter you'll learn how to embellish paths with shapes and textures using Illustrator's four types of brushes: Calligraphic, Scatter, Art, and Pattern. You'll learn how to create and edit custom brushes; add, modify, and remove brush strokes from existing paths; open and create brush libraries; and duplicate, move, and delete brushes from the Brushes palette.

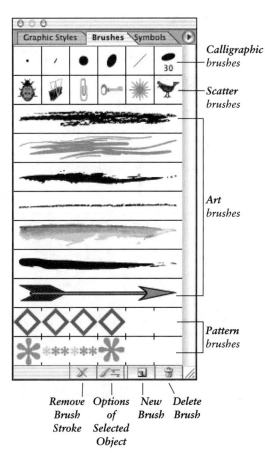

Calligraphic brushes

Scatter brushes

Art brushes

Pattern brushes

Remove Brush Stroke Options of Selected Object New Brush Delete Brush

1 *Press F5 to open/close the* **Brushes** *palette.*

Using brushes

Illustrator's brushes are an illustrator's dream. They combine the ability to draw variable, freehand brush strokes or apply a pattern or objects to a path with all the advantages of vector graphics—small file sizes, resizability, and crisp output.

There are two ways to work with brushes. You can either choose the Paintbrush tool and a brush and draw a shape right off the bat with a brush stroke built into it, or you can apply a brush stroke to an existing path.

To change the contour of a brush stroke, you can use any tool or command you'd normally use to reshape a path, such as the Reshape, Pencil, Smooth, Erase, Add Anchor Point, or Convert Anchor Point tool.

The brushes come in four flavors: **Scatter**, **Calligraphic**, **Art**, and **Pattern**, and they're stored on and accessed from the Brushes palette (F5) **1**. Any brushes that are on the Brushes palette will save with the document. If you modify a brush that was applied to any existing paths in a document, you'll be given the option via an alert box to update those paths with the revised brush. You can also create your own brushes.

As an introduction to the brushes, grab the Paintbrush tool, click one of the brushes on the Brushes palette, and draw (see the instructions on the following page).

If you use a stylus and a pressure-sensitive tablet, the **Paintbrush** tool will respond to pressure. The harder you press on the tablet, the wider the stroke or shape will be.

To draw with the Paintbrush tool:

1. Choose the Paintbrush tool (B), 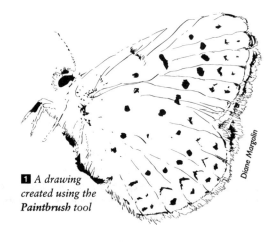 and choose a fill of None.

2. Show the Brushes palette (F5), then click any Calligraphic, Scatter, Art, or Pattern brush.

3. To create open paths, draw freehand lines **1**–**2**. Or to draw closed paths, drag, then Option-drag/Alt-drag for each separate path (release Option/Alt last).

   For quick reshaping, use the Pencil or Paintbrush tool (see page 125). For precise reshaping, use the Direct Selection tool.

Preferences you choose for the Paintbrush affect only future (not existing) brush strokes. You'll learn how to choose options for individual brushes later in this chapter.

To choose preferences for the Paintbrush:

1. Double-click the Paintbrush tool 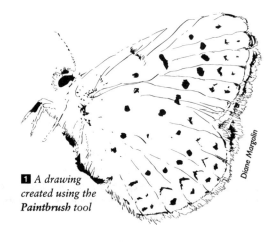 (or choose the tool, then press Return/Enter).

2. Choose a Fidelity value (0.5–20 pixels) **3**. At a low Fidelity setting, more anchor points will be created and the path will follow the movement of your mouse. At a high setting, the path will have fewer anchor points and will be smoother, but will only loosely follow your mouse.

3. Choose a Smoothness value (0–100%). The higher the Smoothness, the fewer the irregularities in the path.

4. Do any of the following:

   Check **Fill new brush strokes** to have new paths be filled with the current fill color.

   Check **Keep Selected** to have paths stay selected right after you draw them.

   Check **Edit Selected Paths** and choose a distance range (2–20 pixels) within which selected paths can be reshaped by the Paintbrush tool (see page 125).

5. Click OK.

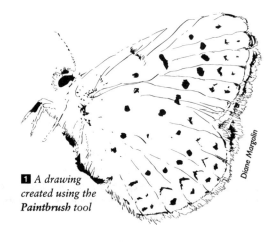

1 *A drawing created using the* **Paintbrush** *tool*

Diane Margolin

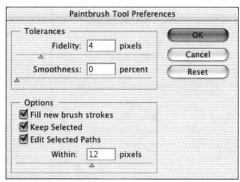

2 *Strokes drawn with an Art brush*

3 *Choose settings for the* **Paintbrush** *in its preferences dialog box.*

Paintbrush Tool

What's the difference?

On the surface, the Pattern and Scatter brushes may look similar, but they have different reasons for being. For a **Scatter** brush, you can make the size, spacing, scatter, and rotation variables more or less random via the Brush Options dialog box. You can't do this with a Pattern brush (they're not called Scatter brushes for nothing). **Pattern** brushes, on the other hand, are made of up to five tiles: Side, Outer Corner, Inner Corner, Start, and End, and they fit more tightly on a path than Scatter brushes.

1 *Select a path.*

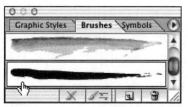

2 *Click a brush on the **Brushes** palette.*

3 *A **Calligraphic** brush stroke is applied.*

You'll learn how to create and modify Scatter, Calligraphic, Art, and Pattern brushes later in this chapter. In these instructions, you'll learn the first step: how to **apply** a **brush stroke** to a path.

To apply a brush stroke to an existing path:

1. Choose Window > Brushes or press F5, if the palette isn't already displayed.

2. Select a path of any kind with any selection tool **1**, then click a brush on the Brushes palette **2**–**7**. You can apply a brush stroke to a type path.
   or
   Click a brush on the brushes palette, then drag the brush onto a path (the path doesn't have to be selected). Release the mouse when the hand pointer is directly over the edge of the object.

➤ If you scale an object that has a brush stroke and the Scale Strokes & Effects option is checked in the Scale dialog box (double-click the Scale tool) or in Illustrator (Edit, in Windows) > Preferences > General, the stroke will resize proportionally. If the Scale Strokes option is unchecked, the brush stroke will scale, but not proportionally.

➤ To select all the paths in an illustration that have brush strokes, choose Select > Object > Brush Strokes.

5 *A **Scatter** brush stroke*

6 *Another **Scatter** brush stroke (made from five birds)*

7 *A **Pattern** brush stroke*

Once an alternate **brush library** is opened, you can apply a brush from that library directly to any path, or you can **add** brushes from the library to the current document's Brushes palette. Also, you can customize any brush from any library.

To add brushes from other libraries:

I. From the Open Brush Library submenu **NEW** on the Brushes palette menu, choose a library name.

or

Choose a library name from the Window > Brush Libraries submenu.

or

To open a library that isn't located in the Adobe Illustrator CS/Presets/Brushes folder, from the Brushes palette menu, **NEW** choose Open Brush Library > Other Library, locate and highlight a library, then click Open.

2. Deselect all the objects in your illustration (Cmd-Shift-A/Ctrl-Shift-A).

3. Click a brush in the library; it will appear on the Brushes palette.

or

Shift-click or Cmd-click/Ctrl-click multiple brushes in the library, then choose Add To Brushes from the library menu **1**–**2**.

or

Drag a brush from the library onto an object in the document window (you don't have to select the object). The brush stroke will appear on the object and the brush will appear on the Brushes palette.

➤ To delete brushes from the Brushes palette, see page 281.

➤ To close a library that's not in a palette group, click its close box. To close a library that's in a group, drag its tab out of the group, then click its close box.

Be persistent

Normally, libraries that you open won't reopen when you relaunch Illustrator. To make a library reopen when you relaunch Illustrator, choose **Persistent** from the library's menu (you need to do this for each library you want to reopen). To save brushes with a document, add them to the Brushes palette by following the instructions at left.

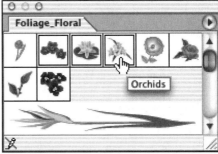

1 *To append multiple brushes, select them, then choose* **Add To Brushes** *from the library menu.*

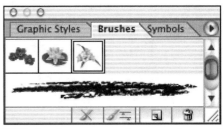

2 *The brushes appear on the current document's* **Brushes** *palette.*

(side margin) **Add Brushes**

1 The original object with a brush stroke

2 The brush stroke is *removed* from the object.

3 The original **brush stroke** on an object

4 The *Expand Appearance* command converted the brush stroke into an object, which is now separate from the original path. (For illustration purposes, we ungrouped the stroke and object and moved them apart.)

When a **brush stroke** is **removed** from a path, you're left with a plain path.

To remove a brush stroke from an object:

1. Select the object or objects from which you want to remove a brush stroke **1**.

2. Click the Remove Brush Stroke button ✖ at the bottom of the Brushes palette **2**.

If you expand a brush stroke (Object > Expand Appearance), it will be converted into editable **outlined paths** and will no longer function as a brush stroke. This means if you subsequently edit the brush, you won't be able to update the brush stroke on that object.

To convert a brush stroke into outlined paths:

1. Select an object that has a brush stroke **3**.

2. Choose Object > Expand Appearance. The brush stroke is now a separate object or objects **4**. The paths will be nested (or double- or triple-nested) in a group sublayer on the Layers palette.

Remove Brush Stroke; Expand Brush Stroke

To choose brush display options:

With **List View** checked on the Brushes palette menu, for each brush there will be a small thumbnail, the brush name, and an icon for the brush type (Calligraphic, Scatter, Art, or Pattern) **1**. With **Thumbnail View** checked, a large thumbnail of each brush's mark or stroke will display, without a name or icon **2**.

To control which **brush types** (categories) display on the palette, choose a brush type from the palette menu (Show...) to check or uncheck that option.

You can **drag** a brush to a different spot on the Brushes palette within its category. To move multiple brushes, select them first (click, then Shift-click a consecutive string or Cmd-click/Ctrl-click them individually).

Creating and modifying brushes

Objects from a **Scatter** brush are placed evenly or randomly along the contour of a path. You can create a Scatter brush from an open or closed path, text character, text outline, blend, or compound path, but not from a gradient, bitmap image (placed or rasterized), mesh, or clipping mask.

To create or modify a Scatter brush:

1. To create a new brush, select one or more objects **3** or a blend, click the New Brush button **⬛** on the Brushes palette, click New Scatter Brush, then click OK. *or*
   To modify an existing Scatter brush, deselect, then double-click the brush on the Brushes palette. Or click a brush, then choose Brush Options from the palette menu.

2. In the Scatter Brush Options dialog box (**1**, next page), enter a new name or modify the existing name.

3. If you're modifying an existing brush that's applied to an object(s) in your illustration, you can check Preview.

4. Each of the four brush properties (Size, Spacing, Scatter, and Rotation) can be set to the Fixed, Random, or Pressure variation via the pop-up menu next to each

Dupe it

To create a variation of an existing brush of any type, either drag the brush over the **New Brush** button on the Brushes palette or click the brush and choose **Duplicate Brush** from the palette menu. Then modify the duplicate.

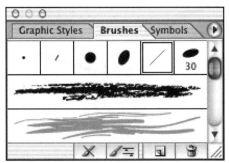

1 *With the **List View** option **checked** on the Brushes palette menu*

2 *With the **Thumbnail** option **checked** on the Brushes palette menu*

3 *The original objects*

Brush Display Options; Create/Modify Scatter Brush

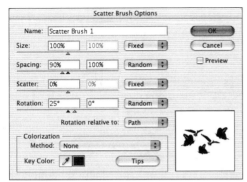

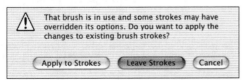

1 *Preview is available in the **Scatter Brush Options** dialog box only if you select a path to which a brush stroke is applied before opening the dialog box.*

2 *The new **Scatter brush** applied to a path*

3 *The same **Scatter brush** after moving the Size sliders apart (Random setting)*

> ⚠ That brush is in use and some strokes may have overridden its options. Do you want to apply the changes to existing brush strokes?
>
> (Apply to Strokes) (Leave Strokes) (Cancel)

4 *This prompt will appear if you **modify** a brush that's currently **applied** to objects in the file.*

option. Choose **Fixed** to use a single, fixed value.

Choose **Random**, then move the sliders (or enter different values in the left and right fields) to define a range within which that property value can vary.

Choose **Pressure** if you're using a graphics tablet. Move the sliders (or enter different values in the left and right fields) to define a range within which that property can respond to stylus pressure. Light pressure will produce a brush property based on the minimum property value (left field); heavy pressure will produce a brush property based on the maximum property value (right field).

Size controls the size of the scatter objects.

Spacing controls the spacing between the scatter objects.

Scatter controls the distance the objects are from either side of the path. When Scatter is set to Fixed, a positive value places all the objects on one side of the path, and a negative value places all the objects on the opposite side of the path. The further the Scatter value is from 0%, the further the objects will be from the path, and the less distinct the path shape.

Rotation controls how much objects can rotate relative to the page or the path. Choose **Page** or **Path** from the **Rotation relative to** pop-up menu for the axis the rotation will be based on.

5. For the Colorization options, see the sidebar on page 281.

6. Click OK **2**–**3**. If the brush was already applied to existing objects in the document, an alert dialog box will appear **4**. Click Apply to Strokes to update those objects with the revised brush, or click Leave Strokes to leave the existing objects unchanged.

➤ You'll find Scatter brushes in the Animals, Decorative, Foliage, Food, Objects, and Sports libraries, and in the Arrows_Standard, Celestial_Stars and ⓝⓔⓦ Sky, Transportation, and Water libraries.

(Continued on the following page)

Create/Modify Scatter Brush

➤ Shift-drag a slider in the Scatter Brush Options dialog box to move its counterpart gradually along with it. Option-drag/Alt-drag a slider to move it and its counterpart away from or toward each other by the same distance from the center.

➤ For a uniform orientation of the scatter objects along a path, set Scatter and Rotation to Fixed, set Scatter to 0°, and choose Rotation relative to: Path **1**–**2**.

1 *The "Fish" Scatter brush, from the Animals_ Animals brush library, applied to a path*

2 *After choosing the Fixed option for Scatter and Rotation and setting Scatter to 0%*

Calligraphic brush strokes vary in thickness as you draw, as in traditional calligraphy media.

To create or modify a Calligraphic brush:

1. To create a new Calligraphic brush, click the New Brush button ▣ on the Brushes palette, click New Calligraphic Brush, (the default setting) then click OK.
or
To modify an existing brush **3**, deselect all objects, then double-click the brush on the Brushes palette **4**.

2. In the Calligraphic Brush Options dialog box, enter a new name or modify the existing name **5**.

3. For an existing brush, check Preview to preview changes on any paths to which the brush is currently applied. The brush shape will also preview in the dialog box.

4. The Angle, Roundness, and Diameter can be set to the Fixed, Random, or Pressure variation via the pop-up menu next to each option.

Choose **Fixed** to keep the value constant.

Choose **Random** and move the Variation slider to define a range within which that brush attribute value can vary. A stroke can range between the value specified for angle, roundness, or diameter, plus or minus the Variation value. For example, a 50° angle with a Random Variation value of 10 could have an angle anywhere between 40° and 60°.

If you're using a graphics tablet, you can choose **Pressure**. Move the Variation

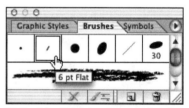

3 *After applying a* **Calligraphic brush** *to a plain object*

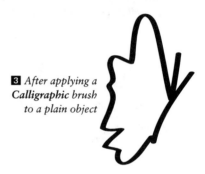

4 *Double-click a brush on the Brushes palette.*

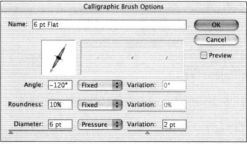

5 *Adjust the settings for a new or existing brush via the* **Calligraphic Brush Options** *dialog box.*

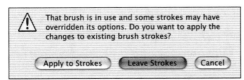

1 *If you modify a brush that has been **applied** to objects in the file, this alert prompt will appear.*

2 *The Angle and Diameter were set to Random in the Calligraphic Brush Options dialog box, and **Apply to Strokes** was clicked when the prompt appeared, causing the brush strokes to update on the object.*

slider to define a range within which that brush attribute can respond to pressure from a stylus. Light pressure will produce a brush attribute based on the value specified for angle, roundness, or diameter minus the Variation value; heavy pressure will produce a brush attribute based on the specified value plus the Variation value.

5. Enter an **Angle** (–180° to 180°), or drag the gray arrowhead in the preview box. The angle controls the thickness of the horizontals and verticals in the stroke. A 0° angle will produce a thin horizontal stroke and a thick vertical stroke; a 90° angle will produce the opposite effect.

6. Enter a **Roundness** value (0–100%), or reshape the tip by dragging either black dot inward or outward on the ellipse.

7. For the brush size, enter a **Diameter** value (0–1296 pt) or drag the slider.

8. Click OK. If the brush was already applied to existing paths in the document, an alert dialog box will appear **1**. Click Apply to Strokes to update the existing strokes with the revised brush, or click Leave Strokes to leave existing strokes unchanged **2**.

Create/Modify Calligraphic Brush

An **Art brush** can be made from one or more objects, including a compound path, but not a gradient, mask, or mesh. When it's applied to a path, an Art brush stroke follows the shape of the path. If you reshape the path, the Art brush stroke will stretch or bend to conform to the new path contour (fun!).

To create or modify an Art brush:

1. To create a new brush, select one or more objects **1**, click the New Brush button **3** on the Brushes palette, click New Art Brush in the New Brush dialog box **2**, then click OK.
   or
   To modify an existing brush, deselect all objects, then double-click that brush on the Brushes palette. Or click an Art brush, then choose Brush Options from the palette menu.

2. For a new brush, enter a name in the Art Brush Options dialog box **3**.

3. Check Preview (available only for existing brushes) to view changes on any paths to which the brush is currently applied.

4. Click a Direction button to control the orientation of the object on the path. The object will be drawn in the direction the arrow is pointing. The direction will be more obvious for objects with a distinct directional orientation, such as text outlines, or for recognizable objects, such as a vase or leaf.

5. Enter a Size: Width to scale the brush. Check Proportional to preserve the proportions of the original object as you change its size.

6. *Optional:* Check Flip Along to reverse the object on the path (left to right) and/or Check Flip Across to reverse the object across the path (up and down).

7. Choose a Colorization option (see the sidebar on the following page).

8. Click OK **4**.

➤ You'll find Art brushes in the Animals, Arrows, Artistic, Decorative, Foliage, Food, Object, Sports, and Transportation sample libraries.

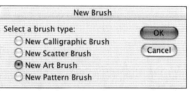

1 *To create a new Art brush, select an object or objects. These objects are text outlines.*

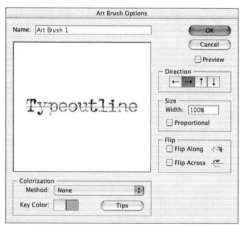

2 *Click New Art Brush.*

3 *Enter a name for a new brush; modify any of the settings for a new or existing brush. Bug: On the Mac, there should be a Key Color eyedropper icon at the bottom of the dialog box; the button is functional even without the icon, however.*

4 *The new Art brush is applied to a path.*

Create/Modify Art Brush

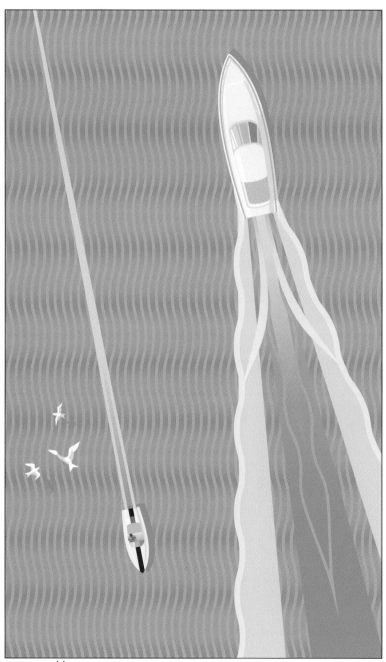

©Nancy Stahl (texture added in Photoshop)

©Nancy Stahl (texture added in Photoshop)

Tyson Foods, Inc.; art director, Steve Pope; design and illustration ©Tom Nikosey

©Tom Nikosey

Thelma's Lemonades; art director, Chris Bohlin, Latitude;
design and illustration ©Tom Nikosey

©Telecom; art director, Julie Albin/
Townsend Agency; illustration, Tom Nikosey

Paramount Farms/California; art director, Brad Donenfeld; design and illustration ©Tom Nikosey

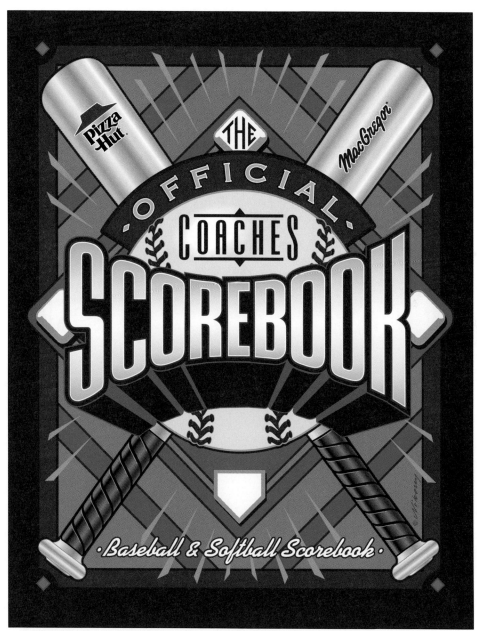

Pizza Hut/MacGregor; design and illustration ©Tom Nikosey

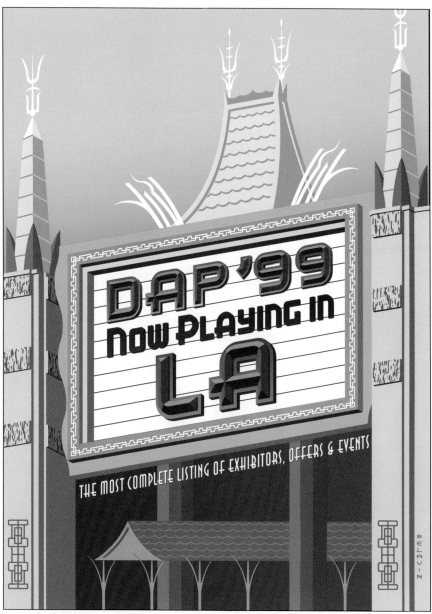

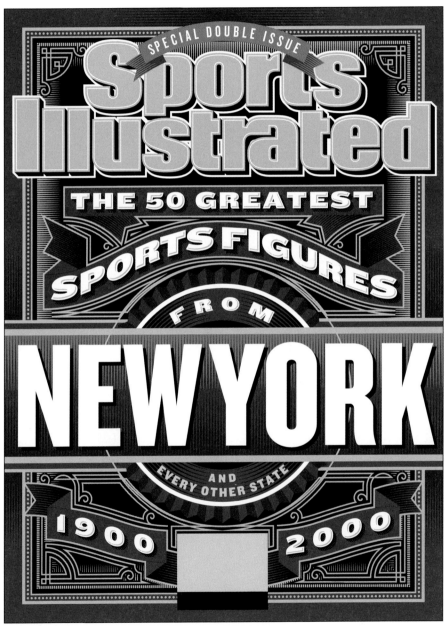

Daniel Pelavin

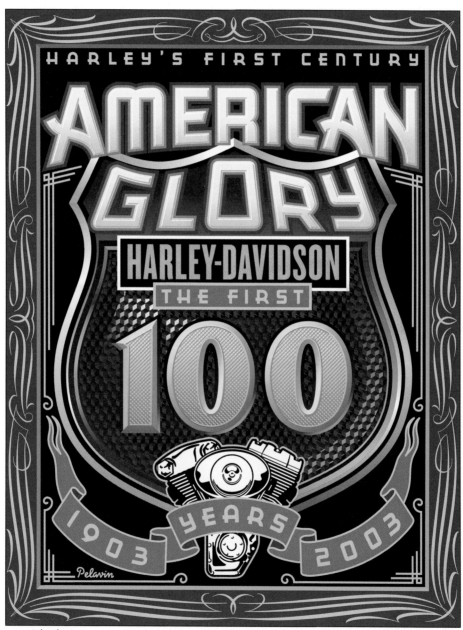

©Daniel Pelavin

Jeanne de la Houssaye

©Dynamic Graphics, illustration by Jeanne de la Houssaye

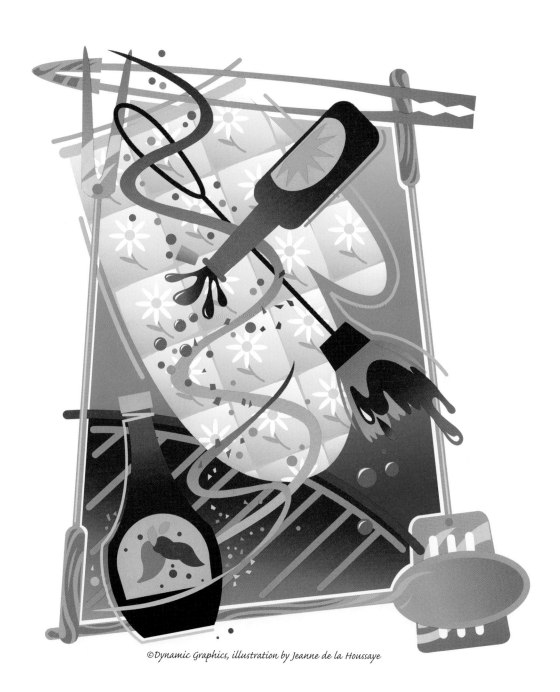

©Dynamic Graphics, illustration by Jeanne de la Houssaye

The American West

As settlers moved west, they came into conflict with American Indians. After the last armed Indian resistance was defeated, the U.S. government moved many tribes to reservations.

The completion of the transcontinental railroad in 1868 opened the West to more settlement. Gold and silver strikes also drew people hoping to get rich.

The railroads helped make the rise of the Cattle Kingdom possible. Cowboys drove huge herds of cattle from ranches to railway stations to be shipped East.

Farmers settled the Great Plains in large numbers. They overcame great hardships to make the Plains the breadbasket of America.

©Kenneth Batelman

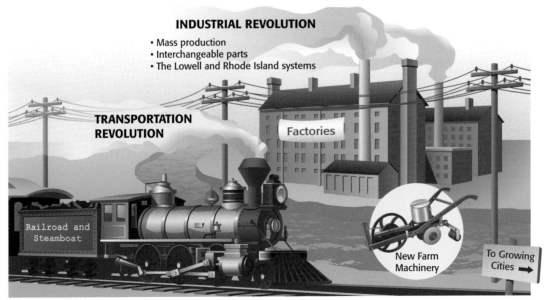

INDUSTRIAL REVOLUTION
- Mass production
- Interchangeable parts
- The Lowell and Rhode Island systems

TRANSPORTATION REVOLUTION

Factories

Railroad and Steamboat

New Farm Machinery

To Growing Cities →

©Kenneth Batelman

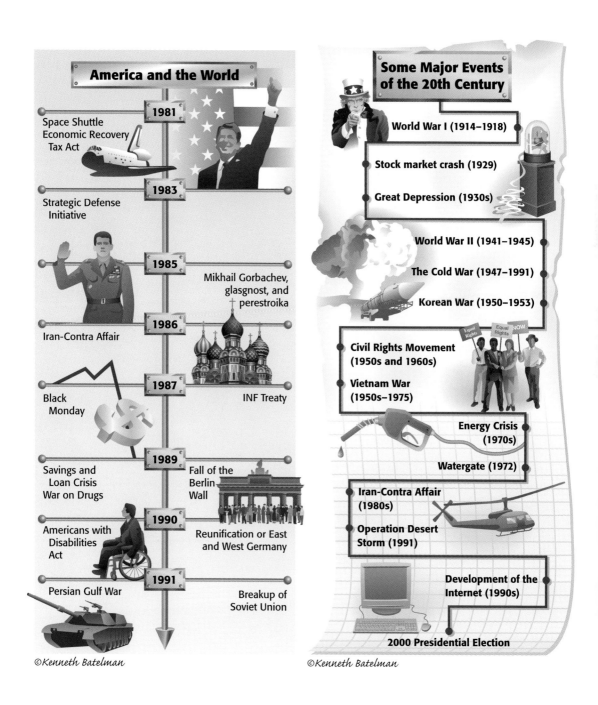

America and the World

1981
Space Shuttle
Economic Recovery
Tax Act

1983
Strategic Defense
Initiative

1985
Mikhail Gorbachev,
glasgnost, and
perestroika

1986
Iran-Contra Affair

1987
Black
Monday

INF Treaty

1989
Savings and
Loan Crisis
War on Drugs

Fall of the
Berlin
Wall

1990
Americans with
Disabilities
Act

Reunification or East
and West Germany

1991
Persian Gulf War

Breakup of
Soviet Union

©Kenneth Batelman

Some Major Events of the 20th Century

World War I (1914–1918)

Stock market crash (1929)

Great Depression (1930s)

World War II (1941–1945)

The Cold War (1947–1991)

Korean War (1950–1953)

Civil Rights Movement
(1950s and 1960s)

Vietnam War
(1950s–1975)

Energy Crisis
(1970s)

Watergate (1972)

Iran-Contra Affair
(1980s)

Operation Desert
Storm (1991)

Development of the
Internet (1990s)

2000 Presidential Election

©Kenneth Batelman

©Kenneth Batelman

©Kenneth Batelman

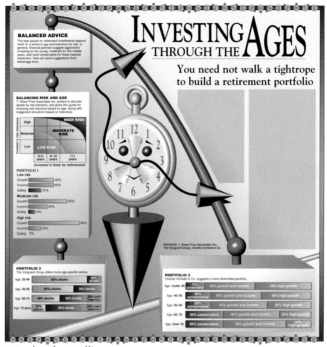

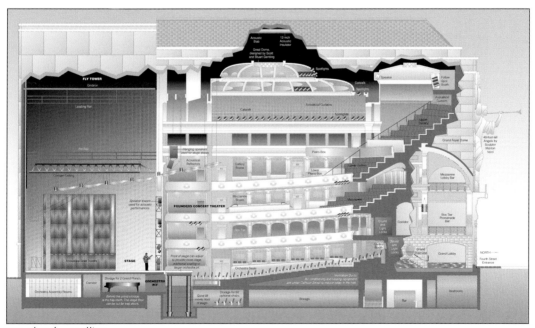

CITY OF ALEXANDRIA, VIRGINIA

Mark Stein

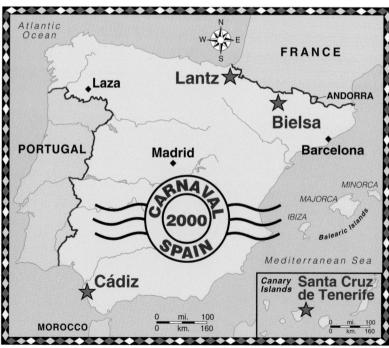

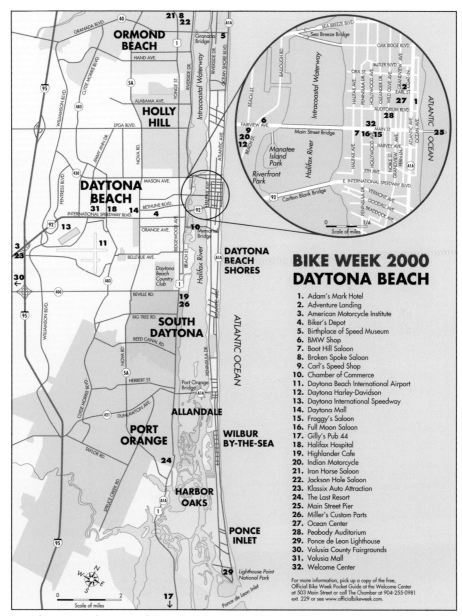

BIKE WEEK 2000
DAYTONA BEACH

1. Adam's Mark Hotel
2. Adventure Landing
3. American Motorcycle Institute
4. Biker's Depot
5. Birthplace of Speed Museum
6. BMW Shop
7. Boot Hill Saloon
8. Broken Spoke Saloon
9. Carl's Speed Shop
10. Chamber of Commerce
11. Daytona Beach International Airport
12. Daytona Harley-Davidson
13. Daytona International Speedway
14. Daytona Mall
15. Froggy's Saloon
16. Full Moon Saloon
17. Gilly's Pub 44
18. Halifax Hospital
19. Highlander Cafe
20. Indian Motorcycle
21. Iron Horse Saloon
22. Jackson Hole Saloon
23. Klassix Auto Attraction
24. The Last Resort
25. Main Street Pier
26. Miller's Custom Parts
27. Ocean Center
28. Peabody Auditorium
29. Ponce de Leon Lighthouse
30. Volusia County Fairgrounds
31. Volusia Mall
32. Welcome Center

For more information, pick up a copy of the free,
Official Bike Week Pocket Guide at the Welcome Center
at 503 Main Street or call The Chamber at 904-255-0981
ext. 229 or see www.officialbikeweek.com.

©Mark Stein, Mark Stein Studios

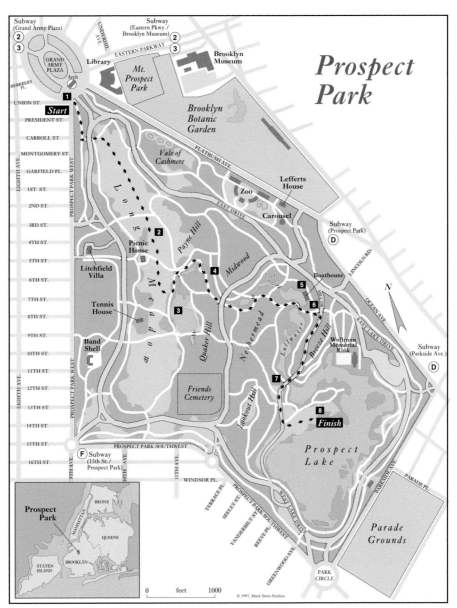

Prospect Park

©Mark Stein, Mark Stein Studios

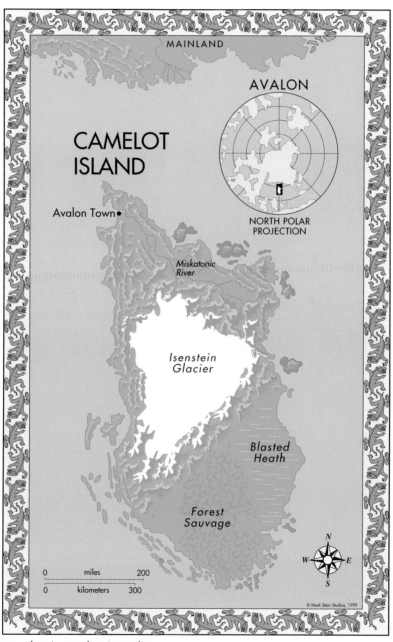

CAMELOT ISLAND

MAINLAND

AVALON

Avalon Town•

NORTH POLAR PROJECTION

Miskatonic River

Isenstein Glacier

Blasted Heath

Forest Sauvage

| 0 | miles | 200 |
| 0 | kilometers | 300 |

N
W E
S

© Mark Stein Studios, 1999

Mark Stein

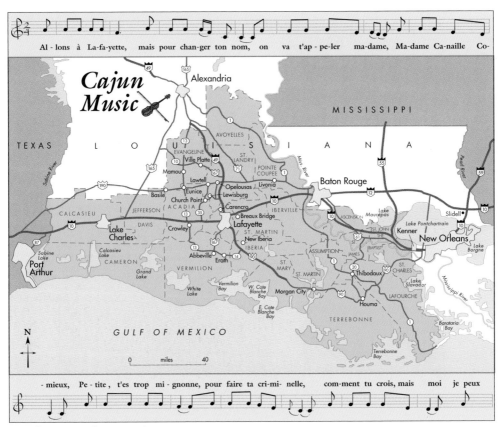

Al - lons à La-fa-yette, mais pour chan-ger ton nom, on va t'ap-pe-ler ma-dame, Ma-dame Ca-naille Co-

-mieux, Pe - tite , t'es trop mi - gnonne, pour faire ta cri-mi- nelle, com-ment tu crois, mais moi je peux

The Colorization options

From the Colorization pop-up menu (available for all brush types except Calligraphic), choose any of these options to change the colors the brush will paint with:

(**None** to leave the colors unchanged.)

Tints to change black areas in the brush stroke to the current stroke color at 100% and non-black areas to tints of the current stroke color. White areas stay white. Use for grayscale or spot colors.

Tints and Shades to change colors in the brush stroke to tints of the current stroke color. Black and white areas don't change.

Hue Shift to apply the current stroke color to areas that contain the most frequently used color on the object (called the key color) and to change other colors in the brush stroke to related hues. Use for multicolored brushes.

If you're editing the brush itself (not a brush stroke), you can click the **key color** eyedropper, then click a color in the preview area of the dialog box to change the key color. (Leetle bug: The Eyedropper icon may not show up, but click where it's supposed to be—it'll work.)

Click **Tips** in the Stroke Options dialog box to learn more **1**.

If you **delete** (from the Brushes palette) a **brush** that's currently applied to any objects in your illustration, you'll be given the option via an alert dialog box to expand the brush strokes or remove them from those objects.

To delete a brush from the Brushes palette:

1. Deselect all objects in your illustration.
2. Click the brush you want to delete.
   or
   To delete all the brushes that aren't being used in the file, choose Select All Unused from the Brushes palette menu.
3. Click the Delete Brush button 🗑 on the Brushes palette, or choose Delete Brush from the palette menu.
4. If the brush isn't currently applied to any objects in the illustration, click **Yes** when the alert dialog box appears **2**.

   If the brush is currently applied to any objects in the current document, click **Expand Strokes** in the alert dialog box **3** to expand the brush strokes (they'll look the same, but won't function as brush strokes), or click **Remove Strokes** to remove them from the objects.

➤ To restore the deleted brush to the palette, choose Undo immediately. Or if the brush came from a library, you can add it again (see page 274).

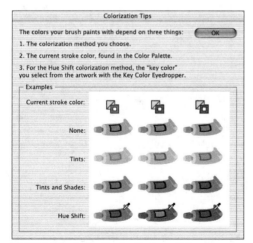

1 *Click **Tips** in the Stroke Options dialog box to read these **colorization tips**.*

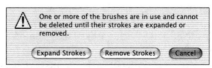

2 *This alert dialog box will appear if you **delete** a brush that isn't being used in the document.*

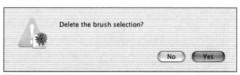

3 *If the brush is currently applied to any **objects** in the current document, this alert dialog box will appear.*

Delete a Brush

Pattern brushes render patterns along the edge of a closed or open path, and can be used to create custom frames, borders, or other decorative elements. You can use up to five different-shaped tile pieces when you create a path pattern: a side tile, an outer corner tile, an inner corner tile, a start tile, and an end tile. Each type of tile adapts to fit its assigned location on the path. Here's how to design your own tiles.

To create tiles for a Pattern brush:

1. Draw closed path shapes for the side pattern tile. Try to limit the tile to about an inch wide, 2 inches at the most. You can resize it later via the Pattern Brush Options dialog box.

2. Because Pattern brushes place side tiles perpendicular to the path, you should rotate any design that happens to be taller than it is wide. To do this, choose the Selection tool, select the shapes for the side tile, double-click the Rotate tool, enter 90° for the Angle, then click OK.

3. Draw separate shapes for the corner, start, and end tiles , if necessary, to complete the design. Corner tiles should form a square, and they should be exactly the same height as the side tile.

4. Choose the Selection tool, then select one of the tiles that you created in the previous step.

5. Drag the selection onto the Swatches palette , then deselect the objects.

6. Double-click the new swatch, then enter a Swatch Name. We suggest typing words such as "side," "outer," "start," and "end" after the tile name to help you remember its placement. Click OK 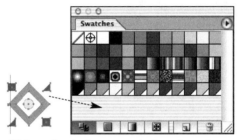.

7. Repeat steps 4 through 6 for the other tiles.

8. Follow the steps on the next page to make the new tiles that you saved to the Swatches palette into a Pattern brush .

➤ When applied to a path, corner tiles will be rotated 90° to follow the path at each point where the path direction changes,

Start tile   *Side tile*   *Outer corner tile*

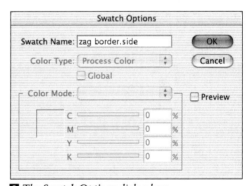

1 *Four of the tiles for a Pattern brush*

End tile

2 *Drag the tile shape onto the **Swatches** palette.*

3 *The **Swatch Options** dialog box*

4 *The pattern tiles made into a Pattern brush and then applied to a path*

speedy recoloring

Apply **global** process fill and stroke colors to your pattern tile shapes, and name the colors appropriately so they can be readily associated with each tile. Then, to recolor the tiles, modify the global process colors.

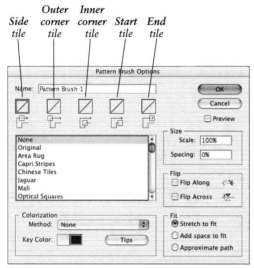

Side tile Outer corner tile Inner corner tile Start tile End tile

1 *The Pattern Brush Options dialog box*

starting after the one in the upper left corner.

➤ To make geometric shapes look more hand drawn, before making shapes into a Pattern brush, apply Effect > Distort & Transform > Roughen at a low setting.

To create a Pattern brush:

1. Create tiles for the Pattern brush (instructions start on the previous page).

2. Click the New Brush button ⬜ on the Brushes palette, click New Pattern Brush in the New Brush dialog box, and click OK.

3. Enter a Name.

4. Click a tile button (along the top) to assign a pattern to that part of a path, then click a pattern name on the scroll list **1**. (The scroll list displays the pattern tiles that are currently on the Swatches palette.) Repeat for the other tile buttons, if desired. The icons under the buttons are there to help you distinguish one type of tile from another. To assign no pattern for a position on the path, choose None. For a round object, you'll need to assign only a side tile.

5. Click OK. Now you can apply the brush to a path. To modify a Pattern brush, see the instructions on the following page.

➤ If you reshape a path that has a Pattern brush stroke, the pattern will reshape along with the path, and corner and side tiles will be added or removed as needed.

➤ Effect menu commands can be applied to objects to be used in a pattern tile, and also to an object to which a Pattern brush stroke is applied.

➤ You'll find Pattern brushes in the Animal, Arrow, Border, Celestial_Stars and Sky, Circular, and Decorative libraries.

To edit a Pattern brush via its options dialog box:

1. Deselect all objects. Then, on the Brushes palette, double-click the Pattern brush you want to modify; or click a Pattern brush, then choose Brush Options from the palette menu.

2. Check Preview to preview changes on any paths to which the Pattern brush is currently applied.

3. To change tile patterns, click a **tile** button, then click a different name on the scroll list **1** (the change won't preview). Repeat for the other tile buttons, if desired. Use the icons under the buttons to distinguish the tiles from one another. To assign no pattern for a tile position, choose None. For a round object, you need to assign only one tile.

➤ To restore the settings to the currently selected tile button (from when the dialog box was opened), click Original on the scroll list.

4. Press Tab as you proceed from field to field as you do any of the following:

Change the Size: **Scale** percentage for the pattern tiles (1–10000%).

To adjust the blank spacing between pattern tiles, change the Size: **Spacing** percentage (0–10000%).

To change the orientation of the pattern tiles on the path, check **Flip Along** and/or **Flip Across**. Be sure to preview this—you may not like the results.

In the Fit area, click **Stretch to fit** to have Illustrator shorten or lengthen the tiles, where necessary, to fit on the path. Or click **Add space to fit** to have Illustrator add blank space between tiles, where necessary, to fit the pattern along the path, factoring in the Spacing amount, if one was entered.

For a rectangular path, if you click **Approximate path,** the pattern tiles will be applied slightly inside or outside the path, rather than centered on the path, in order to make the tiling more even.

5. For the **Colorization** option, see the sidebar on page 281.

6. Click OK. If the Pattern brush is currently applied to any paths in the file, an alert dialog box will appear. Click Apply to Strokes to update the existing strokes with the revised brush, or click Leave Strokes to leave them unchanged.

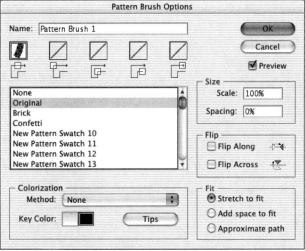

1 *Using the* **Pattern Brush Options** *dialog box, you can reassign different tiles and adjust the Size, Flip, Fit, and Colorization options.*

1 *The original Pattern brush stroke*

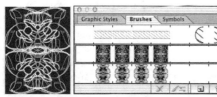

2 *Drag the brush from the Brushes palette onto the artboard. (On the palette, pattern tiles are arranged from left to right in this order: outer corner, side, inner corner, start, and end.)*

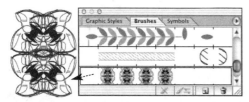

3 *Edit the pattern manually...*

4 *...and then update the brush on the Brushes palette.*

5 *The edited Pattern brush stroke*

In addition to editing a brush via its options dialog box, you can **edit a brush** by reshaping or recoloring it **manually**.

To edit a Scatter, Art, or Pattern brush manually:

1. Deselect all objects, then drag a brush from the Brushes palette onto a blank area of the artboard **1**–**2**.

2. To recolor or transform the entire brush, select it using the Selection tool, then perform your edits **3**. To recolor or transform individual objects within the brush or individual Pattern brush tiles, select them using the Direct Selection tool or the Layers palette. For a Pattern brush, ungroup it before editing it.

3. For a **Scatter** or **Art** brush:

Choose the Selection tool (V), and select the modified brush object or objects. Start dragging the objects onto the Brushes palette, hold down Option/Alt when you pass over the Brushes palette, then release the mouse when the pointer is over the original brush icon and the icon is highlighted. The options dialog box will open for that brush. Proceed to step 4.

➤ To make the revised object(s) into a new brush, separate from the original, drag it (or them) into the palette without holding down Option/Alt.

For a **Pattern** brush:

Start dragging each new pattern tile shape (corner, side, end, etc.), hold down Option/Alt as you pass over the Brushes palette, and release the mouse when the new tile is over a specific tile slot to replace only that highlighted tile **4**. The tile slots are arranged in the following order: outer corner, side, inner corner, start, and end. The Pattern Brush Options dialog box will open with the new tile in the chosen tile position.

4. Click OK. If the brush is currently applied to any paths in the file, an alert dialog box will open. Click **Apply to Strokes** to update the brush stroke on the palette **5**.

By organizing brushes into a **library,** you'll be able to locate them easily and also use them in other files.

NEW **To create a new brush library:**

1. Create brushes in a document or move them to the current document's Brushes palette from other libraries.

2. From the Brushes palette menu, choose Save Brush Library.

3. Enter a name. On the Mac, leave the location as Applications/Adobe Illustrator CS/Presets/Brushes. In Windows, leave the location as Win: Program Files\Adobe\Illustrator CS\ Presets\Brushes.

4. Click Save.

5. The new library can be opened from the Open Brush Library > Other Library submenu on the Brushes palette menu.

1 *To create this pattern, Diane Margolin turned on the "Stretch to fit" option, and used side, outer corner, and inner corner tile shapes.*

2 *A pattern applied to an oval*

1 *Select an object or objects to which a brush has been applied.*

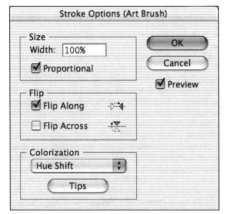

2 *Choose **Stroke Options** for the brush.*

3 *The **brush stroke** is altered on the **object**.*

If you edit a brush, every object to which that brush has been applied will update to reflect the changes. If you want to **modify** a **brush stroke** on a selected object or objects without editing the brush itself, follow these instructions instead. The Colorization option is fun to play with.

To change the stroke options for an individual object:

1. Select one or more objects to which the *same* brush is currently applied **1**.

2. If you want to recolor the brush stroke, choose a stroke color now.

3. Click the Options of Selected Object button on the Brushes palette.

4. Check Preview **2** (see also **1**–**2**, next page).

5. For a Scatter brush stroke, follow step 4 starting on page 276.

   For a Calligraphic brush stroke, follow steps 4–7 on pages 278–279.

   For an Art brush stroke, follow steps 5–6 on page 280.

   For a Pattern brush stroke, follow step 4 on page 284.

6. From the **Colorization** pop-up menu (this is *not* available for Calligraphic brushes), choose:

   None to leave the colors unchanged.

   Tints to change black areas in the brush stroke to the stroke color at 100% and nonblack areas to tints of the current stroke color. White areas stay white.

   Tints and Shades to change colors in the brush stroke to tints of the current stroke color. Black and white areas stay as they are.

   Hue Shift to apply the current stroke color to areas containing the most frequently used color on the object (the key color) and to change other colors in the brush stroke to related hues.

   Click Tips if you want to see an illustration of the Colorization options.

(Continued on the following page)

7. Click OK (**3**, previous page). Only the selected object or objects will change; the brush itself on the Brushes palette will not.

➤ To restore the original brush stroke to the object, select the object, click a different brush on the Brushes palette, then click back on the original brush.

The **Duplicate Brush** command allows you to create a variation of an existing brush— a slimmer or fatter version, for example.

To duplicate a brush:

1. Deselect all objects, then click the brush you want to duplicate **3**.

2. Choose Duplicate Brush from the palette menu.
or
Drag the selected brush over the New Brush button **⬜**.

The word "copy" will be appended to the brush name **4**. To modify the brush, see the individual instructions for that brush type earlier in this chapter.

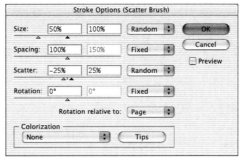

1 *Stroke Options for a Calligraphic brush*

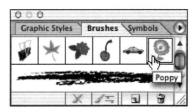

2 *Stroke options for a Scatter brush*

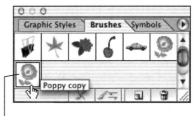

3 *Click the brush you want to duplicate.*

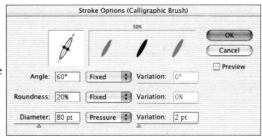

4 *The duplicate brush appears after the last brush icon in the same category.*

In this chapter you'll learn how to work with symbols, which are objects that are stored on the Symbols palette. You'll learn how to place symbol instances into a document either by dragging or by using the Symbol Sprayer tool and how to edit those instances using the Symbol Shifter, Scruncher, Sizer, Spinner, Stainer, Screener, and Styler tools. You'll also learn how to create, rename, duplicate, edit, and delete symbols.

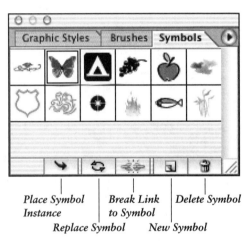

Place Symbol   Break Link   Delete Symbol
Instance   to Symbol
     Replace Symbol   New Symbol

1 *Use the Symbols palette to save and delete symbols and place and replace symbols instances.*

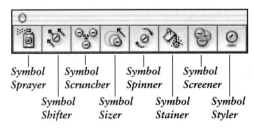

Symbol   Symbol   Symbol   Symbol
Sprayer   Scruncher   Spinner   Screener

     Symbol   Symbol   Symbol   Symbol
     Shifter   Sizer   Stainer   Styler

2 *The symbolism tools*

Using the Symbols palette

Any object that you can create in Illustrator can be stored on the **Symbols** palette (Shift-F11) **1** and reused in any document. To place an **instance** of a symbol onto the artboard, all you have to do is drag it out of the Symbols palette.

To place multiple instances of a symbol, drag or hold the mouse down with the **Symbol Sprayer** tool **2**. A collection of instances in its own bounding box, called a **symbol set,** will be created. With symbols, you can create complex art quickly and easily. Spray a tree symbol, spray a grass symbol, then spray a flower symbol to create a flowering forest meadow with just a few mouse clicks.

Using any of the other symbolism tools (**Symbol Shifter, Scruncher, Sizer, Spinner, Stainer, Screener,** or **Styler**), you can change the density, position, stacking order, size, rotation, transparency, color tint, or style of multiple symbol instances in a selected symbol set, while still maintaining the link to the original symbol. Because of this link, if you edit the original symbol, any instances of that symbol in the document will update to reflect the change automatically. Also, you can apply styles, effects, or tranformations to a single instance or to a whole set.

(Continued on the following page)

Symbols Palette

Another advantage of using symbols is that each time you create an instance, Illustrator uses the original symbol instead of creating individual objects multiple times. For example, say you draw a boat, save it as a symbol in the Symbols palette, and then drag with the Symbol Sprayer to create multiple instances in a symbol set. Even though 50 instances of the boat may appear in the symbol set, Illustrator defines the object in the document code only once. This not only saves you time, it also keeps the illustration file size down. When outputting files to the Web in SVG (Scalable Vector Graphics) or SWF (Flash) format, file size is critical. Because each symbol is defined only once in the exported SVG image or Flash animation, the size of the export file is kept small, significantly reducing its download time.

When you drag a symbol out of the Symbols palette, a copy of the symbol (called an **instance**) is made automatically; the original symbol remains on the palette. To begin with, you can use the default symbols on the Symbols palette. On page 292, you'll learn how to create your own symbols.

To place symbol instances into a document one at a time:

Drag a symbol from the Symbols palette onto the artboard **1**–**2** (Shift-F11 opens and closes the palette).
or
Click a symbol on the Symbols palette, then click the Place Symbol Instance button ➘ on the palette. The instance will appear in the center of the document window.

Repeat to add more instances. Each instance is automatically linked to its original symbol. To demonstrate this point, select an instance on the artboard, then look at the Symbols palette; its original symbol will be selected automatically. You'll learn how to preserve or break this link later in this chapter.

➤ To duplicate an instance, Option-drag/ Alt-drag the instance on the artboard. To place many instances of a symbol quickly, it's much more efficient (and fun) to use the Symbol Sprayer tool (see page 296).

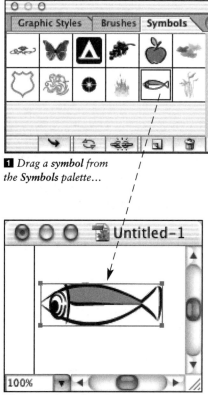

1 *Drag a symbol from the Symbols palette…*

2 *…onto the artboard.*

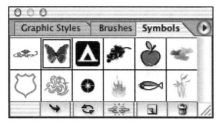

1 *The Symbols palette in Thumbnail View*

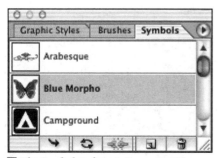

2 *The Symbols palette in Small List View*

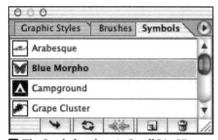

3 *The Symbols palette in Large List View*

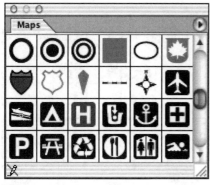

4 *The Adobe Illustrator* **Maps** *symbol library*

To change the Symbols palette display:

From the palette menu, choose:

Thumbnail View 1 to display symbols as swatches. Use tool tips to learn the names.
or
Small List View 2 to display symbols as small swatches with their names listed.
or
Large List View 3 to display symbols as large swatches with their names listed.

➤ Choose Sort by Name from the palette menu to sort the symbols alphabetically by name.

Already bored with the default selection on the Symbols palette? Take a peek at some of the Adobe **symbol libraries.**

To use symbols from other libraries:

1. From the Open Symbol Library submenu **NEW** on the Symbol palette menu (or the Window > Symbol Libraries submenu), choose a library. A library palette will open **4**–**5**.

2. Click a symbol on the library palette to add it to the Symbols palette. Or to add multiple symbols, click the first symbol in a series of consecutive symbols, then Shift-click the last symbol in the series (or Cmd-click/Ctrl-click nonconsecutive symbols), then drag them to the Symbols palette.

➤ If you drag a symbol from a library into your document, the symbol will appear on the Symbols palette automatically.

➤ To save a symbol library, see page 293.

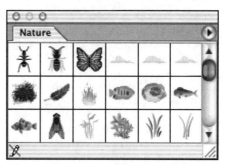

5 *The Adobe Illustrator* **Nature** *symbol library*

Symbols Palette Display; Other Libraries

When you apply a **different symbol** to an existing instance in a document, any transformations, transparency, or effects that were applied to the instance will also appear in the replacement.

To apply a different symbol to an existing instance:

1. Choose the Selection tool, then click an instance in your document .

2. On the Symbols palette, click a symbol.

3. Click the Replace Symbol button ⟳ on the palette 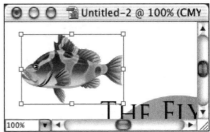.
   or
   Choose Replace Symbol from the palette menu.

Now that you're acquainted with the Symbols palette, it's time to get personal and start **creating your own symbols.** Any Illustrator object—path, compound path, mesh, embedded raster image, text, group of objects, or even another symbol—can be made into a new symbol. Within reason, that is. If you're going to use the Symbol Sprayer to spray a gazillion instances of a symbol, it's probably wise to create the symbol out of an object that's not overly complex.

Note: If the object (to become a symbol) contains a brush stroke, blend, effect, style, or other symbols, those attributes will become fixed parts of the new symbol, which means they can't be reedited in a linked instance of that symbol (see page 294).

To create a symbol from an object in your artwork:

1. Create an object, scale it to the desired size, and leave it selected. Or select an existing object in your document ❸.

2. Choose the Selection tool, then drag the object onto the Symbols palette ❹.
   or
   Click the New Symbol button ◱ at the bottom of the palette.
   or
   Choose New Symbol from the palette menu, type a name, then click OK.

To rename the new symbol, follow the instructions on the next page.

Replace Symbol; Create New Symbol

❶ *Click an **instance** in your document,...*

❷ *...click a different symbol on the Symbols palette, then click the **Replace Symbol** button on the palette. The fly is replaced with the fish.*

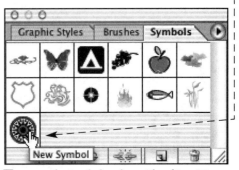

❸ *Drag an object or group from the document...*

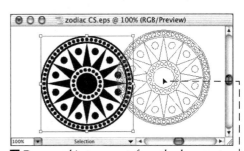

❹ *...onto the Symbols palette. The object (**New Symbol**) appears on the palette.*

What's in a name?

Symbol names are visible when the Small List view or List view is chosen as the display option for the Symbols palette. You'll also see a name (tool tip) if you move the pointer over a symbol icon. To **rename** a symbol, double-click a symbol on the Symbols palette, change the name, then click OK.

You can **save** the symbols currently on the Symbols palette into a **library.**

To save a symbol library: NEW

1. Choose Save Symbol Library from the Symbol palette menu.

2. Type a new name for the library in the Save As field, choose a location for it, then click Save.

3. To open the library you saved or any other custom library, from the Symbols palette menu, choose Open Symbol Library > Other Library (or choose Window > Symbol Libraries > Other Library), locate and click the library you want to open, then click Open.

If you **delete** a **symbol** that's linked to instances on the artboard, an alert dialog box will appear. At that point you can choose to expand the instances, delete the instances, or cancel the deletion.

To delete a symbol:

1. Drag the symbol you want to delete over the Delete Symbol button 🗑 at the bottom of the palette.
   or
   Click a symbol on the Symbols palette, click the Delete Symbol button 🗑 at the bottom of the palette, or choose Delete Symbol from the palette menu, then click Yes.

2. An alert dialog box will appear if the document contains any linked instances of the symbol being deleted **1**. Click Expand Instances to expand the linked instances into standard, nonlinked objects, or click Delete Instances to delete the linked instances (or click Cancel to cancel the whole thing).

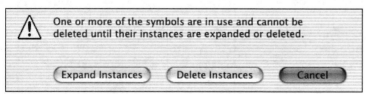

1 *This prompt will appear if you try to **delete** a symbol that's **linked** to instances on the artboard.*

To modify instances:

Modifications that are made to an instance or set have no effect on the symbol or the link to the symbol the instance originated from. You can modify an instance or set in the following ways **1**–**2**: move it; transform it (via the Transform palette, by dragging its selection handles, or via an Object menu > Transform command); change its opacity; change its blending mode; or apply styles or effects to it. You can't recolor it directly.

To modify any live effects that were applied to an instance or set after it was placed into the artwork, double-click the effect on the Appearance palette, then change the settings.

You can also use the Symbol Shifter, Symbol Scruncher, Symbol Sizer, Symbol Spinner, Symbol Stainer, Symbol Screener, or Symbol Styler tool to modify instances or sets. You'll learn about these tools later in this chapter.

➤ Expanding an instance breaks the link between the instance and the original symbol (see page 308).

On the next page you'll learn how to edit a symbol (we're talking there about editing the original symbol—not an instance). When you do this, you may want to work on a **duplicate** of the **symbol** rather than the original.

To duplicate a symbol:

On the Symbols palette, drag the symbol that you want to duplicate over the New Symbol button ▣ at the bottom of the palette **3**–**4**.
or
Click the symbol that you want to duplicate, then choose Duplicate Symbol from the palette menu.

The duplicate symbol will appear after the last symbol.

➤ You can drag a symbol icon to a different position on the palette.

➤ Option-drag/Alt-drag one symbol over another to copy the first symbol and remove the second symbol.

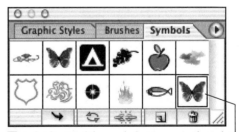

1 *The original* **instance** *of a symbol*

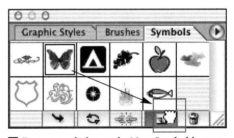

2 *After* **enlarging** *the instance, lowering its* **opacity**, *and applying the Drop Shadow* **effect** *to it*

3 *Drag a symbol over the* **New Symbol** *button.*

4 *A* **duplicate** *of the symbol appears on the palette.*

1 *The original* **instance**

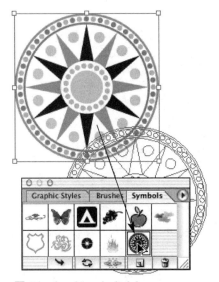

2 *After* **breaking** *the* **link** *between the instance and the original symbol, the former instance is* **edited** *(recolored, in this case), and then Option/ Alt dragged over the original symbol.*

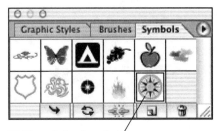

3 *The* **redefined** *symbol*

To edit a symbol, the first step is to break the link between the symbol and one of its instances. Next, you'll modify the former instance. And finally, you'll use that object to **redefine** the original **symbol.**

Beware! Every instance is linked to its original symbol. If you redefine a symbol, those changes will be applied to any and all instances in the document that originated from that symbol. This makes for efficient document editing, of course, but it can also wreak havoc if you don't keep it in mind.

To redefine a symbol:

1. Create an instance of a symbol (or a duplicate of a symbol) in the artwork **1** and keep it selected. To duplicate a symbol, see the previous set of instructions.

2. Click the Break Link button ⚌ at the bottom of the Symbols palette.

3. Modify the resulting object (former instance) to your liking, as you would any object.

4. With the object still selected:

   Option-drag/Alt-drag the object over the symbol you want to redefine on the Symbols palette **2**–**3**.
   or
   Click a symbol on the palette, then choose Redefine Symbol from the palette menu.

   All instances that are currently linked to the now redefined symbol will automatically update to reflect the changes that were made to the symbol. And any transformations, effects, opacity values, brush strokes, etc. that were applied to those instances before the symbol was redefined will be preserved.

➤ To create a new symbol instead of redefining an existing symbol, drag the object onto a blank area of the Symbols palette.

Redefine Symbol

Using the symbolism tools

There are eight symbolism tools 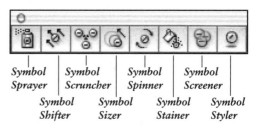. If the Adobe gang couldn't think of a name for a tool that began with the letter "S," the tool got scrapped (just kidding; no e-mails on this, please).

The Symbol Sprayer tool is used to quickly spray multiple instances of the same symbol onto the artboard. Each time you use this tool, the objects that result are grouped together into what is called a **symbol set.** The Symbol Sprayer can also be used to delete instances from a set.

The other symbolism tools (Symbol Shifter, Symbol Scruncher, Symbol Sizer, Symbol Spinner, Symbol Stainer, Symbol Screener, and Symbol Styler), which are discussed individually on the following pages, are used to modify the position, size, orientation, color, transparency, or style of a symbol instance or symbol set while preserving the link to the original symbol.

First, the **Symbol Sprayer.** You can choose from a slew of options for this tool, but before you get into that, do some spraying.

To use the Symbol Sprayer tool:

1. Choose the Symbol Sprayer tool (Shift-S) (looks like a can of spray paint).

2. Click a symbol on the Symbols palette.

3. Do any of the following:

   Click once; or click and hold the mouse in the same spot **2**; or drag across the artboard (**2**–**3**, next page). As you drag, a wireframe representation of the instances will display on the artboard. When you release the mouse, the fully drawn instances will appear in a set with a bounding box around it.

   To remove any instances, select the set, then Option-click/Alt-click or Option-drag/Alt-drag inside the set.

➤ To move a whole symbol set on the artboard, drag one of the objects in the set with the Selection tool. To transform all the instances in a symbol set, drag any of the handles on its bounding box (see page 105).

1 The **symbolism** tools, shown on a tearoff toolbar

Symbol Sprayer	*Symbol Scruncher*	*Symbol Spinner*	*Symbol Screener*
Symbol Shifter	*Symbol Sizer*	*Symbol Stainer*	*Symbol Styler*

2 These multiple instances were placed on an artboard by **holding down** the Symbol Sprayer tool in one spot. When we created the original symbol, we gave it an opacity of 50%. You can also drag with the tool.

The **Symbolism Tools Options** dialog box lets you choose global settings that apply to all the symbolism tools, as well as settings that apply only to individual tools. Individual tool settings are covered in the instructions for each tool on the following pages.

To choose global properties for the symbolism tools:

1. If you're going to adjust the Density for the Symbol Sprayer, you may want to select a symbol set in your document now. That way, you will be able to preview the Density changes while the dialog box is open.

2. To open the Symbolism Tools Options dialog box, double-click any symbolism tool.

3. To choose a default size for all the symbolism tools, enter a value in the **Diameter** field or press the arrowhead and drag the Diameter slider .

4. To adjust the rate at which the tools apply their effect, choose an **Intensity** value (the higher the Intensity, the more quickly an effect is applied). Or to have a stylus control this option instead, check Use Pressure Pen.

5. To specify how close instances will be to each other when applied with the Symbol Sprayer tool, choose a **Symbol Set Density** value ❷–❸. The higher the Symbol Set Density, the more tightly the instances will be packed within each set. This option will preview in any sets that are currently selected in your document.

6. Check **Show Brush Size and Intensity** to have the current Diameter and Intensity settings display onscreen inside the cursor when a symbolism tool is used. The Intensity setting is expressed as a shade in the brush cursor: black for high intensity ❹, gray for middle intensity, and light gray for low intensity ❺.

7. Click OK.

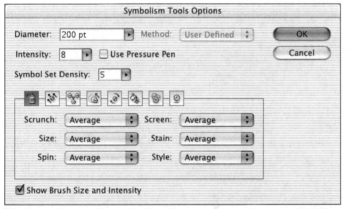

❹ *High Intensity cursor*

❺ *Low Intensity cursor*

❶ *Choose global and individual properties for the symbolism tools in the* Symbolism Tools Options *dialog box.*

❷ *The Symbol Sprayer tool used with low Intensity and Symbol Set Density values*

❸ *The Symbol Sprayer tool used with high Intensity and Symbol Set Density values*

Global Symbolism Tool Options

To choose Symbol Sprayer tool options:

1. Double-click the Symbol Sprayer tool.
or
Double-click a symbolism tool, then click the Symbol Sprayer (first) button in the Symbolism Tools Options dialog box.

2. Choose **Diameter, Intensity,** and **Symbol Set Density** settings **1** (see the previous page for definitions).

3. The Scrunch, Size, Spin, Screen, Stain, and Style pop-up menus define the parameters for instances that are placed by the Symbol Sprayer tool:

Choose **Average** from a property's pop-up menu to add instances based on an average sampling from neighboring instances in the set within the diameter of the brush cursor in its current location.
or
Choose **User Defined** from a property pop-up menu to add instances based on a predetermined value (see the sidebar).

Note: The setting chosen for each of the six individual tool pop-up menus has no relationship to the Method setting, which applies to the other symbolism tools.

4. Click OK.

User Defined defined

For the Symbol Sprayer tool, you can choose either Average or User Defined for each property. If you choose User Defined, the properties will be based on the following variables:

Scrunch (density) and **Size** are based on the original symbol size.

Spin is based on the mouse direction.

Screen is based on 100% opacity.

Stain is based on the current Fill color at a 100% tint.

Style is based on whichever graphic style is currently selected on the Graphic Styles palette.

➤ For more information, read about the peculiarities of each tool on the following pages.

➤ When you use a symbolism tool (such as the Symbol Shifter, Scruncher, or Sizer) to modify instances in a symbol set, keep these two seemingly conflicting tendencies in mind: Instances try to stay as close as possible to their original position in the set in order to maintain their original set density, but at the same time they also try to stay apart.

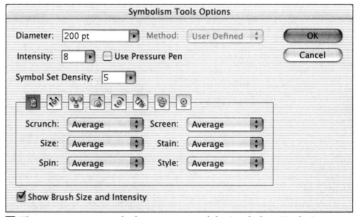

1 *The pop-up menus in the lower portion of the **Symbolism Tools Options** dialog box appear when the **Symbol Sprayer** tool is chosen.*

For all the symbolism tools

When you use a symbolism tool, you can maximize your control by interactively readjusting the brush size and intensity (e.g., a small brush will affect a handful of instances; a large brush will affect a larger number of instances).

To **increase** a brush's **intensity** interactively as you use a symbolism tool, press Shift-]; to **decrease** brush's intensity, press Shift-[.

To **enlarge** a brush interactively as you use a symbolism tool, press]. To **shrink** it, press [.

The effect of the symbolism tools is strongest in the center of the brush cursor and fades toward the edge of the cursor. The longer the mouse button is held down, the stronger the effect.

You can't **add symbols** to an **existing set** by using the Place Symbol command, but you can do so using the Symbol Sprayer tool. Similarly, you can't select or delete instances in a set using the Selection tool, but as we showed you on page 296, you can delete instances by Option/Alt clicking or dragging with the Symbol Sprayer tool.

To add instances to a symbol set:

1. Choose the Selection tool, then click a symbol set in your document.

2. Choose the Symbol Sprayer tool.

3. The icon for the symbol that was last sprayed in a symbol set will become selected on the Symbols palette when the set is reselected. You can either continue to spray with that symbol or click a different symbol on the palette. Drag inside the selected set **1**.

➤ If a selected set contains instances that originated from two or more different symbols and you click one of those symbols in the Symbols palette, modifications will be limited to only the instances of that one symbol. If you want to modify instances of different symbols in the same set, first make sure no symbols are selected by clicking an empty area of the Symbols palette.

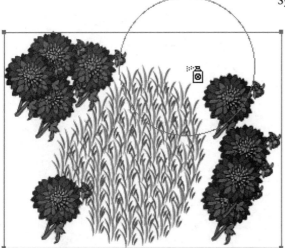

1 *To add instances of a different* **symbol** *to a* **set***, select the set, click a symbol on the Symbols palette, then drag inside the set.*

Add to Symbol Set

With the exception of the Symbol Sprayer, the function of all the symbolism tools—Shifter, Scruncher, Sizer, Spinner, Stainer, Screener, and Styler—is to modify the position, size, orientation, color, transparency, or style of individual symbol instances or all the instances in a set.

The **Symbol Shifter** tool shifts instances in a symbol set sideways based on the direction you drag the cursor. The tool can also change the stacking order (front-to-back position) of instances within a set, bringing an instance forward or sending it back behind other instances. For example, if a symbol set contains trees and figures where the trees obscure the figures, you could use the Symbol Shifter tool to move the trees closer together to create a forest, then bring the figures forward in front of the trees.

1 *The Symbol Shifter tool is used (with Shift held down) on this symbol set...*

To use the Symbol Shifter tool:

1. Select a symbol set in your document.

2. Choose the Symbol Shifter tool.

3. Drag inward where you want to pull instances **together,** or drag outward to move instances **apart.** The tool will try to preserve the current density and arrangement of instances as it does its job.
   or
   Shift-click an instance to bring it in **front** of adjacent instances **1**–**2**.
   or
   Option-Shift/Alt-Shift click an instance to send it **behind** adjacent instances.

2 *...to **shift** the plovers into a more naturalistic front-to-back order.*

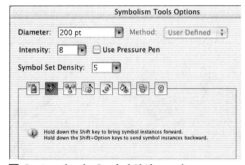

3 *Options for the Symbol Shifter tool*

To choose Symbol Shifter tool options:

1. Double-click the Symbol Shifter tool.

2. Choose a brush Diameter **3**.

3. Choose an **Intensity** value for the rate of shifting and the amount of space the tool will create between shifted instances. The higher the Intensity, the greater the space and shifting.

4. Choose a **Symbol Set Density** value to specify how much the tool will try to keep the instances together.

5. Click OK.

One method for all

The current choice on the **Method** pop-up menu applies to all the symbolism tools except the Symbol Sprayer and Symbol Shifter.

1 *Option/Alt dragging across a symbol set with the Symbol Scruncher tool*

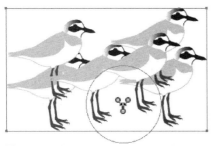

2 *The plovers are moved apart.*

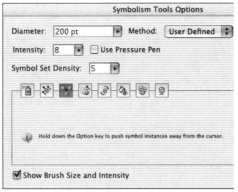

3 *Options for the Symbol Scruncher tool*

The **Symbol Scruncher** tool pulls symbol instances closer together or pushes them apart. A symbol set of birds, for example, could be contracted (scrunched) to move the birds closer together or expanded to create more space between the birds. You can either drag the mouse with the tool or hold the mouse button down in one spot.

To use the Symbol Scruncher tool:

1. Select a symbol set in your document.

2. Choose the Symbol Scruncher tool.

3. To move instances closer **together,** either click and hold in one spot or drag inside the set.
or
To push symbol instances **away** from one another, Option-click/Alt-click or Option-drag/Alt-drag **1**–**2**.

To choose Symbol Scruncher tool options:

1. Double-click the Symbol Scruncher tool.
or
To change the density in an existing set, click the set, then double-click the Symbol Scruncher tool.

2. Choose a brush **Diameter** and choose a **Symbol Set Density** value to specify how much the tool will try to keep the instances together **3**.

3. Choose an **Intensity** value to control how much the tool changes the density, and how quickly it produces the change.

4. For the Method:
Choose **User Defined** to gradually increase or decrease the amount of space between symbol instances based on the way you click or drag.
or
Choose **Average** to even out and make more uniform the amount of space between instances based on an average of the existing density of instances. This method will produce a minor effect if the spacing is already averaged.
or
Choose **Random** to randomize the amount of space between instances.

5. Click OK.

The job of the **Symbol Sizer** tool is to reduce or enlarge instances within a symbol set. The Symbol Sprayer tool creates instances only of a uniform size, so this tool comes in handy for resizing individual instances within a set.

To use the Symbol Sizer tool:

I. Click a symbol set in your document.

2. Choose the Symbol Sizer tool.

3. Click on or drag over instances to **increase** their size ■.

or

Option-click/Alt-click or Option-drag/Alt-drag over instances to **reduce** their size.

Note: If very little happens when you use this tool, change the Method to User Defined or Random (see step 6, below).

➤ Use a small brush Diameter to select instances with more precision.

To choose Symbol Sizer tool options:

I. Double-click the Symbol Sizer tool.

2. Choose brush **Diameter** and **Symbol Set Density** values ■.

3. Choose an **Intensity** value for the rate and amount of resizing. The higher the Intensity, the wider the range of scale changes.

4. *Optional:* Check Proportional Resizing to resize instances without distortion.

5. *Optional:* Check Resizing Affects Density to force instances to move away from each other when they're scaled up or move closer together when they're scaled down, while maintaining the current set density. With this option unchecked, more overlapping of instances can occur.

6. For the Method:

Choose **User Defined** to gradually increase or decrease the size of instances based on the way you click or drag.

or

Choose **Average** to make the instances more uniform in size. If the sizes are already near uniform, this method will produce little effect.

or

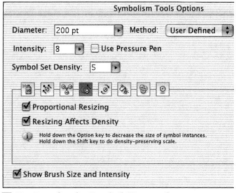

■ *Instances scaled using the Symbol Sizer tool*

■ *Options for the Symbol Sizer tool*

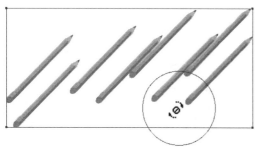

1 *Dragging across a symbol set with the Symbol Spinner tool with Method: Random chosen*

2 *The pencils are rotated randomly.*

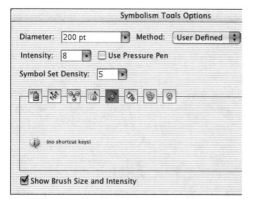

3 *Options for the Symbol Spinner tool*

Choose **Random** to randomize scale changes within the brush diameter.

7. Click OK.

➤ With Average or Random chosen as the brush Method, Shift-click or Shift-drag to scale instances while maintaining (if possible) the current density.

The **Symbol Spinner** tool changes the orientation of instances within a symbol set.

To use the Symbol Spinner tool:

1. Click a symbol set in your document.

2. Choose the Symbol Spinner tool.

3. Drag a symbol instance or instances in the direction you want them to rotate, using the arrows as an orientation guide **1**–**2**. Clicking and holding has no effect.

➤ If the arrows are hard to see, change the selection color for the layer the set is on.

➤ The smaller the brush's diameter, the easier it will be to isolate individual symbol instances for rotating.

To choose Symbol Spinner tool options:

1. Double-click the Symbol Spinner tool.

2. Choose brush **Diameter** and **Symbol Set Density** values **3**.

3. Choose an **Intensity** value for the rate and amount the instances can be rotated. The higher the Intensity, the sharper the angles of rotation using the least amount of mouse movement.

4. For the Method:

Choose **User Defined** to rotate the symbol instances in the direction of the cursor.
or
Choose **Average** to gradually even out and make uniform the orientation of all instances within the brush's diameter.
or
Choose **Random** to randomize the orientation of instances.

5. Click OK.

Like the Colorization: Tints and Shades option for brushes, the **Symbol Stainer** tool colorizes symbol instances with varied tints of the current fill color. It changes solid fills, but not patterns or gradients. Use it to vary the shades of green in foliage, the shades of brown in buildings, and so on.

Note: The Symbol Stainer tool increases file size and decreases performance, so don't use it if you're going to export your file in the Flash SVG format, or if memory is a concern.

To use the Symbol Stainer tool:

1. Select a symbol set in your document.
2. Choose the Symbol Stainer tool.
3. Choose a fill color to be used for the staining.
4. Click on an instance to apply a tint of the current fill color to the current object color. Continue clicking to increase the amount of colorization, up to the maximum amount.
   or
   Drag across the symbol set to colorize any instances within the brush's diameter **1**–**2**. Drag again to intensify the effect.

➤ Option-click/Alt-click or Option-drag/Alt-drag to decrease the amount of colorization and reveal more of the original symbol color.

➤ Shift-click or Shift-drag to tint only instances that have already been stained, while leaving unchanged instances that haven't been stained.

To choose Symbol Stainer tool options:

1. Double-click the Symbol Stainer tool.
2. Choose brush **Diameter** and **Symbol Set Density** values **3**.
3. Choose an **Intensity** value for the rate and amount of the tint the Stainer applies.
4. For the Method:
   Choose **User Defined** to gradually tint symbol instances with the current fill color.
   or

1 Dragging across a symbol set with the **Symbol Stainer** tool

2 The fireworks are **tinted** gradually.

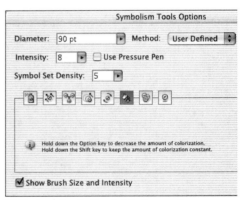

3 Options for the **Symbol Stainer** tool

1 *Holding the mouse down on an instance (the beetle) with the **Symbol Screener** tool*

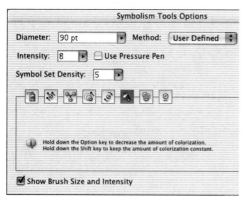

2 *The beetle is **screened**.*

3 *Options for the **Symbol Screener** tool*

Choose **Average** to even out the amount of existing colorization among selected instances without applying new tints.
or
Choose **Random** to randomize the colorization for a more naturalistic effect.

4. Click OK.

The **Symbol Screener** tool increases or decreases the opacity of instances within the brush's diameter. Use this tool to fade instances and make them more transparent.

To use the Symbol Screener tool:

1. Select a symbol set in your document.

2. Choose the Symbol Screener tool.

3. Click and hold on or drag across instances to make them more **transparent** **1**–**2**.
or
Option-click/Alt-click on or Option-drag/Alt-drag across instances to make them more **opaque.**

Note: If nothing happens when you use this tool, change the Method to User Defined or Random (see step 4, below).

To choose Symbol Screener tool options:

1. Double-click the Symbol Screener tool.

2. Choose brush **Diameter** and **Symbol Set Density** values **3**.

3. Choose an **Intensity** value for the rate and amount of transparency that is applied. The higher the Intensity, the more quickly and intensely instances will fade out.

4. For the Method:

Choose **User Defined** to have transparency increase or decrease gradually.
or
Choose **Average** to even out and make more uniform the amount of transparency among instances within the brush's diameter.
or
Choose **Random** to gradually add transparency in a random fashion.

5. Click OK.

The **Symbol Styler** tool applies the currently selected style to instances in a set. By selecting a different style on the Graphic Styles palette, you can apply one or more styles to a symbol set. The tool can also be used to remove styling.

To use the Symbol Styler tool:

1. Select a symbol set in your document.

2. Choose the Symbol Styler tool. 🖉

3. Click a style on the Graphic Styles palette **1**. *Note:* Be sure to choose the symbolism tool first. If you choose a style while a nonsymbolism tool is selected, the style will be applied to the entire symbol set.

4. Click and hold on, or drag across, an instance or instances to **apply** the selected style within the brush's diameter **2** (and **1**, next page). The longer you hold the mouse down, the more intensely the style will be applied. Pause for the screen to redraw. This can take some time even on a fast machine.
   or
   Option-click/Alt-click or Option-drag/ Alt-drag to **undo** the styling.

➤ Shift-click or Shift-drag to gradually apply the currently selected style to instances that have already been styled, while keeping unstyled instances unchanged.

To choose Symbol Styler tool options:

1. Double-click the Symbol Styler tool.

2. Choose brush **Diameter** and **Symbol Set Density** values.

3. Choose an **Intensity** value for the rate and amount a style is applied. The higher the Intensity, the more intensely and quickly the styling will be applied.

4. For the Method:
   Choose **User Defined** to gradually increase or decrease the amount styling is applied.
   or
   Choose **Average** to even out the amount of applied styling among instances within the brush diameter without applying new styling.

1 *Choose the Symbol Styler tool, then click a style on the Graphic Styles palette.*

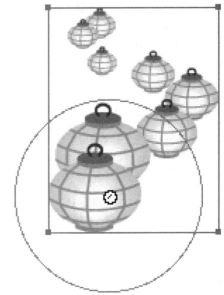

2 *Clicking an instance with the Symbol Styler tool*

When saving

When saving a file containing symbols, we recommend using Save As and unchecking **Create PDF Compatible File** in the Illustrator Options dialog box. This will significantly reduce the file size and speed up the save and open operations.

Saving a file that contains symbols as an EPS will result in a large file size. Consider saving the file as a PDF instead.

or

Choose **Random** to apply styling gradually and randomly.

5. Click OK.

Note: To view the attributes used in an applied style, click the symbol set, choose Object > Expand, check Fill and Stroke, then click OK. On the Layers palette, click the target circle for one of the expanded instances, then look at its appearance attributes on the Appearance palette.

1 *To produce this illustration, various **styles** were applied to **different** instances. Compare with **2** on the previous page.*

The **Expand** command can be used for two different purposes. If it's applied to a symbol set, it breaks the set apart without changing the instances themselves or their link to the original symbol. The instances will be nested inside a group on the Layers palette.

If the Expand command is applied to an individual instance (an instance that wasn't placed using the Symbol Sprayer tool), it does break the link to the original symbol. The individual paths from the former instance will be nested inside a group on the Layers palette.

To expand an instance or a symbol set:

1. Select a symbol set, an instance, or multiple individual instances in your document.

2. Choose Object > Expand (or Object > Expand Appearance if the instance has an effect applied to it).

3. Check Object and Fill ■, then click OK.

4. If you expanded a symbol set, you can now use the Direct Selection tool or Group Selection tool to move the individual instances apart, if desired. They are still linked to the original symbol.

If you expanded an individual instance, it will now be a group of paths. Select any path using the Layers palette to modify it.

➤ If the original symbol artwork contained any live appearances or effects, they will be editable once an individual instance from that symbol (not from a set) is expanded. Use the Layers palette to select any individual path. The applied effects will be listed on the palette, and are editable. To use the edited object to redefine a symbol, see page 295.

Select all instances

To select all the individual instances of a particular symbol in your document that aren't in a set, click the symbol on the Symbols palette, then choose **Select All Instances** from the palette menu.

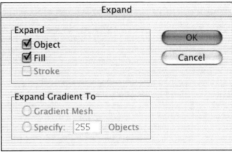

■ *Check* ***Object*** *and* ***Fill*** *in the* ***Expand*** *dialog box.*

COMBINE PATHS | 17

In this chapter, you'll first learn about the shape mode commands, which create editable compound shapes. Second, you'll learn about the pathfinder commands, which form a new flattened, closed object or compound path by dividing, merging, cropping, outlining, etc. Finally, you'll learn how to join two or more objects into a compound path, add objects to a compound path, reverse an object's fill in a compound path, and release a compound path.

shop and compare

For a comparison between compound shapes and compound paths, see page 314.

Add to *Shape Area*

Subtract from Shape Area

Intersect Shape Areas

Exclude Overlapping Shape Areas

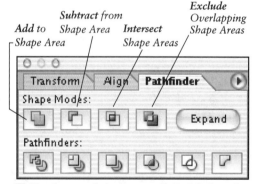

1 *The shape mode buttons on the Pathfinder palette*

Daniel Pelavin

Shape modes

The **shape mode** buttons **1** on the Pathfinder palette produce a compound shape from selected, overlapping objects. And like appearances and effects, compound shapes are editable and reversible. The original objects are nested as individual objects within a <Compound Shape> layer on the Layers palette, making it easy to select them for editing. Individual objects within a compound shape can be moved, restacked, or reshaped, and the overall compound shape adjusts accordingly. And finally, if a compound shape is released, the objects are restored to their original appearances.

A few rules to keep in mind:

➤ Shape modes can be applied to multiple paths, compound paths, groups (nesting is preserved), blends, envelopes, editable text, or even other compound shapes.

➤ Shape modes can't be applied to a group alone, but they can be applied to a group that's selected along with an individual object.

➤ With the exception of the Subtract from Shape Area command, the color attributes of the topmost selected object (or the topmost object in a selected group) are applied to the entire compound shape.

➤ Effects in the original objects are preserved, but only distort and warp effects will be visible in the compound shape.

(Continued on the following page)

309

➤ Shape modes can't be applied to rasterized images, mesh objects, placed objects, or text paths.

The shape mode buttons

Add to Shape Area ▮: Joins the outer edges of selected objects into one compound shape, hiding interior object edges (see also page 133). Open paths are closed.

Subtract from Shape Area ▮: Subtracts the objects in front from the backmost object. Only the paint attributes from the backmost object are preserved.

Intersect Shape Areas ▮: Preserves areas that overlap; hides areas that don't overlap. Works best when used on two objects that partially overlap.

Exclude Overlapping Shape Areas ▮: Areas where objects overlap become transparent.

➤ You can apply a shape mode to an object that's already in a compound shape. Select the object with the Direct Selection tool, then click a shape mode button. Try clicking, say, Subtract from Shape Area to make an object disappear.

➤ A compound shape that's copied from Illustrator and pasted into Adobe Photoshop (click Shape Layer in the Paste dialog box) will show up as a shape layer containing multiple paths. A shape layer containing two or more paths that's copied from Photoshop into Illustrator will show up as a compound shape.

When a **compound shape** is **expanded,** the result is a single path, unless the compound shape had cutouts, in which case the end result is a compound path. Compare this with the Release Compound Shape command, which is discussed on the next page.

To expand a compound shape:

1. Select the compound shape with the Selection tool.

2. Click the Expand button on the Pathfinder palette (Shift-F9).
or
Choose Expand Compound Shape from the palette menu.

▮ *The original objects: The leaf is the topmost object.*

Add to Shape Area

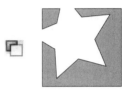

▮ *The frontmost object will be cut out of the object behind it.*

Subtract from Shape Area turns it into a compound shape.

▮ *The original objects*

Intersect Shape Areas: Only areas that originally overlapped other objects remain.

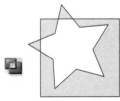

▮ *The original objects*

Exclude Overlapping Shape Areas: areas where the objects overlapped become a cutout.

Shape Mode Buttons; Expand

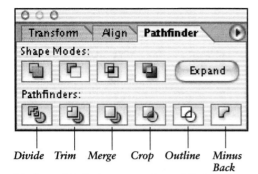

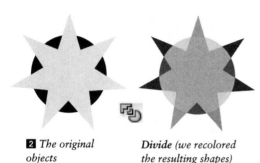

Divide Trim Merge Crop Outline Minus
Back
1 *The pathfinder buttons on the Pathfinder palette*

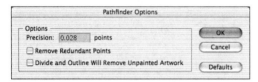

2 *The original objects*

Divide *(we recolored the resulting shapes)*

3 *The Pathfinder Options dialog box*

Pathfinder Options

Options
Precision: 0.028 points
☐ Remove Redundant Points
☐ Divide and Outline Will Remove Unpainted Artwork

OK
Cancel
Defaults

Pathfinder options

To open the Pathfinder Options dialog box **3**, choose Pathfinder Options from the Pathfinder palette menu.

The higher the **Precision** value (.001–100), the more precisely a command is applied—but the longer it takes to process.

With **Remove Redundant Points** checked, any anchor points with a duplicate in the same location will be deleted when a pathfinder command is applied.

For Divide and Outline Will Remove Unpainted Artwork, see the Note at right.

Releasing a **compound shape** restores the original objects used within the compound shape, with their original appearances.

To release a compound shape:
1. Select the compound shape with the Selection tool (V).
2. Choose Release Compound Shape from the Pathfinder palette menu.

Pathfinders

The **pathfinder** commands determine where selected paths overlap and then divide, trim, merge, crop, outline, or subtract from them to produce nonoverlapping (flattened) closed paths or lines. Object colors and appearances are preserved, and the resulting paths are put into a group. The pathfinder commands, like the shape mode commands, are applied using the Pathfinder palette **1**.

Here are a few guidelines:

➤ Unfortunately, the original objects can't be restored after applying a pathfinder command, except by choosing Undo. Make a copy of your objects first!

➤ We like to apply the pathfinders to closed paths. If applied to an open path, Illustrator may close the path for you before performing the command. To control how a path is closed, see page 313.

➤ Pathfinders can be applied to an object that has a pattern fill, brush stroke, or applied effect.

➤ To apply pathfinders to type, first convert the type into outlines.

(To apply pathfinders via Effects menu commands, see page 387.)

Note: If Divide and Outline Will Remove Unpainted Artwork is checked in the Pathfinder Options dialog box (choose Pathfinder Options from the palette menu), the Divide and Outline commands will delete any nonoverlapping areas of selected paths that have a fill of None.

Divide: Each overlapping area becomes a separate, nonoverlapping object **2**.

(Continued on the following page)

Release Compound Shape; Pathfinders

➤ After applying the Divide command, click away from all objects to deselect them, choose the Direct Selection tool, click any of the objects, and apply new fill colors or effects; or apply a fill of None or transparency to make an object see-through; or remove an object to create a cutout.

Trim ❶: The frontmost object shape is preserved; parts of objects that are behind it and overlap it are deleted. Adjacent or overlapping objects of the same color or shade remain separate (unlike the Merge command). Stroke colors are deleted (unless effects were applied to the original objects).

Merge ❷: Adjacent or overlapping objects with the same fill attributes are united. Stroke colors are deleted (unless effects were applied to the original objects).

Crop ❸: Areas of selected objects that extend beyond the edge of the frontmost object are cropped away, and the frontmost object loses its fill and stroke. Stroke colors are removed (unless effects were applied to the original objects). Crop works like a clipping mask, except in this case you can't restore the original objects except by choosing Undo.

Outline ❹: All the selected objects turn into stroked line segments (zero width), with the fill colors of the original objects becoming the stroke colors. Transparency settings are preserved; fill colors are removed. The resulting strokes can be scaled and recolored individually.

Minus Back ❺: Objects in back are subtracted from the frontmost object, leaving only portions of the frontmost object. The paint attributes and appearances of the frontmost object are applied to the new path. The objects must at least partially overlap for this command to produce an effect.

Shortcuts to remember

Apply **last-used** Pathfinder   Cmd-4/Ctrl-4
   command to any objects

Turn shape mode command   Option-click/Alt-
into **pathfinder** command   click the button

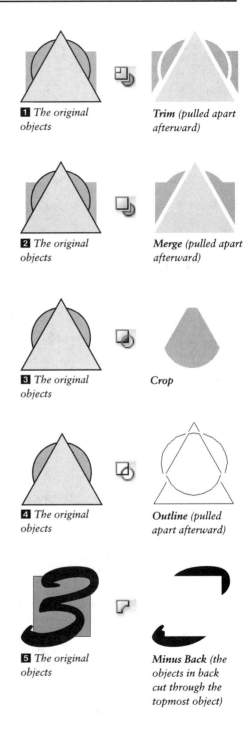

❶ *The original objects* — *Trim (pulled apart afterward)*

❷ *The original objects* — *Merge (pulled apart afterward)*

❸ *The original objects* — *Crop*

❹ *The original objects* — *Outline (pulled apart afterward)*

❺ *The original objects* — *Minus Back (the objects in back cut through the topmost object)*

1 *Select an object that has a stroke. To produce the button shown below, we applied a gradient fill and a stroke to the object before applying the Outline Stroke command.*

2 *The Outline Stroke command converted the stroke into a compound path. We selected the outer ring with the Selection tool, applied a gradient fill to it, then dragged the Gradient tool downward across it to make it contrast with the gradient fill in the inner circle. Finally, we selected the gradient in the inner circle using the Layers palette, then modified that gradient.*

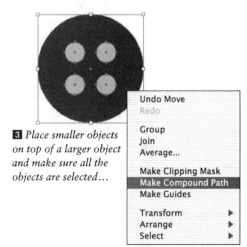

3 *Place smaller objects on top of a larger object and make sure all the objects are selected...*

4 *...then Control-click/ right-click and choose* **Make Compound Path** *from the context menu.*

If you're going to apply a pathfinder command to an open path, you can use the **Outline Stroke** command first to turn the stroke into a filled object instead of letting the pathfinder command close it for you. Another reason to use this command is to convert a line or a stroke into a closed path so it can be filled with a gradient or so it can be prepared more easily for trapping.

To turn a stroke or an open path into a filled object:

1. Select an object that has a stroke color **1**.

2. Choose Object > Path > Outline Stroke. The new filled object **2** will have the same width as the original stroke. Any fill from the original object will be preserved as a separate object.

Compound paths

The **compound path** command joins two or more objects into one object—that is, until or unless the compound path is released. Where the original objects overlapped, a transparent hole is created, through which shapes or patterns behind the object are revealed. Regardless of their original paint attributes, all the objects in a compound path are painted with the attributes of the backmost object, and they form one unit.

To create a compound path:

1. Arrange the objects you want to see through in front of a larger shape **3**. Closed paths work best. The paths can have brush strokes.

2. Select all the objects, using the Selection tool (V) or Lasso tool.

3. Choose Object > Compound Path > Make (Cmd-8/Ctrl-8).
   or
   If the objects aren't grouped, you can Control-click/right-click on the artboard and choose Make Compound Path from the context menu **4**.

(Continued on the following page)

Outline Stroke; Create Compound Path

The frontmost objects will cut through the backmost object like a cookie cutter **1**–**2**. The words "<Compound Path>" will appear on the Layers palette, but the original objects will no longer be listed as separate objects; they'll be part and parcel of the compound path object. (Compound shapes, in contrast, are preserved as individual objects and are listed as such on the Layers palette.)

The fill and stroke attributes of the backmost object will be applied to areas of objects in front of it that overlap it or that extend beyond the edge of it.

If the holes don't result, see the second set of instructions on the following page.

➤ Regardless of which layers the objects were on originally, the compound path will be placed on the layer of the frontmost object.

➤ Don't overdo it. To avoid a printing error, don't make your compound paths from very complex shapes or create too many compound paths in the same illustration.

1 *The objects are converted into a compound path.*

2 *We placed a background object behind the compound path and applied a white stroke to the black circle.*

Compound shapes	*Compound paths*	*How they're the same*
Subpaths are listed as **separate** objects on the Layers palette.	Subpaths are part of a <Compound Path> layer.	Use the **Selection** tool to select or move a whole compound shape or compound path.
Click with the **Direct Selection** tool to select a whole subpath within a compound shape.	**Option-click/Alt-click** with the Direct Selection tool to select a whole subpath within a compound path.	**Reshape** any subpath within a compound shape or compound path by the usual methods (e.g., add points, delete points, move points).
There are **four** shape mode buttons to choose from. And after a compound shape is created, additional shape modes can be applied to individual objects within it.	There is only **one** kind of compound path: Overlapping areas are subtracted from the backmost object, period.	Only one **fill color** can be applied to a compound shape or compound path at a time.
When released, the objects' **original** appearances (e.g., effects, opacity, blending modes) are restored.	When released, the objects take on the appearances of the **compound path**, not their original appearances.	

1 *Click an object in a compound path.*

Use Even-Odd Fill Rule

Use Non-Zero Winding Fill Rule

2 *Reverse Path Direction Off* **3** *Reverse Path Direction On*

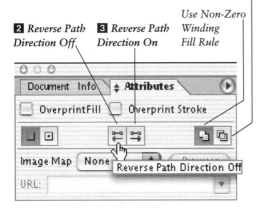

4 *The color of two of the buttonholes is reversed.*

To add an object to a compound path:

1. Move the object you want to add in front of the compound path. If it's in the back, its attributes will be applied to the compound path. Using the Selection tool or the Lasso tool, select both the compound path and the object you want to add to it.

2. Choose Object > Compound Paths > Make (Cmd-8/Ctrl-8).

You can remove the fill color of any shape in a compound path, making the object transparent, or vice versa, by flipping the **Reverse Path Direction** switch on the Attributes palette.

To reverse an object's fill in a compound path:

1. Deselect the compound path (Cmd-Shift-A/Ctrl-Shift-A).

2. Choose the Direct Selection tool (A).

3. Click the edge of the object in the compound path that you want to reverse the color of **1**.

4. Show the Attributes palette (F11).

5. Click the **Reverse Path Direction Off** button or the **Reverse Path Direction On** button—whichever button isn't currently highlighted **2**–**4**.

➤ If the Reverse Path Direction buttons have no effect, it means you have selected the whole compound path. Select only one path in the compound and try again.

The fill rules

In case you're wondering what those buttons are on the right side of the Attributes palette, here's a brief explanation:

Non-Zero Winding Fill Rule is Illustrator's default rule for combined paths. The Reverse Path Direction buttons (discussed above) are available only when this button is clicked.

The **Use Even-Odd Fill Rule** button makes every other overlapping shape within a compound transparent. It produces more cutouts than the Non-Zero Winding Fill Rule.

Add To, Reverse Object Fill in Compound Path

You can **release** a **compound path** back into its individual objects at any time.

To release a compound path:

1. Choose the Selection tool, then click on the compound path .

2. Choose Object > Compound Path > Release (Cmd-Option-8/Ctrl-Alt-8). (*Note:* at the time of this writing, the shortcut isn't working on the Mac.)
or
Control-click/right-click the artboard and choose Release Compound Path from the context menu.

   All the objects will be selected, and they will be painted with the attributes, effects, and appearances from the compound path—not their original, precompound appearances 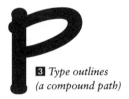. You can use Smart Guides (Object Highlighting) to figure out which shape is what.

➤ The released objects will all be nested within the same top-level layer that originally contained the compound path.

➤ A compound path is created automatically when the Type > Create Outlines command is used on a type character that has a counter (interior shape). If you release this type of compound path, the counter will become a separate shape with the same paint attributes and appearances as the outer part of the letterform 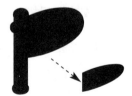–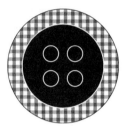.

1 *Click on the compound path.*

2 *The compound path is released. The buttonholes are no longer transparent.*

3 *Type outlines (a compound path)*

4 *The compound path is released into separate objects. (We moved the counter of the "P.")*

Release Compound Path

GRADIENTS 18

A gradient fill is a gradual blend between two or more colors. In this chapter you'll learn how to fill an object or objects with a gradient; create and save gradients; edit a gradient using the Gradient palette; and change the way a gradient fills an object or objects by using the Gradient tool.

You'll also learn how to use the Mesh tool, the Create Gradient Mesh command, and the Expand command to create painterly gradient mesh objects, and how to modify mesh objects by adding, moving, deleting, or recoloring mesh points and lines.

Daniel Pelavin

Gradient basics

Gradients are used to create volume in realistic objects or to soften abstract shapes. The simplest gradient fill consists of a starting color and an ending color, with the point where the colors are equally mixed together located midway between them. A gradient can be **linear** (side to side) or **radial** (outward from the center). You can apply a gradient fill to one object or across several objects. A set of predefined gradients is supplied with Illustrator, but you can also create your own gradients by using the **Gradient palette** (F9).

Once an object is filled with a gradient, you can use the **Gradient tool** to modify how the fill is distributed within the object. You can change the direction of the gradient, or change how quickly one color blends into another. You can also change the location of the center of a radial gradient fill.

You'll be using the Color, Gradient, and Swatches palettes for the instructions in this chapter.

You can apply a gradient that's supplied with Illustrator or, even better, create your own gradients. Follow these instructions to apply an **existing gradient** to an object. Follow the instructions that begin on the next page to create your own gradient.

To fill an object with a gradient:

1. Select an object, then click a gradient swatch on the Swatches palette **1**–**2** or on any open gradient library (see the sidebar).
   or
   Drag a gradient swatch from the Swatches palette or the Gradient Fill box on the Gradient palette (F9) **3** over a selected or unselected object.

2. *Optional:* If the object contains a Linear gradient, you can select it and then change the Angle on the Gradient palette.

➤ If a selected object has a solid color or pattern fill, but it previously had a gradient fill, you can reapply the gradient by clicking the Gradient Fill box on the Gradient palette, or by clicking the Gradient button on the Toolbox, ■ or by pressing "." (period).

➤ You can't apply a gradient to a stroke, but here's a workaround: Make the stroke the desired width, apply Object > Path > Outline Stroke to convert the stroke into a closed object (see page 313), then apply the gradient.

➤ To fill type with a gradient, first convert it into outlines (Type > Create Outlines). Or select the type, choose Add New Fill from the Appearance palette menu, then click a gradient swatch.

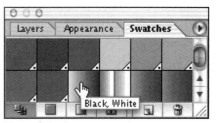

1 *Click a gradient on the Swatches palette.*

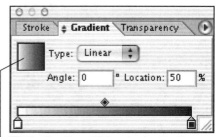

2 *An object filled with a radial gradient*

3 *The Gradient Fill box on the Gradient palette*

More gradients NEW

To access the other gradient libraries that are supplied with Illustrator, from the Swatches palette menu, choose **Open Swatch Library > Other Library,** open the Adobe Illustrator CS/Presets/Gradients folder (Mac) or the Adobe\Illustrator CS\Presets\Gradients folder (Windows), click the library you want to open, then click Open. Any gradient that you click on in a library palette will appear at the bottom of the Swatches palette.

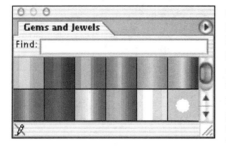

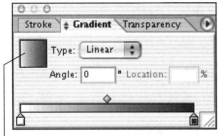

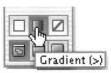 **1** *First click the **Gradient Fill** box on the Gradient palette...*

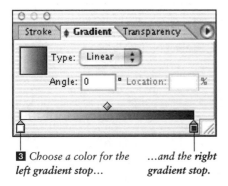

2 *...or on the Toolbox.*

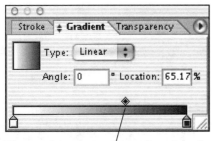

3 *Choose a color for the left gradient stop...* ...*and the **right** gradient stop.*

4 *Move the **midpoint diamond** to adjust the amount of each color.*

A **custom gradient** can be composed of all CMYK colors, all RGB process colors, tints of the same spot color, or multiple spot colors.

To create and save a two-color gradient:

1. Display the full Gradient palette (F9), with its options panel.

2. Click the Gradient Fill box on the Gradient palette **1**.
   or
   Click the Gradient button ■ on the Toolbox or press "." (period) **2**.

3. Drag a solid-color swatch from the Swatches palette over the left gradient stop on the Gradient palette **3**.
   or
   Click the left gradient stop on the Gradient palette. Then use the Color palette to mix a solid color; or Option-click/Alt-click a solid-color swatch on the Swatches palette; or choose the Eyedropper tool and Shift-click a color anywhere in the document window.

4. Repeat the previous step to choose a solid color for the right gradient stop.

5. From the Type pop-up menu on the Gradient palette, choose Linear or Radial.

6. *Optional:* Move the midpoint diamond to the right to produce more of the starting color than the ending color, or to the left to produce more of the ending color than the starting color **4**. Or click the diamond, then change the Location value.

7. *Optional:* For a Linear gradient, you can change the Angle.

8. If you select another object or swatch now, the new gradient will be lost—unless you save it. To save the gradient:

   Drag the Gradient Fill box from the Gradient palette onto the Swatches palette.
   or
   Click the Gradient Fill box on the Gradient palette, then click the New Swatch button ■ at the bottom of the Swatches palette.
   or

   (Continued on the following page)

Create Two-Color Gradient

To name the gradient as you save it, click the Gradient Fill box on the Gradient palette, Option-click/Alt-click the New Swatch button 🔳 on the Swatches palette, enter a name, then click OK.

➤ To swap the starting and ending colors or any other two colors in a radial or linear gradient, Option-drag/Alt-drag one stop on top of the other.

➤ To delete a gradient swatch from the Swatches palette, drag it over the Delete Swatch button. 🗑

It's hard to tell whether a gradient is going to look good until it's been applied to an object. Luckily, gradients are easy to edit. You can either recolor a gradient in an object and leave the swatch alone, or you can **assign new colors** to a **gradient** swatch, with or without recoloring any objects that the gradient is currently applied to.

To assign new colors to a gradient:

1. Choose the Selection tool (V), then click an object that contains the gradient you want to edit. For editable type, click the type, then click the Fill attribute on the Appearance palette that has a gradient icon, if it isn't already active.
or
Click the gradient swatch on the Swatches palette that you want to edit. In addition, you may also select any objects that contain that gradient.

2. On the Gradient palette (F9), click the gradient stop that you want to recolor. Then choose a color from the Color palette or Option-click/Alt-click a solid color on the Swatches palette.
or
Drag a solid-color swatch from the Swatches palette over a gradient stop.

3. To resave the edited swatch, Option-drag/ Alt-drag from the Gradient Fill box over the swatch.

start from something

To use an existing gradient as a starting point for a new gradient, click a gradient swatch on the Swatches palette, choose **Duplicate Swatch** from the palette menu, click the duplicate swatch, then edit the gradient as per the instructions on this page.

Color-separating gradients

➤ To color-separate a gradient that changes from a spot color to white on one piece of film (one plate), create a gradient with the spot color as the starting color and **0%** tint of the **same color** as the ending color.

➤ If you're going to color-separate a gradient that contains **more than one** spot color, get some advice from your prepress specialist. He or she may tell you to assign a different screen angle to each color using File > Print > Output Panel (Convert All Spot Colors to Process should be unchecked). See page 457. If you need to convert each spot color to a process color, click the spot color square on the Color palette, then choose a process color model from the Color palette menu.

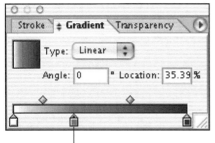

1 *Click below the **gradient slider** to add a new stop, then choose a color.*

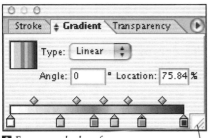

2 *Four new shades of gray were added to this gradient.*

*You can drag the **resize** box to widen the palette if your gradient contains a lot of colors.*

3 *Multicolored gradients*

A gradient can contain over 100 colors. The colors can be changed and color stops can be **added** or removed at any time.

To add colors to a gradient:

1. Follow the steps starting on page 319 to produce a two-color gradient.
   or
   On the Swatches palette, click an existing gradient swatch.

2. On the Gradient palette (F9), click below the gradient bar to add a gradient stop **1**. Then use the Color palette to mix a color or Option-click/Alt-click a swatch on the Swatches palette.
   or
   Drag a solid-color swatch from the Swatches palette to the gradient bar (but not on top of an existing stop) on the Gradient palette. A new stop will be created automatically.

3. *Do any of the following optional steps:*

   Move a stop to the left or to the right to change how abruptly that color spreads into adjacent colors.

   Move the midpoint diamond that's located above the gradient bar to the left or right of the new color to adjust the amount of that color.

   ➤ To remove a stop, drag it downward out of the Gradient palette.

   Repeat step 2 to add more colors **2**–**3**.

4. If you edited an existing swatch, Option-drag/Alt-drag from the Gradient Fill box on the Gradient palette over the swatch.
   or
   If you created a multicolored gradient from scratch, or if you want to save your modified gradient as a new swatch instead of saving over the original, drag it to the Swatches palette without holding down Option/Alt. Also remember to save your document!

   ➤ To make a gradient appear in every new Illustrator document, save it in either or both of the two Illustrator Startup files (see page 439).

   ➤ Option-drag/Alt-drag a stop to copy it.

Multicolored Gradients

You've already learned how to edit a gradient swatch. Now you'll learn how to adjust the angle and location of a gradient in an object using the **Gradient tool.** You can change how abruptly the colors blend, change the angle of a linear fill, or change the center location of a radial gradient fill. On the next page, you'll learn how to apply a gradient across a series of objects.

To use the Gradient tool:

1. Apply a gradient fill to an object, and keep the object selected.

2. Choose the Gradient tool (G).

3. Drag across the object in any direction (e.g., from right to left or diagonally):

   To blend the colors abruptly, drag a short distance **1**–**3**. To blend the colors more gradually across a wider span, drag a longer distance.

   To reverse the order of the colors in a linear gradient, drag in the opposite direction.

   For a radial gradient, position the pointer where you want the center of the fill to be, then click or drag **4**–**5**.

   ➤ You can start dragging or finish dragging with the pointer outside the object. In this case, the colors at the beginning or end of the gradient fill won't appear in the object.

4. If you don't like the results, drag in a different direction. Keep trying until you're satisfied with the results.

➤ If you use the Gradient tool on an object and then apply a different gradient to the same object, the Gradient tool's effect will be applied to the new gradient.

➤ To restore the original gradient to the object, make sure the object is selected, then click the swatch on the Swatches palette. If you edited the gradient by using the Gradient palette, you may need to click the swatch more than once.

1 The original linear gradient fill

2 Dragging a short distance with the **Gradient tool**

3 After using the Gradient tool as shown in the previous figure

4 The original radial gradient fill

5 After we dragged outward from the center of the rose with the **Gradient tool,** the center of the gradient is in a new location.

To spread a gradient across multiple objects:

1. Select several objects, and fill all of them with the same gradient **1**.

2. Choose the Gradient tool (G). ▪

3. Drag across all the objects **2**. Shift-drag to constrain the angle to a multiple of 45° (actually, to a multiple of the current Constrain Angle in Illustrator [Edit, in Windows] > Preferences > General).

➤ Once multiple objects are filled with the same gradient, don't combine them into a compound path, or you may change how the gradient looks. Also, the resulting object may be too complex to print.

1 *In the original gradient fill, the gradient starts anew in each type outline.*

2 *After we dragged across all the objects using the Gradient tool in the direction shown by the arrow, the gradient starts in the first type outline and ends in the last type outline.*

Gradient meshes

What is a gradient mesh?

A **gradient mesh** is an object that contains multiple gradients in various directions and locations with seamless transitions between them **1**. Using the gradient mesh features, you'll be able to easily render and modify photorealistic or painterly objects and complex modeled surfaces, such as skin tones, objects of nature, or machinery.

Both the **Mesh tool** and the **Create Gradient Mesh command** convert a standard object into a mesh object with lines and intersecting points. A gradient mesh can be produced from any path object or bitmapped image, even a radial or linear blend. To produce a mesh from a compound path, text object, or linked image, you must first rasterize it.

After you create a mesh object, you'll assign colors to mesh points or mesh patches. Then you can add or delete gradient colors or sharpen or soften color transitions by manipulating the points and lines. It's like a watercolor or airbrush drawing with a flexible armature above it. Reconfigure the armature, and the colors beneath the armature will shift right along with it.

Mesh building blocks

A mesh object consists of anchor points, mesh points, mesh lines, and mesh patches **2**. The mesh can be reshaped by manipulating its anchor points, mesh points, or mesh lines.

➤ **Anchor points** are square. You can add, delete, or move them or pull on their direction lines in order to reshape the object, as in nonmesh objects.

➤ **Mesh points** are diamond shaped and appear where two mesh lines intersect. You'll use them to assign colors to gradients. Like anchor points, they can be added, deleted, or moved.

➤ **Mesh lines** crisscross the object to connect the mesh points and act as guides for placing and moving points.

➤ A **mesh patch** is an area that's defined by four mesh points. You can move these, too.

Mesh another way

The Object > Envelope Distort > **Make with Mesh** command can also be used to produce a mesh. It will have the same components, and can be edited using the same techniques, as a mesh created by using the Mesh tool or the Create Gradient Mesh command (see pages 325–326).

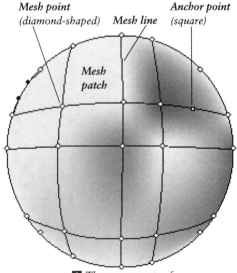

1 *Danny Pelavin used* **gradient meshes** *to render the glossy surfaces and complex shading in this illustration.*

Mesh point (diamond-shaped)   Mesh line   Anchor point (square)

Mesh patch

2 *The components of a* **gradient mesh** *object*

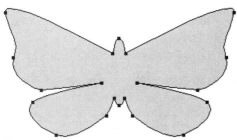

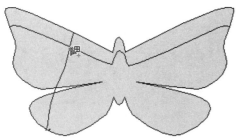

2 *Click the object—it will convert immediately into a gradient mesh object.*

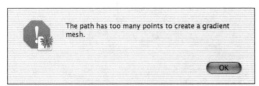

3 *If you get this alert dialog box, it means you must remove points from the path before you can convert it into a gradient mesh.*

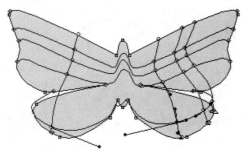

4 *Continue to click to create additional sets of mesh lines.*

You can convert a standard object into a gradient mesh by using either the **Mesh** tool or the **Create Gradient Mesh** command. To convert a complex object into a gradient mesh, your best bet is to use the Create Gradient Mesh command. To convert simpler objects, you can use either the Create Gradient Mesh command or the Mesh tool. The Create Gradient Mesh command creates more regularly spaced mesh points and lines than the Mesh tool.

Beware! The only way a mesh object can be converted back to a path object is by choosing Undo.

To convert an object into a gradient mesh using the Mesh tool:

1. Select an object (not a text object, compound path, or linked image) and apply a solid-color fill to the object if it doesn't already contain one **1**. The object can have an applied brush stroke, but the brush stroke will be removed by the Mesh tool. You can use a bitmap image.

> ➤ To preserve a nongradient mesh version of the object, copy it before proceeding.

2. Choose the Mesh tool (U).

3. Click on the object to place a mesh point. The object will be converted into a mesh object containing the minimum number of mesh lines **2**.

If an alert dialog box appears **3**, it means you need to remove points from the path before you can convert it into a gradient mesh. You can do this with the Delete Anchor Point tool or the Smooth tool.

4. The gradient mesh doesn't look very interesting yet. To start the process of building the mesh, you can click in the object to create a few additional sets of mesh lines **4**.

5. Proceed to page 327 to learn how to apply colors to the mesh.

In these instructions, you'll learn how to create a gradient mesh using the **Create Gradient Mesh** command. Complex gradient meshes increase file sizes and require a significant amount of computation, so try to keep them as simple as is reasonably possible. To avoid printing errors, build your drawing from a few smallish mesh objects rather than one large, complex one.

To convert an object into a gradient mesh using a command:

1. Choose the Selection tool (V), select an object (not a text object, compound path, or linked image), and apply a solid-color fill to the object, if it doesn't already have one. The object can have an applied brush stroke, but the brush stroke will be removed by the Create Gradient Mesh command. You can use an embedded bitmap image.

   ➤ To preserve a nonmesh version of the object, copy it before proceeding.

2. Choose Object > Create Gradient Mesh.

3. Check Preview **1**.

4. Enter the desired number of horizontal Rows and vertical Columns for the mesh grid.

5. From the Appearance pop-up menu, choose **Flat** for a uniform surface with no highlight; **To Center** for a highlight at the center of the object; or **To Edge** for a highlight at the edges of the object.

6. If you chose the To Center or To Edge Appearance option, enter an intensity percentage (0–100%) for the white Highlight.

7. Click OK **2**–**4**. To apply colors to the gradient mesh, follow the instructions on the following page.

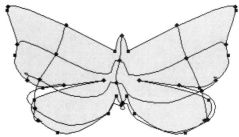

1 *The* **Create Gradient Mesh** *dialog box*

2 *Create Gradient Mesh command, Appearance: Flat*

3 *Create Gradient Mesh command, Appearance: To Center*

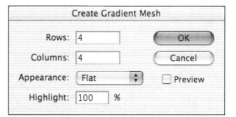

4 *Create Gradient Mesh command, Appearance: To Edge (shown here on a dark background so you can see the highlight on the edge)*

Create Gradient Mesh

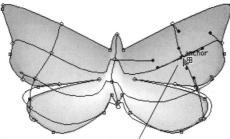

1 *Click an existing mesh point.*

2 *The point is recolored.*

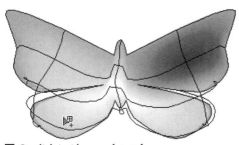

3 *Or click inside a mesh patch.*

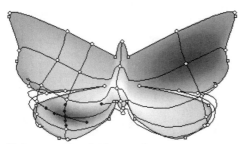

4 *A new mesh point is created.*

Each mesh **point** and mesh **patch** can be assigned a different **color,** and each color will blend into its surrounding colors. Click a mesh point to assign a color to a small area, or click a mesh patch to spread a color across a wider area.

To recolor a gradient mesh:

1. Zoom in on a mesh object (you should still see the entire object in the document window, though) and deselect it.

2. Choose the Direct Selection tool (A), then click the edge of the mesh object.

3. Do any of the following:

   Click a mesh point **1** or Shift-click multiple points, then choose a fill color from the Color palette or Swatches palette **2**.

   Drag a color from the Swatches palette over a mesh point or mesh patch.

   Click a mesh patch, then choose a fill color from the Color or Swatches palette. The four mesh points that surround the patch will be recolored.

➤ Deselect the gradient mesh as you work any time you need to start afresh.

➤ You can also recolor mesh points by using the Mesh tool (U). Select the object first using the Direct Selection tool (A). To select a mesh patch with the Mesh tool without adding a mesh point, Cmd-click/Ctrl-click the patch.

You can use the Mesh tool to **add mesh points** or **lines,** and thus more colors.

To add mesh points or lines:

1. Deselect all, and make sure smart guides are on (Cmd-U/Ctrl-U), with Object Highlighting (Preferences > Smart Guides & Slices).

2. Choose the Mesh tool (U).

3. Choose a color from the Swatches palette or Color palette, then click inside a mesh patch **3**–**4**. A new mesh point with connecting mesh lines will appear, and the current fill color will be applied to that point.
   or

(Continued on the following page)

Recolor Mesh; Add Mesh Points, Lines

Choose a fill color, then click an existing mesh line to add a new line perpendicular to it **1**–**2**.

or

Shift-click a mesh line to add a mesh point using the existing color from that line.

4. *Optional:* To recolor a new mesh point with a color from elsewhere in the same object, keep the point selected, choose the Eyedropper tool (I), ✐ then Shift-click a color.

➤ You can also recolor a gradient mesh by using Filter > Colors > Adjust Colors, Convert to CMYK (or Convert to RGB), Invert Colors, or Saturate.

Follow these instructions to **add** or **remove** square-shaped (not diamond-shaped) **anchor points** from a **mesh object.** You'll use these points to reshape the mesh object—not to add colors or push colors around on the mesh. If you want to add diamond-shaped mesh points with their connecting mesh lines, follow the previous set of instructions instead.

To add or remove square points:

I. Choose the Direct Selection tool (A), then click the edge of a mesh object. Zoom in on it, if you need to.

2. To add an anchor point, choose the Add Anchor Point tool (+), ✒ then click the outer edge of the mesh object or click a mesh line inside the object **3**.

or

To delete a user-created anchor point, choose the Delete Anchor Point tool (-), ✒ then click the point **4**.

Recoloring tips

To select and recolor multiple instances of the same color, choose the Direct Selection tool, click a mesh point or patch that you want to recolor, choose Select > Same > **Fill Color,** then choose a new color from the Color palette or the Swatches palette.

To make a color area **smaller,** add more mesh lines around it in a different color. To **spread** a color, delete mesh points from around it or assign the same color to adjacent mesh points.

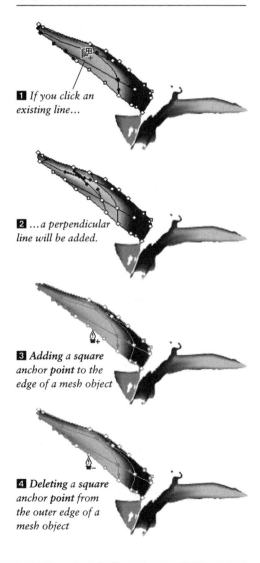

1 *If you click an existing line...*

2 *...a perpendicular line will be added.*

3 *Adding a square anchor* **point** *to the edge of a mesh object*

4 *Deleting a square anchor* **point** *from the outer edge of a mesh object*

Add, Remove Square Points

1 *Option-click/Alt-click a mesh point to delete it.*

2 *The point is deleted.*

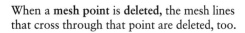

3 *Drag a direction line.*

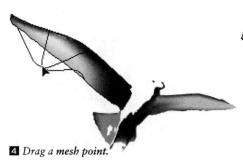

4 *Drag a mesh point.*

When a **mesh point** is **deleted,** the mesh lines that cross through that point are deleted, too.

To delete mesh points:

1. Choose the Direct Selection tool (A), then click the edge of the gradient mesh object.

2. Click the mesh point that you want to delete, then press Delete/Backspace.
or
Choose the Mesh tool (U), then Option-click/Alt-click the point that you want to delete (a minus sign will appear next to the pointer) **1**–**2**.

Next, you'll learn how to **push mesh colors around**—it's like electronic sculpting!

To reshape the mesh:

1. Choose the Direct Selection tool (A), then click the edge of the gradient mesh object.

2. Click a mesh point or anchor point.

3. Do any of the following:

Lengthen or rotate either of the point's direction lines to reshape its adjacent mesh lines **3**. To constrain the line angle to a multiple of 45° (or the current Constrain Angle in Illustrator [Edit, in Windows] > Preferences > General), start dragging the line, then Shift-drag.

Drag a mesh point **4**, mesh patch **5**, or anchor point. You can drag it outside the object.

Shift-drag a mesh point to drag it along an existing mesh line.

To convert a mesh point into a corner point with direction lines that move independently of each other, choose the Convert Anchor Point tool (Shift-C), click the point, then drag either one of its direction lines.

Delete Mesh Points; Reshape Mesh

5 *Drag a mesh patch.*

To expand a standard gradient into separate objects:

1. Select an object that contains a standard gradient (not a gradient mesh) **1**.

2. Choose Object > Expand.

3. Click Expand Gradient To: Specify, then enter the desired number of objects to be created **2**. To print a gradient successfully, you'll need to enter a number that's high enough to produce smooth color transitions.

4. Click OK **3**. *Note:* The resulting number of objects may not match the specified number of objects if there were minimal color changes in the original gradient.

➤ You could also use the Expand command to simplify a gradient fill that won't print.

➤ To expand a gradient using the last-used "Specify [ ] Objects" setting, hold down Option/Alt as you choose Object > Expand.

This is another, albeit less useful, method for creating a gradient mesh—the **Expand** command.

To expand a radial or linear gradient into a gradient mesh:

1. Select an object that contains a radial or linear gradient **1**.

2. Choose Object > Expand.

3. Click Expand Gradient To: Gradient Mesh.

4. Click OK **4**. The resulting expanded objects can be a little confusing. What you get is a clipping path object that limits the gradient color area, with the mesh object below it. Use the Layers palette to view the nested groups, clipping path, and mesh.

Bird by Diane Margolin

1 *The original object contains a* ***linear gradient.***

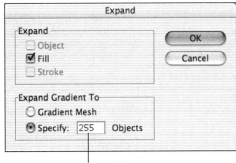

2 *In the* ***Expand*** *dialog box, specify the number of objects the gradient is to be expanded into.*

3 *After applying the* ***Expand*** *command, the gradient is converted into a series of separate rectangles, grouped with a clipping mask. Each rectangle is a different shade.*

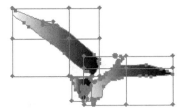

4 *This is the original object after expanding it into a* ***gradient mesh.***

APPEARANCES/STYLES 19

In this chapter you'll learn how to create, apply, copy, modify, and remove appearance attributes, which are editable strokes, fills, effects, transparency settings, etc. You'll also learn how to use the Graphic Styles palette to save appearance attributes as graphic styles; apply graphic styles to an object, group, or layer; and copy, edit, merge, and delete graphic styles.

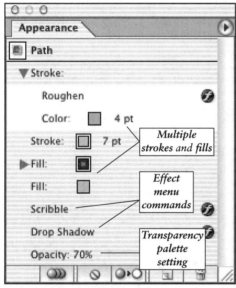

Multiple strokes and fills

Effect menu commands

Transparency palette setting

1 Use the **Appearance** palette to apply, restack, and remove **appearance attributes** from layers, sublayers, groups, objects, and graphic styles. This screenshot shows the appearance attributes for an **object**.

Using appearances

Appearances provide a whole new approach to object editing. Before appearances arrived on the scene, you could apply only one stroke and fill to an object. With appearances, you can apply multiple fills and strokes to the same object, and to each stroke or fill you can apply a different opacity level, blending mode, or Effect menu command. Furthermore, although appearance attributes change how an object looks, they don't actually alter its underlying path. Appearances add flexibility—and complexity—to object editing.

Because appearance attributes change only an object's appearance, not its actual underlying path, you can save, close, and reopen an illustration, and you'll still be able to re-edit or remove any appearance attributes in the saved file. When an object is selected, its appearance attributes are listed on the Appearance palette **1**. You can also use this palette to reedit, restack, and remove appearance attributes.

➤ Copy an object several times, then experiment with different appearance attributes for each copy. No commitment, no obligation. Create a handful of variations on a basic shape, and then gradually hone in until you achieve a combination of appearance attributes that you're satisfied with.

➤ Once you learn about the Appearance palette, read the Effects & Filters chapter to learn how to apply editable effects.

Appearances and layers

Any attributes that are applied to an object beyond just the run-of-the-mill stroke and fill are called **appearance attributes.** When an object contains appearance attributes, its listing has a gray **target circle** on the Layers palette **1**.

You can either apply appearance attributes to individual objects one by one or you can target a whole top-level layer or group for appearances. In the latter case, the appearance attributes that you choose will apply to all the objects that are nested within the targeted layer or group. For example, if you target a layer and then modify its opacity or blending mode, all objects nested within that layer will adopt that opacity or blending mode; that attribute can be reedited simply by retargeting the layer.

These are the basic techniques:

➤ To **select** an **object** or **group,** click the selection area or the target circle on the Layers palette. Clicking either of these icons will also cause that object or group to be targeted for appearance attributes.

➤ To **select** (but not target) a **layer,** click the selection area. To target a layer, click the target circle (see the sidebar on this page).

➤ To **view** and **modify** the existing **appearance attributes** for an object, group, or layer, click the gray target circle; Shift-click the gray circle to deselect that object, group, or layer.

To target appearances to a group or layer:

To target appearance attributes to a whole group or top-level layer, click its target circle on the Layers palette. A ring will appear around the circle, indicating an active target, and all the objects in that group or on that layer will become selected in the illustration. (Shift-click the ring to untarget.)

Layers and appearances

Although selecting and targeting both cause objects to become selected in your illustration, they're not interchangeable operations when you're working with whole layers. If you **target** a top-level layer by clicking its target circle and then apply appearance attributes (e.g., fill color, Effect menu command, Transparency palette values), those attributes will be applied to, and will be listed on the Appearance palette for, the layer as a whole.

If you click the **selection** area for a top-level layer instead of the target circle and then apply appearances, those attributes will be applied separately to each object or group in that layer, not to the layer as a whole. In this case, you won't see an itemized list of appearance attributes on the Appearance palette—you'll just see the generic words "mixed appearances" at the top of the palette. Nor will they be listed if you subsequently target the layer.

*This layer is **active** but **not targeted,** and it doesn't contain appearances.*

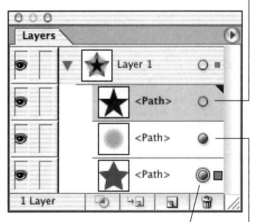

*This object is **targeted,** and it already contains appearances.*

1 *This path object **contains appearances,** but it's not currently targeted.*

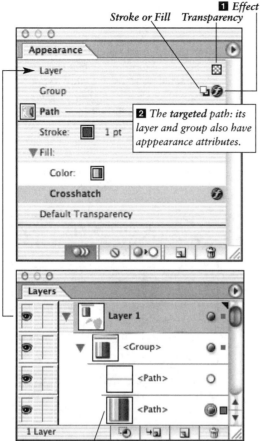

Stroke or Fill **1** *Effect* *Transparency*

2 *The targeted path: its layer and group also have apppearance attributes.*

3 *This targeted object is nested within a group and a layer, all of which have appearance attributes.*

The Appearance palette icons

One of three icons may display in the upper portion of the Appearance palette (Shift-F6) to the right of the word "Layer" or "Group" **1**:

➤ ⌑ means an additional stroke or fill attribute is applied to a layer or group.

➤ 🄵 means an effect is applied to a layer or group.

➤ ▨ means transparency is applied to a layer or group.

The generic name for the currently targeted item (e.g., Layer, Group, or Path) is listed in boldface at the top of the Appearance palette. If an object is targeted and that object is nested within a layer and/or group to which appearance attributes have been applied, the word(s) "Layer" and/or "Group" will also appear above the word "Path" at the top of the palette **2**–**3**.

If the selected object is a mesh, the word "Mesh" will appear instead of the word "Path." The same holds true for type ("Type"), an image ("Image"), a symbol ("Symbol"), an envelope ("Envelope"), a compound shape ("Compound Shape")—you get the idea.

When you **apply appearance attributes,** your object adopts a new look that can be modified or removed at any time, even after the file is saved, closed, and reopened.

To apply appearance attributes:

I. In the document window, select the object whose appearance attributes you want to modify.
or
On the Layers palette, click the gray circle for a layer, group, or object to target that item for appearance changes.

2. Display the Appearance palette (Shift-F6).

(Continued on the following page)

Palette Icons; Apply Appearance Attributes

3. On the Appearance palette, do any of the following 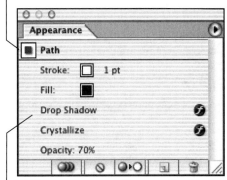:

Click **Stroke** to select the Stroke square on the Color palette, then modify the stroke color and/or stroke width via the Stroke palette.

Click **Fill** to select the Fill square on the Color palette, then modify the fill color.

Double-click **Default Transparency** (or the current transparency appearance attribute) to show the Transparency palette, then modify the Opacity value and/or change the blending mode.

Choose a command from a submenu on the **Effect** menu (for starters, try applying an effect from the Distort & Transform or Stylize submenu), modify the dialog box settings, then click OK. The Effect command will be listed in the attributes area of the palette. (Read more about effects in Chapter 22.)

Note: Remember to choose appearance commands from the Effect menu, not the Filter menu. Filter menu commands will permanently alter an object, whereas Effect menu commands, because they're vector effects, can be reedited or removed at any time without permanently changing the object. Some of the vector filters, for which there are Effect menu equivalents, are illustrated on pages 393–395.

Working with attributes

If a layer or group is targeted, the word **Contents** will appear on the attributes list on the Appearance palette; if an individual text object is targeted, you'll see the word **Type;** if an object with gradient mesh fill is targeted, you'll see the words **Mesh Points.**

The item that the appearance attributes are being targeted to is listed in boldface (e.g., Layer, Group, or Path).

■ The appearance attributes are listed in this part of the palette.

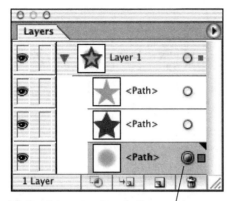

1 *A path is targeted on the Layers palette.*

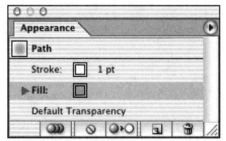

2 *The Fill attribute is clicked on the Appearance palette.*

3 *Attributes are applied to the Fill attribute; the Fill list expands automatically.*

Aside from merely listing appearance attributes, the Appearance palette can also be used to open palettes and other dialog boxes (e.g., Effect menu, Stroke) for previously applied appearance **attributes** in order to **edit** them.

To edit or restack appearance attributes:

1. In the document window, select the object whose appearance attributes you want to modify.
or
On the Layers palette, click the gray circle for a layer, group, or object to target that item for appearance changes.

2. On the Appearance palette, double-click any appearance attribute to open its dialog box or show its palette, and make modifications.
and/or
Drag any appearance attribute (except Opacity) upward or downward on the list. Its location will change on the list, and thus change how the object looks. For example, if you drag a stroke below a fill attribute and then lower the opacity of the fill attribute, the stroke will then show through the fill.

To edit an object's stroke or fill appearance attribute:

1. Target an object **1**. (To apply a stroke or fill to a layer or group, see the next page.)

2. On the Appearance palette, click Stroke or Fill **2**.

3. Change the opacity or blending mode using the Transparency palette, and/or apply an Effect menu command. These attributes will apply only to the selected stroke or fill—not to the whole object. The list for the attribute you're modifying will expand automatically **3**. You can click the triangle at any time to collapse the list.

A brush can be applied to a stroke. The brush name will appear next to the Stroke attribute on the Appearance palette. Double-click the brush name to open the Stroke Options dialog box.

To remove a brush stroke from a stroke attribute:

1. Target a layer, group, or object.

2. Show the Brushes palette (F5), then click the Remove Brush Stroke button ✕ at the bottom of the palette. Any prior stroke will be restored.

or

Click the Stroke attribute on the Appearance palette, then click the Delete Selected Item button 🗑 at the bottom of the palette. The stroke becomes None.

To apply multiple stroke or fill attributes:

1. Target a layer, group, or object ◼.

2. Choose Add New Fill (Cmd-/; Ctrl-/) or Add New Stroke (Cmd-Option-/; Ctrl-Alt-/).

or

Click an existing Stroke or Fill listing on the Appearance palette, then click the Duplicate Selected Item button 🗐 at the bottom of the palette ◼ (or drag the Stroke or Fill icon over the button).

Note: For text (as in our example), choose Add New Stroke, adjust the stroke width and color, then either add another stroke attribute or duplicate the first one.

3. A second Stroke or Fill attribute will appear on the palette ◼–◼. Now modify its attributes so it's different from the original.

➤ Make sure narrower strokes are stacked above wider strokes on the palette list. If the narrower strokes are on the bottom, you won't see them. Similarly, apply opacity and blending modes to the upper fill attributes, not the lower ones.

➤ If a layer, group, or object has multiple fills or strokes, be careful about clicking the attribute you want to modify.

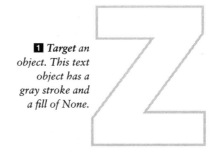

◼ *Target an object. This text object has a gray stroke and a fill of None.*

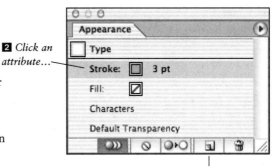

◼ *Click an attribute…*

*…then click the **Duplicate Selected Item** button.*

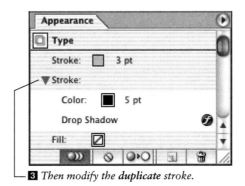

◼ *Then modify the **duplicate** stroke.*

◼ *After **duplicating** the stroke, widening the duplicate, and applying the Drop Shadow effect to the duplicate*

1 *Target a layer, group, or object, then click the **Reduce to Basic Appearance** button at the bottom of the Appearance palette.*

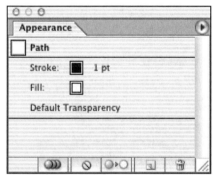

2 *All appearance attributes are **removed** from the targeted entity.*

To duplicate an appearance attribute:

1. Target a layer, group, or object.

2. Choose Duplicate Item from the Appearance palette menu.
or
Click an attribute, then click the Duplicate Selected Item button 🔲 at the bottom of the palette. Or drag an attribute over that button.

To remove an appearance attribute:

1. Target a layer, group, or object.

2. On the Appearance palette, click the attribute you want to remove.

3. Choose Remove Item from the palette menu.
or
Click the Delete Selected Item button 🗑 at the bottom of the palette (or drag the attribute over the button).

➤ The last remaining Fill and Stroke appearance attributes can't be removed. Clicking the Delete Selected Item button 🗑 for either of these appearance attributes will produce a fill or stroke of None.

To remove all appearance attributes from an item:

1. Target an object, layer, sublayer, or group.

2. To remove **all** the appearance attributes and apply a stroke and fill of **None,** click the Clear Appearance button ⊘ at the bottom of the Appearance palette.
or
To remove all the appearance attributes and keep only a **single stroke and fill** listing, click the Reduce to Basic Appearance button ⦿▸⦿ at the bottom of the Appearance palette **1**–**2**.

➤ If you target a layer or group, any appearances that were applied directly to nested paths within that layer or group won't be removed by the commands used in the instructions above. To remove appearances from a nested path, you need to target that path, not the path's layer or group.

To choose appearance options for future objects:

If the **New Art Has Basic Appearance** command on the Appearance palette menu has a check mark or you click the **New Art Has Basic Appearance** button  at the bottom of the palette, newly created objects will have only one fill and one stroke. With this option unchecked in either location, the currently displayed appearance attributes will apply automatically to new objects.

Blends and appearances

If you blend objects that contain different appearance attributes (e.g., effects, fills, or strokes), those appearance attributes will be in full force in the original objects and will have sequentially less intensity in the intermediate blend steps **1**. The Object > Blend > Make command automatically nests blend objects on a Blend sublayer.

If you blend objects that contain different blending modes, the blending mode for the topmost object will be applied to all the intermediate blend steps. The <Blend> sublayer on the Layers palette will have a gray target circle, indicating that an appearance attribute is applied to the objects. Also, the Knockout Group option will be checked on the Transparency palette by default. This prevents the blend steps from blending with or showing through each other when a blend object has an opacity below 100% or has a blending mode other than Normal. Uncheck Knockout Group if you want the blend steps to show through or blend with each other. Regardless of whether Knockout Group is on or off, though, objects behind the blend will be visible if the blend objects have an opacity below 100% or a blending mode other than Normal.

To attach appearance attributes to, and view the Transparency palette options for, an entire blend, first click the target circle for the <Blend> sublayer on the Layers palette, or select the blend in the document window with the Selection tool.

1 *The **Drop Shadow** effect was applied to the bottommost horse but not to the topmost horse, so the drop shadow fades gradually between the intermediate objects.*

1 *The default **Graphic Styles** palette for RGB documents*

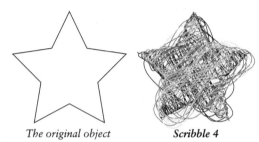

The original object   *Scribble 4*

RGB Denim   *Motion Trail Long*

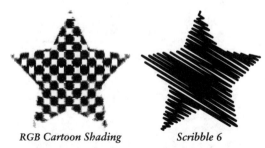

RGB Cartoon Shading   *Scribble 6*

2 *We applied a few Illustrator **graphic styles** to a star, just to give you an inkling of what styles can do.*

Using graphic styles

Graphic styles are used to quickly apply sets of attributes to objects. Any kind of appearance attributes can be saved in a graphic style, such as colors, gradients, patterns (stroke and fill), stroke attributes (weight, dash pattern, etc.), blending modes, transparency settings, and live effects. Even Attribute palette overprint options can be saved to a style. In short, any appearance attribute that can be applied to an object can also be saved as a graphic style.

Graphic styles are created, saved, and applied via the **Graphic Styles** palette (Shift-F5) **1**–**2**. Each graphic style's individual attributes, however, are listed on the Appearance palette, and the Appearance palette is also used to create or modify those attributes.

There are three main advantages to working with graphic styles:

➤ By applying a graphic style, you can apply many attributes at once with the click of a button.

➤ Like appearance attributes, graphic styles change the way an object looks without changing the underlying path. This means a graphic style can be turned on or off easily, and a different style can be applied at any time.

➤ If you edit a graphic style, the style will update on any objects to which it's already linked. This streamlines object editing and helps make object styling more consistent.

Graphic styles differ in one significant way from paragraph and character styles, which we discussed in Chapter 13. If you modify an attribute directly on an object to which a graphic style is already applied, that modification breaks the link between the selected object and the style. The object's style attributes won't be removed, but if you subsequently edit the style, that object's appearance won't change, because it's no longer associated with that style. This "local styling" has no effect on the original style, nor on any other objects that may be linked to that style.

(Continued on the following page)

Using Graphic Styles

There are a couple of rules you must keep in mind when applying and creating graphic styles:

➤ Graphic styles can be applied to layers, sublayers, groups, or objects. When applied to a layer or group, styles are associated with all the objects in the layer or group, as well as any new objects that are added to a layer or group after the style is applied.

➤ Only one graphic style can be associated with a layer, sublayer, group, or object at a time.

Graphic styles remain associated with the objects to which they're **applied,** even if you close and reopen the file.

To apply a graphic style to an object:

I. Choose the Selection tool (V), then select an object or objects in the document window.
or
On the Layers palette, click the target circle for an object **1**–**2**.

Remember, for a top-level layer, selecting and targeting have different functions! See page 182.

2. Click a style name or thumbnail on the Graphic Styles palette (Shift-F5) **3**–**4**.
or
Drag a style name or thumbnail from the Graphic Styles palette over a group or object in the document window. The object doesn't have to be selected.

➤ To access other Illustrator graphic style **NEW** libraries, choose from the Open Graphic Style Library submenu on the Graphic Styles palette menu.

➤ The name of the graphic style that's applied to the currently selected object will be listed at the top of the Appearance palette.

➤ To produce dramatic results on a placed image or rasterized object, apply a graphic style that contains raster effects (from the lower portion of the Effect menu). These effects can also be applied to vector objects.

1 *The original text object*

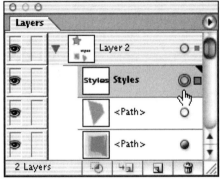

2 *The text object is **targeted** for an appearance change on the **Layers** palette.*

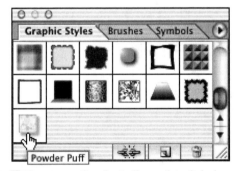

3 *Our custom Powder Puff **swatch** is clicked.*

4 *The graphic style appears on the **object**.*

1 *A graphic style is applied to a* ***group.***

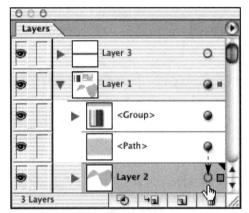

2 *Moving existing appearances from a <Path> to a sublayer (Layer 2, in this case)*

3 *Drag this* ***icon*** *from the* ***Appearance*** *palette over an object.*

If you **apply a graphic style** to a layer or a group, that style will be applied to all the current and subsequently created objects in that layer or group.

To apply a graphic style to a layer, sublayer, or group:

1. On the Layers palette, click the target circle for a layer, sublayer, or group.

2. Click a style name or thumbnail on the Graphic Styles palette **1**.

➤ To choose a different view for the Graphic Styles palette, from the palette menu, choose Thumbnail View, Small List View, or Large List View.

To copy or move appearance attributes from one object or layer to another:

To **copy** appearance attributes, Option-drag/Alt-drag the target circle from the item that you want to copy onto the target circle for another layer, group, or object. Pause for the appearances to copy.

or

To **move** appearance attributes from one item to another, drag a target circle from one layer, group, or object to another without holding down any keys **2**. The appearance attributes will be removed from the original layer, group, or object.

To copy all the attributes of a graphic style from one object to another:

1. Choose the Selection tool (V), then click an object whose graphic style or appearance attributes you want to copy.

2. Drag the square thumbnail from the top left corner of the Appearance palette over an unselected object **3**.

If you **break the link** between an object and a graphic style, the object's style attributes won't be removed, but if you subsequently edit the style, the object's appearance won't change because it no longer has any association with that style.

To break the link between a graphic style and a layer, sublayer, group, or object:

1. Choose the Selection tool (V), then select an object or objects in the document window, or click the target circle for an object on the Layers palette.
   or
   If the style was applied to a group or layer, click the target circle for a layer, sublayer, or group on the Layers palette.

2. Click the Break Link to Graphic Style button ⟨image⟩ at the bottom of the Graphic Styles palette .
   or
   Change any appearance attribute for the selected item (e.g., apply a different fill color, stroke color, pattern, gradient, or effect).

   The graphic style name will no longer be listed at the top of the Appearance palette for the selected item.

Next, we offer two methods for creating a new graphic style. In the first set of instructions, you'll **create a style** based on a styled **object.** This method will probably feel the most natural and intuitive, especially if you're going to experiment with various settings for the new style. To create a new graphic style from a duplicate style, follow the instructions on the next page instead.

To create a new graphic style by styling an object:

1. Target an object that has the attributes you want to save as a graphic style. Use the Appearance palette to create other attributes you want the style to have 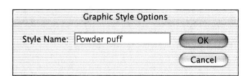.

2. From the Graphic Styles palette menu, choose New Graphic Style, enter a name for the style, then click OK . The new

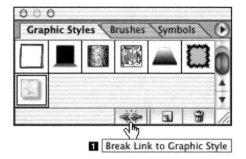

1 Break Link to Graphic Style

2 *Click the object whose attributes you want to save as a graphic style.*

3 *Give the new graphic style a* **name.**

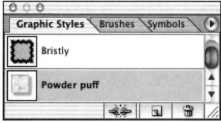

4 *The* **new** *style swatch appears at the bottom of the Graphic Styles palette.*

Break Link; New Graphic Style from Object

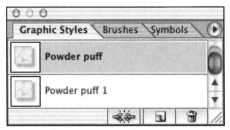

1 *Our Powder puff graphic style is duplicated.*

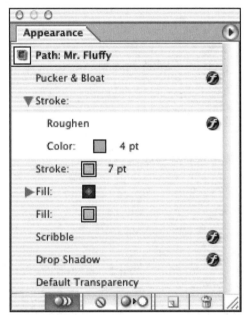

2 *The duplicate style is renamed, and then its attributes are edited via the Appearance palette. The graphic style name is listed at the top of the palette.*

style will appear at the bottom of the list or below the existing swatches on the Graphic Styles palette (**4**, previous page).
or
Drag the thumbnail next to the item name from the top of the Appearance palette onto the Graphic Styles palette, or drag the object onto the Graphic Styles palette. Double-click the new style swatch, type a name for it, then click OK.

To duplicate a graphic style:

1. On the Graphic Styles palette, click the style swatch or name that you want to copy.
2. Click the New Graphic Style button or drag the swatch over the button. The number "1" will be added to the existing style name **1**.
or
Choose Duplicate Graphic Style from the Graphic Styles palette menu, double-click the duplicate, type a name for the style, then click OK.
3. Click the duplicate graphic style swatch or name, then use the Appearance palette to edit the style so that it contains the desired attributes **2**.

Beware! If you **edit** a **graphic style,** the style will update on any objects it's currently applied to. If you don't want this to happen, duplicate the style instead (see the previous page) and then edit the duplicate.

To edit a graphic style:

1. In order to preview your changes, apply the graphic style you want to edit to an object 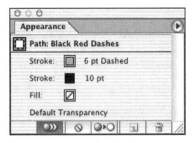.

2. Via the Appearance palette (Shift-F6), edit or restack the existing appearance attributes or add new attributes .

3. Choose Redefine Graphic Style "[style name]" from the Appearance palette menu.
   or
   Option-drag/Alt-drag the object thumbnail from the top left corner of the Appearance palette over the original style swatch on the Graphic Styles palette.

   Regardless of which method you use, the style swatch will update to reflect the modifications , and any objects to which the style is currently applied will update automatically .

➤ While editing a graphic style, don't click on other styled objects or style swatches, or you'll lose your current appearance attributes settings.

1 *Start by **applying** the graphic style that you want to edit to an object.*

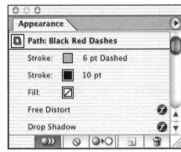

2 *Edit the style on the object, via the **Appearance** palette.*

3 *The style is replaced on the **Graphic Styles** palette.*

4 *The graphic style also **updates** automatically on other objects to which it was previously applied.*

Edit Graphic Style

What stays, what goes

Attributes are listed on the Appearance palette in the order in which they're applied. When graphic styles are merged, the final order of fill attributes on the Appearance palette follows the top to bottom order of the styles that were selected for merging on the Graphic Styles palette. The fill of the topmost selected style on the Graphic Styles palette will be listed above other fills on the Apperance palette in the merged style. Of course, if you merge graphic styles that contain fully opaque fills, only the topmost fill will be visible.

To achieve different results using the same fills, edit their opacity and/or blending modes or restack them on the Appearance palette list (and thus change the order in which they are applied).

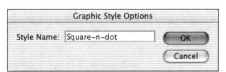

1 *Two styles are clicked, then Merge Graphic Styles is chosen from the palette menu.*

2 *The merged style is **renamed**.*

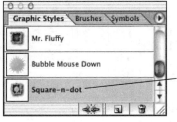

3 *The newly **merged style** appears on the Graphic Styles palette.*

If you have **two graphic styles** whose attributes you want to combine into one, you can **merge** them into one new (additional) style. The original swatches won't be altered. Before proceeding, please read the sidebar at left.

To merge graphic styles:

1. Cmd-click/Ctrl-click two or more style swatches or names on the Graphic Styles palette **1**.

2. Choose Merge Graphic Styles from the Graphic Styles palette menu.

3. Enter a name for the new merged style, then click OK **2**. A new style swatch will appear at the bottom of the list of names or below the existing swatches, depending on the current palette view **3**.

If you **delete** a **graphic style** that's associated with any objects in your document, the object's appearances will remain. However, the objects will no longer be associated with the style, since it no longer exists.

To delete a style from the Graphic Styles palette:

1. On the Graphic Styles palette (Shift-F5), click the style you want to remove.

2. Click the Delete Graphic Style button 🗑 on the palette.
   or
   Choose Delete Graphic Style from the Graphic Styles palette menu.

3. Click Yes.

➤ Oops! Change your mind? You can Undo the deletion of a graphic style.

Merge, Delete Graphic Styles

Graphic styles from Illustrator's predefined **style libraries** or any other Illustrator CS files can be **added** to the current document's Graphic Styles palette. Graphic styles can't be deleted or edited directly from the library, but they can be edited once they're copied into the Graphic Styles palette.

To add graphic styles from a library or another file to the Graphic Styles palette:

1. Open the Graphic Styles palette (Shift-F5).

2. If the graphic style library that you want to add styles from is already in the Adobe Illustrator CS/Presets/Graphic Styles folder (e.g., a graphic style library from Adobe), choose from the Open Graphic Style Library submenu on the palette menu **1**–**4**.

(NEW)

or

If the graphic style library is in a location other than the Adobe Illustrator CS/Presets/Graphic Styles folder, choose Open Graphic Style Library > Other Library from the palette menu, then locate and open the library. You can also use this command to open any Illustrator CS file, and then use that file's Graphic Styles palette as a library.

(NEW)

3. To add a graphic style by styling an object, select an object, then click a style thumbnail in the library. Or drag a style thumbnail from the library over any object, selected or not. In either case, the new style will appear on the Graphic Styles palette.

or

To add a style to the Graphic Styles palette without styling an object, deselect all, then click a style thumbnail in the library.

or

Shift-click consecutive styles or Cmd-click/Ctrl-click individual styles on the library palette, then drag the selected styles onto the Graphic Styles palette or choose Add to Graphic Styles from the library palette menu.

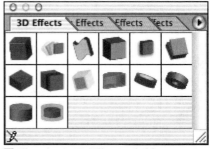

1 *Illustrator's **3D Effects** style library*

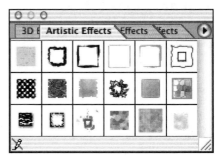

2 *Illustrator's **Artistic Effects** style library*

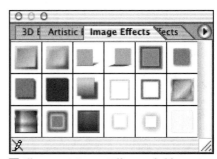

3 *Illustrator's **Image Effects** style library*

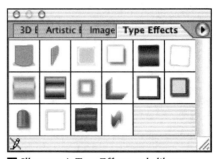

4 *Illustrator's **Type Effects** style library*

To create a graphic style library: NEW

1. In a new Illustrator document, create objects with the desired appearance attributes, and save those appearances as styles on the Graphic Styles palette.

2. *Optional:* If you want to remove all styles from the Graphic Styles palette that aren't currently applied to objects in the document, choose Select All Unused from the Graphic Styles palette menu, click the Delete Graphic Style button 🗑 on the palette, then click Yes.

3. From the Graphic Styles palette menu, choose Save Graphic Style Library, enter a name for the library file (the Presets/ Graphic Styles folder in the application folder will be chosen automatically as the location), then click Save.

4. Quit/Exit Illustrator, then relaunch. The new style library will be listed on, and can be opened from, the palette menu's Open Graphic Style Library submenu.

➤ Any brush that's used in a style in a graphic style library but that isn't present on the document's Brushes palette will be added to the document's Brushes palette if that style is applied to an object in the document.

➤ To restore the default graphic style thumbnails to the Graphic Styles palette, from the palette menu, choose Open Graphic Style Library > Default_RGB or Default_CMYK, then add the needed thumbnails (follow step 3 in the instructions on the previous page).

Create Graphic Style Library

When you **expand** an object's **appearances,** the paths that were used to create the appearances become separate objects and can be edited individually. This command is also helpful when exporting files to other applications that can't read appearances per se. Note that this command creates dozens of new path objects.

To expand an object's appearance attributes:

1. Select an object that contains the appearances (or graphic style) that you want to expand **1**–**2**.

2. Choose Object > Expand Appearance **3**. On the Layers palette, you'll see a new <Group> (or a nested series of groups) containing the original object and the effects and appearance attributes, which will be listed either as paths or images.

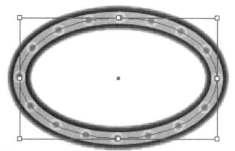

1 *Select an object to which a graphic style is applied.*

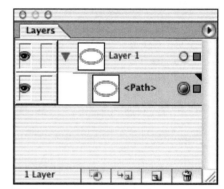

2 *The Layers palette **before** choosing the* ***Expand Appearance*** *command: the <Path> object is targeted.*

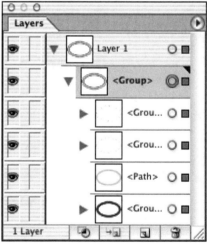

3 *The Layers palette **after** choosing the* ***Expand Appearance*** *command*

MASKS/TRANSPARENCY 20

In this chapter you'll learn how to create a clipping mask, which works like a picture frame, and then you'll learn how to restack, select, copy, lock, edit, or add objects to a clipping set.

You'll also learn how to use the Transparency palette to apply opacity levels and blending modes to a layer, group, or object; restrict those effects to specific objects; use the transparency grid; create, reshape, and use opacity masks; and apply the Feather command.

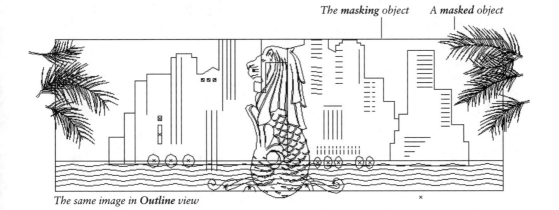

The **masking** object   A **masked** object

*The same image in **Outline** view*

Clipping sets

In Illustrator, a **clipping mask** works like a picture frame or mat. While it's in effect, it hides (clips) parts of an illustration that fall outside its borders; only parts of objects within the confines of the masking object will be visible. Masked objects can be moved, restacked, reshaped, or repainted.

To create a clipping set:

1. Arrange the object or objects to be masked **1**. They can be grouped or not. To avoid a printing error, don't use very intricate objects.

2. Put the masking object, which we call the "clipping path," in front of the objects it will be masking. If you need to restack it, on the Layers palette, drag its name upward on the list. The clipping path can be an open path or closed path. It can have a brush stroke, but remember, the path itself—not the brush stroke—will be used as the clipping path. You can use type as a clipping path without having to convert it to outlines, and you can also use a compound path as a clipping path.

3. Choose the Selection tool (V).

4. Select the clipping path and the object or objects behind it that are to be masked.

5. Choose Object > Clipping Mask > Make (Cmd-7/Ctrl-7) **2**. The clipping path will now have a stroke and fill of None, and all the objects will remain selected. The words "<Clipping Path>" (underlined) will appear on the Layers palette (unless text was used as the clipping path, in which case the text character[s] will be underlined instead). Also, the clipping path and masked objects will be moved into a clipping set <Group> in the top-level layer of the original clipping path object.

   Note: To recolor the stroke or fill of a clipping path, see page 353.

➤ Don't let the inconsistency between the command name ("Clipping Mask > Make") and the listing on the Layers palette ("Clipping Path") confuse you. They refer to the same thing.

Clipping sets and layers

The **Make/Release Clipping Mask** button at the bottom of the Layers palette can be used to clip objects, groups, and even other clipping masks that are nested within the currently active top-level layer. A **clipping set** will be created, but it won't be in a group. We recommend putting all the objects to be masked on one top-level layer before clicking this button.

The instructions on pages 351–354 in this chapter also apply to clipping sets that are made with objects nested within one top-level layer, except here, instead of working with a group, you'll be working with the layer.

If you export your file using File > Export and choose Photoshop (psd) format, keep the following in mind: A clipping set in a layer will export to Photoshop as a layer with a vector mask, whereas a clipping set within a group will export to Photoshop as a layer without a vector mask.

1 *The original objects: a standard type character on top of a placed bitmap image*

2 *After selecting both objects and applying Object > **Clipping Mask** > Make*

1 *The object to be added (the star) is moved over the clipping set (the banner shape) to the desired x/y location.*

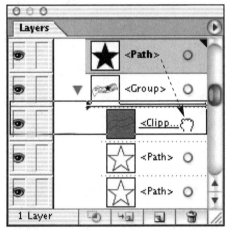

2 *A path is moved downward into the **clipping set** <Group>.*

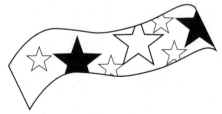

3 *The object has been **added** to the clipping set.*

We'll refer to a clipping mask and the objects it's masking as a **clipping set.**

To select a whole clipping set:

On the Layers palette (F7), click the selection area for the layer or group containing the clipping set.

or

Choose the Selection tool (V), then click the clipping path or one of the masked objects in the document window.

To select an individual clipping path or masked object:

On the Layers palette, click the selection area for the clipping path or a masked object.

or

Choose the Direct Selection tool (A), then click the clipping path or a masked object in the document window. You can use smart guides to help you locate the objects (check Object Highlighting in Illustrator [Edit, in Windows] > Preferences > Smart Guides & Slices).

To select all the clipping masks in your illustration:

Deselect all objects, then choose Select > Object > Clipping Masks. (With the Selection tool, Shift-click the edge of any masking object you don't want selected.) *Note:* This feature won't select type if the type is being used as a clipping mask.

To add an object to a clipping set:

1. Choose the Selection tool (V).

2. In the document window, move the object to be added over the clipping set **1**.

3. On the Layers palette, expand the list for the clipping set <Group> or layer.

4. Drag the object to be added to the set upward or downward into the <Group> **2** or layer, and release when the object name is in the desired position **3**.

➤ To change the stacking order of an object in a clipping set, drag it upward or downward on the Layers palette.

Select Objects in, Add Objects to Clipping Set

Basic stacking techniques are explained on pages 190–191.

To restack a masked object within its clipping set:

On the Layers palette (F7), drag the object name upward or downward to a new position within the group or layer 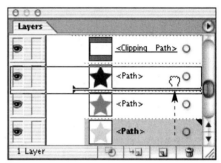–.

To copy a masked object:

1. On the Layers palette, click the selection area for the object you want to copy.

2. Option-drag/Alt-drag the selection square upward or downward, and release it somewhere within the same clipping set <Group> or layer.

3. The copy will be in the same *x/y* location as the original object, so you'll probably want to reposition it. You can use the Direct Selection tool to do this. Or select the masked object via the Layers palette, then move it using the Selection tool.

➤ If you drag an object's selection square or name outside its group or layer, it will no longer be in the clipping set.

Using the Layers palette, you can lock any object within a **clipping set** or lock an entire group to prevent it from being moved.

To lock a clipping set or an object within it:

To lock the whole clipping set, click the blank box in the second column for the <Group> or layer.

or

To lock one object in the group or layer, expand the clipping <Group> list on the Layers palette, then click the blank box in the second column for the clipping path or a masked object.

➤ To unlock a clipping set or object, click its padlock icon (the padlock will disappear).

1 *The original **clipping set**, masked by a rectangle*

2 *The lightest star <Path> is dragged **upward**...*

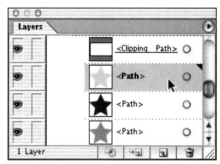

3 *...to the **top** of its clipping set.*

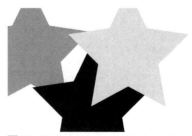

4 *The lightest star is now in **front** of the other masked objects.*

1 *Select the object you want to unmask.*

2 *The object is **unmasked** and repositioned.*

3 *The original clipping mask*

4 *After applying a black **fill** to the clipping mask object and recoloring the masked objects*

It's easy to **unmask** an object. All you gotta do is drag it outside its group or top-level layer on the Layers palette.

To unmask one object:

1. Expand the clipping set list on the Layers palette.
2. *Optional:* For the object you want to unmask, click the object name on the Layers palette. Or choose the Direct Selection tool (A), then click the object in the document window **1**.
3. On the Layers palette, drag the nested object upward or downward out of the group or layer **2**.
➤ To simultaneously unmask an object and delete it from the illustration, select it, then press Delete/Backspace.

To recolor a clipping path:

1. Select the clipping path by clicking in its selection area on the Layers palette.
2. Apply color as you would to any object **3**–**6**. The fill and stroke will be listed as attributes on the Appearance palette.

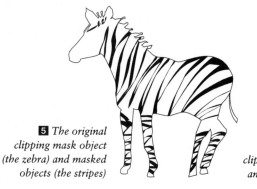

5 *The original clipping mask object (the zebra) and masked objects (the stripes)*

6 *The recolored clipping mask object and masked objects*

Unmask One Object; Recolor Clipping Path

353

If you **release** a clipping set, the complete, original objects will redisplay. The former clipping path will be listed as a standard path on the Layers palette. If you created the clipping set via Object > Clipping Mask, use Method 1 below; if you created the clipping set via the Layers palette, use Method 2.

To release a clipping set:

Method 1 (via a command)

1. Choose the Selection tool (V).

2. In the document window, click any part of the clipping set **1**.
   or
   On the Layers palette, click the selection area for the clipping set group you want to release.
   or
   On the Layers palette, click the selection area for the clipping path.

3. Choose Object > Clipping Mask > Release (Cmd-Option-7/Ctrl-Alt-7) **2**. The <Group> listing for the clipping set will disappear from the Layers palette.

Method 2 (via the Layers palette)

1. On the Layers palette (F7), click the name of the top-level layer that contains a clipping set, or click the selection area for that layer.
   or
   Select a group that contains a clipping path.

2. Click the Make/Release Clipping Mask button 🔲 at the bottom of the Layers palette. The <Group> listing for the clipping set will remain on the palette.

   Note: A whole clipping set, if created via the Layers palette, can't be selected using the Selection tool; you have to use the Layers palette.

➤ The stroke and fill were removed from the clipping path when the mask was created, so unless you recolored it, it will still have a stroke and fill of None. If you want to recolor it, use the Layers palette to select it first.

Learn from the masters

Once you've mastered the basics, we recommend Sharon Steuer's four-color ***The Adobe Illustrator CS Wow! Book*** (Peachpit Press), which features advanced tips and techniques from Illustrator pros.

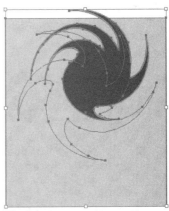

1 *The original **clipping set***

2 *After choosing Object > Clipping Mask > **Release***

Exporting transparency

Exporting a file that contains transparency to another application involves choosing options in the File > Export dialog boxes and in the Document Setup dialog box. Read about these options in Chapter 26. Outputting transparency can be very problematic!

1 *A variety of opacities and blending modes were applied to the objects in this illustration.*

Transparency

Using Illustrator's transparency controls **1**, you can add a touch of realism to your drawings. Study a real object on your desk for a minute, such as a lamp, or your keyboard if it's in one of the jelly colors. When a lamp is on, the shade looks semitransparent rather than solid. You might say "The shade is white" when you describe it. In reality, though, it's not a dense, solid white, but rather various permutations of white—especially when a light bulb is projecting light through it. Objects in real life have different densities, depending on what material they're made of. If you have tools or commands for rendering light filtering through various materials, you can create a sense of realism.

If you draw a window, for example, you can then draw a tinted, semisheer, diaphanous curtain on top of it. If you draw a vase on a table, you can create a realistic shadow for the vase that feathers softly into the table color.

In Illustrator, the opacity of any kind of object can be changed at any time, even the opacity of editable type. You can also choose a blending mode for any object to control how it blends with objects below it.

Yet another way to work with transparency in Illustrator is to turn an object into an opacity mask. In this scenario, the lights and darks of the top masking object will mask (control the visiblity of) the objects below it.

First we'll show you how to change an object's opacity and blending mode.

The Opacity slider on the Transparency palette controls the transparency of each object; the blending modes control how an object's color is affected by the colors in underlying objects. When a group or layer is targeted, the transparency settings affect all the objects in that group or layer. Objects that are added to a group or layer adopt that group or layer's transparency settings.

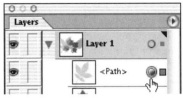

1 *On the Layers palette, click the **target** circle for an object, group, or layer.*

To change the opacity or blending mode of an object, group, or layer:

1. Show the Layers palette (F7), then select, or click the target circle **1** for, an object whose opacity or blending mode you want to change. For an image that was pasted, or dragged and dropped, target the <Image>. To edit the appearance of all the objects on a group or layer, you must click that group or layer's target circle.
   or
   Select some type characters with a type tool, or select a whole type object using the Selection tool.

2. Show the Transparency palette (Shift-F10). A thumbnail for the selected layer, group, or object will display on the palette.

3. Move the Opacity slider (0–100%) **2**–**3**.
   and/or
   Choose a different blending mode from the pop-up menu (see "The blending modes" beginning on the next page).

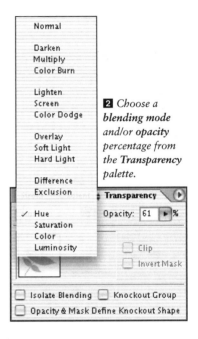

2 *Choose a **blending mode** and/or **opacity** percentage from the **Transparency** palette.*

To change the opacity or blending mode of only an object's fill or stroke:

1. Click the target circle for an object on the Layers palette. To change a type object's stroke or fill separately, see the sidebar on page 358.

2. On the Appearance palette (Shift-F6), click Fill or Stroke.

3. On the Transparency palette (Shift-F10), move the Opacity slider **4** and/or choose a different blending mode. Attribute changes will be nested under the targeted object's Fill or Stroke attribute on the Appearance palette.

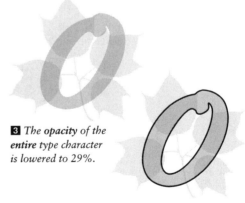

3 *The **opacity** of the entire type character is lowered to 29%.*

4 *The type **Fill opacity** is lowered to 29%; the Stroke opacity is left at 100%.*

Applying blending modes

➤ To change the blending mode for an individual object, first **target** the **object,** then choose a blending mode from the Transparency palette.

➤ Or to ensure consistency, **target** a **group** or **layer** before choosing a blending mode. The mode you choose will apply to all existing and future objects that are nested within that group or layer.

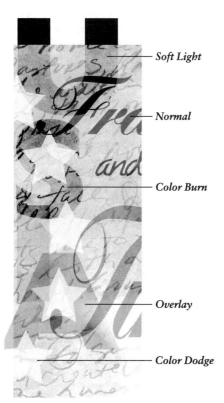

Soft Light

Normal

Color Burn

Overlay

Color Dodge

1 *Text objects in front of an image object, using five different blending modes*

The blending modes

You can choose from 16 **blending modes** on the Transparency palette (Shift-F10)—the very same modes that you may already be familiar with if you use Photoshop **1**. The blending mode that you choose for an object affects how that object modifies underlying colors (the "base color").

NORMAL

All base colors are modified equally. At 100% opacity, the object color will be opaque.

DARKEN

Base colors that are lighter than the object color are modified; base colors that are darker than the object color are not. Use with an object color that is darker than the base colors you want to modify.

MULTIPLY

A dark object color removes the lighter parts of the base color to produce a darker base color. A light object color darkens the base color less. Good for creating semi-transparent shadows.

COLOR BURN

A dark object color darkens the base color. A light object color tints the base color slightly.

LIGHTEN

Base colors that are darker than the object color are modified; base colors that are lighter than the object color are not. Use with an object color that is lighter than the base colors you want to modify.

SCREEN

A light object color removes the darker parts of the base color to produce a lighter, bleached base color. A dark object color lightens the base color less.

COLOR DODGE

A light object color lightens the base color. A dark object color tints the base color slightly.

OVERLAY

Multiplies (darkens) dark areas and screens (lightens) light base colors. Preserves luminosity (light and dark) values. Black

(Continued on the following page)

Blending Modes

and white areas aren't changed, so details are preserved.

SOFT LIGHT

Lightens the base color if the object color is light, darkens the base color if the object color is dark. Preserves luminosity values in the base color. Creates a soft, subtle lighting effect.

HARD LIGHT

Screens (lightens) the base color if the object color is light, multiplies (darkens) the base color if the object color is dark. Heightens contrast in the blended color areas. Good for creating glowing highlights and composite effects.

DIFFERENCE

Creates a color negative effect on the base color. When the object color is light, the negative (or inverse) effect is more pronounced. Produces marked color changes.

EXCLUSION

Grays out the base color where the object color is dark. Inverts the base color where the object color is light.

HUE

The object color's hue is applied. Saturation and luminosity values aren't changed in the base color.

SATURATION

The object color's saturation is applied. Hue and luminosity values aren't changed in the base color.

COLOR

The object color's saturation and hue are applied. The base color's light and dark (luminosity) values aren't changed, so detail is maintained. Good for tinting.

LUMINOSITY

The base color's luminosity values are replaced by tonal (luminosity) values from the object color. Hue and saturation aren't modified in the base color.

Changing a type object's stroke or fill

Before you can change the opacity of a type object's stroke separately from its fill, or vice versa, you must either convert the type to outlines or, if you want to keeps the type editable, follow these instructions:

1. Select the type object using the Selection tool.

2. Choose **Add New Fill** or **Add New Stroke** from the Appearance palette menu, then choose fill and stroke colors and a stroke weight. Make sure the type is large enough for both the fill and stroke to be visible.

3. Double-click the word "Characters" on the Appearance palette; all the characters in the object and a type tool will become selected.

4. Choose a fill and stroke of None for each Stroke and Fill attribute on the Appearance palette.

5. Click the word "Type" on the Appearance palette, then click the Fill or Stroke attribute.

6. Modify the Fill or Stroke attribute by moving the Opacity slider and/or choosing a different blending mode on the Transparency palette.

1 *The original objects (an image and a group of squares): Each square's own blending mode and opacity interacts with **all** the underlying layers.*

2 *With **Isolate Blending** on for the group of nested squares, the blending modes affect only objects **within** the group (where the objects in the group don't overlap each other, though, you can still see through to the globe below the group).*

If you apply a blending mode to multiple selected objects, that mode will become an appearance for each of those objects. In other words, the objects will blend with one another and with underlying objects below them. Checking the **Isolate Blending** option, discussed below, "seals" a collection of objects so the blending modes will affect only those objects—not underlying objects below them.

Note: The Isolate Blending option has no effect on opacity settings, which means underlying objects will still show through any object that isn't fully opaque.

To restrict a blending mode effect to specific objects:

1. On the Layers palette (F7), click the target circle for a group or layer that contains nested objects to which a blending mode or modes are applied **1**.

2. Check Isolate Blending on the Transparency palette **2**. Nested objects within the group or layer will blend with each other, but those objects won't blend with any underlying objects outside the layer or group.

   Note: To reverse the effect, retarget the group or layer, then uncheck Isolate Blending.

➤ Isolate Blending can also be used on individual objects that have overlapping strokes and/or fills. Each stroke or fill can have a different blending mode.

➤ If Isolate Blending is checked for objects nested within a group or layer and the Illustrator file is exported to Photoshop (via File > Export, with the Photoshop [psd] format chosen), the group will be preserved as a separate layer within a layer set and each layer will keep its blending mode setting from Illustrator.

Isolate Blending

The **Knockout Group** option on the Transparency palette controls whether or not objects nested in a group or layer will show through each other (knock out) where they overlap. This option affects only objects within the currently targeted group or layer.

To knock out objects:

1. Nest objects in the same group or layer and arrange them so they partially overlap each other. In order to see how the Knockout Group option works, apply an opacity value or values below 100% and/or a blending mode or modes other than Normal to some or all of the nested objects.

2. On the Layers palette (F7), target the group or layer that the objects are nested within **1**.

3. On the Transparency palette (Shift-F10), keep clicking the Knockout Group box until a check mark displays **2**. With this option checked, objects won't show through each other, and if their opacities are below 100%, you'll still be able to see through them to objects below them.

➤ If both Knockout Group and Isolate Blending are checked, nested objects will look as if they have a blending mode of Normal, regardless of their actual blending mode.

➤ To apply the Knockout Group option to an object or outline type that has only transparency applied to its stroke, select the object, click Default Transparency on the Appearance palette to target the whole object, then check Knockout Group. The object's stroke will no longer be transparent to its fill **3**–**4**.

To turn off the Knockout Group option:

1. Target the group or layer to which the option is applied.

2. On the Transparency palette (Shift-F10), keep clicking the Knockout Group box until the check mark disappears.

When to put it in neutral

Objects whose opacity is below 100% will show through each other whether the Knockout Group icon is blank (unchecked) or **neutral.** Neutral is represented by a dash on the Mac ▬ and by a green square in Windows. ▣ Choose the neutral setting for a group of objects nested within a larger group if you want to make the nested group independent of the Knockout Group setting for the larger group.

1 *The original group of nested objects on top of an image, with Knockout Group off*

2 *With Knockout Group on, objects are no longer transparent to each other and no longer blend with each other.*

3 *Knockout Group off: Half the stroke is transparent to the object's fill.*

4 *Knockout Group on: The stroke knocks out the object's fill.*

Knockout Group

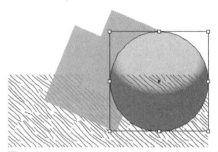

1 *With* **Knockout Group** *on, the opacity mask covers shapes that are nested in the same layer.*

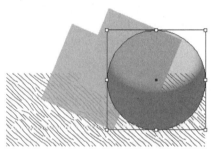

2 *After* **Opacity & Mask Define Knockout Shape** *is checked, shapes nested in the same layer are revealed through the opacity mask.*

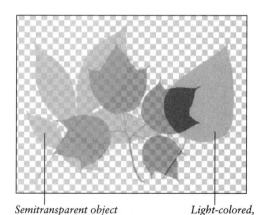

Semitransparent object   *Light-colored, opaque object*

3 *With the* **transparency grid** *showing, you can easily see which objects are opaque and which are not.*

If the **Knockout Group** option is on for a group or layer and that group or layer contains an **opacity mask**, Knockout Group will prevent any nested group or objects from displaying through any transparency in the mask. To reveal nested objects below the opacity mask, do as follows.

To use an opacity mask within a knockout group or layer:

1. On the Layers palette (F7), target a group or sublayer that contains an opacity mask as well as other nested objects below the mask. Make sure the Knockout Group option is checked for the group or sublayer.

2. Target the opacity mask object or group (look for the dashed underline).

3. On the Transparency palette (Shift-F10), check Opacity & Mask Define Knockout Shape **1**–**2**. Any objects in the same nested group that are below the opacity mask object will now show through areas of transparency in the opacity mask.

➤ Regardless of whether Opacity & Mask Define Knockout Shape is on or off, objects on lower layers will always show through transparent or semitransparent areas in the opacity mask.

Once you start working with semitransparent objects, it may be hard to distinguish between objects that have a light but solid tint and those that are semitransparent. With the **transparency grid** on, you'll be able to see the gray and white checkerboard behind any object whose opacity is below 100%.

To show/hide the transparency grid:

Choose View > Show Transparency Grid (Cmd-Shift-D/Ctrl-Shift-D) **3**. To turn this feature off, choose View > Hide Transparency Grid or press the shortcut again.

Mask in Knockout; Transparency Grid

You can change the transparency grid **colors** or **size** to make the grid contrast better with colors in your artwork.

To choose preferences for the transparency grid:

1. Choose File > Document Setup (Cmd-Option-P/Ctrl-Alt-P) 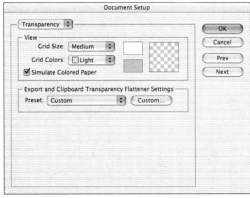.

2. Choose Transparency from the first pop-up menu.

3. Choose the desired Grid Size: Small, Medium, or Large.

4. To choose Grid Colors:

   From the pop-up menu, choose the Light, Medium, or Dark grayscale grid or choose one of the preset colors.
   or
   To choose custom colors, click the top color swatch (this color will also be the artboard color when no transparency grid is showing), choose a color from the color picker, then click OK. Click the second swatch, click a second color, then click OK again.

5. *Optional:* Check Simulate Colored Paper if you want objects and placed images in the illustration to look as if they're printed on colored paper. The object color will blend with the "colored paper" (the paper color being the color chosen for the top color swatch). Hide the transparency grid to see the full effect.

6. Click OK.

1 *Choose preferences for the transparency grid in the* **Transparency** *pane of the* **Document Setup** *dialog box.*

Flatten selectively?

Object > **Flatten Transparency** can be applied to selected semitransparent objects that overlap other objects. This command prepares such objects for print output by flattening the overlapping areas into separate, nonoverlapping objects **2**–**3**. The semitransparent look is preserved; the transparency is no longer editable. In contrast, Transparency Flattener settings chosen in either File > Document Setup or File > Print (Advanced panel) affect the whole document. Read more about printing and exporting transparency on pages 461–465.

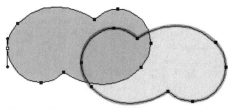

2 *Two objects are selected. The object that has a stroke color is transparent; the object behind it doesn't have a stroke color.*

3 *After the* **Flatten Transparency** *command is applied, the paths now number five instead of two. (We pulled the paths apart to show you.)*

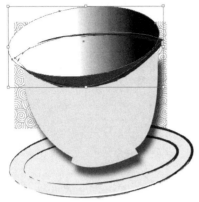

1 *Two objects are selected: the oval top of the cup and a gradient oval directly above it.*

2 *After applying the Make Opacity Mask command*

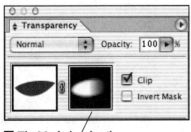

3 *The Mask thumbnail*

Opacity masks

An **opacity mask** is an object whose shape and fill controls the opacity (transparency) of the objects it masks. The topmost object in a selection of objects works as the opacity mask. The masking is controlled by the value level (grayscale equivalent) of the top object's fill. In the mask, black or dark values will make the underlying masked object(s) totally transparent (see-through); white or very light values will make the underlying masked object(s) opaque; and shades of gray (mid-range color values) will make the underlying masked object(s) partially transparent.

To create an opacity mask:

1. Place the object to be used as the mask above the object or objects to be masked, then select them all **1**. As the mask, you may use editable text, a placed (linked or embedded) image, an object containing a pattern or gradient, or a mesh.

2. Choose Make Opacity Mask from the Transparency palette menu **2**. The Make Opacity Mask command links the object(s) and the mask. On the Transparency palette, a thumbnail of the object(s) being masked will appear on the left and a thumbnail for the mask will appear on the right, with the link icon between them **3**. (If the thumbnails aren't visible, choose Show Thumbnails from the Transparency palette menu.)

   If you used only two objects in step 1, those objects will be combined into one; if you used more than two objects, they will be nested within a <Group>. The new object or <Group> name will have a dashed underline, indicating the presence of an opacity mask.

➤ The object/mask combination can be transformed, recolored, or assigned transparency attributes, effects, or graphic styles—like any object.

You can control whether or not an opacity mask **clips** parts of an object(s) that extend beyond its edges.

To turn clipping on or off for an opacity mask:

1. Choose a selection tool, then select an opacity mask object by using the Layers palette .

2. Check or uncheck Clip on the Transparency palette –.

➤ To have future opacity masks be clipped by default, make sure the New Opacity Masks Are Clipping command on the Transparency palette menu has a check mark.

The **Invert Mask** option reverses the value levels in the masking object.

To invert an opacity mask:

1. Choose a selection tool, then select the opacity mask object  by using the Layers palette.

2. Check Invert Mask on the Transparency palette –. (Uncheck the box to uninvert the mask.)

➤ To have future opacity masks be inverted by default, make sure the New Opacity Masks Are Inverted command on the Transparency palette menu has a check mark.

1 *The original objects*

2 *After choosing **Make Opacity Mask** with the **Clip** option on...*

3 *...and with the **Clip** option off*

4 *A photographic image is being used as an **opacity mask** (a graphic style was applied to the background object).*

5 *Check **Invert Mask** on the **Transparency** palette.*

6 *The opacity mask is **inverted**.*

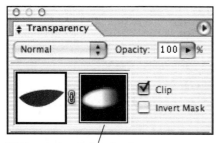

1 *Opacity mask thumbnail*

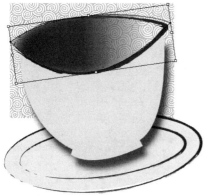

2 *An opacity mask, positioned at the top of the cup, is selected.*

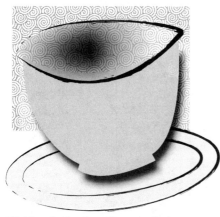

3 *After the Feather effect is applied to the masking object, the opaque part of the mask is reduced and the edges of the mask create a softer transition.*

Follow these instructions to edit a **masking object** separately from the masked objects.

To reshape or edit an opacity masking object:

1. Select the opacity mask object by using the Layers palette.

2. Click the mask thumbnail (on the right) on the Transparency palette **1**. If necessary, select the masking object by using the Layers palette.

3. Do any of the following: Use any path reshaping tool to change the contour of the mask; transform the object; change its color, pattern, or gradient fill; change its opacity; or apply an effect or style to it.

4. When you're done, be sure to click the object thumbnail on the Transparency palette.

➤ Option-click/Alt-click the opacity mask thumbnail on the Transparency palette to toggle between viewing just the masking object and the full illustration in the document window.

➤ When the opacity mask thumbnail is active, all you'll see on the Layers palette is an <Opacity Mask> layer containing a nested object or objects. You can target the layer or individual objects for appearance changes. To go back to the normal Layers palette display, click the object thumbnail on the Transparency palette.

Stylize > **Feather** is only one of the many Effect menu commands that can be applied to a masking object.

To feather the edge of a masking object:

1. Target an opacity mask object by using the Layers palette **2**.

2. Click the mask thumbnail on the Transparency palette.

3. Choose Effect > Stylize > Feather.

4. Check Preview, then choose a Feather Radius value for the width of the feathered area.

5. Adjust the Feather Radius, if desired, then click OK **3**.

If you want to **reposition** a masking object relative to the masked object(s), you first have to **unlink** the mask.

To move mask objects independently:

1. Choose a selection tool, then select the opacity mask object.

2. On the Transparency palette (Shift-F10), click the link icon between the object thumbnail and the mask thumbnail **1**.
   or
   Choose Unlink Opacity Mask from the Transparency palette menu.

3. Click the object or mask thumbnail, then move either object in the document window **2**–**3**.

4. Make sure the object thumbnail is selected, then click again between the thumbnails to relink the mask. The link icon is accessible only when the object thumbnail is selected.

To temporarily disable a mask:

1. Select the opacity mask object via the Layers palette.

2. Shift-click the mask thumbnail on the Transparency palette.

   A red "X" will appear over the thumbnail and the mask effect will disappear from view.

3. To reinstate the mask, Shift-click the mask thumbnail again.

If an opacity mask is **released,** the masked object(s) and the masking object will become separate objects. Any modifications that were made to the mask will be preserved, along with the objects' original appearances.

To release an opacity mask:

1. Select the opacity mask object using the Layers palette.

2. From the Transparency palette menu, choose Release Opacity Mask. The opacity mask thumbnail will disappear from the Transparency palette.

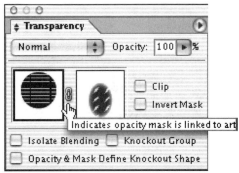

1 *Click the* **link** *icon to unlink (not unmask!) the masking and masked objects.*

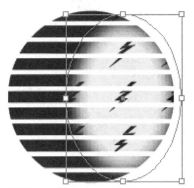

2 *The masking object is selected…*

3 *…and then moved.*

Unlink Mask Objects; Disable, Release Opacity Mask

DISTORT 21

In this chapter, you'll learn about the tools that do strange things—Warp, Pucker, Bloat, Twirl, Scallop, Crystallize, and Wrinkle—and about envelopes, which are used for sculpting whole objects.

Warp (Shift-R) distorts by pushing or pulling an edge

Twirl distorts in a spiral fashion

Pucker distorts inward toward the cursor

Bloat distorts outward from the cursor

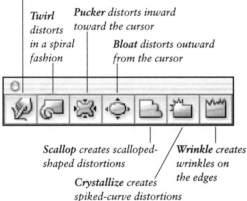

Scallop creates scalloped-shaped distortions

Wrinkle creates wrinkles on the edges

Crystallize creates spiked-curve distortions

1 *The tearoff toolbar for the seven **liquify** tools*

Liquify tools

The seven liquify tools **1**—Warp, Twirl, Pucker, Bloat, Scallop, Crystallize, and Wrinkle—produce distortion on the edges of individual objects or groups of objects. You push and pull on an object's edges with the brush's circular cursor, much as you would sculpt a piece of clay by pushing and pulling the clay. Each tool offers different sculpting controls, and each can be customized.

To use one of the liquify tools, first you specify option settings for the particular tool, then you drag across an object. You don't have to select the object or group of objects first, but doing so will help prevent other nearby objects from becoming distorted.

The distortions produced by the liquify tools depend on three factors:

➤ The **size** and **angle** of the tool cursor

➤ The tool's **Intensity** setting

➤ The length of **time** the cursor is clicked and held over an object and/or the **distance** the cursor is dragged

As with any feature that offers a lot of options, you'll need to spend some time working with the liquify tools in order to discover how they can be of service to you or how you can achieve the desired effect—or degree of effect. Feel free to experiment with different global brush dimensions and individual tool options settings.

(Continued on the following page)

Liquify Tools

367

As usual, first we'll give you a few ground rules so you can get your bearings:

➤ The liquify tools can be used on an individual object, a multiobject selection, a group, or any combination thereof.

➤ The liquify tools can be used on an object that contains appearances, effects, brush strokes, or styles.

➤ To use a liquify tool on a pattern fill, the fill must be expanded first (Object > Expand).

➤ To use a liquify tool on text, the text must be converted to outlines first (Type > Create Outlines).

➤ To use a liquify tool on a symbol instance or set, the instance or set must first be unlinked from the original symbol (click the Break Link to Symbol button 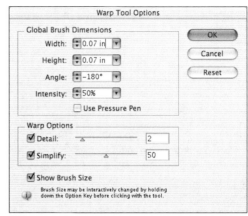 on the Symbols palette).

1 *The* **Global Brush Dimensions** *and* **Show Brush Size** *options, shown here in the* **Warp Tool Options** *dialog box, are present in the options dialog box for all the liquify tools.*

Every liquify tool has an options dialog box in which you can choose **Global Brush Dimensions** settings **1**, among other options. The global settings—the dimensions and angle of the cursor as well as the intensity of the liquify effect—apply to all the liquify tools and remain in effect until they're changed in any of the tool option dialog boxes. (To choose nonglobal settings for an individual liquify tool, see page 370.)

To choose global brush dimensions:

1. Double-click any liquify tool to open that tool's options dialog box. To choose a value for the cursor, enter a value in the appropriate field; or choose a value from the pop-up menu; or click the up or down arrowhead to the left of a field to increase/decrease (nudge) the current value **2**. For Angle and Intensity, each click of an arrow nudges the existing value up or down by 1.

➤ Shift-click a nudging (up/down) arrowhead to change the value by larger increments.

➤ Click a keyboard arrow, alone or in combination with Shift, to nudge the

	Click	**Shift-Click***
Points	±1 pt	±6 pt
Picas	±p3	±1p
Inches	±1/8"	±1"
Millimeters	±1 mm	±10 mm
Centimeters	±0.1 cm	±1 cm
Pixels	±1 px	±10 px

2 *The* **nudge** *value changes for a cursor's Width and Height*

* The first click rounds off the value in the current meaurement units, then the next Shift-click raises or lowers the value by the quantity shown above.

1 *Two liquify tool **cursors**: The cursor on the left is ½ in. x ½ in.; the cursor on the right is 1 in. x ½ in. at a –30° angle.*

value in the currently active entry field upward or downward.

2. Enter Width and/or Height values in any unit of measure.

3. Choose the Angle for the cursor **1**. The Angle is measured in a counterclockwise direction from the vertical axis.

4. Choose an Intensity (1–100%) for the rate of change and amount of pull or push the tool exerts on the edges of an object(s). At 5%, edges will hardly be distorted. At 100%, the edges will follow the cursor exactly as it's dragged **2**.

5. To have a pen or graphics tablet control the Intensity, check Use Pressure Pen.

6. Click OK. To choose individual liquify tool options, see the instructions on the following page.

➤ Click Reset to restore the options settings for the current tool and all global dimensions to their default values.

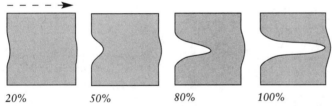

20%   50%   80%   100%

2 *The **Warp** tool is used with increasing **Intensity** on a square. In each case, the cursor was dragged from the left to the right edge of the square. At 20% Intensity, distortion was minimal. At 100%, the distortion followed the cursor almost all the way to the right edge.*

In contrast to the Global Brush Dimensions discussed on the previous page, the options in the lower portion of a liquify tool's options dialog box affect only that tool. In other words, you could choose different Detail and Simplify settings, say, for the Warp tool than for the Bloat tool.

The options that are present in all or most of the options dialog boxes (**Detail**, **Simplify**, and **Show Brush Size**) are discussed below. Some tools also have additional options, such as the Complexity setting for the Scallop tool. These options are mentioned, where applicable, in the instructions for the individual tools, which begin on the next page.

To choose options for an individual liquify tool:

1. Double-click a liquify tool to open its options dialog box.

2. All the liquify tools have a **Detail** option **1**–**2**, which controls the spacing of points that are added in order to produce distortion. To use this option, check the box, then enter a value (1–10) or drag the slider. The higher the Detail value, the closer the added points will be to one another. With Detail unchecked, distortion will be produced using only the existing points on the path, and no new anchor points will be added.

3. The **Simplify** option **3**–**4**, which is available only for the Warp, Twirl, Pucker, and Bloat tools, smooths the distorted path by reducing extraneous points. Enter a value (0.2–100) or drag the slider. The higher the Simplify value, the smoother the curve. With Simplify unchecked, the resulting distortion will have many more anchor points than are necessary or desirable.

4. Check **Show Brush Size** to have the cursor display as an ellipse using the current Global Brush Dimensions (width, height, and angle) so you can see the cursor dimensions relative to the object(s) you're distorting. If unchecked, the familiar crosshairs cursor will be used instead.

5. Click OK.

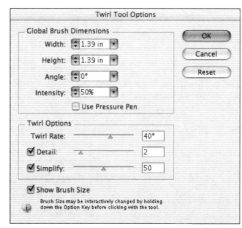

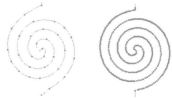

1 Use the **Detail** and **Simplify** options in any liquify tool options dialog box to control the spacing of added points and the smoothness of the distortion.

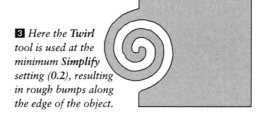

2 At left, the **Detail** for the **Twirl** tool was set to 1; at right, to 10 (with Simplify unchecked for both). Note how many points were added and how close together they are.

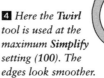

3 Here the **Twirl** tool is used at the minimum **Simplify** setting (0.2), resulting in rough bumps along the edge of the object.

4 Here the **Twirl** tool is used at the maximum **Simplify** setting (100). The edges look smoother.

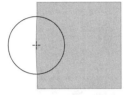 **1** *Distortion produced by the* **Warp** *tool*

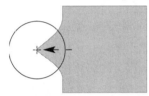

2 *First the cursor for the* **Pucker** *tool is positioned along one side of the square. Then it's dragged to the left, causing that side of the square to pucker out.*

3 *The original object*   **4** *After dragging toward the middle of the screw with the* **Pucker** *tool*

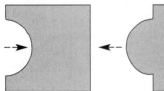 

5 *After dragging* into *a square with the* **Bloat** *tool*   **6** *After dragging* away *from the square with the* **Bloat** *tool*

In the instructions that follow, we'll discuss the **Warp, Pucker,** and **Bloat** tools. The Warp tool **1** produces distortion by pushing a portion of an object's edge in the direction the cursor is dragged. It works like the Bloat tool, except the results are softer.

The Pucker tool acts like a magnet to squeeze an object's contour. As the tool nears the edge of an object, a point on the path moves toward the center of the brush cursor **2**–**4**.

The Bloat tool expands the edge of an object outward from the center of the cursor, filling the cursor's circumference. If you drag the tool into an object, it will look as though the cursor cut a chunk out of it **5**. If you drag the tool away from an object, it will bulge out and look as though the cursor shape was added to it **6**.

To use the Warp, Pucker, or Bloat tool:

1. Double-click the Warp (Shift-R) 🖊, Pucker 🔧, or Bloat ⊙ tool.

2. Choose Detail and/or Simplify options (see the previous page). *Note:* The Detail setting seems to make little difference for the Pucker or Bloat tool.

3. Click OK.

4. *Optional:* Select an object or group to prevent the tool from editing other nearby objects.

5. Click and hold, or drag, the tool over an object or objects.

➤ A bulge or indentation produced by the Bloat tool can't extend outside the circumference of the tool cursor.

Resize/reshape cursor interactively

To **resize and reshape** the cursor interactively, check the Show Brush Size option in the tool options dialog box, then Option-drag/Alt-drag away from the cursor to enlarge it, or drag diagonally toward the lower left to reduce it. To **resize** the cursor **proportionally,** Option-Shift-drag/Alt-Shift-drag away from or toward the center of the cursor. *Beware!* Both shortcuts establish a new global cursor size for all the liquify tools!

Warp, Pucker, Bloat Tools

The **Twirl** tool twirls a whole object from its center—if used with a large brush cursor. If this tool is used with a small brush cursor, each edge of an object will be twirled separately.

To use the Twirl tool:

1. Double-click the Twirl tool.

2. Under Twirl Options, choose or enter a **Twirl Rate** (–180° to 180°). A positive value will produce a counterclockwise twirl; a negative value will produce a clockwise twirl. The Twirl Rate controls the speed at which the spiral is created and the amount of twirl. The higher the value (the further the slider is moved from 0°), the greater the distortion.

   ➤ To decelerate the rate of distortion, lower the Intensity setting.

3. Choose **Detail** and/or **Simplify** options (see page 370).

4. Click OK.

5. *Optional:* Select an object, group, or combination thereof.

6. Click and hold, or drag, the Twirl tool over an object –**2**.

   ➤ Hold down Option/Alt after you start dragging to reverse the direction of the twirl.

Next, we'll discuss the **Scallop**, **Crystallize**, and **Wrinkle** tools. The Scallop tool produces curves or spikes that move toward the center of the cursor. Try using it to produce soft folds or gathers **3**. For a sharper-edged distortion, try using the Crystallize tool. It produces spiked curves that move away from the center of the cursor **4**. And finally, for a more random, wrinkled-edge distortion, try using the Wrinkle tool (**1**, next page). As with the Twirl tool, the longer the Wrinkle tool is clicked and held over an edge, the stronger the effect.

To use the Scallop, Crystallize, or Wrinkle tool:

1. Double-click the Scallop, Crystallize, or Wrinkle tool.

1 *The original object*

2 *After using the Twirl tool: Intensity 50%, Twirl Rate –59°, Detail 5, Simplify 60*

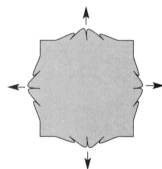

3 *To produce this shape, we moved the Scallop tool away from each edge of a square in the direction shown by the arrows.*

4 *To produce this shape, we moved the Crystallize tool from the left edge of the square toward the center of the square.*

Twirl, Scallop, Crystallize, Wrinkle Tools

1 *Distortion produced using the* **Wrinkle** *tool: The cursor was placed at the middle of the left edge, then moved to the left, away from the object.*

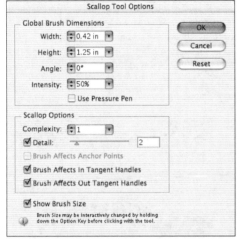

2 *The Scallop Tool Options dialog box*

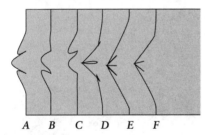

A   B   C   D   E   F

3 *How the different "Brush Affects" check boxes affect the distortion produced by the* **Scallop** *tool:*

A: Brush Affects In Tangent Handles and Brush Affects Out Tangent Handles checked

B: Brush Affects In Tangent Handles checked

C: Brush Affects Out Tangent Handles checked: note the reflected direction of distortion between B and C

D: Brush Affects Anchor Points checked

E: Brush Affects Anchor Points and Brush Affects In Tangent Handles checked

F: Brush Affects Anchor Points and Brush Affects Out Tangent Handles checked

2. Choose a **Complexity** value (0–15) **2**. The higher the Complexity, the more curves or spikes will be generated. At a Complexity setting of 0, only existing anchor points will be modified; no new points will be created.

3. Choose a **Detail** setting. In addition to the spacing between points, this option also controls the number of curves or spikes generated by the tool.

4. For the Scallop or Crystallize tool, check one or two of the available **Brush Affects** options. For the Wrinkle tool, you can check one, two, or all three of these options. Brush Affects Anchor Points repositions anchor points; Brush Affects In Tangent Handles and Brush Affects Out Tangent Handles change the control handles of added points **3**.

Note: To preserve the current position of the anchor points, don't check Brush Affects Anchor Points.

➤ When using the Scallop tool, if only one Brush Affects Tangent Handles option is checked and Brush Affects Anchor Points is unchecked, distortion won't be pulled to the center of the cursor, and the effect will be more subtle (fingerlike).

5. Click OK.

6. *Optional:* Select an object, group, or combination thereof.

7. Click and hold, or drag, the tool over an object or objects.

Scallop, Wrinkle, Crystallize Tools

373

Envelopes

To use the **Envelope Distort** commands, first you create a container, called an "envelope," for one or more objects. Then you distort the envelope shape, and the object within the envelope conforms to that distortion. Envelopes can be created by using any of these three commands on the Object > Envelope Distort submenu **1**–**3**:

➤ **Make with Mesh** command: Creates a mesh, then you manipulate it

➤ **Make with Warp** command: Uses a preset, but editable, warp

➤ **Make with Top Object** command: Converts a user-drawn path into an envelope

Regardless of which method you use to create the envelope, both the envelope and the object will remain fully editable, both while the object is contained in the envelope and after it's expanded. If you're familiar with using gradient meshes, you'll be way ahead of the game here because envelopes are really meshes, and they work the same way. The only difference is that envelope meshes are used to distort shapes, whereas gradient meshes are used to apply color areas.

Envelopes can be applied to just about any kind of Illustrator objects, including paths (simple and compound); placed (embedded) images; images rasterized in Illustrator; text; clipping masks; objects with applied effects, styles, or brush strokes; and symbol instances.

When you're done using an envelope to distort an object, you have two choices: You can either expand the result, leaving the distorted object but deleting the envelope, or you can release the result, thus creating two separate objects—the envelope shape on top of the original, undistorted object.

➤ Editable text can be contained within an envelope, and it will remain editable. However, if the envelope is expanded, the text will convert automatically to outline paths.

Another way to warp

You can also create envelopes using the commands on the **Effect > Warp** submenu, but with one notable disadvantage. When an envelope is applied via an effect, the only way to edit the envelope is via the Warp Options dialog box, which you can reopen by double-clicking the Warp effect listing on the Appearance palette. You won't be able to manipulate the points or segments on the warp shape itself.

If you use the **Envelope Distort** commands, on the other hand (discussed at left), you'll have the option of readjusting the mesh points and segments at any time.

Illustrator

1 *The original object*

2 *A **warp** envelope distortion produced by using a horizontal arc with a 50% bend and a –50% horizontal distortion*

3 *A **mesh** envelope produced by using a 3x3 grid that was then distorted manually*

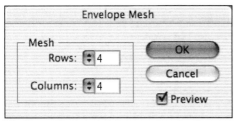

1 *Choose Rows and Columns values for the envelope mesh in the **Envelope Mesh** dialog box.*

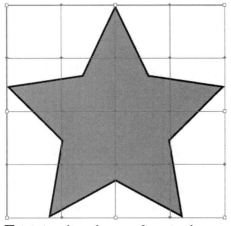

2 *A 4x4 mesh envelope on a five-pointed star*

➤ When enveloping a placed image, if the Envelope Distort commands are dimmed, it means the image must be embedded in the file prior to being enveloped (to embed images, see page 265). A linked TIFF image can be enveloped, and if the envelope is expanded or released, the TIFF will remain linked to the file.

➤ An envelope for a clipping path will be scaled automatically in order to cover both the visible and clipped parts of the objects.

In the following instructions you'll create an **envelope** as a **mesh**. Because all envelopes essentially are meshes, we think working with a mesh first will help you get a handle, in visual terms, on how the distortion process works.

To create a mesh envelope:

1. Select an object or group.

2. Choose Object > Envelope Distort > Make with Mesh (Cmd-Option-M/ Ctrl-Alt-M).

3. Check Preview **1**.

4. Enter the desired number of Rows and Columns, or click an up or down arrowhead.

5. Click OK. An envelope will be created in a grid, using your specifications, overlaying the object **2**. To edit the envelope mesh, see page 378.

➤ The arrowheads change the existing values by ±1. With Shift-click, the arrowheads change the existing values by ±10.

Mesh Envelope

Another way to create an envelope is to use a preset shape, such as an arc, arch, shell, fish, or fisheye, to produce the distortion. You're not limited to the preset shape, though. With the **Warp Options** dialog box open, you can apply distortion to the envelope, and then you can further customize it after closing the dialog box.

To create a warp envelope:

1. Select an object or group.

2. Choose Object > Envelope Distort > Make with Warp (Cmd-Option-Shift-W/ Ctrl-Alt-Shift-W).

3. Check Preview **1**.

4. Choose one of the 15 preset Styles.

5. Click **Horizontal** or **Vertical** for the warp orientation.

6. Enter a **Bend** value (–100 to 100) or move the slider to the desired value to control the extent of the Warp style **2**.

7. Enter or choose Horizontal and Vertical **Distortion** values (–100 to 100) to specify how much additional horizontal and vertical distortion the chosen warp style will contain.

8. Click OK. A warp grid will now overlay the object(s), using the specifications from the Warp Options dialog box **3**. To edit the envelope path, see page 378.

➤ To change the current warp style used for the envelope, select the envelope, then choose Object > Envelope Distort > Reset with Warp again.

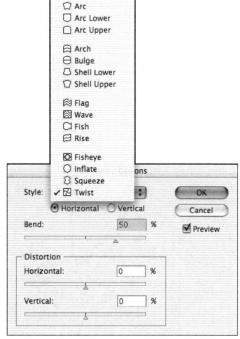

1 In the **Warp Options** dialog box, the first step is to choose a preset **Style**. Then, if you like, you can customize the distortion either by using the dialog box or by manipulating the mesh after closing the dialog box.

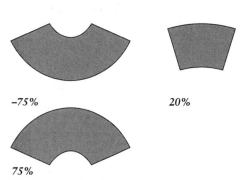

–75%

20%

75%

2 Various Bend settings

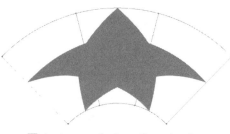

3 An **Arc**, enveloping a five-pointed star

(sidebar, left margin) **Warp Envelope**

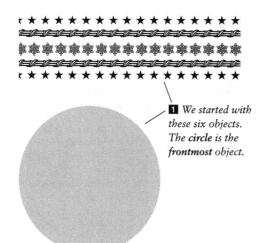

1 *We started with these six objects. The* **circle** *is the* **frontmost** *object.*

2 *After choosing Object > Envelope Distort >* **Make with Top Object**

3 *After* **adding mesh points** *and* **moving them around**

And finally, a third way to create an envelope is to produce it from your own **path**. Be creative!

To create an envelope from a user-created path:

1. Create a path to use for the envelope. The path can be open or closed. Don't worry about whether it has a fill or stroke; both will be removed automatically.

2. Make sure the path to be used as the envelope is on top of the objects to be put into the envelope (it makes a difference!). If necessary, you can choose Object > Arrange > Bring to Front (Cmd-Shift-]/ Ctrl-Shift-]) or restack the object on the Layers palette.

3. Select the path and the object(s) to be enveloped. They can overlap each other, but they don't have to. When you choose the Make with Top Object command (the next step), the objects will be sucked into the envelope like a vacuum cleaner. Watch.

4. Choose Object > Envelope Distort > Make with Top Object (Cmd-Option-C/ Ctrl-Alt-C). The objects will be moved into, and will be scaled automatically to fit, the envelope **1**–**3**. To edit the envelope, see the next page.

➤ If you use an open path for the envelope, it won't stay open. When you choose Make with Top Object, the path will be closed automatically.

➤ To use a text character for an envelope, it first has to be converted to outlines, released from its compound path, and ungrouped. You can use only one character at a time.

Envelope from Path

As we said before, envelope meshes work like gradient meshes (a mesh is a mesh is a mesh). If you're not familiar with meshes yet, no big deal; they're easy to work with. The techniques for **editing** meshes are summarized in the following instructions. For more detailed instructions on editing meshes, see pages 327–329.

To edit an envelope:

1. Make sure smart guides are showing so you'll be able see the envelope and anchor points without selecting the envelope (View > Smart Guides or Cmd-U/ Ctrl-U).

2. The envelope will be listed as Envelope on the Layers palette **1**. To select it, click its target circle.

3. Do any of the following (have some fun!):

   Use the Add Anchor Point tool (+) to add mesh points to existing mesh lines. Option/Alt-click with the Add Anchor Point tool to delete mesh points that don't have lines crisscrossing through them.

   Use the Mesh tool (U) to add mesh points with mesh lines that crisscross through them. Option-click/Alt-click with the Mesh tool to delete mesh lines or points. Or drag with the Mesh tool to move mesh points.

   Use the Direct Selection tool (A) to move mesh points or mesh patches.

   Modify the mesh points or lines using a transform tool, such as Scale, Rotate, or Move, or push them around using a liquify tool, such as Warp, Bloat, or Wrinkle.

➤ To edit the contents of an envelope but not the envelope itself, follow the instructions on the next page.

Back to square one

To reset a **warp** envelope to its state prior to any manual point or line additions or changes being made, choose Object > Envelope Distort > **Reset with Warp** (Cmd-Option-Shift-W/Ctrl-Alt-Shift-W), then choose options in the Warp Options dialog box.

To reset an edited **mesh** envelope, choose **Reset with Mesh** (Cmd-Option-M/Ctrl-Alt-M), then choose options in the Reset Envelope Mesh dialog box **2**. Check Maintain Envelope Shape to reset the inner mesh points while preserving the envelope's outer shape, or uncheck this option to reset the entire envelope to a rectangular mesh.

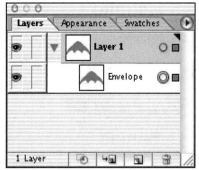

1 *An envelope listed on the Layers palette*

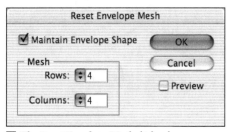

2 *The Reset Envelope Mesh dialog box*

Edit Envelope

Keeping up with appearances

The Appearance palette lists different attributes depending on which part of an envelope is currently being edited. If you edit the envelope itself, attributes or applied effects for the envelope, if any, will be listed. If you edit the contents, attributes for the object will be listed. Merely toggling between the Edit Contents and Edit Envelope commands doesn't target the correct object. To avoid confusion, before adding or editing appearances, be sure to **target the correct object!**

In these instructions, you'll learn how to edit objects within an envelope without changing the envelope itself. You can toggle back and forth between **editing objects** and editing the **envelope** whenever you need to. With the envelope selected, you can switch to editing the object's contents; with an object selected, you can switch back to editing the envelope.

To edit objects in an envelope:

1. With an envelope selected, choose Object > Envelope Distort > Edit Contents (Cmd-Shift-V/Ctrl-Shift-V).

2. An expand arrowhead will appear next to the Envelope listing on the Layers palette. Click the arrowhead to expand the list, then click the target circle for an individual path to target the path for editing. You can edit the object contents as you would any nonenveloped object. The Appearance palette will update.

3. When you're done editing the objects, choose Object > Envelope Distort > Edit Envelope (Cmd-Shift-V/Ctrl-Shift-V). The envelope will recenter itself on the edited object automatically. If you click the target circle for the "Envelope," any appearances you apply now will affect the envelope—not its contents.

Once you're done editing the object and envelope, you can use either the Release command or the Expand command.

The **Release** command is useful if you have an envelope that you like, and you think you might want to use it again. If you've taken a preset warp style and fiddled with it, for example, you can release the envelope and preserve it as a separate object so it can be used as an envelope for other objects (with the Make with Top Object command).

To release an envelope:

1. Select an envelope with a selection tool.

2. Choose Object > Envelope Distort > Release. This command will leave the original object(s) unaltered, with the former envelope object on top **1**. On the Layers palette, you'll see a <Mesh> listing for the envelope and one or more <Path> listings for the objects **2**.

Use the **Expand** command as a final step once you're satisfied with the distortion. To choose expand options for both raster images and vector objects, see the following page.

To expand an envelope:

1. Select an envelope. The Expand command will delete the envelope, so make a copy of it for safekeeping, if desired.

2. Choose Object > Envelope Distort > Expand. The distortion will be applied to the object **3**. The envelope will be discarded and can't be retrieved, except by choosing Undo. A <Group> containing the distorted object(s) will be created (Layers palette) **4**. To learn how Illustrator expands different kinds of attributes, such as live effects, appearances, and styles, see the following page.

➤ If an envelope containing a mesh object is expanded, the mesh will remain a mesh.

➤ If an envelope containing a symbol or brush stroke is expanded, the symbol or brush stroke will be converted to standard paths.

➤ If text is expanded, it's converted automatically to outline paths.

1 *After Object > Envelope Distort > Release is chosen, the envelope is placed on top of the object; the object is unchanged. (We changed the opacity of the envelope to 75%.)*

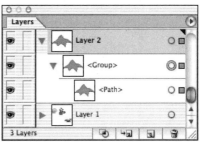

2 *The Layers palette after choosing the Release command*

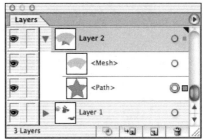

3 *After the Expand command is chosen, the envelope distortion is applied to the star, and the envelope itself is discarded.*

4 *The Layers palette after applying the Expand command*

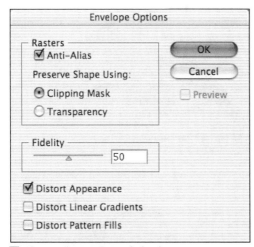

1 *The Envelope Options dialog box*

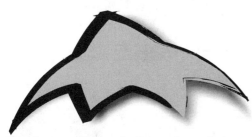

2 *A five-pointed star with effects is distorted using a 70% Bend, Horizontal Arc Warp. Then **Distort Appearance** is checked in Envelope Options.*

3 *The same five-pointed star with **Distort Appearance unchecked** in Envelope Options*

Envelope Options control how content (appearances, gradients, and patterns) is distorted, as well as what happens to that content when the envelope is expanded.

To choose envelope options:

1. To change the settings for an existing envelope, select it now (or select multiple envelopes).
   or
   To choose settings for subsequently created envelopes, deselect all.

2. Choose Object > Envelope Distort > Envelope Options.

3. Check Preview (if an envelope is selected).

4. For raster images (placed images or images rasterized in Illustrator), check **Anti-Alias** **1** to smooth the edges. This option can increase the processing time.

5. For Preserve Shape Using:
   Click **Clipping Mask** to place a raster image in a clipping mask if it's expanded.
   or
   Click **Transparency** to make the background of the expanded raster image transparent by use of an alpha channel.

6. Enter a **Fidelity** value (0–100) for the number of new anchor points to be added to a path to make it fit the envelope shape. The higher the Fidelity value, the more points will be added.

7. Check **Distort Appearance** to have an object's appearances (live effects, brushes, styles, etc.) be distorted by the envelope **2**. If the envelope is expanded, each appearance will also be expanded into a plain path or group, which will become a separate listing on the Layers palette. For example, if an appearance consisting of two strokes was applied to the object, when the envelope is expanded each stroke will become a separate listing on the Layers palette.

   Uncheck Distort Appearance to distort the object, but not any appearances. Any appearances will be applied after distortion **3**. If you then expand the envelope,

(Continued on the following page)

the appearances will remain applied to the object and the resulting group will contain only one object.

Note: If appearances are applied to an envelope, those appearances won't be applied to the objects within the envelope. However, if the envelope is expanded, the appearances will be applied to the resulting group.

8. When Distort Appearance is checked, these two additional options become available:

Check **Distort Linear Gradients** to have a linear gradient fill be affected by an envelope distortion. If the envelope is then expanded, the gradient will become a mesh nested within a sequence of nested groups. If Distort Linear Gradients is off and the envelope is expanded, the linear gradient will be part of the resulting <Path>.
and/or
Check **Distort Pattern Fills** to have pattern fills be affected by an envelope distortion –. If the envelope is then expanded, the pattern will become a sequence of nested groups containing components of the pattern. If Distort Pattern Fills is off and the envelope is expanded, pattern fills will remain undistorted and will be a part of the resulting <Path>.

9. Click OK.

1 *Distort Pattern Fills off: The pattern does* **not** *conform to the envelope distortion.*

2 *Distort Pattern Fills on: The pattern conforms to the envelope distortion.*

22

This chapter begins with a comparison between effects and filters, and a how-to section for applying them. Second, we provide specific instructions for applying a few effects and filters, such as Twist, Scribble, and Object Mosaic. For easy reference, we've included a complete illustrated compendium of all the raster filters. And finally, don't miss our instructions for applying the new 3D Extrude & Bevel, 3D Revolve, and 3D Rotate effects!

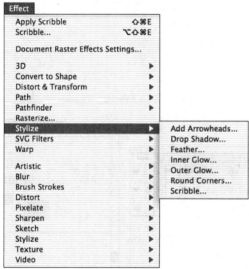

1 *The Effect menu has two sections: mostly vector effects (and a few raster effects) at the top, and raster effects on the bottom.*

Effects and filters

Illustrator's effects and filters are used for applying distortion, texture, color adjustment, 3D, artistic, and stylistic changes to objects and images, with results ranging from subtle to marked. Many of the filters on the Filter menu have a matching counterpart under the Effect menu **1**. In fact, the Filter and Effect menus are so interdependent, settings used for a command on one menu become the settings for its counterpart on the other menu.

However, there are significant differences between effects and filters, in terms of both the kind of objects they can be applied to and whether the results are editable after the command is applied. We'll discuss some of those differences next.

Using effects

Filter menu commands change the path of the underlying object and aren't reeditable, whereas **effects** change only the appearance of an object—not its underlying path— and are fully editable. Because they can be reedited or deleted at any time without affecting the object they're applied to (or any other applied effects or appearance attributes), effects lend themselves to experimentation. What's more, if you reshape the underlying object's path, the effects adjust accordingly. In other words, effects are live!

(Continued on the following page)

Using Effects

On the top portion of the Effect menu you'll find vector commands that have counterparts on the Filter menu, such as Drop Shadow and Roughen, as well as some commands that are not found on the Filter menu, such as Feather, Inner Glow, Outer Glow, and Convert to Shape (see pages 389 and 391). All the raster effects on the lower part of the Effect menu have counterparts on the Filter menu. These effects can be applied to any kind of object, not just to images!

➤ Raster effects become rasterized (do not remain vector) when exported to a vector format such as SVG. Also, remember that this increases the file size.

Effects can be applied to **any** kind of object, even editable text (it doesn't have to be converted into outlines first), and the text will remain editable. In fact, if you opt to use the Outline Object effect to convert text into outlines, the underlying text will remain editable, as long as its font is available in your system.

Like object attributes, applied effects are listed individually on the Appearance palette; each object has its own listing **1**. If an effect is applied to a **targeted** layer, sublayer, or group, that effect will be applied automatically to all existing and future objects on that layer, sublayer, or group. Furthermore, since effects display on the Appearance palette along with other attributes, they can also be saved in a graphic style. You can reedit any effect that's contained in a style, at any time.

Using filters

Unlike effects, commands on the Filter menu **2** do alter an actual object's path. Filters that are designed primarily for use on vector (path) objects are grouped in submenu categories in the upper portion of the menu. Some of these filters are discussed individually in this chapter.

Filters that are designed for use on bitmap images and rasterized objects are grouped in ten submenu categories at the bottom of the Filter menu: Artistic, Blur, Brush Strokes, Distort, Pixelate, Sharpen, Sketch, Stylize, Texture, and Video. If you're a Photoshop

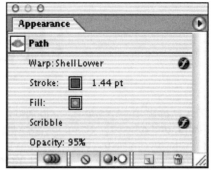

1 *The* **Appearance** *palette, listing the Warp and Scribble* **effects**

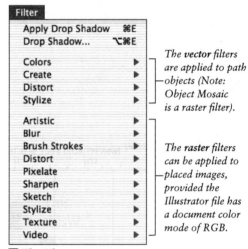

2 *The Filter menu*

The **vector** *filters are applied to path objects (Note: Object Mosaic is a raster filter).*

The **raster** *filters can be applied to placed images, provided the Illustrator file has a document color mode of RGB.*

From effect to graphic style

To make all the attributes that are listed on the Appearance palette into a single **graphic style,** drag the square thumbnail from the top left corner of the Appearance palette onto the Graphic Styles palette (see pages 342–343).

Using Filters

Quickly reapply

Reapply last effect using the same settings	Cmd-Shift-E/ Ctrl-Shift-E
Reopen last effects dialog box	Cmd-Option-Shift-E/ Ctrl-Alt-Shift-E
Reapply last filter using the same settings (no dialog box opens)	Cmd-E/Ctrl-E
Reopen last filter dialog box	Cmd-Option-E/ Ctrl-Alt-E

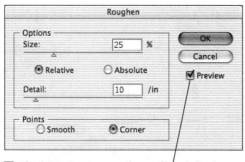

1 *Check* **Preview** *in any effect or filter dialog box that offers this option to monitor changes in the document window.*

2 *Other effect and filter dialog boxes have a* **preview window** *inside the dialog box.*

user, you may already be familiar with them. The raster filters are discussed and illustrated in the latter part of this chapter.

➤ Most of the raster filters are inaccessible when the Illustrator file has a document color mode of CMYK.

Applying effects and filters

Some effects and filters are applied simply by choosing the command from a submenu; others are applied via a dialog box in which special options are chosen. To make things easier, we recommend memorizing the shortcuts listed in the sidebar at left.

➤ Some filters are memory-intensive, but using lower or different settings in a filter dialog box can help speed things up.

Many vector effect and filter dialog boxes have a Preview option **1** that allows you to preview the result in your illustration as you choose settings. If you enter a value in a field, press Tab to update the preview.

Raster effect and filter dialog boxes have a preview window inside the dialog box **2**. In most dialog boxes, you can drag inside the preview window to move the image inside it. Click the + button to zoom in on the image in the preview window, or click the – button to zoom out. A line will flash below the preview percentage while the preview is rendering.

➤ In a raster effect or filter dialog box, you can hold down Option/Alt and click Reset to reset the slider settings to what they were when the dialog box was opened.

Note: Some Illustrator filters are covered in other chapters. For other page locations, look up the filter name under "Filters" in the index.

Applying Effects and Filters

In these instructions, you'll **apply** an **effect** directly to a layer, sublayer, group, or object. In the instructions on page 388, you'll add to, or edit an effect in, a style.

To apply an effect:

1. On the Layers palette (F7), target a layer, sublayer, group, or object . (The target circle should have a double border.)

Note: To limit an effect to only an object's stroke or fill, select the object, then click the Stroke or Fill attribute on the Appearance palette.

2. Choose an effect from a submenu on the Effect menu.

3. Check the Preview box, if there is one, to preview the effect as you choose options, then choose options **2**.

4. Click OK **3**. If you applied the effect to only a stroke or fill, the effect name will be nested below the Stroke or Fill attribute on the Appearance palette.

To edit an effect:

1. On the Layers palette (F7), target the layer, sublayer, group, or object to which the effect you want to edit is applied. If the effect was applied to only an object's stroke or fill, select the object, then expand the Stroke or Fill attribute listing on the Appearance palette.

2. Double-click the effect name or icon 🎯 on the Appearance palette **4**.

NEW

3. Make the desired adjustments, then click OK.

1 *The original* **targeted** *object*

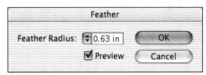
2 *A value is chosen in the effect dialog box.*

3 *The* **Feather** *effect is applied.*

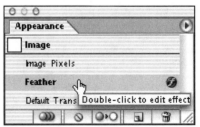
4 *Double-click an effect name or icon on the* **Appearance** *palette to* **edit** *that attribute.*

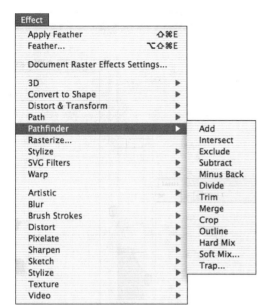

Effect	
Apply Feather	⇧⌘E
Feather...	⌥⇧⌘E
Document Raster Effects Settings...	
3D	▶
Convert to Shape	▶
Distort & Transform	▶
Path	▶
Pathfinder	▶
Rasterize...	
Stylize	▶
SVG Filters	▶
Warp	▶
Artistic	▶
Blur	▶
Brush Strokes	▶
Distort	▶
Pixelate	▶
Sharpen	▶
Sketch	▶
Stylize	▶
Texture	▶
Video	▶

Pathfinder submenu:
Add
Intersect
Exclude
Subtract
Minus Back
Divide
Trim
Merge
Crop
Outline
Hard Mix
Soft Mix...
Trap...

1 *The **Pathfinder** commands can be applied as effects via the **Effect** menu.*

Pathfinder effects

The Pathfinder commands that are available on the Pathfinder palette are also available as effects on the **Effect > Pathfinder** submenu **1**. Unlike the commands, the Pathfinder effects modify an object's appearance, not its path. You can delete a Pathfinder appearance attribute at any time without affecting the actual objects.

A couple of other differences are worth noting. First, unlike the commands, the Pathfinder effects don't create compound shapes. And second, the Divide, Trim, and Merge effects don't break up objects' over-lapping areas into separate objects, as their counterparts on the Pathfinder palette can.

Here are a few guidelines for applying Pathfinder effects:

➤ Before applying a Pathfinder effect, you must collect the objects that you want to apply the effect to into a sublayer or group, and then **target** that **sublayer** or **group** (that's target—not select).

➤ Pathfinder effects can be included in a **style.**

➤ Objects can be **moved** within, into, and out of any group or sublayer after the effect is applied.

➤ Pathfinder effects can be **removed** at any time. To remove an effect, on the Appearance palette, drag the effect name over the Delete Selected Item 🗑 button.

➤ Double-clicking an effect name on the Appearance palette opens the **Pathfinder Options** dialog box, where you can pre-view other Pathfinder effects and change which Pathfinder effect is applied to the currently selected group.

➤ If a Pathfinder effect is **expanded** (Object > Expand Appearance), the result will be either a path shape or a compound path.

Pathfinder Effects

We've told you that graphic styles are flexible. Any of the effects used in a style can be modified, and new effects can be added. To learn more about styles and appearances, see Chapter 19.

To add an effect to, or edit an effect in, a graphic style:

1. Click a style name or swatch on the Graphic Styles palette **1**, or select an object that uses that style so you can preview your edits. The style name will appear at the top of the Appearance palette.

2. To **add** an effect, choose an effect from a submenu on the Effect menu, then choose options. Check Preview if you selected an object in the previous step.

or

To **edit** an existing effect, double-click the effect name or icon on the Appearance palette **2**.

3. Click OK.

4. Choose Redefine Graphic Style "[style name]" from the Appearance palette menu to update the style.

You can **remove** an **effect** from a layer, object, or style as easily as you can add one. Easy come, easy go.

To remove an effect from a layer, object, or graphic style:

1. On the Layers palette, target the layer, sublayer, group, or object that contains the effect you want to remove.

or

On the Graphic Styles palette, click the style name or swatch that contains the effect you want to remove.

2. On the Appearance palette, click the effect name or icon.

3. Click, or drag the effect name to, the Delete Selected Item button 🗑 on the Appearance palette.

4. If you're removing an effect from a style, choose Redefine Graphic Style "[style name]" from the Appearance palette menu to update the style.

1 *Click a style on the **Graphic Styles** palette.*

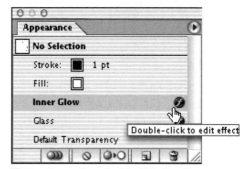

2 *To edit an effect, double-click the effect name or icon on the **Appearance** palette.*

Effect in Style; Remove Effect

1 *The original object*

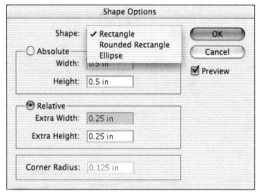

2 *Choose shape and scale options in the Shape Options dialog box.*

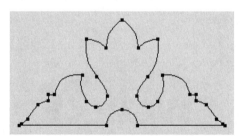

3 *A rectangular shape appearance attribute is added to the object; the underlying path is unchanged.*

4 *Rectangle is listed as an effect on the Appearance palette.*

In these instructions, you'll use the **Convert to Shape** effects, which are found only on the Effect menu. Like all effects, they change an object's shape without changing the actual underlying path.

To apply a Convert to Shape effect:

1. Select or target an object or objects in the document window or via the Layers palette **1**.

2. Choose Effect > Convert to Shape > Rectangle, Rounded Rectangle, or Ellipse. *Note:* Any of these three options can also be chosen from the Shape pop-up menu once the dialog box is open **2**.

3. Check Preview.

4. Click **Absolute,** then enter the total desired Width and Height values for the shape's appearance.
   or
   Click **Relative,** then enter the Extra Width or Extra Height that you want added to or subtracted from the object's current shape. Enter a positive value to expand the shape or a negative value to contract it.

5. *Optional:* For the Rounded Rectangle shape, you can change the Corner Radius value.

6. Click OK **3**–**4**.

➤ To simply round off sharp corners on an object, use Effect > Stylize > Round Corners.

Convert to Shape

Next we'll show you how to use the "live" aspect of effects, using text as an example.

To use live shapes with text:

1. Select a type block by using the Selection tool .

2. Choose Add New Fill from the Appearance palette menu. *Note:* The original fill or stroke color will be listed on the palette if the type is selected using a type tool, but not (at least not initially) if the Selection tool was used.

3. Click Fill on the Appearance palette, choose a color from the Color or Swatches palette, and leave the Fill listing selected.

4. Click the Duplicate Selected Item button ▣ at the bottom of the Appearance palette.

5. Click the lower of the two Fill attributes on the Appearance palette, then choose a different color for it ▣.

6. Apply an effect from the Effect > Convert to Shape submenu to the new Fill attribute, using the Relative option (see step 4 on the previous page) ▣.

7. To see how the live effect works, add or delete some type characters or resize the type. The new fill shape will resize accordingly ▣.

It's a hard mix

To simulate overprinting, target a group or layer that contains two or more objects (they can be type objects) that at least partially overlap one another, then choose Effect > Pathfinder > **Hard Mix**. The highest C, M, Y, and K, or R, G, and B values from each of the original objects will be mixed in areas where they overlap. The greater the difference between the original colors, the more marked the resulting effect will be. This effect will remove any stroke color.

effect

1 *The original text*

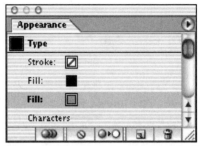

2 *A new **Fill** attribute is created and duplicated, and a different color is chosen for it.*

effect

3 *After applying the **Convert to Shape** effect to the duplicate Fill (Shape: Ellipse; Relative: Extra Width 13 pt, Extra Height 3 pt)*

liveffect

4 *Here's the point: When more characters are **added** to the text, the **shape enlarges** to accommodate it.*

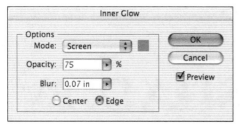

1 *The original group of objects*

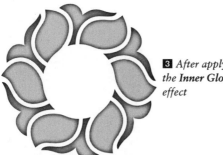

2 *Options in the* **Inner Glow** *effect dialog box are chosen.*

3 *After applying the* **Inner Glow** *effect*

4 *After applying the* **Outer Glow** *effect*

5 *Both* **Glow** *effects applied*

The **Inner Glow** effect applies a color glow that spreads from the edge of an object toward its center. The **Outer Glow** effect applies a color glow that spreads from the edge of an object outward.

(To apply the Drop Shadow effect, see the following page.)

To apply the Inner Glow or Outer Glow effect:

1. Select or target a layer, sublayer, group, or object **1**.

2. Choose Effect > Stylize > Inner Glow or Outer Glow.

3. Check Preview **2**.

4. Do any of the following:

   Click the **Color** square, then choose a different glow color.

   Choose a **blending Mode** for the glow color from the pop-up menu.

   Choose an **Opacity** for the glow color.

   Click the **Blur** arrowhead, then move the slider to adjust how far the glow extends inward or outward from the edge of the object. The higher the Blur value, the wider the glow.

   For Inner Glow, click **Center** to have the glow spread outward from the object's center, or click **Edge** to have the glow spread inward from the object's edge to its center.

5. Click OK **3**–**5**.

Inner Glow; Outer Glow

The **Drop Shadow** command creates soft, naturalistic shadows, and it can be applied either as a filter or as an effect. The Drop Shadow filter creates a new shadow object, separate from the original object. The filter dialog box has a Create Separate Shadows option that nests the object and the shadow into a new <Group> on the Layers palette.

Unlike the filter, the Drop Shadow effect has a Preview option, and it becomes an appearance on the original object. One advantage of applying a shadow as an effect is that you can double-click the Drop Shadow effect listing on the Appearance palette to reopen its dialog box at any time and edit any of the settings, including the color. The shadow effect can also be removed at any time.

To create a drop shadow:

1. Select one or more objects. The Drop Shadow command can be applied to editable type (it doesn't have to be converted into outlines).

2. Choose Filter > Stylize > Drop Shadow or Effect > Stylize > Drop Shadow. If you chose the command from the Effect menu, check Preview.

3. In the Drop Shadow dialog box, do the following:

   Choose a blending Mode ◼.

   Choose an Opacity value for the shadow.

   Enter an X Offset for the horizontal distance between the object and the shadow and a Y Offset for the vertical distance between the object and the shadow.

   Enter a Blur value (0–144 pt) for the width of the shadow.

   Optional: Click Color, click the color square, then choose a different shadow color from the color picker. Or click Darkness, then enter a percentage of black to be added to the shadow.

4. Click OK ◼.

➤ Highlight the current Opacity (or Blur) value, then press the up or down arrow on the keyboard to change it.

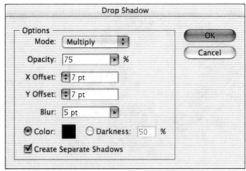

◼ *Sometimes we're satisfied with the default settings in the* **Drop Shadow** *dialog box, as shown here; at other times we might change the opacity or blur value.*

SHADOW

◼ *After applying the* **Drop Shadow** *filter to editable type*

1 *The original object*

2 *Choose Scribble Options.*

A few vector effects and filters

The **Scribble** effect makes an object's fill and stroke look as though it was drawn with a felt-tip marker or pen. It can be applied to any object, even editable type.

To apply the Scribble effect: NEW

1. Select a path object or objects **1**.

2. Choose Effect > Stylize > Scribble.

3. Check Preview **2**. As a start, choose a preset from the Settings pop-up menu. Follow the remaining steps if you want to choose custom settings for the preset.

4. Enter an **Angle** value or rotate the dial to change the angle of the sketch lines.

5. Choose a positive **Path Overlap** value to allow the sketch lines to extend beyond the edge of the path, or a negative value to keep them inside the path. Choose a high **Variation** value to produce random variations in line lengths and a wilder, more haphazard look, or a low Variation for more uniform lengths.

6. For Line Options, do any of the following:

   Choose a **Stroke Width** for the lines.

   Choose a **Curviness** value to control whether the lines angle more sharply or loop more loosely where they change direction. The **Variation** slider controls the degree of random variation in these direction changes.

   Choose a **Spacing** value to cluster sketch lines more tightly or to spread them apart. The **Variation** slider controls how much random variation occurs in the spacing.

7. Click OK **3**. Scribble will become an object attribute listing on the Appearance palette. Double-click the listing to edit the attribute at any time.

➤ If you make Scribble setting changes and then choose a preset from the Settings pop-up menu, your custom settings will be deleted. You can't save your presets for inclusion on the Settings menu—yet.

3 *After applying the Scribble effect*

Scribble

The **Roughen** filter makes an object look more hand-drawn by adding anchor points and then moving them.

To apply the Roughen effect or filter:

1. Select a path object or objects , and choose View > Hide Edges (Cmd-H/ Ctrl-H), if you like, to make previewing easier.

1 *The original object*

2. Choose Effect > Distort & Transform > Roughen or Filter > Distort > Roughen (it's on the top portion of the menu).

3. Check Preview **2**.

4. Choose a **Size** percentage to specify how far the object's anchor points can be moved. Use a very low Size percentage to preserve the object's basic shape.

5. Click **Relative** to move points by a percentage of the object's size, or click **Absolute** to move points by a specific amount.

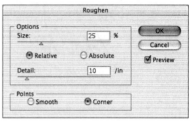

2 *The **Roughen** dialog box*

6. Choose a **Detail** amount for the number of points to be added to each inch of the path segments.

7. Click **Smooth** to produce curves, or click **Corner** to produce points.

8. Click OK **3**.

To apply the Twist effect or filter:

1. Select a path object or objects **4**. If two or more objects are selected, they will be twirled together.

3 *After applying the Roughen filter (or eyeing a dog)*

2. Choose Effect > Distort & Transform > Twist, or Filter > Distort > Twist (it's on the upper part of the menu).

3. Enter a positive Angle to twirl the path(s) clockwise or a negative number to twirl it/them counterclockwise (–360 to 360).

4. Click OK **5**. Only an object's outer shape will be twisted, not a pattern or gradient fill.

➤ For comparison, try using the Twirl tool (see page 372).

4 *The original object*   **5** *After applying the **Twist** effect*

gothic horror

1 *The original type. You will need to convert type to outlines before using the filter.*

2 *After applying the **Pucker** part of the filter (or effect)*

3 *The original object*

4 *After applying the **Bloat** filter (or effect)*

To apply the Pucker & Bloat effect or filter:

1. Select an object or objects **1**. Effect > Pucker & Bloat can be applied to editable text.

2. Choose Effect > Distort & Transform > Pucker & Bloat or Filter > Distort > Pucker & Bloat.

3. Check Preview.

4. Move the slider to the left toward **Pucker** to move anchor points outward and curve segments inward **2**, or move the slider to the right toward **Bloat** to move anchor points inward and curve segments outward **3**–**4**.

5. Click OK.

➤ To intensify the Pucker or Bloat, prior to applying the filter or effect, add points to the path by applying Object > Path > Add Anchor Points one or more times. See also figures 1–3 on page 122.

Raster effects and filters

These are the important rules to remember:

➤ All the raster filters are available for a rasterized object or a placed bitmap image, provided the Illustrator document itself is in RGB Color mode.

➤ Only the Blur, Sharpen, and Pixelate filters and effects are available for an embedded image or rasterized object in a document that's in CMYK color mode.

➤ Raster effects are available for vector objects and for embedded bitmap images.

➤ Raster filters are available for embedded bitmap images.

Some raster effects and filters introduce an element of randomness or distortion that would be difficult to achieve by hand. Others, such as the Artistic, Brush Strokes, Sketch, and Texture filters, are designed to make an image look a little less machine-made, more hand-rendered. When a raster filter or effect is applied to a large, high-resolution bitmap image, a progress bar may display while the

(Continued on the following page)

Pucker & Bloat; Raster Effects and Filters

filter is processing. To cancel a filter or effect in progress, click Stop or press Return/Enter.

In the dialog boxes for some effects and filters, such as Rough Pastels and Grain, you can choose a texture type from the **Texture** or **Grain Type** pop-up menu **1**–**2**. Move the Scaling slider to enlarge or reduce the size of the texture pattern, and move the Relief slider, if there is one, to adjust the depth and prominence of the texture on the image's surface. In some dialog boxes, you can load in a bitmap image saved in the Photoshop format (files with the ".psd" extension) to use in lieu of a preset texture. To do this, choose Load Texture from the Texture pop-up menu, click the bitmap file you want to use, then click Choose.

In addition to the raster filters, other filters that you can apply to a raster image include Colors submenu > Adjust Colors, Convert to Grayscale, Convert to CMYK or Convert to RGB (depending on the current document color mode), Invert Colors, and Saturate. There are no effects equivalents for these filters.

1 *Some commands have a **Texture** (or **Grain Type**) pop-up menu.*

2 *Rough Pastels filter/effect, Burlap **Texture***

Before experimenting with the raster filters, you should learn about Illustrator's **Rasterize** command, which converts a vector (path) object into a bitmap image. You can apply any raster filter to an object, provided it's been rasterized using the proper settings. (*Note:* All the effects work on vector objects; they don't have to be converted.)

To rasterize a path object:

1. Select a path object or objects or target them on the Layers palette.

2. Choose Object > Rasterize or Effect > Rasterize. The Effect is reversible and editable; the Object menu command is permanent.

3. Choose a **Color Model** for the object 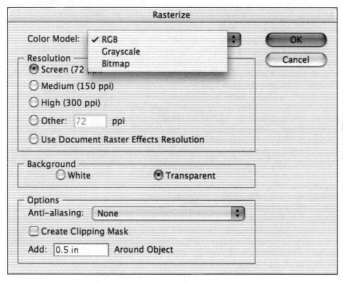. Depending on the current document color mode, you can choose either CMYK for print output (only the Blur, Sharpen, and Pixelate raster filters and effects will be available) or RGB for video or onscreen output (all raster filters and effects will be available); or Grayscale for shades of black and white (all raster filters and effects will be available); or Bitmap for only black-and-white or black-and-trans-parent (no raster effects or filters will be available).

4. Click a **Resolution** setting: choose Screen for Web or video output; or choose High for imagesetter output; or enter a resolution in the Other field; or click Use Document Raster Effects Resolution to use the global resolution settings as specified in Effect > Document Raster Effects Settings.

5. Click **Background:** White to make the transparent areas in the object opaque white, or click Transparent to make the background transparent (see the sidebar on the following page).

6. Under Options:

   Choose **Anti-Aliasing:** Art Optimized (Supersampling) to have Illustrator soften the edges of the rasterized shape. This option may make text or thin lines look

(Continued on the following page)

1 *Choose a Color Model in the Rasterize dialog box.*

Rasterize an Object

blurry. Choose Type Optimized (Hinted) for a type object. Edges will be jagged if you choose None.

Check **Create Clipping Mask** if you want Illustrator to generate a clipping mask for the shape so its background will be transparent (see the sidebar).

To have Illustrator add pixels around the object for padding (the bounding box will become larger), enter a value in the **Add [ ] Around Object** field.

7. Click OK.

➤ Once a solid color object is rasterized, its color can be changed by using Filter > Colors > Adjust Colors.

➤ If you rasterize an object that contains a pattern fill and you want to preserve any transparency in the pattern, click Background: Transparent and choose Anti-aliasing: Art Optimized.

Transparent versus clipping mask

Both the **Background: Transparent** and **Create Clipping Mask** options in Object > Rasterize remove an object's background. Unlike Create Clipping Mask, the **Transparent** option creates an alpha channel in order to remove the background, and the resulting image stays as an individual listing on the Layers palette. Any blending mode or opacity settings are removed, but the object keeps any transparency appearances. Blending modes and opacity can be applied to the targeted image at any time. The alpha channel effect will be preserved if the file is exported to Photoshop.

Create Clipping Mask, on the other hand, produces a nested group composed of a clipping path and the image, and the clipping path preserves any transparency appearances. Blending modes and opacity for the object can be adjusted for the targeted <Image>, but not for the <Clipping Path>.

If you choose the Transparent option, you don't need to create a clipping mask. Effect > Rasterize preserves blending and transparency. The SVG format also preserves the appearance of blending and transparency. The SWF format preserves only the appearance of transparency, not blending.

1 *The original image*

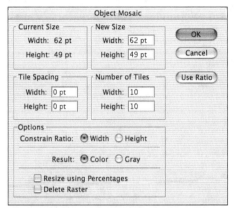

2 *The Object Mosaic dialog box*

3 *The Object Mosaic filter applied*

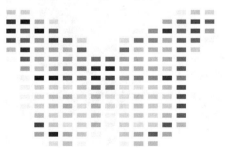

4 *The Object Mosaic filter applied to the original image (**1**) with spacing between the tiles*

The **Object Mosaic** filter breaks up a raster image into a grid of little squares. Each of the squares is a separate object that can be moved or recolored individually. There is no effect version of this filter.

To apply the Object Mosaic filter:

1. Click on a rasterized object or an embedded bitmap image **1**.

2. Choose Filter > Create > Object Mosaic.

3. *Optional:*

   Change the New Size: Width and/or Height values **2**. (The Current Size field displays the width and height of the image in points.) If you want to enter dimensions in percentages relative to the original, check Resize using Percentages at the bottom of the dialog box; the Width and Height fields will switch to percentage values.
   or
   Enter a New Size: Width (or Height), click Constrain Ratio: Width (or Height) under Options to lock in that dimension, then click Use Ratio to have Illustrator automatically calculate the opposite dimension proportionate to the object's original dimensions.

4. Enter the desired Number of Tiles to fill the Width and Height dimensions. If you clicked Use Ratio, the Number of Tiles will be calculated automatically.

5. *Optional:* To add spacing between the tiles, enter Tile Spacing: Width and Height values.

6. *Optional:* When it's applied to a bitmap image, the Object Mosaic filter affects a copy of the image that's made automatically, and the original is left unchanged. Check Delete Raster if you want the original image to be deleted.

7. Click Result: Color or Gray.

8. Click OK **3**–**4**. The mosaic object is listed as a group on the Layers palette.

Object Mosaic Filter

The raster filters illustrated
Artistic filters

Artistic Filters

Original image

Colored Pencil

Cutout

Dry Brush

Film Grain

Fresco

Neon Glow

Paint Daubs

Palette Knife

Artistic filters *(continued)*

Original image

Plastic Wrap

Poster Edges

Rough Pastels

Smudge Stick

Sponge

Underpainting

Watercolor

Artistic Filters

Blur filters

Original image

Radial Blur

Gaussian Blur

Brush Strokes filters

Original image

Accented Edges

Angled Strokes

Crosshatch

Dark Strokes

Ink Outlines

Blur Filters; Brush Strokes Filters

Brush Strokes filters *(continued)*

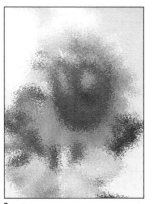

Spatter

Sprayed Strokes

Sumi-e

Distort filters

Original image

Diffuse Glow

Glass (Blocks)

Ocean Ripple

Pixelate filters

Original image

Color Halftone

Crystallize

Mezzotint (Short Strokes)

Mezzotint (Medium Dots)

Pointillize

To learn about the Unsharp Mask filter, see our Visual QuickStart Guide on Photoshop!

Pixelate Filters

Sketch filters

Original image

Bas Relief

Chalk & Charcoal

Charcoal

Chrome

Conté Crayon

Graphic Pen

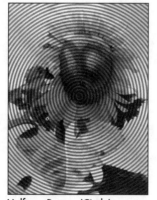
Halftone Pattern (Circle)

Halftone Pattern (Dot)

Sketch Filters

Sketch filters *(continued)*

Original image

Note Paper

Photocopy

Plaster

Reticulation

Stamp

Torn Edges

Water Paper

Sketch Filters

Stylize filter

Original image

Glowing Edges

Texture filters

Original image

Craquelure

Grain (Enlarged)

Grain (Horizontal)

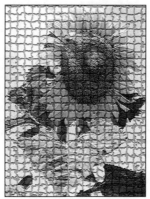

Mosaic Tiles

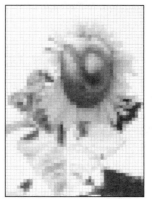

Patchwork

Stylize Filter; Texture Filters

Texture filters *(continued)*

Original image

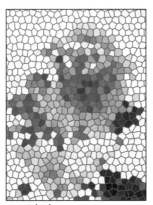

Stained Glass

Texturizer

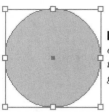

The original 2D object: a 100 pt diameter circle with a light gray fill and no stroke

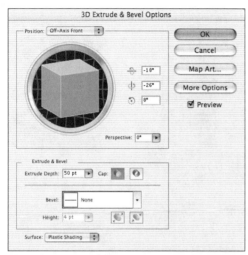

Use the 3D Extrude & Bevel Options dialog box to choose depth, position, and perspective options; add beveling; and, by clicking More Options, also choose Surface and Lighting options.

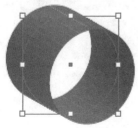

After applying 3D Extrude & Bevel at an Extrude Depth of 100 pt.

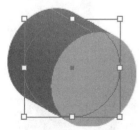

The Extrude Cap Off button is clicked, creating a hollow appearance.

3D effects NEW

The **3D Extrude & Bevel**, **3D Revolve**, and **3D Rotate** effects on the Effect > 3D submenu enable you to, with very little effort, make 2D (two-dimensional) objects, even type, look 3D (three-dimensional). You can bevel edges; change perspective, lighting, and shadow color; adjust surface reflectivity; and even map artwork onto your 3D objects.

Once applied, 3D effects are listed on the Appearance palette and can be edited or saved as styles for use with other objects, or removed at any time. For information about creating and editing effects using the Appearance palette, see pages 331–338. First, 3D Extrude & Bevel.

The **3D Extrude & Bevel** effect creates a three-dimensional appearance by adding depth to an object along its *z*-axis (the axis that's perpendicular to the object's front surface). A solid or hollow appearance is achieved by capping or uncapping extruded objects. Bevels can be used to reshape an object's edges, and to add facets.

To apply the Extrude & Bevel effect: NEW

1. Select an object .

2. Choose Effect > 3D > Extrude & Bevel.

3. Check Preview ❷. Working with Preview on is useful for getting to know the 3D effects but may result in long rendering times between steps.

4. You can start by fiddling with the track cube. The front surface of the object is represented in the track cube by cyan, the sides by medium gray, the back by dark gray, and the top and bottom by light gray.

   To rotate the object in **any direction**, move any flat surface of the cube (four-way arrow pointer), then drag.

   Shift-drag to rotate the object around a fixed horizontal or vertical axis.

   To rotate the object on a **relative** axis, drag one of the edges of the cube (two-way arrow pointer). The edge highlight

(Continued on the following page)

color represents the axis around which the object will rotate (red for *x*; green for *y*; blue for *z*). (See also pages 412–413.)

5. In the Extrude & Bevel pane, do the following:

    Enter or choose an **Extrude Depth** value (0–2000 pt) to adjust the depth of your object along its *z*-axis (**3**, previous page).

    Click the **Cap On** button ⬤ to create a solid object, or click the **Cap Off** button ⬤ to create a hollow object (**4**, previous page).

6. To bevel **1** the object's edges along its *z*-axis, choose a design from the **Bevel** pop-up menu and choose or enter a **Height** value (1–100 pt); use low values.

    Click the **Bevel Extent Out** button 🔳 to have the bevel extend outward from the original shape, or click the **Bevel Extent In** button 🔳 to have the bevel carve into the shape.

7. *Optional:* To choose Surface options, click More Options (see pages 414–415).

8. Click OK **2**–**3**.

➤ You can create your own custom bevel shapes. Open the Bevels.ai file (located in the Adobe Illustrator CS Plug-ins folder) and follow the instructions in the file.

➤ Try extruding objects with multiple strokes to create interesting 3D effects— but be prepared for prolonged rendering times! Avoid applying brush strokes!

The **3D Revolve** effect creates a three-dimensional appearance by spinning a path in a circular direction around a *y* (vertical) axis. This effect is useful for creating cylindrical shapes, such as spheres, chess pieces, vases, bottles, etc.

Revolve rotates a path in a circular direction around a *y*-axis, either touching or outside of the object's left or right edge. For instance, a circular path **4** revolved 360° around a *y*-axis along its left edge results in a doughnut, or "torus" shape **5**. Similarly, an S-shaped path

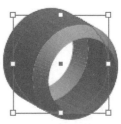

1 The **Classic** bevel, applied at a bevel height of 10 pt

2 The original path: a 200 pt letter with a gray fill

3 After applying **3D Extrude & Bevel** at an Extrude Depth of 50 pt, and a Tall-Round bevel of 1 pt

4 The original object: a circular path with a gray fill and no stroke

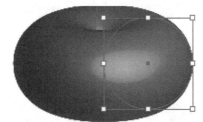

5 After the **3D Revolve** effect is applied, revolving the object around its left edge

revolved 360° around a *y*-axis along its left edge is transformed into a vase **1**–**2**.

To apply the Revolve effect: (NEW)

1. Select a closed object that has a fill color and a stroke of None, or a path that has a stroke color and a fill of None. The object should consist of one side (half) of a symmetrical shape **1**.

2. Choose Effect > 3D > Revolve.

3. Check Preview, if desired **3**.

4. To rotate the track cube, see step 4 on page 409 (see also pages 412–413).

5. In the Revolve area, specify the number of degrees the object is to be revolved by moving the **Angle** dial or by entering a value (0°–360°).

6. Click the **Cap On** button ⬤ to create a solid object or the **Cap Off** button ◐ to

create a hollow object (less evident on objects rotated less than 360°).

7. Choose or enter an **Offset** value (0–1000 pt) to widen the radius of revolution (and thus widen the 3D object), and from the pop-up menu, choose whether this distance will be measured from the Left Edge or Right Edge of the 2D object.

8. *Optional:* To choose Surface options, click More Options (see pages 414–415).

9. Click OK **2**.

➤ In order to revolve multiple objects around a common *y*-axis, you must group or layer the objects first, and then target the group or layer. For more information about applying effects to groups and layers see page 386.

➤ Applying this effect to a closed path that has a stroke color may produce irregular effects and increase the rendering time. Applying it to an open path that has a fill will cause the fill to be revolved along with the object's path, which may produce irregular effects.

1 *The original object: an S-shaped path*

2 *After the 3D Revolve effect is applied, revolving the object around its left edge*

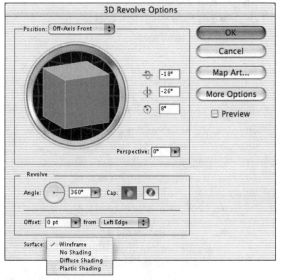

3 *The 3D Revolve Options dialog box*

You can use the **3D Rotate** effect to alter the perspective of a two-dimensional object in 3D space, as if you were to tilt a piece of paper. In other words, the object remains two-dimensional, but is thrust into 3D space.

NEW **To apply the Rotate effect:**

1. Select the object to be rotated .

2. Choose Effect > 3D > Rotate.

3. Check Preview.

4. To rotate the track cube, see step 4 on page 409 (and see also the next set of instructions).

5. *Optional:* To choose Surface options, click More Options (see pages 414–415).

6. Click OK **2**.

➤ Don't use 3D Rotate to change the position of an existing 3D object. Instead, reopen the original 3D effect by double-clicking its listing on the Appearance palette, and change the Position settings.

3D position, surface, lighting, and mapping

In the remaining pages of this chapter, we'll show you how to use the more advanced features of the 3D effect dialog boxes, starting with the **Position** options.

NEW **To choose custom position settings:**

1. Select an object, then open any 3D effect dialog box.

2. A feature that you've already explored is the **track cube.** If you have a mind for this sort of thing, here's a more detailed description of how it works:

   To rotate the object in **any direction,** move any flat surface of the cube (four-way arrow pointer), then drag.

   To rotate the object around one axis, hold down the Shift key to constrain rotation. The cursor appears as an *x–y* axis-shaped pointer. Drag the pointer up and down (or left and right) for rotation around the global *x* (or *y*) axis. For the global *z*-axis, release the Shift key and

Fresh start

To reset the settings in any open 3D effect dialog box, hold down Option/Alt and click **Reset** (the Cancel button changes to a Reset button).

1 *The original object: a star-shaped path with a gray fill and no stroke*

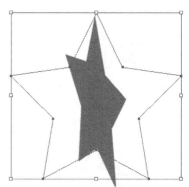

2 *After applying the **Rotate** effect, using the preset Off-Axis Right position*

position the cursor in the cyan ring surrounding the cube. The cursor becomes a
z–axis pointer and movement is con-
strained around the global z-axis.

To rotate the object on a **relative** axis 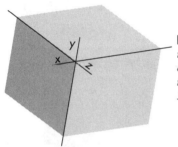,
drag one of the edges of the cube (two-
way arrow pointer). The edge highlight
color represents the axis around which
the object will rotate (red for x; green for
y; blue for z).

3. Another option is to use a **preset** as a
starting point, and then customize it by
using other options in the Position area.
From the Position pop-up menu in the
Position area **2**, choose a preset plan
and elevation, off-axis, or isometric view.

4. *Optional:* In the fields to the right of the
track cube, you can enter how many
degrees you want the object to be rotated
from each axis, as represented by the x-,
y-, and z-axis colors.

5. To create the appearance of three-point
perspective (a single vanishing point),
move the **Perspective** slider or enter a
lens distortion value from 0° (similar to
a telephoto lens) to 160° (similar to a
wide-angle lens).

➤ Separate objects can't share a common
vanishing point, but you can group
some 2D objects first and then apply
Perspective to the targeted group. Be
prepared for prolonged rendering times.

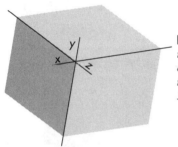

1 *This diagram shows
the relative x-y-z axes
on the **Position** cube
that you see in all of the
3D effect dialog boxes.*

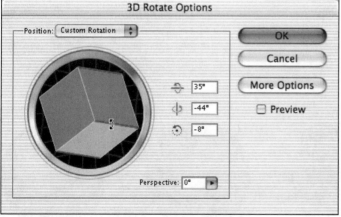

2 *In the **Position** area of all the 3D effects dialog boxes, you can choose a
preset position, drag the track cube, enter a degree of rotation for each axis,
and add three-point perspective.*

In the Surface area of the 3D Extrude & Bevel and 3D Revolve options dialog boxes, you can choose from preset surface settings, edit lights on the lighting sphere, make lighting and surface texture adjustments, and adjust the shading color behavior and other options to change your object's appearance. For the 3D Rotate effect, you can choose from a more limited number of surface options.

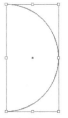

1 *The original object: a semicircular open path*

NEW

To apply Surface options:

1. Select an object **1**.

2. Apply an effect from the Effect > 3D submenu.

or

Double-click an effect on the Appearance palette to reopen that dialog box.

3. If the Surface options aren't visible in the dialog box, click More Options.

4. Choose a rendering setting from the **Surface** pop-up menu **2**: Wireframe **3** shows the object's edges outlined with transparent surfaces; No Shading **4** uses only the surface properties of the original 2D object; Diffuse Shading **5** creates a soft light reflection; Plastic Shading **6**, the default setting, creates a highly reflective, glossy effect.

In the 3D Rotate Options dialog box, only the Diffuse Shading Surface setting is available, and for some, but not all, position options.

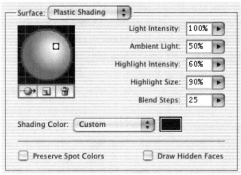

2 *This **Surface** area is found in the 3D Extrude & Bevel and 3D Revolve options dialog boxes.*

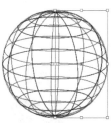

3 *The **3D Revolve** effect applied using the Surface: Wireframe option; the object is revolved around its left edge.*

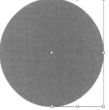

4 *Using the **No Shading** Surface setting*

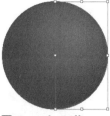

5 *Using the **Diffuse** Shading setting*

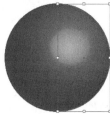

6 *Using the **Plastic** Shading Surface setting*

Creating complex objects

Each object created with 3D effects inhabits its own 3D space and can't be merged with other 3D objects (such as setting a sphere partly inside a cube). Individual 3D objects do not share axes of revolution, lighting sources, or perspective vanishing points, unless they're grouped or layered first, and then the 3D effect is applied to the targeted group or layer. Complex 3D objects are best formed by creating individual 3D shapes such as cylinders, cones, cubes, and spheres, which can then be edited and stacked on the artboard to build more intricate constructions. To learn more about targeting groups or layers, see page 332.

1 *This is* **6** *on the previous page after changing the Ambient Light to 20%, changing the Highlight Intensity to 100%, repositioning the first light, and adding a second light in the back.*

5. Using the **lighting sphere**, you can create and position lights on an object, control background lighting, and specify light intensity, highlighting, and size for all lights. A light source appears on the sphere as a black hollow circle, changing to a hollow circle in a black square when selected. *Note:* The lighting settings aren't available for the Wireframe or No Shading surface rendering settings.

Do any of the following **1**:

On the lighting sphere, click a light to select it, then **drag** it to a new position.

To move a selected light source to the **back** of the object, click the Move Selected Light to Back of Object button; click the button again to move the light to the front.

To **add** a light source, click the New Light button below the lighting sphere. Objects must have a minimum of one light source.

To **delete** a light, click on it, then click the Delete Light button.

6. On the right side of the dialog box, you can choose:

A **Light Intensity** value (0–100%) to control the brightness of the selected light.

An **Ambient Light** value (0–100%) to control the uniform brightness of all surfaces.

A **Highlight Intensity** (0–100%) to control the object's reflectivity. *Note:* This feature isn't available for the Diffuse Shading surface rendering setting.

A **Highlight Size** (0–100%) to control the uniform size of highlighted areas. *Note:* This option isn't available for the Diffuse Shading surface rendering setting.

7. Click OK.

➤ To display an object's outline in Wireframe view in a color other than black, apply a 3D effect (with Surface set to Wireframe), choose Object > Expand Appearance, then change the stroke color.

3D Surface Options

415

Here we explore advanced surface options in the 3D Extrude & Bevel and 3D Revolve effects dialog boxes.

NEW **To apply other 3D surface options:**

Click More Options, then do any of the following:

1. Adjust the **Blend Steps** value (1–256) to control the smoothness of shading across the object **1**–**2**. Higher settings produce smoother shading, but with a significant increase in rendering time.

2. Specify how the dark parts of an object are shaded by choosing from the **Shading Color** pop-up menu:

   None uses the object color for shading. Spot colors aren't affected.

   Black applies only black ink over the original color to create shading. Use this option to preserve any spot colors in objects and mapped artwork.

   Custom displays the Shading Color window. Click the window to open the color picker. When Preserve Spot Colors is checked, the Custom option is disabled and the Black option is automatically chosen.

3. Check Preserve Spot Colors to prevent any spot colors in the selected object from being converted to process colors. To observe this shading, View > Overprint Preview must be checked.

   Note: Gradients made with spot colors are converted to process colors when 3D effects are applied.

4. Check Draw Hidden Faces to enable rendering of surfaces that, though normally hidden from view, may become visible in transparent or expanded objects. This feature isn't available for the Wireframe rendering setting.

➤ A metallic look on surfaces can be created by rendering with high-contrast gradient fills and high light intensity settings.

Editing and saving 3D effects

Once a 3D effect has been applied, it's listed as an attribute on the Appearance palette and can be edited by double-clicking the attribute listing. Effects are listed in the order in which they were applied. Attributes can be restacked, edited, duplicated, or deleted. Drag the icon at the top of the Appearance palette into the Graphic Styles palette to save the 3D attribute(s) as a style. To learn more about attributes and the Appearance palette, see pages 331–338.

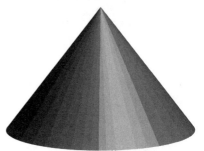

1 *A revolved cone with a Blend Steps setting of 8*

2 *A revolved cone with a Blend Steps setting of 256*

Advanced 3D Surface Options

1 *The original object: a pentagon, after applying 3D Extrude & Bevel at an Extrude Depth of 150 pt*

You can take any artwork—object, path, text, image, mesh object, or group that you have saved as a symbol—and map, that is, apply, reposition, scale, and rotate it onto any **surface** of a 3D object. Symbol instances remain editable and automatically update on the surfaces they're mapped to.

To map artwork to a 3D object: NEW

1. Create and select a 3D object **1**.

2. Double-click an existing 3D Extrude & Bevel or 3D Revolve effect on the Appearance palette to reopen the dialog box for that effect.

3. Click Map Art; the Map Art dialog box opens. The surface window shows elevations of the object's surfaces, one at a time **2**. Visible surfaces are displayed as light gray, hidden surfaces as dark gray.

4. Check Preview (or leave it unchecked to avoid rendering time).

5. Using the **Surface** arrow buttons or numeric field, choose which surface of the object you want mapped. In the preview in the document window (if enabled), the surface you chose will be outlined in red. (To hide the object in the

(Continued on the following page)

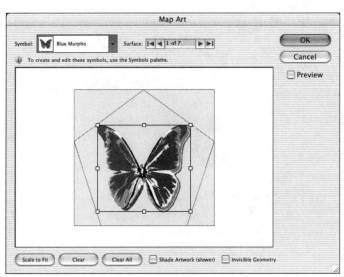

2 *The Map Art dialog box, showing Surface: 1 of 7. A symbol is chosen, and its size is adjusted.*

Map Artwork to 3D Object

preview and display only the chosen surface as a red outline, check Invisible Geometry.)

6. From the **Symbol** pop-up menu, choose the artwork to be mapped. (The symbols that are currently on the Symbols palette will be listed on the menu. To learn how to create symbols, see page 292.)

7. Do any of the following optional steps:

   Reposition the symbol by dragging inside its bounding box.

   Scale the symbol by dragging any corner or side handle.

   Rotate the symbol by dragging outside its bounding box.

   ➤ If the shape of a surface is edited, mapped artwork will be repositioned relative to the new center of the surface of the object.

   To have the artwork conform to the surface's shape, click **Scale to Fit.**

   To have the artwork's lighting and shading match the surface on which it's mapped, check **Shade Artwork (slower).**

   At any time, you can click Clear to remove artwork from the surface displayed or click Clear All to remove artwork from all surfaces.

8. Click OK twice to apply the mapped artwork to the object ◼.

Changing sides

Illustrator assigns each side of a 3D object a numeric value. Artwork can be mapped to any of an object's sides. If the number of sides of an object is later reduced or the effect is applied to an object that has fewer sides than the original, any artwork that was mapped to discarded sides will also be discarded.

◼ *After using **Map Art** to apply a symbol to a surface of the pentagon*

PRECISION TOOLS 23

There are many tools you can use to position or move objects with exact precision. In this chapter you'll learn how to use rulers, guides, and grids to align and position objects; move an object a specified distance via the Move dialog box; use the Measure tool to calculate distances between objects; use the Transform palette to move, scale, rotate, or shear objects; and use the Align palette to align or distribute objects.

Smart guides are precision tools, too, but they're so helpful and so easy to use, we discussed them early in the book (see pages 90–91, 99, and 170). Also, the Transform Each command is discussed on page 107, and the Transform Effect on page 108.

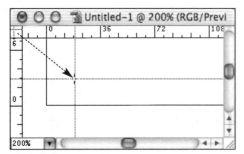

1 To change the **ruler origin**, drag diagonally away from the intersection of the rulers.

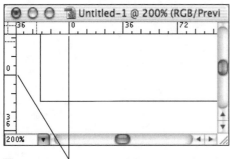

2 Note the new position of the zeros on the rulers.

Ruler and object guides

The rulers are located at the top and left edges of the document window. Location measurements (e.g., the X and Y readouts on the Transform and Info palettes) are read from the ruler origin, which is the point where the zeros of both rulers meet. By default, the **ruler origin** is positioned at the lower left corner of the page, but it can be moved to a different location in any individual document to help you measure or position objects. The current pointer location is indicated by a mark on each ruler.

To move the ruler origin:

1. If the rulers aren't displayed, choose View > Show Rulers (Cmd-R/Ctrl-R); or deselect all objects, then Control-click/right-click the artboard and choose Show Rulers from the context menu.

2. Drag the square (where the two rulers intersect) to a new position **1**–**2**. The ruler origin will stay in the new location if you save, close, and reopen the file.

➤ If you move the ruler origin, pattern fills in any existing objects may shift position.

419

To restore the ruler origin to its default location:

Double-click where the two rulers intersect at the upper left corner of the document window.

➤ Control-click/right-click either ruler to open a context menu from which you can choose a different unit of measure for the document. This setting will override the units setting in Illustrator (Edit, in Windows) > Preferences > Units & Undo.

For most purposes, smart guides work quite well for arranging objects (see pages 90–91). If you need **ruler guides** that stay on the screen, however, you'll need to create them using either method described below. Ruler guides don't print.

To create ruler guides:

1. To make sure the guides will be visible, choose View > Guides > Show Guides (Cmd-;/Ctrl-;). If the command is Hide Guides, leave it as is.

2. *Optional:* Create a new top-level layer expressly for the guides.

3. If the rulers aren't visible, choose View > Show Rulers (Cmd-R/Ctrl-R).

4. Drag a guide(s) from the horizontal or vertical ruler onto your page ◾. The guide will be locked and will be listed on the Layers palette as <Guide> in the currently active layer. If View > **Snap to Grid** is on, as you create or move the guide, it will snap to the nearest ruler tick mark. (*Note:* If Pixel Preview is on, Snap to Grid won't be available.)

   If View > **Snap to Point** is on, as you drag an object near a guide or anchor point, the black pointer will turn white and the part of the object that's under the pointer will snap to the guide or point. You can change the **Snapping Tolerance** (the maximum distance between object and target) in Illustrator (Edit, in Windows) > Preferences > Smart Guides & Slices.

➤ Option-drag/Alt-drag from the horizontal ruler to create a vertical guide, or from the vertical ruler to create a horizontal guide.

snap to pixel

If View > **Pixel Preview** is on, View > Snap to Grid becomes View > **Snap to Pixel,** and Snap to Pixel is automatically turned on. With Snap to Pixel on, any new objects you create or any existing objects you drag will snap to the pixel grid, and anti-aliasing will be removed from any horizontal or vertical edges on those objects.

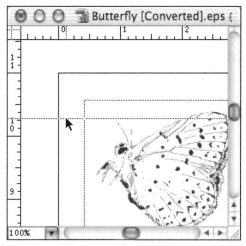

◾ *Drag a **guide** from the horizontal or vertical ruler.*

1 *An object is selected, and then View > Guides > Make Guides is chosen.*

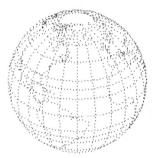

2 *The object is now a guide. The former "path" object will now be listed as "guide" on the Layers palette.*

So far we've shown you how to work with two kinds of guides: smart guides and ruler guides. Now you'll learn how to convert standard Illustrator paths into guides. **Object guides** are reversible, meaning they can be converted back into standard objects at any time.

To turn an object into a guide:

1. Select an object, a group of objects, or an object within a group (not a symbol or an object in a blend) **1**. You can copy the object and work off the copy, if you want. *Note:* If the object you turn into a guide is part of a group, the guide will also be part of that group.

2. Choose View > Guides > Make Guides (Cmd-5/Ctrl-5) **2**.
or
Control-click/right-click and choose Make Guides from the context menu.

➤ You can transform or reshape a guide object, as long as guides aren't locked (see the following page). Object guides can be selected using the Layers palette (look for <Guide>). Relock them when you're done.

Back we go—reversing object guides.

To turn all object guides back into objects:

1. If guides are locked, Control-click/right-click and choose Lock Guides from the context menu to uncheck that option.

2. Choose the Selection tool (V).

3. Select one guide or marquee or Shift-click multiple guides.

4. Choose View > Guides > Release Guides (Cmd-Option-5/Ctrl-Alt-5).
or
Control-click/right-click and choose Release Guides from the context menu.

The guide will revert to an object, with its former fill and stroke.

To turn one guide back into an object:
Cmd-Shift-double-click/Ctrl-Shift-double-click the edge of the guide.

Object Guides

To select or move guides, whether standard or object, they must first be **unlocked.** By default, the Lock Guides command is on.

To lock or unlock all guides:

Choose View > Guides > Lock Guides (Cmd-Option-;/Ctrl-Alt-;) to check or uncheck the command.

or

Deselect all objects, then Control-click/right-click the artboard and choose Lock Guides from the context menu.

To lock or unlock one guide:

1. Make sure View > Guides > Lock Guides doesn't have a check mark. You can also access this command by deselecting all objects and then Control-clicking/right-clicking the artboard.

2. On the Layers palette, click in the lock column for any guide you want to unlock.

Note: Make sure the selection color for a <Guide> (Layers palette) is different from the guide color; otherwise you won't be able to tell whether the guide is selected.

To remove one guide:

1. Make sure either all guides are unlocked or the guide you want to remove is unlocked.

2. Choose the Selection tool (V), then click the guide.

3. On the Mac, press Delete. In Windows, press Backspace or Del.

4. *Optional:* To relock all the remaining guides, deselect all objects, then Control-click/right-click the artboard and choose Lock Guides.

To remove all guides:

Choose View > Guides > Clear Guides.

Guide control

You can hide/show or lock/unlock individual guides, because each one is listed as a separate item on the Layers palette (<Guide>).

➤ After guides are created, drag all of them into one layer or sublayer. Then if you hide/show or lock/unlock that layer, all those guides will be affected simultaneously. You'll still be able to lock and unlock individual guides.

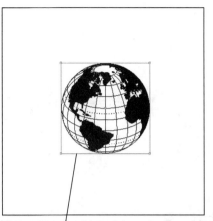

1 *Drag a rectangle around an object to define the guide area.*

To place guides around an object or create evenly spaced guides:

1. Choose the Selection tool (V), then select a rectangular object. Make sure the rectangle is on the printable page. *Beware!* If you use a nonrectangular shape, the shape will be converted to a rectangle!
   or
   Choose the Rectangle tool, 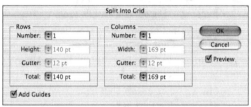 then drag a rectangle to define a guide area **1**.

2. Make sure the ruler origin is in the default location.

3. Choose Object > Path > Split Into Grid. **NEW**

4. Check Add Guides and check Preview **2**.

5. To encircle the object with guides without dividing the object, leave the Number and Total for Rows and Columns as is.
   or
   To divide the object and create guides around each section, choose a Number above 1 for the Rows and/or Columns, and enter Width and Gutter values.

6. Click OK **3**.

7. The guides will be listed as a <Group> (of paths) on the Layers palette. Click the <Group>, then choose View > Guides > Make Guides (Cmd-5/Ctrl-5) **4**.

8. *Optional:* Delete the rectangle that was used to create the guides.

2 *Choose options in the **Split Into Grid** dialog box (formerly called Rows & Columns).*

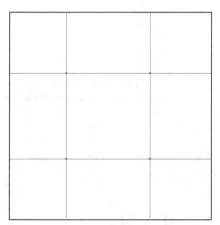

3 *Lines appear around the rectangle.*

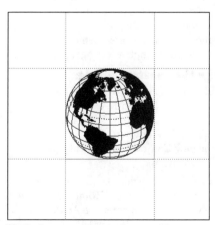

4 *The lines are **converted** into guides.*

Split Into Grid

Using the grid

The grid is like nonprinting graph paper. You can use it as a framework to help you arrange objects, either by eye or using Snap to Grid. Start by showing the grid.

To show/hide the grid:

Choose View > Show Grid (or Hide Grid) (Cmd-"/Ctrl-") 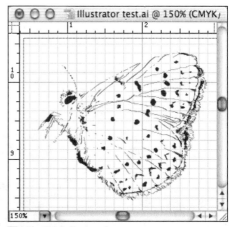 **1**.

or

Deselect, then Control-click/right-click and choose Show Grid (or Hide Grid) from the context menu.

You can change the grid style (lines or dots), color, or spacing in Illustrator (Edit, in Windows) > Preferences > **Guides & Grid** (see page 444). Check Grids In Back in that dialog box to have the grid appear in back of all objects instead of in front.

To use Snap to Grid:

Choose View > Snap to Grid (Cmd-Shift-"/Ctrl-Shift-"). Now if you move an object near a gridline, the edge of the object will snap to the gridline. This works whether the grid is displayed or not.

The default **Constrain Angle** is 0°—the horizontal/vertical *(x/y)* axes. When you change the Constrain Angle, any new object that you draw will rest on the new axes, and any new object that you move or transform with Shift held down will snap to the new axes. This setting affects the whole application, both future documents and existing ones—whether those documents are open or closed when the Constrain Angle is changed.

To change the Constrain Angle:

Choose Illustrator (Edit, in Windows) > Preferences > General (Cmd-K/Ctrl-K), change the Constrain Angle (–360 to 360), then click OK **2**–**3**. The grid will change to conform to the new Constrain Angle (display it to see what we mean).

➤ To establish a Constrain Angle based on an object rotated using the Rotate tool, ↻ select the object, then enter the Angle readout ∠ from the Info palette as the Constrain Angle.

1 *The Grid displayed*

What the Constrain Angle affects

➤ Text objects

➤ Rectangle, Ellipse, and Graph tools

➤ Transformation tools (Scale, Reflect, and Shear, but not Rotate or Blend)

➤ Gradient tool and Pen tool when used with Shift held down

➤ Moving objects with Shift held down or by pressing an arrow key

➤ Grid

➤ Smart guides

➤ Info palette readouts

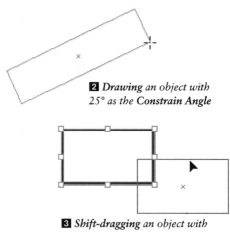

2 *Drawing an object with 25° as the Constrain Angle*

3 *Shift-dragging an object with 25° as the Constrain Angle*

shifting patterns

If you move an object that contains a pattern fill manually or by using the Move dialog box, and **Patterns** is unchecked in the Move dialog box, the object will move but not the pattern. If Patterns is checked but **Objects** is not, and you use the Move command, the pattern position will shift but not the object.

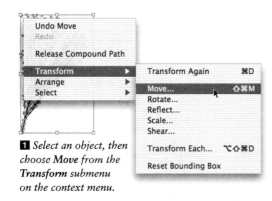

1 *Select an object, then choose* **Move** *from the* **Transform** *submenu on the context menu.*

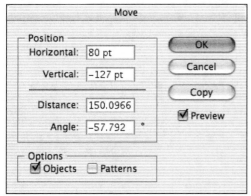

2 *In the* **Move** *dialog box, enter Horizontal and Vertical values or enter the Distance and Angle you want the object to move.*

Transforming using numbers

You can precisely reposition an object by entering values in the **Move** dialog box. Move dialog box settings remain the same until you change them, move an object using the mouse, or use the Measure tool, so you can repeat the same move as many times as you like using the Transform Again shortcut (Cmd-D/Ctrl-D)—even on another object.

To move an object a specified distance:

1. *Optional:* Choose a lower zoom level for your illustration so the object won't disappear from view when it's moved.

2. Choose the Selection tool (V).

3. Select the object you want to move.

4. Double-click the Selection or Direct Selection tool.
   or
   Control-click/right-click and choose Transform > Move from the context menu **1**.
   or
   Choose Object > Transform > Move (Cmd-Shift-M/Ctrl-Shift-M).

5. In the Move dialog box, check Preview **2**.

6. Press Tab to preview these changes:

   Enter positive **Horizontal** and **Vertical** values to move the object to the right and upward, respectively; enter negative values to move the object to the left or downward; or enter a combination of positive and negative values. Enter 0 in either field to prevent the object from moving along that axis. You can use any of these units of measure: "p," "pt," "in," "mm," "q," or "cm."
   or
   Enter a positive **Distance** and a positive **Angle** between 0 and 180 to move the object upward; enter a positive Distance and a negative Angle between 0 and –180 to move the object downward. The other fields will change automatically.

7. *Optional:* Click Copy to close the dialog box and move a copy of the object (not the object itself). For the Options, see the sidebar on this page.

8. Click OK.

Use the **Transform** palette to move, scale, rotate, or shear an object or objects based on exact values or percentages.

To move, scale, rotate, or shear an object using the Transform palette:

1. Open the Transform palette (Shift-F8).
2. Select an object or objects.
3. Choose the reference point from which you want the transformation to be measured by clicking one of the nine square **Reference Point** handles on the left side of the palette **1**.
4. From the Transform palette menu, choose **Transform Object Only, Transform Pattern Only,** or **Transform Both** (to transform objects and patterns).
5. If you're going to scale the object(s), decide whether you want the **Scale Strokes & Effects** option to be on or off (palette menu). With it on, the object's stroke and appearances will scale proportionately. This option can also be turned on or off in Illustrator (Edit, in Windows) > Preferences > General.
6. To apply any of the following values, use one of the shortcuts listed in the sidebar on this page:

   To **move** the object horizontally, enter a new X position. Enter a higher value to move the object to the right, and a lower value to move it to the left.

   To **move** the object vertically, enter a new Y position. Enter a higher value to move the object upward, a lower value to move it downward.

   To scale the object, enter new **width** and/or **height** values. You can enter a percentage instead of an absolute value. If you want to scale the object proportionally, click the Link button (a bracket will appear next to the button). NEW

   Enter a positive Rotate value to **rotate** the object counterclockwise or a negative value to rotate it clockwise. Or choose a preset angle from the pop-up menu.

Applying Transform palette values

Exit the palette	Return/Enter
Apply a value entered in a field and highlight the next field	Tab
Apply a value and rehighlight the same field	Shift-Return/ Shift-Enter
Clone the object and exit the palette	Option-Return/ Alt-Enter
Clone the object and highlight the next field	Option-Tab (Mac only)
Repeat last transformation	Cmd-D/ Ctrl-D

*The x and **y axis** locations of the currently selected Reference Point: Enter new values to position the object's Reference Point at that value on the x or y axis.*

*The selected object's **height***

*The selected object's **width***

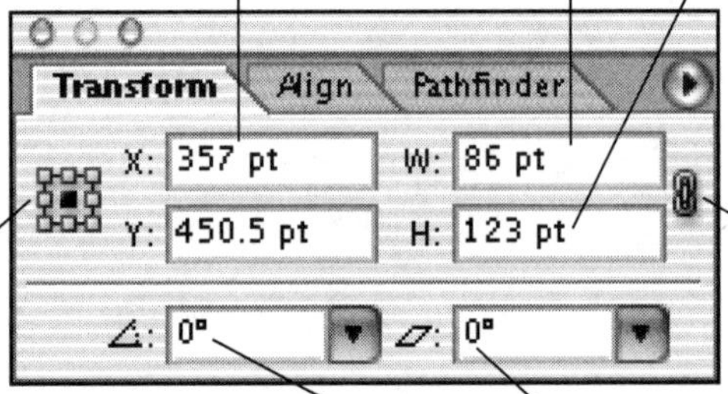

***1** **Reference Point** (the part of the object from which Transform palette values are calculated)*

***Rotate** field for rotating the object*

***Shear** field for shearing the object*

***Link** button for scaling objects proportionally*

Let the palette do the math

In the W or H field on the Transform palette, you can perform simple math to scale an object. Try using any of the following methods:

➤ After the current number, type an asterisk ***** and then a **percentage** value. For example, to reduce an object's scale by half, click to the right of the current value, then type "*50%" (e.g., 4p would become 2p).

➤ Replace the entire field with a **percentage.** Enter "75%," for example, to reduce the W or H to three-quarters of its current value (e.g., 4p becomes 3p).

➤ Enter a **positive** or **negative** value to the right of the current number, as in "+2" or "-2", to increase or decrease, respectively, the current value by that amount.

Press **Tab** to apply the math and advance to the next field, or press **Return/Enter** to apply the math and exit the palette.

To **shear** the object to the right, enter or choose a positive Shear value. To shear an object to the left, enter or choose a negative Shear value.

7. From the palette menu, you can also choose **Flip Horizontal** or **Flip Vertical.**

➤ To apply a transformation as an editable and removable effect, see page 108.

➤ If Use Preview Bounds is checked in Illustrator (Edit, in Windows) > Preferences > General, the full dimensions of an object, including its stroke and any effects, will display on the Width and Height fields on the Transform and Info palettes.

Transform Palette

Aligning and distributing

Buttons, point type blocks—anything that's lined up in a row or column—will require aligning and distributing in order to look neat and tidy. With the **Align** palette **1**, it's easy to do.

To align or distribute objects:

1. To align, select two or more objects or groups; to distribute, select three or more objects. Display the Align palette (Shift-F7).

2. Turn **Use Preview Bounds** on from the Align palette menu or in Illustrator (Edit, in Windows) > Preferences > General to have Illustrator factor in an object's stroke weight and any effects when calculating alignment or distribution. Turn this option off to have Illustrator ignore the stroke weight and any effects. The stroke straddles the edge of the path, halfway inside and halfway outside.

3. *For occasional use:* Choose **Align To Artboard** from the palette menu to align the objects along the top, right, bottom,

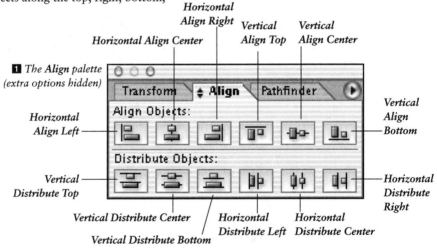

1 *The Align palette (extra options hidden)*

Horizontal Align Center

Horizontal Align Right

Vertical Align Top

Vertical Align Center

Horizontal Align Left

Vertical Align Bottom

Vertical Distribute Top

Horizontal Distribute Right

Vertical Distribute Center

Vertical Distribute Bottom

Horizontal Distribute Left

Horizontal Distribute Center

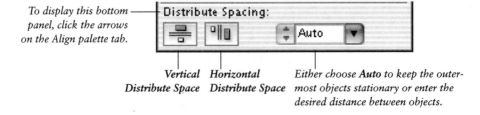

To display this bottom panel, click the arrows on the Align palette tab.

Vertical Distribute Space

Horizontal Distribute Space

Either choose **Auto** to keep the outermost objects stationary or enter the desired distance between objects.

Align and Distribute

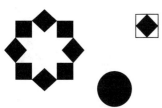

1 *The original objects*

Vertical Align Center

Horizontal Align Center

2 *The original objects*

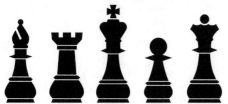

3 *After clicking* **Vertical Align Bottom***...*

4 *...and then clicking* **Horizontal Distribute Center.**

5 *The original objects*

Horizontal Distribute Space

or left edge of the artboard, depending on which Align Objects button is clicked. If Align to Artboard is on and objects are distributed vertically, the topmost object will move to the top edge of the artboard, the bottommost object will move to the bottom edge of the artboard, and the remaining objects will be distributed between them. If objects are distributed horizontally with this option on, objects will be aligned between the leftmost and rightmost edges of the artboard.

4. *Optional:* By default (with Align To Artboard turned off), the topmost, bottommost, leftmost, or rightmost object will remain stationary, depending on which Align Objects button you click. To choose a nondefault object to remain stationary, Cmd-click/Ctrl-click that selected object now (that is, after all the objects are selected and before you click an align button). To go back to the default object, choose **Cancel Key Object** from the palette menu (the command will become dimmed).

5. Click an **Align Objects** button **1** and/or a **Distribute Objects** button **2**–**4** on the Align palette.

   Or for **Distribute Spacing 5**, choose Auto from the pop-up menu to keep the two objects that are farthest apart stationary (topmost and bottommost or leftmost and rightmost) and redistribute the remaining objects evenly between them, or enter an exact distance you want between objects (the outermost objects will probably move); then click either of the two Distribute Spacing buttons.

➤ If you change your mind and want to apply a different Align palette option, first Undo the last one.

Align and Distribute

429

You can use the **Measure** tool to calculate the distance and angle between two points in an illustration. When you use the Measure tool, the amounts it calculates are displayed on the Info palette, which opens automatically when the tool is used.

The distance and angle calculated using the Measure tool also become the current values in the Move dialog box, which means you can use the Measure tool as a guide to mark a distance and direction, then use the Transform Again shortcut to move any selected object.

To measure a distance using the Measure tool:

1. Choose the Measure tool (it's on the same pop-out menu as the Eyedropper tool).

2. Click the starting and ending points that span the distance and angle you want to measure **1**–**2**.
   or
   Drag from the first point to the second point.

   Distance (D) and angle readouts will now display on the Info palette **3**.

3. *Optional:* To move any object the distance and angle you just measured (until those values are changed), select the object, then press Cmd-D/Ctrl-D.

➤ Shift-click or Shift-drag with the Measure tool to constrain the tool to a multiple of 45° or to the current Constrain Angle.

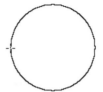

1 *Click a starting point. The Info palette will open.*

2 *Click an ending point. The distance between clicks will display on the Info palette.*

Horizontal distance from the x-axis

Horizontal distance from the starting point

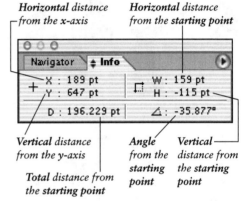

Vertical distance from the y-axis

Total distance from the starting point

Angle from the starting point

Vertical distance from the starting point

3 *After clicking a starting and ending point with the Measure tool, distance and angle values display on the Info palette. The X and Y positions are measured from the ruler origin.*

In this chapter you'll learn how to record a sequence of edits and commands in an action. You'll also learn how to edit an action using various methods and replay an action on one document or on a batch of documents.

1 *The Actions palette in Button mode*

An actions set

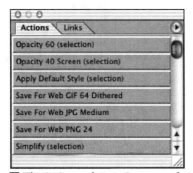

Expand/
collapse
list

Toggle
dialog
box pause
on/off

Toggle
item
on/off

A *recorded action*
A *recorded command*

Stop *(playing/ Record Play New New Delete*
recording) Set Action Selection

2 *The Actions palette in List mode*

Creating actions
Actions and the Actions palette

An action is a recorded sequence of tool and menu events. When an action is replayed, the same series of commands is executed in exactly the same sequence in which it was recorded. Actions can be simple (as short as a single command) or complex—whatever your work demands. And they can be replayed on any Illustrator document. What's more, actions can be edited, reorganized, and traded around among Illustrator users.

Actions are recorded, played back, edited, saved, and deleted by using the Actions palette (Window > Actions). The Actions palette has two modes: Button and List (choose either one from the palette menu). Only the action name is listed in **Button mode 1**, so this mode is used only for playback. Actions can be assigned keyboard shortcuts for fast access in Button mode. To turn Button mode on or off, choose Button Mode from the Actions palette menu.

In **List mode** (Button mode turned off), the commands that the action contains are displayed in sequential order on the palette **2**. Use this mode to record, play, edit, save, and load actions.

Note: For the instructions in this chapter, put your Actions palette into List mode.

Actions are organized in **sets**, which are represented as folder icons on the Actions palette.

To create an actions set:

1. Click the New Set button  at the bottom of the Actions palette.
   or
   Choose New Set from the Actions palette menu **1**.

2. Enter a Name for the set **2**.

3. Click OK. A new folder icon and set name will appear on the palette **3**. (To save the set, see page 437.)

Until you become familiar with using actions, you should practice **recording** them on a duplicate file. Figure out beforehand what the action is supposed to accomplish, and run through the command sequence a few times before you actually record it.

To record an action:

1. Open an existing file, or create a new one.

2. On the Actions palette, click the name of the actions set that you want the new action to belong to. (To create a new set, follow the previous set of instructions on this page).

3. Click the New Action button 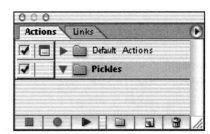 at the bottom of the Actions palette.

4. Enter a Name for the action **4**.

5. *Optional:* Choose a keyboard shortcut for the action from the Function Key pop-up menu, and click the Shift and/or Command/Control box. Choose a color for the action name in Button mode from the Color pop-up menu.

6. Click Record.

7. Create and edit objects as you normally would. Any tool and menu commands that are recordable will appear on the action command list.

8. Click the Stop button 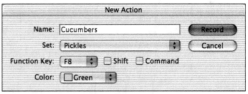 to end recording.

1 *Choose New Set from the Actions palette menu (or click the New Set button at the bottom of the Actions palette).*

New Action…
New Set…
Duplicate
Delete
Play

Start Recording
Record Again…
Insert Menu Item…
Insert Stop…
Insert Select Path
Select Object…

Action Options…
Playback Options…

Clear Actions
Reset Actions
Load Actions…
Replace Actions…
Save Actions…

Button Mode

Batch…

2 *Enter a Name for the new set.*

3 *A new set folder appears on the Actions palette.*

4 *Use the New Action dialog box to change an action name or keyboard shortcut, or to change its button display color for Button mode.*

Create Actions Set; Record Action

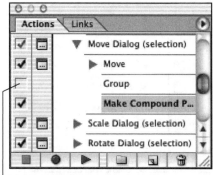

1 *Click in the first column to exclude/include a command from playback. Note: A dimmed check mark signifies that at least one of the commands in that action is turned off.*

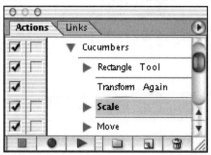

2 *Click the command that you want the new command to follow.*

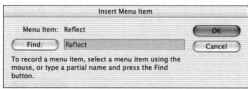

3 *After opening the Insert Menu Item dialog box, we chose Object > Transform > Reflect.*

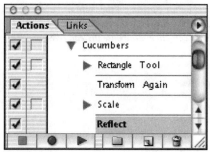

4 *The new command appears on the palette.*

Playing back actions

The first time you **play back** an action, do it on a duplicate file or on a file that you don't care about preserving.

To play back an action on an image:

1. Open the Illustrator file on which you want to play the action, and select any objects, if necessary.

2. If the Actions palette is in List mode, make sure the check mark is present for the action that you want to play back. Click the name of the action you want to play back, then click the Play button.▶

➤ You can temporarily **exclude** commands you don't need from playing back. Click the check mark ☑ in the leftmost column to disable that command **1**, or click in the blank spot to enable it.

Editing actions

You may find that an action needs to be enhanced or modified from its original recorded version. There are several techniques you can use to edit actions, starting with **inserting a menu item.**

To add a menu command to an action:

1. Put the Actions palette in List mode (turn off the Button Mode option).

2. If the list for the action into which you want to insert the menu item isn't expanded, click the right-pointing triangle.

3. Click the command on the action list that you want the new command to follow **2**.

4. Choose Insert Menu Item from the Actions palette menu.

5. Choose the desired menu command from the menu bar. The command name will appear in the dialog box **3**.
   or
   Type the command name into the Find field, then click the Find button.

6. Click OK **4**. The command you added will appear on the action list.

If you **insert a stop** into an action, the action will pause during playback. At that point, you can perform a manual operation, such as entering type or selecting an object, then resume the action playback.

To insert a stop in an existing action:

1. Put the Actions palette in List mode, and expand the action into which you want to insert a stop.

2. Click the command after which you want the stop to be inserted 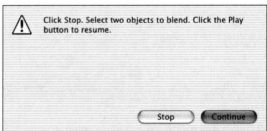.

3. Choose Insert Stop from the Actions palette menu.

4. Type an instructional message in the Record Stop dialog box to tell the user which operations to perform during the stop. At the end of the message, tell users to click the Play button on the Actions palette when they're ready to resume playback (e.g., "Click the Play button to resume") **2**.

5. *Optional:* Check Allow Continue to permit the user to bypass the pause.

6. Click OK **3**. A Stop listing will appear within the action.

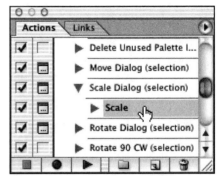

1 *Click the command that you want the stop to appear* **after.**

2 *Type an* **instructional message.**

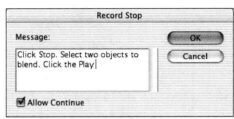

3 *In this example of a* **pause** *dialog box, the user is instructed to press* **Stop**, *select two objects for blending, and then click the Play button on the Actions palette to resume the action playback. If the two objects are already selected, the user can click* **Continue** *instead of Stop.*

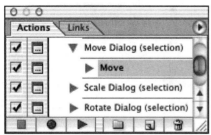

1 *Click the command that you want new commands to appear after.*

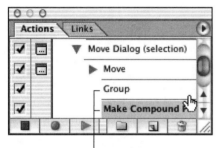

2 *Two new commands are added.*

In much the same manner as you would insert a menu command, you can record **additional commands** into an existing action.

To record commands into an existing action:

1. Put the Actions palette in List mode, and expand the action into which you want to insert a command or commands.

2. Choose the command you want the new command(s) to follow **1**.

3. Click the Record button. ●

4. Make modifications to the file as you would normally, using the commands you want inserted in the action.

5. Click the Stop button ■ when you're ready to stop recording. The command(s) you just recorded will be listed below the chosen insertion point on the Actions palette **2**.

For any command or tool that uses a dialog box that requires pressing Return/Enter (known as a "modal control"), you can insert a **pause** to enable the user to change any of the dialog box settings during playback.

To turn on a command's dialog box pause:

If a recorded command uses a dialog box, it will have a pause icon ▦ for toggling that command on and off. Click the icon to disable the dialog box pause and use the prerecorded input instead, or click the blank space to enable the command's dialog box pause and allow user input.

A red pause icon next to an action name means that at least one command within that action has been turned off.

To rerecord a command that uses a dialog box:

1. Put the Actions palette into List mode.

2. Expand the list for the action that contains the command that you want to rerecord.

3. Select an object in your illustration, then double-click the command that you want to rerecord **1**. It must have a dialog box icon (or a blank box for the icon).

4. Change any of the dialog box settings, then click OK. The next time this action is played back, the new parameters that you entered will be used.

To delete an action or a command:

Click the action or command that you want to delete, click the Delete button 🗑 at the bottom of the Actions palette, then click Yes.
or
To bypass the prompt, drag the action or command over the Delete button; or click the command, then Option-click/Alt-click the button. You can't undo this.

➤ Beware of the Clear Actions command on the palette menu, which clears all actions from the palette (you'll get a warning prompt, and you can also use the Undo command immediately afterward, if you need to). Only slightly less perilous is the Reset Actions command, which lets you either replace all the existing actions with the default actions or append the default actions to the palette.

You can **restack** and **move** action commands, just as you would restack layers on the Layers palette. *Note:* Before rearranging things, you should save the actions set that contains the actions you're working on (see the next page).

To restack a command or move it to another action:

In List mode, drag any command upward or downward to a new location in the same action, or into another action.

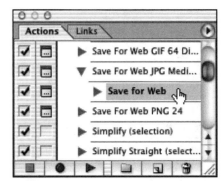

1 *Double-click the command that you want to rerecord.*

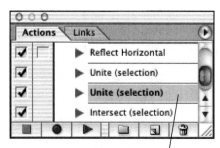

1 *The* **duplicate** *command appears.*

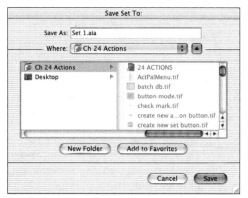

2 *Enter a Name in the Save Set To dialog box.*

To copy a command:

1. In List mode, click the action command that you want to copy.

2. Option-drag/Alt-drag the command upward or downward in the same action or into another action list.
or
Drag the command name over the New Action button at the bottom of the Actions palette **■**,**⬗** then drag the duplicate command to any location on the palette.

Managing actions sets

One of the handiest things about actions is that you can share them with other Illustrator users. To do this, you must **save** the set that contains them. Try to keep your actions and actions sets well organized—and perform frequent backups!

To save an actions set:

1. Click the actions set that you want to save.

2. Choose Save Actions from the Actions palette menu.

3. Type a name in the Save As field (keep the .aia extension) **2**, and choose a location in which to save the set. You can save the set in Illustrator CS\Presets\Actions.

4. Click Save.

To load an actions set:

1. Choose Load Actions from the Actions palette menu.

2. Locate and click the actions set that you want to load, then click Open. The actions set will appear on the palette.

Copy Command; Save, Load Actions Set

437

Batch processing

Actions are a great way to optimize work-flow, and being able to perform an action on a designated **folder full of files** gives you even more power.

Note: Batch processing will end if it encounters a stop command in an action. You should remove any inserted stops from the action that you're going to use for batch processing.

To play an action on multiple files:

1. Make sure all the files to be batch-processed are in one folder. The folder can contain subfolders, but only one main folder can be chosen at a time.

2. From the Actions palette menu, choose Batch.

3. Choose a set from the **Set** pop-up menu 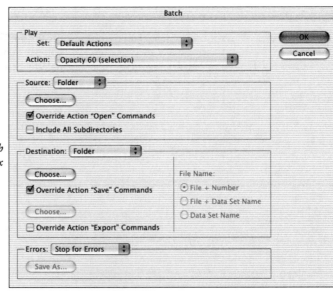 and an action from the **Action** pop-up menu.

4. Choose **Source:** Folder, click Choose, then locate the folder that contains the files that you want to process.

   Check **Override Action "Open" Commands** to open files from the chosen folder, thus ignoring any Open commands in the recorded action.

   Check **Include All Subdirectories** if you also want to process folders within the folder you've chosen.

(For information about working with data sets as the source, see Illustrator Help.)

5. Choose **Destination: None** to have the files remain open after processing; or **Save and Close** to have the edited files be saved over and closed; or **Folder** to have the files be saved to a new folder (click Choose to specify the destination folder).

6. *Optional:* If you chose Folder for Destination, check **Override Action "Save" Commands** to have the files save to the folder designated in step 5, should a Save command occur in the action.

7. *Optional:* Check **Override Action "Export" Commands** to override any Export command destination used in the action (click Choose to specify the new destination folder).

8. *Optional:* By default, Illustrator will stop the batch processing if it encounters an error. If you choose Error: Log Errors to File, the batch processing will continue and error messages will be sent to a text file. Click Save As, then give the error log file a name and destination. If this option is chosen, an alert message will inform you of any errors.

9. Click OK.

1 *The Batch dialog box*

438

PREFERENCES 25

The first skill you'll learn in this chapter is how to customize your startup file. Then, using the various panes in the Preferences dialog boxes, you'll learn how to choose dozens of default command, tool, and palette settings for current and future documents, such as type options, units, display performance, display options, smart guides and slices options, scratch disks, and the Constrain Angle.

The startup files

The startup files—**Adobe Illustrator Startup_CMYK.ai** and **Adobe Illustrator Startup_RGB.ai**—are stored in Adobe Illustrator CS/Plug-ins.

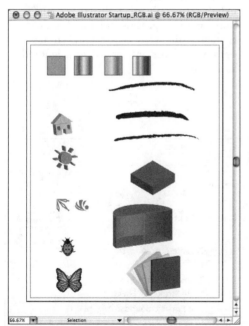

1 The Adobe Illustrator *Startup* file will be blank until you add stuff to it. Here, we've added objects that contain gradients, brush strokes, symbols, graphic styles, and effects.

By creating a custom CMYK and/or RGB startup file containing the colors, patterns, gradients, and document settings that you work with regularly, you can have those elements be part of every new document.

To create a custom startup file:

1. For safekeeping, duplicate the existing startup file, and move the copy to a different folder (see the sidebar at left).

2. Double-click either of the two Adobe Illustrator Startup file icons.

3. Do any of the following **1**:

   Create new colors, patterns, or gradients, and add these new items to the Swatches palette. For a visual reminder, apply swatches to separate objects in the file.

   Drag-copy swatches from any open swatch libraries to the Swatches palette.

   Create custom brushes, symbols, or graphic styles, and apply them to objects as a visual reminder.

   Choose Document Setup and Print dialog box settings.

   Choose ruler and page origins.

   Choose a document window size, scroll positions, and View menu settings.

4. To help Illustrator launch quickly, delete whatever items you don't need in the startup file (e.g., delete unnecessary brushes from the Brushes palette).

5. Save over the file in the Plug-ins folder using the same name, as listed in the sidebar at left.

General Preferences

*Choose Illustrator (Edit, in Windows) > Preferences > General (**Cmd-K/Ctrl-K**).*

Keyboard Increment
This value is the distance (0–1296 pt) a selected object moves when an arrow key is pressed on the keyboard.

Constrain Angle
This is the angle (–360 to 360°) for the x and y axes. The default setting is 0° (parallel to the edges of the document window). Tool operations, dialog box measurements, and the grid are calculated relative to the current Constrain Angle (see page 424).

Corner Radius
This value (0–1296 pt) controls the amount of curvature in the corners of objects drawn with the Rounded Rectangle tool. 0 produces a right angle. Changing this value updates the Corner Radius field in the Rounded Rectangle dialog box, and vice versa.

Object Selection by Path Only **NEW**
With this option checked, in order to select an object, you must click a path segment or anchor point with the Selection or Direct Selection tool. With this option unchecked, you can select a filled object in Preview view by clicking with a selection tool anywhere within the object's bounding box.

Use Precise Cursors
When this option is checked, the drawing and editing tool pointers display as a crosshair instead of as the tool icon. To turn this option on temporarily when the preference is off, press Caps Lock.

Show Tool Tips
When this option is checked and you rest the mouse on a palette button, tool, icon, or option, a one-line description of that feature will pop up onscreen.

Anti-aliased Artwork
When this option is checked, edges of existing and future vector objects (not placed images) look smoother onscreen. It has no effect on print output.

Select Same Tint %
When this option is checked, the Select > Same > Fill Color and Stroke Color commands select only other objects with the same spot (not process) color and tint percentage as the selected object. When this option is off, the tint percentage is ignored as a criterion.

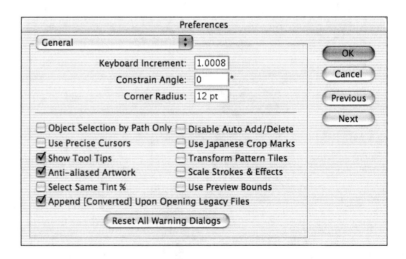

Fast track to the Preferences

Use the shortcut that opens the General Preferences dialog box (**Cmd-K/Ctrl-K**), then choose from the pop-up menu at the top of the dialog box.

Legacy files

Illustrator CS provides support for such new text features as Unicode, OpenType, and character and paragraph styles, and because of this, text from any earlier version of Illustrator must be updated before it can be edited. When you open a file containing text that was created in a previous version of Illustrator, you can opt to have Illustrator update the text immediately, or you can opt to update it later.

When text is updated, some changes may occur in leading, tracking, and kerning; words may shift to the next line in an area type object; and words may overflow from an area type object or shift to the next threaded text object.

If you opt not to update the text (leave it as legacy text), you'll be able to view, move, and print it, but not edit it. **Legacy text** has an "x" in its bounding box when selected, and is listed as "Legacy Text" on the Layers and Appearance palettes.

Append [Converted] Upon Opening
Legacy Files
With this option checked, when updating text in a file that was created in a previous version of Illustrator, Illustrator will append the word "[Converted]" to the file name. See "Legacy files" at left.

Disable Auto Add/Delete
Checking this option disables the Pen tool's ability to change to the Add Anchor Point tool when the pointer passes over a path segment, or to the Delete Anchor Point tool when the pointer passes over an anchor point.

Use Japanese Crop Marks
Check this box to use Japanese-style crop marks when printing separations. Preview this style in the Separation Setup dialog box.

Transform Pattern Tiles
If this option is checked and you use a transformation tool on an object that contains a pattern fill, the pattern will also transform. You can also turn this option on or off for any individual transformation tool in its own dialog box, in the Move dialog box, or on the Transform palette.

Scale Strokes & Effects
Check this box to allow an object's stroke weight and appearances to be scaled when you scale an object by using its bounding box, the Scale tool, the Free Transform tool, or the Effect > Distort & Transform > Transform command. This option can also be turned on or off in the Scale dialog box and the Transform palette.

Use Preview Bounds
If this option is checked, an object's stroke weight and any effects are factored in when an object's height and width dimensions are calculated or the Align palette is used. This option changes the dimensions of the bounding box.

Reset All Warning Dialogs
Click this button to allow any warning in which you checked "Don't Show Again" to redisplay if an editing operation causes it to appear.

For the Pencil tool preferences, see page 80.

General Preferences

Type & Auto Tracing Preferences

Choose Illustrator (Edit, in Windows) > Preferences > Type & Auto Tracing.

Type Options

Size/Leading; Baseline Shift; Tracking
Selected text is modified by this increment each time a keyboard shortcut is executed for the respective command.

Greeking
This value is the point size at or below which type displays on the screen as gray bars (greeked) rather than as readable characters. Greeking speeds up screen redraw. It has no effect on how a document prints.

NEW Type Object Selection by Path Only
With this option checked, to select type you have to click right on a type's path. With this option unchecked, you can select type by clicking with a selection tool anywhere within the type's bounding box.

NEW Show Asian Options
Check this option to access options for Korean, Japanese, and Chinese type on the Character palette, Paragraph palette, and Font menu.

Show Font Names in English
When this option is checked, two-byte font names display in English on the font pop-up menu. When this option is unchecked, two-byte font names display in two-byte script.

Number of Recent Fonts
Choose the maximum number of fonts (1–15) to be listed on the Type > Recent Fonts submenu.

Font Preview Size NEW
Check this option to have font family names display in their fonts (WYSIWYG), for easy identification on the Type > Font menu and the Find Font dialog box (and the Character palette in the Mac). Also choose a size for the font display: Small, Medium, or Large.

Auto Trace Options

Auto Trace Tolerance
This value (0–10) controls how closely the Auto Trace tool traces a path. Enter a low value to have the tool follow the path closely; enter a high Auto Trace Tolerance to have the tool ignore minor irregularities on the path's contour.

Tracing Gap
When tracing the contour of a bitmap image, the Auto Trace tool will ignore gaps that are equal to or less than the number of pixels (0–2) specified in this field. The smaller the gap, the more closely an image will be traced, and the more anchor points will be created.

Type & Auto Tracing Preferences

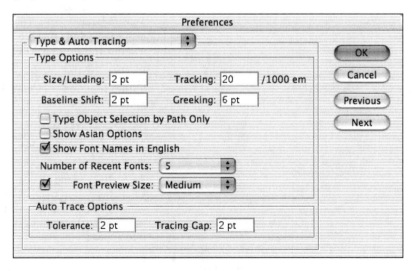

Units & Display Performance Preferences

Choose Illustrator (Edit, in Windows) > Preferences > Units & Display Performance.

Units
General
This unit of measure is used for the rulers, dialog boxes, and Transform and Info palettes for the current document and all new documents.

➤ For the current document, the Units chosen in File > Document Setup (under Artboard: Setup) override the Units chosen in this preference dialog box.

Stroke
This unit of measure is used on the Stroke palette.

Type
This unit of measure is used on the Character and Paragraph palettes. (We use Points.)

Asian Type (NEW)
This unit of measure is used for Asian type.

Numbers Without Units Are Points
If this option is checked, Picas is chosen as the Units: General, and you enter a value in points into a field, the value won't be converted into picas. For example, if you enter "99," instead of being converted into "8p3," it will stay as "99."

Identify Objects By
When creating dynamic objects associated with variables, you can specify whether variables are assigned the Object Name or an XML ID number. Consult with your Web developer regarding this option.

Display Performance (NEW)
Hand Tool
Drag the Hand Tool slider to the left toward Full Quality for better onscreen display when the illustration is moved in the document window with the Hand tool; or move the slider to the right toward Faster Updates to allow the illustration to be moved more quickly, but at a lower display quality while it's being moved.

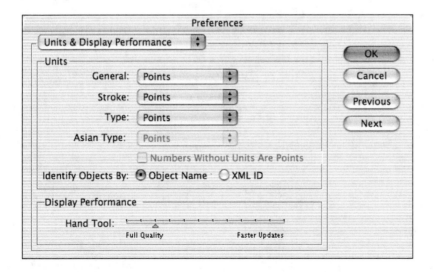

Guides & Grid Preferences

Choose Illustrator (Edit, in Windows) > Preferences > Guides & Grid.

Guides

Color

For Guides, choose a color from the Color pop-up menu. Or choose Other or double-click the color square to open the System color picker and mix your own color.

Style

Choose the Lines or Dots Style for the guides.

➤ To help differentiate between guides and gridlines, choose the Dots style for guides.

Grid

Color

For the Grid, choose a color from the Color pop-up menu. Or choose Other or double-click the color square to open the System color picker and mix your own color.

➤ If View > Snap to Grid is on, guides will snap to the gridlines as you create or move them.

Style

Choose the Lines or Dots Style for the Grid. Subdivision lines won't display if the Dots Style is chosen.

Gridline every

Enter the distance (.01–1000 pt) between gridlines.

Subdivisions

Enter the number of Subdivision lines **1**–**2** (1–1000) to be drawn between the gridlines when the Lines Style is chosen for the grid.

Grids In Back

Check Grids In Back to have the grid display behind all objects. With the grid in back, you can easily tell which objects have a fill of None because the grid will be visible underneath them.

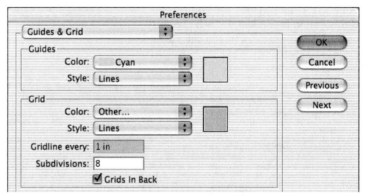

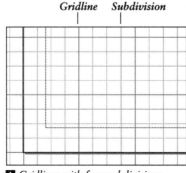

Gridline   Subdivision

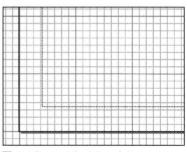

1 *Gridlines with **four** subdivisions*   **2** *Gridlines with **eight** subdivisions*

Smart Guides & Slices Preferences

Choose Illustrator (Edit, in Windows) > Preferences > Smart Guides & Slices.
To turn on smart guides, choose View > Smart Guides (Cmd-U/Ctrl-U).

Display Options

Text Label Hints
These labels display as you pass the pointer over an object, an anchor point, etc.

Construction Guides
Check this option to have angle lines display as you draw or drag an object ∎. Choose or create an angles set in the Angles area (see below).

Transform Tools
Check this option to have angle lines display as you transform an object using a transformation tool or the object's bounding box ∎. Choose or create an angles set in the Angles area (see below).

Object Highlighting
Check this option to have an object's path display as you pass the pointer over it ∎. This is helpful for locating unpainted paths (e.g., clipping masks) or paths behind other paths. Hidden paths won't highlight.

Angles

If Smart Guides is on and you drag an object or move the pointer, temporary angle lines will display relative to other objects in the illustration. Choose a preset angles set from the Angles pop-up menu or enter custom

angles in any or all of the fields. If you enter custom angles, "Custom Angles" will appear on the pop-up menu. If you switch from Custom Angles to a predefined set and then later switch back to Custom Angles, the last-used custom angles will reappear in the fields.

Snapping Tolerance
This is the distance (0–10 pt) within which the pointer must be from an object for smart guides to display. The default is 4 pt.

Slicing

Show Slice Numbers
Check this option to have slice numbers display onscreen. From the **Line Color** pop-up menu, choose a color for those numbers and for the lines that surround each slice.

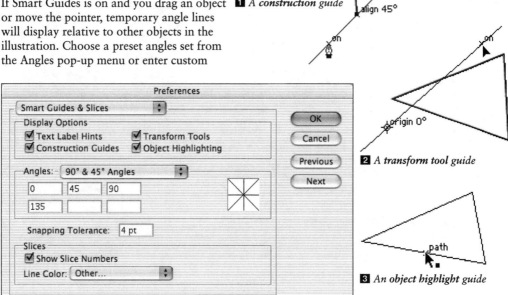

∎ *A construction guide*

∎ *A transform tool guide*

∎ *An object highlight guide*

445

Hyphenation Preferences

*Choose Illustrator (Edit, in Windows) >
Preferences > Hyphenation.*

Default Language

Choose the language dictionary for
Illustrator to use when it inserts hyphen
breaks. You can choose a different hyphenation language dictionary for the current
document from the Language pop-up menu
on the Character palette.

Exceptions

Enter words that you want hyphenated in a
particular way. Type the word in the New
Entry field, inserting hyphens where you
would want them to appear (or enter a word
with no hyphens to prevent Illustrator from
hyphenating it), then click Add. To remove a
word from the list, click it, then click Delete.

Resetting preferences

To restore all the default Illustrator preferences,
trash the Adobe Illustrator Prefs/AIPrefs file:

➤ On the Mac, it's stored in Startup drive/Users/
[user name]/Library/Preferences/Adobe
Illustrator CS Settings.

➤ In Windows, it's stored in C:\Documents and
Settings\[username]\Application Data\Adobe\
Adobe Illustrator CS Settings\AIPrefs.

Whatever you do, don't delete the whole
Preferences folder! You need everything else
that's in there in order to run other applications
and utilities.

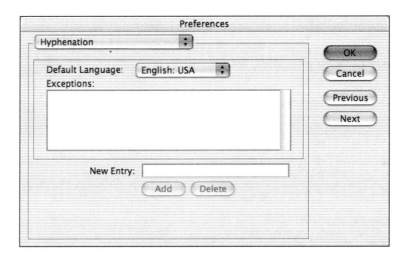

Hyphenation Preferences

(sidebar) **Hyphenation Preferences**

Plug-ins & Scratch Disks Preferences

Choose Illustrator (Edit, in Windows) > Preferences > Plug-ins & Scratch Disks.
For changes made in this dialog box to take effect, you must quit/exit and
relaunch Illustrator.

Plug-ins folder

Illustrator comes with core and add-on plug-in files that provide additional functionality to the main application. These and other plug-in files are placed in the Plug-ins folder in the Adobe Illustrator CS folder. If for some reason you need to move the Plug-ins folder, you must use this Preferences dialog box to tell Illustrator the new location of the folder.

The current Plug-ins folder location is listed in the Plug-ins Folder area. To change the plug-ins location, click Choose, locate and click the desired folder name, then click Choose. The new location will now be listed.

Scratch Disks

Primary
The Primary scratch disk is used as virtual memory when available RAM is insufficient for image processing. Choose an available hard drive—preferably your largest and fastest—from the Primary pop-up menu. Startup is the default.

Secondary
As an optional step, choose an alternate Secondary hard drive to be used as extra virtual memory when needed. If you have only one hard drive, of course, you can have only one scratch disk.

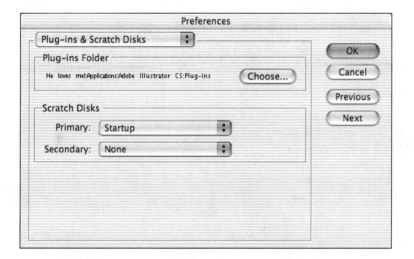

File Handling & Clipboard Preferences

Choose Illustrator (Edit, in Windows) > Preferences > File Handling & Clipboard.

Version Cue and Files

 Check **Enable Version Cue** to utilize the Adobe Version Cue Workspace features, which let you control file security, organize files into private or shared projects, and search and review file information and file statuses among the Adobe Creative Suite applications (e.g., GoLive, Photoshop). For more information, click Tell Me More to access Adobe Version Cue Help, or read the VersionCueHelp.pdf file on the Illustrator CD.

If you're working with a lot of linked files, you can enhance performance by checking **Use Low Resolution Proxy for Linked EPS**; placed images will display as bitmap proxies. With this option unchecked, placed images will display at full resolution and vector objects will display in full color.

To specify how linked images are updated when the original files are modifed, from the **Update Links** pop-up menu, choose:

Automatically to have Illustrator update linked images automatically whenever the original files are modified.

Manually to leave linked images unchanged when the original files are modified. You can use the Links palette to update links.

Ask When Modified to display a dialog box when the original files are modified. (In the dialog box, click Yes to update the linked image, or click No to leave it unchanged.)

Clipboard on Quit

The Clipboard can be used to transfer selections between Illustrator and other Adobe programs, such as Photoshop, GoLive, and InDesign. When a selection is copied to the Clipboard, it's copied as a PDF and/or AICB, depending on which of the following Copy As options you choose:

PDF preserves transparency information in the selection. PDF is designed for use with Adobe Photoshop, InDesign, and future Adobe applications.

AICB (no transparency support), a PostScript format, breaks objects into smaller opaque objects, preserving the appearance of transparency through flattening. Check **Preserve Paths** to copy a selection as a set of detailed paths, or check **Preserve Appearance and Overprints** to preserve the appearance of the selection and any overprinting objects. **NEW**

Note: If you check both PDF and AICB, the receiving application will choose its preferred format. Fills and effects will copy and paste more accurately, but the copying time will be longer and the memory requirements higher.

➤ If you're unable to paste a selection into Illustrator, try using drag-and-drop to acquire the selection instead.

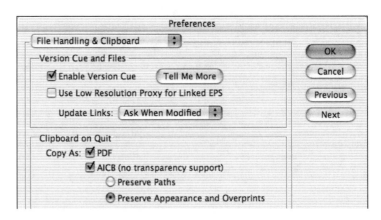

OUTPUT/EXPORT | 26

Although Illustrator objects are described and stored as mathematical commands, when they're printed, they're rendered as dots. The higher the resolution of the output device, the more smoothly and sharply lines, curves, gradients, and continuous-tone images are rendered. In this chapter you'll learn to print an illustration on a PostScript black-and-white or composite color printer; print an oversized illustration; output and export transparency; create and edit presets; and create a crop area and crop marks. You'll also learn about saving files for export to other applications, and how to manage color in your documents using the Color Settings dialog box. For Web output, see the next chapter.

Charles, Nancy Stahl

Norah, Nancy Stahl

General and Setup panels

You'll use the **Print** dialog box to choose settings for printing an illustration, such as tiling, page size, printer marks, color management profiles, and flattening. The dialog box has seven panels. First, we'll take a look at the General and Setup panels.

NEW **To print to a black-and-white or color PostScript printer:**

1. Before outputting to a color printer, from the File > Document Color Mode submenu, choose the correct color mode for your printer.

2. Choose File > Print (Cmd-P/Ctrl-P).

3. From the **Printer** pop-up menu , choose from the list of printers your system is connected to. The PPD pop-up menu will automatically display the PPD (PostScript printer description file) for the chosen printer. If it doesn't, choose the appropriate PPD from the pop-up menu.

4. Click **General** on the options list on the left side of the dialog box to display that panel.

5. In the **Copies** field, enter the desired number of print copies.

   In the **Media** area, choose a paper **Size**.

   Click an **Orientation** button to print vertically or horizontally on the paper.

6. In the Options area, from the **Print Layers** pop-up menu, choose which layers will print:

   Visible & Printable Layers to print only the visible layers for which the Layers palette's Print option was checked. (To prevent individual objects from printing, place them on a layer for which the Print option is unchecked before choosing File > Print.)

   Visible Layers to print only those layers that aren't hidden.

   All Layers to print all layers.

1 *The **Print** dialog box, **General** panel*

Options list

Preview window

Save your print settings!

With all the options in the Print dialog box, you'll want to save your settings as a preset so you don't have to reenter them each time you print in a particular output setting. To create a print preset of the current print settings, click **Save Preset** at the bottom of the Print dialog box, enter a name for the preset, then click OK.

Saved presets can be chosen from the **Print Preset** pop-up menu at the top of the Print dialog box. To edit a print preset, see pages 466–467.

7. Click **Do Not Scale** to print the illustration at its current size; or click **Fit to Page** to have the illustration be scaled to fit the current paper size; or click **Custom Scale,** then enter a Width or Height value to scale the document proportionally. Or to scale nonproportionally, deselect the chain icon, then enter separate Width and Height values.

8. Click **Setup** on the options list on the left side of the dialog box to display that panel (**1**, next page).

9. From the **Crop Artwork to** pop-up menu, choose Artboard.

10. Leave the **Tiling** choice as Single Full Page, unless the document is large and needs to be tiled onto multiple pieces of paper (see the next page).

11. Click a corner or side point on the **Placement** icon to position the illustration on that corresponding part of the paper; click the center point if you want to recenter the illustration on the paper.
or
Enter Origin X and Origin Y values to specify the position of the upper left corner of the illustration on the paper.
or
Place the pointer over the preview window and drag to reposition the illustration on the paper. Only the parts of the illustration that are visible in the preview window will print. Dragging the preview actually repositions the page borders on the artboard!

12. Click Print to print the illustration, or click Done to save the current settings with the document without printing.

➤ Although you can access the system's printer driver dialog boxes from the Print dialog box by clicking the Page Setup or Printer button on the Mac, or the Setup button in Windows, we think you're better off ignoring those buttons and choosing all your print settings from within the Print dialog box. This way, you'll be utilizing Illustrator's print capabilities when outputting your illustration.

Print: General and Setup Panels

Options in the Setup panel control the position of the document on the printable page. You can use this panel to tile a large document onto multiple pages, or via cropping, control which objects will print.

NEW **To print (tile) an illustration that's larger than the paper size:**

1. Choose File > Print (Cmd-P/Ctrl-P), then click **General** on the left side of the dialog box.

2. Choose **Media** (page) **Size** and **Orientation** settings, and under Options, click **Do Not Scale**. (If you choose Fit to Page, the Tiling pop-up menu that you'll choose from in step 5 won't be accessible.)

3. Click **Setup** on the options list **1**.

4. From the **Crop Artwork to** pop-up menu:

   If all the objects to be printed lie within the artboard, choose **Artboard**.
   or

Honey, I shrunk...

Another solution for printing an illustration that's larger than the printer's paper size is to reduce the output size. To do this, go to the General panel in the Print dialog box, and in the Options area, click **Fit to Page**. In this case, the Tiling pop-up menu options won't apply.

If you want to print all the objects in the illustration, even objects that extend beyond the edge of the artboard, choose **Artwork Bounding Box**. Illustrator will create a bounding box that surrounds all the objects in the illustration.
or
If you've already created crop marks in the illustration to limit which objects will print, choose **Crop Area** (**1**, next page). To create a crop area, see page 468.

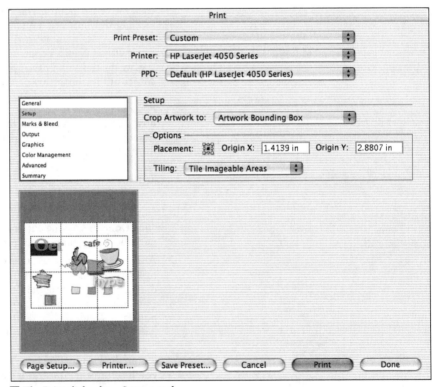

1 *The* **Print** *dialog box,* **Setup** *panel*

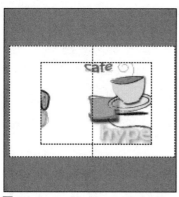

1 *Tile Imageable Areas with the Crop Artwork to: Crop Area settings, viewed in the preview window*

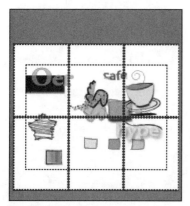

2 *Tile Full Pages setting, viewed in the preview window*

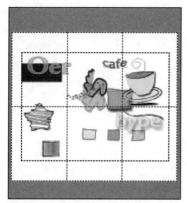

3 *Tile Imageable Areas setting, viewed in the preview window*

5. From the **Tiling** pop-up menu, choose:
   Tile Full Pages 2 to divide the artwork into whole pages (the printer media size that you chose in step 2).
   or
   Tile Imageable Areas 3 to divide the artwork into a grid of pages as per the printer media size.

   Note: These two options may produce similar tiling previews.

6. Click a point on the **Placement** icon to position the illustration on that corresponding part of the paper; click the center point if you want to recenter the illustration.
   or
   Enter **Origin** X and **Origin** Y values to specify the position of the upper left corner of the illustration on the paper.
   or
   Place the pointer over the preview window and drag to **reposition** the illustration on the grid of pages. Dragging the preview will reposition the page borders on the artboard (just as the Page tool does).

7. To print all the tiled pages, in the General panel, leave the **Pages: All** button chosen and check Skip Blank Pages to prevent any blank tiled pages from printing. Or to print select tiled pages, click **Range,** then enter the range of pages in the field, separated by a hyphen.

8. Choose any other print settings. Click Print to print out the illustration, or click Done to save the current settings with the illustration without printing.

Tile Oversized Document

Marks & Bleed panel

Use the **Marks & Bleed** panel to create printer's marks at the edge of the printed artwork. A press shop uses crop marks to trim the final printout, registration marks to align printing plates, and color bars to help them evaluate the print colors.

NEW **To include printer's marks in your printout:**

1. In the Print dialog box, click **Marks & Bleed** on the options list (**1**, next page).

2. Check **All Printer's Marks** to include trim marks, registration marks, color bars, and page information.
   or
   Check **Trim Marks** to add thin lines extending from the horizontal and vertical edges of the illustration's bounding box to designate where the printout is to be trimmed. The current choice on the Crop Artwork to pop-up menu in the Setup panel determines what Illustrator considers to be the illustration's bounding box.

   Registration Marks to add a small circle outside each corner of the bounding box.

   Color Bars to add color swatches outside the bounding box.

   Page Information to add a text label above the top edge of the printout that contains print specs for the press shop.

3. Choose a printer mark style from the **Printer Mark Type** pop-up menu: Roman or Japanese.

4. Choose a thickness for trim marks from the **Trim Mark Weight** pop-up menu.

5. Enter or choose an **Offset** value (0–72 pt) for the distance between trim marks and the bounding box.

➤ The Object > Crop Area command creates nonprinting trim marks. If you use this command, you'll still need to check Trim Marks in the Print dialog box to create trim marks on the actual printout.

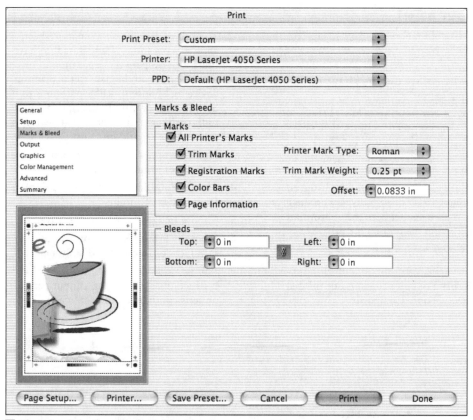

1 *The* **Print** *dialog box,* **Marks & Bleed** *panel*

The **bleed** area is the area just outside the edge of a printed document. You can position objects in the illustration so that they extend into the bleed area to ensure that they'll print to the very edge of the final trimmed page. Have your print shop advise you as to what bleed values are required for their specific print setting.

To choose bleed values: (NEW)

1. In the Print dialog box, click **Marks & Bleed** on the options list.

2. In the Bleeds area **1**:

   For asymmetrical bleed values, deselect the link icon, then enter Top, Left, Bottom, and Right values (0–1 inch, or

0–72 pt). Enter a low bleed value to move the trim marks closer to the edges of the printed illustration or a higher bleed value to move them farther away.

Or click the link icon, then enter a single bleed value to be used for all four sides of the illustration.

➤ The bleed settings have no effect on the size of the final output.

➤ Click Save Preset to save the current settings as a print preset (see the sidebar on page 451). Click Done to exit the dialog box and save the current printer settings with the document without printing.

Output panel

The **Output** panel lets you choose options for printing process colors and spot colors as a composite print or as **separations**.

NEW **To print colors on one sheet or as separations:**

1. Make sure your file is in CMYK Color mode, choose File > Print, then click **Output** on the options list **1**.

2. From the **Printer** pop-up menu, choose whichever high-end PostScript printer your system is connected to. If the chosen printer's PPD doesn't display on the PPD pop-up menu, choose the appropriate PPD from the pop-up menu.

    For steps 3–6, ask your print shop for advice.

3. From the **Mode** pop-up menu:

    To print out all colors on one printed sheet, choose **Composite**.

or

To print each color on a separate sheet, choose **Separations (Host-Based)** to have Illustrator prepare the separation information and send the data to the printing device; or choose **In-RIP Separations** to have Illustrator send PostScript data to the printer's RIP to have that device perform the separation.

Available options will vary depending on the type of printer you chose in step 2.

4. Choose **Emulsion:** Up (Right Reading) or Down (Right Reading).

5. Choose **Image:** Positive or Negative.

6. From the **Printer Resolution** pop-up menu, choose a combined halftone screen ruling (lpi)/device resolution (dpi).

Instructions for choosing Output panel options continue on the next page.

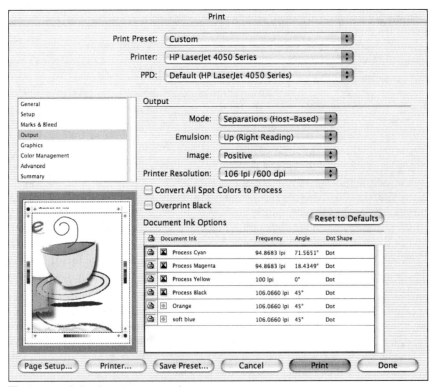

1 *The **Print** dialog box, **Output** panel*

Overprinting

Normally, Illustrator automatically knocks out any color below an object so the object color won't mix with the color beneath it on press. If you check Overprint Fill or Overprint Stroke on the Attributes palette, the fill or stroke color will overprint colors underneath it instead. That is, where colors overlap, the inks will mix and a combination color will be produced. Colors will overprint on a printing press, but not on a PostScript color composite printer.

When the **Overprint Fill** or **Overprint Stroke** option is checked for a selected object, you can see how a spot color fill or stroke will look when it overprints underlying objects by choosing View > Overprint Preview **1**–**2**. When this option is checked, "Overprint Preview" appears in the document window title bar.

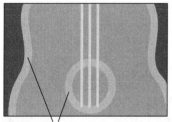

1 *Two objects with their strokes set to overprint*

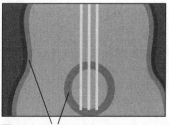

2 *With **Overprint Preview** checked, the overprint strokes simulate ink mixing with objects below.*

If a Separations option is chosen from the Mode menu in the **Output** panel of the Print dialog box, Illustrator will create and print a separate sheet for each process and spot color used in the illustration. You can use this panel to turn printing on or off for individual colors or convert individual spot colors into process colors.

To choose colors to print and/or ⟨NEW⟩ convert to process:

1. Choose File > Print, then click **Output** on the options list.

2. In the **Document Ink Options** area **3**, you'll see a listing for each color used in the illustration. For each process or spot color you don't want to print, click the printer icon 🖨 next to the color name. (Click again to redisplay the icon.)

3. Check **Convert All Spot Colors to Process** to convert all spot colors in the document into process colors.
   or

   For each spot color that you want to convert into a process color, uncheck Convert All Spot Colors to Process, then click the spot color icon ⊙. The process color icon ⊠ will display.

4. Choose other print settings, then click Print.

➤ Don't change the other Ink Options settings in the Output panel unless you're advised to do so by your print shop. The desired values will vary depending on the type of output device being used. If necessary, you can click Reset to Defaults to restore all the default ink settings.

➤ To have black fills and strokes overprint background colors, check Overprint Black (see also the sidebar at left).

3 *The Document Ink Options area of the Output panel*

This spot color **won't print.**
This spot color will print as a **spot color.**

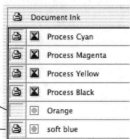

🖨 Document Ink		
🖨	⊠	Process Cyan
🖨	⊠	Process Magenta
🖨	⊠	Process Yellow
🖨	⊠	Process Black
	⊙	Orange
🖨	⊙	soft blue

457

Graphics panel

The precision with which objects are printed from Illustrator is determined by the **Flatness** setting in the Print dialog box. This setting affects every object in the current document. If your document doesn't print, raise the Flatness setting, then trying printing again.

NEW **To change a document's Flatness setting to facilitate printing:**

1. Open the file that stubbornly refuses to print, choose File > Print, then choose **Graphics** from the options list 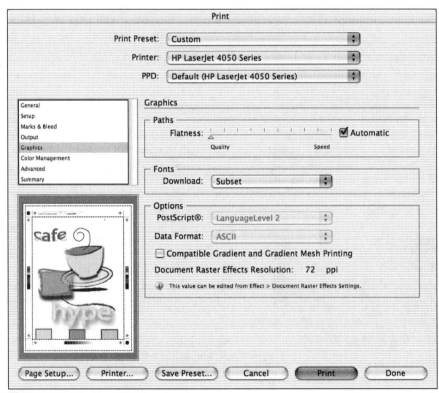.

2. Drag the **Flatness** slider slightly to the right, then click Print. If it prints, but with noticeable jaggedness on the curve segments, it means you've raised the

Flatness setting too much; lower the setting by dragging the slider to the left, and try printing again.

or

Check **Automatic** to have Illustrator choose an optimal Flatness value for the chosen printing device.

➤ A Flatness setting of 2 is appropriate for most printers. To see a numeric display (tool tip) of the current Flatness settings, rest the mouse on the slider.

1 *The Print dialog box, Graphics panel*

Flatness versus flattening

Don't confuse Illustrator's process of **flattening** overlapping shapes in order to preserve the look of transparency with **flatness,** which is the printing device resolution divided by the output resolution. The Flatness setting controls the degree to which a printed path follows an object's curve segments. For any given printer, raising the Flatness value lowers the output resolution. The higher the Flatness value (or the lower the output resolution), the less precisely curve segments will print.

Illustrator got smarter NEW

Normally, you won't have to choose PostScript LanguageLevel or Data Format options in the Print dialog box (Graphics panel). Illustrator now automatically sets these options for you based on the chosen printer. However, if your printer supports more than one option in these two categories, the above-mentioned settings become available and you'll need to select one of them (decisions, decisions!).

To download fonts and print meshes: NEW

1. To manage how fonts are downloaded to the printer, in the **Fonts** area of the Graphics panel, from the **Download** pop-up menu, choose one of these options:

   None to have no fonts download. This is the preferred setting when fonts are permanently stored in the printer.

   Subset to have only the characters (glyphs) used in the illustration download.

   Complete to have all the fonts used in the illustration download at the beginning of the print job. This is effective when printing multiple pages that use the same fonts (Illustrator files are usually one-page printouts, though).

2. To improve gradient fill printing on an older PostScript imagesetter or printer, check **Compatible Gradient and Gradient Mesh Printing.** Any mesh objects will be converted to JPEG format. Don't check this option if your gradients are printing well, as it may slow printing.

3. Click Print or click Done.

PostScript is a language that describes images for output to printers and other output devices. PostScript Level 2 can process grayscale vector graphics and grayscale bitmap images; it supports RGB, CMYK, and CIE color and offers compression techniques for bitmap images. Level 3 adds the ability to print gradient mesh objects to a PostScript 3 printer.

To print to a PostScript file: NEW

1. Choose File > Print.

2. Choose Adobe PostScript® File from the Printer pop-up menu.

3. Click **Graphics** on the options list. If necessary, choose the desired LanguageLevel from the PostScript pop-up menu, and a format from the Data Format pop-up menu (■, previous page). For more about this pop-up menu, see the bottom sidebar.

4. Choose other printer settings, then click Save to open the Save dialog box. Choose a location, enter a file name, then click Save.

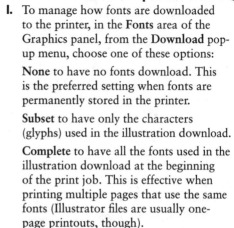

Print: Graphics Panel

Color Management panel

Use the **Color Management** panel to choose the appropriate device profile for your selected printer. Using a profile will help you achieve good-quality color conversion from Illustrator to your printer. (*Note:* If you don't know anything about profiles and Color Settings yet, first read "Color Management" on pages 479–485.

NEW **To print using color management:**

1. Choose File > Print, then click **Color Management** on the options list **1**.

2. Choose a **Print Space** profile from the **Profile** pop-up menu:

   Choose **Same As Source** if a profile has already been assigned to the document via Edit > Assign Profile. This profile name will display in the source space area.

or

Choose an appropriate profile for the type of output printer you're using (e.g., a Web, SWOP, or Sheetfed profile for a CMYK press; or an Epson Stylus or HP DeskJet profile for an RGB inkjet).

3. Leave the **Intent** menu option on the default Relative Colorimetric setting unless you or your output specialist have a specific reason to change it. To learn more about intents, see pages 483–484.

4. Choose other print options. Click Print to print the document, or click Done to save the current settings without printing.

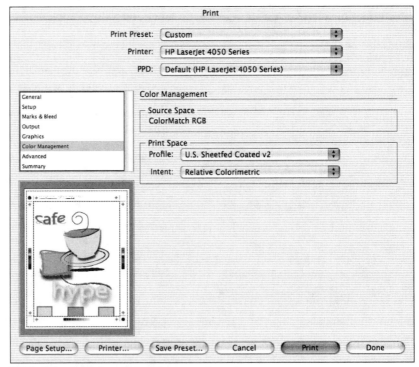

1 *The Print dialog box, Color Management panel*

Non-PostScript printers, anyone?

When printing an illustration to a non-PostScript or low-resolution printer, check **Print as Bitmap** in the Advanced panel in the Print dialog box. This option helps when an illustration contains complex objects that are made with gradients or meshes or soft-edge effects that may cause print errors if printed as vectors. Note that the chosen printer's driver determines whether this option is available, and most Mac printer drivers don't include it.

1 *The Print dialog box, Advanced panel*

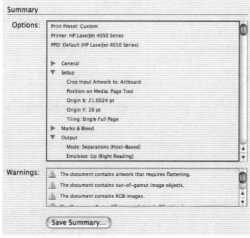

2 *The Print dialog box, Summary panel*

Advanced panel

The **Advanced** panel lets you choose options for processing overprinting fills and strokes for color-separations or composite printing.

To choose overprint and flattening options for output:

1. In the Print dialog box, click **Advanced** on the options list.

2. Choose an option from the **Overprints** pop-up menu **1**:

   Preserve to maintain the file's overprint settings in printers that support overprinting (usually separation printers).

   Discard to ignore a file's overprint settings in the printout.

   Simulate to create the visual effect of overprinting in the composite printout. When printing a composite, Illustrator always flattens areas that are set to overprint.

   Note: The Overprints setting doesn't override Overprint Fill or Stroke settings chosen via the Attributes palette.

3. To determine how transparent objects are **flattened** for printing, choose a preset from the Preset pop-up menu (see the sidebar on the next page), or click Custom to create and save a custom preset that saves with the file (see page 463).

4. Choose other print settings, then click Print.

Summary panel

Use the **Summary** panel to view a summary of the current Print dialog box settings.

To view a summary of the current print settings:

1. In the Print dialog box, click **Summary** on the options list **2**.

2. Scroll down the **Options** window to view the settings, and read any alerts in the **Warnings** window.

3. *Optional:* Click Save Summary to save the current settings to a file.

NEW Printing and exporting transparency

Transparency settings (nondefault blending modes and opacity levels) in objects, groups, or layers are preserved when a document is saved in either of the native Illustrator formats: Adobe Illustrator CS or Adobe PDF (Compatibility: Acrobat 5 or 6). When a file that contains Transparency palette settings is exported in a nonnative format or is printed, Illustrator uses transparency flattener settings to determine how objects will be flattened and rasterized in order to preserve the look of those transparency settings.

In the process of flattening, Illustrator breaks up overlapping objects that contain transparency and converts each overlapping and nonoverlapping area into a separate, nonoverlapping, opaque shape.

Illustrator tries to keep these flattened shapes as vector objects. However, if the look of transparency settings can't be preserved in a flattened shape as a vector object, Illustrator will rasterize the shape instead. This will happen, for example, if two gradient objects with nondefault transparency settings overlap. The resulting flattened shape would be rasterized in order to keep the look of transparency in this complex area.

To determine how transparency is flattened for exported files:

Choose File > **Document Setup,** then choose **Transparency** from the topmost pop-up menu **1**. In the Export and Clipboard **NEW** Transparency Flattener Settings area, choose a preset from the Preset pop-up menu (see the sidebar at right), then click OK.
or
Click Custom to create a custom preset that saves with the file (see the following page).

Print and Export Transparency

Default transparency flattener presets

[High Resolution] can be used for high-quality separation printouts and film-based color proofs.

[Medium Resolution] can be used for printouts and proofs from desktop PostScript color printers.

[Low Resolution] can be used for printouts from black-and-white desktop printers or for illustrations that will be viewed on the Web.

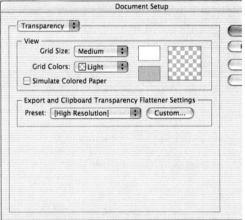

1 *The Document Setup dialog box (Transparency panel), where you can choose an existing transparency flattener preset, or create a custom preset*

To choose custom transparency flattener options: NEW

If you click Custom in either the Document Setup dialog box (Transparency panel) or the Print dialog box (Advanced panel), the Custom Transparency Flattener Options dialog box will open **1**. Do any of the following:

Raster/Vector Balance: Move the Raster/Vector Balance slider to control the percentage of flattened shapes that will remain as vectors versus the percentage of shapes that will be rasterized. Raster/Vector Balance settings apply only to flattened shapes that represent transparency. Vector shapes print with cleaner, higher-quality color and crisper edges as compared with rasterized shapes.

Higher values (to the right) produce a higher percentage of flattened shapes as vectors, though complex flattened areas may be rasterized. A higher percentage of vector shapes will result in higher-quality output, but at the expense of slower, more memory-demanding output processing.

The lowest value (to the left) won't necessarily produce poor output quality. In fact, if an illustration is very complex and contains a lot of transparency effects, this may be the only setting that produces adequate output. Low settings are usually used to produce fast output at a low resolution.

Line art and text: The rasterization process requires resolution settings to determine output quality. To specify the resolution for line art and text that are rasterized, enter a **Line Art and Text Resolution** value. As a general rule of thumb, the resolution of line art should equal twice the line screen (lpi) for that output device. The default is 300 ppi. Transparent text is flattened and preserved as text objects. Clipping and masking are used to preserve the look of transparency.

Text that is stroked, filled with a pattern, or used as a clipping mask will be converted to outlines. When path strokes are converted to outlines, the filled "strokes" may be wider than the original stroke by one or two pixels. To prevent this thickening, move the **Raster/Vector Balance** slider to 100 (far right) or 0 (far left). At 100, all strokes will be converted to outlines and thickening will be uniform; at zero, all objects will be rasterized. For rasterized text, enter a Line Art and Text Resolution value of 600 ppi or higher. Another option is to check **Convert All Text to Outlines,** which makes text widths print uniformly within a chosen font.

Gradient and mesh objects: When printed on a PostScript level 3 printer, mesh objects print as vectors. When mesh objects are printed to a PostScript level 2 printer or saved in an EPS format that is PostScript Level 2 compatible, both vector data and rasterized data are saved in the file, allowing the output device to choose which set of

(Continued on the following page)

1 Use the **Custom Transparency Flattener Options** dialog box to choose custom settings for the current file.

Custom Transparency Flattener Options

data to use. Specify the resolution for the rasterized mesh object in the Gradient and Mesh Resolution field. The default value is 150 ppi; 300 ppi would be considered a high value.

Placed or embedded images: When the Raster/Vector Balance slider is below 100, Illustrator rasterizes placed images at the resolution specified in the Gradient and Mesh Resolution field. This value will be used only for portions of an image that overlap a transparent object; the remainder of the image will print at the image's original resolution. To keep things simple, always choose a Gradient and Mesh Resolution that's equal to or higher than the original resolution of the placed image.

For an EPS image that overlaps an object that contains transparency, embed the image into the Illustrator document via the Embed Image command on the Links palette menu. This will ensure an accurate printout of the image and the transparency effect.

Strokes: Strokes are converted into filled objects. The width of the object will equal the weight of the original stroke. With the Raster/Vector Balance slider at 0, all strokes (and all objects, for that matter) will be rasterized. A high setting in the Line Art and Text Resolution field ensures high-quality output.

With the Raster/Vector Balance slider between 10 and 90, any strokes that overlap an object with transparency will be converted to outlines. Very thin strokes may be thickened slightly and may look noticeably different from parts of strokes that don't overlap transparency.

Check **Convert All Strokes to Outlines** to convert all strokes in an illustration to outlines. This preserves the look of a stroke for its entire length, but results in a larger number of paths in the file. An alternative to using this option is to apply Object > Path > Outline Stroke to selected strokes in the illustration.

When an output file contains an object that's flattened into rasterized shapes next to vector

Flatten a selection

To control the flattening of just a selection in a document, choose Object > **Flatten Transparency,** then adjust the Raster/Vector Balance slider, the Line Art and Text Resolution value, and the Gradient and Mesh Resolution value.

Don't stop here

You can use the **Flattener Preview** palette to show where flattening due to transparency will occur in an illustration. To preview what image areas will be flattened, open the Flattener Preview palette and click Refresh. Choose Show Options from the palette menu; move the Raster/Vector Balance slider, if desired; check Options; then click Refresh again. You can save your settings as a preset by choosing Save Transparency Flattener Preset from the Flattener Preview palette menu. For a more information about flattening and the Flattener Preview palette, see Illustrator Help.

shapes, there may be a visible discrepancy among the flattened shapes that share the same color. An example of this would be a complex, transparent, smaller object (which must be rasterized when flattened) that overlaps a larger, solid-color object. The solid color in the flattened vector shapes that represent the large solid-color object may not perfectly match the background color of the flattened rasterized shape that represents the transparent object. This is called "stitching," and it's most likely to occur when the Raster/Vector Balance slider is between 1 and 30. At 0, the entire document is rasterized, and no stitching occurs. Check **Clip Complex Regions** to make any boundaries between raster and vector flattened shapes fall on object paths. This helps to lessen the signs of stitching, but also produces complex paths that slow down printing.

When you're done choosing transparency flattener options, click OK.

Custom Transparency Flattener Options

NEW Creating and editing presets

Illustrator CS lets you create a preset of transparency flattener and Print dialog box settings. Presets help ensure consistency when applying flattening to a series of illustrations or when outputting a series of illustrations to the same printer. Presets can also be exported as files for use by other users.

The custom presets you can create in the Print dialog box (Advanced panel) and the Document Setup dialog box (Transparency panel) are for use only with the current file. The presets you save using the Print dialog box can be edited using the Print Presets command. You can also use this command to create a new print preset.

To create presets for display on the Preset pop-up menus in the Document Setup dialog box (Transparency panel) and in the Print dialog box (Advanced panel) for any file, use one of the **Presets** commands found on the Edit menu instead.

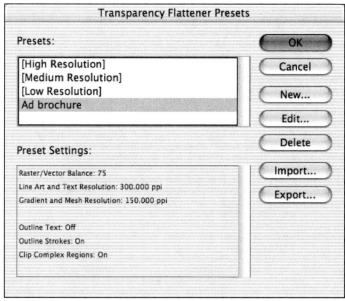

1 *The Transparency Flattener Presets dialog box*

Create, Edit Presets

To create a transparency flattener, print, or PDF preset: NEW

I. Choose Edit > Transparency Flattener Presets.
or
Choose Edit > Print Presets.
or
Choose Edit > PDF Presets.

2. Click New to create a new preset (**1**, previous page).
or
Click an existing preset, then click New to create a variation (copy) of that preset.

3. In the Transparency Flattener Preset Options dialog box **1**, enter a Name, choose settings for the various options (see pages 463–465), then click OK.
or
In the Print Presets Options dialog box, enter a name, choose settings as you would in the Print dialog box (see pages 450–461), then click OK.
or
In the PDF Presets Options dialog box, enter a name, choose settings as you would in the Adobe PDF Options dialog box (see pages 52–54), then click OK.

4. *Optional:* For a summary of the current settings, click a preset name, then view the settings in the lower window of the dialog box.

5. *Do any of the following optional steps:*
Click a user-created preset name, click **Edit,** modify any of the settings, then click OK.

Click **Delete** to delete a user-created preset.

Click **Export** to save the settings as a separate file.

Click **Import** to locate and open an exported settings file.

Note: You can edit the [Default] print preset, but you can't edit any of the default transparency flattener presets or default PDF presets.

6. Click OK.

➤ There is a transparency flattener Preset pop-up menu in the Advanced panel of the New/Edit PDF Preset dialog box (Edit > PDF Presets, then click New or Edit), and in the Adobe PDF Options dialog box (accessed via the Save As command) when Compatibility: Acrobat 4 (PDF 1.3) is chosen.

Create Transparency Flattener, Print, PDF Preset

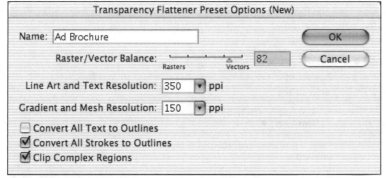

1 *The Transparency Flattener Preset Options dialog box*

Creating custom crop marks

Crop marks are short perpendicular lines around the edge of a page that a print shop uses as guides to trim the paper. Illustrator's **Crop Area** command creates visible, non-printing crop marks around a rectangle that you draw.

To create a crop area:

1. Choose the Rectangle tool (M).

2. Carefully draw a rectangle that encompasses some or all of the objects in the illustration **1**.

3. With the rectangle still selected, choose **NEW** Object > Crop Area > Make **2**. The rectangle will disappear, and crop marks will appear where the corners of the rectangle were.

➤ If you don't create a rectangle before choosing Object > Crop Area > Make, crop marks will be placed around the entire artboard.

➤ Only one set of crops can be created per illustration by using the Crop Area command. If you apply Object > Crop Area > Make a second time, new marks will replace the existing ones. To create more than one set of crop marks in an illustration, use the Crop Marks filter instead (see the following page).

Crop marks that are created via the Crop Area command limit what part of the illustration is going to print.

NEW ### To limit the printout to the crop area:

1. Follow the steps in the previous set of instructions to create crop marks in the illustration.

2. Choose File > Print, then click **Setup** on the options list.

3. From the Crop Artwork to: pop-up menu, choose **Crop Area.** The crop area will display in the preview window.

4. Choose any other print settings, then click Print to print the illustration.

1 *A rectangle is drawn.*

2 *After choosing the Crop Area > Make command*

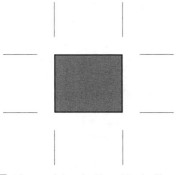

1 *After applying the* **Crop Marks** *filter*

To remove crop marks created with the Crop Area command:

Choose Object > Crop Area > Release. The (NEW) selected rectangle will reappear, with a fill and stroke of None. Toggle to Outline view or use smart guides (with Object Highlighting option checked in Preferences > Smart Guides & Slices) to locate it. You can recolor it or delete it.

➤ If crop marks were created for the entire page, the released rectangle will have the same dimensions as the artboard.

The **Crop Marks** filter places eight crop marks around a selected object or objects. You can create more than one set of Crop Marks in an illustration.

To create crop marks for an object:

1. Select the object or objects that you want to create crop marks for.

2. Choose Filter > Create > Crop Marks. (NEW) Crop marks will surround the smallest rectangle that could be drawn around the selection **1**.

➤ Group the crop marks with the objects they surround so you can move them in unison. On the Layers palette, crop marks are listed as nested objects within a group.

➤ To move or delete crop marks, select them first with the Selection tool or via the Layers palette.

➤ The Crop Artwork to: menu in the Print dialog box (Setup panel) doesn't recognize crop marks that are generated via the Create > Crop Marks filter. Illustrator treats such crop marks as artwork.

➤ Similarly, the Marks & Bleed panel trim marks are aligned with the edge of the entire printed illustration, and are independent of marks created by the Crop Marks filter.

Raster settings for effects

Some Effect menu commands must be rasterized when printed or exported. The default resolution setting is 72 ppi, a rather low setting that's suitable only for onscreen output.

To choose a higher resolution, choose Effect > **Document Raster Effects Settings** 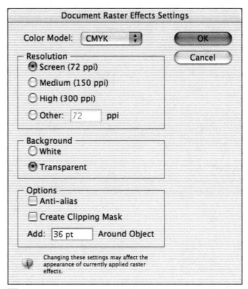, then click another resolution option, or click Other and enter a custom resolution setting. The higher the resolution, the slower the output processing time.

➤ Leave the resolution for effects at the default 72 ppi while working on an illustration, then increase the resolution before printing or exporting the file. A new resolution setting will affect all objects with applied effects that will rasterize, as well as resolution-dependent filters, such as Crystallize and Pointillize.

➤ For information on the options in the Document Raster Effects Settings dialog box, see pages 397–398.

➤ The current Raster Effects Resolution setting displays in the Graphics panel of the Print dialog box.

What gets rasterized

All the effects in the lower half of the Effect menu will **rasterize** upon export or output, including the Artistic, Blur, Brush Strokes, Distort, Pixelate, Sharpen, Sketch, Stylize, Texture, and Video effects. These effects on the Stylize submenu will rasterize, too: Drop Shadow (if the Blur value is greater than 0), Inner Glow, Outer Glow, and Feather.

1 *The Document Raster Effects Settings dialog box*

1 *The Document Info palette with Document information displayed. This information is always available—whether the Selection Only option is on or off.*

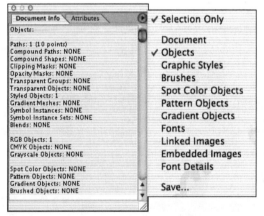

2 *The Document Info palette with the Selection Only and Objects options checked on the palette menu*

Document Info palette

To display information about an object or a document:

1. *Optional:* Select the object (or objects) about which you want to read info.

2. Display the Document Info palette (Window > Document Info) **1**.

3. To display information about a currently selected object, on the palette menu, make sure Selection Only has a check mark **2**.
   or
   To display information pertaining to all the objects in the illustration, uncheck Selection Only.

4. Choose Objects from the palette menu to have the palette list the number of paths, clipping masks, compounds, opacity masks, transparent groups, transparent objects, styled objects, meshes, and objects that contain brush strokes in the selection, as well as color, font, and linking info about the selection.
   or
   Choose another category from the palette menu to see a listing of styles, brushes, spot color objects, pattern objects, gradient objects, fonts, linked images, embedded images, or font details (PostScript name, font file name, language, etc.) in a selection or in the entire document.

5. *Optional:* If the Selection Only option is checked on the palette menu, you can click any other object in the document to see info for that object in the currently chosen category.

6. *Optional:* Choose Save from the palette menu to save the currently displayed information as a text document. Choose a location in which to save the text file, rename the file, if desired, then click Save. Use the system's default text editor to open the text document. You can print this file and refer to it when you prepare your document for imagesetting.

Exporting files

In order to open an Illustrator file in other graphics programs that won't recognize the Illustrator CS format, you may need to save it in an earlier Illustrator format. You won't be able to preserve Illustrator CS features, but in some situations this might be your only option.

NEW **To export a file as an earlier version of Illustrator:**

1. Choose File > Export.

2. On the Mac, choose Illustrator Legacy (ai) from the Format pop-up menu, then click Export.

   In Windows, choose Illustrator Legacy (*.ai) from the Save as Type pop-up menu, then click Save.

3. In the Illustrator Legacy Options dialog box, from the Version menu, choose an earlier version of Illustrator **1**.

4. Choose Fonts and Options settings (follow the steps on pages 46–47).

5. Click OK.

NEW **To export as EPS in an earlier version of Illustrator:**

1. Choose File > Export.

2. On the Mac, from the Format pop-up menu, choose Illustrator Legacy EPS (eps), then click Export.

   In Windows, choose Illustrator Legacy EPS (*.eps) from the Save as Type pop-up menu, then click Save.

3. In the Legacy EPS Options dialog box, from the Version menu, choose an earlier version of Illustrator.

4. Choose Preview, Fonts and Options settings (see the steps on pages 50–51).

5. Click OK.

AI, PDF, EPS, SVG

To learn how to save a file in other formats:

Illustrator	See pages 46–47
Adobe PDF	See pages 52–54
Illustrator EPS	See pages 49–51
SVG	See page 511

If you save back to Illustrator 8...

...you'll need to choose a Transparency option:

Click **Preserve Paths (discard transparency)** to preserve your objects' paths and eliminate all transparency effects (e.g., blending modes and opacity masks). Or click **Preserve Appearance and Overprints** to preserve the appearance of transparency and overprints by rasterizing objects that contain these attributes.

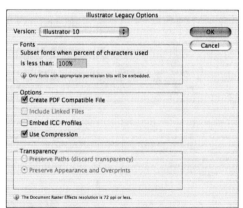

1 *Choose an earlier version of Illustrator from the* **Version** *pop-up menu in the* **Illustrator Legacy Options** *dialog box.*

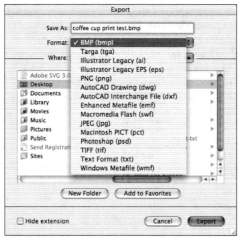

1 *On the Mac, choose from the* **Format** *pop-up menu.*

2 *In Windows, choose from the* **Save as type** *pop-up menu.*

It doesn't all end in Illustrator. An Illustrator file can be saved in a variety of file formats for **export** into other applications. Some of these formats are discussed on the following five pages.

To export a file:

1. With the file open, choose File > Export.

2. If you don't want to use the original file name, enter a new name in the Save As/ File Name field.

   When saving a file, Illustrator automatically appends the proper file extension to the name (e.g., .ai, .eps, .tif) based on the chosen file format.

   Optional: On the Mac, extensions will be hidden if you check Hide extension.

3. Choose from the Format **1**/Save as type **2** pop-up menu.

4. Choose a location in which to save the new version.

   Optional: To create a new folder for the file on the Mac, click New Folder, enter a name, then click Create. In Windows, click Create New Folder, then enter a name.

5. Click Export/Save. Choose settings in any secondary dialog box that opens, then click OK. Some of these dialog boxes are discussed on pages 474–478.

Export a File

Secondary export dialog boxes
Rasterize

When exporting a file, if you choose a raster (bitmap) file format, such as BMP, the Rasterize Options dialog box will open . Choose a Color Model for the resulting file color. For file Resolution, choose Screen (72 dpi), Medium (150 dpi), or High (300 dpi), or enter a custom resolution (Other). Check Anti-Alias to smooth the edges of objects (pixels will be added along object edges).

Bitmap (BMP)

BMP is the standard bitmap image format on Windows and DOS computers. If you choose this format, you'll also need to choose the Windows or OS/2 format for use with those operating systems, specify a bit depth, and choose whether you want to include RLE compression.

NEW Photoshop

Exporting to the Photoshop format helps preserve transparency effects. If you choose the Photoshop file format, the Photoshop Export Options dialog box will open 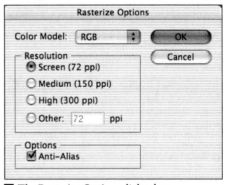. Choose a Color Model, and a Resolution (preset or custom).

To export Illustrator layers to Photoshop, in the Options area, click Write Layers and check Maximum Editability. Although the Write Layers option preserves the stacking appearance of objects nested within a layer, only the top-level layers will become layers in Photoshop. Any hidden layers in the Illustrator file will become hidden layers in Photoshop. (If you click Flat Image, Illustrator will flatten layers, and the illustration will appear as one layer in Photoshop.)

If the Illustrator file contains text that doesn't have a stroke or effects applied to it, you can check Preserve Text Editability to keep the text editable in Photoshop. Text must be stacked as individual objects within a top-level layer, and the layer must be near the top of the Layers palette.

And finally, turn the Anti-alias option on or off, and choose whether to embed an ICC profile in the Photoshop document if you've assigned one to your Illustrator file.

Layer upon layer

If you keep layers intact when you export files to Photoshop, you'll then have the opportunity to apply Photoshop filters to those individual layers. You can also drop a native Photoshop PSD file containing Illustrator layers into Adobe ImageReady, where you can convert the layers to animations. (ImageReady is used for creating and optimizing raster graphics, rollovers, and animations for the Web.)

1 *The Rasterize Options dialog box.*

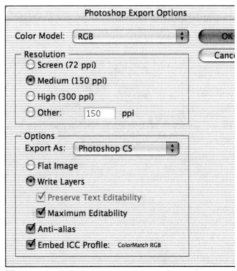

2 *The Photoshop Export Options dialog box*

Photoshop and Illustrator

➤ If you open a Photoshop file in Illustrator, the file's blending modes, transparency, and vector masks will be preserved, and layers can be converted to separate Illustrator objects.

➤ If you export an Illustrator file to the Photoshop format, opacity masks, layers, and editable type that doesn't have a stroke or effects will be preserved. The appearance of blending modes and transparency will be preserved in Photoshop, although on the Layers palette the blending mode of the imported layers will be listed as Normal, Opacity 100%.

If an Illustrator layer contains an object (e.g., one that contains a stroke and effects) that Photoshop can't easily import, that layer and any layers below it will be merged into one Photoshop layer.

➤ Layer masks from Photoshop will be converted to opacity masks in Illustrator, whereas opacity masks from Illustrator will be converted to layer masks in Photoshop.

➤ Compound shapes can be traded back and forth between Illustrator and Photoshop.

To learn more about Photoshop and Illustrator, see pages 267–268.

Tagged-image file format (TIFF)

TIFF is a bitmap image format that's supported by virtually all paint, image-editing, and page-layout applications. It supports RGB, CMYK, and grayscale color schemes, as well as the lossless LZW compression model. You can specify a color space and resolution when you create TIFF files.

If you choose the TIFF file format, the TIFF Options dialog box will open **1**. Choose a Color Model. Choose a Resolution: Screen (72 dpi), Medium (150 dpi), or High (300 dpi), or type in a custom resolution. And turn the Anti-Alias option on or off. Check LZW Compression to compress the file. This type of compression is lossless, which means it doesn't cause loss or degradation of image data. Choose your target platform in the Byte Order area. And check Embed ICC Profile if you've assigned such a profile to your file.

JPEG

JPEG format is a good choice if you want to compress files that contain placed, continuous-tone bitmap images or objects with gradient fills. JPEG is also used for viewing 24-bit images via the Web. (The JPEG format for Web output is discussed on pages 492 and 505–506).

When you choose an Image Quality, keep in mind that there's a tradeoff between image quality and the amount of compression. The greater the compression, the greater the loss of image data and the lower the image quality. To experiment, export multiple copies of a file, using a different compression setting for each copy, and then view the results in the target application. Or use Illustrator's Save for Web command to preview different compression settings (see page 487).

(Continued on the following page)

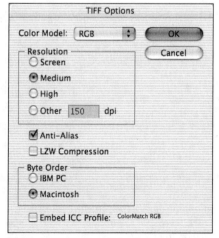

1 *The TIFF Options dialog box*

If you choose the **JPEG** file format in the Export dialog box, the JPEG Options dialog box will open ▮:

To export a JPEG file:

1. Choose an **Image Quality:** Enter a numeric value (0–10); or move the slider; or choose Low, Medium, High, or Maximum from the pop-up menu.

2. Choose a **Color Model:** RGB, CMYK, or Grayscale.

3. Choose a Format **Method: Baseline (Standard); Baseline Optimized** to optimize color and slightly reduce the file size; or **Progressive.** A progressive JPEG will display at increasingly higher resolutions as the file downloads on the Web. Choose the number of **Scans** (iterations) you want displayed before the final image appears. This type of JPEG isn't supported by all Web browsers and requires additional RAM in order to be viewed.

4. Choose a Resolution **Depth:** Screen, Medium, or High. Or choose Custom and enter a Custom resolution (dpi).

5. In the Options area:

   Check **Anti-Alias** if you want your image to have smooth edges.

   If your file contains objects linked to URLs, check **Imagemap** and click **Client-side** or **Server-side.** For Client-side, Illustrator saves the JPEG file with an accompanying HTML file that holds the link information; both files are required by your Web-creation application in order to interpret the links correctly. For Server-side, Illustrator saves the file for use on a Web server.

   Check **Embed ICC Profile** to embed the file's Color Settings profile.

6. Click OK.

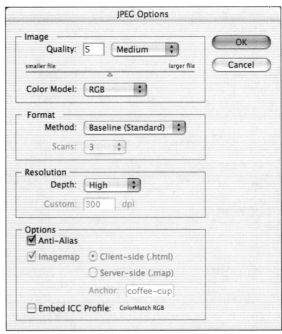

▮ The JPEG **Options** dialog box lets you tailor your image for a number of uses, whether it's optimizing it for fast downloading on the Web or preserving enough resolution to output a crisp print.

Macromedia Flash (swf)

The **Macromedia Flash** (swf) format is another vector graphics format for the Web. This format is commonly used for animations, as SWF files are compact and scale well. Using Illustrator, you can create frames for an animation on separate layers and then export the layers to a Flash file to create an animation.

Keep in mind that the Flash format doesn't support such transparency appearances as blending modes and opacity masks. Also, gradients that encompass a wide range of colors will appear as rasterized shapes. Patterns will also be rasterized.

And finally, Flash supports only some kinds of joins. For example, beveled or square joins and caps will be converted to rounded joins.

To export a Flash file:

1. Choose File > Export.

2. In the Export dialog box, choose a location and type a name for your file.

3. Choose Format/File Type: Macromedia Flash (swf), then click Export/Save.

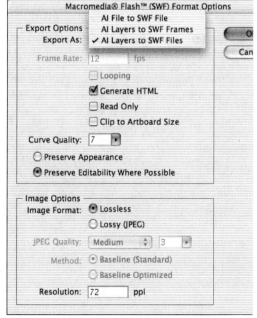

1 *The Macromedia® Flash™ (SWF) Format Options dialog box*

4. From the Export Options: Export As pop-up menu **1**, choose **AI File to SWF File** to export your entire Illustrator file as one Flash frame; **AI Layers to SWF Frames** to export each layer in your Illustrator file to a separate Flash frame within a Flash document; or **AI Layers to SWF Files** to export each Illustrator layer to a separate Flash file composed of one frame.

5. Choose a **Frame Rate** (in frames per second) for your Flash file if you chose AI Layers to SWF Frames in the previous step.

Then check any of the following options:

Looping if you want the animation to loop, or leave it unchecked if you want the animation to play once and then stop.

Generate HTML if you want an HTML file to be created for the exported SWF file. The HTML file will be put in the same location as the exported SWF file.

Read Only to prevent users from modifying the Flash file.

Clip to Artboard Size to export only the artwork that is inside the artboard.

6. Choose a **Curve Quality** value (0–10) to control how accurate the Bézier curves will be in your Flash file. The higher the Curve Quality value, the more accurate the curves (and the larger the file size).

7. Click **Preserve Appearance** to maintain (NEW) the look of an object's effects and opacity. *or*
Click **Preserve Editability Where Possible** to keep objects as vector shapes when the document is exported.

8. Under Image Options, click an **Image Format**. **Lossless** is useful for images that contain large areas of solid color or for images that are to be edited later, whereas **Lossy (JPEG)** is useful for bitmapped images, but it lowers the image quality.

(Continued on the following page)

Export Flash

If you clicked Lossy (JPEG), choose a **JPEG Quality** to determine the amount of compression in your placed bitmaps. As quality increases, so does file size. Also choose a compression Method. Click **Baseline** (**Standard**) for standard compression, or click **Baseline Optimized** for standard plus additional compression.

9. Enter a **Resolution** value (72–600 ppi) for your bitmap images. As the resolution increases, so does the file size. If you plan to export rasterized images and scale them up in Flash, choose a higher resolution than 72 ppi so the scaled images won't appear pixelated.

10. Click OK.

➤ Choose Release to Layers from the Layers palette menu to put nested objects onto their own layers before exporting them to the Flash format.

⬤NEW Microsoft Office

Choose File > Save for Microsoft Office to save your illustration in a PNG format that can be placed into Microsoft Word, PowerPoint, or Excel. Choose a location, enter a file name, then click Save. *Note:* Any existing transparent areas in your file will become opaque when saving in this format.

Text (TXT)

You can export any text in your Illustrator file in a text-only format that other applications can read and use as text (path information isn't included). Select the text that you want to export, choose File > Export, type a name for the new text file, choose Text Format (txt), choose a location in which to save the file, then click Export. In the Text Export Options dialog box, choose a Platform (PC or Macintosh), and an Encoding method (Default Platform or Unicode) for the exported file, then click Export.

Animation

To animate a transition from one shape into another, use Illustrator's Blend tool to create intermediate steps between two objects. In the Blend Options dialog box, use a specified number of steps (say, around 10 or 15) to limit the number of layers that will be created in the export program. Expand the blend, ungroup it, and then use the Layers palette's Release to Layers (Sequence) command on the objects' top-level layer. Finally, export the file.

AutoCAD Drawing (DWG) and AutoCAD Interchange File (DXF)

DWG is the standard AutoCAD file format. DXF is a tagged data representation of the information contained in an AutoCAD drawing file. If you export a document in either of these formats, you'll also need to choose an AutoCAD version, the number of colors you wish to include, and a raster file format.

Windows metafile (WMF) and Enhanced metafile (EMF)

A metafile describes a file and functions as a list of commands for drawing a graphic. Typically, a metafile is made up of commands for drawing objects such as lines, polygons, and text, and commands to control the style of these objects.

WMF is a 16-bit metafile format that's used on Windows platforms.

EMF is a 32-bit metafile format that's used on Windows platforms. It can contain a wider variety of commands than a WMF file.

Microsoft Office, TXT, DWG, DXF, WMF, EMF

Color management

Problems with color can creep up on you when various hardware devices and software packages you use treat color differently. If you open an image in several different imaging programs and in a Web browser, the colors in the image might look completely different in each case, and thus may not match the color of the picture you originally scanned in. Print the image, and you'll probably find that your results are different yet again. In some cases, you might find these differences to be slight and unobjectionable, but in other cases, such color changes can wreak havoc with your design and turn a project into a disaster.

A color management system can solve most of these problems by acting as a color interpreter. Such a system knows how each device and program understands color, and adjusts colors so your images look the same as you move them from one program or device to another. It achieves this by using color profiles, which are mathematical descriptions of each device's color space. Both Illustrator and Photoshop use the standardized ICC (International Color Consortium) profiles to tell your color management system how specific devices use color.

Illustrator's color management features will probably seem complex to you at first. But it's well worth the investment of time to learn about them because they've been adopted by the latest versions of other Adobe programs, such as Photoshop. You can find most of Illustrator's color management controls in Edit > Color Settings. This dialog box gives you access to predefined management settings for various publishing situations, including prepress output and Web output.

Illustrator supports color management policies for RGB and CMYK color files. These color management policies govern how Illustrator deals with color when opening images that do or don't have an attached color profile.

(Continued on the following page)

If you plan on using the same graphics for different purposes, such as for the Web and for printed material, you may benefit from using color management.

➤ Consult with your prepress service provider, if you're using one, about color management to ensure that your color management workflows work together smoothly.

Calibration

The first step toward achieving color consistency is to **calibrate** your monitor by adjusting the contrast and brightness, gamma, color balance, and white point. The Adobe Gamma utility is installed with the Windows version of Illustrator CS, whereas the Mac version relies on the operating system's monitor calibration utility in the Displays option (Color tab) in System Preferences.

Both the Adobe Gamma and Displays control panels generate an ICC profile that Illustrator can use as its working RGB space in order to display the colors in your artwork accurately. To generate a more complete profile, use a hardware calibrator.

You have to calibrate your monitor and save the settings as an ICC profile only once; thereafter, the profile will be available to all applications.

For more information about calibration, see Illustrator Help or our *Photoshop CS: Visual QuickStart Guide.*

To choose a predefined color management setting:

1. Choose Edit > Color Settings (Cmd-Shift-K/Ctrl-Shift-K).

2. Choose a configuration option from the Settings pop-up menu 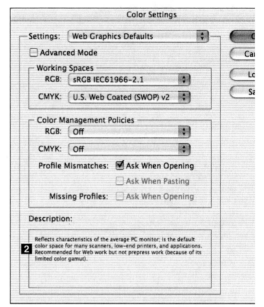:

   Color Management Off emulates the behavior of applications that don't support color management. This is a good choice when preparing projects for video or onscreen presentation.

   ColorSync Workflow (Mac only) manages color using the ColorSync color

Point and learn!

The Color Settings dialog box has a Description area **2** that displays valuable information about options the mouse is currently over. Make use of this great feature!

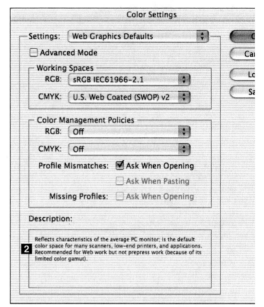

1 *The* **Color Settings** *dialog box with the* **Web Graphics Defaults** *setting chosen*

management system. Profiles (including any monitor profile you may have created using the Apple Display Calibrator Assistant) are based on those in System Preferences > ColorSync. This setting is a good choice if you need to keep color consistent between Adobe and non-Adobe applications on the Mac.

Emulate Acrobat 4 uses Acrobat 4.0's color handling. To access this setting, Acrobat must first be installed.

Emulate Photoshop 4 uses the same color workflow as the Mac version of Photoshop 4 and earlier versions. This setting doesn't recognize or save color profiles.

North American General Purpose **NEW** **Defaults** tries to keep colors consistent among Adobe products.

Photoshop 5 Default Spaces uses the same working spaces as the default settings found in Photoshop 5.

U.S. Prepress Defaults manages color using settings based on common press conditions in the U.S. In the European or Japanese prepress setting, the CMYK working space is changed to a press that's standard for that region.

Web Graphics Defaults manages color for content that's going to be published on the Web.

(Choosing Emulate Adobe® Illustrator® 6.0 makes all the settings inaccessible and turns color management off.)

At this point you can click OK to accept the predefined settings or you can proceed with step 3 to choose custom settings.

3. Next, you can choose color working spaces, which define how RGB and CMYK color will be treated in your document. For CMYK settings, you should ask your output service provider which working space to choose.

The following **RGB** settings are available:

Monitor RGB [current monitor name]: This choice sets the RGB working space

to your monitor's profile, and is useful if you know that other applications you'll be using for your project don't support color management. Keep in mind, however, that if you share this configuration with another user, the configuration will use that user's monitor profile as the RGB working space, and color consistency may be lost.

Adobe RGB (1998): This color space produces a wide range of colors and is useful when converting RGB images to CMYK images, but it's not a good choice for Web work.

Apple RGB: This space is useful for files that you plan to display on Mac monitors, as it reflects the characteristics of the older standard Apple 13-inch monitors. It's also a good choice for older desktop publishing files (e.g., Adobe Photoshop 4.0 files).

ColorMatch RGB: This space produces a smaller range of colors than the Adobe RGB (1998) model, but it matches the color space of Radius Pressview monitors and is useful for print production work.

sRGB IEC61966-2.1: This is a good choice for Web work, as it reflects the settings on the average computer monitor. Many hardware and software manufacturers are using it as the default space for scanners, low-end printers, and software. It shouldn't be used for prepress work; use Adobe RGB or ColorMatch RGB instead.

ColorSync RGB [current ColorSync default]: (Mac only) Use this color space to match Illustrator's RGB space to the space specified in System Preferences > ColorSync > Default Profiles. This can be the profile you created using System Preferences > Displays. If you share this configuration with another user, it will utilize the ColorSync space specified by that user.

4. Click OK.

Color Settings

You can choose a **customized** color management policy that will tell Illustrator how to deal with artwork that doesn't match your current color settings.

To customize your color management policies:

1. Choose Edit > Color Settings (Cmd-Shift-K/Ctrl-Shift-K).

2. From the Settings pop-up menu, choose any predefined setting other than Color Management Off or Emulate Acrobat 4, or chose your own custom Working Spaces settings.

3. From the pop-up menus in the Color Management Policies area **1**:

   If you choose **Off**, Illustrator won't color-manage color files that are imported or opened.

   Choose **Preserve Embedded Profiles** if you think you're going to be working with both color-managed and non-color-managed documents. This will tie each color file's profile to the individual file. Remember, in Illustrator, each open document can have its own profile.

   Choose **Convert to Working Space** if you want all your documents to reflect the same color working space. This is usually the best choice for Web work.

   For Profile Mismatches, check **Ask When Opening** to have Illustrator display a message if the color profile in a file you're opening doesn't match your selected working space. If you choose this option, you can override your color management policy when opening documents.

   Check **Ask When Pasting** to have Illustrator display a message when color profile mismatches occur as you paste color data into your document. If you choose this option, you can override your color management policy when pasting.

   For files with Missing Profiles, check **Ask When Opening** to have Illustrator display a message offering you the opportunity to assign a profile.

4. Click OK.

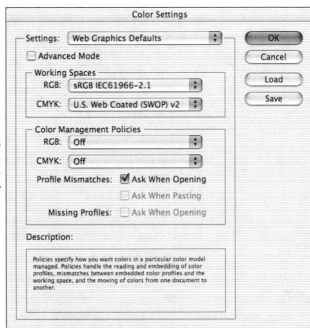

1 *Color Management Policies options are chosen from the middle portion of the Color Settings dialog box.*

To customize your conversion options:

1. Choose Edit > Color Settings (Cmd-Shift-K/Ctrl-Shift-K).

2. Check Advanced Mode **1**.

3. Under Conversion Options, choose a color management Engine to be used to convert colors between color spaces: **Adobe (ACE)** uses Adobe's color management system and color engine; both **Apple ColorSync** and **Apple CMM** use Apple's color management system; and **Microsoft ICM** uses the system provided in Windows 98 and later systems. Other color engines can be chosen to fit into color workflows that use specific output devices.

4. Choose a rendering **Intent** to determine how colors will be changed as they're moved from one color space to another:

Perceptual, the default intent for all predefined "General Purpose" settings, changes colors in a way that seems natural to the human eye, although the color values actually do change. It's appropriate for continuous-tone images.

Saturation changes colors with the intent of preserving vivid colors, although it compromises the accuracy of the color; it's good for charts and business graphics.

Absolute Colorimetric keeps colors that are inside the destination color gamut unchanged, but the relationships among colors outside this gamut are changed in an attempt to maintain color accuracy.

Relative Colorimetric is the same as Absolute Colorimetric, except that it compares the white point, or extreme highlight, of the source color space to

(Continued on the following page)

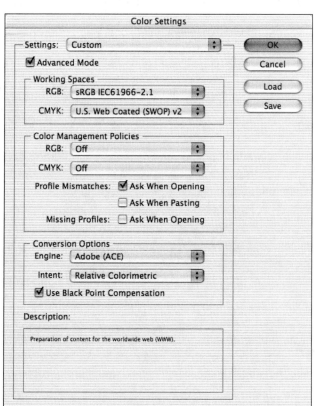

1 *When Advanced Mode is checked in the Color Settings dialog box, the Conversion Options become available.*

the destination color space and shifts all colors accordingly. The accuracy of this intent depends on the accuracy of white point information in an image's profile.

Note: Differences between rendering intents are visible only on a printout or upon a conversion to a different working space.

Check **Use Black Point Compensation** if you want adjustments to be made for differences in black points between color spaces. When this option is chosen, the full dynamic range of the source color space is mapped into the full dynamic range of the destination color space. If you don't choose this option, your blacks may appear as grays. We recommend that you check this option for an RGB-to-CMYK conversion, but consult your print shop before checking it for a CMYK-to-CMYK conversion.

5. Click OK.

Save your settings

To save your custom settings for later use, click **Save** in the Color Settings dialog box. If you want your custom file name to display on the Settings pop-up menu on the Mac, save the file in Users/[CurrentUser]/Library/Application Support/Adobe/Color/Settings. To do the same thing in Windows, save it in the default location, which is Program Files\Common Files\Adobe\Color\Settings.

When you're ready to reuse the saved settings, choose the file name from the Settings pop-up menu. To locate a settings file that isn't saved in the Settings folder (and thus doesn't appear on the Settings menu), click **Load** in the Color Settings dialog box.

In the Save As dialog box, when you save a file in a format that supports embedded profiles, such as Illustrator or Adobe PDF, you can check **Embed ICC Profiles** to embed a profile with the document, if one has been assigned.

You may decide later that you want to change or remove a document's color profile. For example, when preparing a document for a specific output device, you may need to switch profiles. You also may need to switch profiles if you change your mind about your color management settings. The **Assign Profile** command reinterprets the color data directly in the color space of the new profile (or lack thereof), and visible shifting of colors can result.

To change or delete a document's color profile:

1. Choose Edit > Assign Profile 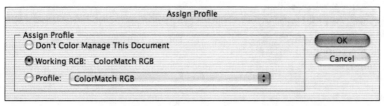.

2. Click **Don't Color Manage This Document** to remove the color profile.
   or
   Click **Working** (plus the document color mode and the name of the working space you're using) to assign that particular working space to a document that doesn't use a profile or that uses a profile that's different from the current working space.
   or
   Click **Profile** to reassign a different profile to a color-managed document; choose a profile from the pop-up menu.

3. Click OK.

   Note: If you save a file in (or export a file to) a format that supports embedded profiles, you'll have the choice to select or deselect the Embed ICC Profiles option. You should keep this option checked unless you have a specific reason to uncheck it.

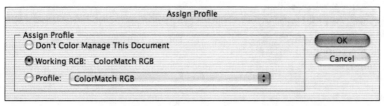

1 *Use the **Assign Profile** dialog box to change a file's color profile. The Profile chosen here will also be listed as the Source Space in the Color Management panel of the File > Print dialog box.*

Assign Profile

Specifying a color management setup is all well and good, but sometimes what you need is to get an idea of how a document is going to look when it's printed or when it's displayed on a website. You can do this by **soft-proofing** your colors. Although this method is less accurate than actually making a print or viewing your Web artwork on different monitors, it can give you a general idea of how your work will look in different settings. You can either choose a preset proof setup or choose custom settings.

To proof your colors:

1. Choose View > Proof Setup. From the submenu, choose which type of output display you want simulated:

   Custom will allow you to create a proofing model for a specific output device via the Proof Setup dialog box 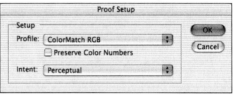. To do this, choose the color profile for your desired output device from the Profile pop-up menu, then check or uncheck Preserve Color Numbers (see the sidebar at right). If you check this option, Illustrator will simulate how the colors will appear if they're not converted to the proofing space. If you uncheck this option, Illustrator will simulate how the colors will appear if they are converted, and you'll need to choose a rendering Intent, as described on page 483. Click OK.
   or
   Choose **Macintosh RGB** or **Windows RGB** to soft-proof colors using a Mac or Windows monitor profile as the proofing space you wish to simulate.
   or
   Choose **Monitor RGB** to use your monitor profile as the space for proofing.

2. View > **Proof Colors** will be checked automatically so the soft proof can be previewed. Uncheck this option if you want to turn off proofing.

If Preserve Color Numbers is dimmed

The **Preserve Color Numbers** option is available only when the color mode of the current file is the same as that of the output device profile currently chosen in the Proof Setup dialog box. For example, if the document color mode is RGB and the chosen proofing profile is an RGB profile, the Preserve Color Numbers option will be available.

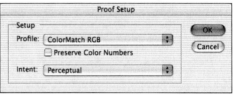

1 *The Proof Setup dialog box*

This chapter covers the preparation of Illustrator files for the Web. You'll learn how to choose an appropriate export format, create and use slices to achieve faster download speeds, choose optimization settings via the Save for Web dialog box, and save a file as SVG.

Illustrator's Save for Web dialog box

The file optimization features in Illustrator CS (borrowed from its sibling program, ImageReady CS) are found in the File > **Save for Web** dialog box **1**. There you'll find Original, Optimized, 2-Up, and 4-Up preview tabs at the top of the main window; a Color Table palette; format, matte, quality, and other options; a Preview in [default browser] button; and a Select Browser menu.

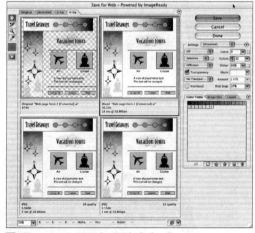

1 *Illustrator's Save for Web dialog box*

Exporting Web graphics

Illustrator excels at creating crisp, tidy graphics—the kind of graphics that are perfect for the Web. Thankfully, the program boasts a number of tools that streamline the preparation of Web graphics.

The basic formula for outputting a file for online viewing may seem straightforward: Design the illustration in RGB color mode and export it in GIF or JPEG format—the file formats used by Web servers and browsers (the applications that combine text, images, and HTML code into a viewable page on the Web). However, when you load and view an image via a Web browser, you may be disappointed to find that not all colors or blends display well on the Web.

What's more, an illustration with a large, placed image may take an unacceptably long time to download and render, due to its large storage size. If an image looks overly dithered (grainy), was subject to unexpected color substitutions, or takes too long to view on a Web page, it means your design isn't outputting well. Some of the key issues that you'll need to address for online output are discussed on the remaining pages of this chapter.

When you're preparing Web graphics, there are four important issues you'll need to address for online output: the pixel size of the image, the color palette, the color depth, and the file format (GIF, JPEG, PNG, Flash, or SVG).

Web Graphics

Image size

To calculate the appropriate image size, you must know the monitor size and the modem speed of your intended viewers beforehand. In most cases, you should be designing your artwork for an 800 x 600-pixel viewing area—the most common monitor size, and a 56 Kbps modem, the most common modem speed (at least for the moment).

The Web browser window will display within these parameters, so your maximum image size will occupy only a portion of the browser window—about 8 inches high (570 pixels) by 7 inches wide (500 pixels). The image resolution should be 72 ppi.

To determine a file's actual storage size, on the Mac, highlight the file name in the Finder, then choose File > Get Info. In Windows, right-click the file in Windows Explorer and choose Properties from the pop-up menu.

If you know the exact size of the compressed image, you can then calculate how long it will take to transmit over the Web. If you use the File > Save for Web dialog box, you can find out exactly how large your JPEG, GIF, PNG-8, or PNG-24 file is and how long it will take to download **1**. To calculate the download time based on file size and modem speed, choose a Size/Download Time from the Preview menu ⊙ at the top of the main window (or Control-click/right-click in the main window, then choose a Size/Download Time).

Saving a file in the GIF or JPEG file format reduces its storage size significantly because these formats have built-in compression schemes. The degree to which these file formats compress a file depends on how compressible the file is **2**–**3**. Both formats cause a small reduction in image quality, but this tradeoff is worthwhile because the image will download faster on the Web. A file size of about 50K traveling on a 28.8 Kbps modem will take about 18 seconds to download, and half that time for a 56 Kbps modem. (No, this isn't a test question!)

Image Size

Create a browser window layer

Take a screen shot of your browser window, place the file into an Illustrator file, then drag it into the bottommost layer. Now you can design your layout for the dimensions of that specific browser window.

GIF
11.91K
3 sec @ 56.6Kbps

1 *The current file's size and download time display in the Info annotation area in the lower left corner of each preview window of the Save for Web dialog box.*

2 *A 20K GIF, from an image with a reduced color table…*

3 *…as compared with a 120K GIF, from a continuous-tone image*

A document with a solid background color and a few solid-color shapes will compress a great deal (expect a file size in the range of 20 to 50K), whereas a large file (over 100K) with many color areas, textures, or patterns won't compress nearly as much. Continuous-tone, photographic images may compress less than flat-color graphics when saved in the GIF format. JPEG is a better format choice for a photographic-type image.

To summarize, if the image must be large (500 x 400 pixels or larger), it ideally should contain only a handful of large, solid-color shapes. If the image is intricate in color or shape, you should restrict its size to only a portion of the Web browser window.

One way to minimize the download time is to use symbols to create repetitive elements for a Web page instead of the usual method of background tiling. Create a symbol set and place it behind other Illustrator objects, use the symbolism tools to modify the symbol set, then export the entire Web page in SVG format.

Another way to handle large illustrations is to slice them into smaller sections so they download faster. Read about slicing on pages 494–499.

Color table

In the early days of the Web, most people using the newfangled Web browsers had computers with pretty basic video hardware —at least by 21st-century standards. If their monitors could display color at all, they were limited to displaying 256 colors at a time.

With such a restricted range of colors available, Web designers learned to plan their graphics around limited collections of colors. If the designers made sure their images used only colors from these collections, they could be relatively sure that their pages would be displayed with the same colors when viewed on another browser or platform. These collections are called "color tables" or "palettes." (Illustrator confusingly uses both terms, as in the marvelously named "Color Table palette.")

(Continued on the following page)

Palette (or Color Table)

Today, most Web surfers have display hardware that can handle thousands or even millions of colors, and designing with a limited color palette is less of a practical necessity. But it's still useful to be able to reduce the number of colors in an image just to make its file size smaller; this technique, called "optimization," is discussed on pages 500–503.

Color depth

Lowering a file's color depth reduces the actual number of colors it contains, which in turn reduces its file size and speeds up its download time on the Web. Color reduction may produce dithered edges and duller colors, but you'll get the desired reduction in file size. You can reduce the number of colors in an 8-bit image to fewer than the 256 colors it originally contained via Illustrator's Save for Web dialog box.

➤ Always preview an image at 100% view to evaluate its color quality.

Dithering

Dithering is the intermixing of two palette colors to create the impression of a third color. This technique is used to make images that contain a limited number of colors (256 or fewer) appear to have a greater range of colors and shades. It's usually applied to continuous-tone images in order to increase their tonal range, but—argh, life is full of compromises—it can also make them look overly grainy.

Dithering usually doesn't produce aesthetically pleasing results in flat-color graphics. This is because, on an 8-bit display, the browser will dither pixels to re-create any color that its palette doesn't contain. It's better to create colors in flat-color graphics by using the Web Safe RGB model on the Color palette with its Web Safe color ramp. Existing flat-color areas should also be selected and Web-shifted to make them Web-safe.

Some continuous-tone imagery looks fine on a Web page without dithering and in a limited range of 256 colors. However, color banding will result if you lower both the

Color depth

Number of colors	Bit depth
256	8
128	7
64	6
32	5
16	4
8	3
4	2
2	1

1 *A closeup of an image with a small amount of dithering*

1 *The same image with a lot of dithering*

2 *GIF is a suitable optimization format for this illustration, because it contains flat color shapes.*

3 *This hybrid illustration, which contains both a sharp-edged element (type) and a continuous-tone element (ducky), is also a good candidate for GIF optimization.*

number of colors in the palette and the amount of dithering when an illustration is optimized. The Dither value is chosen in Illustrator's Save for Web dialog box. The higher the Dither value, the more seamless the color transitions will appear, but the more grainy the image may also appear **1** (and **1**, previous page). You can decide which of these two evils appears lesser to your eye.

One more consideration: Dithering adds noise and additional colors to the file, so compression is less effective when dithering is turned on than when it's off. With dithering enabled, you may not be able to achieve the desired level of file compression. As is the case with most Web output, you'll have to strike an acceptable balance between aesthetics and file size.

File Formats
GIF

GIF (Graphics Interchange Format) is an 8-bit file format, meaning a GIF image can contain a maximum of 256 colors. It's a legacy from the days when a majority of Web users had 8-bit video hardware that could display a maximum of 256 colors. GIF is still a good choice for illustrations that contain solid-color areas and shapes with well-defined edges, such as type **2**–**3**.

To save an illustration in the GIF format and see how it will actually look when it's viewed via the browser, use File > Save for Web (we'll show you how to do this later in this chapter).

To prevent unexpected dithering, consider optimizing your illustration using the Web palette in the Save for Web dialog box. Or Web Snap 30–50 percent of the colors using Save for Web, and then manually shift the critical solid-color areas into the Web-safe gamut. (You'll read more about these methods later.) Color substitutions will be particularly noticeable in solid-color areas.

➤ If you want to apply a gradient fill to a large area of an illustration and you're going to use the GIF format, create a

(Continued on the following page)

top-to-bottom gradient. Top-to-bottom gradients produce smaller file sizes than left-to-right or diagonal gradients.

Consider also creating a slice to define a gradient object, and then optimize that slice for export in SVG format (see pages 509–511).

JPEG

The JPEG format may be a better choice for preserving color fidelity if your artwork is continuous-tone (contains gradations of color or is photographic) and if your viewers have 24-bit monitors, which have the capacity to display millions of colors **1**.

An advantage to using JPEG is that it can take a 24-bit image and make it as small as the GIF format can make an 8-bit image.

JPEG does have some shortcomings. First, a JPEG file has to be decompressed when it's downloaded for viewing on a Web page, which takes time. Second, JPEG isn't a good choice for flat-color graphics or type because its compression methods tend to produce artifacts along the well-defined edges of these types of objects **2**–**3**.

And third, not all Web viewers use 24-bit monitors. JPEG images will be dithered on an 8-bit monitor, although this will be less noticeable in continuous-tone areas than in flat-color areas. To see a preview of how an image will look in an 8-bit setting, choose Browser Dither from the Preview menu in the Save for Web dialog box. If it doesn't contain type or objects with sharp edges, the JPEG image will probably survive the conversion to 8 bits.

You can also choose the Progressive option when optimizing a file as JPEG. With this option enabled, the image will display in increasing detail as it downloads onto a Web page.

If you choose JPEG as your output format, you can experiment in Illustrator's Save for Web dialog box by optimizing an illustration and then using the 4–Up option to preview several versions of it in varying degrees of compression. Decide which degree of compression is acceptable by weighing the file size versus diminished image quality.

1 *JPEG optimization is suitable for continuous-tone images like this one.*

2 *JPEG isn't a great choice for optimizing sharp-edged graphics. Note the artifacts around the type.*

3 *The word "Duck" looks crisper in this GIF.*

Dress down your bitmaps

One way to reduce the number of pixels and lessen the color complexity in a bitmap image before placing it is to use an image-editing program such as Photoshop to **scale** the image to the actual size needed for the Web page. You can also reduce the image resolution to 72 ppi.

You can also use Illustrator's Rasterize command to reduce the pixel **resolution** of a placed image (check the Anti-Alias option).

To reduce color complexity, try **posterizing** a continuous-tone image down to somewhere between four and eight levels in Photoshop before placing it into Illustrator. The result will be a smaller file size—albeit with noticeable color transitions.

In Illustrator, you can save an optimized file separately and keep the original file in reserve for potential future revisions.

PNG-8 and PNG-24

The two PNG formats save partially transparent pixels (such as soft, feathered edges) using a method called alpha transparency. With alpha transparency, a pixel can have any one of 256 levels of opacity, ranging from totally transparent to totally opaque. The PNG-8 format is limited to a maximum of 256 colors in the optimized image, and is similar to the GIF format. The PNG-24 format allows for millions of colors in the optimized image and is similar to the JPEG format. The PNG formats use a lossless compression method (it doesn't cause data loss).

There are a couple of drawbacks to using PNG: Animation can't be done in the PNG format (animation can be done in the GIF format), and PNG-24 files are larger in size than equivalent JPEGs. However, PNG is now supported by all the major Web browsers (as of this writing, Internet Explorer versions 4.0 and later directly support PNG).

The SVG format is discussed on pages 509–511. The Flash format is discussed on pages 477–478.

Anti-aliasing

Anti-aliasing blends an object with its background by adding pixels with progressively less opacity along the edge of the object. When imagery is composited or montaged, anti-aliasing helps to smooth the transitions between shapes. With anti-aliasing turned off, the edges of an object will look sharp because no extra pixels will have been added.

If you create an object, save it for the Web, and later place it against a colored background, an unattractive fringe of pixels, sometimes called a halo, may be visible. To avoid halos, follow the instructions for creating background matting for the GIF, PNG, and JPEG formats. This will determine how partially transparent pixels (the kind of pixels that are created by anti-aliasing) are treated.

Slicing

Slicing involves dividing an illustration into smaller pieces for more efficient downloading . When exporting an illustration using the Save for Web dialog box, you can choose different optimization formats and settings for each slice in order to achieve faster download speeds. A separate export file is generated for each slice that contains the object or objects within the slice area. Slices also determine how an exported illustration is translated into a valid HTML table for display as a Web page within a browser. Slices created in Illustrator can be edited in Adobe Photoshop or Adobe ImageReady, and Illustrator slices can be read by Adobe GoLive. In Illustrator, you'll work with four types of slices: object slices, text slices, user slices, and auto slices.

An **object** slice is defined by the smallest rectangle that could completely enclose an object. If the object is moved or resized, or an effect is applied to it, the slice resizes automatically to accommodate the modified object. A group can also be made into an object slice and, as with an object, the slice will resize to accommodate changes made to the group.

A **text** slice is based on the bounding box of selected text. When a text slice is exported, the text is converted to HTML text with all its format and character settings intact.

A **user** slice is one that is created manually using the Slice tool. User slices can be moved and resized using the Slice Selection tool. Each user slice is listed as a separate <Slice> on the Layers palette.

Auto slices are described in the sidebar.

Before you begin to slice up your Illustrator document, make sure slices are showing.

To show/hide slices:

Choose View > Show Slices. (To hide slices choose View > Hide Slices.)

➤ To view slices in the Save for Web dialog box, click the Toggle Slice Visibility button ▣ in the upper left corner. To hide slices, click the button again.

Automatic slices

Illustrator creates **automatic** slices that divide up the remaining rectangular areas around any object or user slices. Automatic slices can't be selected or edited by hand, although they can be selected for optimization in the Save for Web dialog box. All the auto slices in a document must use the same optimization settings. Auto slices are redrawn and renumbered automatically whenever an object or user slice is edited. That way a valid HTML table will be created for the exported illustration. They display as lighter lines with a vertical link symbol (to show that they're linked together) to the right of the slice number icon, in the upper left corner of the slice.

1 *An Illustrator file containing slices*

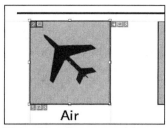

 An **object slice** is created for a selected rectangular object.

 An **object slice** is created for a selected rectangular object.

2 Drag with the **Slice** tool over the area to be **defined** as a slice.

Object slice

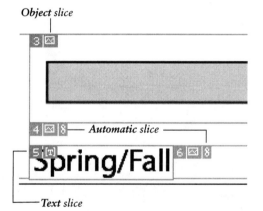

Automatic slice

Text slice

3 A **sequence number** displays on each slice. An icon also displays next to the number to signify what type of slice it is.

4 A selected **user slice**

To create an object or text slice:

1. On the artboard, select an object, multiple objects, or a group.

2. Choose Object > Slice > Make **1**. The new slice will be defined by a rectangle that snaps to the boundaries of the object.

3. *Optional:* To create a text slice, follow steps 1–2 above, select the object, choose Object > Slice > Slice Options, then choose HTML Text from the Slice Type pop-up menu (read about Slice Options on pages 498–499).

User slices are selected, moved, resized, divided, combined, duplicated, aligned, and restacked by way of the slice commands. (Object slices, by contrast, resize automatically if the object inside them is resized or moved.)

To create a user slice:

1. Choose the Slice tool.

2. **Drag** over the area of the artwork to be defined as a slice **2**. A rectangle will surround the selected object or area you marqueed.

➤ Shift-drag to constrain a slice to a square. Option-drag/Alt-drag to create a slice from the center.

➤ If you want slices to be created from existing guides in the artwork, choose Slice > Create Slice from Guides. But beware, this command deletes all existing slices!

A rectangle surrounds each area or object that has been designated as a **slice,** and each slice has a sequence number in its upper left corner **3**. The slice in the upper left corner of the illustration is assigned the number 1, with the remaining slice numbers increasing in ascending order from left to right and top to bottom.

To select a slice:

1. Choose the Slice Select tool (it's on the Slice tool pop-out menu).

2. Click a user slice or object slice **4**. Shift-click if you want to select additional slices.

Unlike object slices, user slices don't resize automatically when objects within the slice area are modified. If you modify or move objects inside a user slice, you'll need to resize the slice afterward.

To resize a user slice:

1. Choose the Slice Select tool, 🖋 then click a slice.

2. Position the pointer over a slice border or corner **1**. When the double-headed border ⇔ or corner arrow ↖ displays, drag to resize the slice **2**.

To move a user slice:

1. Choose the Slice Select tool, 🖋 then click a slice.

2. Position the pointer inside the slice, then drag to reposition it.

To duplicate a user slice:

1. Choose the Slice Select tool, 🖋 then select a user slice.

2. Choose Object > Slice > Duplicate Slice. A copy of the slice will appear, offset from the original slice **3**–**4**.

➤ A selected slice can also be copied and pasted within the current document or into another document.

To combine two or more user slices into one:

1. Choose the Slice Select tool, 🖋 and then, holding down the Shift key, select two or more user slices. The selected slices can overlap each other, but they don't have to.

2. Choose Object > Slice > Combine Slices. One larger user slice will be created that encompasses the slices you selected **5**–**6**.

Align it

To align user slices precisely, select them, then apply any of the **Align** palette commands. This will help to streamline the overall layout of objects, eliminating any small, unnecessary slices that may have been generated automatically, and thus produce a simpler HTML table.

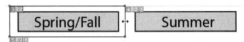

1 *Position the Slice Selection tool over the border of a selected slice...*

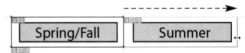

2 *...then drag with the tool to resize the slice.*

3 *A user slice is selected...*

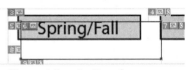

4 *...and then duplicated.*

5 *Several user slices are selected...*

6 *...and then combined into one slice.*

1 *A user slice is selected.*

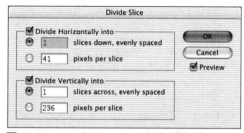

2 *Options are chosen in the **Divide Slice** dialog box*

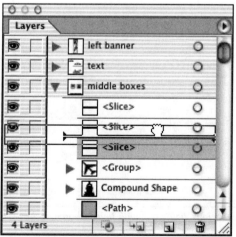

3 *The user slice is **divided** into four separate user slices.*

4 *A user slice is **restacked** using the Layers palette.*

To divide a user slice into smaller slices:

1. Choose the Slice Select tool, 🔪 then select a user slice **1**.

2. Choose Object > Slice > Divide Slices **2**.

3. Check Divide Horizontally Into and/or check Divide Vertically Into to specify where the division will occur, then for either or both options, click the first button and enter a value to divide the slice into equal-sized parts, or click the second button and enter an exact number of pixels for the divided parts.

4. Check Preview to preview the divisions.

5. Click OK **3**.

To restack a user slice:

1. Choose the Slice Select tool, 🔪 then select a user slice.

2. Locate the <Slice> you want to restack on the Layers palette, then drag it upward or downward **4**.

The **Lock Slices** and **Release** commands apply to any type of slice.

To lock all slices:

Choose View > Lock Slices. The Slice commands aren't available when slices are locked.

To release a slice:

1. Select any type of slice, or select an object inside an object slice.

2. Choose Object > Slice > Release. Any object or user slices will be removed; the original artwork objects will remain.

Beware! If you **delete** an object slice, the artwork object inside it will also be deleted.

To delete a user slice:

1. Choose the Slice Select tool, 🔪 then select a user slice.

2. Press Delete/Backspace.

➤ To remove all slices, choose Object > Slice > Delete All.

You can use the **Slice Options** dialog box to categorize the content of a slice for browser viewing and to assign a URL and an Alt tag for the display of substitute text.

To choose slice options:

1. Choose Object > Slice > Slice Options.
   or
   Double-click a slice in the Save for Web dialog box.

2. From the **Slice Type** pop-up menu 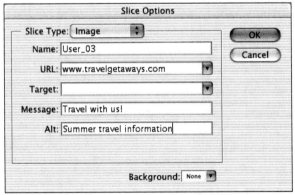, choose a category for the slice content: **No Image, Image,** or **HTML Text.**

3. Follow the steps under the appropriate category below for the Slice Type you chose:

   For the **Image** Slice Type:

   Leave the default slice name as is or enter a **Name** (with no spaces). This name will be used for the separate slice file.

   Enter a URL or choose a previously used URL from the pop-up menu. Viewers will be linked to this URL if they click the slice area in a browser.

   Optional: Enter a frame **Target** or choose a standard frame from the pop-up menu. Linked content will load into the chosen frame target: _blank opens a new browser window for the link contents; _self loads the new link contents into the HTML frame for the current slice; _parent replaces the current HTML frames with the new link contents; and _top loads the new link contents into the entire browser window (this is similar to the _parent option). The Target field is available only when information is entered into the URL field.

Enter a **Message** to have text appear on the browser's status bar at the bottom of the browser window when the user's pointer is over that slice.

Enter **Alt** text to be displayed while the actual image downloads or if a user's browser is set to display without images. This text is also spoken by browser-installed voice recognition software for visually impaired users.

Choose a **Background** color to be displayed in the slice in a browser. (This color choice won't display in Illustrator.)

1 *The Slice Options dialog box with **Image** chosen as the Slice Type*

or

For the **No Image** Slice Type 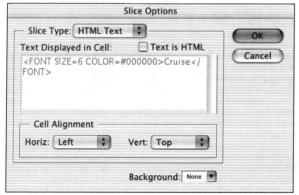:

Enter **text** to be displayed in the slice when viewed in a browser. (This text won't display in Illustrator.) Standard HTML formatting tags can be entered to control the text styling. The text you enter must fit within the slice area.

Under **Cell Alignment,** choose Horiz and/or Vert pop-up menu options to align the text inside the slice.

Choose a **Background** color to be displayed inside the slice in a browser. This color choice won't display in Illustrator.

or

For the **HTML Text** Slice Type 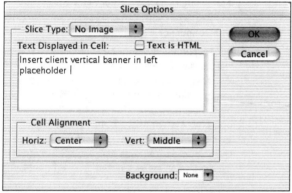:

Under **Cell Alignment**, choose Horiz and/or Vert pop-up menu options to align the text within the slice.

Choose a **Background** color to be displayed in the slice in a browser. This color choice won't display in Illustrator.

4. Click OK.

➤ If text in a text object is changed, any text slice made for that object will resize to reflect those changes.

1 *The Slice Options dialog box with No Image chosen as the Slice Type*

2 *The Slice Options dialog box with HTML Text chosen as the Slice Type*

Slice Options

Optimization

Optimization is the process by which file format, storage size, and color parameters are chosen for a document in order to preserve as much of its quality as possible while still enabling it to download quickly on the Web. Illustrator provides a variety of choices and options for optimization. In this section, you'll learn the basic steps. Your overall goal is to reduce the file size until the quality of the optimized image reaches its reduction limit (starts to degrade). Keep this goal in mind as you choose various palette options.

First, you'll need to choose a file format. **GIF** and **JPEG** are the two most commonly used file formats for displaying graphics on the Web. GIF is recommended for optimized images that contain elements with sharp edges, such as solid-color areas, line art, or type. The **PNG-8** format, which is similar to GIF, uses the same Optimize palette options, with practically the same results. An optimized GIF or PNG-8 file can contain up to 256 colors. You can view the color table for GIF and PNG-8 files and manipulate individual colors in the optimized image. You could also use the SVG format to output Illustrator objects as vectors (without rasterization).

When designing artwork for the Web, it's best to choose **RGB Color mode** for your document. You can do this either when you create your document, or at any time via the File > Document Color Mode submenu.

There's one more thing to keep in mind. While you're working in Illustrator, your vector drawings will appear crisp and smooth. But if you save your illustration in the GIF or JPEG format, Illustrator will rasterize it at 72 ppi. Any rasterized objects that don't precisely align with the pixel grid will have edges that appear jagged or blurry due to **anti-aliasing.** You can preview how your illustration will look in a Web browser by choosing View > Pixel Preview. Your artwork will display as if it had already been rasterized, allowing you to see the impact of anti-aliasing.

Web color palette

If you've ever created an illustration on a monitor that can display millions of colors and then viewed it on a monitor that can display only thousands (or hundreds) of colors, you have some idea of how drastically colors can change in different onscreen settings and what Web-safe colors are all about.

No matter how few—or how many—colors a monitor is capable of displaying, all monitors that have at least 8 bits of color can render **256** specific **colors** without dithering. This is because 8 bits of color can be expressed as 2 to the 8th power, or 256 (each bit has one of two possible values). Subtract 40 for the colors that the Mac and Windows systems reserve for other uses, and you're left with 216 colors that you can use with confidence in your Web graphics.

But keep in mind that not even these 216 colors will display in the same way on every machine. Windows and Mac systems use different color gamma values, and each monitor may be calibrated somewhat differently. The Windows operating system uses a higher gamma value than the Macintosh operating system, so an illustration created on a Mac will appear darker on a Windows system than on the Mac.

Saving your settings

To save the current optimization settings to the current Illustrator file without actually exporting the file, click **Done** in the Save for Web dialog box.

1 *View > Pixel Preview unchecked (off)*

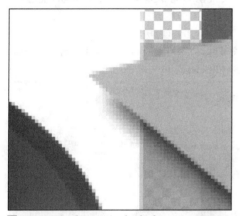

2 *View > Pixel Preview checked (on)*

3 *Choose an optimization preset from the Settings pop-up menu in the Save for Web dialog box.*

With View > Snap to Pixel selected, any artwork you create while your document is in Pixel Preview mode will automatically snap to a pixel grid, and this will prevent any horizontal and vertical edges in your artwork from being anti-aliased. To work in Pixel Preview mode, choose View > **Pixel Preview** **1**–**2**. With Pixel Preview chosen, you can choose View > Snap to Pixel, if desired.

GIFs and JPEGs can't preserve the transparency of soft-edged shapes. If you want an optimized image to fade into a solid-color background, create two layers in your Illustrator document: a lower layer containing a solid Web-safe color that will be used on the full Web page, and a layer above it that contains an overlapping object to which a soft, feathered effect (such as Drop Shadow or Outer Glow) has been applied.

For a hybrid illustration that contains solid-color areas or type combined with photographic imagery, the best approach is to create separate **slices** for the different elements in the illustration, then use the Save for Web dialog box to assign different optimization formats and settings to each slice. This way, the solid-color areas will remain Web-safe and the continuous-tone areas will render reasonably well.

To optimize an illustration or a slice using a preset:

1. Save your file, then choose File > Save for Web.

2. Click the **2-Up** tab above the preview windows to display both the original and optimized previews of the image simultaneously. To optimize just a slice, select it now in the preview window.

3. Choose a named, preset combination of optimization settings from the **Settings** pop-up menu **3**, and don't change any of the optimization settings. Click Save, then choose Format/Save as Type: HTML and images. Change the file name, if desired, but leave the extension as is. Click Save again.

Pixel Preview; Optimizing with Presets

To optimize an illustration in the GIF or PNG-8 format:

1. Save your file, then choose File > Save for Web.

2. Click the **2-Up** or **4-Up** tab above the preview windows to display both the original and optimized previews of the image simultaneously. To optimize just a slice, select it now in the preview window.

3. From the **Optimized file format** pop-up menu, choose GIF or PNG-8.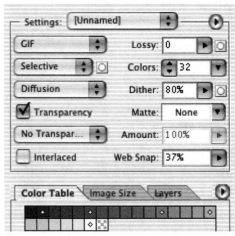

4. For GIF only, drag the **Lossy** slider or enter a value to allow the compression scheme to eliminate pixels from the image, thus reducing file size. The lossy effect will display in the selected preview window. *Note:* You can't use the Lossy option with the Interlaced option, or with the Noise or Pattern Dither algorithms.

5. Choose a color reduction method from the next pop-up menu (see the sidebar on the next page), bearing in mind that the GIF and PNG-8 formats restrict a file to a maximum of 256 colors. **Perceptual, Selective,** and **Adaptive** render the optimized image using colors from the original illustration, whereas Web shifts all colors to Web-safe. Web isn't the best choice if the illustration contains continuous-tone areas, blends, or gradients. Custom optimizes colors based on a palette that you've previously saved.

6. If you want to choose a specific number of colors, choose that value from the **Colors** pop-up menu, or enter a value in the field, or click the arrows to arrive at the desired number of colors.

7. From the next pop-up menu, choose a **Dither** method: No Dither, Diffusion (and choose a dither value using the slider), Pattern, or Noise.

8. If the illustration contains transparency that you want to preserve, check **Transparency.** Fully transparent pixels will be preserved as transparent; partially transparent pixels will be filled with the Matte color or will be converted to

No halos

When creating GIF or PNG-8 files, you can create a hard-edged transparency effect. This will cause all pixels that are more than 50% transparent to be fully transparent and pixels that are less than 50% transparent to be fully opaque. This type of transparency will eliminate the halo effect that can occur when the matte color is different from the background color in the original illustration.

To create hard-edged transparency:

1. Open an illustration that contains **transparency.**

2. Choose File > **Save for Web,** then choose **GIF** or **PNG-8.**

3. Check **Transparency.**

4. Choose **None** from the **Matte** pop-up menu.

5. Click **Save** to save the file.

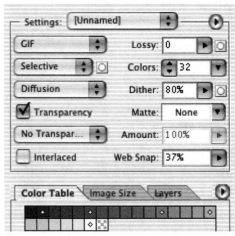

1 *Use the* **optimize** *panel to choose custom settings for a GIF export.*

Four GIF *color reduction methods*

Perceptual

Generates a color table based on the colors currently in the illustration, with particular attention paid to how people actually perceive colors. This method's strength is in preserving overall color integrity.

Selective

Generates a color table based on the colors currently in the illustration. The Perceptual and Selective options are similar, but the Selective option leans more toward preserving flat colors and Web-safe colors.

Adaptive

Generates a color table based on the part of the color spectrum that represents most of the color in the illustration. This choice produces a slightly larger optimized file.

➤ If you switch among the Perceptual, Selective, and Adaptive methods, any Web-safe colors currently on the Color Table palette are preserved.

Web

Generates a color table by shifting image colors to colors that are available on the standard Web-safe palette. This choice produces the least number of colors and thus the smallest file size, though not necessarily the best image quality.

Where exported image files go

By default, when the Save for Web dialog box saves a Web page as a set of multiple image files, it places them in a new **images** folder in the same folder as the exported HTML file. To rename this folder, click Save in the Save for Web dialog box, then choose Other from the Settings pop-up menu. The Output Settings dialog box appears. Choose Saving Files from the second pop-up menu from the top. In the Optimized Files area, change the folder name in the **Put Images in Folder:** field, then click OK.

fully transparent or fully opaque pixels, depending on which Matte option you choose.

If you don't check Transparency, both fully and partially transparent pixels will be filled with the Matte color.

9. To control how partially transparent pixels along the edges of the optimized image (such as the edges of anti-aliased or rasterized elements) will blend with the background of a Web page, choose a **Matte** option.

Choose Other to set the Matte color to any color you wish. If you're not sure what color the graphic will be displayed against, set Matte to None (this will result in hard, jagged edges). Both options eliminate halo effects along the edges of optimized images when they're displayed on the Web. Any soft-edged effect (such as Drop Shadow or Feather) on top of transparency will be filled with the current Matte color.

10. From the next pop-up menu, choose a method by which transparent pixels will be dithered with opaque pixels in order to simulate semitransparency: **No Transparency, Diffusion, Pattern,** or **Noise.** Only the Diffusion option makes use of the accompanying 0–100% Amount slider.

11. *Optional:* Check **Interlaced** to have the GIF or PNG image display in successively greater detail as it downloads on the Web page.

12. *Optional:* To automatically shift colors to their closest Web palette equivalents, drag the **Web Snap** slider or enter a value. The higher the Web Snap value, the more colors will be shifted.

13. Click Save, then choose Format/Save as Type: **HTML and images.** This format creates all the necessary files to use the image as a Web page. The appropriate file format extension will be appended to the file name. Change the name, if desired, then click Save again. (See "Where exported image files go" at left.)

Optimize as GIF or PNG-8

Let's say you have an illustration that you're going to optimize in the GIF format using the Perceptual, Selective, or Adaptive palette, but the illustration has solid-color areas that aren't **Web-safe.** Before outputting the image online, you can make the solid-color areas Web-safe.

To make solid-color areas Web-safe:

1. Open the file and optimize it in the GIF format, using File > Save for Web.

2. Choose the Eyedropper tool.

3. Click a solid-color area to be made Web-safe.

4. If the Color Table panel isn't showing, click the Color Table tab. The color you just clicked will be the highlighted swatch **1**.

5. Click the Shift Selected Colors to the Web Palette button at the bottom of the palette. A diamond with a diagonal line will display on the selected swatch to signify that the color was shifted to a Web-safe equivalent. The swatch is also automatically locked. See the next step.

6. *Optional:* Click the Lock Selected Color button to preserve the currently selected swatch even if the number of colors in the GIF palette is reduced. A small square will display in the lower right corner of the swatch.

➤ Shift-click with the Eyedropper tool on other areas in the Optimized preview to select more than one color, then Web-shift all the selected colors at once.

➤ Click a Web-shifted color swatch, then click the Shift Selected Colors to Web Palette button again to unshift the color out of the Web-safe range.

A highlighted swatch

*A swatch that was **shifted** to a Web-safe color*

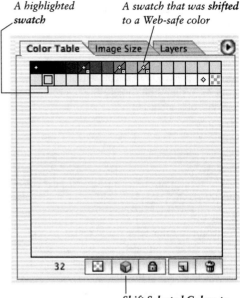

Shift Selected Colors to the Web Palette button

1 *The Color Table panel in the Save for Web dialog box, with a color swatch highlighted*

JPEGs and Web-safe colors

JPEG compression adds compression artifacts to an image. Because of this, Web-safe colors in a JPEG image are rendered non-Web-safe after compression. This is acceptable because the JPEG format is usually used to optimize continuous-tone imagery, and on this type of imagery, browser dither isn't objectionable. Don't try to match a color area in a JPEG file to a color area in a GIF file or on the background of a Web page, though, because the JPEG color will shift and become dithered when the artwork is compressed.

1 *An optimized image with* **Browser Dither** *unchecked*

2 *An optimized image with* **Browser Dither** *checked: Soft edges and transparent areas are dithered.*

Those few souls who will view your website using 8-bit, 256-color displays will find that any colors that aren't on the Web-safe palette will be dithered. Follow the steps below to **preview browser dithering** in an image.

To preview potential browser dither in an optimized image:

1. With the illustration open, choose File > Save for Web, then click the 2-Up or 4-Up tab.
2. Choose Browser Dither from the Preview menu **1**–**2**.

JPEG is the format of choice for optimizing continuous-tone imagery (photographs, paintings, gradients, blends, and the like) for display on the Web. If you optimize to JPEG, the file's full color depth will be preserved, and the colors will be seen and enjoyed by any Web viewer whose monitor is set to 16-bit or 32-bit color. Keep in mind, however, that JPEGs are optimized using a lossy compression method, meaning it causes image data to be eliminated.

The PNG-24 format is similar to JPEG, except PNG allows for multiple levels of transparency along edges and employs a nonlossy compression method. PNG-24 files are larger than equivalent JPEGs.

To optimize an illustration in the JPEG format:

1. Open the original Illustrator file, choose File > Save for Web, then choose one of the JPEG settings from the **Settings** pop-up menu or choose JPEG from the next pop-up menu (the "Optimized file format" pop-up menu, if you're using tool tips) (**1**, next page).
2. Click the **2-Up** or **4-Up** tab at the top of the main window to display the original and optimized previews of the illustration simultaneously. To optimize a slice, select it now in the preview window.
3. In the optimize panel, choose or enter a **Quality** value for the optimized image. *or*

(Continued on the following page)

Browser Dither; Optimize as JPEG

Choose **Low, Medium, High,** or **Maximum** from the compression Quality pop-up menu to the left. A higher setting preserves more color information but makes the file size larger. Experiment with this setting to achieve an acceptable balance between file size and file quality.

4. *Do any of the following optional steps:*

Check **Progressive** to have the image render in stages as it downloads onto the Web page.

Increase the **Blur** value to lessen the visibility of JPEG artifacts that arise from the JPEG compression method and also reduce the file size. Don't overblur the image, though, or details in the artwork will become too soft. The Blur setting can be lowered later in order to reclaim image sharpness.

Check **ICC Profile** to embed an ICC profile in the optimized image. To utilize this option, the document must have had a profile assigned to it in Illustrator (see the sidebar on this page).

5. Choose a **Matte** color to be used for areas of transparency in the original document. If you choose None, transparent areas will appear as white.

Note: The JPEG format doesn't support transparency. To utilize the Matte color option to simulate transparency, choose Matte: Other and then choose the solid color that matches the background color of the Web page.

6. *Optional:* Check Optimized to produce the smallest file size.

7. Click Save, then choose Format: **HTML and images.** The appropriate file format extension will be appended to the file name. Change the name, if desired, then click Save once more.

check your profiles

An embedded profile will slightly increase a file's size. As of this writing, Internet Explorer for Mac versions 4.01 and later support color profiles and ColorSync. On the Mac, ColorSync makes sure the browser and the operating system know the viewer's monitor profile. This helps to ensure consistent color between the monitor and JPEG files. As color management support and profile automation improve, embedded profiles will become standard. Windows has a bit of catching up to do in this area. For the moment, use your own judgment when deciding whether to embed profiles.

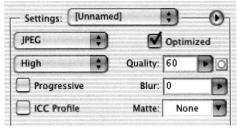

1 *The optimize panel with settings chosen for a JPEG export*

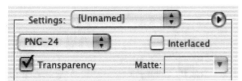

1 *The optimize panel with settings chosen for a PNG-24 export with transparency preserved*

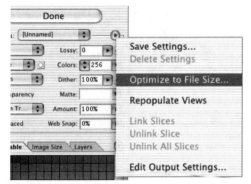

2 *Choose Optimize to File Size from the pop-up menu.*

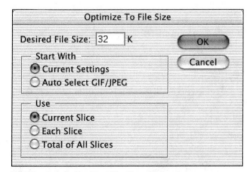

3 *The Optimize To File Size dialog box*

You can preserve up to 256 levels of transparency in PNG-24 images by using a feature called alpha transparency. Not all browsers can display this feature, however.

To preserve multilevel transparency in PNG-24 images:

1. Open the Illustrator file, then choose File > Save for Web.

2. Choose PNG-24 from the Optimized File Format pop-up menu **1**.

3. *Optional:* Check Interlaced to have the PNG image display in successively greater detail as it downloads on the Web page. This option increases the file size.

4. Check Transparency to preserve transparent pixels.

5. Click Save to save your file.

By **saving** your optimization **settings**, you'll be able to apply them to other files.

To save your Save for Web settings:

1. In the Save for Web dialog box, choose Save Settings from the Optimize menu.

2. Name the settings file. By default, it will be saved in Adobe Illustrator CS/Presets/ Save for Web Settings/Optimize folder.

3. Click Save. Your new settings will appear on the Settings pop-up menu, if they were saved in the default location.

You can have Illustrator pick your optimization settings based on the desired **file size**.

To optimize to a desired file size:

1. Open the Save for Web dialog box, then press the arrowhead in the circle and choose Optimize to File Size **2**.

2. Click a **Start With** option. **Current Settings** uses your current optimization settings; **Auto Select GIF/JPEG** tells Illustrator to choose either GIF or JPEG, depending on the program's analysis of your output image **3**.

3. Enter a value for the Desired File Size.

4. Click one of the buttons in the Use area to specify whether the file size limit

(Continued on the following page)

should be applied to the size of the current slice, each individual slice, or the combined size of all the slices.

5. Click OK.

You can **resize** the optimized image directly in the Save for Web dialog box. Note: To make best use of this option, size your artboard before opening the Save for Web dialog box.

To resize your output image:

1. Open the File > Save for Web dialog box, then click the Image Size tab 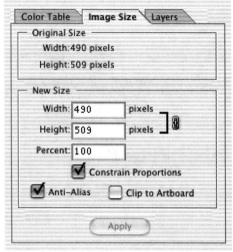.

2. Check **Constrain Proportions** if you want to maintain the relative width and height of your output image.

3. Enter a **Percent** value if you want to make the new image a specific percentage of the original size.
   or
   Enter specific Width and/or Height values.

4. *Optional:* To clip the exported illustration to the size of the document's current artboard, check **Clip to Artboard.** This can be useful for clipping artwork to an artboard that's the size of a banner ad.

5. Click Apply to preview the clipping effect on the image. (If you need to undo Clip to Artboard, uncheck the option, then click Apply again.)

6. *Optional:* Check the Anti-Alias option to keep the image smooth.

7. Click Save or Done.

1 *The Image Size pane in the Save for Web dialog box*

Resize Output Image

SVG

The SVG (Scalable Vector Graphics) format lets you incorporate interactivity into an optimized image and also lets you scale objects on a Web page. Unlike the bitmap formats (GIF, JPEG, and PNG), which save as large files that require a large bandwidth for Web viewing, SVG, a vector format based on XML, lets you store shapes, paths, text, SVG filter effects, and color quality support in a small, efficient file. Currently, Web surfers must download an SVG plug-in in order to view graphics in this format. Keep in mind that many people won't bother to do this and will miss out on seeing your artwork.

SVG is a native Illustrator format, so Illustrator can open and save SVG files. We'll explore several aspects of Illustrator and SVG, such as work guidelines that improve SVG performance, using Save for Web to optimize a file or a slice area as SVG, and saving to the SVG format.

Guidelines for using SVG effectively

Keep the following guidelines in mind when preparing illustrations for the SVG format:

➤ Each layer in the illustration will become a group element in the SVG file; nested layers will become nested group elements. Plan your SVG groups by organizing your layers.

➤ Let each object have its own transparency setting; don't change the transparency value for the whole layer the objects reside in.

➤ When the SVG file is exported, any linked images used in the illustration that don't have an alpha channel will export in the JPEG format; any linked images that do have an alpha channel will export in the PNG format.

➤ All of the commands listed in the lower half of the Effects menu will produce a raster object in the SVG file. Gradient mesh objects are also rasterized by the SVG format. Bear in mind that rasterization increases the file size and download time of an SVG file.

When you use an **SVG filter effect**, you avoid the rasterization that the other Effect menu commands produce. SVG filter effects are rendered to the object in the browser, not in Illustrator, and this helps to reduce a file's download size. In Illustrator, you'll see only a preview of the SVG filter effect.

To apply an SVG filter effect to an object:

1. Select an object.

2. Choose Effect > SVG Filters > Apply SVG Filter **1**.

3. Check Preview.

4. Choose a filter from the scroll list.

5. Click OK.

➤ To prevent an SVG effect from becoming rasterized, it must be listed at the bottom of the Appearance palette, just above the Transparency listing. Drag it downward to move it to the correct position, if necessary.

Optimizing files as SVG

The Save for Web dialog box includes SVG as one of the available optimization formats. This format can be applied to the entire file or to a selected slice within the illustration.

SVG format options display in the optimize panel of the Save for Web dialog box **2**. As listed in top-to-bottom order, the pop-up menu options are: File Format, Font Subsetting, Image Location, CSS Properties, and Character Encoding (these names will be visible if you use tool tips). On the right side, you'll see the Compressed option for creating a compressed SVGZ file, as well as the Decimals option.

The Font Subsetting and Image Location options are also found in the SVG Options dialog box, and the CSS Properties, Character Encoding, and Decimals options are found in the Advanced portion of the SVG Options dialog box. For more about the SVG options, see the following page.

More about SVG

SVG format saves objects as vectors, and preserves gradients, animation, and SVG filter effects as efficient vector shapes. The browser requires the SVG plug-in in order to display SVG files. An SVG file can be opened and displayed in Internet Explorer 5 and later or Netscape Navigator 4.6 and later.

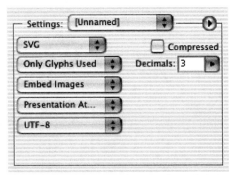

1 *The Apply SVG Filter dialog box*

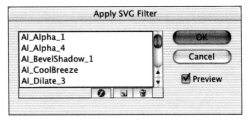

2 *The optimize panel in the Save for Web dialog box, with settings chosen for SVG export*

Link or embed?

Link a font or an image if you're going to share the font or image file with multiple SVG files.

Embed a font or image to guarantee that the font or image will be available. This option increases the file size.

Worth the squeeze?

If you choose SVGZ in the Export dialog box, your file will be compressed; a compressed file can't be edited using a text editor.

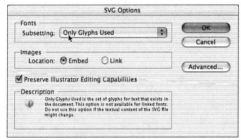

1 *The SVG Options dialog box*

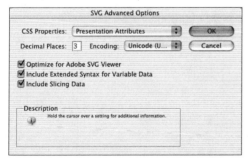

2 *The SVG Advanced Options dialog box*

To save a file in SVG or SVGZ format:

1. Choose File > Save or Save As.
2. Choose a location and file name for the file.
3. Choose Format/Save as Type: SVG (svg) or SVG Compressed (svgz), then click Save.
4. In the SVG Options dialog box **1**, choose a **Fonts: Subsetting** option to embed the specific characters of the fonts you used in your document. **Only Glyphs Used** (the default) includes only the set of glyphs for text used in the document (not including linked fonts); **Common English** and **Common Roman** include only English or Roman characters (each of these two options is also combined with the Glyphs Used option); **All Glyphs** includes every font character, including non-Roman characters.

   All of these choices (except the Only Glyphs Used option) allow for changes in text content in dynamic text (as in data-driven graphics for the Web).

   ➤ Rest the cursor over any option or pop-up menu choice in the dialog box, then read information about it in the Description area.

5. Click **Images Location: Embed** to embed rasterized images in the file, or click **Link** to link the file to the exported JPEG or PNG images from the Illustrator file.
6. Check **Preserve Illustrator Editing Capabilities** to include Illustrator-related data in the file. This permits the saved SVG file to be edited by designers even after a developer's code is added to it.
7. *Optional:* Click Advanced to choose additional options in the SVG Advanced Options dialog box **2**—but only if you have a thorough understanding of the SVG format.
8. Click OK.

Export CSS layers

If you build your web page using **CSS** (**cascading style sheets**), the page can contain layers (similar to layers in Illustrator). Each layer is an object that is defined by HTML, and can be stacked, moved, hidden, and revealed. Layers can be used to create interactive elements on a page, such as pop-up menus. (Adobe GoLive calls these items "floating boxes.")

The **Export As CSS Layers** option in the Save for Web dialog box does just what you would think: It causes Illustrator layers to be converted to CSS layers. Each layer is exported as a separate image file.

To export Illustrator objects as CSS layers:

1. Use the Layers palette in Illustrator to arrange objects on separate layers, then choose File > Save for Web.

2. Click the Layers tab in the Save for Web dialog box **1**.

3. Check **Export As CSS Layers.**

4. Choose a layer from the **Layer** pop-up menu.

5. Click **Visible, Hidden,** or **Do Not Export** to determine how that layer's display will be handled in the exported HTML file.

6. Choose optimization settings from the optimize panel for the objects on the currently selected layer.

7. Choose other layers from the Layer pop-up menu, and repeat steps 5 and 6 for each one.

8. Click Save, then click Save again to export the layers as separate optimized files. The files will be collected in the folder name designated in the Output Settings dialog box under the Saving Files option. The default folder name is "images" (see the bottom sidebar on page 503).

➤ Check Preview Only Selected Layer to preview only the layer chosen in step 4 in the Save for Web previews.

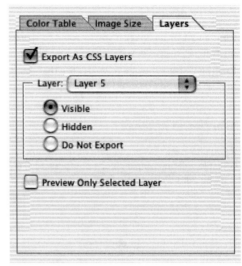

1 *The Layers panel in the Save for Web dialog box*

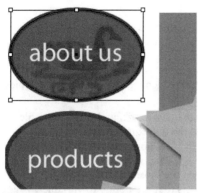

1 *Select the object to which you want to assign a URL...*

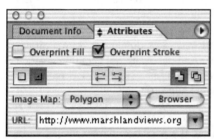

2 *...then enter a URL for the selected object on the Attributes palette.*

Image maps

The **Image Map** option lets you attach a URL to any object you create in Illustrator.

To create an image map:

1. Select the object to which you want to attach a URL **1**.

2. Choose Window > Attributes (F11).

3. From the **Image Map** pop-up menu, choose one of the following: **Rectangle** to create a rectangular image map around the object (the image map boundaries will be similar to the object's bounding box); or **Polygon** to create a map that follows the object's irregular contour.

4. Type a URL into the URL field **2** or choose a URL from the pop-up menu.

5. You can verify the URL location by clicking the Browser button on the palette to launch your system's default Web browser (assuming you have one loaded on your system and your computer is currently connected to the Web).

6. When you're ready to export the file, use the Save for Web dialog box to optimize it. Click Save when you're done, and in the Save Optimized As dialog box, choose Format: **HTML and images** to save the necessary HTML file, complete with the image map and URL links.

   The HTML file, the folder that contains the optimized image file, and the other images being used in the document must be kept together in the same folder when the image map is imported into your Web-page creation program. The HTML file contains the URLs, image name, dimensions, and necessary code to display the image on a Web page.

Image Maps

Data-driven graphics

This page contains a brief synopsis of how the **Variables** palette is used. For more information, refer to *Real World Adobe Illustrator CS* by Steve Kurth (Peachpit Press) or Illustrator Help.

A Web server can connect with a database in order to download text and graphics for inclusion in a Web page. Using Illustrator, a Web page designer can control which objects in an illustration can receive changes from a server. Each element the designer decides can be changed is assigned (bound) to a **variable** via the Variables palette **1**. Then, once the Illustrator object and a variable are bound together, they become dynamic and will update automatically whenever the server software accesses the database and downloads new data to the variable. Only objects bound to variables will change.

You can use the Variables palette to turn object attributes into variables. You can work with four types of variables: **Graph Data, Linked File, Text String,** and **Visibility.** A Graph Data variable updates a graph with new graph data; a Linked File variable replaces one placed image with another; and a Text String variable replaces text. The Visibility variable controls whether an object is visible, and can be changed for any object. The objects that are bound (to variables) serve merely as placeholders in the illustration, displaying whatever data the database and the server send down to that variable.

Variables and their currently displayed data can be captured into a **data set.** Each data set can contain the same variables, but with different object content. Sets are listed on the Data Set menu at the top of the Variables palette.

To edit the data associated with a variable, you edit the object in the artwork to which that variable is bound. A Visibility variable is edited by hiding or displaying its associated object via the Layers palette. After editing the objects that are bound to variables, you can use the Variables palette to capture those edits into a new data set. You can switch between data sets on the Variables palette in order to preview how the changeable objects will look on the page.

Let's say you have a template for a Web page that displays a picture and text for a different car each week. It could contain several different data sets, with each set containing a Linked File variable bound to a picture of a car, and Text String variables that display text objects containing a text description of each car. If you change the car images and text descriptions and capture those changes to a new data set, as you display each data set, the image and text content will update on the Web page.

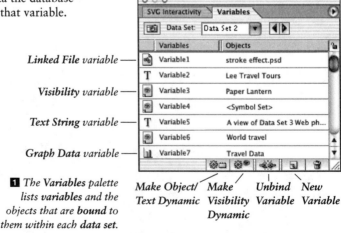

Linked File *variable* —
Visibility *variable* —
Text String *variable* —
Graph Data *variable* —

1 *The Variables palette lists **variables** and the objects that are **bound** to them within each **data set**.*

Make Object/ Make Unbind New
Text Dynamic Visibility Variable Variable
Dynamic

KEYBOARD SHORTCUTS A

	Mac	Windows
Files		
New Document dialog box	Cmd-N	Ctrl-N
New Document from Template	Cmd-Shift-N	Ctrl-Shift-N
Open dialog box	Cmd-O	Ctrl-O
Close	Cmd-W	Ctrl-W
Save	Cmd-S	Ctrl-S
Save As dialog box	Cmd-Shift-S	Ctrl-Shift-S
Save a Copy dialog box	Cmd-Option-S	Ctrl-Alt-S
Document Setup dialog box	Cmd-Option-P	Ctrl-Alt-P
Revert (to last saved version)	F12	F12
Quit/exit Illustrator	Cmd-Q	Ctrl-Q
Tools		
Selection	V	V
Direct Selection	A	A
Magic Wand	Y	Y
Lasso	Q	Q
Pen	P	P
Type	T	T
Line Segment	\	\
Rectangle	M	M
Ellipse	L	L
Paintbrush	B	B
Pencil	N	N
Rotate	R	R
Scale	S	S
Reflect	O	O
Warp	Shift-R	Shift-R
Free Transform	E	E
Symbol Sprayer	Shift-S	Shift-S
Column Graph	J	J
Mesh	U	U

To assign custom shortcuts, see pages 526–528

	Mac	Windows
Gradient	G	G
Eyedropper	I	I
Paint Bucket	K	K
Blend	W	W
Slice	Shift-K	Shift-K
Scissors	C	C
Hand	H	H
Zoom	Z	Z
Add Anchor Point	+	+
Delete Anchor Point	-	-
Convert Anchor Point	Shift-C	Shift-C

Dialog boxes

	Mac	Windows
Highlight next field/option	Tab	Tab
Highlight previous field/option	Shift-Tab	Shift-Tab
Cancel	Cmd-. (period) or Esc	Esc
OK	Return	Enter
Convert Cancel button to Reset button	Option	Alt

Open/Save dialog boxes

	Mac	Windows
Desktop	Cmd-D	
Up one folder level	Cmd-left arrow	

Palettes

	Mac	Windows
Show/hide all palettes	Tab	Tab
Show/hide all palettes except Toolbox	Shift-Tab	Shift-Tab
Apply value in palette field	Return	Enter
Apply value in field, keep field selected	Shift-Return	Shift-Enter
Highlight next field (pointer in palette)	Tab	Tab
Highlight previous field (pointer in palette)	Shift-Tab	Shift-Tab

Open/close individual palettes

	Mac	Windows
Align palette	Shift-F7	Shift-F7
Appearance palette	Shift-F6	Shift-F6
Attributes palette	F11	F11
Brushes palette	F5	F5
Character palette	Cmd-T	Ctrl-T
Color palette	F6	F6
Gradient palette	F9	F9
Graphic Styles palette	Shift-F5	Shift-F5
Info palette	F8	F8

	Mac	Windows
Layers palette	F7	F7
OpenType palette	Cmd-Option-Shift-T	Ctrl-Alt-Shift-T
Paragraph palette	Cmd-Option-T	Ctrl-Alt-T
Pathfinder palette	Shift-F9	Shift-F9
Stroke palette	F10	F10
Symbols palette	Shift-F11	Shift-F11
Tabs palette	Cmd-Shift-T	Ctrl-Shift-T
Transform palette	Shift-F8	Shift-F8
Transparency palette	Shift-F10	Shift-F10

Views

	Mac	Windows
Preview/Outline view toggle	Cmd-Y	Ctrl-Y
Pixel Preview view on/off	Cmd-Option-Y	Ctrl-Alt-Y
Overprint Preview view on/off	Cmd-Option-Shift-Y	Ctrl-Alt-Shift-Y
Toggle crosshair pointer on/off (drawing tools)	Caps Lock	Caps Lock
Show/hide edges	Cmd-H	Ctrl-H
Display entire artboard	Double-click Hand tool	Double-click Hand tool
Fit in window	Cmd-0	Ctrl-0
Minimize window	Cmd-M	
Actual size	Double-click Zoom tool	Double-click Zoom tool
Actual size and center artboard in window	Cmd-1	Ctrl-1
Zoom out from tool position (Zoom tool selected)	Option-click	Alt-click
Zoom in at tool position (any tool selected)	Cmd- + (plus) or Cmd-Spacebar-click	Ctrl- + (plus) or Ctrl-Spacebar-click
Zoom out from tool position (any tool selected)	Cmd- – (minus) or Cmd-Option-Spacebar-click	Ctrl- – (minus) or Ctrl-Alt-Spacebar-click
Adjust zoom marquee position	Drag with Zoom tool, then Spacebar-drag	Drag with Zoom tool, then Spacebar-drag
Zoom in on specific area of artboard	Drag Zoom tool or Cmd-drag in Navigator palette	Drag Zoom tool or Ctrl-drag in Navigator palette
Use Hand tool (any tool selected)	Spacebar	Spacebar
Hide selected objects	Cmd-3	Ctrl-3
Hide all unselected objects	Cmd-Option-Shift-3	Ctrl-Alt-Shift-3
Show all	Cmd-Option-3	Ctrl-Alt-3
Show/hide template(s)	Cmd-Shift-W	Ctrl-Shift-W

	Mac	Windows
Show/hide bounding box	Cmd-Shift-B	Ctrl-Shift-B
Show/hide transparency grid	Cmd-Shift-D	Ctrl-Shift-D
Standard screen mode/full screen mode with menu bar/full screen mode	F	F

Undo, redo

Undo last operation	Cmd-Z	Ctrl-Z
Redo last undone operation	Cmd-Shift-Z	Ctrl-Shift-Z

Create objects

Draw object from center using Rectangle, Rounded Rectangle, or Ellipse tool	Option-drag	Alt-drag
Draw square with Rectangle or Rounded Rectangle tool; circle with Ellipse tool	Shift-drag	Shift-drag
Move object as you draw with Rectangle, Rounded Rectangle, Ellipse, Polygon, Star, or Spiral tool	Spacebar	Spacebar

Polygon, Star, Spiral tools

Constrain orientation 90° as you draw with Polygon, Star, or Spiral tool	Shift	Shift
Add or subtract sides as you draw with the Polygon tool, points as you draw with the Star tool, or segments as you draw with the Spiral tool	Up or down arrow	Up or down arrow
Align shoulders as you draw with Star tool	Option	Alt
Increase or decrease outer radius as you draw with Star tool, or decay as you draw with Spiral tool	Cmd	Ctrl

Select, copy

Repeat last Select menu command	Cmd-6	Cmd-6
Use last-used selection tool (any non-selection tool chosen)	Cmd	Ctrl
Toggle between Group Selection and Direct Selection tools	Option	Alt
Select all	Cmd-A	Ctrl-A
Deselect all	Cmd-Shift-A	Ctrl-Shift-A
Select hidden objects sequentially	Cmd-Option-[	Ctrl-Alt-[
Add to selection with Lasso tool	Shift-drag	Shift-drag
Subtract from selection with Lasso tool	Option-drag	Alt-drag

Move

Open the Move dialog box (object selected)	Double-click Selection tool or Cmd-Shift-M	Double-click Selection tool or Ctrl-Shift-M

	Mac	Windows
Drag copy of object with Selection or Direct Selection tool	Option-drag	Alt-drag
Drag copy of object (any tool)	Cmd-Option-drag	Ctrl-Alt-drag
Move selected object the current Keyboard Increment (Preferences > General)	Any arrow key	Any arrow key
Move selection 10x Keyboard Increment	Shift-arrow key	Shift-arrow key
Constrain movement to multiple of 45°	Shift	Shift

Clipboard

	Mac	Windows
Cut	Cmd-X	Ctrl-X
Copy	Cmd-C	Ctrl-C
Paste	Cmd-V	Ctrl-V
Paste in Front	Cmd-F	Ctrl-F
Paste in Back	Cmd-B	Ctrl-B

Transform

	Mac	Windows
Set origin, open dialog box for Rotate, Reflect, or Shear tool	Option-click	Alt-click
Transform object along multiple of 45° for Rotate, Shear tools; 90° for Rotate tool	Shift-drag	Shift-drag
Scale object uniformly (Scale tool dragged diagonally or by using Free Transform)	Shift-drag	Shift-drag
Transform again	Cmd-D	Ctrl-D
Transform pattern fill, not object, with Rotate, Reflect, or Shear tool	~ drag	~ drag
Transform copy of object with Rotate, Reflect, or Shear tool	Start dragging, then Option-drag	Start dragging, then Alt-drag
Transform copy of object (Transform palette)	Modify value, then press Option-Return	Modify value, then press Alt-Enter
Scale object uniformly (Transform palette)	Modify W or H value, then press Cmd-Return	Modify W or H value, then press Ctrl-Enter
Transform Each dialog box	Cmd-Option-Shift-D	Ctrl-Alt-Shift-D

Bounding box

	Mac	Windows
Scale object uniformly using bounding box (Free Transform or Selection tool)	Shift-drag handle	Shift-drag handle
Resize object from center using bounding box (Free Transform or Selection tool)	Option-drag handle	Alt-drag handle
Scale object uniformly from center (Free Transform or Selection tool)	Option-Shift-drag corner handle	Alt-Shift-drag corner handle

Blends

	Mac	Windows
Blend > Make	Cmd-Option-B	Ctrl-Alt-B
Blend > Release	Cmd-Option-Shift-B	Ctrl-Alt-Shift-B

	Mac	**Windows**
Free Transform tool		
Transform selected object from center	Option-drag a handle	Alt-drag a handle
Distort selected object	Start dragging corner handle, then Cmd-drag	Start dragging corner handle, then Ctrl-drag
Distort selected object in perspective	Start dragging corner handle, then Cmd-Option-Shift-drag	Start dragging corner handle, then Ctrl-Alt-Shift-drag
Shear selected object along side axis	Start dragging side handle, then Cmd-drag	Start dragging side handle, then Ctrl-drag
Shear selected object around center axis	Start dragging side handle, then Cmd-Option-drag	Start dragging side handle, then Ctrl-Alt-drag
Drawing		
Temporary Smooth tool (Pencil tool chosen)	Option	Alt
Close path while drawing with Pencil or Paintbrush tool	Drag, then Option-release	Drag, then Alt-release
Add to existing open path using Pencil tool	Cmd-click to select, then drag from endpoint	Ctrl-click to select, then drag from endpoint
Move anchor point while drawing with Pen	Spacebar-drag	Spacebar-drag
Reshape		
Add Anchor Point and Delete Anchor Point tool toggle (either selected)	Option	Alt
Use Add Anchor Point tool (Scissors tool selected)	Option	Alt
Use Convert Anchor Point tool (Pen tool selected)	Option	Alt
Constrain direction line angle to multiple of 45° with Direct Selection or Convert Anchor Point tool	Shift-drag	Shift-drag
Join two selected endpoints	Cmd-J	Ctrl-J
Average two selected endpoints	Cmd-Option-J	Ctrl-Alt-J
Average and Join two selected endpoints	Cmd-Option-Shift-J	Ctrl-Alt-Shift-J
Cut in a straight line with Knife tool	Option-drag	Alt-drag
Cut in 45° increment with Knife tool	Option-Shift	Alt-Shift
Fill and stroke		
Default fill/stroke	D	D
Eyedropper and Paint Bucket tool toggle (either one selected)	Option	Alt

	Mac	Windows
Fill/Stroke box toggle (Toolbox and Color palette)	X	X
Apply last-used solid color	, (comma)	, (comma)
Apply fill/stroke of None	/	/

Color palette

	Mac	Windows
Cycle through color models	Shift-click color spectrum bar	Shift-click color spectrum bar
Swap fill/stroke	Shift-X	Shift-X

Swatches palette

	Mac	Windows
Set options for new swatch	Option-click New Swatch button	Alt-click New Swatch button
Create new spot color	Cmd-click New Swatch button	Ctrl-click New Swatch button
Create new global process color	Cmd-Shift-click New Swatch button	Ctrl-Shift-click New Swatch button

Layers

	Mac	Windows
Expand/collapse all sublayers and groups in a layer	Option-click arrowhead	Alt-click arrowhead

Grouping

	Mac	Windows
Group selected objects	Cmd-G	Ctrl-G
Ungroup selected objects	Cmd-Shift-G	Ctrl-Shift-G

Restacking (keyboard)

	Mac	Windows
Bring to front	Cmd-Shift-]	Ctrl-Shift-]
Send to back	Cmd-Shift-[	Ctrl-Shift-[
Bring forward	Cmd-]	Ctrl-]
Send backward	Cmd-[	Ctrl-[

Select

	Mac	Windows
Select layer, sublayer, group, or object	Click selection area or Option-click name	Click selection area or Alt-click name
Add to selection	Shift-click selection area	Shift-click selection area
Copy selection to new layer, sublayer, group	Start dragging selection square, then Option-drag	Start dragging selection square, then Alt-drag

Views

	Mac	Windows
Hide/show all other layers	Option-click eye icon	Alt-click eye icon
View a layer in Outline/Preview view	Cmd-click eye icon	Ctrl-click eye icon
View all other layers in Outline/Preview view	Cmd-Option-click eye icon	Ctrl-Alt-click eye icon
Lock/unlock all other layers	Option-click blank box in second column	Alt-click blank box in second column

Keyboard Shortcuts

	Mac	Windows
Create top-level layers		
Create layer above currently selected layer	Cmd-L	Ctrl-L
Create layer at top of list	Cmd-click New Layer button	Ctrl-click New Layer button
Create layer, open Layer Options dialog box	Option-click New Layer button	Alt-click New Layer button
Create layer below currently selected layer, open Layer Options dialog box	Cmd-Option-click New Layer button	Ctrl-Alt-click New Layer button
Lock/unlock objects		
Lock selected object	Cmd-2	Ctrl-2
Lock all unselected objects	Cmd-Option-Shift-2	Ctrl-Alt-Shift-2
Unlock all	Cmd-Option-2	Ctrl-Alt-2

Type

	Mac	Windows
Show hidden characters	Cmd-Option-I	Ctrl-Alt-I
Hard return	Return or Enter	Enter
Soft return	Shift-Return or Enter	Shift-Enter
Highlight font field on Character palette	Cmd-Option-Shift-M	Ctrl-Alt-Shift-M
Create outlines from selected type	Cmd-Shift-O	Ctrl-Shift-O
Type tools		
Use Area Type tool (Type tool selected, over open path)	Option	Alt
Use Path Type tool (Type tool selected, over closed path)	Option	Alt
Switch to vertical/horizontal type tool equivalent as you create type	Shift with any type tool	Shift with any type tool
Switch to Type tool when selecting type block	Double-click with any selection tool	Double-click with any selection tool
Show/hide text threads	Cmd-Shift-Y	Ctrl-Shift-Y
Selecting type		
Select a word	Double-click	Double-click
Select a paragraph	Triple-click	Triple-click
Select all the type in a block	Cmd-A	Ctrl-A
Move insertion pointer left/right one word	Cmd-left/right arrow	Ctrl-left/right arrow
Move insertion pointer up/down one line	Up/down arrow	Up/down arrow
Move insertion pointer up/down one paragraph	Cmd-up/down arrow	Ctrl-up/down arrow
Align		
Align left	Cmd-Shift-L	Ctrl-Shift-L
Align center	Cmd-Shift-C	Ctrl-Shift-C
Align right	Cmd-Shift-R	Ctrl-Shift-R

	Mac	Windows
Justify	Cmd-Shift-J	Ctrl-Shift-J
Justify all lines	Cmd-Shift-F	Ctrl-Shift-F

Point size

Increase point size of selected type	Cmd-Shift->	Ctrl-Shift->
Decrease point size of selected type	Cmd-Shift-<	Ctrl-Shift-<

Leading

Increase leading	Option-down arrow	Alt-down arrow
Decrease leading	Option-up arrow	Alt-up arrow
Set leading to current font size	Double-click leading button on Character palette	Double-click leading button on Character palette

Scaling

Reset horizontal and vertical scale to 100%	Cmd-Shift-X	Ctrl-Shift-X

Kerning and tracking

Highlight kerning field (cursor in text) or highlight tracking field (type object selected)	Cmd-Option-K	Ctrl-Alt-K
Increase kerning/tracking	Option-right arrow	Alt-right arrow
Decrease kerning/tracking	Option-left arrow	Alt-left arrow
Increase kerning/tracking 5x	Cmd-Option-right arrow	Ctrl-Alt-right arrow
Decrease kerning/tracking 5x	Cmd-Option-left arrow	Ctrl-Alt-left arrow
Reset kerning/tracking to 0	Cmd-Option-Q	Ctrl-Alt-Q

Baseline shift

Increase baseline shift	Option-Shift-up arrow	Alt-Shift-up arrow
Decrease baseline shift	Option-Shift-down arrow	Alt-Shift-down arrow
Increase baseline shift 5x	Cmd-Option-Shift-up arrow	Ctrl-Alt-Shift-up arrow
Decrease baseline shift 5x	Cmd-Option-Shift-down arrow	Ctrl-Alt-Shift-down arrow

Smart quotes

'	Option-Shift-]	Alt-0146
'	Option-]	Alt-0145
"	Option-Shift-[	Alt-0148
"	Option-[	Alt-0147

Numeric keypad only

Spelling

Check spelling	Cmd-I	Ctrl-I

	Mac	**Windows**
Combine paths		
Compound Path > Make	Cmd-8	Ctrl-8
Compound Path > Release	Cmd-Option-8* *Bug: shortcut not working on the Mac*	Ctrl-Alt-8
Pathfinder commands		
Repeat last-used Pathfinder command	Cmd-4	Ctrl-4
Turn shape mode button into pathfinder button	Option-click button	Alt-click button
Gradients		
Reapply last-used gradient	**.** (period)	**.** (period)
Reset gradient palette to black and white	Cmd-click Gradient square on palette	Ctrl-click Gradient square on palette
Duplicate color stop	Option-drag color stop	Alt-drag color stop
Apply swatch color to active color stop	Option-click swatch	Alt-click swatch
Meshes		
Move mesh point along one of its lines without reshaping perpendicular line	Shift-drag with Mesh tool	Shift-drag with Mesh tool
Add mesh point using adjacent mesh color	Shift-click with Mesh tool	Shift-click with Mesh tool
Remove mesh point	Option-click with Mesh tool	Alt-click with Mesh tool
Appearances		
Add new fill	Cmd-/	Ctrl-/
Add new stroke	Cmd-Option-/	Ctrl-Alt-/
Clipping masks		
Clipping Mask > Make	Cmd-7	Ctrl-7
Clipping Mask > Release	Cmd-Option-7	Ctrl-Alt-7
Transparency		
View only opacity mask in mask edit mode (toggles on/off)	Option-click mask thumbnail	Alt-click mask thumbnail
Disable/enable opacity mask	Shift-click mask thumbnail	Shift-click mask thumbnail
Change opacity in increments of 10 (for increments of 1, omit Shift)	Click field, then Shift-arrow	Click field, then Shift-arrow
Envelope distort		
Make with warp	Cmd-Option-Shift-W	Ctrl-Alt-Shift-W
Make with mesh	Cmd-Option-M	Ctrl-Alt-M
Make with top object	Cmd-Option-C	Ctrl-Alt-C

	Mac	Windows
Effects and Filters		
Apply last effect	Cmd-Shift-E	Ctrl-Shift-E
Last effect (reopen last effect dialog box)	Cmd-Option-Shift-E	Ctrl-Alt-Shift-E
Apply last filter	Cmd-E	Ctrl-E
Last filter (reopen last filter dialog box)	Cmd-Option-E	Ctrl-Alt-E
Precision tools		
Show/hide rulers	Cmd-R	Ctrl-R
Show/hide guides	Cmd- ;	Ctrl- ;
Make [convert selected objects to] guides	Cmd-5	Ctrl-5
Release [object] guides	Cmd-Shift-double-click guide	Ctrl-Shift-double-click guide
Convert ruler guide between horizontal/vertical orientation	Option-drag new guide	Alt-drag new guide
Lock/unlock guides	Cmd-Option-;	Ctrl-Alt-;
Lock/unlock one guide	Cmd-Shift-double-click guide	Ctrl-Shift-double-click guide
Show/hide grid	Cmd-"	Ctrl-"
Snap to grid if Pixel Preview is off; Snap to pixel if Pixel Preview is on	Cmd-Shift-"	Ctrl-Shift-"
Snap to point	Cmd-Option-"	Ctrl-Alt-"
Smart guides	Cmd-U	Ctrl-U
Constrain Measure tool to multiple of 45°	Shift-drag with tool	Shift-drag with tool
Preferences		
General Preferences dialog box	Cmd-K	Ctrl-K
Export, print		
Save for Web dialog box	Cmd-Option-Shift-S	Ctrl-Alt-Shift-S
Print dialog box	Cmd-P	Ctrl-P
Color Settings dialog box	Cmd-Shift-K	Ctrl-Shift-K
Keyboard shortcuts		
Keyboard Shortcuts dialog box	Cmd-Option-Shift-K	Ctrl-Alt-Shift-K
Help		
Illustrator Help (HTML Help files)	F1 or Help key	F1

Keyboard Shortcuts

Customizing shortcuts

If you don't like Illustrator's default shortcuts for commands and tools, or if you want to assign a shortcut to a command that has none, you can assign your own. Shortcuts are organized into keysets.

To assign your own shortcuts:

1. Choose Edit > Keyboard Shortcuts (Cmd-Option-Shift-K/Ctrl-Alt-Shift-K). The Keyboard Shortcuts dialog box opens (**1**, next page).

2. To edit an existing keyset (set of shortcuts), choose a keyset name from the Set pop-up menu. To create a new keyset, ignore this step (you'll create one later).

3. Choose Menu Commands or Tools from the next pop-up menu.

4. If you chose Menu Commands, click the arrowhead next to a menu name. To access some commands (e.g., the Type submenu under the Window menu), you'll need to click yet another arrowhead.

5. In the Shortcut column next to the command that you want to assign a shortcut to, click in the blank area if the command doesn't have a shortcut (hand pointer), or click an existing shortcut.

6. Press the desired shortcut key.

   If that key is already assigned to another command or tool, an alert message will appear in the dialog box, and the shortcut will be removed from the previous command or tool. To assign a new shortcut to the command or tool from which you just removed a shortcut, click Go To, then press a shortcut.
   or
   If you change your mind, click Undo in the dialog box. The shortcut will be reassigned to its original command or tool. To clear a shortcut altogether, click Clear.

7. *Optional:* In the Symbol column, enter the keyboard symbol you want to appear on the menu or tool tip for the command or tool.

8. Repeat steps 4–6 for any other shortcuts you want to assign.

9. As soon as one user-defined shortcut is entered in the dialog box, the word "Custom" appears on the Set pop-up menu. To create a new keyset to include your new shortcuts, click Save, type a name for the new keyset, click OK, then click OK again to exit the dialog box. The new keyset name will appear on the Set pop-up menu.
or
To save your changes to the currently chosen keyset, click OK.

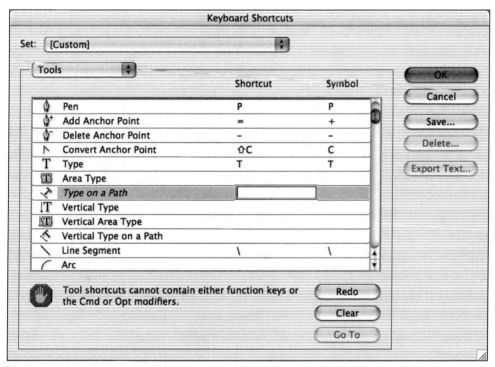

1 *The Keyboard Shortcuts dialog box*

To choose, delete, or print a keyset:

1. Choose Edit > Keyboard Shortcuts
   (Cmd-Option-Shift-K/Ctrl-Alt-Shift-K).

2. Choose a keyset from the Set pop-up
   menu.

3. To use the chosen keyset, click OK.
   or
   To delete the chosen keyset, click Delete,
   then click OK.
   or
   To print the chosen keyset, click Export
   Text, choose a location in which to save
   the file, type a name for the keyset, click
   Save, then click OK to exit the dialog
   box. Open the new SimpleText (Mac)/
   Notepad (Win) file and print it.

Choose, Delete, Print Keyset

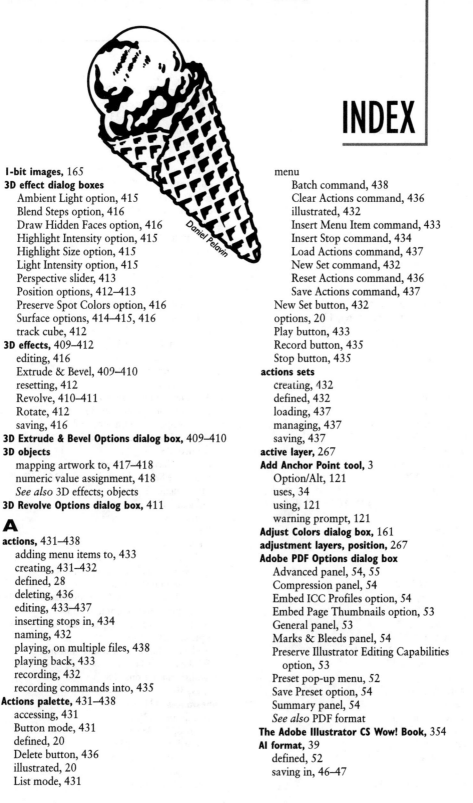

INDEX

Index

Daniel Pelavin

Chris Spollen

Index

Index

Index

Index

Index

Index

Index

Index

Index

Index

Daniel Pelavin

Index

Index

Daniel Pelavin

Index

Index

Daniel Pelavin

Index

Z

Chris Spollen

Index